8/03

Voice of America

VOICE OF AMERICA

A History

ALAN L. HEIL, JR.

COLUMBIA UNIVERSITY PRESS

NEW YORK

Columbia University Press
Publishers Since 1893
New York   Chichester, West Sussex

Library of Congress Cataloging-in-Publication Data
Heil, Alan L.
        Voice of America : a history / Alan L. Heil, Jr.
        p. cm.
        Includes bibliographical references and index.
        ISBN 0-231-12674-3 (cloth : alk. paper)
        ISBN 0-231-12675-1 (paper : alk. paper)
        1. Voice of America (Organization)—History. 2. International
broadcasting—United States—History. I. Title

HE8697.45.U6 H44 2003
384.54'0973—dc21   200204109

⊗

Columbia University Press books are printed on permanent and
durable acid-free paper.
Printed in the United States of America
c 10 9 8 7 6 5 4 3 2 1
p 10 9 8 7 6 5 4 3 2 1

To my beloved family
and
to those dedicated souls of the Voice of America,
past and present, all of whom made this account possible

Contents

Acknowledgments

This book seeks to reflect the spirit of the Voice of America and its dedicated journalists and engineers over more than three generations. The intention has been to blend the perspectives of scores of U.S. professional international broadcasters and their loyal listeners who have been united over the airwaves since the founding of America's Voice in 1942. To them, I owe much. Through their craftsmanship, journalistic curiosity, and reactions to the broadcasts, I have been taught much about what the late astronomer Carl Sagan once described on VOA's *Talk to America* as "a pale blue dot . . . and on that pale blue dot is all of us."

It would be impossible to cite each and every one of the scores of individuals who have encouraged, at times prodded, gently counseled, and generously shared nuggets of wisdom with the author. Any errors or omissions, of course, are mine—not theirs. This has been a somewhat daunting labor of love; there has been no comprehensive history of the Voice since the mid-1980s. This mirror of a great, relatively unknown national institution is really a series of stories that attempt to fill only some of the gaps. It could never have been framed, however, without the insights and support of many—in America and abroad.

I would like to thank principal manuscript readers and editors Eva Jane Fritzman, Claude B. Groce, and Barbara Schiele, each in his or her own right a master historian of the Voice. Other valuable contributors to this history include Brian Armstead, Scott Cohen, Frank Cummins, Ray Ewing, Morand Fachot, Bob Goldmann, Michael Gray, Ed Gursky, Jay Henderson, Sam and Kate Hilmy, Philomena Jurey, Bernard H. Kamenske, John Lennon, John Lindburg, Negussie Mengesha, Graham Mytton, Joseph D. O'Connell, Jr., Walter Roberts, Holly Cowan Shulman, Connie Stevens, Myrna Whitworth, Barry Zorthian, and, in the technical fields, Terry Balazs, Vicki Brimmer, George Jacobs, and Fred Wulff. Martin Manning of the Department of State Public Diplomacy Research Center and the staff of the IBB/VOA Office of

External Affairs, including Lesley S. Jackson and art director Tuleda Poole Johnson, have been generous in providing indispensable archival material. My superb editors, Stephen Q. Shannon and, at Columbia University Press, Irene Pavitt, also deserve particular thanks, as does Sara Sams, who did so much to proof and produce the original manuscript.

Over the years, and in encouraging this book, I have been fortunate to have had the counsel and valued friendship of VOA's former directors Mary G. F. Bitterman, Richard W. Carlson, Geoffrey L. Cowan, Kenneth R. Giddens, Sanford Ungar, and Charles (Chase) Untermeyer. Deans Douglas Boyd of the University of Kentucky and Richard Cole of the University of North Carolina School of Journalism and Mass Communication also have been instrumental in inspiring this work. I owe much, as well, to Radio Canada International. RCI brought together international broadcast professionals from throughout the world in biannual Challenges conferences (1990–2000) and has continued to include me in these gatherings since my retirement in 1998.

No listing of support for this book would be complete, however, without mention of three remarkable generations of Heils. My beloved parents, Eddi and Alan Heil, often entertained overseas guests during my teen years in Montclair, New Jersey. They instilled in me an appreciation and understanding of other cultures, introduced me to a fascinating, wider world, and encouraged and supported my journalistic endeavors— wherever those might lead. My wife, Dot, has unfailingly supported VOA and our association with it over the years. She moved our three preschool children to four different posts in six and a half years during our time in the Middle East. She patiently adapted to every travel need of this former foreign correspondent, and entertained many other VOA correspondents and their bosses in our home. She is a self-styled "news junkie" after listening to America's Voice all these years and observing at close hand the triumphs and reverses at a VOA that John Chancellor once fondly christened the citadel of "ramshackle excellence." She has read every word of this history, contributing valuable editorial suggestions and research assistance. She has been a loving partner and confidante every step of the way through this book, and our life journey as well.

Finally, it is likely our three daughters—Wendy Packer, Dr. Susan Cheatham, and Nancy Knor—have heard more about the Voice and its adventures over the years than any in their generation should be expected to endure. But they and their husbands have supported the Voice and the writing of this history with uncommon love and patience. Nancy once spoke during a Peace Corps assignment in Belize of spreading "idea seeds" through a library she helped her village build. Broadcasting knowledge, nurtured by the love of pursuing it, is in fact what the Voice is all about—its lasting gift to the nation and to the world.

September 1, 2002

Voice of America

Introduction

Let Facts be submitted to a candid World.
　　—Thomas Jefferson, Declaration of Independence

The Voice of America . . . says here is the news, and even
Walter Cronkite wouldn't be ashamed to read it.
　　—James Reston, "The Voice of America"

In the mid-1950s, I landed my first job as a paid journalist with the former *Newark Evening News* in New Jersey. That was nearly five years before my first encounter with America's Voice. I can recall distinctly, as an overnight copy clerk with the *News*, stripping the wires and finding time on my hands around 3:00 A.M., when I sauntered into the office of the Old Man, the publisher, who seldom kept such hours, of course. There, in the piercing beam of a distant street light, the words of John Ruskin were framed in a plaque above the Old Man's desk:

Upon a thought, there fell a drop of ink
And made not hundreds, but thousands think.

Little could I have imagined then that I would spend most of my professional life at an organization that reaches not hundreds, not thousands, but tens of millions of listeners each week. That global network, the Voice of America, had then and continues to have today a nearly universal reach. Its daily "piercing beam of light" is its determination to present straight-arrow news, public-service programming, and enlightened comment of value to people everywhere. It is Jeffersonian in its resolve "to let facts be submitted to a candid world."

This book attempts to tell the story of America's Voice as I saw it. It is the nation's largest and only global, publicly funded international broadcasting organization. VOA was listened to at the beginning of this century in more than fifty languages by more than 90 million people weekly. Because it operates around the clock, every day of the year, its central newsroom literally never sleeps.

I observed VOA closely from 1962 to 1998. The Voice is a great, at times heroic, but fragile and often endangered national institution that deserves to be more widely understood and supported by American citizens than it is. I spent thirty-six years there, beginning as a newswriter trainee and retiring as deputy director. This account takes the reader to the Voice's sixtieth anniversary.

The real "magic of the Voice," said its eleventh director, the late distinguished NBC anchor John Chancellor, is the daily contact that a thousand people, who put the programs on the air, have with its listeners. Scores of engineers who beam its signals abroad are magicians, too. What follows is actually their story, from the perspective of one who watched closely much of its twentieth-century activity.

My most fulfilling moments were when I was in the trenches with them: cutting tape, transcribing speeches, covering wars abroad, writing and voicing reports under tight deadlines. There's a sort of ramshackle majesty about

- A VOA correspondent running, gazelle-like, a couple of miles through the streets of Rawalpindi to make a four o'clock feed that would break news of the creation of Bangladesh in 1971
- A VOA contract reporter getting the story of Israel's Entebbe raid before anyone else had it, and a newsroom shift supervisor rushing breathlessly up a confounded, nonmoving escalator to a studio just past one in the morning to score a world beat
- A Turkish Service staff member calling the central newsroom to positively identify Mehmet Ali Agca as Pope John Paul II's assailant before any other international news agency had it
- A VOA reporter huddled next to an open phone line in a villa adjacent to Tehran's airport, watching that plane full of American hostages at dusk on January 20, 1981, and shouting on the phone to the newsroom in Washington, "Liftoff!"
- A VOA technician scaling the heights of the Capitol rotunda on a freezing January morning so that nine VOA languages could

broadcast Ronald Reagan's second inaugural address live to millions around the world

- A VOA special events officer, drenched under a wind-broken umbrella in a deluge near Beijing, waiting to badger her way with Voice reporters into a packed conference hall at the United Nations women's conference
- A VOA traffic manager working with Master Control to arrange hundreds of circuits on U.S. election night, and running like a jackrabbit from patch to patch, studio to studio, to ensure that it went like clockwork
- A VOA team of radio and television producers applauding as one, as the first viewer to their inaugural radio–TV simulcast call-in program to Iran is asked if he wants a prize. He tells the Farsi (Persian) Service host: "No need, you've just given me the greatest gift of all!"

The Voice is often perceived as America's official international broadcasting organization. It is that and more. It is America's town crier to the world. During a visit to Africa in the late 1970s, an Ivory Coast broadcaster told me that he doesn't view VOA as "an official radio." Rather, he said, VOA is a reflector of "an American optic." He said its credibility and determination to "tell the news straight" (Americans are famous for that) is the real reason it is believed in faraway places. "A veritable alarm bell of civilization," VOA News chief Bernard H. Kamenske once called it.

Today, America's Voice speaks in more languages than any other public broadcaster on the planet. Its transmission power, provided by the International Broadcasting Bureau, adds up to more than 36 million watts, enough to light a small city.

Atop the Voice's massive stone headquarters building and multimedia news center in Washington, D.C., is a giant satellite dish that beams those languages to distant places. It is located at the foot of Capitol Hill, within easy sight of the halls of Congress. Yet some there scarcely recognize its name because of post–World War II legislation forbidding its dissemination in the United States. Nor is the public at large aware of how it sends news and information about the nation and the world all over the Earth, in microseconds. A VOA relay station manager has noted the irony, calling the Voice "America's best kept secret."

The need for VOA news and programming is, in the view of Czech Republic president Václav Havel, even greater in the world today than it was during the Cold War. Many of the new democracies are themselves struggling to survive. In the twenty-first century, the planet continues to be plagued by disasters caused by humans and nature: terrorism, nuclear proliferation, ethnic cleansing, regional wars, poverty, disease, AIDS, and environmental and natural calamities.

International broadcasting specialist Doug Boyd cites four principal reasons that nations broadcast across borders to others: "(1) to enhance national prestige, (2) to promote national interests, (3) to attempt religious or political indoctrination, and (4) to foster cultural ties."[1] I believe that America's Voice can continue to enhance national prestige in an increasingly dangerous world, promote the national interest, and foster cultural ties with others if it keeps its covenant with its listeners "to tell it straight."

VOA is a full-service, digital-age broadcasting network, informationally, via many delivery systems (radio, television, the Internet, and 1,500 or more FM and TV partner stations). I've watched it—read on and you'll experience it—evolve from a regional shortwave enterprise into a global multimedia giant.

It has been written that the Voice suffers from a split personality, that it stands at the crossroads of journalism and diplomacy. As its charter says, it must be an accurate, objective, and comprehensive source of world and U.S. news. If not, it will not be listened to, watched, or believed. The charter also requires VOA to reflect America, not any single segment of American thought and opinion, and to present the policies of the United States as well as debate about those policies.

Some see the several functions as incompatible. I disagree. As a veteran of many policy wars, I am convinced that America's diversity, dynamism, and debates over policy in the world of the twenty-first century can be accommodated and reported within accepted Western journalistic norms. With the unceasing vigilance of professionals committed to those norms, this can be done without sacrificing VOA's accuracy, integrity, or credibility.

To quote *New York Times* columnist James Reston in a 1978 dispatch from Damascus: "It is an honest service, reporting our national failures as well as our virtues, which also troubles those who want it to produce nothing but propaganda. But heard over here, a long way from home, it seems worth the money and even makes you proud."[2] The VOA Charter, after all, is the source of the first three principles governing all the nation's publicly funded overseas networks supervised by the United States Broadcasting Board of Governors.[3]

Information of quality, based on firsthand news gathering and reporting, is difficult for any network, particularly a federal government network, to produce. Often, VOA is underfunded. And over the years, there have been pressures—at home and abroad, in administrations and in Congress—to shape Voice programming content: political intrusions, congressional investigations, reorganizations, budget cuts, purges of its leaders, and changes in directors an average of every two and a quarter years. Other governments have jammed VOA, expelled or detained its correspondents, attacked its content in local media, and from time to time put pressure on Washington officialdom to alter its broadcasts to the world in ways wholly inconsistent with American journalistic practice. As President John F. Kennedy told the staff in 1962, less than three weeks after I joined the Voice of America, "its burden of truth is not easy to bear."

Thousands of men and women have borne that burden since VOA first went on the air on February 25, 1942. You'll meet many of them in this book. Their goal, usually but not always achieved, is a "struggle to get it straight," as television producer and writer Harry Miles Muheim put it in an award-winning fiftieth-anniversary documentary about VOA. To get it straight, around the clock every day of every year, for listeners in four-fifths of the world who still are denied completely free media by their own governments. The struggle is never ending in a terrorism-plagued world, at home and abroad.

In the chapters that follow, we examine many facets of the Voice's history, focusing primarily on events that spanned the period from the 1960s onward. VOA reported epochal events during those years: the worst act of terrorism in U.S. history as thousands perished on September 11, 2001; the Cold War and its dramatic conclusion; Vietnam; presidential scandals, including Watergate and the Lewinsky affair; the five-week Bush–Gore impasse ending the 2000 presidential race; conflicts in the Middle East (including the Gulf War); ethnic cleansing in the Balkans and Rwanda; and the first footsteps on the moon. VOA reported them all, in addition to miraculous breakthroughs in science, technology, medicine, and the human spirit: the civil rights revolution in the United States and the growing focus on human rights violations the world over.

In many ways, the men and women of VOA have had a front-row seat for all these events. This account of the first six decades of America's Voice opens with a glimpse at how VOA witnessed and covered the dramatic developments in China during the spring of 1989, a curtain-raiser of sorts for the end of the Cold War and the years beyond.

1

Tiananmen

THE BURDEN OF TRUTH

Radio, if it is to serve and survive, must hold a mirror up to the nation and the world. The mirror must have no curves, and be held with a steady hand.
——Edward R. Murrow, in
Voice of America Programming Handbook

The government has accused me of inciting turmoil and counterrevolutionary rebellion. That's not what I do. What I do is report the news.
——Al Pessin, in Muheim and Krell, *The Voice*

Imagine the sound of a million voices. A million people clamoring for a dialogue with their government and democratic reforms. It's just past dusk in Tiananmen Square in the heart of the Chinese capital of Beijing. It's a sultry May evening in 1989, and many of the demonstrators in the huge plaza are camped out in tents or makeshift shelters. They've been here for days as their numbers have swelled to epochal proportions.

From the ancient Forbidden City overlooking the square, one can see smoke curling skyward from bright campfires on the dark cobblestones in the vast plaza. These splotches of crimson flame are for cooking, and for warmth in the gathering coolness of night. There's the din, a kind of roaring hum, of those million voices. It is punctuated, from time to time, by leaders with megaphones at the heart of the square. The epicenter of the demonstration, you see, is not far from the towering handmade statue of the goddess of democracy. It is a somewhat imperfect likeness, but it is intended to remind the world of the great Statue of Liberty looming above a harbor half a world away.

Suddenly, there is a hush over some sectors of the plaza. Scores of transistor radios seem to materialize out of nowhere, aerials pointed skyward. In the tents. By the campfires. Out in the open. The signature tune sounds from those radios, "Yankee Doodle," mingling with the hum of humanity. It's 9:00 P.M., and the Voice of America Chinese Branch is on the air.[1]

AROUND THE EARTH ON ELECTRONIC WINGS

The latest news is a lifeline of up-to-the-minute information on the revolution, which is centered in this teeming plaza. A reality check. Hourly newscasts chronicle what is happening throughout China, and for many right there, what is happening almost within their sight, in the square. Around the clock, live reports from VOA correspondents in Chinese and English stationed in Beijing surge through busy phone lines to Washington. Within minutes, and sometimes live in split seconds, they speed back around the Earth on electronic wings via the miracle of international radio to eager ears at Tiananmen. And America's Voice, as we shall see, reaches millions more in China beyond Tiananmen and around the globe during the Beijing spring of 1989.

Today, a multimedia Voice is ranging far beyond its shortwave origins. Its continued success, however, rests on maintaining its reputation for credibility. News, English-language lessons, glimpses of the history and culture of the United States, and honest reportage about China itself laid the foundations for the extensive and loyal following it had in Beijing in 1989.

VOA first went on the air on February 25, 1942, seventy-nine days after the attack on Pearl Harbor. In the years since, there have been dozens of tests of its ability to level with its listeners, none in the modern era more challenging, perhaps, than Tiananmen. This pitted straight news from America delivered by megawatt transmitters into the heartland of the world's most populous nation against the authoritarian might of a regime conditioned for a half century to snuff out or distort the truth.

The demonstrations in Beijing began on April 15, 1989, as students first marched on the square and in the streets during the funeral of former Chinese Communist Party leader Hu Yaobang. They regarded Hu as something of a reformer and initially wanted to show solidarity with the late leader. But the movement struck surprising sparks. Greater numbers

"I Owe My Life to You!"

About four years before the Beijing spring of 1989, then chief of VOA News Don Henry paid a visit to China. He took an internal flight from Shanghai to Beijing. He was seated next to a Chinese gentleman wearing glasses, and struck up a conversation. It turned out that his fellow passenger was a professor from Fudan University in Shanghai. He had suffered greatly during the Cultural Revolution of the mid-1960s to mid-1970s in the People's Republic of China (PRC). He recalled that as the Red Guards penetrated the university campus and came in the front door of his faculty's library, he fled out the back door with as many books as he could carry. Soon afterward, he was banished to a farm in southwestern China for some years before he could return to Shanghai and resume his university post. The professor then turned to Don Henry and asked, "And what is it that you do?"

"I'm the head of the Voice of America newsroom in Washington."

"You are from V-O-A? I owe my life to you."

"How's that . . . why is that?"

When I was about ten, I started listening to your Chinese-language broadcasts and the English lessons on them. Then I graduated to the very slowly delivered simple form of English you broadcast, called Special English [a 1,500-word vocabulary, a single idea per sentence]. Special English opened up a whole new world to me: American history, science, space news, literature, as well as daily news from everywhere on Earth.

I then moved up what I call a ladder of learning, once again, to your standard English broadcasts, which kept me up to date on everything under the sun. By the time I turned sixteen, I had pretty well mastered English, and had learned a great deal more, too. I took an entrance exam to the university—only 1 to 2 percent of us go to a university in my country—and I passed it easily. I graduated, was hired as an assistant professor of literature. I later became the head of my department. You are from V-O-A? I owe my life to you!*

The professor's experience—getting the latest news, accurate and complete, and learning "a great deal more" as well—is familiar to listeners of many nationalities in many other places.

*Don Henry, briefing to Voice of America staff, 1986.

than expected flocked to Tiananmen and, eventually, to plazas in many cities throughout China. After all, as Shen Tong (one of the movement leaders) later told a Smithsonian Institution–VOA symposium in Washington, there had been smaller student demonstrations in the provinces every year throughout the 1980s.[2] The revolution was already there; international broadcasters such as VOA simply provided a communications link among its many parts.

The people of VOA tracked the expanding wildfire. They double-checked each event in a burgeoning movement, which ultimately attracted workers as well as students, seasoned Chinese journalists as well as Communist Party functionaries, farmers as well as city dwellers. Overnight, after mid-April of that Beijing spring, the Voice's news bureau in the Chinese capital suddenly found itself filing reports from early dawn until after midnight to Washington[3] for broadcast back into China and to all areas of the world, including Eastern Europe and the Soviet Union.

NO "BACK-ALLEY GOSSIP," PLEASE

The Voice's staff in Washington also kept pace to sort out fact from fiction. This was essential in China, where *xiao dao xiao xi* (back-alley gossip or little road news, a gentle term for rumors) was in full flower in the spring of 1989. Two particular groups of VOA experts worked around the clock together to get it straight in Washington before broadcasting accounts of the day's events.

The *Central News Division* screened thousands of words daily: international wire-service files, reports of its own correspondents, advisories from the Chinese Branch, monitored transcripts of official broadcasts from China, reaction from world capitals, briefings at the White House and State Department, hearings on Capitol Hill. The VOA's time-honored two-source rule was standard practice. Unless witnessed or verified on the scene by a field reporter or coming from an official statement at home or abroad, the newsroom insisted, as it had for years and does to this day, on two independently corroborating sources before broadcasting the information. Texts of newsroom-produced items or incoming correspondent reports and backgrounders then were transmitted electronically in English to VOA language services located in widely dispersed offices within the Washington headquarters building.[4]

The *Chinese Branch* accessed this central file on its personal-computer workstations, translating and adapting the latest texts from the central newsroom and adding its country and audience expertise to the final product. Here, too, the two-source rule was paramount, as the branch winnowed through voiced reports phoned in by its own correspondents and stringers in Beijing and throughout China. During the Beijing spring, the Chinese Branch received scores of unsolicited telephone tips on events in the capital and far-flung cities of its audience area. It sorted through these tips, painstakingly cross-checking the accounts with those of the newsroom, before stepping into nearby Studio 10 to broadcast the information to a Chinese-speaking world hungry for news.

GEARING UP FOR A SUMMIT, AND MUCH MORE

Within a few days after April 15, events in China accelerated at an all-consuming pace. All consuming, that is, for demonstrators in dozens of Chinese cities; for the Chinese government, which was about to host a summit with Soviet leader Mikhail Gorbachev; and for the VOA team in Washington and Beijing.

In the Chinese capital, there was a serious-looking foreign correspondent with a trademark pair of glasses and a neatly trimmed dark beard soon to be tinged with gray, VOA bureau chief Al Pessin. Pessin was a seasoned journalist by 1989, having served VOA in New York, Islamabad, and Hong Kong. He and his assistant, a tireless and irrepressible freelance reporter, Heidi Chay, almost single-handedly took on the early challenge of field reporting. They were on the front lines of a revolution. A diary of its events might read like this:

April 22, 1989: "In the morning," Pessin recalls,

I would go out to the campuses to learn of the student protesters' plans. After covering the early part of their day, I'd return to the bureau to begin preparing reports for VOA's evening broadcasts. Meanwhile, Heidi would head for the campuses or accompany the protest marchers, or later, go to Tiananmen Square to talk with the strikers. Later in the day, she would phone the office with highlights of interviews she had done as well as "on the street" features and news reports. In the evening, I'd drive around checking roadblocks that Chinese citizens had set up to protect the students on Tiananmen Square from arrests by the army or police.[5]

April 25, 1989: Pessin's apartment overlooks Chang An Boulevard, the main thoroughfare leading through the center of Beijing to Tiananmen Square. From there, he sees exuberant and expanding crowds, surging down the boulevard, and banners with news in Chinese characters beginning to appear. Many of them quote VOA news directly, despite the fact that the *People's Daily* and other Chinese media are still, at the end of April, reporting the daily developments. "Yet the crowds kept swelling," Pessin recalls. "There were streams and streams of humanity . . . two kilometers long . . . I remember that most vividly. . . . I abandoned any thought of taxis to get to the square, and rented a bicycle to get to and from the scene of the action to the bureau."[6]

REINFORCEMENTS FOR A BEIJING SPRING

April 27, 1989: The VOA newsroom in Washington, headed by News and English Broadcasts editor in chief and former White House correspondent Philomena Jurey and Chief of News Diane Doherty, dispatches reinforcements to aid the twenty-four-hour-a-day Beijing bureau operation. VOA correspondents David Dyar from Bangkok and Phil Kurata from Tokyo are the first to take up successive assignments there. Several weeks later, Pessin's predecessor as chief of the Beijing bureau, veteran VOA correspondent Mark Hopkins, is flown in from Boston.[7]

April 30, 1989: VOA expands its on-site reportorial strength even more. It sends Chinese and Russian Branch correspondents to Beijing to cover the student demonstrations and to position themselves for the Sino-Soviet summit in mid-May. Betty Tseu of the Chinese Branch and Nik Sorokin of the Russian Branch add to the team of foot soldiers filing reports by telephone back to Washington.

May 2, 1989: Tseu visits Shanghai and notes what she called "the grassroots nature" of the movement. Teachers join their students. Army helicopters fly overhead, but some troops on the ground appear to support the demonstrators. "When the workers began to join in," Tseu recalls, "that's when the government really began to get scared."[8]

HUMANITY PARTS LIKE WATERS OF THE RED SEA

May 4, 1989: Back in Beijing, the demonstrators seize on a key anniversary, the date of the first Chinese student protests of 1919, to build their ranks to unprecedented proportions. In these days, a half decade before the advent of lightweight portable satellite telephones, Tseu, too, rents a bike to get to and from Tiananmen Square to the bureau. She gathers the news, records interviews, and phones them back to Washington from the bureau. She straps her Sony 5000 recorder on the back of the bike. Chinese by birth, she initially blends into the outer edges of the crowd, a virtual unknown. But once her identity as a VOA reporter spreads through the plaza, the sea of humanity parts like the waters of the Red Sea,[9] permitting Tseu easy access to the very heart of Tiananmen. That is the loudspeaker platform of the uprising leaders, among them Wang Dan, Shen Tong, Chai Ling, and Wu'er Kaixi.

May 10–14, 1989: In Washington, the captains of the Chinese-language broadcasts begin planning contingencies. They are Ivan Klecka, chief of the East Asia and Pacific Division, and David Hess, chief of the Chinese Branch. The two U.S. foreign service information officers are constantly debating the next possible turns in the Tiananmen story. Hess says: "Stability is everything to Deng Xiaopeng and the leaders; if they lose Beijing, they lose it all." Klecka sets up an alert system, reinforces contract staff, and pounds on the doors of his bosses in the program director's office to get resources for expansion of the Chinese broadcast schedule beyond eight hours a day, if needed.[10]

"A RADIO TO THEIR EARS"

"Nothing we can say," according to Klecka,

> is as compelling as a crowd of Beijing students cheering a VOA reporter, or driving up and down toward Tiananmen Square, a radio to their ears, shouting VOA news bulletins to their compatriots, or transcribing VOA newscasts on big-character posters hung all over town. The *Washington Post* the other day quoted a Chinese worker saying he heard two versions of events, one from VOA and another from Chinese People's Radio, so he decided to make the four-hour trip to see for himself. Once he got to Beijing, he realized the VOA coverage was accurate. He stayed to join the demonstration for press freedom.[11]

May 15, 1989: Mikhail Gorbachev arrives for a four-day state visit to China, the first Sino-Soviet summit since the rupture of relations between the two Communist giants in the late 1950s. This reinvigorates the demonstrations, which had lagged a bit after the May 4 anniversary. The demonstrators are blocking the streets of the capital well beyond Tiananmen. Initially, they organized to protest corruption and lack of openness in government. Now, with the international press on hand, they increasingly blend prodemocracy themes with their demands for Chinese government reforms and a dialogue. The resulting chaos, as some army and police units help the students, disrupts the summit.

May 18, 1989: It has been more than a month since the movement began. The square is becoming squalid, with the seemingly never-ending vigil generating piles of trash, and the leaders now on an extended hunger strike at the center of the action. Popular support is growing for the demonstrators. Bellhops and waitresses in Beijing hotels, Betty Tseu recalls, are organizing convoys of fresh water and food to students at Tiananmen. Even village peasants flocking to Beijing are bringing in pastries on bikes, and others nearby are carrying in *man tou*, steaming hot buns, to feed the masses.[12]

GLASNOST IN THE HEART OF BEIJING,
A LABYRINTH OF TUNNELS UNVEILED

VOA Beijing correspondent Al Pessin is assigned as a pool reporter for all the networks to cover a famous handshake between host Deng Xiaoping and visiting Soviet president Mikhail Gorbachev in the Great Hall of the People. He is among a small contingent of news people present for the arrival of the official guests. The group is able to hold a conversation with Raisa Gorbachev, wife of the Soviet leader. Asked if the official party had trouble getting from venue to venue because of the demonstrations, Raisa Gorbachev replies: "Oh no, we haven't seen much because we've been riding around in the tunnels." Before her comment, the existence of a network of tunnels linking various government buildings in the Chinese capital had been suspected, but was considered a state secret.*

*Alan Pessin, interview with author, Washington, D.C., September 14, 2000.

May 19, 1989: A moderate in the government's hierarchy, prime minister and reform architect Zhao Ziyang, meets at 4:00 A.M. in Tiananmen Square with demonstration leaders in an unsuccessful last-minute effort to get them to call off their protests. The world learns from secret documents published in 2001 that Zhao later that morning requested three days' sick leave.[13] This evolved into a permanent house arrest. The regime hardliners thus end his once-promising political career.

AN OMINOUS PHONE TIP

May 20, 1989: The number of phone calls to the Beijing bureau and to the Chinese Branch in Washington from Chinese men and women in the streets has now swelled to at least a hundred per day, including tips about what is going on in communities across the land. Such citizen advisories, under VOA's two-source rule, could not be accepted uncritically and broadcast back to China; they had to be matched by on-scene observations of journalists or contract reporters. But in the wee hours of the morning, Al Pessin recalls, a farmer phoning the bureau from the northwestern outskirts of Beijing reported that People's Liberation Army (PLA) units were moving toward the city.[14] It was just eight hours before the first signal that the government's patience had run out: a formal declaration of martial law.

May 21, 1989: Back at the Washington headquarters, irrepressible Frequency Division officer Phil Goodwin gets on the phone in his fourth-floor warren and places an urgent call to the office of the program director. He barks: "I've got something you'll want to hear. It may even make your day, or maybe break it!" He hastens downstairs to the third-floor executive suite to play a cassette of an evening broadcast of VOA Chinese monitored in Hong Kong. It begins with the famous "Yankee Doodle" signature tune, and then a reading of the news. About eighteen seconds in, a telltale noise begins to creep in behind the female newscaster's reading. The noise sounds like a cross between a buzz saw and a woodpecker with weak tonsils. At first it is faint, barely audible. But then the obnoxious sound swells. The announcer's voice becomes steadily more difficult to hear. Ten seconds later, it is inaudible. The People's Republic of China (PRC) is jamming America's Voice for the first time since shortly before Sino-American relations were established in 1979. Martial law one day, jamming a few hours later. The hardliners seem to be gaining the upper hand. (Those secret Party documents that reached the West a decade later quote China's de facto leader, Deng Xiaoping, as saying about this time: "We have to be decisive. . . . How can we progress if things are in an utter mess?")[15]

May 22, 1989: Monitors report that jamming of three of VOA's five frequencies in morning and evening Chinese broadcasts is nearly total in some areas of the PRC.[16] But this skywave jamming, the most intense and most effective, fails to hinder reception in many cities where prodemocracy advocates assemble. Richard Baum, a professor at the University of California, Los Angeles, was in Nanjing at the time. Eight years later, he recalled for an audience at the Annenberg School for Communication, University of Southern California:

> I remember vividly being in the city of Nanjing at the town square twenty-four hours after martial law was declared, when the Chinese government had imposed a news blackout on all the official central radio, so that there could be no contradictory stories about what was going on in Tiananmen. And during those days, young boys, teenage youths in Nanjing, would climb up in the top of shade trees in the town square with their boom boxes. They had recorded the latest VOA broadcasts in Chinese, and played them on their boom boxes to tens of thousands of people below. And people in the crowds, in the outer edges of the crowds, would write down the commentaries and put them on posters so that people passing by could read them. It was an extraordinary example of the power of unofficial voices in a place like China.[17]

BEYOND THE INNER KINGDOM, OTHER WALLS TO TOPPLE

May 23, 1989: The news from China is having an impact far beyond its borders. So, evidently, is the reporting of VOA Russian Branch reporter Nik Sorokin, now on temporary duty in Beijing.

In Washington, President George Bush receives Wan Li, chairman of the standing committee of the Chinese National People's Congress, at the White House. The two leaders meet from 2:30 to 3:30 P.M. Li briefs the president on the Sino-Soviet summit and on the prodemocracy demonstrations in China. Bush, according to a White House statement, reiterates the U.S. commitment to democracy around the world and adds: "I urge nonviolence and restraint in your present situation. I urge that the Voice of America not be jammed, and that reporters be given open access."[18]

May 24, 1989: In the ionosphere over and around China, the game of electronic cat and mouse begins in earnest. To counter jamming, VOA adds to its five frequencies assigned to Chinese, scheduling three new ones: two on shortwave, and, for a half hour daily, one on the powerful 1,000-kilowatt (1 megawatt) medium-wave transmitter in the Philippines. That Poro Point medium-wave signal is available on the standard broadcast band in car radios in southeastern China. These technical enhancements are intended to strengthen the eight and a half program hours daily in Mandarin Chinese, and the half hour daily of Cantonese, beamed to the mainland. The PRC jammers do not catch on for a few hours, but some of the new shortwave frequencies are tracked and blocked about nineteen hours after they are introduced.[19]

TRIMMING THE TRUTH ABOUT TIANANMEN

In Moscow, Soviet media are saying as little as possible about the story. A brief one-minute report on Vremya TV does concede, in this era of glasnost, that 1 million demonstrators from all strata of Chinese society and all regions of the country are now demanding an end to martial law. A leading Izvestia commentator, however, pulls no punches. Alexander Bovin characterizes what he called "poor Soviet media coverage of the prodemocracy demonstrations" in a country visited by Soviet leader Mikhail Gorbachev little more than a week earlier. "We are not showing the unprecedented scale of events," Bovin tells his viewers. He adds that details are lacking in Soviet media about the latest demands for the resignation of Deng Xiaoping and other Chinese leaders, a statement issued by Chinese army generals questioning martial law, and about what Bovin called "the danger of an uncontrolled chain reaction occurring." He adds that because of their scale, the events in China, unlike those in Poland, Yugoslavia, and Hungary, may have "a concrete effect on us."* Bovin should get a medal for prophetic powers. It is less than six months before the dismantling of the Berlin Wall.

*Quoted in Sergei Markov, "Soviet Media Say Little About Events in China" (USSR Division content analysis, May 23, 1989), 1.

In a Beijing-datelined dispatch, Jay Mathews of the *Washington Post* writes: "The Chinese language Voice of America broadcasts, because of their detail and balance, 'each day win more and more respect,' said one member of the movement for democracy, a son of a high Communist Party official. In the last few days, the Chinese government has paid them the backhanded compliment of resuming jamming on some frequencies."[20]

May 26, 1989: The temporary visas issued to Betty Tseu and Nik Sorokin are about to expire, and there is no way Chinese authorities will renew them. They leave China for Hong Kong or the United States, a little less than a week after the declaration of martial law.

May 27–30, 1989: An eerie calm settles on the capital city as the second week of martial law takes hold. It is "standoff time." The government has not yet deployed troops in massive numbers in Beijing. The student-led demonstrators are weary beyond measure. The perimeter of the Tiananmen crowd is shrinking. Audiences to international broadcasts (VOA and the BBC) surge as real news disappears from the internal media and announcers warn of the consequences to any citizen breaching martial-law regulations. Yet there is a tentativeness about it all, as the government continues to prepare for its next move.

THE GLOBAL MARKETPLACE OF NEWS AND INFORMATION

On May 30, 1989, *Boston Globe* assistant editor H. D. S. Greenway writes:

> The Voice of America has sixty million listeners in China. Chinese turn to the VOA because their own state-run news organizations are reluctant to report anything that may be politically sensitive. "Some news takes a long time to get to us, and some news we never hear," a student told the *New York Times*. "VOA helps us understand what's going on in our own country." There are several first-class international services, but none have the global reach or the reputation of the BBC and the VOA. The faith and trust that millions of people all over the world put into these two services is as touching as it is revealing.*

*H. D. S. Greenway, syndicated column, *Lexington (Kentucky) Herald*, May 30, 1989.

June 1, 1989: In the evening, Pessin ventures out onto Tiananmen Square, where the number of demonstrators has diminished to a few thousand hardy souls since the declaration of martial law. "The Deng–Gorbachev summit was well past," Pessin recalls, "and so was a meeting of the Asian Development Bank just completed in Beijing. I was out there on the square with a *Wall Street Journal* correspondent, and I remember remarking to her: 'This is a stupid place to be . . . we should be out on the edge of the square in case something happens.'"

June 2, 1989: Even more ominous for Pessin and other foreign correspondents, the Chinese government has tightened regulations governing their coverage of demonstrations or military movements. They are also prohibited from making appointments with any Chinese citizens and from receiving any information that could be seen as "inciting citizens" under martial law. VOA News and English Broadcasts editor in chief Jurey issues a note to the newsroom staff that says, in part: "VOA will continue to cover the news developments in China. We must be extremely careful to maintain our accuracy, integrity and credibility. If Chinese authorities notice one (even minor) error in our broadcasts, they could use it as an opportunity to take some action against VOA or Al Pessin. Our reports have been balanced and accurate so far. Let's keep them that way."[21]

THE MOMENT OF TRUTH IS AT HAND

June 3, 1989: In the early evening, Pessin receives a call from "a frantic young woman" informing VOA that she has been injured by soldiers who piled out of their vehicles, part of a hundred-truck convoy east of Beijing. The convoy, the anguished victim reports, had forced its way through a wall of people blocking the street, headed straight for Tiananmen Square. That was the first indication that the final assault was imminent. A few minutes later, the assignments desk in the VOA newsroom in Washington phones Pessin to alert him that some wire services are reporting troops on the move. They are moving in from the north, west, and east of Tiananmen, close to Pessin's apartment, and in a western central city neighborhood called Mu Shu Di. Military units now fill the streets and prevent Pessin from getting to the square.

June 4, 1989: Around midnight, Central China Time, gunfire erupts in the heart of the Chinese capital. Pessin keeps running on adrenalin and files reports copiously for each hourly deadline, well beyond the usual eighteen-hour day. There is panic in the streets. Someone brings a sobbing woman to the VOA bureau. She's shocked and very upset. When Al calms her down a bit, she tells him what happened as the square was cleared, and in neighborhoods surrounding it. There was shooting by soldiers, she confirms. She herself had dropped down on the square, and crawled off, with bullets buzzing overhead.[22] Pessin reports to Washington and to the world that the crackdown is now well under way.

In Washington, it is Saturday afternoon. The newsroom is alive with activity, as the news wires are hot with descriptions of the expanding carnage in Beijing. Extra news writers and editors are brought in to evaluate and write thousands of additional words about the events in Beijing. Chinese Branch chief David Hess is on the phone to the program director's office, pleading immediately for additional airtime for his service. "It's imperative," he says, "to get on the air even before our early-morning broadcast starts at 5:00 A.M. Beijing time to let our listeners know what is going on." Hess has mobilized his staff, canceled broadcasts in Cantonese, and brought in an extra dozen broadcasters to handle the programming expansion. I contact Director of Programs Sid Davis, who authorizes expanded airtime and frequencies. As his deputy, I go to work with VOA historian and programming specialist Barbara Schiele, who had urged the use of the Poro medium wave, and Goodwin, who consults his encyclopedic book of charts and sets the wheels in motion. VOA English news offers minute-by-minute updates. At 4:00 A.M., China time, VOA's Chinese Branch is on the air with translations of Pessin's reports and initial reactions from around the globe.[23]

UNCOMMON VALOR, ON CHINA'S OWN AIRWAVES

Back in Beijing, the state-controlled media are going into high gear, denouncing the student leaders as renegades and alleging that the troops fired in self-defense. That is, with the exception of the English Service of Radio Beijing, the official international broadcaster of the People's Republic of China. A courageous announcer goes on the air with this announcement:

> This is Radio Beijing. Please remember June 3, 1989. The most tragic event happened in the Chinese capital, Beijing. Thousands of people, most of them innocent civilians, were killed by fully armed soldiers when they forced their way into the city. Among

the killed are our colleagues at Radio Beijing. The soldiers were riding on armored vehicles and used machine guns against thousands of local residents and students who tried to block their way. When the army convoys made a breakthrough, soldiers continued to spray their bullets indiscriminately at crowds in the street. . . . Radio Beijing's English department deeply mourns those who died in a tragic incident and appeals to all its listeners to join our protest for the gross violation of human rights and the most barbarous suppression of the people.

(Later, we learn that the announcer was apprehended by the authorities almost immediately and detained for several years in a villa near Beijing, where he was separated from his family and underwent an extended "reeducation" campaign.)[24]

THE BRIDGE OVER THE RIVER YANGTZE

June 4, 1989: Despite the crackdown, the situation in China remains fluid this Sunday, the morning after Tiananmen. Can Deng Xiaoping and the hardliners count on support of People's Liberation Army units throughout the country? Do they have enough units to quell adverse reactions to the massacre in Beijing? The special VOA Mandarin "hot line" for phone tips from China remains active. Today, the service receives a call from several very excited listeners in Wuhan, the huge industrial city in the heart of the country. The callers say that thousands of citizens have crowded for twelve hours onto the strategically important Yangtze River bridge linking northern and southern China at Wuhan to block all traffic (including PLA tanks moving northward toward Beijing). Chinese Branch chief Hess feels bound by the two-source rule. He waits for several hours before news agency reports confirm the caller's tip, and then inserts a recording of the eyewitness account into the next news bulletin.[25]

Despite jamming and the Tiananmen massacre, the calls on the hot line continue. John Harbaugh of the Chinese Branch reports:

We have received many calls from the PRC—Chengdu, Changsha, Nanchang, Shenyang, Hangzhou, Nanjing, Zhejiang province and several from Wuhan. The operator tells us many other calls are backed up. The callers all claim they are having great difficulty receiving our signals, but we are getting through. . . . The callers express shock and disbelief and great anger that the army and government have done this. Many state that they know of this tragedy only through VOA. Over and over, they thank us for informing them about these events, even as their voices break into sobs. They stress that we are the only source of news they can trust.[26]

THE DESPERATE LISTENERS REWARDED

June 5, 1989: During the weekend, the News Division reinforces its Beijing staff by quickly authorizing travel there by VOA correspondents whose multiple entry visas had been approved weeks or months earlier by PRC embassies in other countries. Phil Kurata of Tokyo and Mark Hopkins, the former Beijing bureau chief now based in Boston, head for the Chinese capital. The office of the program director works with the Frequency Division to expand the broadcasts. The decision is made to add two hours a day in Mandarin Chinese, and to restore a separate Cantonese stream of programming. VOA's Chinese Branch is now on the air for eleven and a half hours a day, up from nine hours daily before the Saturday-night crackdown.[27]

June 6, 1989: There are indications of continuing unease in some sectors of the PLA, with clashes reported between units on the outskirts of Beijing. The *New York Times* reports that units of the Twenty-seventh Army, supporting hardline Chinese leaders, are taking up defensive positions. It notes that the Chinese Thirty-eighth Army refused earlier to attack student demonstrators and that news of the violence in Beijing by now has spread to most cities in China via shortwave broadcasts of VOA and the BBC. The *Times* quotes a Western diplomat as saying: "The threat of a civil war can no longer be excluded."[28]

The American embassy in Beijing estimates that there are about 2,000 television receiver dishes in various military installations throughout the country. If they can be reached with news of the massacre and the worldwide condemnation that followed, then some in the army might be hesitant to assist the hardliners in tightening their grip on China. VOA director of programs Davis and the Chinese Branch consult with Worldnet Television, the United States Information Agency's global TV network, about putting pictures of VOA newscast readers along with text and voice up on a satellite for possible reception at these critically important Chinese military outposts. Worldnet swings into action.

June 7, 1989: At ten o'clock this Tuesday morning, the area outside the VOA newsroom is alive with activity. VOA Chinese-language broadcasters are reading from scripts in the adjacent Studio 29. Outside, Chinese-character texts of their newscasts are being scrolled by hand by other Chinese staff to match their words as delivered. They are shown, teletext style, across the base of the TV screens on which the readers can be seen. This is so speakers of other Chinese dialects, who can read standard *putonghua* Mandarin Chinese but have difficulty understanding the words, can fully comprehend what is being said. The images, and words, are beamed more than 98,000 miles through a series of electronic paths via an Indian Ocean satellite to the heart of China. Production is primitive, but, overnight, Tiananmen has thrust VOA into the television age.[29]

PIERCING THE BAMBOO CURTAIN, AS SETBACKS MOUNT

There is no way of knowing how many Chinese military personnel are watching, but as an added way around jamming, VOA and Worldnet Television beam the entire eleven and a half hours daily of Chinese-language broadcasts in audio on a TV subcarrier; it can be received, even if images are not shown, via the TV receive-only dishes in Chinese military and government installations. Ten hours of VOA English also reach China each day via shortwave, unjammed, as do broadcasts in Chinese and English from the powerful VOA medium-wave megawatt transmitter in the Philippines. Try as it might, China cannot hide from its own citizens the facts about the postmidnight massacre at the square and surrounding neighborhoods.

June 8, 1989: Despite the technical blitz and reports that as many as 3,000 may have been killed during the massacre in the heart of Beijing, the People's Liberation Army appears to be consolidating its hold on the country. In Washington, calls received via the "hot line" in the Chinese Branch begin to decline; a week after the massacre, they cease altogether. In Beijing, phone calls received by the VOA news bureau turn nasty. Instead of providing news tips and cheering the correspondents on, the callers spout obscenities at the correspondents, often in similar, obviously scripted sentences. They accuse VOA of spreading "counterrevolutionary propaganda."[30] The secret documents released years later quote a State Security Ministry report as saying: "Right from the founding of our People's Republic, VOA's Chinese-language service has been an instrument of the U.S. government's psychological warfare against our country."[31]

All this, as the state-controlled Chinese media escalate an information barrage of their own, one that Pessin describes later as "perhaps the most flagrant propaganda campaign ever inflicted on any populace anywhere." He quotes some typical passages: "A serious counterrevolutionary rebellion took place in the capital last night. . . . No one was killed in Tiananmen Square. . . . Soldiers never fired at civilians."

"The Chinese propaganda apparatus outdid itself," Pessin adds,

> manufacturing evidence to support the party line. Videotapes were edited to show outraged citizens committing violence against troops and military vehicles, without showing what had provoked the attacks. The burned and disemboweled body of one soldier was shown on television repeatedly, his eyes fixed in an agonized gaze, a military hat perched on his head. A front-page editorial in the *People's Daily* attacks VOA. The brain-bending propaganda blitz was strong enough to sow doubt even in the minds of some eyewitnesses. . . . One young teacher who had taken food and medicine to students on the square told a colleague a few days after the massacre that it had never happened.[32]

TIME FOR A BREAK?

June 9, 1989: Pessin continues to file virtually around the clock, but the arrival of Hopkins and Kurata eases his burden a bit after days of unrelenting deadlines and little sleep. Pessin evacuated his wife, Audrey, and infant son, Sam, to Bangkok three days earlier. (Many months before the crisis, Audrey had broken the gloom of Beijing by starting an exercise class, two play groups, and a homemade ice cream business. And when the shooting started, Audrey braved the streets to take Sam to safety, the day before the Chinese army shot up a building next to the Pessins' apartment in a residential compound. The real loss to friends, Pessin commented later, was Audrey's ice cream.)[33]

Pessin is now able to take a lunch break at Jian Guo Hotel in the center of Beijing. Time to relax. But he can't help overhearing a conversation that an American professor is holding at an adjacent table. The professor is giving a friend an eyewitness account of what had occurred

"It Was Just Something . . .
Something They Couldn't Really Believe"

PESSIN: The professor and his friends moved on to the bridge at Mu Shu Di, the site of one of the bloodiest confrontations that night. As they approached the bridge, they took cover along the banks of a canal.

PETERSON: We could see the soldiers going over the bridge, firing into the people. . . . We couldn't see at that point what they were firing at, but once we got to the bridge, we could climb up the bank. We saw them shooting at the people. It was pretty scary there.

PESSIN: When the soldiers had passed, and the shooting had stopped, Professor Peterson and his friends climbed up on the bridge, where they saw a sight they will not soon forget. The professor did not count the bodies, but he watched them being piled onto ambulances, and on trucks, and taken away. After a while, all that was left was the carnage. The professor said that one thing that stood out in his mind was the reaction of the people on the Mu Shu Di bridge.

PETERSON: People there, they were standing there just expressionless, just like they were zombies, sort of paralyzed, you know, because nobody thought they would shoot into the people. They thought they would shoot over their heads. It was just something . . . something they couldn't really believe.*

*Alan L. Heil, Jr., transcript of Alan Pessin's award-winning report, VOA News Branch, June 15, 1989.

in one of the many neighborhoods surrounding Tiananmen in the early morning of June 4. Pessin approaches the professor a few minutes later, introduces himself, and asks if his new acquaintance, Sheridan Peterson, would be willing to repeat the account for VOA. Indeed he would.

June 10, 1989: Central Chinese Radio and the state-run Xinhua News Agency jointly attack VOA's credibility. Pessin telexes the following account to Editor in Chief Jurey:

FYI, Chinese radio broadcast this morning the text of an alleged letter from a university teacher, as follows:

"During the last several days, I was very angry after listening to VOA broadcasts. Disregarding press morality, VOA fabricated various kinds of lies to deceive the masses who did not know the truth, and especially the fabrication of the rumor that the army used machine guns to kill over three thousand people and that many people were killed by tanks which ran over them. . . . I am an eyewitness of the incident and stayed the whole night of June 3 in Tiananmen Square. In the whole process of clearing the square, the PLA men did not open fire on the crowd of people on the square. . . . VOA's irresponsible lies can only fan up greater antagonism and hatred. I believe that anyone hoping for calmness in society and showing concern for the future of the motherland cannot tolerate such deception. The facts will expose their lies."[34]

A RENDEZVOUS WITH SUPPRESSION

June 14, 1989: The telephone rings in the VOA Beijing bureau, shortly after noon. Al Pessin recounts:[35]

A woman speaking excellent English informed me I was "summoned to an interview" at the Foreign Affairs Office of the Beijing Municipal People's government at 4:30 that afternoon.

At the appointed hour, a young official met me outside the gate of the city government's tree-shaded compound, just a block from Tiananmen Square. I was ushered into a high-ceilinged, wood-paneled reception room, where I was momentarily blinded by the light of a television camera. I was introduced to Mr. Li Jiyuan, deputy chief of the city's Foreign Affairs Office. He did not offer to shake my hand and there was none of the usual pouring of tea. I was directed to a sofa on the far side of the room, facing the one on which Mr. Li sat.

Seeing their television camera, as well as a tape recorder and a photographer taking still pictures, I took my tape recorder out of my pocket, put it front of me on the coffee table and turned it on.

High Drama in City Hall, Chinese Style

"Mr. Pessin," Mr. Li began, speaking Chinese. An interpreter translated sentence by sentence. "I am authorized, today, to summon you here and announce a decision to you."

Mr. Li said I had "engaged in illegal news gathering" under martial law, which had been declared more than three weeks earlier. Reading from a prepared statement, he accused me of "distorting facts, spreading rumors and instigating turmoil and counterrevolutionary rebellion." He said my reporting was a "brazen" violation of martial law regulations, which virtually prohibited all news gathering and reporting. Mr. Li said my alleged crimes had caused "grave consequences."

Then he came to the point.

"I am hereby authorized to make the following announcement to you: You are ordered to leave China within seventy-two hours, starting from now."

I found myself thinking, "So this is what it's like behind the scenes when something like this happens." I also found myself taking note of the surroundings for future reference: the dark wood paneling, the high, white ceiling, the shabby, tan-colored sofas, Mr. Li's beige safari suit, open at the neck. . . . Mr. Li brought me back to reality by asking, "Did you hear me clearly?"

A Correspondent Under Fire Responds

"Yes, I heard you clearly," I responded. And I proceeded to ask several questions: Would my wife . . . be allowed to return to China to pack our things? Would I be allowed to return to China sometime in the future? What evidence was there for the charges against me?

Mr. Li could not answer the first two questions. In response to the third, he brandished a two-day-old newspaper, which carried an anti-VOA commentary.

I also asked how the Beijing city government could expel me from all of China, especially since I was in the country under press credentials issued by the Foreign Ministry. Mr. Li said that, in effect, under martial law the city government was empowered to do anything it wanted to control foreign correspondents. He also said he didn't want to answer any more questions.

I requested permission to make a brief statement, and he agreed. I told him the Chinese press accounts of VOA programs were "inaccurate and distorted."

"As is well known [a favorite phrase of Chinese officials] to our tens of millions of listeners in China and around the world," I continued, "VOA does not report rumors. We report the best, most accurate, the fairest and the best-balanced news we possibly can.

"The only motive that we have is to tell the truth as best we can," I said. And, making a point of looking directly at him, I added, "Governments do not always like that."

In a brief response, Mr. Li rejected my statement, repeated parts of his, told me VOA had made many Chinese people "angry" and ended the meeting.

(Security police at the encounter insist on confiscating a tape that Pessin made of the proceedings. Pessin refuses. He stalls them by saying that he has to call his superiors, and then has to wait for them to call back. During the intervening moments, he quickly transcribes the tape, and then, at the insistence of the Chinese, hands it over shortly before leaving for his office.)

ONLY IN CHINA

Later the same evening, Pessin follows the instructions of Li's assistant and presents his passport and residence permit at the Public Security Bureau. The residence card is confiscated, and his visa, valid for another month, is replaced with a stamp valid for seventy-two hours. "I had to laugh," Pessin later wrote, "when the woman behind the counter charged me the equivalent of $5.50 for the new stamp. This is the country which charges families for the bullets used to execute convicted criminals."

June 17, 1989: Chinese security men (and Western television crews) film Pessin's departure for Hong Kong with John Pomfret of the Associated Press, who also was expelled. The two journalists are shown pushing baggage carts through customs. On arriving in the Crown Colony, Pessin is asked by waiting reporters to make a statement: "The [Chinese] government has accused me of inciting turmoil and counterrevolutionary rebellion. That's not what I do. What I do is report the news."[36]

THE POST-TIANANMEN BALANCE SHEET

And so, just two weeks after the massacre, the Deng Xiaoping regime appeared to have scored a decisive victory over the prodemocracy activists. The government had restored "order" throughout the world's most populous country, at a heavy cost. But had it, in the long run, stamped out all the sparks generated by the information beamed to the activists from abroad during and after the Beijing spring of 1989? Hardly.

Hours after the expulsion order, VOA director Richard W. Carlson expressed outrage at Pessin's removal. "They're mad at the messenger. . . . They're trying to jam us intellectually as well as technically," he told Reuters. "Neither approach is going to work."[37] Years later, VOA East Asia and Pacific Division director Kelu Chao, an editor in the Chinese Branch in 1989, remarked: "Tiananmen aroused the branch, which then was a sleeping lion. It was transformed overnight . . . live broadcasts, newsmaker interviews, scrapping of many prerecorded programs . . . everyone working hard around the clock."[38]

The Beijing bureau never closed. Hopkins continued to report until the Chinese expelled him, too, on July 8. But then Chay, who rushed back from a vacation break in Alaska, continued to file. Correspondent Stephanie Mann Nealer was accredited five and a half months later as VOA's Beijing bureau chief.

Back in Washington, VOA programming and technical specialists teamed up to get even more programming and facts into the People's Republic of China. By June 26, VOA hired a dozen new Chinese-language broadcasters and expanded its Mandarin broadcasts to twelve hours a day. Later that summer, frequencies were added from transmitters in southern Germany to increase the challenge to jammers. In subsequent years, America greatly strengthened its broadcast voice to Asia by

- Establishing the Tibetan Service in 1991, heard daily by the Dalai Lama and hundreds of thousands of listeners in the kingdom and surrounding areas of the PRC and northern India (chapter 14).
- Inaugurating a weekly VOA and TV simulcast call-in program, China Forum, in 1994, the first of seven weekly programs added in the next seven years. By 2000, VOA's Chinese Branch—its largest foreign-language unit—had completely reshaped and reenergized its operations. It was a multimedia operation (radio, television, and Internet). Its twelve-hour daily schedule included expert interviews and in-depth reports on Chinese, global, and U.S. events—all backed by a research information center.
- Creating a Mandarin-language Web site containing texts of VOA newscasts twice daily, which, according to East Asia and Pacific Division program manager Jay Henderson, received 100,000 hits a day by the turn of the century.[39] The weekly radio audience was estimated

at 8 to 10 million, despite China's continued jamming of many VOA frequencies carrying Mandarin Chinese broadcasts and the government's blocking of VOA, CNN, the *New York Times*, and others from the public Internet server in the PRC.

WU'ER KAIXI IN "THE DEVIL'S DEN"

All this activity, accompanied by America's establishment in the mid-1990s of the separate Radio Free Asia, can be traced back to Tiananmen. After the massacre, there were authentic voices on the lasting impact of VOA's reportage from the people who mattered most, those in the Chinese audience. Wu'er Kaixi, one of the students who rallied activists from the now-famous platform at the heart of the plaza, escaped his homeland and visited VOA's Chinese Branch on August 2, 1989. He had this exchange with the staff:

> WU'ER KAIXI: I believe that the Voice of America truly strives for freedom of the press. It truly does tell the Chinese people the whole, true story. I believe that VOA did not "agitate." VOA is quite neutral. I wish VOA would broadcast reports that are more partisan toward the People's movement. However, I must admit that your attitude of neutrality is even more admirable.
>
> VOA STAFF MEMBER JACKSON CHOU: The Chinese government accuses us of creating rumors. Do any of our staffers look like devils to you?
>
> WU'ER KAIXI: I think it's very strange that their media are going to such great lengths to try to describe just how VOA spreads rumors. All they accomplish is to give VOA some free advertising. Overall, VOA's credibility will grow even higher because of this campaign to discredit it.[40]

A PHONE CALL FOR THE AGES

Wu'er Kaixi's comments suggest that no authority can imprison peoples' curiosity, or their hopes and dreams for a better life. At an awards ceremony in December 1989, Al Pessin recalled one of his last phone conversations at the VOA Beijing bureau when another voice spoke out for the soul of China:

This call came the day after I was ordered to leave, while I was packing the things from my desk, as a matter of fact. It began, as had the angry anti-VOA calls of the last few days, with the caller asking whether he had reached the Voice of America. Thinking it was another obscene call, I almost hung up.

But I didn't. The excited caller went on to make sure he had *me* on the telephone and then, after a nervous pause, he said: "Don't be discouraged."

Here was a young man risking his freedom, perhaps his life, to call me to urge me not to be discouraged. I had only been expelled from China, sorry to leave but heading for freedom, family, and friends. The young man on the telephone, who wisely identified himself only as a student at a university in Beijing, had just seen his friends gunned down, arrested, or forced into hiding and his hopes impaled on the bayonets of the People's Liberation Army.

And *he* was telling *me* not to be discouraged.

I was at a loss for words. After what seemed like a long time, I finally managed to say: "Don't *you* be discouraged."

He needed no time to collect his thoughts for a response. His instantaneous reply was, "We will *never* be discouraged."[41]

After Tiananmen, VOA veteran and China specialist Jerry Stryker remarked that "1989 showed how far the Voice has come. In the old days, it never would have covered an event that thoroughly, that completely."[42] The Voice's transformation from a wartime propaganda agency, at its birth, to a respected news source half a century later is a remarkable story. How better to begin than with a glimpse at the early years.

2

The Struggle to
Get It Straight

THE EARLY YEARS

We bring you Voices from America. Today, and daily from
now on, we shall speak to you about America and the war. The
news may be good for us. The news may be bad. But we shall
tell you the truth.
—William Harlan Hale, first VOA broadcast, in Pirsein,
The Voice of America

We are not in the business to amuse, entertain or simply
inform our listeners. Nor are we in business because news is an
end in itself. The United States is in the midst of a serious
struggle for the mind of mankind and the only purpose of the
News Branch as well as the entire Voice of America is to contribute toward winning that struggle.
—*This Is Your Job*, VOA News Branch stylebook

During the first decade, the struggle to get it straight was chaotic and at
times heroic. The Voice of America went on the air seventy-nine days
after the attack on Pearl Harbor and the entry of the United States into
World War II, the very reason for VOA's creation. Then, after the
century's most terrible war, there was demobilization and the advent of
the nation's longest struggle "for the mind of mankind," the Cold War.
The Voice survived its first dozen years, severely battered but intact.

The pressures on the Voice were intense:

• Internal pressures, as independent-minded, but extraordinarily
talented journalists, war refugees, dramatists, poets, philosophers, theater

producers, radio announcers, musicians, artists, linguists, and bureaucrats suddenly were thrust together overnight in crowded, makeshift offices and studios in New York City. They and their early successors had before them a fundamental goal: to win the war. How best to do it? Was the Voice primarily a purveyor of policy or straight news? Both approaches produced strong cross currents during the first dozen years and beyond.

• External pressures, fueled by rivalries among wartime and postwar agencies with an assortment of information policy agendas. At times their disputes aired on the front pages of major U.S. dailies and in the full glare of primitive early TV lights in congressional hearing rooms. America was the last major power to broadcast internationally. It was entering uncharted waters, finding its "sea legs" on the world's airwaves. By 1942, the Soviet Union had been at it for two decades; Britain, a decade; and France and Germany, nearly a decade.

THE WAR YEARS

This chapter in no way pretends to be a comprehensive history of VOA's first dozen years. But the times are worth recounting, because the broadcasters of the Voice then were the first in a procession of characters who forged its soul in the decades that followed.

• Playwright Robert Sherwood was a speechwriter for President Franklin D. Roosevelt. As early as 1939, he wrote: "There is a new decisive force in the human race, more powerful than all the tyrants. It is the force of massed thought, thought which has been provoked by words, strongly spoken."[1] A year later, Roosevelt named Nelson Rockefeller as the Coordinator of Inter-American Affairs (CIAA). Rockefeller, called the "grandfather of VOA,"[2] was charged in 1940 with broadcasting programs to Central and South America. The CIAA thus produced the first U.S. overseas broadcasts, even before the Voice went on the air. In mid-1941, Sherwood was named director of the new Foreign Information Service (FIS), which in the beginning was part of the Office of the Coordinator of Information (COI), VOA's first parent organization.

• Commentator Elmer Davis, a CBS news analyst and former *New York Times* editorial writer, was appointed by Roosevelt to create and direct a new agency called the Office of War Information (OWI). That was in June 1942, four months after VOA went on the air. OWI combined four existing government agencies and set up overseas and domestic branches. Sherwood reported to Davis and headed the overseas branch, the FIS, in New York.[3]

• Hollywood and Broadway producer, author and director John Houseman, another VOA pioneer and its first director, was famous for his production of *Julius Caesar*, with his Mercury Theater collaborator Orson Welles. The two were even better known for their radio adapta- tion of *The War of the Worlds*, so realistic in portraying a Martian landing on Earth that the program frightened listeners across the nation in the late 1930s into thinking that an actual invasion was under way. In later years, Houseman was famous for his portrayal of crusty old Professor Kingsfield in *The Paper Chase* television series. Houseman was named the head of FIS radio production in New York City—in effect, the first direc- tor of what was to become known in 1942 as the Voice of America. At VOA's fortieth-anniversary festivities, Houseman treated the staff to an amusing and lively account of VOA's early years.[4]

• *New York Herald Tribune* foreign news editor Joseph Barnes was head of the FIS Radio News and Features Division in New York and other cities. Educated at Harvard and a graduate of the London School of Economics and its Institute of Slavonic Languages, Barnes studied Russian in preparation for assignments successively as a *Tribune* foreign correspondent at posts that included Berlin, a *Tribune* foreign news editor, and, finally, head of all FIS newsrooms.

• Scripps-Howard newspaperman Edd Johnson had in the early 1940s monitored and analyzed foreign news for CBS. He was recruited by Barnes to join the overseas branch of FIS to set up a control desk, a style master responsible for a last-minute check on scripts before broadcast. That desk reviewed nearly all news and politically oriented scripts and had frequent disputes with the language desks.

• Presidential adviser James Warburg also was a major figure in the early years of the Voice. He was Sherwood's deputy in charge of psychological-warfare policy. Historian Holly Cowan Shulman has written: "Strong and driving, opinionated and sure of himself, Warburg possessed deep convictions about the nature and goals of the war, and with that, the goals of U.S. international propaganda."[5] Warburg became the key link between Washington, where wartime policy was made, and New York, where VOA broadcasts were produced. He took the train weekly to the nation's capital to attend meetings and bring the word back to Manhattan. Because of Warburg's domineering personality, and New York's distance from Washington, conflicts inevitably arose about the specifics of VOA's mission. As Shulman described it: "The leaders of the New York office were suspicious of Davis, the State Department, and the military."[6] The feeling was mutual.

Too Many Cooks?

The struggles extended far beyond executive branch departments in the New York–Washington channel. "Men from the Departments of State, War and Navy," Shulman explained, "met with the leaders of the Office of War Information at regular intervals. British propaganda leaders sent representatives to work in the OWI as well as political guidances to steer American propaganda toward British political goals.

"Congress reviewed the workings of the OWI and established limits beyond which the OWI was not to go. The Bureau of the Budget kept a watchful eye over the administration of the propaganda operation, and the Office of Strategic Services, the OSS, competed with the OWI for leadership in the field of propaganda. All this," Shulman concluded, "led inevitably to a second war, a domestic battle for control" of the U.S. overseas information program, including the Voice of America. Which would dominate: news with a twist or news that was, in the context of the times, more straightforward?

The Case Against "Weaseling"

"In reality," said John Houseman on VOA's fortieth anniversary,

> we had little choice. Inevitably, the news that the Voice of America would carry to the world in the first half of 1942 was almost all bad. As Japanese invasions followed one after another with sickening regularity and the Nazi armies moved ever deeper into Russia and the Near East, we would have to report our reverses without weaseling. Only thus could we establish a reputation for honesty that we hoped would pay off on that distant but inevitable day when we would start reporting our own invasions and victories.[7]

The Romanian-born Houseman and his colleagues worked for several weeks in early 1942 to put the first Voice broadcast in German on the air. Like much else about the Voice, there was, to quote John Chancellor, "a fine, antic sense of madness about the place." Only two studios were functional, at 270 Madison Avenue, New York. A few programs were prerecorded by the German-language staff (two editors and a secretary) in early February and transmitted by transatlantic cable to London for rebroadcast later over seven transmitters by the BBC's European Service. Others were put on acetate disks and flown across the Atlantic for retransmission.

Finally, the order came to go on the air, live and direct, from New York. William Harlan Hale, an author and international banker who spoke German with a slight American accent, was tapped for the first broadcast, point to point to London for relay to occupied Europe. VOA still celebrates its anniversary on February 24 because the first fifteen-minute program was largely prepared on that day. But it did not all come together in the studio until 2:30 A.M. on February 25, prime morning time in Europe. Hale recalled:

> By a strange irony, it so happened that before the broadcast, I had an invitation to dinner and a ballet and I was dressed accordingly for the occasion. Peter Kappel [another member of the German Service] was also in a dinner jacket because he previously had to attend a convention. It was the last ballet I saw during the war, but it was a strange affair to appear before the microphone speaking to the enemy fully dressed. . . . Some BBC people who were in the studio thought that we let them down. They said: "You didn't tell us that this was a black tie affair."[8]

Reinforcements were added quickly. Veteran commercial German shortwave broadcaster Robert Bauer recalls an all-night train ride on February 24/25 from Cincinnati. He and Italian shortwave broadcaster Georgio Padovano from station WLWO in Ohio had been drafted into government service. They arrived in New York late and weary, at ten o'clock in the morning on February 25. They stowed their bags, and were pressed immediately into the business of writing and producing the first shortwave program. They broadcast at noon, less than ten hours after Hale and Kappel's program.[9] Houseman recalled: "We went on the air . . . with no name, out of a cramped studio, on borrowed transmitters, with absolutely no direction from anyone as to what we should broadcast other than the truth."[10]

Hot Seats, Hot Words

The German broadcasts were followed, in the next day or so, by fifteen-minute programs in French, Italian, and English. Limited studio space at first forced announcers of different services to engage in what was later called "rat racing," switching out of and into still-warm chairs in front of studio microphones with only thirty seconds to spare between broadcasts. "I remember," veteran broadcaster and U.S. diplomat Walter Roberts recalled, "one hilarious situation at the three quarter hour when the French announcers left the studio and the Italian announcers walked in. Obviously, there must have been some kind of incident. Somebody must have stepped on someone's foot, or whatever. Anyway, five letter words in French were uttered, and these were replied to by words in Italian, which I'm sure were not overly flattering."[11]

Those early programs, although dedicated to offering facts as they were, reflected Houseman's own creative production skills. Veteran broadcaster Gene Kern recalls one program that Houseman often personally produced known as the *ACE, America Calling Europe*. This half-hour program had a narrator report the main aspects of that day's news, and other voices provide related details or quotes—unique among international broadcasters at the time.[12] The quarter-hour rotating newscasts in English, German, French, and Italian also followed Houseman's innovation of using multiple voices:

> VOICE 1: Laval is back in power in Vichy [Nazi-occupied France]. The American government will only make its position known when the composition of the Laval cabinet has been officially announced.
>
> VOICE 2: On the Russian front, Soviet troops have won several successes.
>
> VOICE 3: During the whole of yesterday, the RAF attacked German installations in Normandy.
>
> VOICE 4: President Roosevelt declared that the present war was a life and death struggle where the fate of our entire civilization was at stake.[13]

TRAVAILS OF A SIGNATURE TUNE

At the beginning, Robert Sherwood and John Houseman decided that the new network should have its own logo, or signature music, to be easily identifiable on the airwaves and to help listeners tuning in over-come German jamming. Fred Waring's Pennsylvanians were enlisted to record a rousing rendition of "The Battle Hymn of the Republic." According to Houseman:

> It sounded glorious, and we were very proud of it—until we were informed, by the British, this was exactly the same tune as an old German marching song. "Laura, Laura" it was called, to which Nazi troops had marched into Norway and the rest of Europe the year before. Sadly, we replaced Fred Waring and his Pennsylvanians with a spritely small band rendition of "Yankee Doodle," which Virgil Thompson orchestrated for us in a hurry, which became the signature of the Voice of America. It had the right spirit, and as we later discovered, the ability to pierce the organized bedlam of jamming.*

*John Houseman, "Excerpts from John Houseman's Speech," *USICA World*, April 1982, 6.

That was part of a VOA French Service newscast on April 15, 1942. A British observer found the station "hammy . . . rather like selling toothpaste, urgently."[14] This was in marked contrast to a lower-key, more straightforward sound that began to emerge about two years after the first Voice broadcast. By then, Houseman and his colleagues had moved on, and the Allies began to liberate populations in Europe and, later, the Pacific islands.

Other Early "Characters" of the Voice

The wartime Voice had incredible talent, as the enterprise swelled over the next two years to more than forty languages and hundreds of hours of broadcasts a week. "It was a wild place," recalled Kern, who later became VOA's New York and Munich bureau chief. "Every week a new language service began." The English features desk was headed by Dorothy Van Doren. Other luminaries scurrying down the corridors of 270 Madison Avenue included Virgil Thompson, Richard C. Hotelett, Roland

Winters, Burgess Meredith, Pierre Lazareff, and Yul Brynner.[15] Houseman was their natural leader. Walter Roberts, years later, remembered Houseman's "royal voice, his regal stride . . . he walked up and down Madison Avenue, as if he owned it."[16]

Among the famous Voice pioneers from other lands was Pierre Lazareff, a distinguished French newspaperman and head of what soon grew to become the hundred-member French Service. Lazareff, historian Holly Cowan Shulman recalled, "created cohesion among members of the desk, and he worked tirelessly to create an authentically French sound." The staff included distinguished French writers, philosophers, novelists, and poets. Among them were intellectuals such as Leon Kochnitzky, who published seven volumes of poetry, translated Shakespeare's sonnets into French, edited *La Revue musicale* as well as newspaper criticism of art and music, and spoke Russian, Polish, Italian, English, and German as well as French. "They all lived," Shulman wrote, "in an intense, hothouse environment in which they did not work five days a week for eight hours a day and then go home, but toiled seven long days a week and lived, ate, and breathed the French desk. They were a world unto themselves."[17]

Austrian-born Walter Roberts was recruited around the time of the first broadcast to be a member of the brand-new Austrian Service, a subunit of the German Service. Not surprisingly, there was some tension between the two. Roberts remembers "a shouting match between Hans Meyer of the German Service and Robert Bauer of the Austrian Service. Meyer said to Bauer that the trouble was that Hitler was an Austrian.

VIVE LA FRANCE

In those first months, the New York staff was nagged by the question that mattered most: Was anyone listening? The obstacles on shortwave were awesome: sun spots, magnetic disruptions in the atmosphere, Axis jamming. After several weeks on the air, there was a letter from Cannes: "You in America cannot imagine how even a few minutes of news from America, heard by a Frenchman, is spread around. An hour after it is heard, hundreds, thousands know the truth."*

*Alan Pessin, "Tape Excerpts (of Houseman address at VOA fortieth anniversary)," e-mail to author, December 19, 1991, 2–3.

Whereupon Bauer answered that the trouble was that while in Austria, Hitler was a paperhanger and as soon as he came to Germany, the Germans made him chancellor!"[18]

Then there was the story of radio producer–perfectionist (and, in private life, gourmet chef) Eddie Raquello. Veteran Ed Goldberger, later the producer of *American Theater of the Air* and head of the New York office, described Raquello as "a terror, a very talented terror. One time," Goldberger said, "there was a trial [air raid] alert in New York City, and Eddie insisted on going up on the roof and recording the silence."[19] Claude B. (Cliff) Groce, later VOA deputy program manager, remembered:

> Eddie asked us in the Washington office to record an hour of clear sound at the Lincoln Memorial. Well, we simply stuck a microphone out of a window in the penthouse of the Interior Department building [where the small VOA Washington office was then located]. When we sent the tape to Eddie in New York, he immediately got on the phone, yelling: "That's not the Lincoln Memorial! There are no streetcars at the Memorial." He was right, of course, and we dutifully sent an engineer to the memorial to record an hour of clear sound.[20]

Almost from the start, there were outside political pressures on the Voice. World War I hero Colonel "Wild Bill" Donovan headed the COI in Washington. Before America's involvement in World War II, the COI consisted of both open and covert information activities. But the British advised that to mix the two made no sense. Donovan wanted to retain control of some overt operations, including VOA, which as the first broadcasts were produced was still nominally within his chain of command. The Roosevelt administration decided, however, to separate the two functions. Donovan had the support of the wartime joint chiefs of staff; Sherwood was backed by the White House. On June 13, 1942, President Roosevelt issued an executive order creating the Office of War Information, separating Donovan's operation from the Foreign Information Service. Clearly, Sherwood had won this first round.

"This Is London"

Another point of pressure was the British. Although relations were by and large civil (the relatively inexperienced international broadcasters on the American staff welcomed British advice), the British did assert themselves from time to time. There was occasional vetting of VOA broadcasts before they were relayed from BBC facilities in London (they even played American popular music to fill in blanks if they deleted programs). BBC representative Leonard Miall and an associate, Mark Abrams, were stationed in Washington and New York. They offered policy guidance directly to the VOA staff, some of which was accepted, some not.[21]

There was a huge buildup of the Voice staff in the summer of 1942 after it became part of the Office of War Information, with the acquisition of many floors in the old Argonaut Building on West Fifty-seventh Street, in Manhattan, and expansion to sixteen studios, several score program lines, and forty transmitters in distant locations. Thus the Voice was ready, in the nick of time, for the first big change in the fortunes of war. On November 7, 1942, Allied forces invaded North Africa. Moments after the troops hit the beaches, VOA broadcast statements by President Roosevelt and General Dwight Eisenhower that "friendly landings" were the first step in the "liberation phase" of the conflict.

Even the British were awed by VOA's handling of those critical invasion hours. BBC liaison officer Miall recalled:

> I was very much impressed by the quiet efficiency with which Barnes managed to keep everything under control. Houseman turned out to be a tower of strength, and managed to reorganize all the transmitters and programs very smoothly and very fast. . . . Barnes and Johnson were writing scripts, Houseman was personally in the studio producing the shows, Warburg was writing the leads for the German section. . . . This is the first time that I have seen people at this level so close to the microphone.[22]

Action on the North Africa front proved to be a decisive turning point in the struggle over programming policy that swirled around the wartime Voice. American force commanders were now occupying areas formerly under German control. They brought with them a renewed determination to control all information available to the local populace in the theater of operations: North Africa at first and, later, Italy and areas of southern Europe. The War Department and the State Department sought opportunities to put those "upstarts" in New York in their place.

The "Second War" Intensifies

Over the next fifteen months, decisive ones in World War II, there were a series of skirmishes between the Washington elements and the overseas branch of the OWI in New York. Looming in the background was "Wild Bill" Donovan, still smarting from his reverses in 1942. Barnes quoted the colonel as confiding to the British that OWI needed to make only one major slip "to be out, with the OSS (Donovan's organization) to take over."[23] Houseman, meanwhile, resigned and returned to Hollywood in mid-1943. That was after the State Department denied him a passport (he had only recently obtained citizenship) for travel to North Africa and Europe to inspect the budding field operations.

Sherwood, Barnes, Warburg, and Johnson carried on. They wanted to enhance the independence of policy setting in New York. VOA, control desk chief Edd Johnson said, must be able to make policy decisions because important news stories had to get on the air quickly if the Voice was to remain credible. There could be no delays, he said, while Washington decided what the policy was. "In radio," he added, "the microphone is boss."[24] Donovan, meanwhile, worked closely with members of Congress to press for OSS control. There was a growing gulf between Washington and a New York operation increasingly inclined to make its own programming decisions.

On July 25, 1943, two weeks after Allied forces landed in Italy, dictator Benito Mussolini resigned. This was significant, the BBC said, because it meant that Italy had turned against Hitler. However, Warburg ordered the New York office to treat the event in a straightforward but neutral tone; after all, King Victor Emmanuel III of Italy was still on the throne, and the new prime minister, Marshal Pietro Badoglio, had stated, on taking office, that Italy would remain an ally of Germany in the war.

Warburg commissioned a commentary on Mussolini's resignation and Victor Emmanuel's role in it. The commentary was written by Samuel Grafton (of the *New York Post*), who stated: "The moronic little King who has stood behind Mussolini's shoulder for twenty-one years has now moved forward one pace. I do not feel in any great sense that history has been made today. This is a political minuet, not the revolution we have been waiting for."[25]

The roundup was played once, and only in English. But that was enough. It was monitored by the *New York Times*. Arthur Krock, the *Times*'s chief correspondent in Washington, wrote a story under a front page headline: "OWI Broadcast to Italy Calls Ruler Fascist and 'Moronic Little King.'" Krock said that the broadcast imperiled both international negotiations with Victor Emmanuel III and the lives of American soldiers.

It was the biggest Voice policy flap of the war. It did not help that Krock also uncovered the identity of John Durfee, an obscure contributor to the VOA press roundups. The anonymous columnist turned out to be none other than James Warburg himself. At a press conference, President Roosevelt said that neither he nor Sherwood nor the State Department had approved the use of Grafton's commentary on Victor Emmanuel III. But the president continued to support the overseas service of the Office of War Information (VOA) during a pause in U.S. government infighting.[26]

OWI survived, but in New York, it was never really the same after the furor over the "Moronic Little King." Barnes, Warburg, and Johnson were forced to resign.[27] Their removals followed a showdown meeting at the White House between Sherwood and his boss, Elmer Davis. The two executives had been caught up in a growing rift over the recalcitrant New York office. Davis, known nationally, held all the cards. Sherwood, with less support outside the government, was forced to yield.

A few weeks later, Sherwood was off to serve as chief OWI liaison officer in London. With Allied advances, he found himself coordinating operations with a new, large London-based operation subject to the orders of the theater commander, General Eisenhower. That organization, which had been in the planning stages for at least two years, went on the air on April 30, 1944, in six European languages, including English (that program was partly produced by the BBC). It was known as the American Broadcasting Station in Europe (ABSIE).[28] ABSIE went on the air a little more than a month before D-Day, the most momentous event of the war. At around 8:00 P.M. on June 5, pioneer German Service broadcaster Robert Bauer, now assigned to London, was alerted along with others to prepare for possible special programs. The ABSIE staff members were taken from their hotel to a heavily guarded Allied military installation. Bauer recalled:

A few minutes after midnight, an American major general and his retinue entered the room; a big map of Normandy was unfolded and the general, looking at his watch, quietly but firmly said, "Gentlemen, in five hours and forty-five minutes Allied Forces will land in Normandy." After a brief silence to enable us to grasp the enormity of the event, we were handed the communiqué by General Eisenhower and statements by President Roosevelt, King George VI and Prime Minister Churchill to be translated for our broadcasts. At about 5:30 A.M., I was driven by jeep to our studios. . . . At 6 A.M., I broadcast the communiqué and statements, providing my own lead-in sentence. "Der Sturm aus dem Westen hat begonnen" [The storm from the West has begun].[29]

A New Team for the Endgame

Under new management in the summer of 1944, the Voice reached its wartime peak: 3,000 employees worldwide, with huge staffs in both New York and Los Angeles, and more than forty languages, not counting ten separate dialects beamed to the Philippines.[30] A new leadership team was in place, consisting of Lou Cowan (Houseman's successor), Edward Barrett (Sherwood's successor), and Wallace Carroll (Warburg's successor). The Allies were closing in on Nazi Germany and beginning to make slow headway in the Pacific theater.

In Burma, General "Vinegar Joe" Stilwell commented that his units "took a hell of a beating" by the Japanese. VOA, over considerable opposition in official Washington, broadcast the remark. That, Barrett said after the war, was "a singularly happy decision. Germans, Italians and Japanese testified that they had come really to believe the Voice of America first when they heard it carry Stilwell's statement. 'We felt if the Americans made such admissions to the world,' said one, 'they must be telling the truth.'"[31] Toward the end of 1944, Allied advances in the Pacific enabled OWI to set up a medium-wave relay transmitter on Saipan to beam additional signals to Japan and East Asia. This was to have a significant impact in the Pacific theater during the closing months of the war. As Elmer Davis noted: "Its effectiveness was made clear by the prompt reaction of the Japanese propaganda office, first in attempting to jam the broadcasts and then in repeatedly warning the population not to listen to them. Indications of the value of this transmitter were so unmistakable that we were preparing to erect two transmitters on Okinawa when the war ended."[32]

Others behind the lines during the long conflict later described how they had relied on the OWI broadcasts to Asia. Veteran VOA announcer William Winter recalled that during his postwar visits to General Douglas MacArthur's headquarters in Leyte and to Manila, Filipino guerrillas and even President Ramon Magsaysay said that they had listened daily to his broadcasts since he went on the air in late 1941.[33]

It was a very different atmosphere, internally and externally at the Voice, than in the darkest days of the war. The Allies were winning, not losing. Shulman wrote that the State Department accepted the new regime in the overseas branch of OWI as it had never accepted the old. "Barrett, Cowan and Carroll," she noted, "professionally accepted American foreign policy even when they disagreed with it."[34] The new management team began to pull politely away from the British. The OSS and Donovan stopped campaigning against the OWI. Even Congress backed off a bit.

And then, in 1945, victory. V-E Day in May, V-J Day in August. On August 25, President Harry Truman signed Executive Order 9608, abolishing the OWI. During the postwar demobilization, there were serious questions about whether VOA would survive. With a three-month death sentence, the Voice was placed temporarily within the State Department until its final fate could be determined.

YEARS OF ECLIPSE

The war was over. Many of the VOA staff left for more promising jobs. They assumed that VOA would go off the air, as scheduled, at the end of 1945. But as early as July that year, a State Department commission of private citizens chaired by Columbia University professor Arthur McMahon had debated the future of the U.S. overseas information program. The commission advised that the United States, after World War II, could not be "indifferent to the ways in which our society is portrayed in other countries."[35]

The McMahon commission seemed to be speaking in a vacuum. The overseas information effort had no constituency. Congress was hesitant to appropriate any funds for what was perceived to be a propaganda organization at odds with U.S. traditions. In early 1946, American daily newspapers railed against any foreign information program. The State Department did not know what to do with what was left of that program.

Enter one of the giants in VOA's history. William Benton, a successful advertising executive and dynamic businessman, was named assistant secretary of state for public affairs barely two weeks after the war ended. Benton owned Encyclopedia Britannica, Muzak, and other ventures; had served as vice president of the University of Chicago; and had founded his own advertising agency, Benton and Bowles. Almost single-handedly, according to Voice historian Robert William Pirsein, Benton "saved the VOA from total extinction."[36]

President Truman had given Secretary of State James Byrnes a choice. The secretary could transfer any or all information activities to other bureaus in the State Department or terminate them. At the same time, the president had said that "the nature of present day foreign relations makes it essential for the United States to maintain informational activities abroad as an integral part of the conduct of our foreign affairs."[37]

Benton seized on that opening. During his two-year tenure, the assistant secretary

- Convinced the State Department leadership to keep the overseas information program going, even though Congress had not formally authorized it
- Kept alive leases of shortwave transmission facilities, due to expire in June 1946
- Fought the Associated Press and the United Press (both of which denied VOA permission to subscribe to their services), when they tried to get the American Society of Newspaper Editors to pass a resolution calling for the abolition of the U.S. government overseas information program
- Lined up support from the Federal Communications Commission and commercial broadcasters to keep the program alive
- Lobbied Congress to prevent a fatal budget reduction in mid-1946
- Proposed, if necessary, the formation of a non-civil-service, government-funded broadcasting organization under the direction of a fifteen-member citizen board of governors
- Organized an advisory committee (chaired by legendary CBS broadcaster Edward R. Murrow and including publisher James Linen) on radio programming to increase the visibility of the Voice and marshal public support

Benton, despite his persuasive powers, had an uphill battle. The State Department remained skeptical, and Congress slashed the budget. By April 1946, nearly two-thirds of the broadcasting staff had been dismissed or had resigned. Broadcasting was cut from a wartime peak of more than forty language services to twenty-three, from 1,176 hours to 446 hours a week. Increasingly, programming was contracted out to the commercial networks. Pirsein has noted that by the end of 1946, the Voice of America was producing 58 percent of its programming; CBS, 22 percent; and NBC, 20 percent.[38]

THE COLD WAR BEGINS

About a year after Benton took charge, the geopolitical tides began to shift as a new kind of conflict, that of ideas, heated up. The Voice's ill fortune began to shift as well. "From Stettin in the Baltic to Trieste in the Adriatic," Winston Churchill told a commencement audience in Fulton, Missouri, in mid-October 1946, "an Iron Curtain has descended across the continent. Behind that line lie all the capitals of the ancient states of central and east Europe: Warsaw, Berlin, Prague, Vienna, Budapest, Belgrade, Bucharest and Sofia."[39]

Within months, Greece was threatened with a Communist takeover, Radio Moscow sharply escalated its attacks on the United States, and VOA launched the Russian Service on February 17, 1947. That was just short of five years to the day after the Voice's inaugural broadcast. The following autumn, a joint congressional committee headed by Senator H. Alexander Smith of New Jersey and Representative Karl Mundt of South Dakota visited twenty-two countries, including a number in Europe, and returned home convinced that America needed to energize its international information program. That program, the mission concluded, was badly lagging behind those of the Soviet Union, Britain, and, in relative terms, even tiny Holland.

It is quite possible that Radio Moscow's virulent attacks on the West had several unintended consequences: saving the Voice of America and enhancing the postwar BBC. The congressional fact-finding mission was decisive. On January 27, 1948, after a postwar hiatus of more than two and a half years, Congress passed and President Truman signed the United States Information and Educational Exchange Act—better known as the Smith-Mundt Act (Public Law 402). It called for the creation of government information and educational exchange activities "to promote a better understanding of the United States in other countries, and to increase mutual understanding between the people of the United States and other countries."[40] At last, the nation's peacetime overseas information program was legal, and the Voice could begin to build again.

The Smith-Mundt Safeguards

Public Law 402 authorized the secretary of state "to provide for the preparation, and dissemination *abroad* of information about the United States, its people, and its policies through press, publications, radio, motion pictures and other information media . . . information centers and instructors." The law made clear, however, that no product of U.S. government agencies, including VOA, could be disseminated within the United States. In 1948, memories of Nazi Germany's propaganda machine were still fresh, and Congress wanted to make certain that no government agency could ever be used to influence American citizens the way Hitler had used his German information services.

The prohibition against dissemination of U.S. government–produced information has been challenged in court several times, but with only limited success. In practice, it severely limits VOA audiences in the United States, reducing the Voice's ability to build a constituency and following. However, VOA, at the turn of the century, was logging hundreds of thousands of hits daily on its Internet text, audio, and video services, including readers, listeners, and viewers in the United States. Moreover, the VOA Charter's pledge of objectivity in news programming provides an additional safeguard against misuse by any political party (chapters 7 and 8). The charter did not exist in 1948.

Smith-Mundt was enacted just in time. The year 1948 was tumultuous, with the Communist takeover in Czechoslovakia and the Berlin blockade, the assassination of Gandhi, the founding of Israel, and the break between Stalin and Tito. George V. Allen, U.S. ambassador to Iran, succeeded Benton as assistant secretary of state for public affairs. Another career diplomat, Charles Thayer, was promoted from chief of the VOA Russian Service to director of VOA, followed in both posts by the distinguished diplomat and Soviet affairs expert Foy David Kohler. Allen added six languages, four of them to the Middle East. He established a small news service in English. A careerist at the State Department, the ambassador helped build confidence in VOA within the department.[41] He recruited and brought many foreign service officers into VOA management circles, a trend for the next half century.

Farewell to the Networks

Allen's tenure of about a year was not always easy. Shortly after Allen assumed office, the chairman of the House Appropriations Committee asked to sample VOA scripts picked at random. The congressman selected a program in Spanish produced by NBC. In it, a visitor from Latin America was being shown around Cheyenne, Wyoming, and was told the history of the state. At the end of the program, the Latin American tourist asked:

"Do you still have Indians in Wyoming?" The guide answered: "Yes . . . our Indian maidens run in races dressed in nothing but feathers." Allen recalled later that the chairman of House Appropriations "read this on the floor of the House and the whole place erupted."[42]

Both the Senate and the House opened investigations of the Voice that assailed the lack of supervision and review of program content. Both NBC and CBS canceled their contracts, and once again VOA was solely responsible for producing all its programs. The staff was expanded, over the next two years, to fill the void left when the commercial networks pulled out.

Jamming of VOA Russian by the Soviet Union escalated in 1948 and 1949, and the tone of Voice broadcasts also began to harden. As VOA German Service head and later central program services chief and news analyst John Albert put it: "As the official statements of the United States leaders took up polemics and attacks on the USSR, so did the VOA. By 1952, our hard-hitting negative approach corresponded to the feelings of the people of Eastern Europe who still had the hope of liberation." Allen later conceded: "Looking back, perhaps our tone wasn't justified. A calm, persuasive tone is much better than a mere calling of names."[43]

THE CAMPAIGN OF TRUTH AND
THE McCARTHY HEARINGS

As the 1950s dawned, President Truman called for a Campaign of Truth to counteract the Soviet Union's "big lie." Congress was highly receptive. Inspired by the outbreak of the Korean War, it appropriated $131.4 million for the overseas information program for the 1951 fiscal year. VOA's budget surged from around $9 million to $13 million. It also received a $50 million appropriation for transmitter construction in what was known as the Ring Plan. The idea was to greatly increase broadcast-signal strength in Asia and counter jamming in Europe.[44] Foy Kohler, who became VOA director in October 1949, proposed an expansion of VOA languages from twenty-five to forty-five.

Decades before the term "mission creep" became popular, VOA's operations spread to at least five buildings in the New York City headquarters. By mid-1951, the Voice had ballooned again to forty-five languages, as Kohler suggested, and nearly 400 hours weekly on the air. It put its first mobile unit on the road to cover America, and commissioned a uniquely outfitted Coast Guard ship, the USS *Courier*, to broadcast programs from the Mediterranean island of Rhodes to the Middle East.

VOA also established a Munich radio center to tap refugees streaming across the border to West Germany, interview defectors from the
East, and monitor media in the region. This was the first successor to
ABSIE overseas, and it began broadcasting in Polish on October 1, 1951.
During its eight-year existence, the Munich center at one time broadcast
directly to Eastern Europe and the Soviet Union in more than a half
dozen languages entirely independent of the U.S. headquarters operations. Its programming, in some instances, was even "harder line" than
that of the Voice at home.

Beware of Alphabet Soup

A series of reorganizations of the international information program
within the State Department occurred in 1951 and 1952. This brought
with it a confusing welter of abbreviations describing the evolving
program (and the Voice as part of it): DIB, OIB, IRP, OIX, OEX, IIA
(referring to the semiautonomous International Information Administration within the department), and IBS (International Broadcasting
Service; that is, the Voice of America). With each turn of the organizational screw, VOA's mission was reexamined. In terms of resources, it
was among the best times in the first dozen years of VOA's history. In
terms of organizational focus, consistency, and top management
defense, it was among the worst.

For one thing, its new leaders had relatively little experience in coping
with the constant pressures from Congress, the media, and political currents toward the end of the Truman administration. Dr. Wilson Compton,
former chief administrative officer of the National Lumber Manufacturers
Association and president of the State College of Washington, was named
administrator of the IIA. He conceded that he was "not a professional
publicist, professional diplomat, or professional foreign service officer."[45]
He was ill-equipped for the nightmare that lay ahead.

In 1952, signs of the gathering storm began to accumulate. Kohler,
still head of the Voice, wanted to continue its rush to expand language
services and used his sharply honed expertise and knowledge of geopolitics to make the case. Compton and some VOA engineering managers
disagreed. When his normal rotation time came in September 1952,
Kohler returned to the diplomatic service. He barely escaped the greatest period of turmoil in the Voice's history, during which there were four
VOA directors in six years.

Between mid-1952 and mid-1953, as a result of lackluster responses by Compton and others to congressional questions, four separate committees began to investigate the operations of the overseas information program. They were the Senate Foreign Relations Committee, the president's Committees on International Information Activities and Government Reorganization, and the Senate Subcommittee on Investigations—better known as the McCarthy hearings.

Within the Voice, too, pressures were building. "There were professional rivalries in the expanding workforce," wrote one staff member at the time. When the Campaign of Truth started, "a very great number of the dispossessed refugees sympathized with McCarthy's views." A few current or former programming and technical staff disagreed with their bosses, on philosophy, priorities, or budgetary decisions. Some, their defenders said, felt sincerely about the issues at hand. Others simply wanted advancement, promotions, or removal of bosses and peers they disliked.[46]

Grievances Go National

Hearings chaired by the junior senator from Wisconsin, Joseph R. McCarthy, provided a perfect platform for VOA employees to air their grievances. In his book *The Communist Controversy in Washington*, Earl Latham wrote: "Although the formal hearings began on February 16, 1953, a publicity buildup had preceded it, of a kind to convince newspaper readers that the Voice harbored an anti-American conspiracy and that infiltration of the agency by subversives was 'appalling.' The hearings that followed were less in the nature of a fact-finding inquiry than a show trial to validate the headlines that went before."[47]

Latham noted that in the printed record of the hearings, there was no indication of any charge to the committee to conduct the inquiry, no statement about the purpose of the proceedings, and no narrative about specific topics to be investigated.

But some disgruntled Voice employees organized themselves informally into what became known as the Loyal American Underground, and began cooperating with McCarthy's investigators, Roy M. Cohn and G. David Schine. Their leader was Paul Deac, a Romanian-born alumnus of OWI who had joined the Voice in 1951. As early as April 1952, he presented a list of other employees whom he maintained should be fired (Kohler investigated, and found charges against them to be groundless). Deac then said that unless they were removed, he would see

THAT INFAMOUS PIGEON

Voice historian Robert William Pirsein has quoted Ed Kretzman, a policy adviser to the Voice in 1953 who was credited with "trying to hold things together":

> It now became clear that the McCarthy staff had invited many disgruntled and frustrated employees at the Voice to use the Committee as a means to air grievances against decisions made [by management] in full knowledge of the facts. . . . Within the Voice factions formed, secret meetings were held, and everyone looked upon everyone else with suspicion and mistrust. Any off-the-cuff remark or innocent wisecrack could be transmitted to the ubiquitous and diligent Cohn, whose mind was quite capable of twisting the context to make . . . softness on communism or something verging on subversion out of any casual comment.*

VOA staff members began to make their own tape recordings of meetings to protect themselves. "I'll never forget," staff member Len Reed said years later. "We were in a meeting [on an upper floor in mid-Manhattan] when a pigeon walked across the window ledge. Someone said: 'Shhhh, [it's] a stool pigeon.'"†

*Quoted in Robert William Pirsein, *The Voice of America: An History of the International Broadcasting Activities of the United States Government, 1942–1962* (New York: Arno Press, 1979), 275, 273.
†Ibid., 236.

that information damaging to the Voice was revealed to the press. Shortly after that, Deac began meeting with McCarthy's aides.[48]

Others followed Deac's lead, including a former senior engineer, a news desk editor, an acting division chief, and the heads of several language services. The hearings lasted from February 16 to March 10, 1953. Compton resigned two days after the proceedings began. The relatively new VOA director at the time, Alfred "Doc" Morton, remained secluded in his New York office, devastated by what he heard. He was transferred to the position of science adviser in the State Department in April 1953.

For three and a half weeks, McCarthy and his committee summoned witnesses to probe VOA engineering, management, and programming practices. They scheduled what they considered "damaging" testimony at prime time, with television cameras on full and the press gallery packed. Often, responses were embellished through innuendo by McCarthy, who also peppered witnesses with follow-up questions containing false accusations. Those in a position to refute the charges were rarely called to present an alternative case. In almost every instance, mitigating testimony was deferred for hours, sometimes days, and then recorded off-camera or after newspaper deadlines.

Taking Aim at the Ring Plan

In the engineering probe, the senator and his staff sought to prove that VOA management aided the Soviet Union by ordering the construction of U.S. transmitting relay stations in the Ring Plan too far north. McCarthy selectively excerpted from internal memos and brought in a disgruntled former engineering employee to testify against the Voice. His thesis was that high-powered transmitters being built near Hatteras, North Carolina (code named Baker East), and Seattle, Washington (Baker West), were intentionally placed too far north for effective year-round signal propagation. In fact, VOA management earlier had consulted the Massachusetts Institute of Technology for advice. Jerome Wiesner of MIT concluded that "insufficient data" existed to reach a definite conclusion and that more tests were needed.

The hearings had tragic as well as practical consequences. The construction of Baker East and Baker West soon was canceled, it was said, for lack of support by the National Security Council. This set back the Voice's technical enhancement effort by nearly a decade. VOA engineer Raymond Kaplan, summoned to testify at the McCarthy panel, committed suicide just a week before the hearings ended. Kaplan, who threw himself in front of a truck in Cambridge, Massachusetts, left a note for his widow saying that he feared "he would be a patsy for any mistakes" and that "once the dogs are set on you everything you have done since the beginning of time is suspect."[49] In no instance was there any proof of sabotage or an effort to aid the Communist cause, despite McCarthy's efforts to imply this.

Going for the Jugular: Programming

On the programming side, the subcommittee also practiced smear techniques employed later during the Army–McCarthy hearings in 1954. Among programming targets were VOA News Branch editing, the background and philosophy of the Voice's religion editor, plans to cancel the new Hebrew Service, and the alleged "soft" content of VOA features programs rebroadcast on radio stations in Latin America. In no case was a conspiracy proven to aid the Soviet Union or its allies.

On February 20, an unhappy Latin America desk chief in the News Branch, Virgil Fulling, testified that scripts prepared in the newsroom were being "watered down" and that some of its editors were "soft" on Communism. Fulling had submitted a news item to the central desk on reaction in Guatemala to President Eisenhower's inauguration a month earlier. In it, he wrote that "anti-communist elements hail Eisenhower." The editor in charge, Fulling said, had changed the item to read "democratic" elements. Responding to a question by McCarthy about whether three senior news editors he identified "were friendly to the communist cause," Fulling replied: "I do believe that." He returned to his desk in the New York newsroom, greeted with disdain.

It was not until sixteen days later that News Branch management got a chance to respond. Bob Goldmann, copy editor for the central news desk, led the charge. Virtually everyone in the newsroom amassed scripts and other evidence for the showdown hearing: Goldmann and shift supervisor Donald Taylor versus the junior senator from Wisconsin. The two were summoned to appear in Washington late on March 5, and had to take a night train to arrive in time for the ten o'clock hearing the next day. "Our crime," Goldmann recalled later, "was that I had changed Fulling's repeated use of the word 'anti-communist,' as it had indeed appeared in an International News Service wire story." The story reported on demonstrations by anti-Communists applauding Eisenhower's election. The demonstrations took place in front of the U.S. embassy in Guatemala, a country at that time governed by an extreme left and anti-American regime. "I made it read that 'citizens' were demonstrating, that they shouted anti-communist slogans, and that they were members of democratic organizations. Using the term 'anti-communist' three times in as many lines was just bad and heavy-handed writing. . . . These small changes had become a mountainous 'pattern' of pro-communism. No other 'evidence' was introduced."[50]

"Practically the entire hearing," Goldmann remembers, "turned into a debate on the meaning and use of the word 'democratic' in what was then the Latin American political context." In his view, "we should never let the communists steal that word from us and use it for their own big-lie campaigns":

McCARTHY: Do you not think they have already stolen that word in South America?

GOLDMANN: I don't think so, Mr. Chairman. For instance, the Chilean law, which forbids and outlaws the Communist Party, is called and referred to commonly as the Law of the Defense of Democracy. . . . I have spent almost a year in Latin America and it is not general usage among people there to identify the word 'democratic' with communism.[51]

Soon afterward, the chairman lost interest. Goldmann and Taylor—other than to correct transcripts of their testimony—never heard again from the committee. Nor did the committee in its final report refer to any of the false charges. After the hearing, they returned to a news desk consumed with extensive reporting on the death of Joseph Stalin. Fulling, a broken and isolated man, later committed suicide.

Two other managers summoned for grilling by McCarthy stood up to him in the full glare of television cameras:

• Robert Bauer, pioneer VOA broadcaster (chapter 1) and in 1953 chief of program placement to Latin America, answered a colleague's charge that his soap-opera series on Communism in the region, *The Eye of the Eagle*, was "soft and of poor quality." He quoted twenty-three U.S. missions in the region praising the programs' effectiveness. He began to read excerpts from the programs, but was cut off by subcommittee member Senator Karl Mundt. The senator said he considered the exercise "ridiculous" and urged the hearing to go on to more important issues.

• Reed Harris, the highest-ranking State Department official summoned to the hearings, was deputy administrator of the IIA. For five days, he endured personal attack after personal attack by McCarthy and his aides, including selective citations of his books and writings (including an article in the *Daily Worker*) written twenty years earlier. These, the committee staff alleged, proved that Harris was pro-Communist. No one higher up defended the IIA official. But Harris spoke on behalf of many when he told the subcommittee: "I resent the tone of this inquiry, Mr. Chairman. I resent it not only because it is my neck, my public neck, that you are, I think, very skillfully trying to wring, but I say it because there are thousands of able and loyal employees in the federal government." Harris resigned the next month, but returned as special assistant to Edward R. Murrow, director of the United States Information Agency (USIA), eight years later.

America's Devastated Voice: Picking Up the Pieces

The subcommittee's hearing finally ended, and policy adviser Kretzman commented that this was the Voice's "darkest hour when Senator McCarthy and his chief hatchet man, Roy Cohn, almost succeeded in muffling it."[52] A year later, columnist Frederick Woltman reflected on the just-concluded Army–McCarthy hearings. In his view, "it will go down as one of the most disgraceful, scatter-brained, inept, misleading and unfair investigations in congressional annals."[53] Or as VOA's tenth director, Henry Loomis, put it: "Watching the IIA being beaten by Senator Joseph McCarthy was like watching a snake trying to eat a mouse."[54]

It was time to pick up the pieces. As noted, three other investigations of the State Department's IIA were under way. Two were within the executive branch, and the other was under the Senate Foreign Relations Committee. Secretary of State John Foster Dulles, new in his job, had no interest in retaining the overseas information program; he wanted to concentrate on implementing policy.

The stage was set for the separation of IIA from the Department of State. The Rockefeller Committee appointed by the incoming Eisenhower administration recommended the establishment of the independent United States Information Agency to report directly to the president and administer both the information and cultural programs. USIA came into existence on August 1, 1953, with a mandate to consolidate all its operations in the same city, Washington, D.C.[55] The creation of VOA's fourth successive parent agency was a principal turning point. It was the most significant reorganization affecting the Voice of America since establishment of the Foreign Information Service a dozen years earlier.

BEGINNING THE LONG CLIMB BACK

The McCarthy hearings marked a low point in VOA's history. It took years after that for the network to recover its footing. A successful news organization must have an inquiring spirit—its ability to move out and develop its own sources of information, the heart of "the struggle to get it straight." In its first dozen years, the Voice seemed to step back from the lofty goal stated in its first broadcast: "The news may be good for us. The news may be bad. But we will tell you the truth." In a newsroom stylebook issued eleven years later and just a week and a half before the McCarthy hearings began, the emphasis had changed: "We are not in the business to amuse, entertain or simply inform our listeners. . . . The United States is in the midst of a serious struggle for the mind of mankind."

Could there be a return to the original principle, one respected in the journalistic community at large? At VOA, a growing cadre of journalists and broadcasters fought for the ideal over the next three generations. In the chapters that follow, we trace, step by step, what VOA News chief Bernard H. Kamenske later called "the struggle for the truth."

3

The 1950s and 1960s

FORGING A MORE CREDIBLE VOICE

As long as our programs are considered or appear to be propa-
ganda, they will not be believed.
—George V. Allen,
"USIA: The Big Problem Is Belief"

The Voice is a delicate instrument. It can easily be destroyed.
Without credibility, it is nothing.
—Henry Loomis, to House
Committee on International Relations

The next dozen years at the Voice were ones of rebuilding in the wake of
the McCarthy debacle. Bob Goldmann, who advanced to become chief
of VOA News during that time, explained: "The journalists began to
gain influence, but we struggled all along against actual or feared State
Department pressures. It was a two-front struggle, really. On one front
was State, the external struggle. The other was internal, against the
mostly Eastern European language services within our own organization
who wanted excessive anticommunist programming at a time we were
emerging from this."[1]

It was a turbulent period. The Eisenhower administration's reorgani-
zation of the overseas information and cultural programs distanced the
Voice from the State Department by placing it within the independent
United States Information Agency (USIA). At the same time, VOA was
drawn physically closer to the center of policymaking because the White
House mandated the move of VOA headquarters from New York to
Washington.

This was viewed with alarm by a number on the New York staff. Shop talk has it that as long as six months after the move took place in 1954 and well into the next year, French-language broadcasters seated in studios within sight of the U.S. Capitol at Fourth Street and Independence Avenue, SW, would open their programs with the words: "Ici la Voix d'Amérique en New York." Inevitably, some of the old staff chose to remain in New York. Others moved south with their jobs.

Veteran USIA executive Abbott Washburn, the first USIA deputy director and campaign aide to President Eisenhower in 1952, recalled those days in a letter to a congressional committee a quarter of a century later. He wrote that the new president, based on his wartime experience, believed deeply in the nation's overseas information activities: "He realized, however, that they just weren't State's bag." Located in the State Department, he went on, managers of the information program had only infrequent access to the secretary and other senior officers. "In such a setting," Washburn said, "it was impossible to achieve the attention and speed demanded of media operations."[2] With the creation of USIA, that changed. A lot of newcomers joined the organization, and by the mid-1950s, a renewal of sorts was in the air.

ARCHITECTS OF REVIVAL

A number of figures involved in the VOA renaissance of the 1950s and 1960s stand out:

• Barry Zorthian was a hard-driving dynamo who ate, drank, and slept the Voice for fourteen years from 1947 until 1961. Zorthian began in the tiny English Service, fresh out of Yale after four years of wartime service in the Marines and a bit of time as a reporter for the *New Haven Register*. He moved over to the News Branch in the early 1950s, advanced quickly to head that unit, then was promoted to chief of policy, before becoming director of programs (then, the position was called program manager) from 1955 until his departure as a foreign service officer in India in the early 1960s. Zorthian was arguably the most "hands-on" program manager in the Voice's history. In many ways, he led its evolution into a professional global news organization in the post-McCarthy period. It was not uncommon for workaholic Zorthian to engage in a phone conversation while dictating a memorandum. He typically took home a briefcase overflowing with wire copy at the end of his workday.

Some of his programming innovations continue to distinguish America's Voice to this day.[3]

• Bob Goldmann, whom we have already met, rose after his encounter with Senator McCarthy to become chief of the News Branch and oversee its transformation into a division of considerable clout at VOA. A German-born Jew who fled with his family as an adolescent in the late 1930s, Goldmann worked initially for the Office of War Information (OWI) German Service during the latter war years, and later returned as an English announcer and writer after graduating from Columbia University in New York. Our paths crossed for a few months after he hired me in 1962 as a newswriter trainee. I still remember this remarkably talented journalist and linguist bounding from his office at the appearance of a major event, racing to the central desk, and pecking out the item on a manual typewriter with one finger, at a breathtaking, machine-gun-like speed.[4]

• Henry Loomis, the Voice director from 1958 until 1965, was the only director to serve under successive U.S. administrations of different political parties: Eisenhower and Kennedy/Johnson. Loomis had been a staff commander in the Pacific theater in World War II and graduated from Harvard in 1946 with a degree in physics. Later, he was an assistant to the president of the Massachusetts Institute of Technology and eventually moved on to the White House Offices for Science and International Information Strategy in the Truman and Eisenhower administrations. Loomis knew engineering as well as programming. He drove daily to VOA in downtown Washington from Middleburg, Virginia, a considerable commute each way in those days. He monitored and critiqued tapes of Voice programs en route. Broadcasters cherished receiving handwritten notes of his personal observations, popularly known as Loomies.[5]

• George V. Allen, the remarkable diplomat cited in chapter 2, seemed far ahead of his time in 1948 to 1950, when he served as assistant secretary of state and head of the overseas information program. Allen returned in 1957 as director of USIA and inherited a much different VOA from the one he had left earlier, but one, he felt, that still needed to solidify its commitment to credibility. Goldmann described Allen as a pivotal figure during his three years as USIA director in advancing the Voice toward that goal. The Allen–Loomis–Zorthian leadership team insisted that VOA could be a fully competitive international broadcaster and match the reputation of the BBC if it unfailingly practiced what it had preached in its first transmission: broadcast the truth.[6]

- Edgar Martin was the director of engineering from the summer of 1953 until the mid-1970s. Under Martin's leadership, a system of giant overseas relay stations began to be built (chapter 5). This crusty and politically savvy engineer cultivated close ties with high-level USIA officials and would-be budget cutters on Capitol Hill. Martin experimented successfully with creative ways of overcoming the increasingly heavy Soviet and Warsaw Pact jamming of Western broadcasts. He also oversaw the construction of the largest radio transmitting facility in the world at the time, the one near Greenville, North Carolina. Ironically, it was located within a half-hour drive of the Cape Hatteras site (Baker East) that had been abandoned following the McCarthy hearings.[7]

- Claude (Cliff) B. Groce, whom we met in chapter 2, was an international broadcasting Everyman in his thirty-year VOA career: writer, editor, announcer, producer, and, from 1968 to 1981, deputy program manager. He was a high-energy, go-go champion of broadcasters across the spectrum, in both the English and the language services. He was a prime mover behind a petition signed by hundreds of staff members advocating VOA independence from USIA, a key event in the Voice's history in the mid-1970s. CBG, as this Texan was fondly known, wore his Phi Beta Kappa key proudly. He was a confident, highly respected "certain trumpet" in judging daily programming of whatever genre: political, economic, or cultural. You always knew in a moment where Groce stood on any issue.[8]

- Bernard H. Kamenske, widely known simply as Bernie or BHK, was a no-nonsense journalist who eventually became chief of VOA News and served in that position for eight years in the 1970s and early 1980s. A nationally known giant in his profession, Kamenske was a huge man who brandished a trademark cane. He joined VOA about a year after the move from New York to Washington in 1954. The cane was necessary because of a severe leg injury Kamenske had sustained in a military accident in the early 1950s. But it didn't dampen his zeal to get it straight, and his unrelenting pursuit of the facts became legendary at the Voice. Bernie served first as Latin American editor in the News Branch, next as a desk chief, then as a shift chief, and finally as chief of the Current Affairs Division (1972–1974) before becoming chief of news. Widely read, witty, and articulate on any subject, Bernie alternately drove and coddled those he led or worked with. His influence extended from stalwarts at the central news desk, to kindred souls in the language services, to far-flung correspondents around the globe at any hour of the day or night, their time or his.[9]

BHK fit right in when he arrived at the Voice. There were the incessant struggles between advocates of information warfare and objective news, but it was also a place of vibrant energy and determined principle. Years later, Bernie recalled: "When you went to work in Barry Zorthian's newsroom, you had better be accurate, you had better be objective, you had better be comprehensive. You had better remember that you do not represent any single segment of American society, but all segments. It wasn't written, but it was understood."[10]

It had taken about a decade, from the end of World War II to the mid-1950s, for all the ingredients to come together for the first stages in a professional "greening" of the Voice in terms of both its news and its programming. In the late 1940s, a cadre of journalists was hired, Zorthian among them, for the small English Service. Eventually, he and perhaps a half dozen others were transferred to the News Branch and began to

---

A HOLE IN THE WALL WITH A BELL TO BOOT

In 1955, during Bernie Kamenske's first months at America's Voice, Barry Zorthian's newsroom was located on Pennsylvania Avenue, NW, in Washington, about a block from the White House. "It was on the second floor," Bernie recalled.

> It was a very large room and on one side was the [USIA] press service, on the other side was VOA. IPS [the press service] had people all around town and they would call in to a big bank of people taking dictation on typewriters. But VOA was so noisy and so obstreperous that the IPS people finally built a wall between us. But then they realized they had a responsibility to give us a copy of what they were taking in. So then they built a hole in the wall with a bell to tell us something was there. It was a newsroom straight out of "The Front Page." And it drove the IPS people right up the wall. These were still the days when people would write a story and yell: "Copy!"*

*Mark Willen, interview with Bernard Kamenske, *Room News* [internal newsletter of VOA News Division], December 30, 1981, 4.

write for the entire organization. More and more individuals with news backgrounds or a commitment to the struggle to tell it straight joined their ranks. Among them were Corinne Conde, Don Taylor, Russell Splane, Ruth Lewis, Jerry Theise, Mark Lewis, and Van Seropian.[11] The branch, after the move to Washington, expanded under Goldmann's leadership into a division. Zorthian and Goldmann were determined to centralize and prescribe fairly tightly written news for the language services (some of which still saw news as an instrument to destabilize the countries from which they had fled or had been forced to leave). That was the internal struggle mentioned by Goldmann at the beginning of this chapter.

A FORMER SOVIET GENERAL SPEAKS OUT

One of the most colorful Voice characters of the second decade was General Alexander Barmine, chief of the Russian Service. He had come to the West after defecting in Athens to escape what he felt was his imminent recall by Stalin for execution or deportation to Siberia. He considered himself the leading expert on the Soviet Union, and often was loath to accept advice on news lineups or other daily details of programming. He would sit in the morning editorial meeting with the *New York Times* in front of his face, and the leadership of the Voice across from him on a raised platform, just ignoring them until they said something that he didn't agree with. And then, he'd put the paper down and say: "Nonsense!" or "Ridiculous!"[12]

Before USIA was established, a chief of policy from the State Department could and did order changes in news and programming of the Voice. Then, when VOA was separated from the State Department as part of the independent USIA, VOA insisted on appointing its own policy chief, who would report directly to the Voice director.[13] This was a significant first step along the road to greater autonomy. Although most policy chiefs from the 1950s until the early 1980s were USIA foreign service officers, many fought for the journalistic integrity of the Voice.

Even before the move from New York to Washington, a major figure in the Voice program manager's office, John Wiggin, established an evaluation mechanism called the program review process to critique Voice content and production. These postbroadcast reviews revealed that some language services rearranged news as offered by the central newsroom, at times omitting important stories or playing up others because they were anti-Soviet. When he became program manager in the late 1950s, Zorthian issued a directive mandating that all services follow the lineup supplied by central news.[14]

Sometimes, the journalists and the language broadcasters fought. At other times, both challenged the Office of Policy. The philosophical struggles reached a peak during 1956, when events in Poland and the Hungarian revolution preoccupied both the Kremlin and the West. Then, VOA and Radio Free Europe were accused of airing inflammatory programming that appeared to offer unwarranted promises of U.S. aid to freedom fighters in Budapest. A thorough postrevolution review of VOA broadcasts cleared it of the charges. After that, Zorthian recalled, policy again "descended on the Voice of America with a vengeance." He was convinced that VOA needed some kind of document, some kind of statement of principles, to shield its broadcasters from constant second-guessing by the State Department and, at times, USIA.[15]

THE BIRTH OF THE CHARTER

Henry Loomis became director of the Voice in 1958. He, too, felt that a document, or charter, would offer the kind of principled programming stability that Zorthian and others had advocated. He was supported by USIA director Allen, and asked several Voice managers to prepare drafts of a charter. "I remember trying my hand at a couple of them," Zorthian recalls. "They ended up being four or five pages, much too detailed, much too tedious."

In 1959, Loomis brought on a new deputy director, USIA foreign service officer Jack O'Brien. O'Brien recalls: "He [Loomis] said: 'The first thing I want you to do as the new deputy director is to take a look at this stack of papers,' and boy, they were a stack, at least eight or ten inches deep. There were some beautiful words and some beautiful thoughts, but as Barry has suggested, they were pretty long-winded. A lot of these papers were developed around the theme of the Cold War, and they were reflecting a point of view of the American government at the time."[16]

O'Brien was fresh from a year's sabbatical at the National War College, where he had taken a longer range, more detached look at America, its policies, and its future. That proved to be crucial. Disregarding the thrust of many of the drafts, O'Brien did not mention the

East–West conflict in the charter. That, it turned out, gave the document enduring value after the Cold War ended.

O'Brien took time off to synthesize the voluminous stack of documents. He went home, stayed up all night, and, about seven o'clock the next morning, came up with a four-paragraph synthesis, "a boil-down," he called it, "of what many others had written. So I brought it to Henry," O'Brien remembered, "and he took a quick look and said: 'It looks okay.' And then, he started to pass it around to others, and finally sent it up to George V. Allen, the director of USIA. It came back, with two or three words changed." Allen counseled VOA not to call it a charter, which, in the late 1950s, might have caused Congress or the administration to scuttle the idea for fear that the Voice was becoming "too independent." The final version of what was instead called a directive was approved by President Eisenhower shortly before he left office.

The charter outlined a few key points:

- The Voice of America must win the attention and respect of its listeners.
- VOA news must be accurate, objective, and comprehensive.
- VOA must represent America, not any single segment of the nation, including "a balanced and comprehensive projection of significant American thought and institutions."
- As an official radio, it must present U.S. policies, and "responsible discussion and opinion on those policies."

Henry Loomis later listed the charter first among achievements of his seven-year tenure as Voice director. "It is my hope, it is my belief," Loomis later told the VOA staff, "that the Charter, like the Constitution, is so fundamental and so represents the realities of the world and the moral principles that undergird this nation, that the Charter will endure for the life of the Voice."[17]

A RESPONSE TO A DECADE OF CRISES

Issued in 1960, the charter, or directive, was forged partly as a response to events of the preceding decade. In addition to Hungary and Suez, VOA reported the riots in Poznań, Poland, in June 1956 and Eisenhower's use of troops in Little Rock, Arkansas, to integrate Central High School in 1957. The civil rights revolution erupted on the nation's

---

SPOT NEWS WHILE BAILING OUT

After Barry Zorthian, VOA's Bob Lasher was sent to Korea for combat reportage, including an account he recorded "on the way down" while parachuting thousands of feet from an aircraft: "Here we go! We're pushing ahead. We're going to go right out. One right after another. Left foot first, left foot first. Here we go! [*sound of rushing wind in freefall, parachute opening*] My chute opened! I'm open! Thank God, it's opened!"*

*Wayne Hyde, "The Voices of the Voice" (transcript of VOA thirty-fifth anniversary special feature, February 16, 1977), 4.

TV screens, and there was the Soviet launching of *Sputnik I,* the world's first Earth-orbiting satellite. In 1958, Marines landed in Lebanon. And in 1959, Fidel Castro consolidated his takeover of Cuba.

The Voice put correspondents out in the field to cover many of these events. Zorthian, the irrepressible journalist, was among the first in the postwar period to report from abroad. He had taken a leave of absence from the International Information Administration (IIA) to cover the Korean War during the winter of 1950.

Another correspondent, Bob Walker, was assigned for a time to Beirut, and Howard Garnish to the United Nations. In addition, the "out of control" Munich radio center, which was directly airing some language programs, was taken off the air in 1958. It was converted into a program center to generate correspondents' reports and other programs for transmission to Washington and review there before broadcast. Production centers for feature programs in Arabic were established in Cairo and Beirut in the latter part of the decade and early 1960s.[18]

Back at headquarters, change was in the air, too. A motion picture and television service was established within VOA in the mid-1950s. Ernest Acquisto, who joined the Voice in 1950 in New York, was among its early managers and helped establish the unit in the basement of the new VOA headquarters after the move to Washington. He recalls going out with a 16-millimeter handheld camera and shooting some events on film for use in a regular half-hour feature shipped to television outlets in Japan.[19] The fledgling TV unit was removed from the Voice in 1963 and became a separate organizational unit in USIA. In the 1980s, the service expanded greatly under agency director Charles Z. Wick as Worldnet Television. It was later reintegrated with the Voice in gradual stages, beginning in 1990 (chapter 16).

AN ERA OF PROGRAMMING INNOVATION

In the late 1950s, VOA's English programming took flight under Loomis and Zorthian, as news operations were enhanced and English features were diversified. New programs, reminiscent of some of the VOA arts and music offerings of the early war years, were produced. Among them was *Music USA*, conceived by John Wiggin and hosted by the celebrated jazz-world icon Willis Conover (chapter 13). This program was launched as the Voice moved to Washington. During his career of more than four decades, Willis built a huge following overseas. His voice was mellow, his syntax simple, his delivery slow. He recorded more than 10,000 programs until shortly before his death in 1996.

Other programs included Eddie Goldberger's *American Theater of the Air*. This was a series of ten classic American plays, such as *Our Town*, *The Glass Menagerie*, *Death of a Salesman*, and *Mister Roberts*. The plays were produced in the VOA studios and acted for radio by such top talents as Florence Eldridge, Fredric March, Rod Steiger, Martha Scott, Walter Abel, and George Grizzard. The industry magazine *Variety* termed the production of *Our Town* "a real upper case show, a sampling of the cultural achievements in our society, and its broadcast by VOA should help to spike notions abroad that the U.S. is culturally barren." Goldberger worked with Zorthian and Voice veteran Gene Kern to produce and broadcast the series. Top talent agreed to perform at $75 an hour.[20]

About this time, Special English was created (chapter 12). Its slow-paced, "limited vocabulary" form of American English included cultural programming as well as news. The slow rate of delivery was designed to more easily penetrate Soviet jamming than the Voice's faster-paced standard English. Loomis, a physicist, didn't believe that it would be possible to explain nuclear fusion in Special English. He listened to a program that did just that, and became a true believer.

Other programming innovations included

- *Panorama USA*, the Voice's first magazine-format program, featuring reports and interviews throughout the United States. Designed to

reflect American history and cultural life, the program was produced
and hosted by Cliff Groce.

- *American Forum*, which evolved into *Forum: A Meeting of the Minds*,
  a series of lectures by and interviews with American intellectuals,
  literary figures, and scientists, which was reproduced in book form
  and distributed around the world.

- *The Breakfast Show*, a conversational, prerecorded morning broadcast
  combining music and features, which went on the air in 1961. The
  long-running program (twenty years) was hosted by Al Johnson
  (succeeded by Bill Reynolds), Phil Irwin, and Pat Gates, who later
  became U.S. ambassador to Madagascar.

- *Press Conference USA*, a weekend interview by a panel of correspondents with a prominent figure in the news, very similar to NBC's *Meet
  the Press*. This program, which was initially anchored and hosted by
  Bill McCrory, had been on the air each weekend for more than forty
  years by the turn of the century, perhaps a record on the international
  airwaves.

- *Issues in the News*, another weekend public-affairs discussion among
  U.S. correspondents and columnists. *Issues*, as its title suggests,
  focused specifically on analyses of events of the week, in America and
  the world. It also remained on the air beyond the turn of the century,
  in a format somewhat resembling that of the PBS program *Washington
  Week in Review*.

By 1961, shortly before he left the Voice to take an overseas post,
Zorthian had reason to be pleased. As he later put it, in a Washington
symposium: "Gradually, by the end of the second Eisenhower term, we
could legitimately say we were a professional radio outfit, or at least
headed in that direction. We began to get into some aspects of modern
radio, audience research, reflection of a variety of American opinions—
less selling of soap, more honest information, a respectable operation, if
you will."[21]

INTO THE 1960S: DECADE OF CHANGE

This bolder chapter in VOA's history, however, was coming to a close.
Hopes were high when John F. Kennedy assumed the presidency in 1961,
and appointed the distinguished radio journalist and documentary producer Edward R. Murrow as USIA director. (In 1963, one of Murrow's

World War II colleagues in Europe, Larry LeSueur, joined the Voice and served as congressional correspondent along with veteran VOA Capitol Hill watchers Rob Lodge and Bob Leonard for some years.)[22] Change again was in the air. Allen retired; Zorthian went overseas; and Loomis, who stayed until 1965, dealt with crisis after crisis until he left, exhilarated by his successes but somewhat dispirited because of policy disputes in his final months at the Voice.

Cuba was the first test of the new decade, and the U.S. response to it spanned both the Eisenhower and Kennedy administrations. In April 1960, Allen told a National Security Council (NSC) meeting that USIA had been under pressure from Congress and the press to expand U.S. broadcasts to Castro's Cuba. He counseled against the use of television transmitted from an aircraft to the island (the military was prepared to fly such a plane, circling over Key West).[23] At the same time, Allen said he would investigate the expansion of shortwave to Cuba and also look into leasing time on Florida radio stations for standard-band medium-wave transmissions. Later, after retirement, the ambassador sharply criticized anti-Cuba crusades. "Nothing," he said, "has served to label USIA as a propaganda agency more indelibly than the anti-Castro campaign, and nothing could have helped Castro more."[24]

Loomis struggled to keep overt VOA programs on Cuba separate and clearly distinct from the covert CIA transmissions from Swan Island in the Florida Keys. In a memo to Murrow written shortly after Kennedy took office, Loomis laid out the distinction:

> VOA short wave broadcasts are aimed at an audience throughout Latin America. They discuss problems of interest to all of Latin America, including the Cuban problem. . . . Their tone is objective and unexcited. . . . Radio Swan is for Cubans to talk to Cubans. Its purpose is to excite listeners and to ridicule and undermine the regime. . . . All evidence points to both VOA and Swan having wide audiences. Many listen to both; to VOA for confirmation; to Swan for titillation. . . . VOA is now doing all it can and should.[25]

To reinforce his plea, Loomis quoted a Cuban defector who had arrived in Mexico the first week in February 1961: "VOA is the only thing we have, now that Radio Swan is being jammed. People spend the whole day waiting for the Voice of America to broadcast. They consider it truthful and completely reliable. We know when the Voice says it, it's true. It is dangerous to be caught listening to the Voice of America, but everybody is doing it."[26]

Then, in April 1961, there was the ill-fated U.S.-backed Bay of Pigs invasion of Cuba. Murrow told Loomis that he had had no advance warning about its timing:

> LOOMIS: I was driving to work, listening to the CBS Morning News, when I heard about it, and I flipped as everyone else did who heard the news. So I speeded up, went through red lights, and got to the Voice as fast as I could. I called Ed Murrow, and he was spitting mad, because no one had told him, either. That's when he made his famous statement: "They expect us [USIA] to be in on the crash landings . . . we had better be in on the takeoffs." So I told him what I planned to do, and he said: "Fine, go ahead." And we went to a twenty-four-hour-a-day broadcast in Spanish. Now, the problem was, in addition to our broadcasting, we had trouble finding out what was going on, on being told the truth about what was going on within the [U.S.] government. But the CIA had a transmitter on Swan Island, and it was transmitting into Cuba in Spanish a very different story [from the reality], that the landing was successful and that everything was going fine.
>
> KAMENSKE: The Voice, on the other hand, carried information contradicting these statements, and that really didn't sit well with the policy office. These folks kept saying: "Well, balance . . . balance . . . let's balance . . . let's get a balanced account." Balance. Well, what is the balance when the events turned bad from the point of view of the policy and the State Department?[27]

The following year, in October 1962, the United States and the Soviet Union came eyeball to eyeball during the nuclear showdown over the deployment of Soviet missiles in Cuba. This time, USIA was fully alerted in advance of President Kennedy's nationwide address announcing the crisis. The agency ordered the Voice to broadcast around the clock in Spanish and mount saturation coverage of the Americas and the world in English as well. USIA deputy directors Tom Sorensen (brother of the presidential adviser) and Donald Wilson were active in insisting that Kennedy's propaganda blitz against Cuba be carried out, down to the last word.[28]

Sorensen, acting in Murrow's stead (the director was recovering from surgery at the time), issued a comprehensive policy guidance the very day, October 22, that the president imposed a naval quarantine on Cuba. "Do not use any comment, regardless of source," Sorensen wrote, "which is not wholly consistent with the lines set forth in the President's speech and this instruction."[29]

Wilson summoned the USIA's assistant deputy director for policy and plans, Burnett Anderson, and told him that he would be "personally responsible for every word that's said on the air [the Voice of America] until further notice." I visited the newsroom during the crisis and saw Anderson, seated at the edge of the central desk near the pass-through window to the Teletype operators, checking every word of copy on Cuba before it was put on the house wire for broadcast. Those of us in Worldwide English worked double shifts at the time to produce airshows (a Voice term for programs) on the crisis. I recall feeling that censorship was unnecessary. The newsroom did an admirable job of in-depth, straightforward, up-to-the-minute reporting of the most dangerous crisis of the Cold War. The commentaries aired by the Voice, however, were predictably harsh, somewhat reminiscent of the darkest days of the Campaign of Truth.

In *Psywar on Cuba*, Jon Elliston has written:

A long-standing conflict between USIA and Voice of America managers over the independence of the Voice had left some officials concerned that VOA Director Henry Loomis might not stick sufficiently close to the White House spin on events. Displacing Loomis by installing a USIA editor in the newsroom, Burnett Anderson commented in an interview, was "the most telling piece of evidence of the concern that the Kennedy administration had for foreign opinion and for broadcasting" during the missile crisis.[30]

The Voice regained form, however, in its programming about several other events in the early 1960s. The civil rights revolution at home gathered steam. In August 1963, there was comprehensive coverage of Martin Luther King, Jr.'s famous "I Have a Dream" address on the steps of the Lincoln Memorial. I wandered out of the VOA headquarters building onto the Mall to absorb the spirit of what was, at that time, one of the largest demonstrations ever held in the nation's capital. The mighty choral renditions of "We Shall Overcome." The unprecedented throngs around the reflecting pool, black and white, young and old, all straining for a glimpse of the microphone atop the steps in the portico of the magnificent memorial.

THE DEATH OF A PRESIDENT

But the event that made me an international broadcaster for life occurred just short of two years after I joined America's Voice. It was a date sadly familiar to most Americans and many citizens of the world: November 22, 1963. My colleague and later program manager Jack Shellenberger and I were wolfing down sandwiches at our desks after our airshows to Europe and Africa at 1:32 P.M., Eastern Standard Time. We had five minutes for lunch before attending what was called a "counterinsurgency" course, mandatory for all U.S. government employees in the dawning years of the nation's involvement in Vietnam. We never made it to class that afternoon.

Shellenberger and I were listening to a speaker called the strowger,[31] which had live sound from Dallas. It was an incoming line, scheduled to carry President Kennedy's address at the Trade Mart in that city. A pool producer gave listeners to the line the first word that there had been shooting at the president's motorcade and that he may have been hit. We were in our twenties and thirties, and fleet of foot. We raced at once to the newsroom around the corner, and the commercial news agency Teletype machines were a chorus of bulletin bells. National newswriter Philomena Jurey (chapter 1) was madly typing the first bulletins, and the newsroom erupted into frenzied activity. Then we hurried around to the tape library, where archivist Harry Weaver took a broom handle and simply cleared an entire shelf of old tapes to make room for the expected deluge of new ones—reports on the Dallas tragedy from ABC, CBS, NBC, and the audio of all the television networks. (On that fateful day, VOA did not have a correspondent with the president in Dallas. White House correspondent Jim Yankauer had remained in Washington and filed a report about the Trade Mart speech based on an advance text, which, of course, was useless. Since November 22, 1963, VOA has had a correspondent accompany every president on every trip outside the nation's capital, at home or abroad.)

We passed by the cafeteria and saw deputy chief of Worldwide English Cliff Groce pull anchor Bill McCrory from his sandwich and hustle him toward a studio. It was to be McCrory's first long shift in a continuous live broadcast on the assassination, which lasted nearly 120 hours.[32] Shellenberger and I then took a quick look into the Special Events Office, which in a few hours would begin to plan lines and flatbed trucks linking VOA reporters at all the funeral sites in Washington with headquarters. Feeling that we might be needed, we then hastened back to our desks and ancient tape-editing machines and began chopping tape and writing lead-ins. We ran them into the studio to McCrory and his producer. They were desperate for material to sustain the special at a time when millions of new listeners were tuning into America's Voice for an authoritative account of events after the loss of its thirty-fifth president.

The Voice "Can't Afford to Be Wrong on This One"

There was no confirmation that John F. Kennedy had been killed until an hour after Lee Harvey Oswald's fatal shot was fired. In Bush House, London, a BBC World Service newswriter grabbed a news agency bulletin several minutes before the confirming announcement that said the president had died. He took it to the senior editor in charge and asked: "Can't we go with this and attribute it to the news agency?" The senior editor turned to him and said: "What does the Voice say? They can't afford to be wrong on this one!"[33] Another evidence of VOA's reach at this time of national tragedy came from Nigeria. A listener wrote afterward that shortwave propagation of the Voice's special reportage was so clear that November weekend that he could hear the hoofbeats of the riderless steed that accompanied the young president's coffin on its slow, solemn passage down Pennsylvania Avenue between the Capitol and the White House.[34] It was freezing outside that Sunday, November 24, and the crowd lining the streets was stone silent.

The assassination in Dallas foreshadowed another national tragedy, the ten-year-long Vietnam War. That conflict signaled a serious reassertion of authority by those determined to control America's Voice, to intrude in its daily news operations as well as shape its commentary to the world. Initially, the key protagonists were Loomis and Murrow's successor as director of USIA, columnist Carl Rowan. Bernie Kamenske recalled: "The Voice of America was sucked into the morass of the Vietnam war much as America was . . . it was something that got more and more consuming."[35]

"GOD DAMMIT, I HAVE MY OWN RADIO"

By the mid-1960s, the nation very quickly deployed up to 500,000 troops in Vietnam. Henry Loomis recalled:

> I'm sure the president [Lyndon Johnson] must've known it wasn't working well. I guess maybe he didn't know what to do, how to stop it. He was a proud man. He had been a success all his life. He didn't want to quit when he hadn't won. But he was getting in deeper and deeper, domestically and overseas. He was talking to a friend, and he was furious at the domestic networks: CBS, NBC, and ABC . . . the way they covered specific incidents [in the Vietnam War]. And he turned to his friend and he said: "I know I can't affect the broadcast companies, I know they won't listen to me, I know they won't help me. But God dammit, I have my own radio. I've got to make that do it right." Well, he was talking about the Voice, so that increasingly, at first imperceptibly, there was more and more pressure from the White House on the agency and more and more pressure from the agency onto the Voice to change a word here, to tone down another word there, to change the normal—in our judgment—the objective way of doing our job.[36]

A turning point occurred in South Vietnam in January 1965. American forces by then had begun to engage Vietcong infiltrators and North Vietnamese soldiers directly, at first in villages and hamlets outside the cities. One such village was Pleiku, where eight U.S. servicemen were killed and sixty-two others injured on February 5 during a Vietcong raid. The Pentagon advised President Johnson to retaliate by bombing sites in North Vietnam for the first time. There was a debate at the National Security Council on Saturday night, February 6, about the wisdom of that action because Soviet premier Aleksey Kosygin was then visiting Hanoi, the North Vietnamese capital. American air action on the North might well be misinterpreted as a direct challenge to Moscow. After some deliberation, the president authorized the air strikes against some military barracks in the North, but U.S. officials would "low key" their anti-Soviet rhetoric for the time being.

USIA director Rowan remembered calling Loomis after a second NSC meeting the following morning. He passed along the guidance and requested the VOA director to ensure that no VOA commentary would suggest there was a challenge to the Soviet Union or in any way imply that the bombings were meant to be an insult to Kosygin. Rowan said he was infuriated on Monday morning to discover that a VOA commentary highly critical of the USSR had been issued. Rowan later wrote in the *Washington Evening Star:* "I told Loomis in some pretty graphic language that he had either been inexcusably irresponsible or was manifesting a futile notion that he could run VOA independent of its parent body the way J. Edgar Hoover supposedly ran the FBI, aloof from the policies of the Justice Department."[37]

Rowan then told Loomis that he, as USIA director, would personally clear all VOA commentaries (not news but editorials) about the Pleiku reprisal and the implications as they related to Kosygin.[38] As the weeks wore on, the heavy hand of the policy people "uptown," as VOA insiders referred to the agency at the time, got heavier. In February and March, a comment in the Paris newspaper *Le Monde* critical of U.S. policy in Vietnam was deleted from a review of the world press. A critical portion of a *New York Times* editorial calling for a fresh presidential statement on Vietnam and appealing for negotiations with Hanoi was edited out. A background analysis on a speech by Senator Frank Church, a critic of the administration's Vietnam policy, was held up for several days until Senator Thomas Dodd's proadministration comments could be included with it.[39] *Washington Evening Star* columnist Mary McGrory summarized the dispute: "In 1960, under President Eisenhower and after much study, the Agency finally received a Charter which gave it the green light to be candid and objective, in the manner of the British Broadcasting Corporation. But since the raids on Pleiku, say Voice officials, they have been chafing under the heaviest censorship in their history."[40]

WARTS AND ALL

Henry Loomis resigned on March 4, 1965, about a month after Pleiku, to take a high-level post at the Department of Education. He delivered a farewell speech to a packed auditorium in the Voice headquarters building. He cited the many achievements of his seven-year tenure, including the charter, and noted that it had been approved not only by Allen, but by USIA directors Murrow and Rowan as well. He quoted from John F. Kennedy's address delivered in the same auditorium three years earlier. The late president, Loomis thought, had stated the same mission as the charter but in different words: "It is your task," Kennedy had said, to tell the story of American life around the world. This is an extremely difficult and sensitive task. On the one hand, you are an arm of the government and therefore an arm of the nation, and it is your task to bring our story around the world in a way which serves to represent democracy and the United States in its most favorable light. But on the other hand, as part of the cause of freedom, and the arm of freedom, you are obliged to tell our story in a truthful way, to tell it, as Oliver Cromwell said about his portrait, "Paint us with all our blemishes and warts, all those things about us which may not be immediately attractive."

Loomis looked to the future of the Voice, and to anyone familiar with what had occurred at VOA after Pleiku, his references were clear:

We are . . . acutely aware of the fact that most of our audience listens to other radios besides the Voice and that they consciously compare what they hear on us to what they hear on others. Some tend to believe that if the Voice does not carry a fact, it will not be known to the world. . . . We, however, remember the huge areas unserved by any unbiased news service and the large numbers of countries whose news is censored by the local government. Perhaps most fundamental of all, we believe our audience judges us as a radio, while some of our colleagues assume that the audience considers a commentary on the Voice as authoritative a statement of United States policy as a statement by the secretary of state or the president. . . . I believe that VOA serves the national interest poorly if its output is equated with diplomatic communications.

I believe VOA serves the national interest poorly if its very stance belies the essence of the society it speaks for—it serves it poorly if it is asked to mold its news, editorial, and feature output to serve tactical policy interests. In doing so, it becomes a propaganda instrument in the bad sense of the word. . . . Conversely, I believe VOA serves the national interest well if it reflects responsibly, affirmatively, and without self-consciousness, that ours is a society of free men who practice what they preach. To do this effectively, we must do it at all times—freedom is not a part-time thing. . . . We must show that the United States derives strength, not weakness, from its diversity.[41]

Loomis's farewell address inspired future generations of Voice broadcasters. As Kamenske remarked on the fiftieth anniversary of the Voice: "The professional skill of the VOA in its proudest sense, was honed by those terrible events in southeast Asia."[42]

THOSE YEARS OF GREENING

Despite zigs and zags, one could look back on the period between the McCarthy hearings and the mid-1960s as a time of phenomenal growth for the Voice and, on balance, a time of considerable promise. During those years, VOA

- Began to build an internal consensus in the central and language services about its charter and how to apply it to day-to-day programming (even while combating pressures from those outside who did not yet subscribe to it)
- Increased the power of its transmitters around the world from 5 to 13 million watts, with an additional 8 million watts under construction
- Achieved a dominant shortwave signal in Latin America, West Africa, and Vietnam, and a reasonably competitive signal in Europe, the Middle East, and the remainder of Africa
- Tripled the amount of airtime in English and created Special English to reach those with limited English-language skills as well as produced innovative programs like *Forum* for English-speaking intellectuals
- Initiated special programs to Africa and created the separate Africa Division, supported by a program center in Monrovia, similar to another established for the Arabic Branch on the Greek island of Rhodes[43]

To what end, this initial growth from acetate disks flown across the Atlantic in World War II bombers to a much-expanded worldwide transmission system?

AN ANTENNA WIRE, OUT THE DOOR
AND UP A TREE

Henry Loomis addressed the National Press Club about midway through his tenure at America's Voice. He recalled a visit a few years earlier to the interior of Tanganyika (now called Tanzania). There, he met a man who spoke broken, but intelligible English. They were sitting under a mango tree at a river ferry landing while waiting for trucks to load up and cross. The man was a daily listener to VOA:

> We discussed world affairs for several hours until all our trucks were across the river and then we gave him a lift to his house a couple of miles down the road. The house was the typical wattle and mud hut—with an antenna wire coming out of the door and up a tree. He wore no shoes but he was the secretary of the local chapter of TANU, the leading political party in Tanganyika. Radio was his window on the world—a window for information, for ideas, for entertainment. He listened to all the radios he could hear. He knew to whom he was listening. He compared. He drew his own conclusions. He was typical of the tough, intellectually curious audience we face in international broadcasting. He was the challenge the Voice faces. The Voice is meeting the challenge.[44]

As we've seen, that challenge has ranged over the years from policy conflicts in Washington to action in faraway places. The next pages tell the story of VOA's far-flung correspondents (chapter 4) and its engineers at remote relay stations ringing the globe (chapter 5).

4

The VOA Correspondent

TO THE ENDS OF THE EARTH

The whine of a bullet is a nasty sound, especially if it's passing over your shoulder while you're running full speed down an unfamiliar street.
— Greg Flakus, in McKinney, "The Voice of America Correspondents Corps Reporting the World"

Because they are so few, correspondents move about with precision timing, goaded by foreign editors who try to make their small bands look like armies. It makes no difference if a correspondent is expected to cover 23 countries at a time, eight of them on the brink of hostilities and half lying along an unstable earth fault. He must be in the right place at least a day before the right time.
— Mort Rosenblum, *Coups and Earthquakes*

I will begin with a personal account from my own years as a VOA foreign correspondent. It was back in the Paleozoic era, journalistically, long before satellite telephones, laptops, or even consistently reliable transoceanic telephone communications in zones of conflict. It was September 1970.

THE BIGGEST STORY I EVER BLEW

My assignment: to travel from home base in Athens to Cairo for coverage of the emergency Arab summit called by President Gamal Abdel Nasser to end the bloody civil war in Jordan between King Hussein's Bedouin army and the Palestinian fedayeen, led by Palestine Liberation Organization (PLO) chairman Yasser Arafat.

The king's men had prevailed, it appeared, in the three-week, house-to-house, street-to-street fighting in the Jordanian capital of Amman and other towns and cities in the Hashemite Kingdom. The Arab leaders now had to construct a cease-fire that would hold in a land roughly half Jordanian, half Palestinian. And, in the wake of what became known as Black September, the fedayeen had to be disarmed.

So it was off to Cairo, and the summit, after another of many farewells in those days to my wife, Dot, and three young daughters: Wendy, Susie, and Nancy. When I got to Cairo, I found a typical scene: reporters staked out the summit, waiting for endless hours in a room conveniently located close to a filing facility where I could feed bulletins and reports back to the VOA newsroom as soon as the communiqué was issued.

Another All-Nighter

Such gatherings were never neat or on schedule. Finally, a framework agreement for the Jordanian–Palestinian cease-fire was worked out, at about four o'clock in the morning of September 28. I rushed to file and discussed with the coverage desk back in the VOA newsroom what the next move might be. Word was that a chartered plane would be leaving from Beirut, Lebanon, for Amman in the next day or so—it would carry foreign correspondents right into the heart of the Jordanian capital for a firsthand look at the war's impact and aftermath. The decision: go straight to Beirut.

I grabbed a bit of sleep and, around ten o'clock, headed for the Egyptian Foreign Ministry, getting a very good briefing on how Cairo saw the uncertain days ahead in Jordan. Then, it was off to Beirut early in the afternoon. The one-hour flight got me there by midafternoon, and I quickly went to the St. George Hotel and put my name on the roster of the press charter plane to Amman. The scheduled time for departure: approximately midnight. Adrenalin pumping, I decided to contact the very well informed U.S. press attaché and former senior VOA Arabic editor Boulos Malik. He invited me to join a number of local journalists he was having in for drinks around 5:00, and theories about the next turn in Jordanian (and Lebanese) politics mingled well with scotches and more adrenalin. Finally, around 6:30, I headed back to the hotel for another quick nap before catching the charter.

It wasn't intended to be a serious slumber, because I felt duty bound to let the family in Athens know where I was, where I was headed. At times, Dot learned of my whereabouts only by listening to VOA. I placed a call to her, and was told that it would be perhaps forty-five minutes or an hour before the overseas call would go through to Greece from the hotel switchboard (see why I called it the Paleozoic era?). I fell dead asleep. Perhaps an hour and a half later, I was jolted awake by the telephone ringing. I was barely coherent when awakened, not at my reassuring best: "Sweet, I'm headed for Amman, where it may not be possible to call, but I may be able to let you know via the coverage desk in Washington."

"Oh great!" Dot said, pondering all the news she had heard on VOA about Black September, the war, the snipers, and the land mines. "Well, let us know what's up when you can."

Break Time?

Maybe I could get a bite to eat before hauling my bags across the street to the van leaving for the airport and the charter. It was now about 9:00. I emerged from the elevator in the lobby, and was startled to see that all the lights were out. The big plate-glass window in front had been smashed. There seemed to be flames in the streets. I ran to the desk and blurted out in my pidgin Arabic: "Shu hayda?" (What's up?)

The instant reply: "Abdel Nasser maet!" (Abdel Nasser is dead). And I had flown from Cairo just seven hours earlier, away from one of the biggest stories during the six and a half years I was stationed in the Middle East! If only I had held on in Cairo one more day, or even another few hours.

But Nasser was dead. He had been stricken with a fatal heart attack, just a couple of hours earlier. I had to file. I grabbed a cab. It skillfully navigated the ten blocks to the Beirut office of the Voice of America within the U.S. embassy, located in those days in the Ain Mreisseh district of town. I say skillfully, because the driver had to weave in and out of pyramids of tires and palms that had been set afire amid the streets in tribute to Gamal Abdel Nasser, the hero of the Arab world.

I had to talk my way past the Marine guard into the office (explaining that I had directed that office a few years earlier). It just so happened that I had a biography of Nasser stuffed in my trench-coat pocket, and now had access to the Reuters wire and files in the office. I called Washington, but again was blocked by overloaded circuits. It seemed as if everyone in the Levant was calling everyone else to see if they had heard the news. So while waiting for the call to go through, I wrote and wrote and wrote and fumbled with my patch cords (called alligator clips) and tape recorder to be ready to tap into the phone for the voice feed, which would be possible once the operator got through. It seemed like an eternity.

The Stampede Changes Direction

I also used the time and a second phone line to check on the charter flight. Not surprisingly, it had been canceled. The "pack" of foreign correspondents all were headed back to Cairo in the morning. I quickly called Middle East Airlines to book a place on the commercial flight the next day. Sorry, the clerk said, it was all filled up. I sweet-talked her into giving me perhaps the last seat.

Finally, the call from Washington came through, and I was able to give the coverage desk and operations studio a reasonably full diet of reports and backgrounders on Gamal Abdel Nasser, including some of my own insights since I first observed him giving a National Assembly address in Cairo in 1965. At the end of the feed, I told the desk: "The Amman charter has been canceled. I've managed to book a seat on MEA in the morning to go back to Cairo."

"Sorry," came the reply. "Hank Grady [VOA's other correspondent in Athens] called in a couple of hours ago, volunteered to go to Cairo, and we assigned him to do the story. We want you to go home to Athens and watch the region from there."

"You've got to be kidding!" I bellowed. "I've watched this guy for the last five or six years and simply *must* be there at the funeral. Please see, when the bosses get in, if we can't double team it." The coverage desk agreed to check. I said that I would get to the airport in a few hours and proceed to Cairo. "Okay," warned the coverage desk in Washington. "But you had better be sure you are cleared to go before you take off." Unpleasant words, at 4:00 A.M., Beirut time.

Back to the hotel, and an hour or so more of sleep. Another cab, to Beirut International Airport. Into the waiting room. I checked my bags through. To hell with Washington, I thought. I'll just hop on this plane and see how they respond when I get to Cairo. We got on the plane, and I felt a smug sense of satisfaction. But Middle East Airlines was running on Middle East time, at a Middle East pace. Engine trouble, and a delay. We were hustled back to the airport lounge. Well, my conscience nagged. Perhaps, after all, I should call Washington.

Penny Pinchers

I headed to the phone booth in the main foyer of Beirut International Airport and placed the call, which, as luck would have it, went straight through this time. "You are *not* to go to Cairo. We appealed it to the bosses, and they can't afford to double team. Go straight back to Athens. That's final!"

Crestfallen, I raced back into the lounge and spotted two veteran correspondents in our "pack"—Wilton Wynn of *Time Magazine,* and Wilson Hall, formerly of NBC News—seated near the window. I had covered events with both of them since coming to the Middle East, and asked them if they would mind reminiscing a bit about Gamal Abdel Nasser. Both had been acquainted with him for years, even when he was still *el bikbashi* (the colonel) before the coup that brought him to power in 1952. I bought Wilson and Wilton beers, and recorded their quite colorful recollections of Nasser. Between them, they painted a wonderful portrait of the man behind the headlines. About seven minutes into the interview, Hall gave me a mildly anguished look and said, "Alan, if we answer one more question, we're gonna miss our plane." The interview ended abruptly. Off they went to Cairo. Off I went to the Middle East Airlines desk to book my flight back home and arrange for my bags—already stashed on the aircraft—to go from Beirut to Cairo to Athens.

I settled down in my seat, and after the plane was airborne over the sparkling blue Mediterranean, I plugged in the tape recorder and transcribed the Hall–Wynn–Heil conversation about the late Egyptian president. Upon landing in Athens, by now late afternoon, I rushed to the VOA news bureau just off Constitution Square. I telexed the entire interview to Washington, and stuck those infernal alligator clips in the phone leads and fed it on the phone as well. "Go home and get some rest," came the word from the coverage desk. "Okay," I growled.

Greater than the Sum of Its Parts

Every so often, things really click at America's Voice, among news bureaus, field offices, and the Washington support staff in the newsroom and language services. Longtime Deputy Program Manager Cliff Groce observed that "VOA is greater than the sum of its parts, especially when the team works together." This was certainly one of those cases.

Someone in the newsroom took a perforated tape (the text of the Hall–Wynn–Heil interview) and gave it to the Near East and South Asia Division. That division, headquarters of the Arabic Branch, put it back on a spindle and relayed it at once to the island of Rhodes, in the eastern Mediterranean. In 1970, all VOA programs in Arabic were prepared and broadcast directly from Rhodes via medium wave to the Arab East, including Egypt.

In Rhodes, the extraordinarily alert and able program center director, Dick Curtiss, immediately took the text of the interview and grabbed three members of the Arabic staff. He had each of them assume one of the roles in the conversation—one was Hall, one was Wynn, one was Heil—and they speedily translated each of our comments or questions from English to Arabic.

On the eve of Gamal Abdel Nasser's funeral (attended by millions, some of whom watched the cortege from atop swaying palms), VOA Arabic broadcast the reenacted Saut Amerika (Voice of America) interview. A day or so later, the leading, semiofficial Cairo daily *Al Ahram* carried portions of the text, highly unusual in a newspaper that during most of the Nasser era had been very critical of the United States.

Well, I had to settle for the crumbs, in a sense, and you'd think that would be the end of the biggest story I ever blew. But not quite. I got home in Athens just in time for supper that September 29, 1970. The kids were chattering about school, and we had a good time catching up on all the family news of the past few days. It was fairly early to bed, at last, for the soundest of sleeps. Or so I thought.

That Confounded (but Enterprising) Coverage Desk

At around midnight, the phone rang. It was the coverage desk in Washington. "Alan, we've booked you onto an Air Force C-130 flying out of the air base in Athens at 3:30 A.M. with relief supplies for a MASH hospital in Amman. Good luck!"

That suffering saint, Dot, drove me to the air base in the dead of night. I seemed to be the sole civilian passenger on the great C-130, and soon was assigned a netted, bucket-like seat in the dark, cavernous, windowless hold, crammed close to jeeps, armored personnel carriers, and boxes and boxes of supplies. Airmen were nowhere to be seen, and it was lonely and quite cold—something akin to being a shivering Jonah in the belly of the great whale. In no time, we were airborne.

Another catnap. The flight pattern was necessarily much longer than in ordinary times. No C-130 could cross Syrian airspace, of course, nor could this flight cross Israel or Israeli-occupied territory. Therefore, we had to fly over Egypt, south of the Gulf of Suez, the western extension of the Red Sea; around Eilath at the tip of the Sinai Peninsula; and back north again on the sea's eastern arm, the Gulf of Aqaba.

From the Belly of the Whale to a Breathtaking View

Suddenly, I was awakened. "Hey, young fella," an officer from up front in the cockpit exclaimed. "Why don't you come up with us?"

I hustled gladly into the cockpit. The plane was now headed north. The dawn was beautiful over the desert hills of the Arabian Peninsula, off to the right, and the Sinai Peninsula, over to the left. The pilot and copilot were enjoying cups of steaming coffee, and offered me one. Then, as I took in the spectacular view in a sweeping panorama, 180 degrees through the front window of the cockpit, I was truly startled when the pilot said: "Here, son, take the stick for a minute." There I was, steering a gigantic transport thousands of feet above the Gulf of Aqaba, feeling its surging power as I maneuvered to climb, then descend, then climb, for all of fifteen seconds.

My hosts had no way of knowing how little sleep I had gotten over the past seventy-two hours. They were plainly amused. They let me have the magnificent spare seat in the back of the cockpit for the rest of the way. In the gathering morning light, we flew over the Jordanian port of Aqaba, adjacent to the Israeli port of Eilath. The C-130 descended farther as we swept north along the length of the inland Dead Sea. It swooped to the east, and within minutes, the giant bird of mercy set down onto the runway of Amman International Airport.

The Detritus of War

Now I had by this time been in scores of airports during my tour as a foreign correspondent, but never one quite like this. Not a soul was to be seen. The gate to customs and immigration was swinging in the wind. No passport control. No taxis. Mine, as it turned out, was one of those jeeps I had been riding with in the skies between Athens and the devastated city of Amman. It rolled down the ramp at the rear of the C-130, and I hitched a ride on it, bound for the MASH facility, the only way into town. We quickly found ourselves in the sloping byways of Amman, that city of seven hills. The once-peaceful fieldstone buildings now had charred windows or roofs blown off. The streets were deserted. Smashed glass on the pavement glistened in the morning sun. There were wrecked cars, frozen in place where they had been destroyed by firebombs or maybe artillery. The telephone and electric wires were severed from their poles, one of them still spouting sparks like the entrails of a mortally wounded dragon. The metal shutters of shops were blown off, some crumpled beyond repair during a conflict just ended. This was Amman, or what was left of it, after Black September.

We made our way to the MASH facility, set up in a school building that had been largely spared in the fighting, save a few blown-out windows. United States Army medics were working feverishly with Jordanian soldiers to help the wounded.

A ten-year-old boy was there. A bit of shrapnel had lodged in his left eye, and the doctors were quite certain that he would not recover sight there, unless this metal splinter of war could be removed fairly soon. One of the Americans asked if anyone could find a nail or metal spike. Not too difficult, in this neighborhood ravaged by war. Within minutes, someone found a four-inch-long steel rod, somewhere out there. The army doctor quickly coiled a wire with current from a MASH generator around the rod, thus fashioning a magnet. It magically pulled that piece of shrapnel right out of the young victim's eye. My tape recorder was running. Comments by the doctors, the boy, and a bit of wraparound description.

Pigeoning in Ancient Days

I stepped into an empty classroom, jotted down notes for a couple of eye-witness reports. No telephone connections in Amman. No electricity, even. The only way to get the news out—a quarter of a century before portable satellite telephones, known in the profession as "satphones"—was to pigeon that information out. That is, quickly pack up the tapes and the hand-printed texts. Give the envelope with this precious bit of cargo to the driver of the truck returning to the airport. He, in turn, handed the tape to the C-130 pilot flying back to Athens. The pilot then phoned the VOA bureau in Athens, and secretary Alkistis hastened to the air base and picked up the tape. Then she telexed it and phone fed it from Athens to Washington. With luck, VOA would broadcast it back to the Middle East in English (and an Arabic translation) perhaps eight or nine hours later.

I met the truck to the airport at least once a day for the next four or five days until power was restored to the war-torn capital and I could feed from the central post office. By pigeoning, it was possible to send a fairly complete account of the deployment of an Arab peacekeeping force authorized at the Cairo summit, the fedayeen stacking of arms, the movement of the Palestinian commandos away from populated areas in preparation for their eventual withdrawal to Lebanon, and the beginnings of reconstruction and restoration of services in the Jordanian capital. It all had to be done by daylight. The city's residential neighborhoods were without power for most of what turned out to be a two-and-a-half-week stay; at night, it was pitch black in the deserted villa where the press was billeted. Only tracer bullets—the dying embers of the civil war—lit the sky from time to time.[1]

A STRUGGLE ON MANY FRONTS

War stories. The history of VOA is studded with them, from the early days until the present. We've seen, in chapter 3, how Barry Zorthian deployed the first Voice correspondents "out there" from 1950 onward. Over the years, the number of VOA correspondents grew from a half dozen in the pioneering era to more than a score of overseas news bureaus and ten bureaus in the United States by the year 2000. The forging of the corps over the years was a struggle on many fronts.

The Struggle for Acceptance by Professional Peers

As you'll recall from chapter 2, news agencies and the commercial broadcast and print media in the United States were uncomfortable with VOA reporters (government employees) working in their midst. Associated Press refused to permit VOA to subscribe to or use its news wires (other than as a tip service) from 1946 to 1978, and United Press imposed a similar ban for many years. VOA correspondents had great difficulty in getting accredited to correspondents' associations in Washington and elsewhere around the world because of the stigma of "government journalist." On Capitol Hill, accreditation in both Senate and House galleries was necessary for full access to the halls of Congress; VOA reporters were denied this certification from the late 1940s until the early 1980s. In New York, police passes were withheld from VOA correspondents for more than two decades, and even overseas, VOA had

---

VICTORY FOR THE VINDICATED

By the 1990s, VOA correspondents had won top posts in foreign correspondents' associations around the world. They had been elected presidents of such groups in South Africa, Switzerland, Kenya, and, most famously, Britain, where the Voice's Gil Butler became president of the Association of American Correspondents in London. It was an office held earlier by such distinguished broadcast and print journalists as Edward R. Murrow, Drew Middleton, Elie Abel, Rod MacLeish, Ray Scherer, and Raymond Swing (the last subsequently a senior news analyst at VOA). Only a few months before his expulsion from Beijing, VOA's Alan Pessin was named vice president of its foreign correspondents' association (chapter 1).*

*Voice of America, *Voice of America Broadcasting for the 90s*, annual report (Washington, D.C.: Voice of America, 1990), 4.

---

difficulty getting full recognition by the foreign correspondents' associations in Brussels and Tokyo.

Gradually, though, the barriers fell. As the first and second waves of VOA correspondents were deployed in greater numbers from the late 1960s onward, many became respected members of the "pack." This translated into support in much of the establishment press and broadcasting industry, particularly among foreign correspondents who listened to VOA to keep up with news in regions they covered. The last huge hurdle fell on Capitol Hill, where the press galleries were the most recalcitrant in refusing access. The breakthrough occurred in 1983. Senator Jesse Helms (Republican of North Carolina) entered a hearing room of the Senate Rules Committee, eyes blazing with anger, and inquired of a gallery correspondents' spokesman why Tass and Izvestia correspondents had full access in the halls of Congress and those of America's Voice did not. That did it.[2]

The Struggle with Foreign Governments that Opposed or Feared VOA News Reporting

Over the years, VOA correspondents have been detained temporarily in foreign jails, refused press accreditation by authorities of other countries, denied entry visas to cover significant events, or expelled (chapter 1). In

Argentina in the 1970s, Bolivia in the 1980s, and the Democratic Republic of the Congo (then known as Zaire) in the 1990s, VOA correspondents were held at airport checkpoints or police stations as U.S. embassies intervened to secure their release. Newsroom correspondent Stephanie Ho was shadowed by Chinese security police and detained three times during a five-year tour in the 1990s. In 1994, VOA Hausa Service reporter Shehu Kura was badly beaten by Nigerian government security forces in Abuja, the capital. Kura was covering a protest demonstration at the trial of M. K. O. Abiola, who had won Nigeria's presidential election a year earlier but later was convicted of treason by the military regime.[3]

In Syria, VOA correspondent Mohamed Ghuneim was detained for twelve hours by police while attempting to enter the country in January 1987. According to American embassy officials there, Ghuneim, an American citizen who filed reports in both Arabic and English, was taken from Damascus International Airport to another location and kept in a tiny, dark cell. He was interrogated repeatedly about ties to Iraq, PLO leader Yasser Arafat, and the U.S. government. After vigorous U.S. embassy intervention with the Syrian Ministries of Foreign Affairs and Information, Ghuneim was released and remained in the Syrian capital for five days. He conducted a half dozen interviews with Syrian educators and cultural figures and hired a contract reporter (or stringer) in Damascus. Syrian officials later apologized to Ghuneim, calling his detention a case of "mistaken identity."[4]

The Struggle with Some U.S. Policymakers in Washington and American Embassies Abroad

There were numerous occasions, over the years, when U.S. ambassadors and other diplomats were less than comfortable with VOA newsgathering in countries where they were stationed. In some instances, chiefs of mission delayed or prohibited the establishment of VOA bureaus in capitals or cities overseas, or refused permission for VOA to send correspondents in to cover specific stories. Eventually, Congress weighed in on the side of VOA journalistic integrity, and the State Department issued new guidelines drafted by the Voice. Under these, VOA correspondents would be treated like all other journalists, with offices separate from embassies and missions, and U.S. envoys were prohibited from editing their reports (chapter 8).

A STAGE OF ENDLESS DIMENSIONS

Despite the obstacles, VOA correspondents, by and large, succeeded in reporting the news and in "getting it straight" for hourly newscasts. They also added an on-scene presence to the news and current affairs programming, an important audience builder from the mid-1960s onward. Many correspondents did this by creating, as radio dramatist Arch Oboler once stated, "a stage of endless dimensions in the imagination of the listener." They reflected important events and the commonplace, in the United States and in the far corners of the Earth. The best of them took full advantage of VOA's format, broadcasting reports or backgrounders that were somewhat longer than the standard thirty- to fifty-second sound bites so frequently heard on American commercial networks. What a News Division correspondent or stringer writes in English often is translated into at least some of VOA's more than twoscore other languages. Here are excerpts from reports of VOA correspondents during the last third of the twentieth century.[5]

Ron Pemstein, Auschwitz, Poland: June 7, 1979

In a place where four million people were exterminated, Pope John Paul talked about life. In a place born of war, he talked about peace. And in a place where man was degraded, the Pope talked about man's dignity and human rights. The place was the former Nazi extermination camp at Auschwitz/Oświęcim. The barbed wire and watch towers remain as reminders of a painful past. But Thursday, the people clinging to the barbed wire were cheering still another contradiction of the past—a Polish Pope from this region. The Pope celebrated mass and gave his address where prisoners were selected for either work or death, at the end of a railroad track. Some of those taking part in the ceremony were dressed in concentration camp uniforms. The Pope paid special tribute to three groups that suffered most in the camp, the Jews, the Russians, and the Poles. Pope John Paul said he could not fail to come back to this place, which he called a giant tomb of the unknown. He gave a contemporary eulogy not just for the four million who died in Auschwitz but also to those, he said, whose rights were violated anywhere in the world.

Elizabeth Arrott, Nazran, Russia: January 16, 1995

ARROTT: In the railyards of Nazran, the only cargo is human. Thousands of refugees from Russia's invasion of Chechnya have come to this barren place, their nights spent sleeping in train cars, their days, trying to find food. A little girl runs across the muddy railroad tracks. Her coat is dirty, her cap askew, a tattered cloth flower is fastened in her braid.

TAPE/GIRL: My name is Margaret.

ARROTT: Margaret, seven years old, arrived with her parents here from the besieged Chechen capital this morning. She stands next to her father, who before the war ran a cultural center in Grozny. He explains Margaret was named for Margaret Thatcher. The former British prime minister visited Moscow when the little girl was born. He pulls out a faded newspaper clipping. It shows Margaret holding an autographed picture of the British politician. The photograph, he says, was a present from Margaret Thatcher.

TAPE/FATHER: Let me show you Margaret's gift from our leader, Boris Yeltsin.

ARROTT: He pulls out a fragment of a bomb. The day before they fled Grozny, Margaret's father went to get some belongings from their apartment. It was across from the presidential palace, he says. It no longer exists. Margaret's mother flips through the pictures. They are from the family's vacation last year in Prague: Margaret playing in a park, the family out to dinner, the parents dressed in evening clothes, ready for the theater. The train finally arrives. Margaret and her parents disappear in the crush of people desperate to find a place. Moments later, Margaret reappears at a window, her face pressed against the glass. The little girl waves as she heads off to her new life.

Steve Thompson, Aboard the Carrier USS *Midway* off Vietnam: April 30, 1975

The helicopter hovered just above the roof of the U.S. embassy and then slowly settled onto the landing pad. A small group of Americans and Vietnamese scrambled aboard. The pilot gunned the engine and the bird lifted off and began a perilous race to Tan Son Nhut airport for transfer of its tense human cargo to a bigger bird for the long flight out to the fleet standing off the coast.

Perhaps for the last time Saigon flashed below. The streets were nearly deserted, thanks to a twenty-four-hour-a-day curfew. But large crowds had gathered around the embassy compound. Some were just curious about all the frantic activity. Others were begging to be taken out. U.S. Marines kept them at bay. Tan Son Nhut was tense. Minutes seemed to pass like hours as the assemblies waited for the larger evacuation helicopters to arrive. All baggage was discarded. A U.S. colonel said the space was needed for people. There were only a few grumbles. Then, barreling in out of the chaos, the evacuation helicopter appeared. The people scurried aboard, women and children first. Door gunners helped direct traffic into the cavernous bird as they kept a keen watch out the side hatches. All were aboard and the machine shot skyward and made its run to the coast. Rice paddies flashed below as Saigon disappeared in the distance. However, there was no joviality. This was unfriendly territory below. The tension was too much for one young mother and her tears quickly spread to others. Some prayed. Most sat quietly, eyes fixed blankly ahead.

Suddenly, the copter was taking fire. Bullets ripped through the rear area, miraculously not hitting anyone. The tail gunner fired a burst at an unseen enemy. It then grew quiet, except for the whine of the Giap engine. Soon water was below and an armada of ships appeared. The flight deck of the aircraft carrier *Midway* slowly grew larger. The nightmare was coming to an end.

Sonja Pace, Faya-Largeau, Chad: April 17, 1987

PACE: The recapture of the Chadian oasis of Faya-Largeau (so remote it is a week-long ride deep into the Sahara Desert) marked the latest in a series of triumphs for Chadian government forces. They expelled occupying Libyan troops and antigovernment rebels. Young soldiers like Lieutenant Rozi Hassaballah are proud of their victory. Faya is his hometown. He was here in 1983 when government troops had to flee the intensive Libyan bombing. Now he has come back to help secure the town. Lieutenant Hassaballah says despite years of fighting and neglect, some things haven't changed.

TAPE/HASSABALLAH: Nothing has changed. Faya will always be Faya. But they [the Libyans] have ruined the town. They have destroyed and broken everything. People will come back. But between here and nine kilometers out of town, there were numerous checkpoints [all those years]. It was worse under Libyan occupation than during the colonial period.

PACE: The town has a long way to go before it can accommodate any large number of people. Right now, the market offers only a few vegetables. A loaf of bread is hard to find, as are other basic goods and services. The major commodities for sale at the moment are used Libyan uniforms and AK-47 rifles.

But Lieutenant Hassaballah is right. Some things seem to have a certain air of constancy, like the hospitality of the local population. There is a woman living on the main street just down from the market who took in three bedraggled and hungry foreign journalists, giving them water and a nourishing meal, and then refusing to take any money. There are the children who crowd around the visitor with wide-eyed curiosity. But to truly appreciate Faya, it must be first seen at night, at the end of a long, hard trek through the desert. Then, as your four-wheel drive vehicle bangs and bumps to the crest of a dune, the oasis seems to appear magically from out of nowhere, its soft white sand and swaying palm trees glistening in the light of the stars. Then, whether for the young lieutenant returning home, or for the first-time visitor, Faya-Largeau, in its calm and quiet, seems like paradise.

Gil Butler, Kuwait City, Kuwait: February 28, 1991

TAPE: (*sound of horns honking in jubilation hours after Kuwait's liberation from Iraqi occupation*)

BUTLER: It is one thing to see maps and photographs of the Persian Gulf covered in black smoke. It is quite another to walk the streets of Kuwait City and experience darkness at noon. From the time you cross the border between Saudi Arabia and Kuwait, the sky becomes dark. The sun is obscured, and it is difficult to see things in the distance. But nothing prepares you for Kuwait City, except perhaps an apocalyptic science fiction novel.

At 2:00 P.M., the dark sky became darker during an interview on the seafront. By 2:30, it was pitch dark. Those who had experienced it before pulled out flashlights to light their way. There are no electric lights in Kuwait City except television lights powered by portable generators. The darkness was compounded by a burning sensation in the eyes and throats from the smoky air. Then it began to rain, a quick, heavy shower that seemed to clear the air, temporarily. Kuwait was no longer in pitch darkness but in a kind of pervading gloom. For people emerging from seven months of hostile occupation, the oil fire is just one more of Saddam Hussein's crimes. But the daylight darkness of Kuwait is a warning of what an environmental disaster can mean.

Douglas Roberts, Jerusalem, Israel: November 6, 1994

Israel's austere and imposing parliament building was under siege throughout the day and far into the night as seemingly endless crowds of Israelis poured through the gates to say farewell to Yitzhak Rabin. The flag-draped wooden coffin was placed in the center of a floodlit plaza just outside the main entrance amid an ever-expanding circle of flowers and lighted candles.

Monday's state funeral on nearby Mount Herzl is expected to draw five thousand dignitaries and foreign guests, including dozens of heads of state. But the vigil outside parliament was open to all, and the mourners came from around the country: men and women, young and old, rich and poor, in military uniforms, business suits, and blue jeans. Many wiped away tears as they filed past the coffin. Some sobbed uncontrollably, others chanted prayers, but most simply stared, seemingly lost in thought at this moment of national grief. The mourners carried candles, flowers, or Israeli flags. Others held banners. One said simply: "Farewell, Rabin." Another proclaimed: "No anger, no war, just peace."

Many in the crowd made it clear they were not supporters of Mr. Rabin's policies. Moshe, a Moroccan Jew and backer of the right-wing Likud Party, said the slain prime minister had given away too much to the Palestinians. But even for those like Moshe, Mr. Rabin's place in the pantheon of past Israeli leaders seemed assured. "There was," said Moshe, "no one like him."

As dawn approached Monday, just hours before the state funeral, mourners were continuing to arrive at the parliament building. Many seemed reluctant to leave, even after they had filed past the coffin. Small groups sat on the pavement, singing and praying under a star-pocked sky, the air heavy with the scent of cedar and pine and the last of the autumn roses.

Eve Conant, Stenkovic Refugee Camp, Macedonia: April 16, 1999

CONANT: Tens of thousands of ethnic Albanian refugees are still crowded into Macedonian holding areas and NATO refugee camps near the border with Kosovo. For those at the Stenkovic camp, there are three material things valued above all else: bread, water, and access to a telephone.

TAPE: (*telephone ringing*)

CONANT: One telephone has been set up for the refugees to contact their loved ones and start the search for their lost ones.

TAPE: (*woman on phone*)

CONANT: As soon as this woman hangs up the telephone, she breaks into tears. People in the crowd around her, anxious for their turn to talk, touch her shoulders gently as she makes her way back to her blanket, or her tent, if she is one of the lucky ones here.

TAPE: (*crowd shouting, pleading*)

CONANT: At the far end of the camp, another crowd has formed. NATO soldiers try to hold back what will quickly grow to be a line of hundreds, pushing and shoving to be the first to receive a loaf of white bread. NATO soldiers lock arms and try to form a corridor to create order.

TAPE: (*more crowd sound, escalating*)

CONANT: On this patch of land, several hundred people are crammed together on woolen mats. The Kosovars in this camp made it across the border. But there are others who were turned away. A Western television used a zoom lens to get a glimpse of the Macedonia–Kosovo border point. The pictures show what appear to be a family of eight being told by Macedonian police to turn back. Each is carrying a bag. Even the three children are wearing backpacks. Behind them is Macedonia. In front of them is Kosovo. Surrounding them is barbed wire. They walk slowly.

Edward Conley, Tumengang, North Korea: May 1, 1992

The twelve-car special train that rolled out of Pyongyang to the strains of patriotic North Korean music carried delegations from

Japan, China, South Korea, and the United States on an eight-een-hour, six-hundred-kilometer trip to the northeastern port of Najim. North Korea wants to turn Najim and two nearby seaports into hard-currency-producing special economic zones.

The highly unusual promotion trip allowed the big group of Western observers to get a close-hand look at the northern border region for the first time. It also gave those on the train the oppor-tunity for at least fleeting glimpses of North Korea not ever seen by many foreigners. As the train passed slowly through the central Puk Dae Vong mountains, we could see small villages and agricultural cooperatives trying to scratch out a hard existence from rocky, hilly terrain. Spring has just come to North Korea and summer crops were planted. The farmland was mostly brown and bare and the only livestock seen were a few oxen pulling carts or plows and some goats and sheep roaming the sparsely vegetated hillside. Occasionally, North Korean soldiers could be seen working in the fields with civilians. Medium-sized villages had neat looking white schoolhouses and sometimes formations of small children were marching in cadence to their classrooms. Each town's railroad station was the same: a whitewashed concrete building with a large portrait of North Korean President Kim Il Sung over the entrance.

The train finally took the foreign visitors to the nearby Tumen River, which serves as North Korea's border. Some international trade experts have proposed that the area be turned into an inter-national special economic zone. The thought of more than a hundred Westerners standing in the center of an old North Korean railroad bridge looking into the nearby territories of China and Russia surely seemed impossible just a few months ago.

Lawrence F. Freund, New York City: November 18, 1997

FREUND: Diana Eck is a professor of religion at Harvard University. About a decade ago, she began to notice changes in her classroom as students reflected the changing ethnic mix in the United States. Religious life in the United States, she realized, was also changing, and she organized the Pluralism Project, an effort to detect those changes and answer some questions.

TAPE/ECK: How many mosques were there in Houston, how many Hindu temples in Chicago, how many Buddhist temples in

Denver? So we essentially set out to map the new religious land-scape of America and to ask not only who is here, but how are these traditions changing as they come to the United States? How is Hinduism changing in the American context, for example? And finally to ask: How is America changing as we begin to create a much more pluralist society?

TAPE: (*music: "Ghanesha Sharanam," performed by the Bhajan group, Sri Ghanesha Temple, Nashville, Tennessee*)

FREUND: The actual sound of that religious diversity is now available on a multimedia CD-ROM produced by the Pluralism Project and designed for use by schools, organizations, and individuals. The teaching tool is called "On Common Ground: World Religions in America."

TAPE/ECK: There are many people who will respond with a certain amount of anxiety and fear, because they simply don't know very much about these religious traditions. And other people, like the multitude of people involved in interfaith councils throughout the United States and in local congregations and Jews and Christians and Muslims that are exploring together some of their common heritage, there are other people for whom this is really an oppor-tunity to learn and to make good on the promise of religious freedom that is so fundamental to American democracy.

FREUND: Professor Eck calls the learning tool a work in progress, an invitation to explore the new complexity of the changing American religious landscape.

Charles Medd, Charleston, South Carolina: December 5, 1986

A former cadet is suing South Carolina's state-run military college, the Citadel, charging that his civil rights were violated during a recent campus incident. The incident, involving five white cadets and a black, has attracted new attention to an old, and for many whites, an almost forgotten problem, the Ku Klux Klan.

On the night of October 23, five white cadets wearing white sheets and hoods like those worn by the Ku Klux Klan entered the room of a black cadet named Kevin Nesmith. The uninvited guests shouted obscenities and racial slurs, and like the Klan of old, burned a cross made of crumpled newspapers. Within weeks, cadet Nesmith resigned from the Citadel. His brother, a graduate of the college and a trustee, resigned from that position. And the normally peaceful and always charming city of Charleston, home of the Citadel, was faced with some harsh questions about race relations.

Oddly enough, Charleston, where the first shots of the Civil War were fired, went through this country's civil rights revolution unscathed. City elders claim there were and are no serious racial divisions, a claim that was far more defensible before the incident at the Citadel. Many whites have dismissed what happened as a youthful prank, and they say the college has acted accordingly, applying the strongest possible discipline short of expulsion. For blacks, however, those remedies fall much too short. They want the offending cadets removed from the Citadel. They also want the college to remove some symbols of the past, the waving of the Confederate flag and the singing of "Dixie," so reminiscent, blacks say, of the southern struggle to protect slavery.

The once-feared Klan, which claimed five million members in 1925, has since crumbled into tiny factions, found largely in the poorest rural pockets of the south. Four years ago, a Klan rally near Washington attracted 300 police officers, 160 reporters, and 24 Klansmen. Today, most white Americans view the Klan with a mixture of embarrassment and bemusement. But that's not the view of the blacks. For them, what happened at the Citadel was no prank. To the contrary, it was a very unamusing reminder of this country's unhappy past and of how the two races still deal with that past.

Paula Wolfson, Washington, D.C.: October 8, 1998

WOLFSON: As they walked into the House chamber, lawmakers knew the legacy of this Congress will be its treatment of Bill Clinton. They seemed mindful of history. During the prevote impeachment debate, some quoted the Founding Fathers. "They are watching us," said one congressman as he pointed to a large marble staircase near the House floor.

TAPE/WELDON: At the top of that staircase there is a large painting, a painting by Howard Chandler Christie, entitled *The Signing: The Constitution of the United States*.

WOLFSON: Florida Republican David Weldon told a story about the man in the center of the painting, Benjamin Franklin.

TAPE/WELDON: . . . and it is reported that he walked out of the constitutional convention and a woman approached him and said: "What kind of government have you given us, Mr. Franklin?" And his response was: "A republic . . . if you can keep it."

WOLFSON: On this October day, a day when the mood in the House chamber matched the stormy skies outside, members talked about their responsibility and the republic. There was passion in their voices, sometimes anger, sometimes fear. They offered opposing opinions on the threat posed to the nation by the president's misbehavior. "He broke the law," argued Republicans. "He lied about an affair," said the Democrats.

Democrats were frustrated by a lack of debate time and the knowledge all attempts to stop the Republicans would fail. Their voices formed a chorus of resentment, with the deep resonance of New York congressman Charles Rangel filling the chamber. He said the plan for an unrestrained inquiry is politically motivated.

TAPE/RANGEL: . . . and the reason for it is because it is the only thing they have to take to the American people before this election. What else are they going to take? Your legislative record?

WOLFSON: After the vote for an unlimited inquiry, many members looked worn out as they left the House chamber. They know the impeachment process is just beginning, and it will be their chapter in history.

Jim Malone, Washington, D.C.: December 1, 2000

MALONE: History and high drama were center stage Friday, as the U.S. Supreme Court cautiously involved itself in the disputed presidential election between Vice President Al Gore and Texas governor George W. Bush.

TAPE: (*sounds of chanting*)

MALONE: Outside the court, it was a chaotic scene of protesters chanting and arguing with each other. Both Bush and Gore supporters were well represented, and with a little effort, you could find yourself easily caught in the middle of a screaming match.

TAPE: (*demonstrators yelling at one another*)

MALONE: Inside the ornate Supreme Court chamber, it was a different scene altogether. Reporters scrambled for chairs behind giant pillars along the side of the chamber, while members of Congress and dignitaries such as Caroline Kennedy were calmly escorted to prime seats with a full view of the court proceedings. In a first for the usually secretive court, audio tapes of the oral arguments were released to radio and television networks for broadcast immediately after the hearing ended. Afterward, Bush attorney Theodore Olson said it was obvious that the justices had done their homework.

TAPE/OLSON: They had read the briefs. They asked very difficult and penetrating questions of the lawyers on both sides, and now we will see what happens.

MALONE: The lead attorney for Vice President Gore, Lawrence Tribe, has had a lot of experience arguing before the Supreme Court. But he says it is always difficult to know how the justices will react to the oral arguments.

TAPE/TRIBE: I have learned from twenty-nine other arguments [before the Supreme Court] that you can't always guess anything about where the justices will come out from exactly what they ask.

MALONE: A court decision siding with the Bush campaign could deal a lethal blow to Vice President Gore's efforts to legally challenge the results in Florida. A ruling in Mr. Gore's favor might buy him more time with the American public to pursue the legal challenges in Florida. Legal observers expect the court to act quickly, but given its deliberative nature, it is likely a ruling will not be announced until early next week.

Ed Gordon, Burbank, California: July 30, 1975

The recipe was simple, a few lemons, a lot of sugar. Then, an old orange crate was hauled to the street corner of Judson Place, a sign was roughly lettered: *Lemonade: Two Cents a Glass*. And you were in business. After an hour, or two, or three, perhaps a grand total of four customers had tasted your wares. If it wasn't a financial success, at least something could be said for it artistically: nothing ever tasted as good as that homemade lemonade. Of course, that all goes back forty years ago or so. And we like to think that throughout the country on scorching summer days, thousands and thousands of boys and girls were setting up their own lemonade stands in their own neighborhoods. Norman Rockwell once captured the scene in a painting for the cover of one of our national magazines.

All this came to mind when Rich Melcombe, a nineteen-year-old student at the University of Southern California, set up his lemonade stand in one of our busy Los Angeles suburban shopping centers at Burbank. The product tasted the same, bringing back warm memories. But while we had only a mother to contend with—who sometimes complained about the lemons disappearing from her fruit basket—Rich Melcombe found himself embroiled in the complexities of bureaucracy. First, he needed a business license from the city clerk's office. Then a $100,000 insurance policy for workman's compensation, in case, for example, a helper cut a finger while slicing a lemon. From the Board of Equalization he had to get information on tax structure and Social Security. He had to register a trademark with the secretary of state of California. He had to file a name for his company—he calls it College Made Lemonaid—and advertise it in an authorized newspaper for four consecutive weeks.

But business is now good. He serves more than forty customers in an hour: children, housewives out on a shopping expedition, executives, old timers who endorse the lemonade as "the real thing." Of course, two-cent lemonade is a thing of the past. Rich sells his for thirty-five cents a glass. Which makes one wonder a bit about inflation.

However, the idea is the same. And if we look back to the simplicity and serenity of four decades ago, and the one little lemonade stand on Judson Place, it is with pure nostalgia and no envy at all. We just wanted to be a small businessman. We never wanted to be a lemonade tycoon like Rich Melcombe.

From a busy shopping center near L.A., to the halls of Congress and the Supreme Court, to a remote oasis deep in the Sahara, VOA correspondents have roamed the world for decades. The AP's Mort Rosenblum put it best: "To report it, you must be there. . . . When the phone rings at midnight, you may be in the air by dawn headed for someone else's baffling mayhem. Minor concerns drop away. Is the washer repairman coming? Are eight people invited to dinner? Does your toe ache? Is tomorrow Christmas? Tough. A fireman only has to put on his pants and extinguish flames. You've got to tell a million people who struck the match and why."[6]

THE MASTERS OF MAYHEM

Over the years, VOA reporters have gone to the front lines the world over to ask, "Why?" Among them were two reportorial giants, each over six and a half feet tall, who sought on-scene exclusives no matter how dangerous or difficult the pursuit. Sean Kelly covered wars in Congo and Vietnam with AP's Mort Rosenblum and was with Rosenblum reporting the Nigerian civil conflict in the late 1960s—ducking Biafran and government bullets. In the 1970s, Kelly and colleagues from the *New York Times* and *Newsweek* accompanied guerrillas of the Western Somali Liberation Front across the Ethiopian border to Somalia in the disputed Ogaden region, much to the consternation of the Ethiopian government. Later, Kelly interviewed a Cuban defector at a garden party in the American embassy in Addis Ababa; his hosts were not amused. Still later, a press vehicle in which he was riding was ambushed on a rural road in Zimbabwe-Rhodesia (as it was called at the time), and he and other journalists narrowly escaped injury.* Kelly also broadcast later in his career from Mexico City and Havana. In Cuba, he conducted an unprecedented and controversial VOA interview with Fidel Castro in 1983.

The other giant was the rail-thin, six-foot-seven Milt Benjamin, a contract reporter who broke the story of the birth of a new nation. On December 16, 1971, India's troops defeated those of Pakistan near the eastern city of Dhaka after a war that had lasted for several months. That day, the Pakistani government capitulated and held a news briefing in Rawalpindi, announcing its reluctant acceptance of the independence of Bangladesh, which had been East Pakistan before the New Delhi–supported rebellion. This was long before satphones, and Benjamin had scheduled a 4:00 P.M. two-way radio feed to VOA Washington at the main post office in the Pakistani capital. The Bangladesh birth announcement was issued at about 3:50, two miles away from the studio. Milt ran to the post office, he recalled, as fast as a gazelle—much faster than any local taxi. He was late, but the studio operators (for once) had held the circuit open. Milt was among the first to broadcast the news, and VOA listeners were among the first to hear it.

*Sean Kelly, e-mail to author, June 2, 2002.

About twenty-five years after the Voice of America went on the air in 1942, an energetic young officer named Bill Haratunian became chief of VOA News and Current Affairs. He recognized the necessity of "being there." In a year or two, he greatly expanded the cadre of correspondents begun in the 1950s by program directors Barry Zorthian, Gene King, and others. He realized, as his predecessors had, that effective international broadcasting required much more than cutting, double-sourcing, and rewriting agency copy for newscasts.

The correspondent corps that Haratunian built by the turn of the century stretched around the globe. VOA correspondents have gone to the far corners of the Earth—not only to Kosovo, Chad, and North Korea, but to northern Iraq, the war- and famine-ravaged Horn of Africa, bloody battlefields in Afghanistan, remote reaches of the Kalahari in Botswana, Cuba, the Arctic, and Antarctica. In verifying accuracy, and lending presence and dimension to events, there is no substitute for being there. For being, at one time or another, nearly everywhere.

A BICENTENNIAL BONUS: THE SCOOP OF THE DECADE

I recall particularly what the corps enabled the Voice to do in the early morning hours of the nation's bicentennial, July 4, 1976. We had deployed correspondents and stringers to every city and many towns in America to supplement the work of a large team in Washington and the bureau chiefs in New York, Chicago, Los Angeles, and Miami. Their mission: to report the flotillas, fireworks, and huge celebrations across the land, to provide live feeds for a ten-hour nonstop worldwide special on Bicentennial Day.

To celebrate, Ray Kabaker of the Current Affairs Division leased a Potomac River liner with a capacity of 500. It set sail on the Saturday evening before the big Sunday bicentennial, crammed to capacity with all those VOA managers, editors, and broadcasters in Washington who would coordinate the work of the correspondents the following day. The voyage climaxed with a fair amount of beer and a French embassy sound-and-light presentation at George Washington's mansion in Mount Vernon dedicated to Voix d'Amérique.

There was an unwritten rule then that when any major story broke, anywhere in the world, news chief Bernie Kamenske (chapter 3) would be called for consultation. Well, on this particular evening during the five-hour voyage, he was on the boat, celebrating with the rest of us. This was before pagers, beepers, faxes, or cell phones. If anything happened, the newsroom would simply have to "go it alone."

Shortly before 1:00 A.M., Washington time, the duty editor on the news desk at the Voice downtown, Jane Gillespie, took a call from a very excited stringer in Jerusalem, Al Potashnik. Al had the scoop of the decade: a complete account of Israel's rescue mission to free hostages in Entebbe, Uganda. He had received it from the Israeli Defense Forces (IDF) spokesman moments before it was released to others. He had simply made a routine call to the IDF to inquire if anything was going on. The spokesman gave Potashnik the story before the announcement was put on the IDF's "all call" system.

Well, Gillespie could hardly contain herself. She had the scoop, and no one to call to consult about using it! Al dictated the story to her, and she typed a lead news bulletin with incredible speed, those racing fingers that veteran journalists cherish when handling big news under a tight deadline. She ran to the escalator (the newsroom was then in the base-ment of the Health, Education, and Welfare Building in southwest Washington). Typically, the confounded 1930s-era escalator either didn't work or had been turned off for the weekend. Jane huffed and puffed up two flights of stairs to the studio, hastened in, and thrust the bulletin into the hands of the startled announcer at 1:02.

Gillespie's survival instinct, and a twinge of conscience, immediately set in. She lost no time in calling Bernie at a downtown hotel right after returning to the desk. He had just arrived back from the bicentennial voyage. As he recalled later, his ample belly shook like jelly. He couldn't stop laughing for what seemed like ten minutes, laughing with pride at his newsroom's achievement. The pros had handled the story, and VOA again had a scoop that never would have been possible without the corps that Haratunian and Zorthian had built.[7]

It was not only the correspondents at the Voice of America who ven-tured "out there" over the decades. Its engineers have had to brave malaria-ravaged jungles, insect-infested islands in the Atlantic and Pacific, volcanic-ash showers in the Philippines, and a bloody civil war in Liberia to give America its voice abroad. Next, the story of these intrepid pioneers, both American and from host countries, who built and ran the VOA relay stations that girdle the globe.

5

From Here to Everywhere

BUILDING A GLOBAL NETWORK

When it comes to radio waves, the iron curtain was helpless.
Nothing could stop the news from coming through—neither
sputniks nor mine fields, high walls, nor barbed wires. The
frontiers could be closed; words could not.
—Lech Walesa, foreword to Nelson,
War of the Black Heavens

From Greenville, North Carolina, to Saipan in the Northern
Marianas, the global network of stations has more than 139
transmitters with a combined power capability of almost 40
million watts, that is enough to meet the power requirements
of more than 34,000 American homes. Over 350 antennas
direct signals to audiences worldwide.
—Vicki Brimmer and Terry Balazs,
"The Technical Magic of the IBB's Office of Engineering"

Take a drive in the countryside southeast of Greenville, North Carolina,
at dawn. Somewhere near Hams Crossroads and the village of Blackjack,
deer occasionally wander out of the woods and onto the meadows, less
than an hour's drive from the Atlantic coast. It's an area of cypress
swamps, tobacco farms, and cotton fields. The Tar River snakes through
the land nearby. As the sun rises above the Piedmont plain, you see
mighty steel towers right in the middle of nowhere looming high in the
heavens above the flatlands. These are high-frequency (HF) shortwave
antennas. Some jut nearly 400 feet into the sky. Pairs of these steel transmission leviathans are linked by miles and miles of spider-web-like wires,

stretched like mammoth curtains between them. These curtain antennas shimmer like gossamer mirages in the morning sun. Until you get close.

Then they become immense testaments to the miracle of international broadcasting. Through these curtains of suspended wire (each strand about as thick as your index finger) 6.5 million watts of electricity surge. The array beams shortwave signals that bounce off the ionosphere and back down to millions of radio receivers in Latin America and Africa. A curtain antenna is slewable, meaning that it can be turned or aimed—in this case, thirty degrees in either direction from its normal heading. Most would assume that this could be done only if an entire pair of towers and the network of wires between them were turned at an angle—say, on a movable railroad track.

Wrong. Simply by charging one side of the "curtain" with high power and reducing the power on the opposite side, the engineers can change the trajectory of the signal. For example, if VOA managers decide to direct more broadcasts to Africa because of wars, crises, or a crucial election on that continent, then the engineers at Greenville can shift the power ratios between one side of the "curtain" and the other, and magically change the transmission angle. Or vice versa, in the event of a natural disaster in Central America or a coup d'état in a country in South America.

The arrays of towers, the meshlike curtain antennas, the guy wires holding them together, and the transmitter buildings at their core are called Sites A and B of the Greenville Relay Station.[1] This technical marvel, sprawling over scores of acres, was constructed originally in the late 1950s and early 1960s, thanks to the efforts of George V. Allen, Henry Loomis, and Ed Martin (chapter 3).

During a long-dreamed-of visit to Greenville in early 1998, I got a close-up glimpse of how a shortwave or medium-wave relay station functions. The sun literally never sets in VOA's global network. Relay stations somewhat similar to that in Greenville operate in places as far flung as Delano in California, Tinang in the Philippines, Udorn in Thailand, Colombo in Sri Lanka, Kuwait City in Kuwait, Kavala in Greece, Ismaning in Germany, Tangier in northern Morocco, Botswana in southern Africa, Punta Gorda in Belize, and the jungle isles of São Tomé in West Africa and Tinian in the western Pacific.[2]

Greenville station manager Bruce Hunter (originator of the phrase "VOA, America's best kept secret") explained how transmitters, built by different manufacturers, within the buildings at his site are tested and

Why Shortwave?

During the Persian Gulf crisis of 1990/1991, in an article entitled "Shortwave Radios: More Powerful, More Portable," the *New York Times*'s Philip Shenon explained a delivery system relatively unfamiliar to Americans but widely used throughout the world:

> Perhaps no one understands the value of shortwave radio better than the thousands of Westerners trapped in Kuwait after the oil-rich sheikhdom was invaded by Iraq. . . . Westerners who have since fled Kuwait report that they depended on portable shortwave radios for much of their news, including information about possible routes of escape. . . . The radio frequencies used for regular AM (standard medium wave) and FM radio cannot reach listeners beyond a few hundred miles. Shortwave signals—the waves are indeed shorter than those used in regular commercial radio—rise high into the sky and then bounce off the ionosphere, returning to the earth thousands of miles from their source, making it possible to beam shortwave broadcasts across continents.*

Veteran broadcast engineer and VOA Frequency Division chief in the 1960s and 1970s George Jacobs adds:

> What is there about shortwave broadcasting that continues to make it attractive in this high-tech age? Shortwave broadcasts freely cross frontiers, span continents, and bridge oceans to reach listeners immediately and directly within their own homes. No electronic device or other potential control or constraint stands between the sender and the receiver. The broadcasts do not require the agreement of the recipient country, nor are they dependent upon relays by satellites or terrestrial facilities. It is this directness, immediacy, and intimacy that makes shortwave broadcasting unique.†

*Philip Shenon, "Shortwave Radios: More Powerful, More Portable," *New York Times*, December 2, 1990, D2.
†George Jacobs, "Why Shortwave?" (address at a symposium of the Center for Strategic and International Studies, Washington, D.C., May 23, 1991).

compared. They are huge, boxlike machines, somewhat resembling metal lift vans. Many have consoles and dials utterly beyond the comprehension of the technically untrained eye. The transmitters are hooked up to a device called a switch matrix. In an amazing series of scheduling miracles, the switch matrix "drives" the towering antennas outside, where the deer graze.

The Greenville Relay Station also has been used over the years as a training center for VOA transmission technicians from around the world. Those from the tiny West African island state of São Tomé (many without even a high-school education and limited English) were said to be particularly eager and adept learners, as were their counterparts from Liberia and the Philippines.

LORD OF THE SKY

One of the most fascinating characters I met during the Greenville visit was a veteran rigger with the unlikely name of Lord Byron Van Wagenen. A rigger is what the title implies. He scales the mighty towers and matrices of curtain antennas and guy wires to install new connections or make repairs. At the time of my visit, Lord Byron had been doing this work for more than thirty-two years, practically since Edward R. Murrow dedicated the relay station in the early 1960s. Muscular and youthful looking for his age, he drives the heavy yellow maintenance truck out onto the soft sand of the Piedmont plain. He then uses a mechanized pulley on the back of the flatbed rear of the vehicle to winch his repair platform, an open-air elevator, skyward.

At times, his colleagues, the curtain antenna technicians, must swing out into free space to work on dipoles or rigging wires suspended between the support towers. They straddle the guy wires, the high wires, like acrobats without a safety net. "The scenery," said one, "is terrific." Lord Byron's journey into the heavens can be equivalent to ascending four-fifths the height of the Washington Monument. I asked him how long it takes to go to the top. The veteran rigger said a typical climb is about thirty-five minutes, "but the younger guys can do it in less time."[3]

Those "younger guys" in the technical business of international broadcasting, of course, have an amazing range of other delivery systems besides shortwave to master these days. Although there were an estimated 700 million shortwave receivers in the world at the turn of the century, medium wave (standard broadcast band), FM radio, television, and the Internet all were transforming the way people received information from beyond the borders of countries where they lived. Bandwidth expansion continued at a breakneck pace. "The future is digital," observed one internationally known broadcast engineer. In 1999, a new generation of Internet was being developed to transfer data at a rate 45,000 times faster than the typical modem of that time. The information superhighway, it was said, would soon be capable of accommodating the transmission of ten encyclopedias around the world in less than a second.[4]

International broadcasting scholar Donald R. Browne wrote a book in 1982 called *International Broadcasting: The Limits of the Limitless Medium*. Those limits, two decades later, clearly are of an entirely new magnitude. In the industrialized world, the consumer is limited by only an embarrassment of communications riches. There, the twenty-first-century user has available texts, audio, video, around-the-clock all-news TV, and Internet access any time of the day or night. In the poorer nations, the obstacles to information in the year 2000 were a matter of economics sadly akin to those of the 1980s; slightly more than half the world's citizens had yet to make their first telephone call. Their window of choice to the outside world remained as it had been two decades earlier. It was an inexpensive shortwave transistor radio, sometimes a windup receiver powered by a clock spring in a rural area where no batteries were to be had. International broadcasters had to serve both audiences.

BUILDING A GLOBAL NETWORK

As early as 1920, V. I. Lenin had ordered experimentation with shortwave as a "newspaper without paper and without distances," a way of reaching all eleven time zones of the Soviet Union.[5] Two decades later, the Voice went on the air, largely on shortwave but also on leased lines to Britain. At times, the World War II pioneers of VOA even recorded their programs on acetate disks (chapter 2). They were flown in bomber bays across the Atlantic, put on BBC transmitters, and beamed to Europe—with luck, seventeen hours later. And they called it news.

Alongside the struggle to get it straight was the struggle to get the programs there, just about anywhere in the world. During the war years, the broadcasts were aimed primarily at Europe and Asia. From the 1950s to the end of the century and beyond, transmissions expanded to Africa, the Middle East, and, in fits and starts, Latin America. The struggle persisted, from shortwave to digital multimedia (including the standard broadcast band, FM affiliates, television, e-mail, and Webcasting in text, sound, and video).

From a United States perspective, three major technical problems had to be resolved in building a global network:

- Overcoming signal deterioration in broadcasting to northern latitudes, the so-called auroral zones so unfriendly to shortwave propagation
- Confronting the vast distances across two oceans, the Pacific and the Atlantic, which separate North America from the huge potential audiences in Eurasia and Africa (all other major international broadcast powers are much less distant, geographically, from most of the world's people)
- Countering jamming, first by the World War II Axis powers, and subsequently by the Communist powers of the former Soviet bloc, China, and Cuba[6]

Starting from Scratch

During the early 1940s, even before the attack on Pearl Harbor, the Roosevelt administration ordered the Coordinator of Inter-American Affairs (CIAA), Nelson Rockefeller, to lease twelve shortwave commercial stations in the United States.[7] The goal: to counter Nazi propaganda in the Americas. Eventually, the Office of War Information (OWI) also leased facilities from NBC, CBS, General Electric, Westinghouse Radio, WRUL in Massachusetts, and Crosley Corporation's Bethany Relay Station in Ohio (the last on the air from 1944 to 1995) to carry direct shortwave transmissions during the war. There were local rebroadcasts in Latin America of these programs, shipments of disks to radio stations there, locally contracted productions, and some programs produced and sponsored by U.S. commercial advertisers.

World War II spurred construction by the government of America's first international shortwave transmitters, all located within the United States. Historian Robert William Pirsein, who wrote the most comprehensive account of VOA's first quarter century, notes that by 1945, nineteen of these transmitters were on the air.[8] Private international shortwave licensees operated them. But planners realized at the end of the war that if the United States really wanted to reach listeners and compete globally, overseas relay stations had to be built. Because of the auroral-zone propagation problem for shortwave, they had to be located below the northernmost latitudes.

Moving Beyond the Seas, and Even on Them

The first relay stations were built or leased in Britain, Algeria, Tunisia, Italy, the Belgian Congo, and Saipan. Wartime transmissions were jammed by both Germany and Japan. The American Broadcasting Station in Europe (ABSIE, chapter 2) had eight transmitters, four short-wave and four medium wave. In the mid- to late 1940s, additional relay stations were built in Germany, the Philippines, Greece, Morocco, and Hawaii.[9] They received programming from thirty-six shortwave stations in the continental United States. They then relayed the pro-gramming to listeners with shortwave receivers, usually within a single hop (2,000-mile) or double hop (4,000-mile) range of the relay station. Under optimal conditions, the shortwave signal could leap halfway around the world, as happens even today from perhaps the most techni-cally sophisticated of all the VOA shortwave relay stations at Delano, California.[10]

In 1950, the Voice began using a ship at sea for a relay station. A U.S. Coast Guard cargo vessel was refitted with a platform for shortwave and medium-wave antennas, diesel-generating capability for transmission power, and a broadcast equipment room. The USS *Courier*, with a crew of ten officers and eighty men, was commissioned by President Harry Truman on March 7, 1952. It began operations off the Greek island of Rhodes about six months later and was on the air until May 1964, when it was replaced by a land-based VOA relay station on Rhodes.[11]

Construction to Combat Jamming

Unquestionably, an important motivation behind the ambitious Ring Plan of the early 1950s was the desire of the United States to counter high-powered Soviet jammers (chapters 1 and 2). The core strategy of the Ring Plan was to encircle the USSR and its satellites with fourteen high-powered transmitters and six more powerful U.S.-based feeder sta-tions. For the first time, VOA designed 1-megawatt (1,000-kilowatt) medium-wave transmitters for overseas sites. A megawatt signal is roughly twenty times that of the most powerful AM-band signals one can hear in the United States on car radios.[12]

WHAT IS JAMMING?

George Jacobs defines jamming as "deliberate and intentional interference with a radio station on the same frequency, either in the form of another broadcast or by placing sophisticated noises on the frequency which not only block out reception of the intended broadcast, but also create a psychological condition where it's impossible to listen."*

Skywave jamming is when a nation uses transmitters to obstruct a shortwave signal reflected off the ionosphere during the final split second of its long journey from abroad to a listener. This produces a noxious noise such as that used by the Chinese during the Tiananmen crisis. This kind of jamming can be effective over a wide area.

Groundwave jamming, on the contrary, is local, usually in a single urban area. A competing program or thick blanket of noise is broadcast on a shortwave or medium-wave frequency in a city and its suburbs reaching thirty kilometers, or just under twenty miles.

Jamming is a violation of numerous international treaties, including the Universal Declaration of Human Rights adopted by the United Nations General Assembly in 1948; the Final Act of the Helsinki Accords, agreed to by the Warsaw Pact and NATO nations in 1975; and the International Telecommunications Convention, signed in Geneva in 1982. Over the years, there has been technically confirmed jamming of VOA broadcasts by the Soviet Union, China, Bulgaria, Poland, Burma, North Korea, Iran, Iraq, Cuba, Czechoslovakia, Axis Japan, and Nazi Germany.

*Quoted in Eugene S. Reich, "The Wall of Noise" (script of VOA *Studio One* documentary, February 1, 1987), 5.

As we've seen, the proposal for building huge shortwave feeder stations in the eastern and western United States was a victim of the McCarthy hearings. Plans to outfit more *Courier*-type sea-based transmitters proved not to be cost effective. Ed Martin, who became chief engineer about five months after the hearings, recalled that the executive branch "moved quietly and practically eliminated the professionals in our engineering staff . . . but fortunately, we held on to a small handful."[13]

"It took until about 1958," Martin added, "'till we could start getting somewhere, to get over the McCarthy period, and complete study

THE "WAR OF THE BLACK HEAVENS"

International broadcasters, including VOA, used a number of techniques to counter jamming. Former Reuters general manager Michael
Nelson addressed them in a landmark book published in 1997. Its title,
*War of the Black Heavens: The Battles of Western Broadcasting in the
Cold War*, originated in a statement that Nelson discovered by an
Izvestia journalist who said that jamming and counterjamming measures
constituted an intensification of the conflict in the airwaves, "jointly
known as the 'black heavens.'" This was a reference to the massing of
transmitters in the West and Western broadcasts shortly after the Soviet
invasion of Czechoslovakia in 1968 and Moscow's effort to turn up the
jammers in response.*

*Michael Nelson, *War of the Black Heavens: The Battles of Western
Broadcasting in the Cold War* (Syracuse, N.Y.: Syracuse University Press,
1997), i. The journalist is identified as Karl Nepomnyashchi, correspondent
of the Novosti News Agency, Izvestia. He made the statement on August 21,
1968, the day the Soviet Union invaded Czechoslovakia and quashed
Prague's attempt to shake off Moscow's dominance.

after study, trying to make people understand the need for transmitters." Martin credited George V. Allen, director of the United States
Information Agency (chapter 3), with breaking the logjam. New shortwave relay stations or powerful medium-wave stations were built in
Germany, Okinawa, and the Philippines. The Baker East plan was
revived at Greenville. Stations were also constructed in Thailand and
in Sri Lanka, then known as Ceylon.

To penetrate jamming, Martin and his associates employed frequencies
on yet a third band, long wave (LW). Many receivers in the Soviet Union
and Warsaw Pact countries could take in long wave, and VOA engineers
constructed a powerful megawatt long-wave transmitter near Munich that
was capable of reaching deep into the USSR. VOA used that facility for
many years. The Soviet Union jammed only Russian and nationality languages, but left English in the clear throughout the Cold War.

During the heyday of Soviet jamming, estimates of the Kremlin's
annual expenditures on the operation of more than 3,000 jamming stations ranged from $500 million to $1.2 billion, far more than any Western

international broadcaster spent on its entire worldwide operation. Massing transmitters and transmitting the same program on many frequencies (also known as barrage broadcasting) was one way to overcome jamming. Another was to take advantage of what was called twilight immunity. In the early evening, when there still was sunlight in the West but darkness in the East, it was possible to more easily broadcast effectively to a jammed area like the Soviet Union. Since the ionospheric layer shrinks in the evening coolness, somewhat like an automobile tire shrinks at the onset of cold weather in the autumn, it was technically more difficult for jammers to intercept the incoming signal "bounced" off the shifting ionosphere. Consequently, more of the programming got through.

A third way to counter jamming was the use of so-called speech clippers. As Martin explained, a clipper is a transmission device that deliberately reshapes the wave form that is going into the transmitter to concentrate the energy on that part of the speech spectrum "most conducive to conveying intelligibility to give literally a greater apparent voice power to the listener." Martin, who retired in the mid-1970s, added that clippers are practical only for speech, "so you disengage them when you have music on the air."[14]

Program producers did their share to help defeat jamming. They repeated entire program blocks, particularly at twilight in the audience area, to increase the chance that listeners might hear them. Aware of the speech clippers, they played music in a single programming block, separate from other materials, and announcers spoke slowly (in Special English and foreign languages) to increase comprehension of jammed radio signals.[15]

"Jamming is really an admission of a bad cause," the BBC said in a statement during the height of World War II. "The jammer has a bad conscience. He's afraid of the influence of the truth."[16] The inventiveness of victims of jamming—listeners on the ground denied "the forbidden fruit" of external broadcasts—is awe inspiring. In the USSR, it included comparing notes on broadcasts with neighbors or traveling to countryside dachas or public parks to improve audibility of what were commonly referred to as "the Voices."

Expanding in the 1960s

Between the late 1950s and mid-1960s, there were profound changes in international broadcasting. Because of development of the transistor, the number of inexpensive, smaller radio receivers doubled throughout the world. After President Kennedy's celebrated American University address in May 1963, offering a new dialogue with the Soviet Union, jamming ceased in Europe except in Bulgaria and East Germany. Since the beginning of the Cold War, VOA had broadcast primarily to Communist countries in Europe and East Asia. Now it had to reach out to other regions, including better educated, better informed, younger listeners with a much greater access to a variety of news and information sources.[17]

Overall, airtime of all the international broadcasters doubled. The United States' share of transmissions in the increasing babble of voices decreased from 6 to 4 percent. The Voice, to help keep America's presence in the marketplace of ideas, had to strengthen its technical and programming reach to Latin America and South Asia and to begin to reach audiences in Africa.

VOA relay stations sprouted like mushrooms in the most remote locations. They included a huge site (six 250-kilowatt and two 50-kilowatt shortwave transmitters) in Liberia, the remote village of Selebi-Phikwe in Botswana, and Quesada in northern Costa Rica.[18] Selecting, negotiating, and constructing the sites often was a Herculean feat. Host governments at times offered choices of swampland or less desirable locations at a high price. These sites often were infested with malaria or other diseases, far from any potable water or power supply.

Over the years, local communities objected to construction for political or presumed ecological reasons, despite rigorous U.S. environmental standards. Some host countries attempted to write programming content restrictions into the long-term relay station agreements. When a site was cleared for construction, contracts had to be let under rigorous U.S. federal competitive bidding rules, which at times delayed project completion by years. Geopolitical changes or in-country politics meant that some projects had to be abandoned after an investment of millions of dollars (the end of the Cold War, along with objections by local ecologists, caused the cancellation of a project in Israel in the 1990s).

The 1970s: Lean Years and the Advent of Satellites

During the 1970s, budgetary constraints and renewed congressional skepticism about the value of international broadcasting adversely affected the Voice's effort to expand and modernize its global network. After the construction of a new Kavala Relay Station in northern Greece in the early 1970s, additions to the $1 billion overseas relay station system slowed significantly.

In the late 1970s, VOA lost its very valuable Okinawa medium wave-relay station, which gave it a powerful reach into mainland China. The Department of State notified VOA management that the facility was being returned to Japan following the reversion agreement. This was an additional weakening of VOA's worldwide delivery system.

Not all the technical news was bad for the Voice in the 1970s, however. In 1977, VOA began to use satellites to transmit programming from the continental United States to relay facilities abroad. Before then, it had been necessary to use shortwave (or occasionally, telephone lines) to reach receiver stations overseas. These shortwave or telephone signals then would be transmitted again from the regional relay stations to the listeners' radios. Often, the quality of the program, as finally heard, was dismal—especially during times of atmospheric disturbances or in areas where programming was jammed. Satellites, with a crystal-clear signal during the first leg of the journey, inevitably improved audibility. Over the next two decades, VOA developed a worldwide satellite distribution system. In 1997, this system was completed, and the headquarters in Washington was linked to all relay stations worldwide, via satellite.

The Modernization Vision of the 1980s

By the early 1980s, then, VOA had built a global shortwave relay station network, a billion-dollar investment, with some powerful medium-wave stations, such as the 1,000-kilowatt (1-megawatt) facilities in the Philippines and Thailand. But many of the transmitters were a quarter century old, or older, including captured Nazi stations at Ismaning, near Munich. At the signing of an agreement between the United States and Morocco in 1984, President Reagan said:

> The Voice of America has been a strong voice for the truth. Despite problems of antiquated equipment and Soviet jamming, the Voice of America has been able to extend its message of truth around the world. Were it not for many years of neglect, the Voice of America could be heard more clearly by many more people around the globe. And that's why our administration has made the same kind of commitment to modernizing the Voice of America that President Kennedy brought to the space program.[19]

A Slumbering Giant, Aroused

In *The History of International Broadcasting,* James Wood observed: "VOA before 1985 might be compared with a slumbering giant: its geographical infrastructure is huge, but its technical muscle is weak. . . . VOA has lagged in the state-of-the-art in such things as frequency agility, super power and new modulation techniques." From 1973 to 1983, the number of high-powered shortwave transmitters in the world (those with a power greater than 200 kilowatts) nearly doubled, from 276 to 470.[20] VOA had only six of them. Clearly, America's Voice had to modernize. Under USIA director Charles Z. Wick, a close friend of President Ronald Reagan, conditions were ripe for the launching of a multiyear $1.3 billion modernization program. It envisioned the construction of approximately a hundred superpower transmitters around the world.

As in the early 1950s, however, construction on a huge scale, all at once, proved more than the federal bureaucracy could handle. The chief VOA engineer hired to direct the early modernization was Maury Raffensperger, a former Defense Department official with a kind of Strangelovian approach to VOA expansion. Under Raffensperger, expenditures and new hiring seemed to know no limits. But contracting to build a hundred superpower transmitters was hugely complex. The blueprint called for the construction of new relay sites (in northern Thailand and Israel) and for substantial upgrades or relocations at other sites (Morocco, Sri Lanka, and Botswana). Within three years after the modernization program was launched with considerable fanfare, Congress began to cut budgets drastically, including the Voice's radio construction program.

Negotiating new or expanded relay station sites, even in countries such as Greece and the Philippines, where VOA had facilities since shortly after World War II, proved to be very difficult. VOA director of modernization Morton Smith said in late 1987 that only $300 million of the $1.3 billion had been appropriated by Congress for the construction of new transmitters, and that $142 million remained unspent because of the slowness in awarding contracts. He added that delays meant a cost increase from $1.3 to $1.7 billion.[21] The USIA inspector general issued a report criticizing VOA for underestimating the scope of the project, ignoring new technologies, and insisting that aspects of modernization first be assessed by outside contractors. Nonetheless, VOA's Office of Engineering, by the end of the decade, had

- Started the construction of ten new superpower shortwave transmitters at the Morocco Relay Station near Tangier
- Completed the design of a mammoth new station at Udorn, northern Thailand
- Begun the operation of a medium-wave facility at Punta Gorda, southern Belize
- Made significant progress in acquiring antennas for the new stations and in building the satellite interconnect system linking Washington with relay stations around the world
- Laid plans for refurbishing aging relay stations in Sri Lanka and Liberia[22]

The management in VOA Engineering was improving. One of the most effective engineering directors of modern times, Walter La Fleur, assumed that post in 1989, and was to stress communications with broadcasters in VOA programming and training of relay station staff of other countries. La Fleur, who retired in July 1993, began reforms that served the Office of Engineering well in the decade ahead.

Rounding Out the Century: Seismic Geopolitical and Technological Changes

At the biannual conference of international broadcasters organized by Radio Canada International in March 1992, the director of Radio France International summed up the changes. As André Larquié put it: "A whole new audio visual landscape is coming into view."[23]

The Cold War was over. The Soviet Union was history. New democracies (or at least new governments) were appearing in Russia, Central Asia, Eastern Europe, the Balkans, Africa, and Latin America. The geopolitical earthquake (it no longer was a bipolar world) was matched by the new ways that people sought and received information. Suddenly, more of them could rely on local media and less on international broadcasters for reasonably reliable news and information about events in their own countries and the world. Television viewing and satellite TV were on the rise, as well as high-quality FM radio. Direct broadcasts via satellite grew, both video and audio. And the 1990s saw the rapid growth of what several analysts called the most important conveyor of information since Gutenberg invented the process of printing by movable type: the Internet. "All the world's a dish," said the *Economist* in the mid-1990s. Five years later, it might have added: "All the world's on-line."

The changes inevitably had an impact on the technical modernization planning at America's Voice and other major international broadcast networks. BBC strategic planner Fritz Groothues observed: "The revolution in communications technology, if we don't adapt, could make shortwave as irrelevant as the clipper ship *Cutty Sark*."[24] That was so in several, but not all, regions. In the developing world, the shortwave world-band radio receiver remained king. At the turn of the century, VOA's largest audiences were in China, Nigeria, Ethiopia, Afghanistan, and Bangladesh.[25]

The United States continued to expand shortwave and medium-wave relay stations. Building on the 1980s modernization program, VOA engineers became part of a new organization called the International Broadcasting Bureau (IBB), which

- Completed ten 500-kilowatt shortwave transmitters in Morocco, moving 10 million cubic feet of earth and pilings to make a coastal swamp site viable.
- Erected seven new 500-kilowatt shortwave transmitters at Udorn, in the jungle of northern Thailand. This facility, with its score of curtain antennas, enhanced VOA's signal in China, Southeast Asia, and some southern-tier former Soviet republics. It is within single-hop shortwave range of 40 percent of the world's population.
- Finished a long-held plan for the construction of four 500-kilowatt and a pair of 250-kilowatt shortwave transmitters in Sri Lanka. There was a devastating fire at this project just after it was completed in 1996. The station was rebuilt and finally became operational three years later, serving China, Southeast Asia, and the Middle East.
- Built, modernized, or expanded eleven high- or moderate-power medium-wave sites in nine countries (the Philippines, Thailand, Kuwait, Greece, Germany, São Tomé, Botswana, Belize, and the Florida Keys).[26]

Medium Wave Emerges

During the last fifteen years of the twentieth century, VOA engineers gradually became convinced that medium wave and FM were essential complements to shortwave. (In 1999, ten of the eleven IBB medium-wave sites around the globe relayed VOA programming, and a number of others were leased.) Regional conflicts and civil wars wracked several world regions in the 1990s. But these wars spawned unexpected requirements for the expansion of VOA delivery systems, notably in the Middle East, the Balkans, and, perhaps most dramatically, Africa. For example,

- After its liberation in the Gulf War in 1991, Kuwait concluded an agreement with the United States for the construction of two medium-wave transmitters (600- and a backup 50-kilowatt facility) for transmissions by VOA to Iraq and Iran in English, Arabic, and Farsi.
- The wars in Croatia, Bosnia, and Kosovo, as well as Slobodan Milosevic's campaign to shut down local independent media in Serbia, caused VOA to launch radio–TV simulcasts in Albanian, Bosnian, and Serbian (regional variants of Serbo-Croatian). During NATO's seventy-eight-day air bombardment of Serbia and Kosovo in 1999, the IBB built or leased five FM stations ringing Serbia. The FM stations were used by VOA, Radio Free Europe/Radio Liberty (RFE/RL), the BBC, Deutsche Welle, and Radio France International—the first such joint venture in the history of international broadcasting.
- The civil war in Liberia caused the closing of the mammoth relay station in that country and spurred the construction of new facilities on the Atlantic island of São Tomé and in the southern African country of Botswana.

WAR AND RESURRECTION: VOA'S AFRICA COMEBACK IN THE 1990S

Liberia

In early 1990, Charles Taylor's rebel bands swept across Liberia, threatening a station that relayed most of VOA's programming to Africa.[27] In April, the evacuation of American supervisors at the Monrovia Relay Station began. By July, they and their families had left the West African country. But Liberian employees heroically kept the station on the air until Sunday, September 17. They carried on as almost 20,000 terrified civilians fleeing the civil war encamped on relay station property.

The Liberian transmitter plant director left in charge, Samuel D. Paye, led a team of about two dozen Liberian stalwarts. They kept the station going for fourteen weeks, near the crossroads village of Careysburg outside Monrovia. VOA engineer and transmission specialist

Gary Wise, one of the last Americans to evacuate, recalls deciding that it was time to go when he could hear Liberian army artillery pounding rebel forces just down the highway. That was in June 1990. The departing Americans turned their residences over to the staff. Just before leaving, they brought in many bags of rice to help sustain Paye, his staff, and their families—who had moved to the safety of the relay station compound. But the food supplies soon ran out. Paye and his team had to scavenge in nearby villages.

Terror in a Relay Site

Throughout much of the time, Paye said, bands of Taylor's National Patriotic Front of Liberia (NPFL) rebels entered the compound and harassed the refugees and station employees. He recalled that they seemed to be uncoordinated. Different commanders made different demands. In one particularly terrifying incident, Paye remembered, "I almost got shot. 'You [VOA broadcasts] are saying negative things about us!' one of Taylor's best known executioners told me, a man named Paul Voye. Then he struck me with a 45-caliber pistol." Pressed by the rebels, Paye refused to supply the names of West Africans of other nationalities working at the station (those employees surely would have been killed).

More civilians crowded into the compound, and the struggle for meager food supplies was chaotic. The wife of Liberia Relay Station employee William Knuckles gave birth to a baby boy. An elderly refugee in the compound died, and a merchant who had brought food in for sale was found murdered in a meadow near the antenna field.

Paye, as the person in charge, said that his most difficult daily task was dealing with both the terrified staff and the refugees. "I was constantly being criticized," he recalled, "for not doing enough to feed them and look after their security. They had heard U.S. Marines were in the country to protect Americans in Monrovia, the capital . . . why not protect Liberian employees?" VOA engineers in Greenville and Washington, meanwhile, had hooked up a high-frequency link with the Liberia Relay Station headquarters building and were in daily contact with Paye to assess the situation and offer encouragement. Paye remembers that they told him to "stay calm . . . keep your safety uppermost. . . . Don't resist if the rebel forces try to take over the station. . . . We'll take it up with Taylor."

Endgame at Careysburg

Then, on Sunday, September 17, it happened. It was six or seven o'clock in the evening, and Paye took a break from his work in the transmitter building and went to his nearby quarters for a brief respite and a bite to eat. He was resting on a couch for a moment when one of his four children (the oldest was ten at the time) told him that there was a knock on the door. Armed rebels came in and ordered Paye to gather the entire staff in the main office. They demanded keys to all facilities and said that they were closing the station.

They then forced the staff onto a bus, took them to the nearby highway crossing of Careysburg, and interrogated the employees late into the evening. All were forced to sleep on a concrete floor, in the home of a man who had been murdered by the militias. The next morning, the interrogation continued. A new commander came to lead the questioning. He accused his fellow Liberians of broadcasting "propaganda." To which Paye replied: "What you're saying is not what we're doing."

Eventually that Monday, the terrified Liberian staff was taken back to the relay station site to pick up their families. All had to make their own way "up country" to home villages or the homes of friends to begin a new life. Taylor's marauding forces, meanwhile, overran and looted the relay station compound. They fought among themselves, Paye said, to seize vehicles there. They stripped copper wiring to try to sell as junk, and smashed all the transmitters in the main building. They completely trashed a $17 million installation. Paye made his way to the Ivory Coast, and the VOA correspondent in Abidjan, Max Ruston, put him in touch with U.S. embassy officials who arranged back pay and helped him get his family out of the northern Liberian village of Ganta, where they had fled. They came to the United States a year later. Paye eventually became an American citizen and an engineer at the Greenville Relay Station.

A year and a half later, a VOA assessment team returned to examine the damage at the Careysburg site. Even then one of its members, Cliff Weese, recalled being questioned menacingly by armed irregulars of various factions at checkpoints en route to the station. The relay facility, he said, was "a total disaster." There was no way, Weese recalled, that VOA could or would ever return.

Throughout Africa, the impact on VOA's audience was disastrous as well. Only twenty-one of seventy-nine hours of VOA programming to the continent could be relayed with anything like a reliable signal from points as distant as Greenville, North Carolina; Bethany, Ohio; Morocco; the Philippines; and a relatively low-power medium-wave facility in Botswana. VOA engineers immediately began to arrange temporary leases of transmission time from other international broadcasters. They pressed ahead with planned enhancements of the Botswana and Sri Lanka Relay Stations. The Monrovia closure was scarcely noticed in the outside world, then preoccupied with Iraq's invasion and occupation of Kuwait.

São Tomé

Less than one month after the last VOA broadcast from Liberia, USIA public affairs officer Jan Hartman in Gabon visited São Tomé and Príncipe. This former Portuguese colony consists of islands that lie about 170 miles off the Atlantic coast of West Africa. Malaria-infested São Tomé, the main island, is largely jungle and home to about 100,000 people. Príncipe, the sister isle, lies a few miles to the northeast. Between October and February each season, the islands are lashed with monsoon rains, so-called horizontal rains, more than 400 inches a year.

A Fortuitous Offer on a Jungle Isle

Hartman, visiting the main isle, paid a call on the president of the Republic of São Tomé and Príncipe, Manuel Pinto da Costa, and his brother, the chief of staff, Henrique Pinto da Costa. She recalled:

> They are both fervent listeners to VOA's Portuguese-to-Africa Service, and one day during my visit that October I was meeting with them in the presidential palace, and they asked why they couldn't pick up VOA any longer. I told them it was because our relay station in Liberia had been burned in local disturbances and was off the air.
>
> The president then said on the spot, "Well, why don't they come here?"
>
> I immediately thought, "Why not?" So I asked them where the VOA might be able to put a relay station, and they suggested the very site where it sits today, which had an old radio installation already on it, long abandoned by the Portuguese. So I told them this was a wonderful idea and I would pursue it.

The Persistent Advocate

Hartman returned to the Gabonese capital of Libreville on the mainland and dashed off a cable to Washington, saying that the president of São Tomé had offered his country as a potential alternative site to Monrovia. The U.S. embassy in Gabon was displeased, to put it mildly, because of the extra administrative burden it might impose. But Hartman persisted. She extended her tour twice in Gabon, staying for four years instead of the usual two "just so I could keep my eye on the VOA project. It's probably one of the best things I've done in the foreign service."

It clearly was one of the best things that happened to VOA in the 1990s. Shortly after Hartman's cable arrived in Washington, engineer Bob Everett, who had learned Portuguese as a USAID officer in Brazil, went to São Tomé to survey the site suggested by President Pinta da Costa. He was driven in a government car to the remote location over pothole-rutted roads, through a mostly abandoned little village, past palm and coconut groves, to a nearby deserted beach. There, a forty- by sixty-foot concrete building stood, abandoned by the Portuguese fifteen years earlier and still linked by a dead power line with a couple of decrepit old antennas. Occasionally, power still crept through the line, but there was no water and no one there, and the generators were filthy, with fuel oil leaking all over the deserted plant. I asked Everett what he thought when he saw all this.

"This is heaven!" he replied.

For an engineer, it was pure paradise. Everett explained: "Here we are on a peninsula, so our transmitting antenna can propagate shortwave nearly perfectly over sea water . . . an extensive, flat, conductive trajectory aimed directly at the most populous area of Africa" (Nigeria, with 120 million people, is just 600 miles to the northeast). Medium wave, Everett noted, was even better. The ocean path extended its range, even during daylight hours.

The Pinheira site, five miles south of São Tomé City, turned out to be perhaps the VOA's prize acquisition in Africa in the 1990s. The United States and São Tomé signed an agreement within two years. VOA broadcasts began in May 1993, along with FM broadcasts produced by the São Toméans. The Pinheira signal, Everett noted, can be heard as far north as Morocco, as far south as Mozambique. It reaches an area inhabited by several hundred million people. It is crystal clear on both medium wave and shortwave in Nigeria, where VOA's adult audience share, thanks to improvements in both signal and programming, grew from 18 to 26 percent during the decade.

Constructing and operating the São Tomé facility was filled with hardships. According to veteran relay station manager Gaines Johnson, nearly every American stationed in São Tomé has had malaria at least once. About 10 percent of the São Toméan staff has the disease. One contractor died of an embolism, because the island has no modern medical facilities. Other relay station sites where VOA engineers have contracted tropical diseases, including dengue fever, are northern Thailand and Belize.

VOA ENGINEERING BECOMES IBB ENGINEERING

The United States Information Agency reorganized in July 1990 by combining (on paper) VOA and its Worldnet Television operations into what was then called the agency's Bureau of Broadcasting. The Office of Engineering served both. Later in the decade, the office was rechristened a second time, as the International Broadcasting Bureau, Office of Engineering and Technical Services.

In the continuing effort to build a global network, IBB Engineering sought to bring its technical property around the world up to standard. The office for the first time had to provide RFE/RL and Radio Free Asia (RFA) transmissions in the mid-1990s. It inherited RFE/RL shortwave facilities in Spain and Portugal and three medium-wave relay stations in Germany (Holzkirchen, Lampertheim, and Biblis). It refurbished or relocated older facilities.

Retooling for a Digital Age

In August 1999, the IBB, VOA's support organization, issued a paper recognizing the need to retool the technical infrastructure of the old era to accommodate the new:

> The history of international broadcasting until now has been dominated by the medium of shortwave. In the past, transmission strategies for international broadcasters focused on the best methods for making the most of shortwave delivery. Over the past decade, however, the methods used by audiences to seek and acquire information from international broadcasters have diversified,

providing a far more complex transmission environment. This broadcast delivery environment now encompasses international shortwave, transnational medium wave, free local affiliations, paid leases and licenses for local rebroadcasting, cable and terrestrial television, direct to home (DTH) radio and television, and Internet webcasting.

Although shortwave and cross-border medium wave continue to be the dominant mediums for international broadcasters, other delivery means are growing in relative importance. The fragmentation of our audience across transmission mediums provides additional opportunities to attract listeners and viewers. But it also constitutes a substantial management challenge to spread a static set of resources over different delivery systems as we work to most effectively carry out our broadcasting mission.[28]

As media delivery systems expand beyond imagining, two twentieth-century anecdotes remind us of a fundamental fact. That is, how listeners (and, lately, viewers and personal computer users as well) value VOA's effort "to get it straight and get it there." And most of all, how precious news and information is for people who are denied it.

Richard W. Carlson, VOA director from 1985 to 1990, recalled:

Dr. Yelena Bonner, wife of dissident Soviet physicist Andrei Sakharov, told me she and her husband would sit in Gorky Park with their portable radio and a note pad, and listen to the news. They would switch shortwave frequencies and write down phrases, getting bits and pieces because they were so heavily jammed. Then they would listen to rebroadcasts later that night and fit all the pieces together to learn what was happening. People used to the sea of information in the United States are hard pressed to understand the efforts that are made to imprison a mind, and how thoroughly remarkable the human spirit is in its effort to keep that mind out of prison and free to get information.[29]

Natalie Clarkson, chief of VOA's Russian Branch, visited Volgograd a year or so after the Cold War ended. Her mission would have been inconceivable much before then. Natalie (or Natasha, as she preferred to be called) went to the city, which used to be known as Stalingrad, to nurture relationships with a powerful medium-wave network in one of

Russia's larger metropolitan areas and to arrange for satellite downlinking of VOA Russian and rebroadcasting to a market approaching 1 million listeners. This was in a country that had jammed VOA Russian intermittently for much of the forty years until it finally ceased in May 1987. The director of the Volgograd radio offered to show Clarkson his station's huge transmitter and antenna farm on a hill overlooking the city. They drove to the site, and Natalie was struck by the fact that it seemed like a family enterprise, run almost like a lighthouse in the United States. Its superintendents were a man, a woman, and an aged mongrel dog. After introductions, Natalie visited with the couple, who remarked about how ironic the visit was.

"You know," they recalled, "this complex used to be a jamming station, and we jammed you day and night." They described how they were part of a nationwide network (indeed, Western experts had identified more than 250 skywave jammers working in tandem with some 3,000 groundwave jammers in the Soviet Union at the height of the Cold War).

"I'm curious about something," Clarkson said. "How was it that from time to time, some of our news and information programming got through?"

"Well," the Volgograd transmitter superintendent replied, "sometimes the program was so interesting, we held off because we wanted to hear it." The friendly banter continued. Natalie couldn't help noting the poignancy of this extraordinary moment. A Soviet jamming transmitter was now relaying VOA Russian programming to hundreds of thousands of listeners. In a sense, the construction of VOA's global network had come full circle. Especially, she recalled later, when she reached down to give a farewell pat to the mongrel, and it licked her hand![30]

6

Into the Citadel of "Ramshackle Excellence"

A PORTRAIT

A little mouse, a little tiny mouse of thought appears in a
room, and even the mightiest potentates are thrown into
panic.
—Winston Churchill

Our assignment is to bring the bright dream of a new day into
the dark corners of the world. . . . That is what the Voice of
America means to me.
—John Chancellor

It is what appears to be an ordinary rainy Monday morning at America's
Voice to the millions. The newsroom that never sleeps is rewriting the
overnight stories as the sun sets in Asia. The broadcast staffs begin to
drift in to prepare the broadcasts for noon, when thirteen languages will
be on the air simultaneously. They "read in" (look at the news already on
the wires) and set about their writing and production labors.

One can almost sense the pulses of a million news bits and information bytes this overcast morning. The reports are coming in from all
continents and across the United States, and are being checked and
cross-checked, refined and rewritten, adapted and polished. Many go via
internal high-speed printers in a mammoth stream from the central
newsroom to the language divisions and worldwide English production
center. Other reports are originated in the services themselves.
Fragments of data course their way, in forty-six languages, through the

world's largest multilingual electronic word-processing system. They race along thousands of miles of circuits and cables, all within the Depression-era VOA headquarters building at Fourth Street and Independence Avenue, SW, Washington, D.C.

Now, and throughout the day, these "idea seeds"—news, features, documentaries, music—will be broadcast to a curious world from forty studios in this headquarters building. To farmers in rice paddies in Asia, mujahideen warriors in Afghanistan, peacemakers in mission schools and hospitals in Africa, religious leaders in towering mosques of the Arab world, businessmen speeding along the autobahns in Germany, and cabinet ministers sipping coffee in Latin America.

A DAY TO REMEMBER

It is February 24, 1992. The morning insight (a listing of upcoming stories) squeaks out on the house wires around the building at 1,200 characters a minute, sounding like a chorus of anguished mice. It is the usual time for the insight, just before 7:30 A.M. The listing tells this day of VOA correspondents traveling to Moscow, Tirana, and Kuwait City. It forecasts the filing plans of those in Washington, New York, Johannesburg, Chicago, New Delhi, Bangkok, London, Vienna, Geneva, Bonn, Cairo, and Jerusalem.

It is soon obvious, though, on this rainy Monday, that this not just another ordinary day. Language service broadcasters are entering the C Street main entrance wearing saris, long capes, fezzes, the garb of their native lands. Many are bearing trays or dishes of cuisine representing more than twoscore cultures. A mammoth potluck lunch is in store. And the heading at the top of the insight on dozens of teleprinters around the building sums it all up: CELEBRATING FIFTY YEARS OF EXCELLENCE IN BROADCASTING TO THE WORLD.[1]

Those intrepid pioneers who put the first German program on the air on February 25, 1942, from a half-built studio in lower Manhattan, would be amazed at the sights and sounds and reach of their organization a half century later. Their first broadcasts, you recall, were relayed by the BBC to Nazi-occupied Europe, and no one knew for some weeks whether anyone was listening. On this golden-anniversary day, VOA has an estimated audience of more than 100 million listeners weekly. It has relay stations of its own girdling the globe with an aggregate power of tens of millions of watts, transmitting programs in microseconds to points as far away as New Zealand. Hundreds of FM and medium-wave affiliates overseas, too, are part of the worldwide network.

Racing Against the On-Air Light

The show goes on, from newsroom to cubicle to office to studio to Master Control to relay stations to the far corners of the Earth. You see an occasional broadcaster racing down a corridor to make a split-second deadline. He or she is navigating unusually crowded hallways this special visitors' day, in contest with the merciless march of time, the irreversible flash of the red "on air" light in one of the broadcast studios. By noon, this somewhat dingy government office building is magically transformed. A fiftieth-anniversary cultural festival is getting under way. Here you can see Burmese art displays on the buff-colored plaster walls. There are Bolivian dancers swirling near a foyer. Around another corner, Ethiopian singers chant their rhythms in the marble-paneled corridors. An American sitar player (you'll meet him in chapter 13) is seated comfortably cross-legged on the floor with a few Pakistani masters. There are Egyptian coffee servers, Texas chili ladlers. There are carvers of a mammoth, steaming, stuffed lamb. They stand behind their tables, these regal chefs in flowing robes and turbans, resplendent in the full regalia of Hausaland in West Africa.

The Tie that Binds

In a packed reception room, Director Chase Untermeyer meets the benefactor of this cultural festival, Zelma Giddens. The elegant Alabama hostess is the widow of one of Untermeyer's predecessors, VOA's thirteenth and longest-serving director, Kenneth R. Giddens. Giddens shakes hands with Untermeyer and makes a surprise presentation. She opens a flat box to unveil a treasured 1970s VOA tie that belonged to her husband. It's much wider than the ties of the early 1990s, embossed with a VOA logo of two decades earlier. Without missing a beat, Untermeyer rips off his contemporary VOA tie and replaces it with the Giddens-era model, literally knotting together the Voice's past and present in less than a minute.

Then Untermeyer escorts his guests to the dim and cavernous first-floor auditorium, bedecked with banks of flowers for the ceremonial highlight of the day. Three broadcasters from 1942 look on proudly from the front row. Untermeyer evokes the Voice's history and reminds the hundreds in attendance of Churchill's "tiny mouse of thought" that makes tyrants tremble. He quotes Thomas Jefferson, too: "If a nation expects to be ignorant and free, it expects what never was and never will be. . . . Enlighten the people generally, and tyranny and oppressions of body and mind will vanish like evil spirits at the dawn of day." This, less than eight weeks after the disappearance of the Soviet Union.

Then the festival resumes in corridors on three levels. It is a fantastic treat for every conceivable palate, rows and rows of tables filled to overflowing. "It's unlikely," according to Marian Burros of the *New York Times*, "that the halls of any government office building ever smelled this good, or this exotic. Spices wafted down the halls from the Indian and Pakistani tables; there was a hint of lemongrass in the air at the Thai buffet; soy sauce and garlic swirled around the Chinese chafing dish, and someone, somewhere, was cooking onions." Perhaps it was Jack Murphy, later to become chief (and master chef) of the Eurasia Division. He has prepared sixteen dishes for the occasion. They include *lobio,* a Georgian red-bean dish, and *mashkitchiri,* an Uzbeki bean dish.[2]

Today, these broadcasters are "up." They are filled with pride about their past and hopeful that the next half century will be as rich and productive as the first fifty years. For a day, at least, they are at peace with the world and with one another. But to understand the many currents rippling through the Voice on more ordinary days, it is necessary to reach back yet a few more years, a flashback to where we left off a few chapters ago—the mid-1960s.

CHANCELLOR'S "TURN AT THE BROOMSTICK"

After wandering the corridors for some months in 1965, VOA director John Chancellor wrote in the *Foreign Service Journal:*

> There's a peculiar kind of ramshackle excellence about the Voice of America. I came to work there with the standard conceptions and misconceptions of an outsider. . . . I did think of it as a calm and dignified group of broadcasters. I thought it was an important enterprise. To my surprise, I found that I had misjudged the spirit, indeed the clamor, that exists inside the Voice.

It was like walking into a stately building to find the residents holding up the walls with broomsticks while carrying on a terrific argument. There is a fine, antic sense of madness about the place, and after a year and a half of taking my turn at the broomstick, I view the Voice and its employees with a feeling of pride and affection.

They understand that microseconds after they speak, what they say is communicating to people in bedrooms, living rooms, tents, cars, caravans as they enter the world of the listener. The corridors of official Washington fade, and the broadcasters are with the listeners. It is essential that this connection be understood, for without this knowledge, no understanding is possible of what I unashamedly call the magic of the Voice.[3]

For two decades, a distinguished-looking diplomat's widow, Margaret Jaffie, led public tours of the Voice with that magic on direct display. Jaffie recalls that Americans and guests from overseas alike were thrilled when she pressed a monitoring button in a studio where English or other language broadcasts could be seen going on the air live. Broadcasters were at their microphones, the very scene that Chancellor described. Jaffie, in leading tourists around the Voice from 1975 to 1995, walked well more than 100,000 miles and learned to do so in comfortable shoes. Near the end of her career, she received the coveted Congressional Award for Exemplary Service to the Public. Her retirement gift, a pair of gold-coated tennis shoes, remained at the Voice for all to see for years afterward.[4]

As you stroll through VOA headquarters, as Jaffie and her visitors did on so many days, you might think that you are in the corridors of the United Nations.[5] It's a babble of languages, as snow-white saris from South Asia blend with embroidered light tan *gallebiyas* from Egypt and brilliant blue flowing robes and turbans from Nigeria.

A GLIMPSE AT A FIRST DRAFT
OF HISTORY IN THE MAKING

Walter Lippmann once called journalism a "first draft of history." The many talents of America's Voice have tried, first and foremost, to get the facts straight and then to broadcast them as quickly as possible to a curious world. VOA in Chancellor's time (and for the three decades that followed) consisted of diverse communities.[6]

- *The language service broadcasters, most of whom were born abroad or were first-generation American citizens, native speakers of their mother tongue.* Many of the language service broadcasters had fled their countries of origin or had been exiled, or perhaps they had come to America with parents who had experienced exile. More than half of these 800 or more employees were noncitizens seeking U.S. citizenship. Some had been high-ranking politicians, physicians, educators, journalists, distinguished artists, or poets in their homeland. Life in the United States, for them, was daunting. In many cases, it meant adjusting to a new profession, journalism, and to peculiarly American (and at times arcane) civil service regulations. It meant working hard for relatively modest civil service salaries and, for the noncitizens, dealing with mountains of paperwork related to getting citizenship or, at times, overcoming immigration hurdles necessary to simply remain in the United States or keep their dependents there. It meant bringing entire families into what for many was a strange new environment, the fast pace of modern urban America.

- *The journalists of the central program services (News and Current Affairs), most of whom were born in the United States and had come from American newspapers, wire services, or radio stations.* Others in the newsroom were graduates of the central desks of dailies in other English-speaking countries. The separate Worldwide English Division also had professional staff with announcing or broadcast production backgrounds. The journalists and the announcers had differing priorities. The former were less concerned about achieving perfection in sound than about getting the news out accurately, quickly, and live. The latter wanted finely polished airshows and felt that beautifully produced, often prerecorded programs were essential to high-quality broadcasting. Some English-language broadcasters and newsroom journalists had little prior multicultural contact, and only limited travel time abroad or linguistic skills. They, like most language service staff and the engineers described in chapter 5, were civil servants. They considered themselves international broadcasting professionals and the principal guardians of the Voice's news integrity. They sought to prove, again and again, that government employees could also be good journalists.

- *The foreign service officers, who typically moved into command or midlevel management positions at the Voice between overseas assignments.* The foreign service officers came from the parent agency, the United States Information Agency (USIA), or from the Department of State.

They were usually assigned, in the 1960s and 1970s, to such key VOA positions as deputy director, director of programs, division or language service chief, head of the Office of Policy, even chief of central services, including the newsroom. Some of these managers were skilled cross-cultural communicators, and a few spoke fluently or could even broadcast the language of the services to which they were assigned. Most brought fresh foreign affairs expertise to the Voice. Some, like Paul Modic and Jerry Stryker, were fully committed to the Voice's professional integrity. Others were simply passing time until their next "real" foreign service field assignment. Most of the foreign service officers were new to broadcasting. Some were, or became, committed journalists; others regarded VOA as primarily a purveyor of U.S. policies and culture (or served in the Voice as watchdogs to ensure that State Department or USIA policies were implemented).

- *The political appointees, usually the director or some of his or her powerful staff assistants.* The appointees' terms usually coincided with that of the president, and at VOA, they occupied a handful of positions at any one time and very few of the thousands of jobs filled by incoming administrations in the executive branch. Some had previous international, academic, or journalistic experience; many moved into their jobs from presidential campaigns or were heavy contributors to those campaigns. Occasionally, congressional pressure influenced the assignment of a political appointee. Like the foreign service officers, their terms were temporary. Some absorbed the culture and relished it; others were suspicious of the civil servants, had their own programming agendas, or dreamed of what they saw as higher callings elsewhere in political Washington. Many resigned in the normal course of events at the end of an administration. Others quit after only brief tenures to pursue other opportunities—some under fire, or in protest.

- *The commercial broadcasters, fewer in number, but who sporadically had significant impact when they arrived at the Voice as either political appointees or professional hires.* As we've seen, the first wave of commercial broadcasters joined VOA during the World War II years. In the late 1960s, the 1980s, and the 1990s at usually brief intervals, commercial broadcasters headed the Voice. From time to time, although fewer in number, professional hires from the private broadcasting industry, whatever their rank, had a significant impact on Voice programming. That was particularly the case in the 1960s and the 1980s, and at the beginning of this century.

SWINGING IN THE SIXTIES

John Chancellor resolved to bring a measure of U.S. commercial net-work pizzazz to VOA's English programming, to introduce a new sound that, as he put it, "would make the Voice swing a little." The new sound bore a striking resemblance to the *NBC Monitor* format of the time, more conversational, interspersing music and lighter features among news reports. It substituted the sprightly "Yankee Doodle" identification music, or logo, for the more formal "Columbia the Gem of the Ocean," which had introduced postwar VOA broadcasts. Half-hour or hour-long programs were split up and became, as Chancellor described it, "one continuous flow of programming elements, built around regularly sched-uled newscasts, which in their spirit, tempo and innate interest, reflect the spirit and the tempo and the excellence of American life."[7]

Enter other principal characters of the late 1960s, 1970s, and early 1980s:

• The four very different USIA directors during those years were Leonard Marks (1965–1969), a powerful Washington attorney; Frank Shakespeare (1969–1973), a staunch conservative who clashed publicly and frequently with the State Department; James Keogh (1973–1977), President Richard Nixon's former speechwriter, who believed in firm policy control over VOA; and John Reinhardt (1977–1981), an Africa specialist and distinguished diplomat who had great respect for the Voice's editorial autonomy.

• The three very different VOA directors included Kenneth R. Gid-dens, a commercial-broadcasting executive from Mobile, Alabama, who became the Voice's longest-serving director, from 1969 to 1977. Giddens was a conservative Nixon appointee and a close friend of Shakespeare who became a tireless fighter for additional resources for America's Voice and a fierce advocate of VOA independence. As such, Giddens became Keogh's archnemesis and a popular and revered hero within VOA. He had wide bipartisan support on Capitol Hill and prevented severe VOA cuts. He was followed by media executive R. Peter Straus of New York, close to the Kennedy and Carter campaigns and intensely interested in a cost-efficient news operation at the Voice with a reduced cadre of correspondents around the world. For eleven months in 1980 and 1981, historian, public broadcaster, and East-West Center executive Dr. Mary G. F. Bitterman of Hawaii served as VOA's first female (and youngest)

JANIE'S REMARKABLE JOURNEY

Janie Fritzman joined the Voice in 1960, at the age of eighteen, as a GS-2 clerk-typist. I first met her when she applied for the job of chief administrative aide in News and Current Affairs. That was just a few months after I had returned from assignments in the Middle East and New York to Washington as acting chief of NCA (chapter 7). Fritzman was brimming with ideas about orderly management of the central services and how we might get moderately tolerable air circulation in what was then a vast, windowless catacomb in the cellar of the VOA headquarters (several years earlier, the newsroom had been moved to this cavernlike area in order to obtain more space).

By the time she joined NCA in late 1973, Janie had served as a key administrative assistant in the Office of Engineering. She knew the regulations, was constantly studying them, and was a wise counselor during every twist and turn of the tumultuous 1970s and early 1980s. Her plunge into programming and reporting of politics and foreign affairs helped her become among the most "street smart" of VOA operatives—that is, able to gauge every nuance, politically, within the Voice, USIA, and beyond.

Eventually Fritzman's expertise and unlimited capacity for work enabled her to advance to become key assistant or confidante to at least six VOA directors. Also, she rose to become director of personnel and administration of the Voice and Worldnet Television. For a time, during the last year of her career before retirement (1996–1997), Janie was acting director of the International Broadcasting Bureau—a senior executive overseeing more than 2,000 multimedia broadcasting employees, including those of America's Voice.*

*Brian Fiel, "The Soul of the Voice of America," *Government Executive*, June 1997, 75–76.

director. She brought a human touch, a scholar's curiosity, and uncommon good taste and style to principled management of the organization at the conclusion of the Carter administration.

• Movers and shakers within the Voice included two deputy directors of particular note: senior foreign service officers Serban Vallimarescu and Hans N. (Tom) Tuch. Both were accomplished linguists. Romanian-born Vallimarescu had come up through the Voice ranks as head of the Romanian Service, European Division chief, and director of programs, before serving briefly at the National Security Council. German-born Tuch became, over the years, one of the foremost advocates of U.S. "public diplomacy" in all its forms (information, culture, broadcasting, exchanges). He had been at the Voice early in his career, but before and after he was VOA's deputy director, Tuch served in U.S. information and cultural posts or as embassy public affairs officer in Frankfurt, Munich, Moscow, Sofia, Berlin, Rio de Janeiro, Brasilia, and Bonn. Tuch was succeeded near the end of the Carter administration by a rapidly advancing senior foreign service officer whom we met earlier, Bill Haratunian.

• Of course, laboring in the trenches for years were midlevel managerial stalwarts, some of them career civil servants, some foreign service officers. You've already met most of them: Cliff Groce, Haratunian, Bernie Kamenske, and Paul Modic. They were ably supported by News and Current Affairs (NCA) administrative assistant Eva Jane (Janie) Fritzman, administrative officers A. Carl Malmi and Robert H. Henry, and budget officer Lenore Hemelt. As Giddens said, "it is family"—in addition, he might have noted, to being a veritable Circus Maximus of clashing cultures and different approaches to international broadcasting.

HUNGRY FOR NEWS

Beginning in 1974, a new senior NCA management team was put together. Bernie Kamenske had been named chief of the Current Affairs Division in 1972, but it was obvious that there was only one job for this man with a relentless appetite for news and information. That was, of course, chief of the News Division. Bernie's lateral transfer within NCA then enabled VOA deputy director Serban Vallimarescu to assign his longtime colleague, award-winning documentary writer Michael A. Hanu, as Kamenske's successor in Current Affairs. Both Kamenske and Hanu were hard-driving executives. Eventually, veteran news analyst and reporter George Halsey succeeded Hanu.

Kamenske rejected a deputy's idea of artificial plants to separate regional desks in the basement newsroom because he wanted to always be able to see "what the writers were up to." His antennae were poised, day and night, to sense what he regarded as conspiracies, far and wide in government, to tamper with VOA News. He cared deeply about the quality of the reporting and constantly coached (and at times coddled) able young talent. Bernie's appetite for new services and new gadgets was insatiable, no matter the cost. He expanded VOA's news sources as never before. They included subscriptions to international news agency regional wires unavailable elsewhere in North America, the special "tip service" of the Foreign Broadcast Information Service (FBIS), the reference service NEXIS, and access to the commercial network "white line" pool covering presidential visits abroad. Bernie worked closely around the clock with a number of central newsroom duty editors or managing editors, the so-called rim masters. Among them were Joe Buday, Chuck Flinner, Jane Gillespie, David Gollust, Phil Haynes, Philomena Jurey, John Linehan, Reg McPherson, Al Riddick, and Chuck Roberts. Jurey and Gollust also distinguished themselves as senior field correspondents.

Over in Current Affairs, Hanu concentrated on documentaries, his forte, at times pulling all-nighters himself in his undershirt to write a documentary and make a deadline. He oversaw the introduction of weekly documentaries called *Closeups*. Occasionally, one could hear the high-decibel Hanu disciplining some cowering staff member from behind closed doors. As Chancellor had once said of all of VOA, "it was mad." Fritzman and I fastened our seat belts and found it to be an exhilarating ride.

Each language division, meanwhile, was a unique universe of its own. Most of the broadcasters in these geographic divisions were beaming programs back to countries of their or their parents' birth. Some had grown up in the United States; others had emigrated in the distant past, yet others, recently. Many had come from closed societies, where journalism's only task was to serve the state. Some had come in waves—for example, from czarist Russia, Communist Russia, and, in the 1990s, post–Cold War Russia; from Taiwan, Hong Kong, and, after 1976, mainland China; from Hungary, before and after the 1956 revolution; and from many other East European countries and the Baltic republics, during and after the Cold War.

THE OLD GUARD VERSUS THE NEW?

Each generation, within each division, had a unique outlook and a unique set of linguistic skills. In the hierarchies of many services, one could sense some of the dynamics. Should recent arrivals be permitted to make suggestions concerning linguistic style and adaptation to their venerable senior editors (whose style might be somewhat rusty and dated)? Conversely, were some of the newcomers as highly educated as their elders and as proficient in adapting contemporary American English into the formal classical language used in, say, Arabic or Farsi? What about the American-born broadcasters in the Russian Branch, whose language often was excellent but not perfect and who still at times were shunned by the "old guard?" The language services were as variegated in character and outlook as those portraits in Edward Steichen's *Family of Man*:[8]

- *East Asia and Pacific.* For years, this was the "don't rock the boat" division, heavily influenced by foreign service caution at both the division and language service levels. After the Tiananmen crisis and the birth of its remarkable Tibetan Service, East Asia and Pacific came into its own, some services literally bursting with energy, innovations, and multimedia talent. Services in the 1970s and 1980s included the giant Chinese Branch (Mandarin and Cantonese); the Vietnamese, Korean, Indonesian, Thai, Burmese, Cambodian, and Lao Services; as well as a feed service in English (Tibetan came along in 1991). The East Asia and Pacific Division was the acknowledged VOA pioneer in English teaching and research. At the beginning of this century, it was by far the largest Voice language division.
- *Near East and South Asia.* This division for much of its existence served more than fifty nations, from the Hindu Kush mountains of eastern Afghanistan to the Atlantic shores of Morocco. Arabic was the flagship unit for years, tested mightily in the Gulf crisis of 1990/1991. Other services were Hindi-to-India, Bangla-to-Bangladesh, Urdu-to-Pakistan, Dari- and Pashto-to-Afghanistan, Farsi (renamed Persian in 2003)-to-Iran, Greek (in the 1960s and 1970s), Turkish (which alternately found itself in two other divisions), and Kurdish (added in the 1990s). The Bangla Service at one time had more than a thousand fan clubs in Bangladesh and west Bengal, India. Some of these listener clubs became active civic and community organizations. They built canals, dug wells, and ran local health clinics, all close-knit associations of VOA listeners.[9]
- *Africa.* Originally a spin-off from Near East and South Asia in 1959, the division's highly regionalized programming was at first shaped almost entirely by foreign service officers or those favoring "feel good" stories about Africa. Later, the Africa Division blazed new trails in

regional news gathering and reporting (chapter 11). In the 1960s, 1970s, and 1980s, the division had its own tailored services in English, French, and Portuguese, as well as the indigenous languages of Swahili (spoken in East Africa), Hausa (spoken in northern Nigeria and Niger), and Amharic (spoken in Ethiopia). During the 1990s, the division added a number of local languages to the Horn of Africa and to the Lakes region of Central Africa.

• *USSR.* During the Cold War, this was the most strategically important division, with services in Russian, Ukrainian, Armenian, Georgian, Azerbaijani, and Uzbek. Many credited it with helping to create an appreciation of freedom and democratic institutions, which hastened the dissolution of the Soviet Union.[10] Its "heavier" long-form programming included *samizdat* (underground literature during the Soviet period) and healthy doses of American life and culture. The Russian and Ukrainian Branches for years broadcast live religious Orthodox or Roman Catholic masses from the United States when these were banned under Communism in the USSR. Factionalism at one time or another plagued nearly every unit in this multifaceted division. Its Ukrainian Branch in 1993 became the first at VOA to work closely with Worldnet Television, which produced a regularly scheduled TV program in the language, *Window on America.*

• *European.* This division broadcast largely to the Warsaw Pact nations of the former Soviet empire (Poland, Hungary, Czechoslovakia, Romania, and Bulgaria), the Baltic republics (Estonia, Latvia, and Lithuania), as well as Yugoslavia, Albania, and, at times, Greece and Turkey. For some years, it had Iberian feed services to Portugal and Spain, and for a brief period in the 1990s, it attempted to restore the German Service. At its peak, the European Division had nineteen language services, the most in any single division at VOA. It led all of VOA in a 1997 broadcast inaugural of the Freedom Forum's Newseum (then in Arlington, Virginia) and created journalistically sophisticated multimedia services to Albania, Serbia, Croatia, Bosnia, and Macedonia during the dissolution of Yugoslavia (chapter 16). There were, however, severe post–Cold War reductions in staff and broadcasting in much of the rest of Europe.

• *Latin America.* Informal, fast-paced, dynamic live programming was characteristic of this language division beamed to the score of nations south of the U.S. border and in the Caribbean. This smallest of the geographic entities had to adapt to the decline of shortwave and the ascendancy of medium-wave and, particularly, FM broadcasting. In 2000, its Spanish, Portuguese-to-Brazil, and Creole units had hundreds of partner stations receiving digital satellite feeds from VOA in Washington. The Latin America Division VOASAT feed service supplied a steady stream of news spots throughout a day-long cycle to commercial-station clients in the hemisphere. In general, broadcasters to this hemisphere tended to concentrate less on regional reportage than did other VOA divisions, and more on U.S. events (political, economic, and cultural).

THE SHOCK OF A LIFETIME

Many language service broadcasters came to the United States and suffered severe culture shock. If they were journalists, they discovered what to many (with the possible exception of Latin Americans) was a new approach to their craft. VOA was mandated to broadcast good news and bad news not only about the countries where their listeners lived but about their adopted homeland, the United States. Frequently, they got mixed signals. The central newsroom insisted on "telling it as it is," as President Kennedy said, "warts and all." At the same time, their own bosses (those in the language services) were, in the 1960s and 1970s, mostly foreign service officers. A majority supported objective news, but some counseled caution about using controversial stories directly affecting their regions or "bad" news about the United States.

Beyond that, there was growing discontent in the language services with a gap in pay. Broadcasters in the central newsroom and Current Affairs had higher pay scales, it was said, because they were in a larger department and they supplied news and programming material to all forty or more language services. Civil service rules meant that supervisors in much smaller units, such as the language services, were classified at lower pay grades. Many of the top jobs were held by foreign service officers (twenty-three of thirty-eight senior positions, according to a 1968 study). In the 1990s, the number of foreign service officers at the Voice declined to practically zero. At last the language broadcasters could move up, and all seven language divisions came to be headed by one-time broadcasters in those divisions, five of them born in their audience areas. Some lacked public diplomacy expertise, but all were professional broadcast journalists.

A second and broader fault line within the VOA family centered on relations between USIA and the Voice. In a 1968 analysis, Deputy

Program Manager Cliff Groce noted that the two organizations, although both in the information business, were bound to clash. That, he said, was because of differences in outlook "inherent in their widely divergent functions." USIA, the parent agency, communicated face to face with individuals overseas, in the field. The Voice of America, as a mass medium, reached many people "out there," elites as well as the general population. Groce noted that there is an important role for both, but added:

> In times of "crisis," when normal "field" access is cut off entirely, the Agency regularly rediscovers the importance of VOA and grinds out volumes of instructions for the Voice's dealing with the new "tactical" situation. . . . They fail to understand that this massive communication instrument cannot simply be turned on and off in terms of function, any more than it can in terms of broadcast hours in a given language in a particular area, without serious damage to its continuing function: providing accurate, up-to-date information about developments throughout the world and most particularly, the United States.[11]

Aside from the perspectives of foreign service officers (mostly from USIA but some from the State Department), there were the sometimes clashing approaches of the language broadcasters and those in the central newsroom described earlier. A language service staff member, as late as 1995, attended a news conference of a foreign official visiting Washington. He identified himself as a VOA reporter, and posed a question that appeared to be more of a political statement favoring one faction in his country of origin than a legitimate inquiry. The incident outraged VOA journalists and led to the drafting of a journalistic code for VOA that included a requirement for absolute impartiality by news gatherers throughout the Voice.

THE JONESTOWN MASS SUICIDE

A test of consistency in VOA's response to a controversial, breaking news story was the Jonestown mass suicide during the weekend of November 18/19, 1978. Deep in the jungle of Guyana, South America, U.S. religious cult leader Jim Jones became alarmed when at least a dozen people in his isolated commune asked to leave with an American congressman who had just toured the settlement on an inspection visit. The delegation was ambushed as it was about to take off from a nearby airstrip. Four were killed, along with Representative Leo Ryan of California. Hours later, Jones ordered more than 900 other followers to drink cyanide-laced punch in the largest mass suicide in U.S. history.[12]

It was a classic test of VOA news handling. The first indicator of trouble, the shooting of the House member and others, broke on Saturday night, November 18. On the overnight shift, the newsroom had relatively few staff members and no correspondent or contract reporter in a country as seemingly inconsequential as Guyana. The language services were at an even lower ebb, with few broadcasters present and no higher-level managers to guide the response.

The story at first seemed obscure, except of course that a U.S. congressman had been killed. The News Division moved a regional item and headlines about it on the house wire to all the language services between 10:00 and 11:00 P.M. that Saturday. Editors at the central desk had verified the slaying at the State Department operations center after seeing news agency reports that Ryan had been killed. Well trained by Kamenske, they had taken this extra precaution even with two news agency sources, to be certain of its accuracy. It wasn't until midday Sunday, however, that the full scope of the tragedy, the mass suicide, began to unfold.

A few days afterward, VOA director R. Peter Straus ordered a survey of News Division and language service handling of the Jonestown story. This revealed that fewer than half the language services had used the story when it broke, and some had waited for hours to pick it up even when VOA News began to lead with the carnage at Jonestown. The author of the analysis, Fred Collins, found in interviews that the story had appeared to be "soft" and "negative" to a number of individual language broadcasters in the European, USSR, and Near East and South Asia Divisions.[13] The broadcasters decided on their own not to use the items and bulletins supplied on the wire by central news.

As a result of the Guyana study, Director of Programs Paul Modic ordered the institution of a news-roundup system placing full responsibility on the newsroom for the content of the top-of-the-hour newscasts and mandating the use of translated roundups by the language services to avoid individual decision making and second guessing on whether or not information was sound. The Voice was not alone among international broadcasters in dealing with clashing perspectives between central and language services; the BBC also grappled with the problem for years. Modic's mandate, which lasted until 1982, was among a number of VOA attempts to forge a consistent standard of accurate, objective, and comprehensive news and in-depth, balanced analysis, housewide.

JOURNALISM IN A MULTICULTURAL NETWORK

Several anecdotes reflect the complexities of journalism in a multicultural environment.

The Execution at Evin Prison

One of the most sensitive, caring, and widely read managers I encountered during three and a half decades at America's Voice was Frank Cummins, who arrived there a few months after I did in 1962. He subsequently was posted by VOA or USIA in Beirut, Islamabad, Kaduna in northern Nigeria, and Munich. At the Voice in Washington, Cummins was deputy director of programs for operations in 1982 and 1983, and also deputy chief in the Near East and South Asia, East Asia and Pacific, and Latin America Divisions. Before retiring in 1997, he was director of the Office of Program Review, where he used his powerful intellect and considerable people skills to help create a community of journalists at VOA.

One day, Cummins was passing by the door of the Farsi Service to Iran. He looked inside and spotted a member of the service, her head up against the wall. She was sobbing uncontrollably. Cummins rushed in, and asked what the matter was. Her eyes dimmed with tears, she turned to the chief of program review and explained: "This morning, the authorities took my brother, who had been in Evin Prison in Tehran, out to the front wall of the place, and executed him, a firing squad. I just got the word." She composed herself slightly, the tears cleared a bit. Then, her eyes narrowing, she looked Cummins straight in the eye and exclaimed: "And you tell us to be accurate, comprehensive and *objective!*"[14]

The Indispensable Tip

At times, language service expertise has paid off handsomely. On May 13, 1981, the newsroom was abuzz. The bulletin bells on the international news agency wires were ringing in a chorus. There were reports that sixty-year-old Pope John Paul II had been shot at close range by an unknown assailant in the heart of St. Peter's Square. The phone at the newsroom's European desk rang just as the editor was putting out the first bulletin. It was a call from the VOA Turkish Service. Service chief Dinjer Aktug and senior editor Taçlan Suerdem had been watching CNN and recognized the first photos of the assailant from stories and photos they had seen in the Turkish press. They identified him as Mehmet Ali Ağca, a member of a Turkish right-wing terrorist organization, long sought by Turkish police. The desk didn't question this tip, and within seconds, VOA News, ahead of most international news agencies, was informing its listeners, in Turkish and many other languages, of the would-be assassin's identity. Aktug and Suerdem had plenty of background on Ağca in their files, and that turned out to be indispensable. The value of an alert VOA language service became manifestly clear.[15]

The "Quick Trip" to Southern Lebanon

Abroad, one of the most active VOA war correspondents of the 1970s was Douglas Roberts, restless for action in the most dangerous of places. Roberts, a bearded, no-nonsense journalist with an infectious sense of humor, relished front-line action. He learned over the years to speak near-perfect Arabic. His journalistic triumphs included a visit in the mid-1970s to the UNITA-held stronghold of Huambo in southern Angola, interviews at the Tindouf camp of the Polisario rebels in the western Sahara, and forays into battle zones between the Israeli army and local Lebanese and Palestinians in southern Lebanon.

In the climate of the 1970s, none of these exploits particularly pleased the U.S. diplomatic community. Nor was VOA director R. Peter Straus thrilled about having to defend VOA correspondents' journalistic activities when embassies complained or when the correspondents got into places of danger or stirred up controversy. In fact, Straus really wanted to contract out more of VOA's overseas reporting and reduce the number of foreign correspondents to save headaches and money. This was the situation when Roberts went to Lebanon to cover the civil war in early 1978.

Roberts was based in Athens, but spent much of his time getting to and from east Beirut via boat from the Cypriot port of Larnaca. The civil war now also included Israel, whose troops and tanks crossed their northern border on March 14, 1978, to bomb and shell Palestinian Fatah guerrillas in southern Lebanon near the Litani River. Israeli forces occupied most of the area south of the river. Correspondents in Beirut took trips south to view the action, interview villagers affected, and file eyewitness reports.

So Near, yet So Far

Roberts, however, was operating under a tight security leash imposed by Washington and the U.S. embassy in Beirut. He was not to travel to the combat zone in the south, where the risks were extreme. The risks included an unpredictable war, the prospect of a stray bullet finding its mark in a correspondent wandering in some Lebanese village, and the possibility of the correspondent being seized and held hostage by one or another faction in the civil war. Roberts recalls sitting in Beirut while his colleagues traveled south, came back, and filed eyewitness reports. He had to rely on his colleagues' readouts, news agency tips, and Lebanese sources to piece together daily reports. It was, for a war-hardened journalist, humiliating. So near the action, yet so far.

Finally, after several days of this, three other journalists one morning offered him a ride on a "day trip" to southern Lebanon. Roberts couldn't resist. He hopped into a car driven by George Semerjian, a photographer for the Beirut newspaper *An Nahar*, along with UPI's Ned Temko and David Hirst of the *Guardian*. Why tell the embassy about a mere day trip, such a brief excursion?

They first went to Nabatieh, nestled in the mountains of southern Lebanon, where there were deserted Palestinian camps on the rugged hills around the town. Their next stop was the ancient port city of Tyre, which Israeli planes had bombed a few hours earlier. The correspondents then drove into the mountains again, and were stopped by three Palestinian guerrillas at a lonely checkpoint just above the village of Hadatha. While checking their credentials, one of the guerrillas said that they had knocked out a couple of Israeli tanks. Roberts recalls: "We asked: 'Can we check it out?'"

On to Hadatha

"Sure," came the reply. The correspondents then drove down into the center of Hadatha and were struck by what they saw. Lebanese villagers poured out of their houses, many in tears. There were wounded residents. Their hamlet had been hit by Israeli tanks, and the brand-new village schoolhouse, which had been painstakingly built over the years, had been badly damaged. It was a surging and angry crowd. The villagers led the correspondents to the schoolhouse. All entered the shattered building. Moments later, there was the roar of gunfire, thunder, and chaos.

Israeli tanks on the outskirts of the village had opened fire again. At least twenty tank shells landed on or near the school, which shuddered under the impact. Screaming, the villagers fled. Photographer Semerjian went with them and got separated from his colleagues. He was so shaken and confused by suddenly finding himself under fire that he thought he saw the corpses of the three journalists later that afternoon (it turned out that he saw bodies in the nearby village of Haris, and it was a case of mistaken identity). Semerjian, frightened out of his wits, hopped in the car and headed north to Beirut!

That left Roberts, Temko, and Hirst huddled in the school (they retreated to a basement latrine) while the shelling continued unabated. Finally—by now it was midday—there was a lull. The trio headed back to where the car had been, only to discover that it had left. The shelling resumed. No choice but to find cover, any cover, and not get caught out in the streets. They found a tiny triangular plot of land, a garden in a sort of crevice nestled between deserted houses, and dived for it. A huge piece of plastic sheeting was there, over at the side. The three frightened newsmen covered themselves with the sheet so they wouldn't be spotted from the sky or the heights around the village and be mistaken for Palestinian fedayeen by Israeli gunners. "We had nothing to do, but sit there and lament . . . and speak non sequiturs and streams-of-consciousness nonsense in our terror," Roberts remembers. He kept saying, to himself and out loud: "I'm gonna get fired," as if that were the worst possible ending to this tale of woe.

All the Comforts of Home

The ordeal lasted for what seemed like an eternity, until about an hour after nightfall. The shelling had stopped. "We walked into the village," Roberts says. "Then we spotted a house apparently lit by an oil lamp, and knocked on the door. A tobacco farmer, Mohammed Fadel, short and unshaven, invited us in. He introduced us to several relatives, including an uncle who was bleeding from a shrapnel wound and lying on a mattress. There were cows and goats on the other side of the room. Mohammed gave us tuna fish, lettuce, and bread," Roberts recalled.

What food they had, Hirst wrote, they served on two large platters, and he later quoted an old woman in the dimly lit room as saying: "You are our children, as dear to us as our eyes. If we die, we die together." After a while, Roberts added, "Mohammed took us to his own house, nearby, and gave us maté, a somewhat spicy Brazilian tea. We bedded down for the night, on bales of tobacco."

The next morning, it was quiet. The three journalists and host Mohammed Fadel walked to the northern edge of the village. As they moved to higher ground, they suddenly encountered up on the next hill what, Roberts recalls, "looked like the entire Israeli army." They begged Mohammed to go with them. The soldiers greeted them and demanded IDs. They were friendly enough to the correspondents. But they went right after Mohammed Fadel, slapping and pushing him, while Roberts remembers that "we watched initially dumbfounded." The correspondents screamed angrily at the soldiers, and then Major Uzi Dayan, nephew of the legendary Israeli general Moshe Dayan, stepped in. He demanded that his soldiers stop the nonsense, apologized to Mohammed Fadel, and had him released to go back to Hadatha.

Back in Washington and Beirut, the phone lines were hot. A day earlier, we had learned that Roberts and the others were missing. It was an agonizing wait. Semerjian of *An Nahar* had returned to the Lebanese capital and reported to the embassy that he had seen the corpses of the three. We received word of that moments later.

Hours of Anguish, End of an Era?

Besides my anguish at the thought that we might have lost a fine correspondent and good friend, I also feared the consequences for the Voice. Roberts's foray was without the knowledge or concurrence of the U.S. embassy, and it seemed probable that if he had been killed, the deployment of all VOA correspondents abroad would end. I made a quick phone call to my old friend Boulos Malik, the embassy public affairs officer in Beirut and former VOA Arabic senior editor on Rhodes (chapter 4). We promised to exchange all information regarding the fate of Roberts and the others, and Malik agreed not to make much of Roberts's unilateral decision "to go south." He was, after all, doing what journalists do, and now there were larger issues to deal with. Bernie Kamenske made calls to his many news agency contacts. Hour after hour passed, and it seemed like an eternity. Still no final word from southern Lebanon.

Chicken Soup for the Liberated Soul

It was around noon, Washington time, more than twenty-four hours after we learned that Roberts and his colleagues were missing. The phone rang, and it was a call from VOA's Jerusalem bureau, the kitchen of correspondent Charlie Weiss and his wife, Harriet. On the other end of the line—Douglas B. Roberts. He was sipping some of Harriet's inimitable chicken soup as he recounted his ordeal. After a six-hour wait, he and the two other correspondents had been bundled into an Israeli military vehicle in Hadatha and driven south across the border. They were turned over to the United Press International bureau chief in Tel Aviv, Jack Payton, who later became assignments editor in the VOA newsroom. Then Roberts made his way to the Weiss residence. His family, his colleagues, and his bosses heaved huge sighs of relief.

But now, in getting instructions how to craft an account of his experience, Roberts had a right to be confused. His recollection is that a much-relieved Heil counseled: "Tell the story, but don't put yourself too much in the middle of it." Minutes later, Kamenske called back and said: "Babe, I want you to put yourself right in the middle of the story, it's a story about you." Roberts, laughing, recalls hitting it "somewhere in between." Initially, we told him to head straight back to Athens and home. He called his wife, Rachida, and said he was safe and would soon be there. The VOA director, although relieved, was furious that the correspondent had "broken the rules" about staying in Beirut. He demanded that Roberts be given a formal reprimand. We worked out a compromise. A stern cable reminding Roberts of the rules and sending him back to Lebanon to debrief the embassy would take care of the matter.

So minutes later, we called Roberts back and instructed him to head back to Beirut via Cyprus to keep VOA's presence in Lebanon intact and debrief the embassy. Right away, he was on the phone to Rachida still another time to say wearily: "I'm not dead, but I'm not coming home just yet!" A familiar sort of ending to yet another war story.[16]

THE CONTENTIOUS CITADEL

Back at the Voice, the broomsticks continued to swing with abandon in the last quarter of the century. At times, the struggles centered on management or labor relations issues, as well as on politics.

In a paper entitled "Words Can Not Explain," VOA English-language broadcaster Charlene Porter in 1995 examined the problems of

THE HARTMAN CLASS-ACTION SUIT

In 1977, Carolee Brady Hartman applied for a job as a writer at USIA and was told by a recruiting officer there that "they were thinking about hiring a man for the position." Hartman filed a formal discrimination complaint. This expanded into a class-action lawsuit encompassing VOA. On April 14, 1989, the U.S. district court advertised in the *Washington Post* outlining procedures permitting women at the Voice (as part of USIA) to join in the suit. Litigation, which had already lasted for more than a decade, centered on the years from 1974 to 1984. About 1,100 women—60 percent of them at VOA—filed claims, alleging discrimination because of their gender in hiring or promotions.

Hundreds of depositions were taken, the agency assembled a team of attorneys, and the case extended yet another decade. Finally, on March 22, 2000, the U.S. government agreed to settle the case. It agreed to pay $508 million to the plaintiffs, each of whom collected an average of $460,000. It was the largest award ever in an employee discrimination case, a final settlement after twenty-three years.*

Although the courts found that some women had been denied hiring or promotion opportunities over the years, others at the Voice fared reasonably well. In the last quarter of the twentieth century, two served as presidentially appointed VOA directors, and another, Myrna Whitworth, was director of programs and twice acting director. Eleven others headed broadcast divisions, a majority supervising more than a hundred employees. In the 1980s and 1990s, three of five VOA News directors were women, as were News bureau chiefs at the White House, the State Department, Congress, and the United Nations, as well as in Beijing, Paris, Hong Kong, Moscow, Tokyo, Cairo, Johannesburg, Lima, Abidjan, and Mexico City. In 2001/2002, the acting director of programs was Kelu Chao, normally director of the East Asia and Pacific Division, VOA's largest language unit.

*Bill Miller and David A. Vise, "U.S. Settles Job Bias Case: A Record $508 Million Is Due Women in USIA Dispute," *Washington Post*, March 23, 2000, A1.

cross-cultural communication and labor relations in what she termed "a workplace that mirrors the world's many faces."[17]

Porter noted that at the Voice, exchanges of broadcasters between the newsroom and the language services and multilingual team coverage of events would help to break down barriers, if there were money to do this. She also borrowed an idea from an Idaho food-processing company. "Facing increasing linguistic diversity in the workplace," she wrote, "this company instituted a buddy system, in which American employees were partnered with non-native English speakers . . . to develop language skills and acclimate them" to the U.S. industrial environment. At VOA, innovative Director of Engineering Walter LaFleur had employed the principle with considerable success in the late 1980s and early 1990s, by bringing foreign national relay station employees to the Greenville Relay Station for training in basic transmitter engineering skills. Samuel K. Paye was one of those employees (chapter 5).

If such a program were put in place at VOA's programming department, Porter said, it "might have even broader benefits. Building relationships and enhancing language skills would help each member of the partnership learn more about the other's work priorities. Central services [newsroom] employees could share their often greater experience in broadcasting and journalism; language service employees could share their insights and understanding of various regions of the globe." Ideally, the program would entail pairing every new VOA staff member (language service or news professional) with a counterpart from the other community. It could be extended to partner professionals at VOA with commercial-broadcasting newcomers or political appointees. Janie Fritzman had particular success partnering with both groups (and learning from them) in the 1980s and 1990s.

There was a growing consensus, from 1970 on, among all the groups about VOA's mission and principles. This continued—in the tradition of Henry Loomis, John Chancellor, Kenneth Giddens, and Mary Bitterman—to emerge during the "mad, exhilarating ride" of the 1950s to early 1980s. It was a quest for more journalistic autonomy, in several forms. That plunge into the center of the arena, the heart of the Circus Maximus, is the subject of the next chapter.

7

The Struggle to
Get It Straight

THE CHARTER AS LAW

Truth will ultimately prevail, where there are pains to bring it
to light.
—George Washington

VOA's most precious possession is, and will be, its credibility.
In these days of explosive communication, may I say, it is sheer
folly to presume one can manipulate, or withhold, information
to make propaganda.
—John Charles Daly, to House
Committee on International Relations

At home and abroad, VOA's struggle to get it straight accelerated in the
late 1960s and the 1970s. As we have seen, there were sustained clashes
over content between the diplomats and the journalists. The conflict
extended to the far corners of the Earth, and as Doug Roberts's experience in southern Lebanon illustrated, it coincided with (some would say
was exacerbated by) the emergence of a much-energized VOA news
operation and the presence of more VOA correspondents abroad than
ever before. Passage of the charter as law was an important landmark.
Gradually, foundations were firming up for the news and programming
autonomy first dreamed of a generation earlier.

During my first decade at the Voice, I had been a distant spectator,
mostly removed from the policy wars, as newswriter trainee, English program editor, foreign correspondent, and, from 1971 to 1973, deputy chief

and chief of the New York bureau. But suddenly, in September 1973, I was assigned as deputy chief (and then as acting chief) of News and Current Affairs (NCA), a department of more than 250 Voice journalists, correspondents, writers, and editors. Now I was no longer a spectator, but right there in the arena with them.

THE WHITE HOUSE GOES FOR TOP NETWORK TALENT

The Circus Maximus was full of ironies. In 1965, President Lyndon Johnson actively courted NBC's John Chancellor to run what LBJ called "my own radio." As the Vietnam War escalated, Chancellor signed on as the eleventh director of VOA. For the first time, it appeared, a president was directly involved in the recruitment, selection, and announcement of a VOA director. But Johnson may not have foreseen that Chancellor, when it came to news, was a man who insisted on standing by his principles as well as rejuvenating the sound of the Voice.

Years later, VOA's twenty-second director, Geoffrey Cowan (son of the second director, Lou Cowan), recalled a visit he had at UCLA with retired anchorman Chancellor, his predecessor of a generation earlier. This was shortly before Cowan was appointed VOA director in 1994:

> John Chancellor gave me many pieces of advice, but the one that was most important was this—he said: "I want to remind you that you have to put your hat by the door, and be prepared to leave if you get a call asking you to do something that you don't think is right."
>
> And he said: "You're going to get calls from ambassadors who are going to say: 'You're about to run a story that is going to embarrass the United States, embarrass one of our allies.' And you're going to say: 'Ambassador, I appreciate that call. I want you to feel perfectly free to call me about that subject if you like. You have your job to do, but I have mine. The story was accurate and balanced, and we have an obligation to run it, and I have an obligation to protect those journalists who did run it.'"

Cowan went on to repeat Chancellor's hypothetical scenario— successive appeals by the secretary of state and even higher not to use a story:

"You may get a call from the White House, and let's assume they're speaking on the authority of the president, you say: 'Appreciate the call . . . if you're telling me that this is your decision, then you have your job, and I have my integrity, and with all respect, I will leave this job because I will never violate the journalistic excellence, integrity, professionalism and independence of the Voice of America.'" And that is the story of the charter of the Voice of America, and that is the reason it was written into law.[1]

"FINALLY, I SAID TO MYSELF:
'HEY, THIS IS THE NATURE OF OUR COUNTRY'"

Paul Modic got more than he bargained for: he became the clearing officer and was responsible for all VOA commentaries—then called news analyses. He dealt directly with the analysts themselves, which meant debating with them daily about their scripts. They were a savvy lot. Ronald J. Dunlavey specialized in the Middle East and almost any other global issue. German-born John Albert, a daily reader of many European newspapers in the original languages, was an expert on East–West and disarmament topics. Harold J. Courlander, a writer and historian, was widely known for his expertise on Africa, and Joseph Sullivan for his knowledge of Asian politics and languages.

"The analysis," Courlander said, "should be characterized by thoughtfulness, and appeal to the listener's interest, and a reasonable amount of candor . . . candor, so that the listener discerns an honesty of approach; interest, so that people will listen . . . and thoughtfulness, so that our audience may discern that what is being said is not just an institutional broadside."*

The analysts' emphases varied. On Vietnam—the paramount issue then—Dunlavey tended to be dovish and included candid reflections of the war from the *New York Times*. Albert, on the contrary, was more hawkish—consistent with Pentagon thinking. Modic, responsible for clearing both, remembers tossing at night: Were listeners getting "mixed messages" on U.S. Vietnam policy? Eventually, Modic recalls, his anxieties eased: "Finally, I said to myself: 'Hey, this is the nature of our country.'"†

*Harold Courlander, memorandum to Serban Vallimarescu (deputy director, VOA), March 25, 1974, 1.
†Paul Modic, telephone interview with author, Bethesda, Md., July 13, 2001.

When Chancellor assumed charge of VOA back in 1965, even he—a seasoned and determined journalist—had reiterated the philosophy of Tom Sorensen and Carl Rowan: "Our task is to make the policies of the government of the United States clearly and explicitly understood around the world, with no misunderstandings."[2]

Apparently, however, Chancellor meant that VOA ought to be trusted, without oversight from the agency, to prepare its own news analyses or commentaries reflecting U.S. policy. United States Information Agency (USIA) foreign service officer Paul Modic, a staunch defender of VOA's journalistic autonomy and later its director of programs, was head of the Voice Office of Policy when Chancellor arrived. Modic requested a private meeting to caution the new director about "uptown" (meaning USIA) kills and unwarranted edits of VOA news analyses. Modic said that on most days, he could successfully defend the scripts. But he appealed to Chancellor to back him up, if necessary. Chancellor's reply: "We're not going to do it that way any more . . . VOA will itself clear all commentaries it writes from now on."[3] That practice lasted throughout Chancellor's tenure.

Chancellor left after two years to return to NBC. He was succeeded by another professional with a commercial network background, John Charles Daly, the moderator of the popular TV panel program *What's My Line?* Daly, too, stood his ground on journalistic principles. Shortly before his confirmation, Daly told AP that he intended to have VOA report "fully and fairly the divisions in the country," including conflicting opinions on Vietnam policy. Representative Charles S. Joelson (Democrat of New Jersey) said that Daly had a mistaken view of his new assignment if he thought it was to broadcast all points of view. "The Voice of America is to promulgate our government's policy," Joelson said.[4] Daly quit after only ten months—in part, he said, "because he could no longer serve as an effective shield for the career news employees against pressures from self-interested policymakers."[5]

CHANGING TIMES, INSIDE AND OUTSIDE THE VOICE

In the late 1960s and early 1970s, the pressures mounted. The Vietnam War ground on, and the nation's overseas information and cultural programs came under fresh scrutiny. Senate Foreign Relations Committee chairman J. William Fulbright questioned the need for U.S. international broadcasting, particularly Radio Free Europe (RFE) and Radio Liberty (RL); he termed all the radios "relics of the Cold War."

Inside the Voice, ambitious young Near East and South Asia Division chief Bill Haratunian (chapter 4) was promoted in the late 1960s to become chief of VOA News and Current Affairs. Almost overnight, Bill stationed a dozen VOA staff news correspondents abroad, attaching them to U.S. embassies or missions. He thus established VOA's global correspondents corps in the only practical and the least expensive way at the time; their office space and communications were supported by embassies or consulates. Correspondents in the United States numbered about a dozen, too, as Haratunian opened bureaus in Miami, Chicago, and Los Angeles. The newsroom itself, a major part of NCA, took advantage of this first global, on-the-scene reportorial capability. About the same time, Cliff Groce and Bernie Kamenske advanced to leadership positions—Groce as deputy director of programs and Kamenske as a shift chief in the newsroom.

Outside the Voice, Congress and various commissions included international broadcasting and VOA in their reappraisal of the nation's overseas public diplomacy programs. At least thirty-one studies of U.S. information or cultural activities abroad were conducted between the mid-1940s and mid-1970s.[6] In 1968, Senator Fulbright called for a high-level commission to study both the Department of State and USIA. A few years later, several other panels joined in the probe. Three major ones were

- The Eisenhower Commission (1972–1973), focusing on RFE/RL, which until that time had been covertly funded by the CIA
- The Murphy Commission (1972–1975), examining mainly nonbroadcasting information and cultural activities
- The Stanton Commission (1974–1975), which recommended, among a number of other changes, that VOA become a separate, independent agency (an idea later endorsed by the Murphy Commission)

Gradually, the policy controls on the Voice were easing. Daily guidances, crafted in both the State Department and USIA, had for years counseled VOA News to stress, soft-pedal, or even omit stories. Morning policy notes, a vestige of World War II days, were routinely posted in the heart of the newsroom to be read by all. One day in 1971, VOA policy

WHY INDEPENDENCE?

There had been talk, in varying degrees, of VOA independence—that is, separation from the State Department or USIA—as early as the 1940s. Independence, from the perspective of advocates inside the Voice and their allies, would mean their unquestioned editorial control over news and programming content and a separate organizational structure, including budget and personnel. As the Stanton Commission put it: "VOA should broadcast the news, and do so objectively, because the strength of America's ideological appeal depends in large measure upon our devotion to the free flow of information."*

Ambassador Charles Yost had noted: "A government agency in this field [broadcasting] faces the insoluble dilemma of either hewing strictly to the official line and losing credibility of much of its audience, or of reflecting the wide diversity of behavior and opinion in the U.S. and thus incurring the wrath of the White House, State Department and Congress."†

John Chancellor, too, cited "over-control" by agency policy officers, but cautioned against what he regarded as "too much independence from policy guidelines" by VOA broadcasters. Both, he said, were suspended in a sort of "civil service aspic" and both "go on for years defining truth in their own terms."‡

*Panel on International Information, Education, and Cultural Relations (Stanton Commission), *International Information Education and Cultural Relations: Recommendations for the Future* (Washington, D.C.: Center for Strategic and International Studies, 1975), 47.
†Quoted in Maureen Jane Nemecek, "Speaking of America: The Voice of America, Its Mission and Message, 1942–1982" (Ph.D. diss., University of Maryland, 1984), 33.
‡Quoted in Michael Nelson, *War of the Black Heavens: The Battles of Western Broadcasting in the Cold War* (Syracuse, N.Y.: Syracuse University Press, 1997), 130.

chief Jerry Stryker, a USIA foreign service officer, decided not to place the guidance notes in the newsroom. A few months later, he let them disappear altogether.[7] It was one of several steps in the 1970s toward greater VOA editorial autonomy.

The decade also saw a struggle for resources. In USIA, VOA frequently was accorded a lower priority (and often lost funding) as the agency prepared its annual budget presentations to Congress or had to make congressionally mandated cuts.[8] The slowdown in construction of new VOA relay stations (chapter 5) reflected VOA's declining influence within USIA. The VOA director, although managing roughly a quarter of USIA's staff and resources, was one of nearly a score of assistant directors of an "uptown" agency located a mile and a half away from VOA's headquarters.

Frank Stanton, a distinguished CBS broadcast executive, was named in 1974 to assemble his study panel, a team of twenty-one citizens and senior officers of the overseas information and cultural agencies. Veteran VOA broadcaster and diplomat Walter Roberts (chapter 2) resigned as an associate USIA director to become the project director. The panel met, held hearings, and interviewed more than a hundred foreign information and cultural specialists over a period of about eleven months. It recommended

- Combining all State Department and USIA information and cultural activities into a single new Information and Cultural Affairs Agency (ICA). At that time, cultural and exchange programs were mainly in the State Department, with some in USIA
- Integrating all State Department and USIA programs that articulated policy into a new Office of Policy Information, located in the State Department and headed by a deputy undersecretary
- Establishing VOA as a separate federal agency, under a board of overseers, with a mandate to broadcast accurate, objective, and comprehensive news as well as to represent American society in its totality, with State Department control over foreign policy articulation[9]

It was one thing to have a respected panel recommend nominal independence for the Voice. But it was quite another to reach that goal because of the turf wars being waged at the time within the U.S. foreign affairs community and on Capitol Hill.

INTO THE ARENA

After comprehensive reportage on the Yom Kippur War in the Middle East in October 1973, the Voice became engulfed in its own bureaucratic war of the roses. It once again involved alliances of insiders and external forces. In essence, it was an assault by USIA on Director Kenneth R. Giddens's management of the Voice. Agency director James Keogh had brought a senior foreign service officer, Serban Vallimarescu, back from the National Security Council as Giddens's deputy to try to control VOA. Keogh then appointed a group of three other USIA foreign service officers (Lewis Schmidt, Ed Schechter, and charter drafter Jack O'Brien) to study VOA management. Their investigation focused at first on Program Manager Nathan Kingsley, a Giddens appointee.

After a week or so, the probe expanded to consider complaints against News and Current Affairs by language division chiefs. Supported by Vallimarescu and Groce, they maintained that NCA was producing too many news and current affairs items and that they often were irrelevant to regional audiences. They maintained that Kingsley rarely communicated with either his deputy, Groce, or the language services. The language chiefs (most of them USIA foreign service officers) felt that the program manager was concentrating on news to the exclusion of other programming.

The group reported back to Keogh in April 1974. It recommended that NCA be split into separate news and current affairs divisions. The organization, it said, was too large and insensitive to the needs of language broadcasters and created "a news-oriented climate wherein longer range features that illuminate the American scene get secondary consideration." Decrying what it called "a strain of feisty dedication to unfettered news," the study group characterized NCA news as "frequently too comprehensive and too fast."[10] Kingsley, for his part, maintained that he had communicated directly with other Voice managers at daily meetings. Within weeks after the report was issued, Kingsley and several of his associates were transferred or removed. Miraculously, NCA survived. Its goal was to improve the quality of its product as it focused on three primary issues: détente, Watergate, and Indochina.

DÉTENTE

The easing of tensions between the United States and the Soviet Union—détente—began with President Kennedy's celebrated American University address in 1963 and was further enhanced by President Nixon's visit to Moscow in 1972. The Soviet Union's jamming of VOA Russian-language broadcasts ceased from September 1973 until shortly after the Soviet invasion of Afghanistan six years later.[11]

Détente led to clashes over information policy within the Nixon and Ford administrations. Some executives favored a "go easy" approach on the Soviet Union. Others advocated a harder edge. VOA journalists simply wanted to play it straight, reflecting what U.S. officials and others said and offering balanced analysis as events unfolded.

Frank Shakespeare, the new USIA director under President Nixon, was among those favoring a harder line. He encouraged VOA news analyses with anti-Soviet references. One such assessment in 1970 was broadcast as the United States was engaged in sensitive talks with the Soviet Union on the preservation of an Egyptian–Israeli cease-fire in the Sinai. A week later, another VOA analysis spoke of "Soviet duplicity." The broadcasts drew a rebuke from Secretary of State William Rogers. He reminded Shakespeare that USIA, although an independent agency, was still obligated to receive formal policy guidance from the State Department.[12] James Keogh succeeded Shakespeare at the beginning of Nixon's second term.

A Change in Tone

Keogh, a former *Time* executive editor and Nixon presidential speech-writer, arrived at USIA less than one year after Nixon's historic May 1972 visit to Moscow. He advocated a less strident approach. Keogh sought to extend this to encompass not only VOA analyses reflecting policy, but other content as well. A major event then was the release on December 29, 1973, of Aleksandr Solzhenitsyn's *Gulag Archipelago*, a devastating indictment of life in Soviet prison camps.

During the first two days after publication, the Current Affairs Division under Bernie Kamenske had issued a dozen *Gulag*-related pieces, including extensive excerpts. These were devoured quickly by the USSR Division and its Russian Branch, translated, and broadcast to the Soviet Union, where the book, of course, was unavailable to the public.

Keogh and agency policy officers questioned whether the Voice should broadcast excerpts. "To read from the book," Keogh said, "would be far outside the normal style of Voice of America programming and would tend to reinforce Soviet charges that the United States is utilizing these events as a political weapon and is intervening in the domestic affairs of the USSR." He denied that USIA had "muted its Voice" but said it would not turn backward to what he called "the old Cold War style of broadcasting."[13]

Keogh's view prevailed as broadcast policy. A VOA internal memo had contended that the *Gulag* excerpts were essential, if listeners in the USSR were to adequately evaluate the facts amid Soviet media distortions of Solzhenitsyn's work.[14]

"Not an International NBC or CBS"

The USIA, during the détente years, also sought to control the reporting of VOA overseas correspondents. In 1974, the agency's area director for Europe, John (Jock) Shirley, instructed United States Information Service (USIS)[15] posts in Eastern Europe to review coverage proposals and texts of reports by VOA correspondents stationed in or visiting their countries.

Keogh defended the policy, saying in a *Time* interview: "The Voice of America is not an international NBC or CBS. Détente has changed what we do in USIA. Our program managers must be sensitive to U.S. policy as enunciated by the president and secretary of state. . . . We're not in the business of trying to provoke revolutions."[16]

Some diplomats and USIA public affairs officers recognized VOA's essential need for credibility and left it to the broadcasters to apply their own rigorous sourcing guidelines. Others, however, insisted on second-guessing VOA correspondents abroad.

The "Interference" Log Grows

In the early 1970s, embassy and USIA officials vetted correspondents' reports, including those of the very active Munich bureau chief, Mark Hopkins (chapter 1). Hopkins teamed up with VOA correspondents Larry Freund and Ron Pemstein to begin developing a series on what Hopkins described as widely known "rampant corruption within Communist Party organizations in the region."[17] The USIA European area office rejected the plan because "if it [the series] had been honest and accurate, it would have been offensive to the governments involved . . . it would have seemed gratuitous and ideologically polemical."[18]

Twice in 1977, the American embassy in Belgrade attempted to prevent broadcasts of interviews by Voice correspondents with Yugoslav dissidents Mihajlo Mihajlov and Milovan Djilas. Both interviews were aired, thanks to the support of Voice senior managers, many of whom were USIA foreign service officers; it was, after all, the year after the

VOA Charter became law. Hopkins flew to Belgrade from Munich to interview Mihajlov on November 26, the day after the famous dissident was released from prison. Two hours after the interview, Ambassador (and later Secretary of State) Lawrence Eagleburger asked Hopkins to recommend that the Voice not broadcast it. Eagleburger said there had been an understanding between the U.S. and Yugoslav governments that if Mihajlov was freed, there would be no publicity. Hopkins said he would pass along the embassy's reservations to Washington. The ambassador acknowledged the existence of the newly enacted VOA Charter but added, "You have your job to do, and we have ours."[19] After considerable debate, VOA authorized the broadcast of Mihajlov's interview two days later on all its services except Serbo-Croatian because of the ambassador's appeal.

In other areas of the world besides Europe—Africa, the Middle East, and Southeast Asia—missions blocked the establishment of VOA bureaus or restricted the travel of Voice correspondents into their countries for diplomatic or security reasons. *Time* reported in late 1974 that tensions in the diplomatic community over VOA news gathering "is one item on the agenda of a twenty-member panel [the Stanton Commission] . . . expected to recommend next month that the Voice be given greater journalistic freedom."[20]

WATERGATE

In a book on her years as VOA's White House correspondent, *A Basement Seat to History*, Philomena Jurey recalls an order from Keogh in June 1973 forbidding VOA News from carrying Watergate stories based on unidentified sources. "The Keogh order," Jurey wrote, "would have foreclosed our picking up many of the newspaper accounts on Watergate, causing a gap in our coverage." But, she added, "we got around it by seeking White House reaction when Watergate revelations based on anonymous sources were published." This way, VOA would start its stories with the White House denial and follow it with the report, attributing it to the original news source, with considerable detail.[21]

Kamenske set up a special newsroom unit (two correspondents, two writers, and tape editors) to be solely responsible for covering Watergate. "It's a complicated story," he said at the time, "so it takes space to tell it."[22] Giddens, in supporting expanded reportage, added: "We're trying diligently to convey the idea that what the world is seeing is the genius of our checks and balances at work." For Giddens, a conservative Republican and Nixon appointee, it was a painful time. His unwavering support for the newsroom as Watergate unfolded showed how far he had traveled, as a supporter of VOA's journalistic integrity, since his first days at the Voice under Frank Shakespeare. Then, he had been quoted as saying: "If you dwell on our warts, people will think you're a warthog."[23]

As the Watergate crisis escalated, USIA backed off. Years later, Program Manager Shellenberger (who succeeded Kingsley about ten weeks before Nixon's resignation) explained: "They could see the handwriting on the wall and didn't want to become part of the coverup late in Watergate when they knew the game was probably up."[24] VOA reported the indictment of senior cabinet officials; Nixon's dismissal of others, including the famous Saturday-night massacre of October 1974; and the House Judiciary Committee hearings on the scandal (broadcast live by VOA). It also reported the Supreme Court ruling that forced the release of critical taped conversations of the president and his aides.

During the final week of the Nixon presidency, the newsroom was alive with activity.[25] On August 5, 1974, the now-famous "smoking gun" tape was released, definitively tying the president to the cover-up. Three days later, the White House announced around midday that Nixon would make a major address at 9:00 P.M. Most everyone suspected then that he would become the first president in U.S. history to resign. How to explain this complex story, which then had been unfolding for a year

---

VOICE OF AMERICA "IS IN THE NEWS BUSINESS"

In May 1974, the *Wall Street Journal*, in a story headlined "At the Voice of America, There's No Cover-up on Watergate News," cited Senator Richard Schweiker's call for Nixon to resign and noted that "it was the American government that put him on shortwave radio for the whole world to hear. Although the liberal Pennsylvania Republican has never been a big ally of President Nixon in the Senate, his open call for resignation was news, and the Voice of America is in the news business."*

*Arlen J. Large, "At the Voice of America, There's No Cover-up on Watergate News," *Wall Street Journal*, May 16, 1974. See also Philomena Jurey, *A Basement Seat to History: Tales of Covering Presidents Nixon, Ford, Carter, and Reagan for the Voice of America* (Washington, D.C.: Linus Press, 1995), 70.

and a half, to a perplexed world? Would it set off a constitutional crisis? Would it signal paralysis in Washington?

On August 8 at 4:00 P.M., Program Manager Shellenberger called a meeting of all VOA division chiefs and NCA. He handed out a dozen strictly embargoed NCA-written scripts on the background of the Watergate scandal. This was necessary because of the volume of material. This was before PCs, and there was no way the creaky, typo-prone, antiquated in-house Teletype system could get the centrally produced scripts around to more than thirty language services by nine o'clock. Besides, the language services needed lead time to translate the scripts. Shellenberger held division managers responsible for ensuring a strict embargo until 9:00 P.M. He placed two news analyses in his top desk drawer. One was to be used if Nixon resigned; the other, in the event the president decided to stay the course and go through impeachment hearings and a Senate trial.

Among the scripts was a Watergate chronology written by VOA correspondent and legal analyst Chris Kern:

> After two long years, the White House scandals known as Watergate have reached a spectacular climax. There was little indication this would happen in June 1972, when a team of burglars was arrested in the Washington headquarters of the Democratic Party. They carried electronic equipment for tapping telephones, and it was obvious that they were there on a mission of some kind of political surveillance.
>
> But surprisingly, it took some time for the press and public to begin asking who had sent them. A series of revelations by the *Washington Post* connected the burglars with President Nixon's campaign for reelection. But few other news organizations followed up the story. And Watergate apparently had no effect on the 1972 presidential election. Mr. Nixon was elected by a landslide in November.

Kern went on to describe how the scandal broke wide open the following March when White House counsel John Dean testified before Congress that he had covered up the burglary with the president's approval. Kern continued:

> It was his word against the president's, and the president denied everything. But then another Nixon aide revealed that Mr. Nixon

had secretly recorded almost all his office conversations. If the president was involved in the cover-up, the tapes would tell.

The tapes did tell, though it took the Supreme Court to force Mr. Nixon to surrender them. The evidence on the tapes—recordings of the president's conversations with his closest aides—was cited again and again by congressmen who last month recommended Mr. Nixon's impeachment. The president, they said, had obstructed justice.

He was also accused of abuse of power, misusing the government agencies that, as president, he directed. And a third charge recommended his impeachment for defying congressional subpoenas for the White House tapes.

But only after Mr. Nixon admitted that he misled the Congress and the public, were the charges overwhelmingly accepted. His resignation now only prevents what was clearly going to be the first removal of a U.S. president from office.

Nine o'clock rolled around, and the newsroom and Current Affairs were fully staffed. Nixon resigned, in a subdued address that lasted for sixteen minutes.

Another Critical Phone Call

Shortly after Nixon's address, the phone rang in the office where Bernie and I had been watching the proceedings on TV. It was a call from higher up.

"Wasn't that a noble speech?" the caller inquired. "I think all of the scripts looked very good, but in view of the tone of that speech, I wonder if we shouldn't pull back the chronology?"

Kamenske, normally larger than life in any case, was predictably thunderous in his response. "It's just after nine on the night he resigned," he bellowed. "It's all over! You're not going to blow it now, surely, and make us part of this?"

There was a pause, probably no more than a couple of seconds, but it seemed much longer. "Okay," replied the senior managerial Deep Throat, "let it go."

Out in the newsroom and Current Affairs, they were working the phones and tearing copy off the source wires, pulling in reaction from throughout the nation and the world. The bulldog editions of the east coast papers hit the streets, with Watergate analysis, praise about a system in which no individual was above the law, and biographies of Gerald R. Ford, soon to be president. The central and language services synthesized all this and broadcast special reports. The Current Affairs writers quickly produced an analysis and a roundup of U.S. editorials.

At around two in the morning, Bernie and I were ready to call it a night and walked out of the building together. In the darkened first-floor corridor, we encountered a senior editor of the Russian Branch. He remarked about how his editors admired the work of the newsroom that longest day. "We used everything," he said, "except that chronology." We gasped, too tired to ask if that had been his idea or someone else's.

The following day, Soviet media analyzed the downfall of Richard M. Nixon. The president, papers in Moscow speculated, was "a victim of those opposing détente." Throughout the crisis, Soviet media had conspicuously ignored the Watergate scandal, responding to "policy" made by Kremlin détentists. Kern's Watergate chronology likely was the most important piece that the Russian Branch could have broadcast, especially in the no-jamming environment of the time. His report did reach the USSR in English. Again, at least to listeners in Russian, America's Voice had shot itself in the foot, after winning what had been a marathon race right up to the finish line.

INDOCHINA

"Watergate and Vietnam," Shellenberger said years later, "were the principal concerns I had as program manager."[26] At times during the Indochina conflict, U.S. diplomats found it inconvenient for VOA, with its considerable audience, to be broadcasting objective news to the region. Sometimes the Voice succeeded, despite the pressures. Other times, it did not. Journalists at VOA, however, tried their best during the Vietnam War to tell it as it was, get it fast, and get it straight—no matter what.

Foreign correspondents like Wayne Hyde engage local reporters to help them get the news. VOA was fortunate to have hired one of South Vietnam's best journalists. Pham Tran, widely known in VOA as P. T., was a syndicated columnist and reporter for papers throughout the country. His combination of journalistic curiosity, contacts, and keen judgment about what was fact and what was fiction helped a succession of fifteen VOA correspondents in Vietnam, right up until the war ended.

"Sergeant, Are You About Ready to Move In Now?"

In the late 1960s, correspondent Wayne Hyde was on the front lines:

HYDE: (*with machine gun fire in the background*) I'm with a platoon of soldiers who've come into this Mekong Delta village tonight to clear out a group of Vietcong. The VC took over the village this noon, but one villager managed to get away late this afternoon and tell the Americans the VC were here. As we came in, only a few minutes ago, the VC opened fire on us.

SERGEANT McWILLIAMS: We got to get a machine gun down!

HYDE: That was Sergeant McWilliams, the platoon sergeant. Sergeant, are you about ready to move in now?

SERGEANT McWILLIAMS: Almost, there's five of them.*

*Wayne Hyde, "The Voices of the Voice" (transcript of VOA thirty-fifth anniversary special feature, February 16, 1977), 5.

A Tip that Paid Off

On August 2, 1971, for example, P. T. heard through the Saigon grapevine about a clandestine incursion by South Vietnamese troops into neighboring Laos, code-named Lam Son 719. He knew that he needed to confirm the information before hard-nosed, hard-driving VOA Saigon correspondent Peter Collins would file it. So P. T. placed a phone call to a close friend stationed with the Army of the Republic of Vietnam (ARVN) on the border. They were accustomed to speaking in code. "I heard some rumors," said P. T., "that some guys broke into your neighbors' house."

"How did you hear about that?" P. T.'s contact asked.

"Never mind," said P. T. "That's not so important. What's important is how many of those guys did it, were there . . . say, about five?" (In previous discussions, he and his friend had worked out the math used in the code—a single person in such situations represented 10,000 troops, and P. T. knew military affairs well enough to guess that between 40,000 and 60,000 troops were probably deployed.)

"Five is correct," the informant replied.

P. T. rushed to the VOA bureau, consulted with Collins, and told him that 50,000 troops were involved. They did a little further digging, extracting added confirmation from other military sources and sharing the news with George Esper of the Associated Press, who checked it out with his contacts. Less than twenty-four hours after the South Vietnamese action began, VOA broadcast the news back into the region, scoring a beat, along with AP, on this story.[27]

The ARVN Collapse in the Central Highlands

On March 10, 1975, Kamenske read a news agency report that the town of Ban Me Thuot in central South Vietnam had fallen to the North Vietnamese. Was this a sign that a final offensive on Saigon might be near? In general, the war was going badly for the South. Bernie had moved Bangkok correspondent Wayne Corey to Saigon in late 1974; now he dispatched Steve Thompson from Washington to "double team" events. The two correspondents worked closely with P. T.

Meanwhile, in neighboring Cambodia, Communist Khmer Rouge forces were advancing on the capital, Phnom Penh. American diplomats were closely monitoring VOA. On March 19, the U.S. ambassador to Cambodia, John Gunther Dean, cabled the Voice, asking it not to report about student demonstrations in Phnom Penh calling for the removal of the faltering government of Prime Minister Lon Nol. The broadcast, he said, "could be construed as a signal that the U.S. government was sympathetic to those demands."[28] On April 6, the U.S. ambassador to South Vietnam, Graham Martin, cabled that any VOA broadcasts on the evacuation of Saigon should be limited to official pronouncements.[29] The newsroom continued to be guided by its two-source rule, at times holding stories for several hours to verify their accuracy. VOA could ill afford to make mistakes in a crisis as serious as this one.

A Journalistic Sin of Omission

Amid growing talk of mass evacuations from the South Vietnamese capital, an interagency task force met in Washington. It debated contingencies. Senior officials of the Departments of State and Defense and of the National Security Council decided at the meeting (also attended by USIA director Keogh and VOA director Giddens) that VOA was not to broadcast any information on the evacuation of civilians from Vietnam except official statements of the White House, State or Defense Department, or congressional votes on the pullout. Bernie and I received that directive on April 14, 1975. It was not, to put it mildly, one of our better days.

We placed the directive, paraphrased, on the clipboard in the newsroom in the form of what was popularly referred to as "a slot note," and faced a near revolution.[30] Editors and writers strongly protested that other media, including other international broadcasters such as the BBC, were free to air news about the evacuation while VOA remained silent.

"The people out there," Bernie told United Press International reporter Cheryl Arvidson as he gestured toward the newsroom, "were brought up in the tradition of American journalism . . . and they don't believe in selective reporting. They know, and I know, that we are an important source of truth in the world, and we destroy the sum total of knowledge if we do less. How inadequate I would be if I said that I wasn't horrified, disgusted, unhappy . . . that we had to moderate, adjust if you will, a Charter principle."[31]

USIA deputy director Eugene Kopp, also interviewed by Arvidson, called the directive "unique" and said that it reflected the volatile situation in Saigon. Speculation about an early evacuation, he added, could have caused panic and endangered American and South Vietnamese lives. Kopp said that the directive was justified even though the commercial television networks, the wire services, and the BBC were carrying reports of the pullout, including congressional calls to speed up the evacuation rather than send more military aid to South Vietnam.[32]

Endgame in Saigon

In Saigon, the situation was turning critical. Corey and Thompson were filing around the clock during April as North Vietnamese troops advanced on Saigon. Hue, Da Nang, Nha Trang, and Cam Ranh Bay fell in rapid succession. P. T. used his contacts to help the correspondents check and double-check the facts in each city or province. Under the slot note directive, there was no point in Corey and Thompson voicing reports about evacuation preparations; nonetheless, they kept a stream of advisories flowing to the VOA newsroom. One advisory was particularly grim. As the U.S. embassy drew up evacuation lists, it excluded P. T., VOA Saigon office assistant My Binh, and their families from consideration, because they were not full-time employees.

"The most dangerous thing," P. T. recalled years later, "was that I worked for VOA, and everyone including the North Vietnamese, knew it . . . there was a 100 percent certainty I would've been put in jail if left behind in Vietnam."[33] Jail, or perhaps worse.

I told senior Voice managers on April 3 that the United States simply must secure a place for the VOA Vietnamese in any evacuation.[34] The bosses did indeed follow up at USIA and the State Department, both on the fate of P. T. and My Binh and their families and, later in the month, on the coverage restrictions. By April 26, media coverage of the impending withdrawal was voluminous. NCA got word to cancel the restriction on evacuation reporting. Kamenske wasted no time in drafting a new slot note, signed by both of us: "In darker days in the life of our nation, we told the world: 'The news may be good. The news may be bad, but we shall tell you the truth.' And it is important to remember that we strive to know the truth and tell it."[35]

In Saigon, embassy aides, reacting to the official entreaties from Washington, relented on the evacuation of P. T. and My Binh and their dependents. They agreed not to stand in the way of their departure, if Corey and Thompson would take on the chore of "wardens"—that is, shepherd a number of dependent and Vietnamese families to be evacuated to Tan Son Nhut airport from their places of residence.

Mad Dash to Tan Son Nhut

On Saturday, April 27, P. T., the tireless newshound, made a routine trip into town from home to check out his sources, at the coffeehouses and on the wires. After a couple of hours sniffing about, he dropped by USIS as part of his rounds, and Public Affairs Officer Alan Carter said: "P. T., where have you been? Wayne Corey and Steve Thompson have been looking for you . . . get straight to your meeting place [a house near the airport], where they and your family are waiting." P. T. hopped in his car, and recalls running twenty red lights to get there.[36]

It was chaotic at Tan Son Nhut. Corey and Thompson, unhappy with their meandering colleague, were filling up rosters for departing aircraft, eagerly looking for vacant seats to accommodate P. T. and his wife, mother, and four young children, as well as My Binh and her sister. "Don't talk to anyone," the correspondents cautioned. P. T. noticed many other Vietnamese families, some not even employed by the embassy but with good connections, desperately clamoring for space on the departing aircraft. Hours passed. Corey and Thompson processed nearly 130 "approved" people for departure. Finally, shortly before 1:00 A.M. on April 28, there was the opening they had waited for. They noticed a dozen empty bucket seats aboard one of the C-130s about to take off. Those designated for the assigned places hadn't shown up. They hustled the VOA families aboard. Minutes later, the giant transport was airborne, bearing P. T.; his wife, Huong Vu; his mother, Tang Pham; his sons Nguyen (four), Phong (three), and Son (one) and daughter, Linh (two) as well as My Binh and her sister, My Trang. There was one more fixed-wing flight from Tan Son Nhut for civilians at 4:00 that morning. At 8:00 A.M., North Vietnamese forces began bombing the airport. The fall of Saigon was imminent.

An Odyssey to Remember

The VOA Saigon families had a remarkable journey. They passed through Clark Air Force Base in the Philippines, had stopovers in Guam and Honolulu, and then arrived at Camp Pendleton in California—frequently finding themselves in packed refugee camps and temporary housing. NCA and the newsroom made certain that at each stop a VOA correspondent was there to cover and to expedite them through the facilities. At the California base, Los Angeles bureau chief Ed Gordon (chapter 4) helped the Tran and Binh families get assigned a tent. The next day, Ed and his wife, Norma, brought in clothes and toys for the children as the Vietnamese prepared to continue their journey. On May 3, barely five days after leaving Tan Son Nhut, the VOA Vietnamese families landed at Dulles International Airport near Washington. P. T. was still clad in the fatigues and rugged sandals of Saigon.

The next task was taking care of our newly arrived colleagues, so suddenly on our doorstep. Bernie Kamenske and Janie Fritzman set to work, arranging for the entire group to stay or be fed at various NCA homes for the next three weeks until Janie, working with news editor Jeff Sandmann and others, could paint and repair an abandoned church-owned home in Virginia to accommodate them temporarily. P. T. and My Binh did well in America. P. T. advanced to senior assignments editor in the VOA newsroom, and My Binh was an assistant in the VOA director's office. She married a Maryland biochemist.

Corey and Thompson remained in Saigon until the last hours of the U.S. presence there. On April 30, both were airlifted by helicopter off the roof of the American embassy (see Thompson's eyewitness description of his chopper flight, chapter 4). That occurred just two weeks after another VOA correspondent, Ed Conley, had been evacuated by helicopter with the last Americans to leave the Cambodian capital of Phnom Penh as the Communist Khmer Rouge swept into that city.

Unveiling a Holocaust

The horrific early months of Khmer Rouge rule, in fact, provided another arena for Wayne Corey to exercise his journalistic talents. VOA, thanks to Corey's dogged pursuit of the facts and Kamenske's checking and cross-checking, coaching and advising, was among the first news organizations to report the scale of the Cambodian holocaust. That happened despite urgent cautions against using the story from the Voice's East Asia and Pacific Division, the USIA area office for East Asia, and other regional specialists in Washington. Bernie's recollection: "I worked long distance cheek by jowl with Wayne on the story, and made it clear, when we finally decided to go with his estimate of a million Cambodians dead or missing, that if he went down, I'd go down with him."[37]

How did Kamenske and Corey work together to sound the "alarm bell of civilization" on Cambodia? Bernie noticed news agency reports of heavy traffic on rural roads there. This indicated that many city dwellers were being deported (chapter 19). Straight-arrow Wayne, intense and unrelenting, engaged Kamenske in nocturnal phone conversations that

---

A JOURNALISTIC "NEVER AGAIN"

Bernie Kamenske recalled how VOA and other journalistic organizations had failed to call sufficient attention to or do probing wartime reporting about the World War II Nazi Holocaust of Jews and other European minorities. In talking to veteran editors after he joined the Voice in 1955, Bernie never found any evidence that VOA had covered the killings in the Nazi death camps before the extent of the horror was revealed during the liberation of 1945. Nor did the *New York Times* and other major U.S. dailies. Bernie vowed that at VOA, failure to report a genocide in a timely manner would never happen again, at least not on his watch.

A "BREATH OF LIFE"

Dr. Haing Ngor, the Cambodian physician who won an Academy
Award as an actor in *The Killing Fields*, spoke of what it was like to be
in Cambodia under the Pol Pot regime. He told VOA director Richard
Carlson that when the Khmer Rouge took power in his native country,
people buried their radios in the ground for fear of being arrested if
caught listening. When the Khmer Rouge were driven out of Phnom
Penh in 1978 by the Vietnamese, Haing Ngor recalled, Cambodians dug
up those radios and found that the batteries were dead. They soaked the
batteries in pans of water and set them out on the sun-baked paving
stones to dry. The batteries were resurrected (at least partially). As
Carlson put it: "They got 15 minutes worth of juice out of them. They
used that precious power to tune in the news on the VOA Cambodian
Service." Ngor described listening to VOA as a "breath of life" for himself and his countrymen. Carlson said: "We supply that 'breath of life' to
people like Dr. Ngor and millions of others around the world who are
denied information. . . . I feel this is the most important thing we do and
is what drives us so hard."*

*Quoted in Patricia Seaman, "Richard W. Carlson: VOA's New Director,"
USIA World, November 1986, 4.

occasionally outlasted even BHK's patience for "talking through" a story.
But Corey was accumulating bits and pieces of information to nail down
his estimates. He recalled hearing from experts at the American embassy
in Phnom Penh before the evacuation that the Khmer Rouge had a reputation for killing, deporting, or starving civilians in areas it occupied
earlier in the war. When he returned to his home base in Bangkok after
the evacuation from Saigon, Corey pursued the story immediately.

"To get information," he remembers,

Supang Povatong [P. T.'s counterpart in Thailand and veteran
VOA office assistant] and I made repeated trips to the
Thai–Cambodian border to interview refugees, Thai border
guards, and anyone else who might have information about what
was going on. One young Cambodian woman, who looked twenty
years older than she actually was, crawled across the border as I
watched her. After she got some food and rested, she managed to

convey, better than anyone else I can recall, the scope of the holocaust as it was occurring in Battambang, then Cambodia's second largest city.[38]

Corey reported in September 1975 that a million Cambodians had died from deliberate killings, starvation, or disease or were missing and unaccounted for. He said that estimate was based on the size of Cambodia's urban population before the Khmer Rouge takeover, the known lack of medical facilities and supplies in the countryside, and refugees' descriptions of dire food shortages. "I had no doubt," Corey added, "that they told the truth because they were so traumatized. Many of those who reached Thailand had gray skin and yellow eyes because of malnutrition and disease, and they seemed close to death." The final estimated toll in Cambodia during the Pol Pot holocaust: more than 1.6 million dead, with thousands of others permanently wounded by land mines.

A BIPARTISAN COMMITMENT TO THE TRUTH

In early 1975, Senator Charles Percy (Republican of Illinois), Senator Lloyd Bentsen (Democrat of Texas and, later, secretary of the treasury), and Representative William Cohen (Republican of Maine and, later, U.S. senator and secretary of defense) wrote letters to Secretary of State Henry Kissinger and USIA director James Keogh. They inquired about press reports that VOA had been censored in connection with events in Eastern Europe and during the evacuation of South Vietnam.

In Cohen's words: "Reports that VOA correspondents in foreign capitals have had to clear their copy through American ambassadors certainly do not seem consistent with the avowed purpose of the Voice of America. . . . Our free and open government, unlike those of authoritarian states, is secure enough to trust the truth. We do not need to stoop to the level of the propagandists of other nations."[39]

In 1974 and 1975, more than 200 cables from U.S. embassies or calls from USIA area or policy offices complained about coverage or sought to hinder VOA news gathering or reporting on nearly every continent.[40] VOA journalists and broadcasters resisted. Many in the Voice's high management were foreign service officers who at times felt they were like deer in the headlights in the dead of night, caught right at the intersection of what John Chancellor called "the crossroads of journalism and diplomacy."

At times, top VOA managers sided with their diplomatic colleagues, but at other times they offered steadfast support for Voice journalists. A few complaints called attention to inaccuracies and were justified. VOA, like any news organization, is not infallible.[41] Other protests, as described earlier, resulted in substantive omissions from a news item or a correspondent's report. Still others resulted in delays ranging from a few hours to several days before scripts were issued, as the newsroom and Current Affairs double-checked their sources and debated the items at issue.

Following a series of press reports about restrictions on VOA, Percy, a leading figure and later chairman of the Senate Foreign Relations Committee, and Representative Bella Abzug (Democrat of New York) became active advocates of unfettered news on America's Voice. In early 1976, Abzug summoned Kamenske to her chambers, and accused VOA, and Bernie specifically, of responsibility for less than candid reportage of Watergate. But Bernie stood his ground. He replied that the Voice's coverage was comparable to or better than that of most other news organizations except for some of the daily newspapers with huge investigative staffs. Abzug seemed convinced. She went on, however, to document policy-imposed omissions in VOA's reportage in Ethiopia, South Africa, Lebanon, Western Sahara, and Indochina. But she didn't blame the Voice, only those in Washington and abroad who pressured it for policy reasons.[42]

Percy and Abzug, working independently, continued to amass evidence of interference. Percy's reasoning: the charter (until then an executive branch directive) would have considerably sharper teeth as a law. In the spring of 1976, about a year after the United States withdrew from Vietnam, Percy's aide Scott Cohen tacked the VOA Charter onto the Foreign Relations Authorization Act for the upcoming fiscal year 1977. The amendment went forward virtually unnoticed, a nearly verbatim text of the Eisenhower directive (the 1959 Allen–Loomis–Zorthian charter). It lacked only the clause "As an official radio . . . ," originally in that directive's third and final operative paragraph.

Who, after all, could object to chartering America's Voice? Its provisions for objective news and broadcasting about American policies appeared innocuous to congressional authorizers, somewhat akin to a Mother's Day resolution—as American as apple pie. Advocates tracked each legislative move. Over several months, the measure was approved in a Senate–House conference committee, and then, on the floor of the Senate and House, by voice votes as part of the fiscal year 1977 appropriations bill. Finally, it was sent to President Ford for signature.

The Stroke of a Pen Heard Round the World (Eventually)

More days passed. The suspense grew. Finally, at about two o'clock in the afternoon on July 12, 1976, a stand-in VOA correspondent at the White House phoned Kamenske. "Just to let you know," he said, "the president has signed the appropriations bill, including the Charter!" It was a singular moment in the history of U.S. international broadcasting.

The Voice of America Charter: Public Law 94-350

The long-range interests of the United States are served by communicating directly with the people of the world by radio. To be effective, the Voice of America (the Broadcasting Service of the United States Information Agency) must win the attention and respect of listeners. These principles will therefore govern Voice of America (VOA) broadcasts:

1. VOA will serve as a consistently reliable and authoritative source of news. VOA news will be accurate, objective, and comprehensive.
2. VOA will represent America, not any single segment of American society, and will therefore present a balanced and comprehensive projection of significant American thought and institutions.
3. VOA will present the policies of the United States clearly and effectively, and will also present responsible discussion and opinion on these policies.[43]

Signed by President Gerald R. Ford, July 12, 1976. Co-sponsored by Senator Charles H. Percy (Republican of Illinois) and Representative Bella S. Abzug (Democrat of New York).

Looking back twenty years later, Barry Zorthian commented that the charter has proved to be "absolutely critical to the reputation, the impact, the credibility of the Voice of America to its listeners."[44] VOA's audience, estimated at approximately 45 million when the charter became law, increased to a peak of 130 million during the following decade. There were two possible reasons: the charter's positive effect on

VOA programming and the Voice's construction of a worldwide tech-nical delivery system at the dawn of the satellite age. Whatever the principal factor, the charter left an indelible mark on the struggle to get it straight. Historian Robert S. Fortner, in his book *International Communications: History, Conflict, and Control of the Global Metropolis*, listed its adoption into law as a significant milestone in the history of media.[45]

8

The Independence Debate

TO THE BRINK AND BACK

Sunlight is the most powerful of all disinfectants.
—Louis Brandeis

And though all the winds of doctrine were let loose to play
upon the earth, so Truth be in the field. . . . Let her and
Falsehood grapple; who ever knew Truth put to the worse, in
a free and open encounter?
—John Milton, *Areopagitica*

Ironically, the VOA Charter, like the institution whose spirit it reflected,
at first was one of America's "best kept secrets." There was quiet jubilation at the Voice on the afternoon it was signed into law. But there
was no media reporting of the event, no mention of it in White House
press releases. It was not until a front-page story in the *Washington Post*
in August 1976 that the charter's significance became widely known.[1]

VOA director Kenneth R. Giddens maintained in that article that
Public Law 94-350 set a new legal standard: "Now we can say: 'This is
the way we see it and we are obligated to say it the way we see it.'" News
and Current Affairs (NCA) Division logs reflected a sharp decline in
prebroadcast attempts to tinker with VOA news during the five years
following the charter's enactment. In the fall of 1976, however, the
document met a severe test, just ten weeks after it was signed into law.

A "ROUTINE" CALL TO CYPRUS

On September 27, the Middle East desk in the VOA newsroom phoned
Jerusalem correspondent Charles Weiss. The desk asked him to check

out news agency reports that a vessel on the Mediterranean Sea carrying
Lebanese leftist leader Kamal Jumblatt to Cyprus had been attacked the
day before by an Israeli warship. Weiss said he would phone both a
Palestine Liberation Organization (PLO) contact he had met recently in
Cyprus and an Israeli military spokesman. Weiss made the calls, one local
and one to Nicosia. Within two hours, he reported back comments from
both sides, including an Israeli denial.

On October 1, Weiss was summoned from his office in Jerusalem to the
American embassy in Tel Aviv and was told by Public Affairs Officer Stan
Moss that he was to make no further contacts with the PLO, including
contacts personally or by telephone with PLO sympathizers or those identified with the PLO on the occupied West Bank; he was to limit travel to
the West Bank, and then only with the approval of Moss; and should he
disagree with the instructions, U.S. ambassador to Israel Malcolm Toon
would take the matter to Secretary of State Henry Kissinger "in a minute,"
if necessary, and order the bureau either shut down or moved from
Jerusalem to Tel Aviv so that Moss could directly supervise Weiss.[2]

The embassy cited a law giving chiefs of mission authority over all
nonmilitary American officials in the country where they are stationed.
The embassy considered Weiss to be "a U.S. official," not a journalist. It
had enforced the "no contact with the PLO" provision on all its staff
for many years on the grounds that the PLO was a terrorist organization.
The provision had been reluctantly agreed to by the VOA newsroom,
although it had never been clear that this directive prevented international phone contacts.

After Weiss reported his conversation with Moss to Bernie
Kamenske, a restatement of the "no contact with the PLO" rule was
posted at the VOA newsroom central desk pending clarification.

Who's the Boss?

News and Current Affairs, through Weiss, reminded Public Affairs
Officer Moss that under news-reporting guidelines in effect at VOA since
1972, correspondents were supervised by the newsroom, not U.S. diplomatic missions. Moss and Toon, however, persisted. The dispute surfaced
in Israeli newspapers, amid speculation that the United States was soft-
ening its position on contacts with the PLO.

The ongoing test of wills then escalated rapidly. On October 9, in a
Washington Post interview prompted by reports of embassy interference

with Weiss's work, Kamenske said: "I don't see how we can operate under the demands made by the Embassy. We cannot remain a journalistic force and be regarded as American officials simultaneously."[3] The term "official radio" was deleted from the charter when it became law, Bernie added. This, he said, showed that Congress wanted to alter VOA's image as a propaganda agency and establish it as an "independent journalistic entity."

The Monday after that weekend interview, there was a long-planned shift in top management at the Voice. Senior USIA foreign service officer Hans N. (Tom) Tuch replaced Serban Vallimarescu (Val) as deputy director. Val, during his last year or so at VOA, had become a relatively consistent defender of Voice editorial autonomy, even though he had been appointed by USIA director James Keogh (as had Tuch) without VOA director Kenneth Giddens's concurrence. Now Val was moving on, and Tuch was the brand-new agency watchdog in VOA's senior management. He had an unprecedented baptism of fire.

Settling In Atop a Volcano

Tuch recalled: "I was just getting myself settled in my office that first day, when I got a call from Mr. Keogh to come uptown to USIA headquarters right away. I was confronted by Mr. Keogh, his deputy, the head of agency personnel, and the general counsel. I was told the first thing I had to do was to fire Kamenske, because the previous day he had gone public" about the dispute with the embassy. Tuch remembers responding: "Look, I could not really as my first task on my first day at the Voice of America, fire the news chief. My credibility in the whole organization would be shot, and I could never reestablish it; I can't do it."[4]

"Well," they said, "you have to do it." Tuch asked for time to look into the matter. He returned to VOA, called Kamenske and me into his office, and heard another side of the story. Bernie, at Tuch's request, agreed in the future to give the new VOA deputy director advance warning if he could not resolve problems internally and felt inclined to complain publicly. Tuch then went back uptown and repeated his resolve not to remove the news chief. "If anybody is going to fire him," Tuch said, "you will have to do it because I will not." Keogh agreed to settle for a letter of reprimand. Tuch pointed out that under regulations, only the USIA director of personnel could sign such a letter. "I left it at that," Tuch said later, "and there was never a letter of reprimand."

An Iron Lady Weighs In

On October 12, Representative Bella Abzug, as chairwoman of the House Subcommittee on Government Operations, wrote a letter to Keogh requesting a progress report on USIA implementation of the charter. She said she was "particularly disturbed" by reports of the prohibition of VOA contacts with the PLO by the embassy in Tel Aviv. "I am sure," Abzug wrote, "you can appreciate the serious impediment such a blanket prohibition presents in terms of checking routine stories filed from the Middle East. The result is that VOA is limited to re-writing stories covered by the major wire services and foreign-dominated news outlets which may or may not be accurate in their reporting." Abzug added: "I have also written Secretary of State Kissinger directing his attention to this outrageous restriction on free reporting."[5]

There were follow-up reports in the *Jerusalem Post*, the *Los Angeles Times*, and the *Financial Times* of London about the "no contact" restriction. *Washington Post* correspondent Richard M. Weintraub on October 27 wrote an article summarizing a classified cable from Keogh to Ambassador Toon obtained from congressional sources. In that cable, according to Weintraub, the USIA director endorsed the embassy's position and said that VOA correspondents "must conform to U.S. government policies." Keogh wrote that he did not see the restrictions as "in any way contravening the law referred to as VOA's Charter, nor do I see it as any form of censorship." He maintained that VOA could have had a contract reporter, or stringer, call PLO representatives and thereby avoid "official" contact.[6] In a letter to President Gerald Ford protesting the ban against a VOA correspondent contacting the PLO, the 1,300-member Radio Television News Directors Association said that such contact "was not only legitimate but essential to any reporter covering the Middle East."

The Tel Aviv controversy, and the election of Democrat Jimmy Carter as president in November 1976, were seized on by Senator Charles Percy and other advocates of VOA journalistic independence. Their ranks were growing, both inside and outside the Voice. In the mid-1970s, VOA correspondents had been forced under State Department pressure to withdraw from Lebanon, although, as we've seen, Doug Roberts later returned on occasional trips. VOA correspondent David Lent, however, lamented embassy orders for him to leave Lebanon, as he put it, "with the women and children being evacuated." A VOA attempt to reestablish an office and news bureau in Cairo was blocked for several years because of objections of U.S. embassy officials.[7]

A JUXTAPOSITION OF EVENTS

The disputes over VOA Middle East news gathering occurred as the Stanton Commission issued its 1975 report on the reorganization of the nation's overseas information and cultural programs. As mentioned in chapter 7, the Stanton panel recommended, among other changes, that VOA be an independent agency under a presidentially appointed oversight board.

President Carter had promised during his campaign to take a serious look at the Stanton Commission's recommendations. Within the Voice, hundreds of broadcasters saw an opportunity, with Giddens's encouragement and USIA director Keogh's impending departure, to "break out" of the agency. The change in administration, the growing media attention to interference in VOA news gathering, and the Stanton Commission's conclusions suggested that the timing might be right for independence.

The natural leader of Voice professionals (its huge majority consisting of journalists, the language broadcasters, and the English producers) was its corporate memory and highest ranking civil servant, Deputy Program Manager Cliff Groce. He drafted a petition, "The Future of the Voice of America," which was signed in November 1976 by more than 600 staff members. "In its nearly thirty-five years," the petition said,

> the Voice has been administratively located in several different "parent" institutions and its mission variously defined and interpreted. In every case, VOA has not merely been placed in a subordinate position; it has been made subservient in every area of management and operations, with repeated unwarranted restrictions on its output, and a generally adverse effect on its ability to perform. . . . Now, in 1976, we of the VOA staff have concluded that an independent status within the foreign affairs community is necessary.

Percy Raises the Ante

The VOA petition was released to the press on November 19, 1976. Eleven days later, Percy announced during a luncheon address at the University of Chicago that he would introduce in the Senate a VOA independence bill the following January. Percy added that the Voice should operate under an independent body similar to the board established earlier in the 1970s to oversee Radio Free Europe and Radio Liberty. "Then," he said, "the Voice will be free to report all the news, in Eastern Europe, the USSR, and elsewhere. I don't want a strident Voice of America," he explained. "I want a Voice of America which keeps its cool. But we need a Voice which is not afraid to tell it like it is."[8]

Much, of course, would depend on the new Carter administration and how it chose to proceed. The Stanton and Murphy Commissions' findings remained valid as guideposts to a reorganization of the nation's overseas information and cultural programs. A few weeks after Carter's inauguration, I had lunch with Paul Henze, the new National Security Council aide directly concerned with international broadcasting. Henze agreed that U.S. embassies often had exceedingly narrow interests and that VOA must somehow be protected from them and insulated from unjustified complaints. However, Henze believed that the Voice should remain part of the agency because, in his opinion, all parts of the overseas information program must be kept together.[9]

It did appear that relations between USIA and VOA might improve. The new agency director under the Carter administration, Ambassador John Reinhardt, was the first career diplomat to occupy the position since George V. Allen. He sought at once to canvass VOA career employees, both management and union, who were unhappy about the USIA–Voice relationship. Reinhardt promised, very early on, to refashion USIA and take many of VOA's concerns into account. He said that the position of Voice director would be elevated to that of one of four associate directors of USIA. The new VOA director would stand much higher in the agency's hierarchy than his predecessor—one of nineteen USIA assistant directors in the previous administration.

Early in the new administration, Senator Percy moved ahead with plans to introduce a VOA independence amendment to the Foreign Relations Authorization Act for the 1978 fiscal year. He scheduled hearings of the Subcommittee on International Operations of the Senate Foreign Relations Committee to press his case. For the session on Friday, April 29, 1977, he called as witnesses Giddens (now free to speak his mind as a former VOA director), Kamenske, and me. Reinhardt readily agreed to let us speak out as we saw fit.[10]

Telling It as It Is

Senator Percy opened the hearing by stating: "We are simply trying to make this the voice of truth and a voice of America that we can all be proud of." Giddens noted that the transistor revolution and manufacture of small portable receivers had, by the late 1970s, "transformed hundreds of millions of people on every continent into interested and sometimes

---

PROFESSOR KAMENSKE'S HISTORY LESSON

Bernie Kamenske followed Kenneth Giddens at the witness table before the Senate Foreign Relations Committee. Lifting the veil on VOA's past, he laid out the case in a typical Kamenske-style oration:

> When we first started broadcasting, we went on the air and said: "We will broadcast to you every day. The news may be good and the news may be bad, but we will tell you the truth." Then General Stilwell came out of Burma just for a moment. He said: "We took a hell of a beating," and that set off a two-day debate at Voice of America on whether we would carry that story. . . . In the end, the quote was broadcast. And everybody concluded, "Well, we have won the battle of credibility, people believe what we say." This is a recurring theme and this is a recurring problem. The burden of truth, John Kennedy told us, was difficult to bear. Edward R. Murrow said: "Let truth be your guide." Henry Loomis said: "The facts are sacred." . . . Henry Loomis was later to resign in protest of tampering with his efforts to present the facts in a balanced account of events in this country. You know, going back before that to 1958 and 1959 . . . Ambassador George Allen and Henry Loomis got together and took the best thinking they both could gather and they formulated what is the VOA Charter and they said: "The battle for truth is won." . . . I think the record will show that it was not completely won. And that is why I personally . . . on the basis of my experience, believe the Voice of America should have a form of independence.*

*Quoted in U.S. Congress, Senate, Committee on Foreign Relations, *Hearings of Subcommittee on International Operations on the Foreign Relations Authorization Act of 1978*, 95th Cong., 1st sess., S. 1190, April 29, 1977, 272.

active participants in world affairs. And it has created climates of opinion that rulers and statesmen must take into consideration."

The former director went on to say that as an appendage of USIA,
where in his view the new media realities were "largely unnoticed and
largely unappreciated," VOA fell to fourth place among international
broadcasters in terms of broadcast hours, lagging behind the Soviet
Union, China, and Egypt. He called for a substantial increase in VOA's
budget, decried interferences in its output, and recommended VOA
independence under a board similar to the BBC model. He added: "I
think that is a smart way for this nation to do it, and I recommend it
without qualification."[11]

Some Test Cases

Under extended questioning by Senators Percy and Joseph R. Biden, Jr.
(Democrat of Delaware), Bernie described the attempts by the U.S.
embassy in Warsaw to limit VOA news about the outbreak of violence
and unrest following an increase in food prices in Poland in June 1976.
The embassy, he noted, had cautioned about overplaying the story or
comparing the latest upsurge of protests with those that had led to the
ouster of Polish Communist Party leader Władysław Gomułka six years
earlier.[12] VOA went with the story despite the warning.

> PERCY: You were put on notice that this is something that might not
> be helpful to us or the Polish government or our relationships with
> the Polish government. Isn't that a form of intimidation? There
> was an attempt to interfere in the case of Poland?

> KAMENSKE: Attempted interference. That's one of the things that's
> a problem. We win a lot of these fights. It takes enormous amounts
> of time to win them. They were going on and on. It was difficult to
> win these fights and [when we do] these indications of success are
> used as examples . . . that we are candid and open in reporting the
> facts.

> PERCY: One of the biggest stories [of last year] was the death of Mao
> Tse-tung. Was there any interference by USIA with VOA in
> reporting of that?

> HEIL: I regret to say that yes, we were not able to provide a lead
> analysis on the day following the death of Mao Tse-tung.

PERCY: Why not?

HEIL: The USIA had ruled that this had been fully covered by us in special programming we had developed at the time, interviews with [Harvard China specialist] John King Fairbanks and others. . . . The president and the secretary of state had addressed it. Their remarks, I should say, were fully reported and reflected in our output. It was just that we could not address Mao's death analytically . . . the fact we did not do so, I think, was conspicuous by its absence.

Percy, drawing on these examples, quoted a BBC official as saying: "It is only on rare occasions that efforts are made to influence the BBC's program output. The BBC's attitude toward such efforts has always been to listen politely, to give due consideration to the views of the Foreign and Commonwealth Office, but to reject them when they are in conflict with the BBC's views of its own editorial obligations."

PERCY: We are known for our belief in the truth—that is why we were founded, in a sense—and isn't that why we should organize VOA in such a way that . . . would insure them to tell the truth no matter how the chips may fall? Mr. Kamenske, you have already said that you favor that structure. I would like the views of Mr. Heil and Mr. Giddens . . .

HEIL: I certainly fully subscribe to independence for the Voice of America. I think you've hit the core of the matter in identifying this as wholly consonant with our traditions as a nation. I can remember [a conversation] not so many weeks ago [with] a foreign correspondent of foreign nationality who has some knowledge of our operations. He was astonished that we should operate in an environment so alien to the traditions of our country.[13] The Declaration of Independence said: "Let facts be submitted to a candid world." The Bill of Rights enshrined the freedom of our communicators from the eighteenth-century town crier to the twentieth-century foreign correspondent . . . the unfettered dialogue in the West is most feared by the closed societies of the East for a very simple reason: it is believed. . . . I have an insight into the care with which and the responsibility with which we view the materials, the editing process, the twin source rule referred to by Mr. Kamenske, the care with which analysts study and bone up on the materials with which they deal. . . . I know for all these reasons that we can do the job and fulfill our responsibilities.

PERCY: Mr. Giddens?

GIDDENS: Senator, I subscribe to that wholeheartedly. The other day I ran across the expression, "The truth serves our interests." I believe it does.

The Markup Begins

The hearing lasted for one hour and forty-five minutes. The Subcommittee on International Operations adjourned until the following Wednesday, May 4. The subcommittee chairman was Senator George McGovern of South Dakota, the unsuccessful 1972 Democratic candidate for president and a close friend of conservative Republican Kenneth R. Giddens. The session, with Percy absent, continued discussion of what was known as the subcommittee markup of the Foreign Relations Authorization Act for fiscal year 1978, including the VOA independence amendment. Then there appeared the first sign of a crack in the drive for independence: McGovern said that he had discussed the issue the evening before with Deputy Secretary of State Warren Christopher, who had "some reservations."[14]

The next day, Thursday, May 5, Percy joined the markup with Senators McGovern and Claiborne Pell (Democrat of Rhode Island) and aides to Senators Howard Baker (Republican of Tennessee) and Hubert Humphrey of Minnesota (the 1968 Democratic presidential nominee). Percy reported at the beginning of the session that Christopher had called him and said that the State Department was opposed to the VOA independence amendment on the grounds that it limited the department's response to proposals for the reorganization of U.S. overseas information and cultural programs.

In the Subcommittee, It Is Unanimous

In Percy's view, the adoption of the amendment would be "the only way, really, that we can fulfill the VOA Charter, which is now a matter of statute. I think this is the time to act before we just let dust grow on these commission reports and simply fail to follow through." The subcommittee approved the amendment with little debate, by a 4–0 vote (Percy, McGovern, Pell, and Biden). Humphrey, absent for the vote, was said to favor the amendment. Senators Pell and Baker, however, said they wanted to discuss it further in full committee.

A fateful five days lay ahead. The full Senate Foreign Relations Committee set its crucial markup session for May 10. Opponents of VOA independence and the Stanton Commission's proposed restructuring of USIA, meanwhile, were working overtime to gut the amendment. During the fact-finding phase of the Stanton panel two years earlier, a key figure in the twenty-one-member study group, former USIA director Leonard Marks, had resigned to protest the panel's decision on VOA independence. As the authorization measure moved in early May from the Subcommittee on International Operations to the Committee on Foreign Relations, Marks, a prominent Washington attorney, along with congressional liaison operatives from the State Department and USIA, approached Senators Humphrey and Frank Church (Democrat of Idaho). Their main message: oppose the Percy amendment on the grounds that the new administration should have the first chance at reorganizing the nation's public diplomacy agencies.[15] In hindsight, this reflected what Henze had said earlier: the Carter team didn't want to fragment the overseas information and cultural program by spinning off VOA.

Nails in the Coffin

As if the lobbying effort were not enough, two documents were issued in rapid succession the first week in May 1977, both with a direct bearing on VOA independence:

May 4, 1977: USIA director Reinhardt sent a memorandum to VOA acting director Tuch declaring that VOA "will be solely responsible for the content of its news broadcasts." The memo also said that although the agency's policy office would continue to provide guidance, there would be no prior script clearance of commentaries and news analyses. It added that VOA would refer anyone seeking direct contact with its staff on policy matters to the agency's policy office. In Reinhardt's words: "I attach the highest importance to the integrity of the Voice of America."[16]

May 5, 1977: The General Accounting Office, watchdog of the U.S. Congress, issued findings on the Stanton Commission's proposals. The report to Congress recommended against independence for VOA and was widely circulated in advance of the crucial Senate Foreign Relations Committee markup debate five days later. Comptroller General Elmer Staats said that the Stanton panel had offered no evidence that VOA broadcasts lack credibility, credence, or listenership. He added: "Audience research by the U.S. Information Agency and others in recent years suggests otherwise."[17]

STAATS VERSUS STANTON

STAATS: How U.S. foreign policy is reported and advocated, especially by fast media and especially in moments of international crisis, can greatly affect the national interest for good or ill. For an agency billed and perceived as "the voice of America," there can be circumstances in which diplomatic needs ought to prevail over journalistic concerns. It should be emphasized, however, that circumstances justifying State Department or White House intervention in Voice of America are highly unusual, and the prerogative should be exercised with restraint and in full awareness of the need to protect professional integrity.*

STANTON: Nothing is more important to the American moral position in the world than that this [VOA] news be objective and free from political alteration by diplomats. The [comptroller general's] draft ultimately argues that corruption of news is essential for reasons of state. I disagree. Government censorship of the news is contrary to our deepest values and grossly misrepresents us overseas. It also destroys our credibility when private news sources, the BBC, and Deutsche Welle are all broadcasting the news we ignore.[†]

*Elmer Staats, *Public Diplomacy in the Years Ahead—An Assessment of Proposals for Reorganization*, Comptroller General's report no. ID-77-21 (Washington, D.C.: General Accounting Office, May 5, 1977), iv.
[†]Frank Stanton to Elmer Staats, April 26, 1977, 9.

Percy Persists to the End

The final markup occurred as scheduled on the afternoon of May 10. Senate Foreign Relations Committee chairman John Sparkman of Alabama, a Democrat from Ken Giddens's home state, presided. Others present were Senators Percy, Humphrey, Pell, McGovern, Church, Jacob Javits (Republican of New York), and Clifford Case (Republican of New Jersey).

Percy led off by quoting Jimmy Carter, immediately after his nomination for president the preceding summer. "The Voice of America," Carter had said, "is entangled in a web of political restrictions imposed by the Department of State."[18] VOA should be given independence, Percy added, "so that they can tell the news to foreign audiences as objectively

as humanly possible, unhampered by the chronic interventions of diplomats and bureaucrats."[19] Percy then reviewed restrictions on VOA
coverage, including early Watergate, *Gulag Archipelago*, the death of Mao
Tse-tung, Poland, and a more recent delay of a VOA background report
on the Strategic Arms Limitation Treaty (SALT) "because USIA policy
officers didn't like a direct quotation in the script of Dr. Fred Iklé [direc-
tor of the Arms Control and Disarmament Agency]."[20]

The votes weren't there. As Percy's aide Scott Cohen recalled years
later, Marks had gotten to Humphrey over the weekend and persuaded
him to oppose VOA independence.[21] Senator Church launched the
attack. "If the Voice of America is not going to be the expression of the
American government in its foreign policy and its objectives abroad,"
Church said, "why do we maintain it? I have a high regard for Mr. [Frank]
Stanton, but the Voice of America is not the CBS and you can't make it
into a CBS. It has an entirely different function."[22] Humphrey repeated
the anti-independence refrain: "Give the administration a chance to
act." He cited the comptroller general's recommendation against independence as another reason to oppose the amendment.[23] The movement
was dead. By consensus, the Senate Foreign Relations Committee agreed
to a watered-down amendment of support for VOA that restated the
principles stated in the charter and the need to strengthen VOA technically but omitted a single vital phrase: "to reestablish VOA as a separate
agency."[24]

How close was it, really? Even if the independence measure had
passed the committee, it would have had to be approved in the Senate,
then in the House, and then by a Senate–House conference committee;
then passed a second time by both houses; and finally signed into law by
the president. Walter Roberts, executive director of the Stanton
Commission, noted years later that Representative Dante Fascell
(Democrat of Florida), chairman of the House International Relations
Committee, opposed many of the panel's recommendations.[25] Fascell
held hearings of his own in May and June 1977, to back up his position.
The influential Florida Democrat preferred to keep USIA with VOA
inside it separate from the State Department, essentially intact.

SAME AGENCY, NEW NAME

President Carter, in his Reorganization Plan Number 2, did restructure
USIA, however, and Director Reinhardt kept his promises. The United

States Information Agency was reorganized into the International Communication Agency (ICA), which brought all the cultural and exchange programs (as Stanton had urged) under its aegis. VOA's new director, R. Peter Straus of New York, became an associate director of broadcasting in ICA, one of the four highest posts under Reinhardt and his diplomat deputy, Charles Bray. Reinhardt's memo of May 4, described earlier, was widely welcomed among VOA professionals as putting flesh and muscle on the charter.

Straus, new on the job, was immediately skeptical, however, about having fifteen VOA correspondents abroad (several of them in messy scrapes with diplomats). In early 1978, he convened a five-member panel to study the situation. The group was headed by Chalmers Roberts, retired senior diplomatic correspondent of the *Washington Post*, and included such other prominent retired journalists as Pauline Frederick of NBC and E. W. Kenworthy of the *New York Times*. They concluded that the real problem was not the number of correspondents, but the restrictions placed on them because of their attachment to embassies abroad and their holding of official passports and dependence on diplomatic missions for support. The panel recommended that VOA correspondents

- Use regular, not official, passports
- Operate from offices outside embassies, using commercial, not official, communications channels
- Apply for the same type of visas as commercial news agency and network correspondents
- No longer use post exchange or commissary facilities frequented by diplomatic mission personnel
- Receive no more and no less information support from missions abroad than their commercial network counterparts[26]

Reinhardt, Straus, and Tuch went to work to obtain concurrence in the State Department to put most of the Roberts panel correspondent guidelines into effect. On June 28, 1978, the guidelines were circulated to missions around the world, cleared by Deputy Secretary of State Warren Christopher. His cable said that agency public affairs officers would no longer supervise the work of VOA correspondents. Nor would the correspondents have any obligation to clear copy with anyone before filing it to the newsroom in Washington.[27] Janie Fritzman, in her masterwork as executive assistant at NCA, drafted and negotiated the

THE VALUE OF BEING THERE . . .
ALMOST ANYWHERE

About three weeks after the Roberts study group began its work, USIA's Office of Research issued a report documenting the effectiveness of VOA correspondents' on-scene coverage. Summarizing a series of sixty group discussions around the world, the research survey concluded that "direct reporting from the scene is the single activity on which virtually all panelists ranked VOA either first or tied with BBC among all international broadcasters." It quoted a listener to VOA Worldwide English in Kuala Lumpur, Malyasia: "Correspondents are supposed to give their actual report from the scene . . . if you get a report they send back to headquarters and it is read over the air, you feel that maybe this report has been censored. I prefer it direct from the scene." A VOA Spanish listener in Medellín, Colombia, added: "Accuracy only happens on the spot." VOA, the research survey said, is the international broadcaster most frequently associated with on-scene reporting.*

About three weeks before the Roberts study group concluded its work, *New York Times* columnist James Reston wrote from Damascus:

In the last three months, I have listened carefully to its [VOA's] English language broadcasts in such diverse places as Japan, Australia, Tahiti, West Germany, Yugoslavia, Italy, Egypt, Jordan and here in Syria. This may seem an extreme statement, but for detailed accounts of the world's news, I believe there is nothing on the commercial networks of the United States that equals its performance.

The Voice may not be quite as effective in the Middle East as the BBC, which produces a clearer signal from the island of Cyprus than the Voice does from its relay transmitter on the island of Rhodes off the coast of Turkey, but it has more reporters in more places than the BBC, and like the BBC, it has learned over the years that the best propaganda is an honest account of the facts. . . . It says here is the news, and even Walter Cronkite wouldn't be ashamed to read it.†

*United States Information Agency, Office of Research, "Listeners' Views on the Use of Correspondents by International Broadcasters," January 31, 1978, 1–2.
†James Reston, "The Voice of America," *New York Times*, March 12, 1978, A22.

complex budgetary and administrative arrangements necessary to separate VOA correspondents from overseas missions. The guidelines were
implemented fully by October 1.[28]

Agency and VOA relations were at a high point, as Reinhardt and
Tuch worked together to resist outside pressures. Tuch recalled the
appearance of Senator Paul Laxalt (Republican of Nevada), an opponent
of the Panama Canal treaty, on VOA's weekly panel program *Press
Conference USA*. It was during the heat of the national debate over the
treaty, which was being pushed by the Carter administration and opposed
by conservative Republicans, including Laxalt and Ronald Reagan. The
day after Laxalt's appearance on VOA, Tuch got a call from National
Security Adviser Zbigniew Brzezinski in the White House:

> BRZEZINSKI: What the hell are you doing over there in the Voice of
> America, giving Senator Laxalt a platform?
>
> TUCH: Well, this is our obligation, under the charter, under the law.
>
> BRZEZINSKI: Well, don't you ever do that sort of thing again.

But VOA did. Several months later, Tuch remembered,

> we asked Paul Nitze, who at that time was chairman of the
> Committee on the Present Danger, to appear on *Press Conference
> USA* in his opposition to the SALT II treaty. The next day, I got a
> call to appear at the White House before Mr. Brzezinski. . . . I called
> up John Reinhardt and he and I went together. We explained that
> the charter of the Voice obligated us to present U.S. policy and
> responsible discussion thereof. We felt that Paul Nitze was probably
> the most responsible person we could find to discuss opposition,
> which was certainly strong in this country. There again, it became
> pretty unpleasant, but we marched out of there and John was with
> me all the way, he was perfect. I've always appreciated that.[29]

The tradition of interference with VOA news or news gathering
died hard. On January 4, 1978, USIA assistant director for Europe,
Jodie Lewinsohn, called for the removal of VOA correspondents from
Europe because, in her view, "the Agency and VOA simply are not getting a cost-effective return on the large investment."[30] She asserted this

opinion in a memorandum to the Roberts panel. Eventually, that panel recommended a redistribution of some correspondents. VOA later shifted two of the news bureaus in Europe to Africa and Latin America. But Tuch, in a memo replying to Lewinsohn, defended the correspondents. He noted that they enhanced a new VOA Current Affairs documentary series, Close-Up, and added: "Daily, the correspondents' presence proves indispensable to speed and accuracy."[31]

A YEAR OF BAD NEWS

The value of VOA's presence was again proved as Iran's Islamic revolution dominated the headlines in 1979. VOA London bureau chief David Williams was on the scene in Tehran to witness the turmoil firsthand. He suddenly was caught in a narrow alley between Revolutionary Guards and the shah's army. Fifty yards down the darkened street, a man raised his loaded rifle and pointed it directly at the lone correspondent. There was no place to hide. Suddenly, Williams felt two tugs at his shirt and found himself pulled into a courtyard next to the alley. "We want you to be safe," two Iranian women exclaimed. They introduced Williams to a French camera crew they had just offered shelter to as well.[32] Two weeks after the shah fled, Ayatollah Ruhollah Khomeini returned in triumph, after fifteen years in exile during which he had used cassette tapes and frequent appearances on the BBC's Persian Service to foment revolution back home.

VOA, for budgetary reasons, had been forced to close its Farsi (Persian) Service twice, in 1946 and in 1960. Now, Near East and South Asia Division chief Allan Baker and his deputy, Frank Cummins, had to hustle to assemble all the former Farsi-speaking producers, who had been reassigned throughout VOA, and reconstitute them in a service that went back on the air on April 8, 1979. An audience had to be rebuilt, too, at a time when America's Voice most needed to reach Iran. The case of the on-again, off-again Farsi Service was cited in later years as a prime example of the cost of abolishing VOA language services to save money.[33]

The decision to restore the Farsi Service came just in time. On November 4, students stormed the U.S. embassy in Tehran and captured its sixty-six occupants. Fourteen of them, many noncitizens and women, were soon released. Fifty-two other hostages were held for the next 444 days. To the credit of both the State Department and the USIA, there was no second-guessing as VOA covered a crisis of utmost sensitivity for many months. Then, at the end of this year of bad news, the Soviet

Union invaded Afghanistan and eventually deployed 100,000 troops in the mountainous Central Asian country known as "Moscow's Vietnam."

CHANGING OF THE GUARD, AGAIN

R. Peter Straus resigned to return to Democratic politics in New York just a week before the hostage crisis in Iran erupted.[34] Tom Tuch became acting director of VOA until the confirmation of the brilliant young historian, educator, and public broadcaster from Hawaii, Mary G. F. Bitterman, who served from February 1980 until January 1981. Tuch then moved on to become U.S. counselor for public affairs in West Germany, and Bitterman chose veteran VOA executive and senior foreign service officer Bill Haratunian as her deputy (chapters 4 and 6). Bitterman spent several months preparing for her confirmation hearings before the Senate Foreign Relations Committee. She read all the available literature and newspaper clippings about America's Voice and interviewed all its senior managers before ever setting foot in her office. She charmed Senator Jesse Helms (Republican of North Carolina) in the committee hearings, and then the VOA staff. She forged a community at America's Voice and stood behind it throughout the crises in Iran and Afghanistan. At a briefing before the U.S. Advisory Commission on Public Diplomacy a week after becoming director, Bitterman displayed a veteran's mastery of programming and engineering detail.

Bitterman combined compassion and sensitivity with a steely determination to defend VOA and its charter. During her eleven months at the Voice, she faced pressures on many fronts. Bitterman worked with a USIA interagency task force to protect VOA engineers displaced by the Liberian civil war (chapter 5). Warsaw Pact countries stepped up jamming of VOA Polish as the Voice covered the rise of Solidarity. Congress pressed VOA to start up Dari and Pashto Services to Afghanistan in response to the Soviet invasion, which the Voice eventually did.[35] The Carter administration launched an intensive, worldwide campaign to expand a boycott of the 1980 Moscow Olympics as a protest against the Soviet occupation of Afghanistan. VOA, however, wanted to deploy correspondents to cover the competition, as it had every four years since the mid-1960s. The administration objected, but Bitterman held firm. She placed her job on the line.[36] VOA applied for visas to send two correspondents to Moscow to cover the event. This time, the Kremlin shot itself in the foot; the visas were denied.

ENTER REAGAN, EXIT THE HOSTAGES

Ronald Reagan was elected president on November 4, 1980. The Carter administration, in its waning weeks, engaged in around-the-clock negotiations with Iran to get the American hostages released. As Inauguration Day approached, Deputy Secretary of State Warren Christopher worked night and day to bring them home during Jimmy Carter's term of office. A deal was reached, early in the morning of January 20, 1981, before the presidential transition. President Carter was informed about the final breakthrough just four hours before the inaugural ceremony. It was midmorning, Washington time. The incoming president went to the White House to be greeted at the portico at 10:30 A.M. by the outgoing one. Shortly after that, the two leaders set out in a big black limousine down Pennsylvania Avenue for the Capitol and Reagan's inauguration as the fortieth president of the United States.[37] In Iran, the hostages were driven to the airport in Tehran to board their flight to freedom. They were loaded aboard the plane, but it stayed on the runway as the final minutes of the Carter administration ticked away.

A High Noon to Remember

Up on Capitol Hill, the inaugural stands filled and VOA reporters in seven languages peered out of the radio platform and adjusted their headphones and mikes in preparation for high noon, the administration of the oaths of office to Ronald Reagan and George Bush, and Reagan's inaugural address. Their words, and the new president's, would begin their remarkable split-second electronic journey to the studios, and then to every corner of the Earth. So would news of the hostages' release, the minute it happened.

There was extraordinary activity in the VOA newsroom. At around twelve minutes past noon, a writer rushed into Bernie Kamenske's office and said he had a bulletin from a major news agency that reported the liftoff of the hostages. Could he issue it on the wire for broadcast based on a single source and attribute it to the news agency? "What's the source? What's the dateline?" we asked. The story was from New York, quoting an air-traffic controller at Kennedy International Airport who was repeating a radio message from his counterpart in Tehran. We said, "There's no way we'll go with that!"

At a quarter past noon, just as Reagan was approaching the end of his inaugural address, the phone rang on the newsroom coverage desk. It was Anne Francis, the VOA stringer in Tehran. She breathlessly explained that she was stationed in a house on the edge of the runway at Mehrabad Airport in Tehran. "The plane's still on the ground," she said. "Hold the phone; keep that line open!" an editor shouted. The aircraft with the hostages aboard was motionless, sitting on the tarmac. It was shimmering in the fading light, early evening, Tehran time. The VOA house wires were carrying bulletin-like takes of Reagan's inaugural address. At 12:26, a shout on the phone from Francis in Tehran: "They're in the air!" The bulletin was ready, released instantly on the VOA wires, just as the news agency machines began to ring bells all around the edge of the room, signaling the liftoff.[38] An acquaintance told a member of VOA's Farsi Service on the telephone after the hostages were airborne that the service's live broadcast of the inaugural was monitored in the main Tehran office of PARS, the Iranian news agency.[39]

A few hours later, the hostages' plane landed in Algiers. VOA correspondent David Williams had flown in from London and was there to meet them. He described in detail the dramatic moment they descended from the aircraft, their first footsteps on freedom's soil.[40]

With the charter and the correspondent guidelines, VOA journalism was enhanced in the 1970s and early 1980s. News bureaus that had been blocked earlier by embassies were established in Johannesburg and Cairo.[41]

The ICA did make one agreement with the foreign affairs policy community that proved fateful just a few years later. It instituted "policy commentaries" designed to "give listeners as clear and accurate an understanding of U.S. policies as is possible through international radio broadcasting." They were to be written by Current Affairs news analysts, but became subject, early in the Reagan administration, to outside (USIA and State Department) prebroadcast clearances.[42]

But on balance, the situation had improved. During one of his periods as VOA acting director, Tom Tuch appeared at a hearing on Capitol Hill before the Senate Foreign Relations Committee. Charles Percy, chairman of the committee, was quoted as saying: "Mr. Tuch, if you let anyone in this government or outside of government, in this country or abroad, interfere with news broadcasts of the Voice of America, you are breaking the law." That, Tuch recalled, "was something that any VOA news editor or VOA director took to heart."[43] After 1976, every USIA director and every VOA director for the remainder of the century prom-ised to uphold the charter. The charter, in fact, eventually formed the first three principles of all publicly funded civilian U.S. international broadcasting.

9

The Tumultuous 1980s

A LOST HORIZON REGAINED

We [VOA] must portray the Soviet Union as the last great predatory empire on earth, remorselessly enslaving its own diverse ethnic populations, crushing the legitimate aspirations of its captive nations, and ever seeking by all means, from subversion to military intervention, to widen the areas it subjugates.
—Philip Nicolaides, memorandum to Charles Z. Wick

The Voice of America has been politicized beyond recognition in the last year and a half . . . its hard-earned and quite fragile reputation as an objective chronicler of America has been battered, and I believe it will get worse. . . . Nothing short of an independent entity can start to build a Voice that can fight off those who would engage in their personal crusades.
—Bernard H. Kamenske, in
"Voice of America at the Crossroads"

One week after the release of the hostages held in Iran and Ronald Reagan's inauguration, there was a warm staff send-off for VOA's last director under the Carter administration, Mary G. F. Bitterman of Hawaii. In her gentle way, she counseled: "If there's one thing the people at the Voice of America have got to concentrate on, it's how good they are, and the importance of their work, and how critical your efforts are to the people of the world, and my strong conviction that you must stand bold and tall. . . . There's an old Irish wish which I wish to all of you. May the wind be at your back and may God hold you in the palm of his hand. Thank you and aloha."[1]

The placid breeze filling the sails of the organization that Bitterman had grown to love became something of a tornado. The early 1980s were the most tumultuous times for America's Voice since the early 1950s. The new director of the United States Information Agency (USIA), Charles Z. Wick, was a Hollywood impresario and close friend of the president who wielded, in USIA terms, unparalleled influence in the executive branch. "I don't know anything about foreign affairs and I don't know anything about journalism," Wick was quoted by *Parade* as saying. "But I know how to make things happen."[2] Wick did deliver. He dictated thousands of action memos during his eight-year tenure as the longest-serving agency director, often from airports and limousines. These earned the sobriquet "Z-grams," after his middle initial. In 1981, he brought with him a number of conservative Reagan supporters determined to reshape the agency's programs, including the Voice.

Among them was Philip Nicolaides, a Texas businessman and advertising manager who had a burning desire to "destabilize" the Soviet Union by using VOA to win what he called "the war of ideas."[3] The new director of the Voice, James B. Conkling, a California recording industry executive, arrived in June 1981 and was quickly consumed by the gathering ideological storm. Voice journalists and English broadcasters fought against attempts by the new political appointees to wage an anti-Soviet propaganda campaign in news and news-related programming. A vocal minority in the language services, mostly Eastern European in origin, agreed with the Reagan appointees that VOA programming should be more strident against the Soviet Union. They believed that central news still placed too much emphasis on events in the United States that they regarded as of little interest to their audiences. The language broadcasters also assailed what they regarded as an unfair system. They complained about being "reduced to translating. It's a feudal system," explained one. He contended that at VOA in 1982, bilingualism for any employee was a liability, adding: "The accent dooms us to serfdom."[4] A few of the language service activists saw an opportunity to enhance their influence or even gain appointment to senior Voice positions.

TRIMMING THE TRUTH OR TELLING IT?

This was the backdrop to a titanic struggle over the Voice's programming philosophy. It was a struggle played out in the nation's media, in the privacy of executive offices in the "new" International Communication

Agency (ICA, soon to be rechristened USIA), and in the executive mansion at the other end of Pennsylvania Avenue. Basically, it centered on the question: Would the Voice continue to focus principally on a free flow of information—accurate, objective and comprehensive programming consistent with the charter—or would it be redirected toward what Carnes Lord of the Reagan National Security Council (NSC) later termed an "ideological struggle" with the Soviet Union?

Lord noted that Reagan came to the presidency uniquely equipped to engage in that contest: "While governor of California he successfully led one of the most ideologically supercharged states in the nation, and as president, his personality and speaking and acting skills would justly earn him the title 'the Great Communicator.' With Reagan, for perhaps the first time since Roosevelt, public diplomacy was securely anchored in the Oval Office."[5]

The NSC aide quoted from a national security decision directive (NSDD 45) that ordered VOA to "take steps to strengthen existing mechanisms for relating program content to current U.S. foreign and national security policy objectives" and to ensure that VOA commentary and analysis incorporated "vigorous advocacy of current policy positions of the U.S. government."[6]

The Birth of a Newsletter

The NSDD, issued in 1982, was classified at the time but reflected an intensified focus on VOA programming content obvious to much of the staff. In May 1981, Mark Willen, a senior duty editor in the newsroom, began putting out an internal newsletter, *Room News*. In the September 9 issue, Willen spoke of a marked upsurge in protests by the Department of State, U.S. embassies, and the NSC about VOA news items or reports. They included

- A complaint to senior agency and VOA officials by National Security Adviser Richard V. Allen about a report by VOA journalist Mark Hopkins that the CIA was supplying arms to Afghan rebels
- A suggestion by an ICA policy officer that VOA news use the term "freedom fighters" or "patriots" rather than "antigovernment guerrillas" to describe the Afghan mujahideen
- A charge by the American embassy in Moscow that VOA had given Soviet spokesman Georgi Arbatov too much airtime by rebroadcasting

a brief excerpt of his English-language interview on National Public
Radio

- A request by the U.S. embassy in Manila that an interagency body
  coordinate Voice news and reportage "to assure that only relevant
  information is disseminated on VOA" concerning the flight of boat
  people from Vietnam

Concern about the boat people stemmed from a pair of articles in the
July 17, 1981, issue of *Far East Economic Review,* a Hong Kong weekly,
alleging that VOA was part of a calculated American policy to "pull"
large masses of refugees from Indochina, especially Vietnam. The *Review*
claimed that VOA news carried accounts of the weather conditions at
sea, the location of rescue ships, and the warmth of welcome in countries
of asylum. Voice management and the newsroom then reviewed dozens
of scripts—both newsroom and Vietnamese Service—to see what had
actually been broadcast. "VOA reports the news," the inquiry concluded.
"It may pick up statements about rescues at sea and official announcements of refugee quotas, but its newscasts and other material also have
reported the hazards of escape from Vietnam by sea, including starvation,
attacks by pirates, cannibalism, and conditions in refugee reception centers."[7] At no time, the study found, were weather forecasts broadcast, or
the location of rescue ships, or suggestions of favorable prospects for
refugees' admission to the United States.

The various attacks on VOA news and programs, according to
Willen, "created a difficult psychological atmosphere which increases
the danger of self-censorship . . . a tendency to avoid the controversial,
play it safe, to lay low until the furore blows over."[8] Willen's comments,
including portions of a transcribed newsletter interview he conducted
with Conkling, were picked up two days later by the *Baltimore Sun.* The
paper reported the internal debate on VOA's purposes and methods in
great detail.[9]

A Peasant Under Glass

Retired agency veteran Fitzhugh Green summarized the character of that
debate:

A top Reagan diplomat speaks off the record of VOA's dilemma
in Latin America. "What's happening," he declaims, "is that

Radio Moscow broadcasts more hours than we do and tells the Latinos that the U.S. Americans are no good; that we are racists, economic imperialists, lovers of oligarchy and dictatorship. Then," the diplomat chuckles coldly, "the VOA chimes in with its compulsive drive to maintain credibility by telling the truth. . . . So what does the Latin American peasant think?" the diplomat asks, "He doesn't give a rap for credibility; he's just interested to discover whether it's better to look to the communists or American-style democracy as the key to his future."

Green went on to quote VOA deputy director Bill Haratunian, who, he said, was amused by this tirade:

One of these days I'm going to bring back that "peasant" that everyone talks about and put him under glass. Then I'll ask him if he really does think we're terrible people for telling the truth about ourselves. I don't think peasants are stupid. They know when they're being snowed. It is useful to compare our system with the USSR's. People were kept in the dark there for forty-eight hours after Alexei Kosygin died. They learned of his death from VOA, BBC, and other outside news sources. When President Reagan was shot in 1981, VOA went on the air live before we knew the end of the story. So when it came out well, the listener had to believe that Reagan was really okay. . . . We are an open society and that is our way and to change will reduce our greatest strength.[10]

A Rhythm Tune Master Makes an Ominous Request

The debate at the Voice intensified during September 1981. Conkling had asked Acting Program Manager Cliff Groce for the names of the Worldwide English broadcaster and editor who had decided to air the excerpt of Arbatov's interview. Groce urged Conkling not to pursue his request, saying that it could be construed as reminiscent of the McCarthy period. Conkling backed off, telling Willen in the widely quoted interview: "I think he [Cliff] misunderstood me. . . . I was glad that Cliff asked me not to get the persons' names because, the way he thought of it at least, it would have been a bad sign. I guess that's the way the rest of the people here would have taken it. The business I'm in [music arranging] you do it all the time. You don't mean that 'I'm going to go out and cut that guy's throat.' You may say, 'I'm not going to use him for rhythm tunes any more.'"[11]

Ten days later, Conkling ordered that a prerecorded broadcast of *Press Conference USA* with Secretary of Defense Caspar Weinberger be postponed, a first in the twenty-three-year history of the VOA weekend panel talk show involving prominent Washington journalists. He did so on the grounds that Weinberger had misstated the U.S. position on chemical and biological warfare (implying that Washington might develop such weapons just as the United States was alleging their use in Cambodia by the Soviet Union). Both the State and Defense Departments requested cancellation of the program. Groce and Deputy Director Haratunian stood firm. They insisted that *Press Conference USA* be aired, even on a delayed basis, without edits. When the complete program finally was broadcast on September 23, it included a Department of Defense statement explaining that the United States had renounced any use of biological weapons and remained in full compliance with a convention governing them.[12]

Events were now on fast forward. The same week as the Weinberger flap, the newly appointed policy adviser on VOA, Philip Nicolaides, fired off a memo to agency director Wick:

The only convincing *raison d'etre* for the VOA is to counter USSR propaganda by portraying it as the last great predatory empire on earth. . . . We must strive to destabilize the Soviet Union and its allies. . . . We should seek to drive wedges of resentment and suspicion between the leadership of the various Communist bloc nations. . . . News should be factually accurate. Credibility is all-important. But we need not expatiate endlessly on stories which tend to put us or our allies in a bad light while glossing over stories which discredit the leadership of the communist nations.[13]

About a month later, Nicolaides sent a second memo to Wick, adding: "The Charter was never designed to shield insubordination or journalistic anarchy. If that is not clear to all the people who work for the Voice of America, reporters and editors, it must be made clear."[14] Nicolaides's first memo to Wick was circulated in Conkling's front office suite, and from there, it was leaked two months later to the *Washington Post*. His second memo heralded purges in 1981 and 1982 that would transform VOA's leadership.

Struggling to Stave Off Disaster

Conkling, Haratunian, Groce, and News and Current Affairs (NCA) attempted, each in his or its own way, to stabilize the Voice during these turbulent weeks. In September, Haratunian succeeded in persuading the agency to permit VOA to establish its own personnel office, separate from that of USIA/ICA one-half mile away. At the outset, the new office streamlined hiring and personnel practices. It strengthened VOA's autonomy. However, it also helped the new political appointees remove key managers and reorganize the Voice.

Now the administration held all the cards. In November, just shy of a year after Reagan's election, the forced transfers or retirements under pressure began. Haratunian was transferred to a foreign service assignment elsewhere in the agency—informed about it by a long-distance telephone call. His assistant Bill Read, who had just collaborated with VOA archivist and strategic planner Barbara Schiele on a comprehensive modernization plan for the Voice, also was moved.[15] Just a few days later, Voice pillar and thirty-year veteran Cliff Groce was summoned to Conkling's office and was told that his new assignment would be as deputy director of USIA Television.

The first wave of transfers did not pass unnoticed:

- The *New York Times* reported that Haratunian's ouster was announced by Conkling, "who has been prodded lately by conservative critics demanding changes in what *Human Events*, the conservative weekly, characterizes as the Voice's already too soft approach behind the Iron Curtain."[16]
- Steve Bell of ABC News on November 19 broadcast what he said was a letter to President Reagan, concluding:

Mr. President, I am sure most of us want VOA to tell the American story and there is plenty of room for commentary outside newscasts or popular entertainment features. But . . . millions around the world seek out VOA's signal often at considerable risk precisely because of its credibility. And because their own countries often try to sell politics like soap, they can be pretty sophisticated listeners. One other thing, Mr. President: some would argue that VOA should change its tune just to compete with the Kremlin's propaganda barrage. But Mr. President, in all my travels, I've never met anyone who tuned to Radio Moscow when they really wanted to find out what was going on.[17]

• Senator Charles Percy said that if the ideas in Nicolaides's memorandum ever became policy, it would violate the law (the VOA Charter). Now chairman of the Senate Foreign Relations Committee, Percy added that he had tried to ensure, five years earlier, that VOA broadcasts would be untainted by propaganda or anyone who might want to distort the news. "We fought that battle," he said, "and we are not about to lose it."[18] Percy then held up confirmation of Reagan's nominee for assistant secretary of state for human rights, Elliott Abrams.

• The Society of Professional Journalists (Sigma Delta Chi) condemned "any effort to politicize the Voice of America and convert its primary mission to that of propaganda." It urged President Reagan to uphold the principles embodied in the VOA Charter.[19]

The Purges Continue

In spite of the publicity and criticism, other key managers were to leave or be transferred as Wick installed a new supervisory team at America's Voice. News chief Bernie Kamenske announced his retirement at the end of December, to take up a post at CNN.[20] I was told in January 1982 that I would be reassigned from NCA chief to a new postition with the mikado-like title of deputy director of programs for program development. Frank Cummins was moved from his job as deputy director of the Near East and South Asia Division, and his boss, Allan Baker, retired after being given a new assignment. The chief of Worldwide English, V. Hobson (Hal) Banks, was transferred to New York, and his deputy, Sherwood Demitz, to agency research. And the Monday morning after I left NCA, newsroom duty editor Mark Willen was assigned as VOA correspondent in New Delhi, a posting he declined a month or so later shortly before resigning. Altogether, in just three months, at least ten senior and midlevel managers at the Voice had retired, been removed, or been transferred.

Kamenske's celebrated paranoia at last rang true. A somewhat muted newsroom Christmas party was held in mid-December 1981 at White

House correspondent Philomena Jurey's home in Washington's fashionable Cleveland Park district. BHK, however, could not and would not sit still. Around mid-evening, alerted by a phone call, he rushed downtown to the newsroom. He had to go there to supervise the editing and writing of news about the imposition of martial law and the arrest of many Solidarity leaders by Poland's Communist government. No one was surprised when Bernie announced his resignation less than a week later. The *New York Times* took note of his departure in an editorial:

> In quitting after twenty-eight years, Mr. Kamenske is being loyally discreet about arguments with the new director, James Conkling, a former show business executive. But those quarrels are common knowledge at the station, as is Mr. Kamenske's importance [in enacting a charter into law] that committed the Voice to "accurate, objective, and comprehensive news." . . . It may be quixotic to expect the Voice to avoid any tilt: no government agency can be wholly objective. Still, the ideal is precious and its value is evident as millions of Poles tune in foreign broadcasts to learn what is happening in their own land. They don't want propaganda. . . . To change the Voice's approach and heighten the ideological pitch will not make it an antidote to Radio Moscow. Only an echo.[21]

Rumors were rife about a Wick–Conkling reorganization of the Voice. Ten days after Haratunian was sacked, Conkling introduced two new deputies to replace him: USIA foreign service officers Terry Catherman and Sam Courtney. Nicolaides, the same week, was formally named VOA deputy director of programs for commentary and analysis. A petition signed by more than a hundred Voice employees asked Conkling to cancel the appointment and dissociate himself from Nicolaides's views. The director never responded to the petition. The new senior management team then named NBC's Frank Scott to fill the long-vacant position of program manager, now called director of programs, and NBC's Gene Pell as my successor in NCA. In another aspect of the reorganization, the language broadcasters were given free rein to select most news items from the central newsroom file to use as they pleased. Gone were the centrally produced roundups of news that had been instituted following the Jonestown debacle.

But outside the Voice, the debate persisted. "Three things remain clear," former State Department spokesman and VOA broadcaster John

Trattner wrote in February 1982. "First, the integrity of its news is the key to the Voice of America's success [he noted that it had, at that time, the largest international broadcast audiences in the Soviet Union, China, and Latin America]. Second, each administration has title to use the government's radio station to present and explain its foreign policy ideas and actions. Third, applying these truths cannot ignore what is most important of all: the overseas audience."

Trattner went on to suggest, first, that the official U.S. line could be presented intelligently in VOA programs, without, as he put it, "clobbering" listeners. Second, he counseled: "Leave the news alone. The Voice's new leadership says that it intends to do just that, but some critics remain unconvinced. Convince them. Make it clear that news can't be improved, changed or otherwise tampered with, that its integrity and relevance to listeners is a permanent, truly invulnerable fact of life at the Voice. Continue to demonstrate to the Voice's listening millions that this is so."[22]

THE DAWN OF RECOVERY

Hollywood's celebrated film producer John Houseman, who, as head of the overseas radio production section at the Office of War Information, could be considered the first VOA director, came back for its fortieth-anniversary celebration on February 24. He reminded the packed auditorium that honest reporting had been the key to the Voice's credibility when the tide turned in the direction of an Allied victory at the end of World War II. That underlying theme sustained VOA through the difficult winter of 1981/1982.

The Law of the Land

The new director of programs, Frank Scott, and the new NCA chief, Gene Pell, both from commercial networks, pledged to maintain the Voice's news integrity. They hired another news professional, Edward DeFontaine of Associated Press and Westinghouse radios, to assist them. DeFontaine, throughout his Voice career, steadfastly insisted on honesty in news and cost effectiveness in administrative matters.

In an interview one year after joining the Voice, DeFontaine put it bluntly: "We are the only news organization in the world that is required . . . to be factual, balanced, and complete, *by law*. If we violate that, we are literally violating the law of the land." Subsequently, as director of broadcast operations, DeFontaine cut programming technicians' over-time substantially and never hesitated to point out what he considered to be excessive expenditures by the Office of Engineering and other support organizations.[23]

Scott and Pell worked with their first newsroom chief, VOA correspondent Bill Marsh, to organize a merger of NCA and the Worldwide English broadcasting division into a new, enlarged News and English Broadcasting (NEB) leviathan. It dwarfed even the smaller NCA, which the USIA study group had deemed too big in 1974. Scott strengthened his office with four new deputies: Pell as his deputy for NEB, Cummins as his deputy for operations, Nicolaides as his deputy for commentary and analysis, and me as his deputy for program development.

More Transfers, More Editorials

The Reagan revolution swept forward with the launching of the USIA Project for Truth and a disinformation alert, designed to combat Soviet propaganda. Like many revolutions, however, this one also was devouring its young. Nicolaides proved too costly for Wick, in terms of negative publicity for the agency. The Texan departed suddenly, from the Voice in February and from the agency in March 1982. But the revolution still had its victims. About the time Nicolaides left USIA, Wick demanded the removal of VOA USSR Division chief Barbara Allen, a foreign service officer. It was one of the last of the purges, designed to placate an ultraconservative congressman from Long Island who considered VOA Russian broadcasts "too soft" and accused VOA of downplaying the views of dissident writer Aleksandr Solzhenitsyn. Conkling himself did not survive the turmoil. About the time of Allen's transfer, he asked for studio time at five o'clock one day and announced his own resignation over the strowger system audible throughout VOA. It was only ten months after the recording executive had arrived in Washington. Catherman and Courtney left and went back to the agency. On his last day at VOA, Courtney said to the staff: "I have every confidence that the Voice can take care of itself."

American media continued to focus attention on the quality and credibility of VOA news. The bipartisan U.S. Advisory Commission on Public Diplomacy, the oversight body for USIA/ICA, issued a report in July 1982. It urged that both VOA and the agency remain free from "stridency and propaganda" and that the agency "take particular care" to broadcast news abroad (meaning VOA news) objectively.[24]

Reagan appointees continued to exert influence, however. They focused less on VOA news (perhaps because of the press attention) than on current affairs and other programming. Several studies showed a resurgence of Cold War, anti-Soviet themes in current affairs scripts, with particular emphasis on the struggle against leftists in Central America, denials of human rights in the Warsaw Pact countries, and events in America with a positive spin. Concurrently, the commentaries became more polemic and were renamed "editorials." For the first time, the new administration removed the writing of commentaries from News and Current Affairs and placed them in the separate Office of Policy (headed initially by Nicolaides but later by conservative intellectual Seth Cropsey). Offerings included such titles as "By Hook or Crook" (an attack on the Kremlin's industrial and economic espionage in the West), "Shave Closer, Sleep Better" (on the shortage of razors and other consumer goods in the Soviet Union), and "Comrade, Can You Spare a Dime?" (a scathing denunciation of an American citizen who was visiting the USSR and lionized for criticizing capitalism in the United States).[25] All services were required to use the editorials a prescribed number of times daily, depending on airtime, whether or not they were relevant to their listeners. Each editorial was labeled as "reflecting the views of the United States government."

In another departure from standard practice, Wick or his colleagues became directly involved in relaying instructions from national security agencies to play musical selections on VOA English, Georgian, or Polish programs. These tunes apparently were meant to send coded signals to dissidents. Reports of at least five such incidents surfaced in the press. Some of them were confirmed in court documents in the late 1980s during an unsuccessful suit against the government by a dismissed Georgian Service employee. Broadcasters and music-show hosts were instructed to play the music, with no further explanations, other than that "instructions" came from "on high." One of the English songs played in the summer of 1982 was Rod Stewart's appropriately entitled "Foolish Behavior."[26]

REGROUPING AND RENEWAL

The Reagan administration, for all the turmoil of the early 1980s, did bring unprecedented resources for the strengthening, technically, of the Voice. As a result of the modernization study undertaken by Bill Read and Barbara Schiele, USIA went forward in 1982 with the $1.3 billion modernization plan to strengthen VOA's worldwide reach (chapter 5). The VOA budget was dramatically increased in 1983 and 1984 to permit the hiring of additional stringers, to expand greatly the travel of news and language service reporters, and to deploy a mobile vehicle, *Voyager*, for live broadcasts and interviews across the United States. Studio and Master Control facilities built when the Voice moved to Washington in 1954 were finally refurbished or replaced.

The Birth of VOA Europe

Bill Haratunian and Bill Read, before their transfers, had discussed a concept known as VOA II. The idea was to launch a contemporary American radio service to Western Europe to attract a new generation increasingly unaware of the role played by the United States in Europe's postwar reconstruction. Haratunian and Read's plan eventually led to the creation in October 1985 of VOA Europe. Its initial purpose was to appeal to the increasingly anti-American generation in Western Europe, and its promotional slogan was "music and more." It was the first English-language, around-the-clock, American commercial broadcasting–style FM program to be satellite fed by VOA to affiliate stations. Later, there were some direct broadcasts of VOA Europe to the Caribbean and other regions, on medium wave and shortwave. The staff consisted largely of broadcasters and part-time contractors from commercial U.S. radio. They labeled themselves the "A team" or the "mother of all networks" and constructed the first digital studios at the Voice of America for their upbeat, disk-jockey presentation of news, music, and features about the United States. The new format was designed on the basis of a $1 million broadcast research project in Western Europe. The fast-paced program stood out in a world of international broadcasting then still dominated by announcers with slow delivery to make listening easier on shortwave and heavier, news-related programming fare. VOA Europe was closed, for lack of funding, after an eleven-year run.

A High-Energy Surge into the Mid-1980s

Frank Scott's tenure as VOA director of programs was "high energy," as one might expect from a former commercial-network operative. Scott was program director for eighteen months before his transfer to Munich as VOA Europe's first director. As one of his Washington deputies, I had a few weeks early in his tenure after my own transfer to wander about the Voice and consider ways to help revitalize and heal it. I gained a new appreciation for the talent and dedication in the very language services that had been so critical of NCA. Some were indeed translation services, used to coasting or operating under foreign service officers inclined not "to rock the boat." But others were straining at the leash to do their own reporting. Several divisions showed a mastery of production skills, particularly the Spanish and Brazilian units with extraordinary on-air talents such as José "Pepe" del Rio (Spanish) and José Amerigo and Pedro Kattah (Portuguese-to-Brazil) and later Sandra Dominique (Creole-to-Haiti) in the Latin America Division. Throughout the house, levels of competence varied. But I felt it was important to seek out the broadcasters' views. If we were to get the Voice moving again, what better source than those closest to listeners everywhere? Scott asked me to

- Take charge of the program review and evaluation process originally established by John Wiggin in the 1950s and shape it to meet the needs of a network of the 1980s
- Hire a VOA executive editor and executive producer with authority to work on new programming projects and jump-start initiatives in some of the language services
- Ensure cost-efficient and solid installation of the world's largest multilingual word-processing system to distribute news and current affairs copy electronically to the language services and English, replacing the creaky, typo-prone antiquated internal Teletype system
- Design and construct the mobile remote studio *Voyager*, the first such vehicle at the Voice since the 1950s
- Establish an awards system to recognize distinguished Voice programming across the house: news, current affairs, and language productions
- Assemble housewide teams for program planning and the writing and editing of the first VOA-wide programming and production handbooks since the 1960s

A Remarkable Team

Suddenly, I was busy again, assembling a small, high-quality team. My key lieutenants were Executive Editor John Lennon, a skilled senior editor in Current Affairs with proven organizational and managerial

A KURALT-STYLE MIRROR OF AMERICA,
IN MORE THAN FORTY LANGUAGES

The red, white, and blue *Voyager* mobile studio was built in 1984 and
dedicated in 1985, and rotating crews within it traversed forty-seven
of the forty-eight continental United States during its brief life in the
mid-1980s. Eight state governors were interviewed in its studio, and
live concerts were broadcast from Nashville, Santa Fe, and other
cities. A typical *Voyager* team consisted of three broadcasters (one
from English, two from the language services), a field engineer/driver,
and a special events coordinator. The sleek, Airstream-like *Voyager*
visited Mount Rushmore and other historic places. At times, it transported members of a language service to an ethnic community of
particular interest. *Voyager* logged thousands of interviews and on-
scene reports during its twenty-two-month run. However, mechanical
problems and a drastic budget reduction forced it off the road in 1987.
Three years later, Director of Programs Sid Davis (chapter 1) succeeded in constructing a second, simpler, updated mobile vehicle, but
it, too, ceased operations after a year or two because of budget cuts.
Voyager II finally was sold to the United Nations and shipped to East
Africa for an overland trip to Central Africa, its VOA logo painted
over and its ultimate fate uncertain.

skills, and Executive Producer Terry Hourigan, a commercial broadcaster
with impressive credentials in team building, special events production,
music, and sports broadcasting. These two dynamos operated initially
from a tiny warren of dingy offices fondly known as The Cellblock. They
wandered about, teaching the services a blend of commercial broadcasting techniques such as format clocks and fast-paced bridges along with
VOA standards of double sourcing, thorough reporting, objectivity, and
balance. They also collaborated on the commissioning of *Voyager*, which
provided VOA listeners (and broadcasters) with perhaps their best close-
up glimpse ever of America's heartland.

The new program development team invited more than eighty broadcasters from throughout the Voice to draft and edit the new handbooks.
Three editions came out between 1982 and 1994; they could not have
been produced without the dedicated assistance of others on the team
such as Barbara Callihan, a genius at publications and a savvy radio

program analyst who learned to play her succession of increasingly sophisticated PCs like a Stradivarius.

Teaching and Learning

The new review system, based on the handbooks, became a housewide tutorial. It improved communications between hitherto isolated services: the newsroom and the English broadcasters. Lennon devised a simple framework to explain the basics for anyone judging a daily program or creating an entirely new one. It was known as the ARC formula, focusing on the *audience* (listeners' interests and the competition in a particular region), *radio* (the latest contemporary production techniques), and the *charter* (the framework for all VOA programming).

During reviews—live monitored spot checks and analyses held initially at any hour of the day or night—the team tracked how quickly services picked up items from the central wire and evaluated, minute by minute, what was available and what the services used. (This was designed to detect Jonestown-style "sins of omission" from newscasts and to ensure that the new latitude given the language services to determine their own news lineups would remain sound and relatively consistent throughout the Voice.) It thus became possible to begin building "a community of journalists," with everyone operating on roughly the same set of journalistic standards. Hourigan's design of a housewide programming awards system, along with the reviews, helped standardize and energize VOA production techniques. Format clocks, long in use at commercial networks, were introduced for the first time at VOA. Housewide circulation of review findings—another first—taught managers from the Voice director to the program development team to the division chiefs much about the universe of audiences they sought to reach.

The Birth of SNAP

At the Voice in the early 1980s, the ancient Teletype system was on the verge of total collapse. Managers recognized the potential of the emerging computer technology to distribute VOA newscasts internally and instantaneously, along with correspondent reports, current affairs scripts, programming advisories, and some administrative messages.

Reporter and lawyer Chris Kern (chapter 7) was captivated by the new technology. He decided to move from a promising journalistic career

---

PUTTING THE CHARTER TO WORK IN THE WORLD

In the early 1980s, Africa Division chief Harry Heintzen was on a trip to southern Africa and met a broadcaster in the tiny country of Lesotho, surrounded by South African territory. The broadcaster asked him: "Why doesn't VOA have a program to teach radio professionals in other countries, like the BBC or Radio Netherlands?" Why not indeed? Heintzen asked himself.

In 1983, Heintzen decided to test the idea, and persuaded USAID to bring six Liberian broadcasters to Washington for training in VOA programming and production. Two years later, Heintzen became director of what was to become the VOA (later International Broadcasting Bureau) International Media Training Center (IMTC). The VOA Charter was the central thrust of much of the training, which encompassed management and advertising skills, technical issues, marketing techniques, and many other aspects of free media. This "journalism school for the fearless," as Colman McCarthy of the *Washington Post* called it,* subsequently trained more than 7,000 journalists from at least 140 countries. USAID eventually contributed $1.2 million annually to this venture.

Heintzen believes that the program was especially valuable in the 1980s and 1990s because it coincided with the emergence after the Cold War of many new independent commercial radio and TV stations. "After journalism," Heintzen adds, "radio management in the commercial sense is the most important training we offer." The International Media Training Center also brought to the United States or regional workshops overseas many active or potential managers of VOA affiliates abroad. It encouraged networks and stations around the world to sign on to VOA.†

*Colman McCarthy, "Willing to Pay the Price for a Free Press," *Washington Post,* June 11, 1996.
†Harry Heintzen, interview with author, Washington, D.C., June 14, 2001.

---

and join a small computing services unit that initially was part of the new program development effort. He helped draft a proposal for what was to become a ubiquitous "internetwork" performing many functions in addition to distributing scripts. Another member of the unit, former broadcast technician and NCA technical specialist Don Barth, suggested a name for the new system acquired under a contract with Xerox Corporation. "It's a System for News and Programming," Barth noted. "Why not call it SNAP?"

Establishing SNAP was a formidable task, because it required contracting for the development of software for the alphabets of more than forty languages as well as what Kern called "a comprehensive, enveloping computer environment." Creating software for such unique alphabets as those of Amharic (to Ethiopia), Georgian (to the Soviet republic of Georgia), and Lao and several other Asian languages proved especially daunting.[27] In five years, the system grew to 1,500 workstations. But SNAP also accommodated thousands of service messages daily and became, during the 1980s, the principal delivery mechanism throughout VOA for ideas, plans, complaints, notices, and program review notes. A few months after receiving her SNAP workstation, one manager told Kern that "it has become my window into the organization." The acronym "SNAP" entered the lexicon of the Voice also as a verb. It became common for broadcasters or managers there to say, "Let me SNAP you a note on that," when sharing a plan for coverage of an overseas event such as a presidential trip or the Olympic Games.[28]

Live from the Cape

VOA also undertook more multilingual live remotes than ever before. This was made possible because of both the resources brought in by the Reagan administration and the Voice's very active and energetic chiefs of special events in the 1980s and 1990s: Nancy Smart and Rosie Hall. There was no coverage challenge they couldn't master, no deal in the field they couldn't make under pressure and at a price VOA could afford. Properly motivated, these team leaders discovered, there was magic when journalists in the central newsroom, broadcasters in the language services, and the technicians who supported them worked together. Smart and Hall tamed a lot of egos in their years on the road.

Whirling Rotors at the Penny Pincher Motel

In the spring of 1981, it had been some years since the *Apollo* lunar landings and manned space flight. VOA had to rehabilitate its trailer at the Kennedy Space Center, Cape Canaveral, Florida, to accommodate a multilingual team for the first in a series of manned liftoffs of the space shuttle *Columbia*. Interest was intense. VOA Special Events, always under orders to save money, put the team in a block of rooms at the Penny Pincher Motel, about fifteen miles inland. Their day of glory arrived. The rented van set out at 4:30 A.M. for the early-morning launch. But thousands of Floridians and visitors from across the land and around the world had the same idea. About an hour before liftoff and airtime, the van got stuck in a monumental traffic jam, miles away from the VOA observation trailer located near the *Columbia* launch pad. "Pile out and run," shouted team leader Smart.

Some of the broadcasters had been in the business for years, senior citizens not too fleet of foot. Nonetheless, even the oldest among them, completely out of breath, made it with seconds to spare before the line from the trailer studio opened to Washington and the world. Hurry up and wait. There was a hold. Then another hold. And finally, a postponement of the mission, for two days.

Smart got on the phone to Washington. "Boss," she exclaimed, "this was Friday morning. The next try will be Sunday morning. If you think the traffic was bad today, imagine it then. What will we do?" The first thought: rent some sleeping bags. But, Bernie Kamenske replied, this is a big story. "You ought to rent a chopper to get them from the motel to the launch site," he snorted. "That's what respectable networks do." If we called it "emergency local transportation," regulations master Janie Fritzman concluded, NCA—in a legal exception to most U.S. government transportation rules—could indeed rent a helicopter on Sunday morning.

And so, just as the sun was rising that Sunday, a chopper set down in the parking lot of the Penny Pincher Motel. It made two runs to ferry the team, consisting of newsroom space specialists; broadcasters from the Portuguese-to-Brazil, Russian, Chinese, and Spanish Services; technicians; and coordinator Smart. What a view! The sun was peeking over the Atlantic horizon, coloring the surf with every hue in the rainbow as it rose. The gantry tower far below was smoking. And on the terrestrial surface, gleaming autos beyond counting were stretched out for miles in gridlock. The team landed in plenty of time on a sandy stretch right next to the broadcast trailer. Everyone was totally relaxed (more or less) just past dawn as the line was cut through to a half dozen broadcast studios in Washington. The liftoff was perfect. Pepe del Rio of the Spanish Branch described the thundering blast beneath the rocket as "an artificial sun." Millions heard the countdown and the thunder, live, on America's Voice.

From Triumph to Tragedy

Nearly five years later, after U.S. space missions had settled into what seemed like a routine, VOA Miami bureau chief Greg Flakus went to Cape Canaveral to cover a launch of the space shuttle *Challenger*. Flakus was on hand to witness the explosion in the sky that, in an instant, snuffed out the lives of seven astronauts. The Miami correspondent later recalled:

> It [the vestiges of *Challenger*] hung in the sky for a long time that morning. It was at once beautiful and repelling. The long white plume of smoke left by the space shuttle *Challenger* reminded spectators of how an exciting event full of promise had turned, before our very eyes, into a numbing tragedy. . . . When the shuttles do begin to fly again, we reporters will be back at the Kennedy Space Center press mound. No doubt the press corps will be much larger than it has been for the most recent launches. We will look at that Florida sky and remember that plume of smoke, the glint of fire, the falling debris—and I doubt that any of us will be thinking of the next flight as in any way routine.[29]

The fatal liftoff was broadcast live by VOA that January 28, 1986, and the network was immediately expanded to cover reaction to the tragedy for listeners in Europe, the Middle East, Africa, and South Asia. In a live statement from the White House, President Reagan said: "The future doesn't belong to the faint-hearted. It belongs to the brave. The *Challenger* crew was pulling us into the future, and we'll continue to follow it. I've always had great faith in and respect for our space program and what happened today does nothing to diminish it. We don't hide our space program. We don't keep secrets and cover things up. We do it all up front and in public. That's the way freedom is, and we wouldn't change it for a minute."[30]

Just about ten months after the *Challenger* tragedy, the story of secret American arms sales to Iran broke. *National Journal* reporter Larry Mosher, aware of earlier reports of Reagan administration pressures on VOA, decided to investigate how the newsroom covered the widening scandal. He spent hours at VOA headquarters, reading scripts and talking to editors and senior managers. Between November 4, 1986, and mid-January 1987, Mosher reported, VOA produced more than a thousand news items, special reports, opinion roundups, editorials, and Special English stories on what he called "the still-unfolding Iran–contra saga." Among them was a quotation from a CBS–*New York Times* poll saying that 47 percent of Americans polled thought the president was not telling the truth when he said that he didn't know about the money transfer at the time it occurred. Mosher quoted the fifth VOA director of the 1980s, Richard W. Carlson, as saying: "The White House does not interfere here . . . we are the only news agency that is required by law to offer balanced news coverage."[31]

Challenges Overcome

VOA had come a long way since the dark days of 1981 and 1982. That was something of a miracle, considering the pressures it faced and its extraordinarily rapid revolving-door leadership. After Conkling, its directors were John Hughes (March–August 1982), Kenneth Tomlinson (December 1982–September 1984), Gene Pell (June 1985–October 1985), and Richard W. Carlson (spring 1986–September 1991), who was the third-longest-serving director after Kenneth Giddens and Henry Loomis.[32] In 1983, as noted in chapter 4, VOA correspondents were accredited to Capitol Hill. This was after a strenuous lobbying effort led by Director Tomlinson, who almost two decades later was sworn in as the third chairman of the Broadcasting Board of Governors.

Through both changing leadership and political pressures, the Voice managed to regain its footing by the end of the decade. Four deputy directors in the late 1980s and early 1990s helped in very different ways to stabilize the network. They were Ambassadors Mel Levitsky and Robert Barry, USIA foreign service officer Robert Chatten, and Robert Coonrod, an agency professional and Carlson protégé who developed into a seasoned broadcast manager. Coonrod, like Carlson, later was president of the Corporation for Public Broadcasting.

Roy Cohn's Litmus Test of the 1980s

Two politically conservative VOA directors with nationally known journalistic or editorial credentials, John Hughes of the *Christian Science Monitor* and Gene Pell of NBC, each left after only about five months on the job. In 1982, Hughes became State Department spokesman, and Pell quit unexpectedly in 1985 to become president of Radio Free

---

CARLSON VERSUS GELB

Richard W. Carlson was a journalist to the core and clashed over several issues with USIA director Bruce Gelb at the end of the 1980s and early 1990s. Carlson cited in particular Gelb's unsuccessful efforts to prevent a VOA interview with Chinese dissident Fang Lizhi shortly after the famous dissident was released from jail and came to the United States. He also noted the agency director's dabbling in 1990 and 1991 with Voice coverage of the Persian Gulf War (chapter 15). "So our policy," Carlson said, "is that the Voice of America director is there, among other things, to protect the integrity of the broadcasting."*

*Richard W. Carlson, interview, Charles Stuart Kennedy oral-history project, Association for Diplomatic Studies and Training, Georgetown University and Foreign Service Institute, Arlington, Va., March 2, 1993, 75, 78–79.

Europe/Radio Liberty. Several months after Pell's resignation, Wick tried to recruit a third prominent journalist and former top U.S. network executive, William Sheehan of ABC News, to head the Voice. He and Sheehan lunched at Washington's Ritz-Carlton Hotel to engage in a "bridge-building" exercise with Republicans who had voiced their criticism of the prospective appointment in the conservative magazine *Human Events*. Ironically, the luncheon was organized by none other than former McCarthy aide Roy Cohn (chapter 2).

Sheehan failed the conservative litmus test, because, he said, he had described himself as a "centrist" determined to run the Voice as "an even-handed news organization." Sheehan dismissed as inappropriate a question by one of his luncheon partners about how he had voted in the 1984 presidential election. After being briefed on the meeting, Senator Jesse Helms of North Carolina informed Wick that Sheehan was unacceptable to him and warned of a protracted confirmation hearing by the Senate Foreign Relations Committee if the former ABC executive's name were put forward. Wick then withdrew the nomination, and named USIA public-affairs chief Carlson, another former journalist, as acting director (later to become director) of VOA.[33] During his tenure, Carlson became a fighter in the Ken Giddens tradition for VOA news and managerial integrity.

A Reporter or Supporter?

In 1993, John Lennon, the VOA executive editor who later served as a European Division manager and acting Worldnet Television director, wrote a master's thesis on a fundamental question: Did VOA News a decade earlier become more of a supporter than a reporter of Reagan administration policies? Lennon sampled from an estimated 4,000 items in the VOA news file issued during the Carter and first Reagan administrations. He compared them with content on equivalent dates in the *New York Times* and Facts on File. Lennon concluded that during the early Reagan years, there was an increase in VOA news stories dealing with the Cold War. The Voice, he wrote, may have been "influenced to reflect standards and goals related to U.S. foreign policy rather than standards of journalism such as those in the VOA Charter." But Lennon noted that there also was an increase in the Voice's reflection of non–Cold War international and U.S. news, compared with slight declines, proportionally, in the *Times* and Facts on File samples. Lennon added that even more study was needed to arrive at a definite conclusion.[34]

The Voice veteran recalled John Chancellor's observation that "the persuasiveness of the commentaries is dependent upon the credibility of the news." In the early 1980s, as he was resigning, Bernie Kamenske had elaborated on that. "The news," Kamenske noted, "cannot be an island in a sea of propaganda."[35]

Clearly there were stark contrasts in the way Republican administrations viewed the Voice between the beginning and the end of the turbulent 1980s. "VOA journalists," Carlson said,

> are the kind of people who used to work at *Time* magazine, or at NBC, or at the *Washington Post*. They are not going to put up with any political interference. There is no way they would, or have to, for long. These are people with friends on the Hill, in the newspapers, and moreover a sense of their own purpose and a sense of wrongness of somebody using them for political purposes. They wouldn't abide it. A new VOA director wouldn't last a week if he tried to do something like that. But the conservatives didn't seem to know that.[36]

As Maureen Jane Nemecek noted: "The Voice of America is American indeed. It is a microcosm of all our frustrations, anxieties, ambiguities and self-doubts. Had there been no Voice of America, we would have had to invent one. Its rhetoric represents four decades of searching for the meaning of America's place in world affairs. . . . In the theme of the contradictory voices, we observe a typically American characteristic of airing our problems in public debate and discussion."[37] The *Christian Science Monitor* wisely put it: "America does not need to sell itself. It needs only to be itself, to make sure its institutions [the reference was to VOA] reflect its values. Then the world is sure to listen."[38]

Correspondent Fred Brown interviews Afghan refugee children in Peshawar, Pakistan, January 1979. (Photo by Barry Shlachter, Courtesy of Voice of America archives)

White House correspondent Philomena Jurey works on site in Aswan during President Jimmy Carter's visit to Egypt, 1978. (Courtesy of Philomena Jurey)

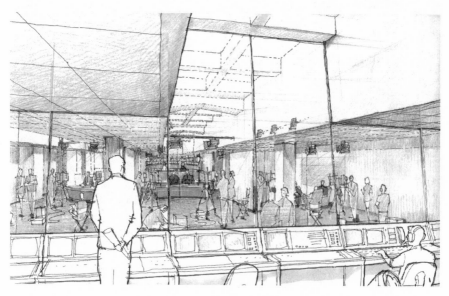

Architect's sketch of the VOA Multimedia Broadcast Center, scheduled for inauguration in 2003 on the first floor of the headquarters building, opposite the Smithsonian Air and Space Museum in Washington, D.C. (Courtesy of Voice of America archives)

A transmission and receive dish (4.5-meter Vertex antenna) atop the VOA studio complex, Washington, D.C., with the Capitol in the background. (Courtesy of Voice of America archives)

The relay station at Tinang, Philippines, with Mount Ayarat in the background. (Courtesy of Voice of America archives)

Engineer Ben Herrick demonstrates how to rig a high-frequency shortwave antenna for maintenance work at the Udorn Relay Station, Thailand. (Courtesy of Voice of America archives)

Chinese Branch broadcaster Shen Hung-hui reads the news during the prodemocracy demonstrations in the People's Republic of China, 1989. (Courtesy of Voice of America archives)

Hausa Service broadcasters Ibrahim Biu (*left*) and Shehu Yusufu Karaye (*right*) confer at a console that receives sound from central audio services, Washington, D.C. (Courtesy of Voice of America archives)

Musicologist Leo Sarkisian (of the Africa Division), sketch of Ghanaian musician Koo Nimo, drawn exclusively for *Voice of America: A History*. (Courtesy of Leo Sarkisian, 2001)

Famed VOA jazz host Willis Conover interviews Louis Armstrong in the 1950s. (Courtesy of Voice of America archives)

President John F. Kennedy addresses the Voice of America staff on the twentieth anniversary of VOA, February 26, 1962. (Courtesy of Voice of America archives)

President Ronald Reagan appears in VOA master control to deliver a message to citizens of the Soviet Union, 1985. (Courtesy of Voice of America archives)

The VOA mobile studio *Voyager*, on the road in New Mexico, 1985. (Courtesy of Voice of America archives)

Geoffrey Cowan, VOA's twenty-second director, is interviewed by host Carol Pearson on the VOA and Worldnet Television weekday worldwide radio–television call-in program, *Talk to America*. (Courtesy of Voice of America archives)

At the Voice of America's forty-fifth anniversary, directors of five decades pose for a photograph. *Left to right:* Mary G. F. Bitterman (1980–1981), Robert E. Button (1956–1958), Henry Loomis (1958–1965), Richard W. Carlson (1986–1991), Kenneth R. Giddens (1969–1977), and James B. Conkling (1981–1982). (Courtesy of Voice of America archives)

During VOA director Robert Reilly's visit to Bangladesh in April 2002, one of the Bangla Service's thousand fan clubs chartered a boat to escort a vessel transporting Reilly and to greet him with banners celebrating the Voice's sixtieth anniversary. On the Buriganga River near the village of Marayanganj, 500 VOA listeners greeted Reilly as he and his party arrived at the town's wharf. On April 4, Reilly cut a ribbon to inaugurate VOA rebroadcasts on an FM station in Dhaka, the capital. To Reilly's right is Bangla Service chief Iqbal Bahar Choudhury; to his left, Information Minister Tariqul Islam; and behind them, Ambassador Mary Ann Peters. (Courtesy of Iqbal Bahar Choudhury)

Veran Matic (*left*), award-winning editor of the independent Serbian radio station B-92, meets with European Division director Frank Shkreli (*right*) and the author (*center*) while on a visit to America's Voice. (Courtesy of Voice of America archives)

The first page of the Arabic Branch Web site, just hours after the terrorist attacks on the World Trade Center and the Pentagon on September 11, 2001. (Courtesy of Voice of America archives)

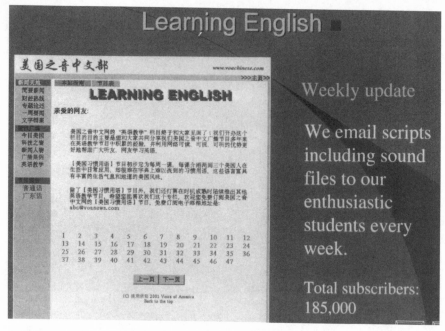

A Web page of the Chinese Branch advertises English lessons in Mandarin. (Courtesy of Voice of America archives)

Roquia Haider of the Bangla Service interviews Mother Teresa at the Missionaries of Charity office in Washington, D.C., August 1987. (Courtesy of Joseph Buday)

The Voice of America
Tibetan Service

ཨེ་མེ་རི་གའི་རྒྱང་སྒྲིང་རླུང་འཕྲིན་ཁང་།
བོད་སྐད་སྡེ་ཚན།

TEN YEARS TO TIBET
March 1991 to March 2001

The cover of special commemorative program marking the tenth anniversary of the Tibetan Service, March 26, 2001. (Courtesy of Voice of America archives)

The VOA Special English logo.

VOA employees get together in a moment away from the microphones to create their own ensemble of sound. *Left to right:* John McNerney, Ernest Acquisto, John Roulet, and Tom Snyder. (Courtesy of Ernest Acquisto and Agnes Timcheck)

Bernard H. Kamenske, VOA News chief (1974–1981) (*right*) and the author at the latter's retirement from America's Voice, January 9, 1998. (Courtesy of James Cowgill)

A gathering of the Heil clan at the author's retirement. *From left to right:* Wendy Heil Packer and Randy Packer; Dorothy Heil and the author; Cary Knor and Nancy Heil Knor; Dr. Susan Heil Cheatham and Mrs. Alan L. Heil, Sr. Missing from the photo are Dr. Michael Cheatham and the Heil grandchildren. (Courtesy of Alan L. Heil, Jr.)

10

The Epochal Years

1969 AND 1989

1969: VOA had the largest audience in radio history [for the moon landing broadcasts]. A woman from Somalia wrote that she named her eleventh child Apollo. A listener from Ecuador cheered the astronauts: "I shared with them the drama and the series of dangers of such a legendary and valiant assignment, vibrating with emotion before and after the splashdown."
—Maureen Jane Nemecek, "Speaking of America"

1989: What did these radios [Western international broadcasters] mean to us until the events of last December? The metaphor of the reeds comes to mind. It was as if we were living underwater and we needed reed pipes for air to breathe. The reeds were the radios of the West. Without them, the entire people surely would have suffocated.
—Nicolae Manolescu, interview with Dorin Tudoran

It was August 1991, nearly two years after the Berlin Wall tumbled and signaled the end of the Soviet empire. VOA's Reuel Zinn, a tall, lanky, ceaselessly energetic radio recording engineer whose belief in America's Voice was total, was on temporary duty in Moscow. It was shortly after the aborted coup against Soviet president Mikhail Gorbachev. One day, Reuel told his taxi driver that he worked for VOA. The driver took him at once to a vast plaza in front of Parliament, known as the Russian White House. There, on the wall near the base of the building, were hand-printed letters in Cyrillic that moved Reuel to tears: "Thank you, Voice of America, for the correct information."[1]

An unknown listener had put into words what the charter had established as a goal. Much of the world turned to America's Voice for an account of two epochal events: the first footsteps on the moon and the collapse of Communist regimes in Eastern Europe.

1969

Hundreds of millions listened as *Apollo 11* made its historic eight-day journey to the moon and back. When Neil Armstrong planted his boot on the lunar soil, VOA had perhaps the largest audience in radio history. Its live broadcast was relayed at that moment by the BBC World Service, nearly all Japanese broadcasting outlets, Radio Australia, Austrian state radio, and many others. During the lunar mission, VOA news and programming was beamed via its own facilities and simulcast at various times by 3,600 stations abroad. The total audience during the *Apollo* adventure was 615 million, according to VOA.

"If estimates were available for the USSR, China, and other communist countries as well as thirty-five others," its Office of Programs summary said, "VOA's total audience might easily have been more than three-quarters of a billion—twenty-seven percent of the world's population outside the United States."[2]

Dress Rehearsal for Destiny

It was one of the Voice's most ambitious news and programming ventures. Preparation for the July mission began in April and involved extensive journalistic and logistical planning. In May, the Voice used *Apollo 10* (with the lunar flyby of astronauts Tom Stafford, Bill Anders, and Gene Cernan) as a "dress rehearsal" of sorts. Based on *Apollo 10's* circumnavigation of the moon and practice in orbit with a lunar landing module, Deputy Program Manager Cliff Groce and Deputy News Division Chief Bill Read engaged in many hours of preparing program schedules and briefing reporters for the big event two months later. They and their assistants ordered additional technical facilities and arranged for live remote teams at the Kennedy Space Center at Cape Canaveral, Florida; at NASA's Johnson Manned Space Flight Center in Houston, Texas; and aboard the USS *Hornet* recovery ship in the Atlantic. It was necessary to arrange hundreds of extra studio bookings and circuits, including ones for reaction recorded by VOA correspondents around the globe.

Finally, July 16—the day of *Apollo's* launch—arrived. VOA Worldwide English anchor Rhett Turner, a licensed pilot and veteran commercial broadcaster who had joined the Voice in 1960, was the lead anchor at Cape Canaveral. Alongside were José "Pepe" del Rio of the Spanish Branch, Stan Grigorovich Barsky of the Russian Branch, and Bing Fong of the Chinese Branch. The remote team included other broadcasters in French and Arabic and technicians Bob Batchelor and Bob Oringle. In advance of the mission, Turner had interviewed the three *Apollo 11* astronauts: Neil Armstrong, Mike Collins, and Edward "Buzz" Aldrin. He had a flight plan in hand, and recorded explanations from each of them to air at all critical phases of the forthcoming eight-day mission. VOA programming was expanded, in English and other languages, to do live reporting of the landing of the *Eagle* excursion module on the moon, the extravehicular activities there, and the critical takeoff of the module from the lunar surface for the return to Earth.

"It Seemed to Sit There, Thundering, for an Eternity"

"It was bedlam at the Cape on launching day," Turner recalls.

> There were thousands of people from all over the world, and traffic jams. The VOA trailer was right in a line with the more elaborate studios of CBS, ABC, and NBC. We were rigged with earphones and a long mike cord, so I could take my mike outside the trailer, listen to the countdown, and describe the liftoff for our listeners, right out there on the sand. When ignition occurred, the gigantic white Saturn rocket five stories high spouted flame and smoke from its base as the huge engines built up thrust. It seemed to sit there, thundering, for an eternity, and you wondered: "Do they have enough thrust to go?" The noise was immense and the ground shook like an earthquake. Then this monstrous thing slowly, so slowly, rose and picked up speed, its rocket plume soon stretching back hundreds of yards in the heavens above.[3]

The VOA remote team waited until the *Apollo* astronauts were confirmed in orbit and on a course to the moon. Then they jumped into waiting cars with the rest of the press for a quick drive along the Beeline expressway to Orlando and a flight to Texas. Within three hours, they were back on the air from the Johnson Manned Space Flight Center in Houston to recount the rest of the mission. "We watched it on three different TV screens," Turner explained. "One had footage from an on-board camera, another had images of the spacecraft's trajectory, and the third displayed mission control timelines."

Descent of an Eagle

Largely on the strength of its *Apollo 11* reportage and cultural programming over the years, VOA won a Peabody Award, broadcasting's most prestigious honor, for the year 1969. The citation was for "radio promotion of international understanding."[4] VOA's Michael A. Hanu wrote and produced a documentary that was a centerpiece of the VOA Peabody submission: *Eagle on the Moon: The Flight of Apollo 11*:

MISSION CONTROL: Hello, Eagle, Houston. We're standing by. Over.

EAGLE: Roger. Eagle is undocked.

MISSION CONTROL: How does it look?

EAGLE: The Eagle has wings! Our radar checks indicate 50,000 feet, our visual altitude checks are about 53,000.

MISSION CONTROL: Roger, copy.

PRESIDENT KENNEDY: I believe that this nation should commit itself to achieving the goal, before this decade is out, of landing a man on the moon and returning him safely to the Earth . . .

MISSION CONTROL: Two minutes, 20 seconds, everything looking good. We show altitude about 27,000 feet.

KENNEDY: We set sail on this new sea because there is new knowledge to be gained, and new rights to be won, and they must be won and used for the progress of all people . . .

MISSION CONTROL: We're now in the approach stage, everything looking good. Altitude 5,200 feet.

EAGLE: Manual attitude control is good.

MISSION CONTROL: Roger, copy. Altitude, 4,700 feet. Houston, you're "go" for landing. Over.

KENNEDY: Space can be explored and mastered without feeding the fires of war, without repeating the mistakes that man has made in extending his writ around this globe of ours . . .

MISSION CONTROL: Sixty seconds.

EAGLE: Lights on, down two and one-half, forward, forward, 40 feet down, two and one-half, picking up some dust, 30 feet, two and a half down, straight shadow, four forward, four forward, drifting to the right a little . . .

MISSION CONTROL: Thirty seconds.

EAGLE: Contact light. Okay, engine stop. Engine arm off, 413 is in.

MISSION CONTROL: We copy you down, Eagle.

KENNEDY: We choose to go to the moon in this decade and do the other things, not because they are easy but because they are hard, because that challenge is one that we're willing to accept, one that we are unwilling to postpone, and one we intend to win . . . (*applause*)

EAGLE: Houston, Tranquility base, here. The Eagle has landed!

NARRATOR: A few short hours after the Eagle landed on the moon, the two men who made the journey on board were ready to take the longest step any man had ever taken. They took it—first one, Neil Armstrong, then the other Edwin Aldrin—in full view of millions and millions of people watching on television.

ARMSTRONG: That's one small step for a man—one giant leap for mankind.

People were watching video in the first transmission of grainy pictures on screens in many places in the world, a decade before the advent of CNN. But even more were listening on radio. When Armstrong made his simple proclamation, VOA was rebroadcast live via the BBC and countless other stations the world over. The global audience at that historic moment was estimated at 450 million listeners. Three days later, just a few hours after Armstrong and Aldrin had returned to Earth, *Eagle on the Moon* captured the majesty of the moment:

NARRATOR: The journey of the Eagle is over. . . . The human spirit, as indefinable as faith or love but as real as the Moon, swept man to another victory in his never-ending quest for accomplishing the impossible, for learning what no one knows, for traveling where no one has ever been. . . . For in the words of one who foresaw it, H. G. Wells, "for man there is no rest and no ending. He must go, conquest beyond conquest. And when he has conquered all the deeps of space and all the mysteries of time, still he will be but beginning."[5]

Apollo 11 united a listening and watching world as no event had since the assassination of John F. Kennedy six years earlier. I was stationed in a distant outpost, Athens, at the time of the lunar landing. Crowds gathered in front of store windows to watch the events unfold during this, the first internationally televised event. Bill Read instructed all his far-flungs to get reactions. I learned that the eminent anthropologist Margaret Mead was in town attending a conference. I reached her at the Grand Bretagne Hotel and requested an interview. She readily agreed. I suggested that I pick her up, take her to the American embassy, and watch the historic moment Neil Armstrong was scheduled to set foot on the moon. The embassy viewing was scheduled to begin around 10:00 P.M., Athens time.

An Unforgettable Tongue-Lashing

Alas, the time of the extravehicular activity (EVA) was then shifted. We waited and waited for some definite word on when Armstrong and Aldrin would exit the lunar module and step down on the moon's dusty surface. Finally, around 3:30 A.M. it was about to happen. I hesitated to awaken the world's greatest anthropologist, now dead asleep.

I called Mead at 5:30, and said that I would pick her up right away to go to the embassy to watch the replay. Her response was swift and sharp and included several quite unladylike epithets. "Replay?" she screamed into the phone, "you should've called me . . . young man, this was *history!*" The Grand Bretagne was only a block away from the VOA bureau. I raced to my car and sped around two corners. In less than five minutes there was Mead, out on the curb in front of the hotel, a diminutive giant in tennis shoes, tapping her feet, glowering, waiting impatiently to be picked up. She gave me the silent treatment during our drive to the embassy. There, the reception room was practically empty by this time, but the TV was on and the great scientist in her thick glasses went up, crouched right before the screen, and watched the replay of the famous Armstrong footstep, again and again. Finally, she turned around and glared at me like an angry schoolmarm, and I quickly said: "Let me treat you to scrambled eggs back at the hotel."

"Let Us Toast the New Era"

"Well, if you insist." We had our breakfast, and the world-famous anthropologist relaxed. She consented, still grumbling just a bit, to a recorded interview. She said: "The mystical quality of man is that he has always sought to break the bonds of his present environment, and now we see that this applies, even in a planetary sense. This is what sets man apart from other creatures. I expect that someday, people will look back on this event and liken it to man's discovery of fire." I hastened back to the bureau and phone-fed the recording. Within an hour, her words were rolling like thunder around the planet, placed in the heavens by America's Voice during the seven-hour worldwide special broadcast, hungry for fresh material.

By then, eight o'clock in the morning, Athens time, I was off to the fifth-story suite of city planner Constantine Doxiadis, halfway up Likavittos Hill, for more reaction. This Magus-like executive, open collar and without a tie or jacket, ushered me into his curtained office, immediately offered champagne, and had the huge wall-to-wall drape pulled aside for a surprise panoramic view of the Acropolis. It was bathed in dawn's golden light. "Welcome," he exclaimed. "Let us toast the new era!"

1989

Two decades later, aided by technology and truth, a new era did dawn, geopolitically. The Cold War ended. By broadcasting straight and accurate news over the decades, VOA and other international broadcasters of the West had helped fuel democratic change in Asia, Africa, and, most notably, the Soviet Union and Eastern Europe. The year 1989 stood out because of the collapse within a dozen weeks of Communist regimes in East Germany, Czechoslovakia, Hungary, Bulgaria, and Romania as reformers moved for the first time to consolidate their dominant position in the Polish government. Albania's Stalinist regime soon was to fall as well.

Former Reuters general manager Michael Nelson, in *The War of the Black Heavens*, wrote: "Why did the West win the Cold War? Not by use of arms. Weapons did not breach the Iron Curtain. The Western invasion was by radio, which was mightier than the sword. Those skilled in war subdue the enemy's army without battle, wrote Sun Tzu, the author of the first known book on warfare."[6]

The Power of Facts

The journalists of the Voice did not see themselves as warriors. They saw themselves as reporters. But the impact of full and fair reportage on the airwaves, for decades before 1989, helped pave the way for the events of that fateful year. "Communism wanted to make everything and everyone the same," Nelson observed. "But the Radios always emphasized individuality, variety, difference. They developed the critical faculties of their listeners."[7] There were many examples during the last half of the century.

• NBC correspondent Irving R. Levine reported from Moscow on November 26, 1956, that Western radio broadcasts "like the VOA" were forcing Soviet authorities "to acknowledge events to their own people that otherwise they would prefer to ignore." He cited the Soviet invasion of Hungary a few weeks earlier and VOA interviews with eight young Hungarians being deported from their country to the Soviet Union; they had "jumped" their prison train and were interviewed by VOA's Hungarian Service shortly thereafter. Their comments were also relayed by VOA's Russian Branch. Soviet media had to report both events, with their own spin. "Russians," Levine reported, "are able to notice that the Soviet version of events comes several days after the broadcasts from Washington or London. Russians are able to note the discrepancies between the reports from overseas and those published here in Russia, and you may be sure the Russians draw their own conclusions about what is truth."[8]

• Vasily Aksyenov, the most popular young novelist of the Soviet Union in the 1960s, listened to VOA regularly before he emigrated to the United States. "It may very well be," he said, comparing its broadcasts to a famous wartime assistance program, "that the forty-year activity of the Voice of America in Russian will be considered by future Soviet historians as a kind of informational Lend Lease of incalculable value."[9]

• David K. Shipler of the New York Times, writing about his years as its Moscow correspondent in the 1970s, recalled how dissidents lacking access to Soviet media were desperate to have their voices heard. He observed what it was like shortly after he arrived at his post: "As time went on, the phones in my apartment and office rang with greater and greater frequency. Unknown voices asked if I would meet them. Usually they would not want to give their names and would not talk on the phone. So I met them, more often than not . . . we would write their stories, the Voice of America would see our articles, and the broadcasters in Washington would translate the stories into Russian, beaming them within hours to the Soviet Union."[10]

• Victor Korchnoi, Soviet chess grandmaster, defected in 1976 while participating in a match in Amsterdam. The news flashed around the world. A short while later, the United Press International correspondent in Moscow saw the bulletin and phoned Korchnoi's wife, who had remained at home in the Soviet capital. She told the correspondent that she had already heard the news on VOA Russian. "But," asked the UPI reporter, "it came to you via the Voice of America. Did you believe it?" To which she replied: "Sir, if I heard it on the Voice of America, I could not help but believe it."[11]

• Vladimir Snegirev, a Soviet journalist, said in 1991, the year the USSR collapsed: "It was sheer stupidity. Our press never talked about the war [in Afghanistan throughout the 1980s], but the Voice of America talked about it every day and people listened in huge numbers. Soviet public opinion about the war in Afghanistan was shaped in large part by Western sources of information."[12]

People in the Soviet Union tuned into the Voice over the years because it could be relied on to provide information, such as Soviet casualties in Afghanistan, that was unavailable on state-controlled media. After the catastrophic accident at the nuclear reactor in Ukraine in 1986, Soviet print and electronic media were silent for many hours. VOA's Russian and Ukrainian Branches, however, told listeners about the disaster as soon as monitors in the West recorded it. Physicians were brought into the studios to advise listeners about how to avoid being victims of that "silent killer, radiation" by not eating fish, fresh vegetables, and fruit.[13]

Key figures in modernizing broadcasts to that part of the world were Natasha Clarkson (chapter 5) and Barbara Cummins, successive chiefs of the Russian Branch. Cummins for a number of years worked twelve- to thirteen-hour days to ensure timely, accurate coverage and was voted VOA's Outstanding Employee of the Year in 1996. I recall vividly

Clarkson and Cummins's deft handling of the live broadcast linking a Washington anchor with Russian Branch correspondent Alec Batchan in Moscow as the Soviet hammer-and-sickle flag was lowered for the last time on Red Square on December 26, 1991, when the USSR ceased to exist. There was an eerie silence and calm on the square, the passing of an empire not with a bang, but a whimper.

An Apparatchik Becomes a Capitalist

VOA's Moscow correspondent at the time, Mark Hopkins (chapters 1 and 7), had watched with fascination as the Soviet Union unraveled. Shortly after arriving in Moscow the previous summer, he made a trip to Volgograd and Samarkand for interviews with regional party officials. One of the second secretaries of the Communist Party, after granting Hopkins a rare interview, apologized that he had run out of the ritual personal cards with his party affiliation and rank embossed on them. Instead, Hopkins recalled, he whipped out a card that said he was the director of a local business enterprise. Thinking back on it, Hopkins realized that this local CPSU (Communist Party of the Soviet Union) apparatchik already was making deals and becoming a bona fide capitalist.

It was a sure signal that the Soviet Union was coming to an end, Hopkins felt. Later that year, he went to Kiev to cover a referendum on independence for Ukraine. Gorbachev, he said, had mishandled that situation by calling for Ukrainians to vote "no" on the eve of the balloting, even though it was obvious that Ukrainians wanted to be rid of Moscow. There was an overwhelming vote for separation, further damaging Gorbachev's standing. Hopkins considered that autumn and winter of 1991 as among the most exhilarating, journalistically, in his VOA career. He had been bureau chief in Belgrade, Munich, Beijing, Boston, Washington, and London as well as Moscow. "It seemed like almost every day, we had a lead story between the unsuccessful coup against Gorbachev and the end of the year," Hopkins said. "It was remarkable," he added, "that the last remaining empire of the preceding century, the Russian/Soviet empire, dissolved without a shot being fired."[14]

The Voice's ability to break news, in fact, attracted the largest international broadcast audience in Soviet Russia during most of the Cold War. In January 1987, Zora Safir-Hopkins of the Russian Branch obtained an extensive telephone interview on prisoners of conscience

A Big Sigh, a Big Story

Glasnost was well established by 1989. Jamming had ceased, and that year, the Soviet government permitted the opening of the first VOA bureau in Moscow. Correspondent (and later news director) Andre DeNesnera was the ideal choice to head it. He could broadcast in Russian and French as well as English. Earlier, he had headed the foreign correspondents' association in Geneva, and now he was setting up shop in Moscow. It was 5:30 on the morning of December 15. There was a phone call from Washington. It was Tom Slinkard, the evening shift editor, who apologized for waking DeNesnera up.

"The Russian Branch here has heard rumors that Andrei Sakharov is dead," Slinkard said. "They say there's talk of it in the Russian community in New York. Can you check it out?"

DeNesnera said of course he would, but felt handicapped. He had just arrived, and his Rolodex was pretty slim. He called the ABC bureau and asked for Sakharov's home number. ABC asked why he needed to reach Sakharov, and DeNesnera promised to get back to ABC's Jim Laurie should he get a good quote or other news.

Home number in hand, DeNesnera called and let the phone at the Sakharov residence ring and ring. No answer. He waited a minute, and called again. A woman picked up the phone, perhaps a cousin or another relative. DeNesnera, speaking perfect Russian, grasped for words. He introduced himself and said: "I understand Andrei Dimitrievich is not feeling well."

There was a big sigh on the other end of the line. "Well, I'm afraid Andrei Dimitrievich has passed away." Sakharov had been stricken the evening before while working on the text of an address to the Soviet Congress of People's Deputies.

DeNesnera hung up and called the desk in Washington with confirmation of the news. VOA broadcast it in the half-hour summary at 6:30 A.M., Moscow time, well ahead of any other medium, electronic or print. DeNesnera then dutifully fulfilled his promise to ABC, giving it confirmation of his scoop. Laurie inserted a bulletin on Sakharov's death into ABC's *Nightline* in the United States, which aired a few minutes later.*

*Andre DeNesnera, interview with author, Washington, D.C., June 4, 2001.

with Nobel laureate and dissident physicist Andrei Sakharov, even before Moscow stopped jamming the Voice.[15] And nearly three years after that interview, VOA was first to tell the world about the death of the famed dissident.

Glasnost in the Soviet Union seemed to stem, in part, from a virus already alive in the nations it dominated. In August 1980, Paul Lendvai of the *Financial Times* recalled, Lech Walesa was head of a small labor union in the Polish port city of Gdansk. It was called Solidarity. The union organized chapters in a few other cities in Poland, including Warsaw, Katowice, and Lódź. Inspired by the Poznań riots of 1956 and the unrest of 1976, Solidarity numbered only a few hundred members that sweltering summer, and was practically unknown in its own country. Solidarity's activities were ignored by Polish state media.

The local chapters began distributing minutes of their meetings to the news agencies, including VOA, BBC, and Radio Free Europe (RFE). Their Polish Services beamed news of the Solidarity meetings back into Poland, often only a few hours later.

In just ten weeks, Lendvai recalled, Solidarity coalesced into a national movement of 10 million members. The radios, he wrote in 1995, were "the bulletin boards of the revolution." Poland's Communist government attempted to crack down on Solidarity, but people power under the Solidarity banner returned, this time to stay. In one of the ironies of 1989, Solidarity won a record number of parliamentary seats in Poland in an election held just a few hours after the Tiananmen massacre in Beijing. A U.S. colonel visiting VOA, when told how simply reporting the news had helped topple politburos in Poland and elsewhere in the region, asked: "How many army divisions would it have taken to do that?"[16] It was a twentieth-century realization of Sun Tzu's ancient admonition.

"Something Fundamental Had Changed"

The events in Poland in June 1989 and the fall of the Communist government in East Germany in early November set off the remaining political tremors of the year. BBC correspondent Misha Glenny witnessed firsthand the events in Prague, the capital of Czechoslovakia. He recalled that in November, "Wenceslaus Square became a shrine to free speech." Just days after the Berlin Wall fell, the Czechoslovak dissident community gathered in the square in force. "None of us, opposition or

The Velvet Revolution and
the Fall of the Old Order

It was early March 1995, scarcely a half decade after the dismantling of the Berlin Wall. VOA director Geoffrey Cowan and I stood on the narrow, sloping Wenceslaus Square, and Jolyon Naegele was our guide. Next to us was the statue of St. Wenceslaus, the man who introduced Christianity to the Bohemians and Czechs in the late fourteenth century. Nearby was the plain marker dedicated to the young Jan Palach, the famed martyr who set fire to himself at that spot in the late 1960s to protest Soviet rule.

One Friday in late November 1989, Reuters and Agence France Presse reported, erroneously it turned out, that two young protesters had been killed by police. VOA and RFE picked up the story and beamed it back into the republic. During the next two days, the streets of Prague filled with tens of thousands of angry Czechs.* The city was ripe with revolutionary fervor that autumn. Naegele pointed out the hotel window from which he had observed the growing crowds in the square that November, and the door at the Finance Ministry above us facing the boulevard where he had interviewed an opposition leader (who told Naegele to leave the ministry by a different door, moments before the dissident was arrested). Naegele described how the crowds had spilled from the square over the old arched bridge spanning the Vltava River to the other bank. It was the first time they had surged beyond the heart of the city and beyond the control of police.

In less than a week, Naegele recalled, the collapse was inevitable, and he watched as dissident playwright and moral leader Václav Havel stood at the upper end of the square to announce the formation of the first free government in Czechoslovakia since 1948.

*Author's notes. Naegele told us that the news agency accounts of the deaths of the two demonstrators turned out to be false. On that Friday, November 17, he was in Berlin covering events after the collapse of the Berlin Wall. He hurried back to Prague forty-eight hours later and learned that on Friday, impostors hired by a disgruntled Communist Party aide had posed as demonstrators supposedly slain by the police, but that no one had been killed. He immediately advised VOA, which broadcast a retraction. By then, however, the regime's collapse was well under way. Naegele left the Voice in the early 1990s and joined RFE as a news analyst in Prague. See also Michael Nelson, *War of the Black Heavens: The Battles of Western Broadcasting in the Cold War* (Syracuse, N.Y.: Syracuse University Press, 1997), 184–186.

officials, believed that ten thousand young people would demonstrate that day," an opposition leader said. "And when [Jolyon] Naegele [VOA East European correspondent] broadcast his piece that night on the Voice of America, people throughout the republic realized that something fundamental had changed." "For the past four years," Glenny wrote, "the impact of Jolyon Naegele . . . on Czechoslovak politics has been greater than most journalists can dream of in a lifetime."[17]

After the Communist government in Prague fell, the revolutions of 1989 continued to sweep through Eastern Europe. Less than six months later, President George Bush addressed the National Association of Broadcasters in Atlanta, Georgia. He marveled at the sudden turn of events. In the Soviet Union, publications that once vilified VOA were now praising it, and the Voice had just established its first news bureau in Moscow. "How did this happen?" President Bush asked:

> It happened in part because of the power of truth. Czechoslovakia's playwright President Václav Havel paid a very personal tribute to this power in his recent visit to Washington. First he came to the White House and told me personally what this broadcasting of the truth had meant to those who were fighting for freedom. And then he visited the Voice of America and met the employees of its Czechoslovak Service. It was a very poignant encounter, for though Havel didn't recognize any of them by face, he knew them all by name the instant he heard them speak. And it's moments like that that convince me of one sure thing: I am determined that America will continue to bear witness to the truth. America must never lose its voice.[18]

For months after the collapse of the Berlin Wall, leaders of Eastern Europe visiting the United States and journalists with them spoke of similar experiences. Among them was Slovakia's reform-minded President Michael Kovac, soon after his country peacefully split off from Czechoslovakia about a year after the tumultuous events in Prague. My longtime associate in the Office of Programs, Barbara J. Tripp, quoted a reporter who accompanied Kovac as saying: "To be a journalist visiting Washington and not to take an opportunity to visit the Voice of America would be as if you were a Muslim visiting Mecca and avoided praying in the mosque. . . . Even President Havel had not bypassed VOA while in the United States."[19]

ECHOES OF 1989

In March 1990, VOA director Richard W. Carlson presided over the annual programming awards ceremony in the Voice auditorium. He told several hundred VOA employees:

> There have been many heroes of the past year. Lech Walesa. Václav Havel. The young man who stopped a column of tanks in Beijing. The Germans who breached the Berlin Wall. The Lithuanians who refused to bow to foreign rule.
>
> Behind these heroes were countless others. People who for years kept alive thoughts and ideas and cultures that governments tried to kill. When the wave of freedom swept through the world, these people kept level heads and stuck to their principles. Among these people were you. You were part of the Revolution of '89.*

*Quoted in Voice of America, Office of External Affairs, *VOA in the News* (Washington, D.C.: Voice of America, Office of External Affairs, 1990), 1.

With the West's Cold War victory won, what next? As it turned out, the contagion of democracy was spreading far beyond the Soviet empire. Freedom House surveys reported that 69 of the world's nations were democracies in 1988; by the year 2000, the number was 119. In Asia, democratically elected governments came to power, dictators were toppled, or opposition leaders were elected for the first time in South Korea, the Philippines, Taiwan, and Indonesia. In Latin America, military leaders were deposed or eased out of office in Argentina, Brazil, and Chile. Mexico's long-dominant Revolutionary Institutional Party (PRI) was ousted from the presidency for the first time in more than seventy years.

The peaceful transition to majority rule in South Africa in 1994 was among the most promising indicators of democratic change anywhere in the world. In the early 1990s, soon after the fall of the Warsaw Pact governments and the dissolution of the Soviet Union, at least a half dozen francophone African countries held constitutional conferences designed to expand the franchise in what had been one-party states. Results were mixed, in a continent afflicted by famine, genocide, and war. But Liberian newspaper editor and publisher Kenneth Y. Best told the House Subcommittee on Africa in 1997:

It was radio and television that helped the post-glasnost democratic movements in Africa, when the broadcast media, especially the BBC and the VOA, brought to Africans the minute-by-minute play of the dramatic changes in central Europe. Africans heard and saw the sounds and images of the fall of the Berlin Wall and of demonstrators demanding freedom and democracy. These dramatic developments prompted them, as they reflected on the widespread and perennial oppression under which they, too, were suffering, to ask themselves the momentous question: "Why not here?" If we could achieve it in South Africa where once it seemed impossible, every place else is within the realm of possibility.[20]

Changes in programming to Africa over several decades were as striking as any at VOA. How the Voice became a credible source in the spread of ideas about pluralist governance and civil society on that continent is the subject of the next chapter.

11

Out of Africa

THE TRIUMPH OF STRAIGHT TALK

VOA has a tremendous impact on human rights violators who feel the eyes of mankind are watching them. This sometimes deters them from committing more atrocities.

—Monique Mujawamaria (Rwandan human rights activist),
in VOA, Africa Division, briefing paper

Ibrahim Babangida, former president of Nigeria, was asked if he listened to VOA Hausa language broadcasts to Africa. He said it not only is the first thing he listens to every morning at five o'clock, but also when he was president he never failed to listen to it before his morning staff briefing. He explained he did that in order to verify that his aides were giving him the correct story on what was going on in his country.

—VOA, Africa Division, briefing paper

Straight talk to Africa from America's Voice evolved over several decades. In early 1962, Edward R. Murrow, director of the United States Information Agency (USIA), traveled throughout Africa and became convinced of the dire need for news and information in a continent just then emerging from colonial rule. The fledgling Africa Division of the Voice, established three years earlier, thus was reinforced because of fresh interest at the top.

I can recall attending meetings of the new division, in my role as a regional editor for Africa in the Worldwide English Division. Our perspectives were quite different. Worldwide English was a global service, with two daily evening programs designed largely to treat world and

U.S. news objectively, with some emphasis on Africa. The new Africa Division, though, focused exclusively on the continent. In its early years, that meant news and programming mainly of a positive nature that would advance USIA information and cultural goals there. The division had a separate English-to-Africa Branch to do so, the only on-air alternative to Worldwide English anywhere in VOA. There was lots of talk in the meetings about covering American educational exchanges in Africa, cultural presentations, United States Information Service (USIS) library openings, and trade fairs. The news about the continent almost invariably was "good" or "official." The idea of probing reportage was virtually nonexistent.

Yet, at century's end, the Africa Division broke the story of the death of a Nigerian dictator and the start of the deadly war between Ethiopia and Eritrea in the Horn of Africa. It focused very early on the HIV/AIDS epidemic. Its broadcasters produced special on-air message services that enabled thousands of family members on the continent to reconnect with their loved ones separated from them by wars or desperate escapes from genocide. How did the division evolve into a respected news and information source about Africa?

A BLEND OF TALENTS

Connie Stephens, former deputy Africa Division chief at VOA, attributes the transformation to recruitment over many years of talented professionals with area expertise.[1] They included

- *Journalists with some knowledge of and interest in Africa.* Among them was Sonja Pace (chapter 4), a tiny, scrappy, no-holds-barred newswoman and war reporter who served in English-to-Africa and later was a foreign correspondent based in Abidjan, Cairo, and Paris before becoming Voice News Division director. Others with previous broadcast or journalistic experience included Barry Maughan, a longtime chief of English-to-Africa; his successor, Rebecca McMenamin, a News Division veteran; Jim Malone, who eventually became assignments editor and national affairs correspondent in the VOA newsroom; and Jennifer Parmalee, a *New York Times* East Africa correspondent who became Horn of Africa Service chief in 2000.

- *Peace Corps volunteers with field experience in Africa.* Stephens herself had served in Niger and learned French and Hausa, a language widely spoken in Niger and northern Nigeria. She came to VOA and was promoted to chief of the Hausa Service before becoming deputy division chief in the early 1990s. Other Peace Corps alumni included Gwen Dillard, Africa Division director at the turn of the century, and founding service chiefs for Hausa David Hofstad and for Swahili David Simonds. Former Peace Corps volunteer David Williams (whom we met in earlier chapters as a VOA foreign correspondent covering the fall of the shah and the hostage crisis in Iran) served as a Nairobi and London correspondent for the Voice and headed the Africa Division in the 1980s.

- *Children of missionaries who had served in Africa.* Steve Lucas, whose parents were American missionaries in West Africa, also later became chief of the Africa Division. Lucas was taught to speak perfect Hausa as a child and regarded the language as his mother tongue. Another missionary youngster and expert on the Congo, Scott Bobb, came to the division and then was assigned as a foreign correspondent in Abidjan and Rio de Janeiro, an assignments editor in the newsroom, and, eventually, News Division director for all of VOA.

- *Scholars specializing in African studies.* Prominent among them were Greg Pirio, a specialist on Angola who headed the Portuguese-to-Africa Service initially and, later, English-to-Africa; Manuel Quaresma, a former priest who also specialized in Portugal's former African colonies; Richard Sigwalt, chief of the Swahili Service and later an Africa regional editor in the newsroom who had done research on eastern Zaire; and division artist-musicologist Leo Sarkisian, whose *Music Time in Africa* was heard throughout the continent by at least two generations of listeners.

- *Linguists or African-born broadcasters with exceptional area knowledge.* Among the most notable over the years were Negussie Mengesha, originally from Ethiopia and the first African-born language service chief who headed VOA Amharic for many years and later was Central Africa Branch chief and division program manager (de facto deputy); Henry Krieger, chief of the French-to-Africa Branch for more than two decades; Neils Lindquist, who came to the division in the 1990s to head Portuguese-to-Africa after having served for some years as Brazilian Branch chief; and Emmanuel Muganda, the first African-born Swahili Service chief.

- *Former USIA foreign service officers with an intense interest in African affairs.* They included Margaret Binda, who had served in Central Africa, later became deputy chief of the French-to-Africa Branch, and eventually rose to division chief; and Harry Heintzen, a former USIA foreign service officer in Morocco and Ethiopia who also became Africa Division chief in the early 1980s and, after that, the architect and director of VOA's international training program (chapter 9).

A GROWING DEMAND

This list, although not nearly complete, samples the range of experience that fueled changes in the Africa Division. In 2002, VOA broadcast in six indigenous African languages: Hausa (spoken by approximately 40 million people in Nigeria and Niger), Swahili (in East and Central Africa); Kinyarwanda-Kirundi (in the Lakes region around and including Rwanda and Burundi), Amharic and Tigrigna (in Ethiopia and Eritrea), and Afan Oromo (in Ethiopia). As it had from the beginning, the division also produced programming in English, French, and Portuguese. These languages of former colonial rulers are widely spoken among educated elites in twenty-two countries in anglophone Africa, seventeen countries in francophone Africa, and five countries in lusophone Africa, which once were Portuguese colonies.

In the 1980s, the growing number of newly hired specialists in the Africa Division began to notice that the commercial news agencies offered only spotty coverage to a continent of nearly fifty nations, if you include Madagascar, Mauritius, the Seychelles, São Tomé and Príncipe, and other offshore island states. Wire services and daily newspapers were cutting costs and closing news bureaus throughout the region.

Driven by Listeners in Need

The programming philosophy of the infant Africa Division also had to change. Listeners were dependent on VOA and other international broadcasters to fill information gaps in a continent where, until the 1990s, nearly all electronic media were state controlled. To be effective, the incoming journalists, scholars, Peace Corps volunteers, and area specialists decided, VOA had to tell it straight—the bad news as well as the good.

Stephens recalls arriving at the Voice's Hausa Service in the mid-1980s after a graduate program in Africa studies at the University of Wisconsin and work managing a USAID literacy program in Niger. Not long after she became Hausa Service chief, a strike erupted in Nigeria.

The service dutifully went about reporting the official version of events, what the Nigerian authorities had to say. "Why not interview the strike leaders?" Stephens asked.[2] The idea was revolutionary at the time and coincided with a similar innovation in the Portuguese-to-Africa Service. It illustrated the awakening of a division that by 2002 had the Voice's largest regional audience—estimated at around 39 million, or four out of ten VOA listeners worldwide.[3]

HOW IT HAPPENED

There were five pillars of the Africa Division's success: (1) credible news reporting from just about anywhere in Africa, (2) the unique presence of an on-air English service in its midst, (3) VOA's improved technical presence in the 1980s and 1990s, (4) innovative public-service, sports, and music programming with popular airshow hosts, and (5) extensive reach, deep into deserts and into the minds of prodemocracy advocates throughout the continent.

Credible News Reporting

The Africa Division had to scramble for accurate news, because of general neglect of the region by others. It did so by training its own reporters in Washington; recruiting a corps of stringers in Africa, which reached a hundred at one time in the 1990s; and making full use of central newsroom correspondents stationed at bureaus in Abidjan, Cairo, Johannesburg, and Nairobi.

Libyan Forces Expelled from Chad

Covering Africa on the scene can be horrendously difficult. On April 5, 1987, VOA Abidjan correspondent Sonja Pace set out from N'Djamena, the capital of Chad, on a week-long trek deep into the Sahara with thirty-six other Western and local journalists. Their mission: to visit a site in the far northern reaches of the country where French-supported Chadian forces with pickup trucks and machine guns had routed Libyan invaders, who were much better equipped. Mu'ammar al-Gadhafi's occupation units had fled and left behind Soviet surface-to-air (SAM-6) missiles for all to inspect. It was one of the decade's most significant military reverses in war-ravaged Africa.[4]

For Pace and her colleagues, it meant seven days in hellish daytime heat, freezing nights sleeping under the stars on the steel platforms of battered trucks, and bumpy rides across dunes (there were few roads on the route north) with reporters groaning and bruised from head to foot. On the second day out, Pace recalls, "we stopped for lunch at a tiny spot in the desert called Ouadi Ouait, where we were shown some Libyan prisoners. But Chadian soldiers did not let us do any interviews. While one of the Libyans tried to speak to me in English, they obviously had been told not to talk with us. However, while the prisoners at least had macaroni to eat, we had to wait patiently while our meal walked by, on all four legs. One hour later, it had been turned into camel stew, of which we all ate relatively little."

The correspondents' Sahara escorts wore the typical headdress of the Goran clan (long scarves wound around the head and face to shield them from the stinging sand, dust, and blistering sun of the desert). Soon, many of the reporters found it expedient to don the same protective outfit. The group finally got its story: the sight, in a sprawling base in the middle of nowhere, of about one-half of the estimated $1 billion worth of Soviet-made equipment destroyed or left behind during the successful three-month Chad army counteroffensive that expelled the Libyans. "The windfall in matériel," Pace reported, "is enough to provide Chad, by World Bank estimates one of the poorest countries in the world, with one of the best-equipped armies on the continent."

The Libyans were still in the air around this vacated installation, however, and two Libyan planes—20,000 feet above—dropped bombs that exploded a mere 300 yards away. All except the TV correspondents dived for cover. The climax of the trip came when the reporters in their bumpy trucks reached the northernmost point of the journey, the oasis of Faya-Largeau (see Pace's account in chapter 4). Residents there said that Libyan soldiers several weeks earlier had simply panicked and fled, before the Chad army retook the occupied outpost without firing a single shot.

Crises in the Lakes Region of Central Africa

The Africa Division also sent reporters from Washington to Africa, and some of them—notably Ferdinand Ferella, Idrissa Dia (French-to-Africa), and Shaka Ssali (English-to-Africa)—became household names in their listening areas and beyond. In Zaire, an official in Kivu Province

"I Don't Know What
Will Happen Later This Night"

Just hours after the plane crash that killed the two Central African chiefs of state, a French-to-Africa staff member was on the phone with a stringer in the Rwandan capital of Kigali, who said: "There are killings going on." It was the first word of the genocide to come. Minutes later, Ferdinand Ferella, who had the home phone number of the first African female prime minister, Agathe Uwinlingiyimana of Rwanda, interviewed her at her Kigali home from his Washington office (she would not go on the air). She said: "It's frightening out there [in the streets]. I don't know what will happen later this night."

Before dawn, Ferella recalls, the Hutu prime minister (who was in danger because she had cooperated with the rival Tutsis) escaped from her home by climbing a wall into the United Nations compound next door. The Hutu-led killers, however, surrounded the compound and demanded that the UN turn over the prime minister and her husband to them for questioning. When a Belgian UN peacekeeper refused, he was shot and killed on the spot. The terrorists then entered the premises and slaughtered Uwinlingiyimana and her husband.

---

told Ferella that residents used their scarce radio batteries for two hours each evening to listen to VOA. In nearby Masisi, one person was designated by the community to make notes on VOA French evening news and put it on a blackboard for all to see.[5] Ferella, Dia, and Ssali covered or conducted one-on-one interviews with African leaders and opposition figures during months of horrible bloodletting in Central Africa in 1994.

On April 6 of that year, a plane crash that killed the presidents of Rwanda and Burundi set off the world's most deadly mass killings since the Cambodian holocaust of the 1970s. Hutu extremists in Rwanda, many wielding machetes, murdered up to 800,000 of their Tutsi compatriots, along with moderate Hutus, Catholic priests, and ten Belgian United Nations peacekeepers. They were spurred on by the Hutu extremist hate broadcaster, Radio des Milles Collines.

Ferella, within days, was off to Rwanda. He joined a small contingent of international reporters who spent time in the bush with the resisting

"And Yes, Bodies that Wait for Justice"

VOA's Johannesburg bureau chief at the time was Alex Belida. His eye-witness account of a second trip to Rwanda that summer reflects the horror of Central Africa in the mid-1990s:

> I have returned to Nyarubuye, a small church parish town in the remote countryside of eastern Rwanda, a place I visited three months ago and where I saw the most horrible thing I have ever seen: evidence of a massacre that had occurred in the middle of April, over five hundred bodies in a churchyard, in the church itself, in school buildings, administration buildings, workshops. And now, three months later, I can tell you that nothing has changed—except the corpses are now in an advanced state of decomposition. Many are just piles of sun-bleached bones, tattered clothing still clinging to the remains. As before in the village of Nyarubuye, there is not a trace of any population. It is an abandoned place.
>
> But will it be forgotten? We have heard that some think this should be preserved, perhaps as a place to remember the slaughter that took place in Rwanda in April, the slaughter of the ethnic Tutsi and moderate Hutus by Hutu extremists. It's also possible, it's suggested to us, that the new government—the Tutsi-installed government in Kigali that won the civil war that began with this terrible bloodshed—may want to pre-serve this site, possibly as a place where forensic experts can gather evidence for their proposed war crimes trials of those responsible for the slaughter. But that is an indefinite time from now. For the moment, the wind blows over this aban-doned site. Rusting gates creak. Birds sing and then peck at the bodies, bodies that wait for that last measure of dignity that is awarded mankind in the form of a decent burial. And yes, bodies that wait for justice.*

Speaking at a communications conference in Finland three days after Belida filed that report, VOA director Geoffrey Cowan observed how international public-service broadcasters uniquely provide services in local languages during humanitarian disasters such as the genocide in Rwanda and its aftermath:

> To take a particularly stark example, international commercial news services are not reaching and have no economic incentive

to reach the hundreds of thousands of men, women, and children in the camps of Goma and the streets of Kigali. That audience has no access to television, and the refugees have no money to spend on the goods and services that advertise on commercial carriers. Nonetheless, the people of central Africa have a desperate need for news and information, about nutrition, weather, the location of relief services, and the threats or opportunities offered [them]. They *can* get that information from radio.†

Cowan noted that the Rwanda tragedy had demonstrated anew the power of hate radio to shape events. "But in the hands of responsible international public broadcasters," he added, "radio has an equal capacity to serve as a voice of sanity, to deliver accurate information, even to save lives."

*Alex Belida, "Rwanda: Massacre Revisited," VOA correspondent report, September 4, 1994.
†Geoffrey L. Cowan, "The Role of International Public Broadcasters in Shaping the Global Information Marketplace" (address presented at the twenty-fifth annual conference of the Institute of International Communications, Tampere, Finland, September 7, 1994), 5.

Tutsi-led Rwandan Patriotic Front (RPF) forces. Ferella's coverage lasted from late April until June 1994. In July, a substantial VOA team returned to cover the flight of refugees from Rwanda: newsroom correspondents Sonja Pace and Larry James from Paris, and Ferella, Dia, Ssali, and Kay Maddux from the Africa Division.[6]

In the refugee exodus, nearly half of the 8 million Rwandans fled their homes, many of them headed for neighboring eastern Zaire (later to be known as the Democratic Republic of Congo, or DRC). In July, the Tutsi-dominated RPF forced the genocidal Hutu leaders from positions of power in the capital city of Kigali. As a result, a second wave of largely militia-led Hutu refugees also fled to Zaire, mixing uneasily with Tutsis already in squalid refugee camps that had sprung up overnight around Goma and other border cities. Amid all this chaos, daily killings occurred in neighboring Burundi, which also had Hutu and Tutsi populations.

Ferella and Dia were on the scene, filing daily and around the clock from Central African locations and Kinshasa, the capital of Zaire. James joined them and e-mailed back: "The recent trip to Africa was a welcome reminder of the kind of impact VOA can make. The French Service will be happy to know they are an important force in eastern Zaire and in Rwanda. As an example of their reach, the hotel staff in Goma seemed truly excited to have someone from VOA staying with them. When I asked for a room for Ferdinand Ferella, they seemed totally starstruck and promised to make room for him even though space was very scarce."[7] Dia drew similar praise.

Family Reunifications on a Mass Scale

The broadcast services of the Africa Division, as its director, Gwen Dillard, explained, "had twin responsibilities in reporting ethnic tensions: to be restrained, and to understand and explain to our listeners the meaning of what was happening."[8] In addition to its reportage, the division had been doing public-service broadcasting for some time. English-to-Africa host Ted Roberts had developed a program called *Missing Link*, recorded messages of refugees in Liberia, Sierra Leone, and other West African countries, which could be aired to help them find lost relatives. The Amharic Service, under Negussie Mengesha's leadership, sponsored a fund-raising drive in Washington in the mid-1980s to provide more than $40,000 for famine relief in Ethiopia, much of it for refugees. In the 1990s, as Cowan suggested, the focus was on Central Africa, where hundreds of thousands of refugees who did not speak English or other European languages desperately sought unbiased news and information. After an extensive search, the Africa Division in the summer of 1996 found six speakers of Kinyarwanda-Kirundi, spoken widely in the Lakes region by many of the dispossessed refugees in the jungles and villages of eastern Zaire. Only two of the new broadcasters had journalistic experience; the division trained the four others. The Kinyarwanda-Kirundi Service began broadcasting on July 16, 1996, made possible by a USAID grant.

The new staff, led by Negussie Mengesha and Etienne Karekezi, knew instinctively that the latest news was vital to thousands of families dislocated after the massacre in Rwanda and the civil war in eastern Zaire. They were hungry for information because thousands of children had been separated from their parents in the desperate flight for their lives. Husbands and wives, brothers and sisters also were unaccounted for. Almost immediately, Negussie and the staff set up a humanitarian hotline similar to Roberts's *Missing Link*. Callers' brief telephone messages inquiring about the whereabouts of family members were recorded in Washington and broadcast back to Central Africa. The messages always included information about where those delivering them were now located.

The results were impressive. Within a year, more than 3,000 families were reunited, and the program was expanded to a full hour on weekends. Later, when the United Nations was trying to locate and regroup an estimated 150,000 Rwandans scattered or hiding in the jungles of eastern Zaire to offer them a way home, the new Kinyarwanda-Kirundi Service broadcast public-service announcements about where international feeding stations were located and even where transportation back to Rwanda was available. The Food and Agriculture Organization (FAO), the International Committee of the Red Cross (ICRC), and the office of the United Nations High Commissioner for Refugees (UNHCR) thanked VOA for broadcasting this lifesaving information. The international agencies also noted a special Harvard University health series adapted on VOA to help refugees cope with the trauma of their unimaginable loss—of loved ones, of homes, and of a life of hope.[9]

The return of the refugees to Rwanda drew correspondent Doug Roberts back to Africa for the first time in more than twenty years; his first overseas assignment had been Abidjan. This time, he witnessed and described an exodus of biblical proportions: "The refugees—men, women, and children, most of them barefoot, meager belongings piled on their heads—plodded along with remarkable discipline and in an eerie silence, broken only by the wailing of infants strapped to their mothers' backs." Their column stretched for thirteen miles or more, Roberts noted. UNHCR spokesman Ray Wilkinson told him: "It almost seemed that the whole of Africa was on that road."[10]

Scott Stearns, originally with English-to-Africa, was named the newsroom's Nairobi bureau chief in the mid-1990s and became one of the most energetic, well-informed young VOA correspondents at a time when broadcasts to Africa were expanding. Scott won the VOA Cowan Award for Humanitarian Reporting in the late 1990s.[11] He specialized in coverage of the forced migrations that plagued the Lakes region in the mid-1990s: refugee crises affecting at least five nations and the remarkably swift drive of Congolese rebels from the eastern part of the sprawling country westward toward the capital of Kinshasa. Stearns, on March 14, 1997, reported visiting the infamous "field of death" at Musenge, Zaire, near the Rwandan border. He and an Associated Press correspondent found more than a hundred corpses there. "The scene is a jumble of skulls, feet and flies," Stearns reported. "Around the bodies are Rwandan identity cards, a few Rwandan Bibles, and food bags distributed by the United Nations."[12] Meanwhile, rebel forces were advancing swiftly to the west in Zaire. This led to the fall of Zaire's dictator, Mobutu Sese Seko, in May 1997 after a corrupt, thirty-year reign.

I remember May 17, when rebel leader Laurent Kabila's forces entered Kinshasa, and Mobutu fled. Ferella was in the capital city and filed eyewitness live reportage into an expanded French-to-Africa broadcast produced in Washington. Acting partly on a tip from Ferella, the Africa Division put French on the air earlier than usual that Saturday, doubling its airtime to nearly five hours throughout the day. French-to-Africa Branch hosts went to Ferella often for live updates. In between news segments, the intrepid reporter then raced to the studios of a relatively new VOA affiliate, independent radio station Raga-FM, and provided Kinshasa citizens with much the same information he had just supplied to Voice listeners throughout French-speaking Africa. That inevitably enhanced VOA's reputation in the Zairean capital; its special transmissions included appeals for calm by Kabila, which helped stabilize a volatile situation.

A Triumph for Democracy

As West African newspaper editor Ken Best had said, if democracy could take root in South Africa, where it once seemed impossible, "everything else is within the realm of the possible." On four days in April 1994, the serpentine lines of voters queuing up in South Africa to exercise their franchise for the first time in their lives added up to an extraordinarily moving sight. The peaceful transition there very likely prevented a gigantic race war between African political parties and the apartheid regime. The election provided the venue for the largest multilingual overseas remote ever produced by the Africa Division.

The division broadcast several extended live specials throughout the election and inauguration of Nelson Mandela. It seemed to have reporters everywhere in South Africa:

- In the black township of Soweto near Johannesburg, stronghold of the victorious African National Congress

- In the beautiful southern city of Cape Town, where former president of the Nationalist Party F. W. de Klerk won the most votes in this first all-race election
- In the coastal city of Durban in eastern Natal Province, which contains South Africa's largest Zulu and Indian populations

Some voters, shaded from the sun by polka-dot umbrellas, had to wait as long as twelve hours in Durban to cast their ballots. One elderly woman told VOA English-to-Africa reporter Deborah Block that it was worth the wait because "it is worth our freedom." Aliyu Mustafa of the Hausa Service reported that some voter queues in Cape Town were as long as two miles and that they "looked like a rainbow of humanity—blacks, whites, and coloreds."[13]

The Struggle for Credibility Back at America's Voice

By the mid-1990s, twenty African states were experimenting with pluralist forms of government. In May 2000, Nigeria elected a civilian president, Olusegun Obasanjo, after sixteen years of military rule. But in much of the continent, the trend was the other way. The elected leaders of Kenya and Zimbabwe turned increasingly authoritarian as the century ended. Politics in Ethiopia confronted the new Broadcasting Board of Governors back in Washington—an early test of its ability to shield the Voice from intense political pressure. How strong was its legally mandated firewall, designed to protect VOA's ability "to tell it straight?"[14]

In Addis Ababa, the Communist government of Haile Mengistu Mariam was ousted in May 1991. Subsequently, a succession of U.S. ambassadors there complained about VOA's broadcasts in Amharic, established nearly a decade earlier. Pressured by the new regime, which was dominated by the Ethiopian People's Revolutionary Democratic Front (EPRDF), embassy aides sent in a barrage of cables critical of the Amharic Service, contending that it unduly focused on opposition views. In mid-1994, the American embassy recommended that VOA Amharic be closed, maintaining that it had outlived its usefulness in the post–Cold War period.

The new government in Ethiopia was trying to establish democracy, the embassy said, and the Ethiopian press was relatively free—that was its assessment—while VOA was "biased and unhelpful." Moreover, according to the embassy, Amharic was the mother tongue of only about

30 percent of the population of Ethiopia. When VOA broadcast in that language, the mission maintained, it subconsciously reflected a tilt toward the Amharas when, in fact, there were other groups such as the Tigreans and the Oromos. The American ambassador, however, simply didn't want *any* broadcasts to Ethiopia; he contended that the Voice might better use its shrinking resources on other projects.

VOA Amharic, like other Africa Division services of the 1990s, was simply reporting the truth. But sometimes the truth was not what the government in Ethiopia wanted to hear. For example, the regime allowed opposition leaders from abroad to return home in December 1994 for a peace and reconciliation conference, and they were promptly picked up at the airport by security police upon entering the country. Five of them were clapped into jail. That was reported by VOA, which was by far the leading international broadcaster in Ethiopia at the time. Surveys indicated that 28 percent of the adult population tuned in at least once a week to the Voice, more than 95 percent of that number to the Amharic Service.

If VOA were to follow the embassy's advice, it would—in effect—go "dark" in the strategic Horn of Africa, that area at the mouth of the Red Sea that encompasses Ethiopia, Somalia, Eritrea, Djibouti, and eastern Sudan. A serious struggle over the fate of the Amharic Service ensued. It lasted for more than a year and a half. The program review staff contracted independent linguists to conduct a six-month study of the service's programming content. They found it to be accurate, balanced, and fair. In the fall of 1995, Amharic Service chief Negussie Mengesha proposed a trip to Ethiopia, and the embassy in Addis Ababa refused to clear it. Mengesha visited neighboring countries and interviewed the chiefs of state of both Eritrea and Sudan, and these interviews were broadcast by VOA's Amharic, Arabic, and English Services.

The embassy in Addis Ababa was uncharacteristically silent after that. It was clear that something was up. Then, in early 1996, the State Department recommended that all forty-seven VOA language services be retained, except Amharic. In rapid succession, the Africa area office of USIA, the National Security Council (NSC), and the House appropriations committee dealing with Africa all called for the termination of the service. The U.S. embassy in Addis Ababa had done a superb job of lobbying. It was tightening the noose and closing in for the kill.

The Broadcasting Board of Governors called a meeting of its subcommittee on Africa for February 6, 1996, to discuss the future of the

Amharic Service. VOA director Cowan set about gathering facts and data. He determined that the Amharic staff had two female broadcasters with unique skills: Tizita Belachew spoke Afan Oromo, and Adanech Fessehaye knew Tigrean. Why not restructure the service, retaining a half hour a day in Amharic (reduced from an hour) and introducing two fifteen-minute programs in the two other languages? Thus the Horn of Africa Service would be born; VOA would stay on the air with exactly the same amount of airtime to Ethiopia, and Tigreans in neighboring Eritrea would benefit as well.

Cowan worked closely with the board in constructing the agenda for the meeting. He suggested bringing all the parties into the room at the same time, to discuss the issues. The fierce critics of the Amharic Service would have their say; Mengesha, smooth and diplomatically persuasive as a latter-day Anwar Sadat, and Veda Wilson, the hard-as-nails Africa Division chief and USIA foreign service officer, would have theirs. The meeting was set. The service's critics were warmly welcomed by Cowan and ushered into the hearing room. They were surprised to see Wilson and Mengesha, smiling, sitting at a conference table directly opposite them.

The VOA director began the testimony calmly and dispassionately. Cowan presented a perfectly balanced list of pros and cons: why the service should be closed, why it should stay open, and how it might be restructured as a compromise to meet some of the objections of its opponents. The NSC and congressional representatives were joined by the Africa area director of USIA for the crucial session. All three of them seemed caught off-guard by having to testify against a division and a service whose chiefs sat right across from them. No harsh criticisms were uttered (unlike the countless cables from Addis Ababa). The opponents advocated closing the service largely on the grounds that it would save money and that it was dominated by Amharas.

Mengesha was calm and professorial, citing his own commitment and that of the staff to accurate, honest reporting. He noted that the EPRDF government in Addis Ababa had refused ever to grant an interview to VOA and had on three occasions blocked him from entering the country by denying him visas. Frank Cummins followed with a summary of the independent program-review findings, which affirmed the service's objectivity. Then Cowan asked Wilson to outline how the Voice might preserve a presence in the region by establishing a three-language Horn of Africa Service. Wilson was crisp, direct, no-nonsense, with fire in her eyes. Somewhat meekly, both the congressional aide and the NSC representative said that they might "live with" the Horn of Africa plan.

What did the board think? Chairman David Burke zeroed in on the central question: What kind of regime does Ethiopia have, and is there a value to the United States in reaching its people? He had been poring over an information packet prepared by Cowan's office and pulled out a press release just faxed in that morning by the Committee to Protect Journalists, based in New York City. The CPJ urged the retention of the Amharic Service because between 1993 and 1995, the Ethiopian government had jailed a hundred journalists, more than any other nation in Africa.

"It doesn't sound like a very free country to me," Burke remarked. He then reminded the gathering that the board has a statutory responsibility to act as a firewall to protect U.S. international broadcasters from—among other things—the whims of those in the foreign affairs community who might wish to placate governments to which they were accredited. The subcommittee approved the compromise. The reconstituted Horn of Africa Service began broadcasting in Amharic, Afan Oromo, and Tigrigna in July 1996.[15]

On-Air English Service

Sonja Pace—an alumna of the Africa Division, a News Division chief, and a foreign correspondent—said she could observe the beginnings of improvement in Africa Division journalistic capabilities as early as 1980 to 1985, when she worked there for a time. She credits English-to-Africa as being the "news driver" of the division, particularly its energetic professional broadcast chief of many years, Barry Maughan.[16]

As we have seen, other services contributed much to VOA Africa reportage, notably the French-to-Africa Branch through the efforts of Ferdinand Ferella, Idrissa Dia, and Idrissa Fall. Mimi Sebhatu of the Horn of Africa Service, while on a ridge near the village of Zalambassa overlooking the arid plains straddling the Ethiopian–Eritrean border in 1998, saw flashes of orange flame and puffs of tank-blown dust. This signaled the start of a terrible two-year war between the two northeastern Africa neighbors, which cost tens of thousands of lives. Sebhatu's tip to the newsroom in Washington enabled VOA to report the outbreak of the conflict before any other news organization.[17]

But English-to-Africa had a distinct advantage. It operated in the lingua franca of the division and the Voice, and its materials—including reports from a dozen stringers in the field as well as correspondents—were instantly available to all in the Africa Division and to the central newsroom. It benefited from, and shared scoops with, the other Africa services at the daily division 9:00 A.M. coverage planning meeting. That session was a daily tutorial on contemporary African affairs.

Improved Technical Reach

The pioneering work done by VOA engineers in the vast continent is described in chapter 5, but one note is worth adding: placement of VOA programs on African radio stations. The field-placement service, headed for many years by Marilyn Silvey, saw to it that hundreds of tapes monthly were shipped to USIS posts throughout Africa for use on local radio stations. Silvey's creativity led to the development of many features on health, hygiene, nutrition, and, very early on, HIV/AIDS. She also packaged programs already aired by the division services for replay on African state radios.

Division chief David Williams made a trip to Africa in 1987 and noticed that USIS posts were beginning to receive video materials via satellite from Worldnet Television in Washington. These satellite feeds had unused audio subcarriers capable of carrying VOA field services features, if only the Voice could use this service. When he returned to Washington, Williams floated a proposal to use the subcarriers. Archivist (and later affiliate relations satellite manager) Barbara Schiele and Williams worked together to enable the Africa Division initially to send five hours a week of audio material via this channel (infinitely more efficient than shipping tapes). Within three years, VOA was transmitting more than 1,200 hours of programming weekly this way to posts and radio stations around the world via TV subcarrier channels.

Innovative Public-Service, Sports, and Music Programming

Thanks largely to the persuasive skills of Greg Pirio and Gwen Dillard, grants from USAID sources enabled the Africa Division to create a number of new public-service and current affairs programs in the 1990s:[18]

- Health programming included radio dramas on family health and public-service announcements on inoculation campaigns to assist

Rotary International and AID in their campaign to eradicate polio by 2005.

- Portuguese-to-Africa broadcasts to Angola were enriched and expanded, including a VOA news bureau in the capital city, Luanda, with daily media training there of local station managers and journalists.[19]
- A Washington conference on child survival was held in April 1998, which brought together broadcasters of VOA, the BBC, Radio France International, and others to share ideas on radio programming to help children in developing countries, especially in Africa.

The Carnegie Corporation gave the Africa Division a two-year grant in the 1990s to send English- and French-speaking broadcasters to report from Rwanda, Burundi, and South Africa on conflict-resolution efforts in those countries.

In 2001, Africa Division director Gwen Dillard observed that new technologies are bringing broadcasters and listeners closer together in the age of globalization. Speaking at a Howard University symposium, Dillard said: "We matter to Africa, and in ways the commercial media do not . . . we are using multimedia to try to understand our listeners, find the best ways through call-ins and interactive programs of keeping our audience in touch with us, and keeping us in touch with our audience. We have to hear their voices as much as they hear our voices."[20]

English-to-Africa chief Barry Maughan reflected the rhythms of a young Africa in broadcasts of his weekday sports program, which covered the Pan-African Games, Africans at the summer Olympics, and world soccer competitions. Maughan was known throughout the continent as the "Emperor," a moniker he developed in connection with this fast-paced, conversational daily program segment. It was a popular feature of the service's evening program, *Africa World Tonight*.

French-to-Africa, inspired by Henry Krieger and Dillard and headed by veteran VOA broadcaster Claude Porsella at the turn of the century, each evening put together a potpourri of news and information in a fresh two-hour program, *Le Monde aujourd'hui* (The World Today). It was among the most appealing programs produced at the Voice, attractively packaging two hours of American, African, and international news and information, including roundups of editorial opinion, features, and much music.

The Africa Division had and has a wealth of music-show personalities who are widely known in the continent, especially to English- and

French-speaking listeners. Among them are Roger Guy Folly, Leo Sarkisian, Rita Rochelle, and Georges Collinet (chapter 13).

Extensive Reach, Deep into Deserts and into Minds

Among other well-known on-air personalities was the Hausa Service's Steve Lucas, who later headed the Africa Division. Lucas, you'll recall, was the son of American missionaries in Nigeria, but he spoke Hausa as his mother tongue because he had been taught it as a child by one of their associates "up country" in West Africa. After he joined VOA in the 1980s, Lucas broadcast in the language every day. He became known in the region as the "white Hausa."

Years later, Lucas traveled to Africa and went by Land Rover to arid northern Nigeria. He and a driver stopped several hundred miles north of the Atlantic coast at an isolated gas station to fill up. It was in the middle of nowhere. There was a little lad offering to sell a sack of boiled peanuts on the side of the road, and Lucas decided to make a purchase. You don't do that in West Africa, however, without bargaining. So Lucas began to haggle. The little boy had only to hear a word or two. He immediately began to whistle the distinctive opening signature tune of the Voice of America Hausa Service!

One of Lucas's many acquaintances in Africa was President Ousmane Mahamane of Niger, the country just to the west and north of Nigeria. Lucas first met Mahamane when the president was still an underground opposition leader; Niger had been ruled by a military regime for much of the time after gaining independence from France in the 1960s until the first free elections in the early 1990s. The regal, turbaned Mahamane visited Washington shortly after taking office and insisted on visiting the Voice and seeing Lucas. He credited VOA and the other international broadcasters with bringing democracy to his country, both by reporting elections and the electoral process elsewhere and by providing education on community building and the rule of law in Hausa and French to his nation of 6 million people. "You nurtured the seeds of change," he told us.

Mahamane recounted how his tiny political opposition group, partly because of international broadcasts, had become a national movement in Niger and a majority party practically overnight.[21] "It reminded us," I wrote at the time, "of what Librarian of Congress James Billington recently told a Washington audience. 'Democracy,' he said, 'is a fire in the minds of men. That fire feeds on constant communication, back and forth, a sharing of information, ideas, skills and experience.'" It reminded us, as well, of one of the least-noticed phenomena of the 1990s, the growth of independent electronic media throughout Africa.

No Slaking That Thirst for the Straight Story

From the beginning of 1993 to September 1994, the number of private, commercial stations between Cairo and Cape Town increased from two to more than fifty. It was an astonishing surge, doubtless traceable in part to the revolutions in Eastern Europe described earlier. Many of the new independent radio enterprises—FM outlets from South Africa to Uganda to Ghana to Mozambique to Mauritius—immediately wanted to become VOA affiliates. The democratic revolution on the continent seemed to stall in the 1990s, a victim of wars, genocide, and disease.[22] But the media revolution, interactive radio, and thirst for radio did not. English-to-Africa introduced a radio–television call-in show with expert guests at the dawn of the twenty-first century. Topics included frank discussions and debates about politics, conflict resolution, and health, including HIV/AIDS. The program immediately attracted dozens of calls and e-mail queries from listeners and television viewers throughout the continent. Its host: Shaka Ssali. Its name: *Straight Talk, Africa.*

12

On Language

WORDS AND THEIR STORIES

Let's talk ballpark figures: a billion babes and dudes under the
sun have what it takes to chew the fat in English.
—Barry Newman, "World Speaks English,
Often None Too Well"

About a thousand million people can speak English.
—VOA, *Special English Word Book*

In early October 1991, Prince Norodom Ranaridh of Cambodia visited
the Voice of America. He met with Director Chase Untermeyer. "If I
am speaking English to you today," he said, "it is due to the VOA." The
prince explained that he had been a faithful listener to Special English
since arriving in exile in Thailand eight years earlier. He added that
he had to learn the language to work with leaders and staff in the
Association of Southeast Asian Nations (ASEAN).[1]

To listeners in much of the world, learning English is a daunting task
because it is a fluid, constantly changing language. It is, Ralph Waldo
Emerson said, "the sea which receives tributaries from every region under
heaven." Among audiences for whom English is a second language, that
vast ocean—spoken and written English—has to be pure and clean.
Broadcasts in the language must be clear, understandable, and free of
idioms and slang. So must VOA's centrally produced English scripts,
which often are the basis for adaptation by twoscore or more other language services for their programs. Beyond that, some services addressing
largely rural audiences with limited or no education must invent words
or phrases to convey new concepts in the twenty-first-century world.

Precision in language matters—in diplomacy and in international broadcasting. You might call it "straight talk, world." Or, to be precise, "straight talk as possible, world."

SPECIAL ENGLISH

What is Special English? As noted in chapter 1, it has a limited vocabulary that has grown over the years to about 1,500 words. It is written in short sentences that contain only one idea. No idioms are used, and Special English is spoken at a slower pace, about two-thirds the speed of standard English in most VOA broadcasts.[2] A briefing paper written in Special English says: "We speak more slowly. Our sentences are shorter. Our words are simpler. But the powerful ideas we communicate are understood. That is why Special English is so popular with listeners around the world."[3]

Special English was conceived in 1959. Program Manager Barry Zorthian remembers that it was developed both to overcome jamming and to ease normal shortwave listening. "A scientific advisory committee," Zorthian said, "urged us to undertake some kind of program that would make it easier to understand a broadcast."[4]

VOA director Henry Loomis and Zorthian discussed how to use radio to open up a wider world to people who were just beginning to speak English. The idea was not to teach the language but to inform listeners. English has a vocabulary of 250,000 words, and VOA managers consulted specialists in universities about the best way to create a simplified vocabulary for broadcast. The response was unanimous: "Don't try it. You'll look foolish."

Zorthian looked around for a skilled young writer who might take it on anyway. He decided on Richard L. (Dick) Borden, a former NBC producer who had come to VOA just a few years earlier.[5] Soon afterward, Borden was joined by a scholar of languages and broadcaster on loan from the BBC, René Quinnault. They decided that this experimental broadcast English should be limited to 1,200 to 1,300 words; be joined in short, simple sentences; and be spoken slowly and carefully.

"Very rapidly what we came to," Borden later recalled, "was to study the scripts of VOA newscasts and other features, other types of broadcasts, and the frequency with which words were used at the time. Many of those words, of course, are current in ordinary, everyday English, but many of them are unique to the information business. . . . In a matter of weeks, we developed a very tentative list of words that might be used."[6]

What to call it? Short English, Basic English, Simple English, American English? None of these names would work. All seemed to suggest that the program was designed for a limited audience or for students, rather than a larger audience of people who simply wanted to be informed. In creating the vocabulary lists, and in conversations with announcers, producers, and managers, the idea of a "different" English came to the fore. It became known as "special English." The label took hold, Borden recalled, almost by default—"for want of something better."

The day of reckoning came. It was Monday, October 19, 1959. Borden had recruited Paul Parks, a barrel-chested announcer with a voice like thunder, to deliver the first ten-minute newscast. "And so, on that fateful day," Borden said later,

> with our hearts in our mouths, we ventured into a VOA studio and . . . on the air we went. I believe it was one or two o'clock in the afternoon, in a broadcast beamed to Europe, the Middle East, and Africa, in what would be their evening hours. I wish I could reproduce that very first broadcast that Paul Parks voiced. . . . What I do vividly recall is that he went on the air with the opening words, "This is the Voice of America broadcasting in Special English." With no more fanfare than that, we were on our way![7]

The first reaction from abroad was immediate and unflattering. The American embassy in Manila led the charge. "Do not beam any of your programs to the Philippines," it warned. "People here speak English. Your programs would be demeaning, an insult." There were similar criticisms, initially, from Africa.

But soon the trend reversed. Worldwide English Division chief Len Reed said it became clear that VOA Special English had a much larger audience of admirers than at first believed. "The thousands of testimonials over the years," former VOA news editor Mark Lewis observed at the end of the century, "show that the program unquestionably has assisted in the expansion and nurture of English as an international language."[8]

Hard-charging Zorthian wanted to build on the early success of the program. He persuaded Hal Berman, a former VOA News chief who was a victim of the McCarthy era, to return in 1961 to direct the Special English newscast operation. Only a few months after Berman arrived, he

WORDS AND THEIR STORIES,
AND A DOLLOP OF AMERICAN HISTORY

Hal Berman, known by some as the "father of Special English," illustrated the concept in a *Words and Their Stories* script on the use of the words "buffalo" and "bulldoze" in contemporary American politics:

> Long before the first Europeans arrived in the New World, a strange animal lived on the rich grasses of the western plains. He looked like some kind of water buffalo. But he had a big hump on his back like a camel. And he had hair like a lion. In 1850, estimates say twenty million buffalo lived on the open plains of the west. They were powerful creatures that ran with great speed. American Indians hunted them for food and clothing. As white settlers moved west, they began to hunt the animals for skins to sell in eastern markets.
>
> The American buffaloes could run at the speed of almost seventy-five kilometers (nearly fifty miles) an hour. It was not easy to get close to them to shoot. Sometimes the hunters were completely unsuccessful in killing any of the animals. They were "buffaloed" by these powerful, speedy creatures who were so hard to control. The expression "to buffalo" soon became part of the speech of the American West. It meant to make someone helpless, to trick them. The meaning is almost the same today.
>
> The expression "to bulldoze" also means to make someone helpless. The term most often is used to describe a powerful machine designed to clear away trees and other big objects. Nothing much can stop it. Americans still use the expression "to bulldoze" but mainly in political situations. For example, a newspaper might comment that a bill that was not popular passed in Congress because the supporters bulldozed the opposition. The force of the supporters' arguments, or perhaps some legislative tricks, buffaloed the opponents.*

*Hal Berman, "Special English Words and Their Stories no. 2368—To Buffalo," April 22, 2001.

was instructed to begin broadcasting features in Special English, an entirely different dimension than news. The first feature was an adaptation of Nathaniel Hawthorne's classic short story "Feathertop." Much to the surprise of its producers, it won an honorable mention in the 1962

Ohio State University programming awards for the best program produced that year in the U.S. broadcasting industry.[9]

It was possible, VOA Special English writers discovered, to convey in vivid colors American short stories such as Stephen Crane's "Red Badge of Courage." That was especially the case in the hands of a master radio storyteller like Walter Guthrie: "As the landscape changed from brown to green, the army slowly awakened. It turned its eyes upon the roads. A narrow river lay at the army's feet. At night, when the stream became black, one could see clear across it. One could see the enemy campfires, red in the distant hills."[10]

In another Special English program series, *Space and Man*, narrator Jack Moyles spoke of how limited the knowledge of the universe used to be before the invention of the telescope. Jack's description, in conversational, storytelling style, was Genesis-like in its simplicity: "For thousands of years the universe seemed so very small to man. He knew only what he could see with his eyes. The Earth. The Sun and Moon. And about five thousand stars. That was the limit of the universe he could see."[11] Over the years, Special English features have informed listeners about life in America and developments in agriculture, literature, science, film, the arts, and history. Titles included *The Making of a Nation, People in America, Science in the News, Environment Report, Agriculture Report, American Short Stories, American Mosaic, In the News* (an explanation of terms such as "gross domestic product" and "Dow Jones industrial average"), and *Words and Their Stories* (a lighthearted survey of the origins of American English words and phrases).

Another longtime chief of Special English, Frank Beardsley, later created a minidrama series, *Tuning in the USA*. It was designed to enhance the conversational skills of listeners who were just starting to learn English. It was a joint project with the publisher Maxwell-Macmillan, which began distributing books to be used at the same time as Special English broadcast by VOA as early as the 1960s. "Special English programs," Beardsley wrote in the *Washington Post*, "are especially popular in Africa and China. Our listeners tend to be young adults interested in developing English language skills for educational and professional advancement."[12]

It wasn't designed to teach, but since it went on the air, Special English has turned out to be a university of the airwaves for millions:

- A Polish professor in Warsaw produced an English textbook and cassette with excerpts from scripts and tapes of Special English programs.

- A company in Japan used Special English news for a correspondence course in English. Students tested before and after the course showed a dramatic improvement in their understanding of spoken English.
- Peace Corps volunteers in Russia, Ukraine, and Central America have requested Special English books to help them in English teaching.
- An Italian textbook author included Special English scripts in an anthology of English literature to be used in Italian secondary schools.
- A Nigerian writer who has been listening to Special English for more than twenty years said it was "the ideal language for shortwave reception because its slower speed and clear pronunciation ensure that words are not lost." Similar sentiments were registered by high-school students and young people in Ethiopia and Zambia.
- Scripts on the history of medicine in Special English were used as a teaching tool at Beijing Medical College and Jiangxi Medical College in the People's Republic of China.
- Special English sent tapes and scripts to professors who teach at several Chinese universities. One professor wrote back that the materials were "more precious than diamonds to me."[13]

As the twenty-first century began, Special English was on the air for more than twenty hours a week to every region of the world. Its logo was a smiling tortoise wearing earphones with an antenna and carrying a transistor radio on its back. "Of course," a teacher in the Philippines wrote, "the slower speed helps very much. People who learn a foreign language need more time to process the words." How did this experiment of 1959 actually affect the lives of listeners? Dobrin Tztozkov of Sofia, Bulgaria, wrote:

> The sounds of Special English fill my room every morning when I wake up and raise the curtains. Your program has become an inseparable part of our daily life—a unique window into the world, a model of clear, exact, and straightforward language, a never failing source of hope, confidence and joy. You enrich the mind with your historical, social and science programs. People often ask me: "Where and when did you and your family learn so much about mankind, earth, space?" My answer is VOA Special English. Thank you![14]

"AN ODE TO SPECIAL ENGLISH"

Even the most polished users of English are avid followers of the Voice's unique form of the language. A. V. B. Menon of Coimbatore, Tamil Nadu, India, was listening early in this century to a broadcast history of Special English and dedicated his poem "An Ode to Special English" to pioneer creators Barry Zorthian and Richard Borden:

> Hail, Thee, Special English!
> Thou art a virgin maiden,
> Uncorrupted, simple, easy.
> Ye ring a familiar tone
> To one and all, learned and wise,
> As much to the uninitiated;
> Simple is beautiful,
> No frills, no twists, nor pretensions.
> Ye wind your way to the heart,
> To strike a familiar chord.
> It's neither the King's nor the Queen's,
> But that of very common folk;
> It is a symphony in prose,
> Long live Special English!*

*A. V. B. Menon to Special English Branch, June 30, 2001.

Special English can seem to be ubiquitous. It is heard in the mornings, in the evenings, and sometimes throughout entire neighborhoods. After a trip to southwestern China, Warren Kozak of the *Washington Post* wrote: "It was a lovely, warm evening, and my wife and I decided to take a stroll in Chengdu, the capital of Szechuan Province. As we walked past the card games under the street lamps and the old people watching their grandchildren, we heard coming from every window a newscast, spoken very slowly in English. It was coming from the Voice of America, and you could walk the length of the street without missing any of it."[15]

WORDS MATTER, IN DIPLOMACY AND INTERNATIONAL BROADCASTING

As Special English illustrates, words matter. Words have power. In VOA language services, translating English scripts for broadcast in foreign

---

Complete Equivalence or Dynamic Equivalence?

Salman (Sam) Hilmy, the veteran chief of VOA's Near East and South Asia Division from the mid-1980s to the early 1990s, notes that in rendering English into another language, the material at hand dictates how this is best done. Official texts and statements demand particular precision in translation. Hilmy calls this "complete equivalence," with a caveat: the translation must not sound so literal that it comes across as stilted, artificial, or awkward—sounding like a "translation" in the mother language. The other variant, known as adaptation, can be used for rendering less sensitive, usually nonpolitical and less formal English scripts into another language. Adapters can employ idioms unique to their language, rearrange sentences, or take other liberties (without violating journalistic rules of accuracy and balance) to make the translated material more readily comprehensible. Hilmy calls this "dynamic equivalence." He adds that some broadcasters are more adept at handling the first category of scripts; others do better with the second. Most VOA language service chiefs, Hilmy notes, assign translations and adaptations based on the natural strengths of individual broadcasters.*

*Sam Hilmy, interview with author, Wheaton, Md., July 5, 2001.

---

languages is a fine art. It is much more complex than would appear at first glance.

Literal translations are almost always noticed by a listener and damage credibility. Moreover, adapters in VOA language services must have a keen knowledge not only of history and culture in their native lands, but of America's past as well. In a major VOA language service, for example, the term "underground railroad" in a script describing the escape routes of slaves from the South to the North during the Civil War came out of the word processor as something more like "subway."

Perfection in the art of adaptation sometimes is difficult, or impossible, to achieve. When President Ronald Reagan called Libyan leader Mu'ammar al-Gadhafi "flaky" at a news conference, that puzzled many adapters at VOA. How do you render that in Lao, much less in Arabic? I can recall once being asked by an expert in the Arabic Branch what the term "down to earth" meant. (The question was posed in the 1960s by a VOA staff member, an Oxford-educated former distinguished Egyptian editor often assigned to adapt the most nuanced news analyses from English into classical Arabic.) A VOA newsroom stylebook cautioned its writers against the casual use of American political terms such as "lobbyist" (difficult to translate into almost any other language), "springboard" (as in a presidential primary victory), "behind closed doors" (as in secret meeting), and, worst of all, "at loggerheads" (a fierce dispute between political opponents).[16]

What Kind of Cousin?

English is not easy to adapt, even if relatively straightforward. In some Middle Eastern languages, it is not sufficient, for example, to say "cousin." One must define whether the person is a cousin on the father's or the mother's side of the family; there is a separate word for each. When an adapter of an English script gets an item from the central newsroom based on news agency dispatches describing a coup leader as a "cousin" of a head of state, it poses a virtually insurmountable linguistic challenge. Language service broadcasters have been known to call the central news desk to inquire about the genealogy of figures such as that murky coup leader. Of course, there is no ready answer.

English, it turns out, is far less precise in some respects than many other languages. Former BBC World Service managing director John Tusa, in *A World in Your Ear*, defines the problem by quoting a Hungarian Service colleague:

> As for the peculiarity of English, most difficulties arise from the sophistication of English in glossing over missing or unwanted information and in mitigating the effect of "sitting on the fence." Although, generally speaking, English has a more rigorous internal logic than Hungarian, a missing piece of information becomes more glaringly obvious in Hungarian, e.g., calling someone a leader instead of giving him a title, or saying "earlier this month" or "later this year." And there is the difficulty of rendering opacity convincingly and of providing a plausible equivalent of waffle. All that is the stuff of compromise; Cervantes thought that a translation was inevitably the wrong side of a tapestry.[17]

In a few languages, adaptation (or translation) is, of necessity, invention. This is the case in broadcasts to isolated countries or areas where literacy rates are low and there has been relatively little contact with modern society. Programming in Hausa to northern Nigeria and Niger offers such a challenge. Hausa Service staff explain that telling stories and employing folklore and fables are essential, even if used to introduce newscasts or to reflect relatively new technical terms to their society. A classic example: How to say "helicopter" in a language that had no term for it? Simply using the English word would only confuse many Hausa listeners. Therefore, the service came up with a substitute that painted a picture, calling a chopper "a sky canoe which ascends and descends like an eagle."[18]

How Do You Say "Junk Bond" in Tibetan?

Tibetan Service chief John Buescher explains that checking to see if modern equivalents exist is like detective work in the language of his specialty:

> Back in Lhasa, I check the two largest bookstores in the city for reference books in Tibetan, especially on science, because at VOA we've had some interesting times making up Tibetan words and expressions to render some English terms that have to be translated: "cholesterol," "junk bond," "ozone layer," "gridlock," and "catalytic converter" are memorable examples. But the stores have no such reference books, only collections of history, politics, poetry, folksongs, and a few reprints of religious texts. Very little effort has been made in Tibet (though some Tibetans in India are working on it) to develop in Tibetan the technical vocabulary necessary for systematically describing the modern world.[19]

The Dalai Lama, who has visited VOA's Tibetan Service in Washington on several occasions, sought its advice on the proper rendering in his own language of the trade term "most favored nation" (MFN). The service supplied the phrase it had coined, *misge tsong don te cha*, and the exiled Nobel laureate later used it in his addresses around the world (chapter 14). It has appeared in Tibetan newspapers as well.[20]

Within language services, there are tricky translation/adaptation challenges also. There are approximately 2,600 languages worldwide, and within the larger ones, there are huge variations in local usage and dialects. I can recall, during my foreign correspondent days, registering

---

TEACHING ENGLISH IN OTHER LANGUAGES

A survey of VOA language services in the year 2000 revealed that about twenty of them were teaching English to their listeners. Several of them used adaptations of *Tuning in the USA*. Publication wizard Barbara Callihan produced promotional puzzle books and catalogs listing them. Some language units developed their own series. Among them was the Vietnamese Service. In one of his *Idioms in the News* scripts, service chief Dick McCarthy explained the expression "to take him out to the woodshed." He said that it applies today broadly to punishment of any sort, but originated in earlier times when woodsheds were detached from homes in the United States, and American fathers who were disciplinarians took their sons out there for a private spanking. "Idioms like these," McCarthy told listeners to the program, "are a problem that men and women who translate the news face almost every day. When they are lucky, they can find a matching idiom in their own language. Otherwise they have to do their best to find another reasonable way to make sense out of the original."*

*Richard E. McCarthy, "Idioms in the News (2)" (script of VOA, East Asia and Pacific Division, *English, American Style*, no. 260, May 11, 1993), 2–3.

---

at the press desk of an Islamic summit in Rabat, Morocco. That is about as far west as you can go in the Arab world, which spans four time zones. Next to me were two well-known Lebanese columnists, who began speaking in eastern Mediterranean Arabic to the Moroccan who was examining our credentials. They quickly switched to French, because their words were incomprehensible in a setting where Arabic is heavily influenced by the Berber language of North Africa. Even in languages spoken in smaller geographic regions, there can be disputes over how dialects are used: Albanian (Tosks and Ghegs), Kurdish (Kurmanji and Sourani), and Tibetan (Kham and Amdo). In the Urdu Service to Pakistan and India, language issues are frequently sorted out in a designated "glossary moment" during daily editorial meetings. The Dari Service to Afghanistan even developed its own dictionary in the late 1980s.

Adapters at VOA are accustomed to using expressions natural to their mother tongues to avoid sounding as if they were simply back-translating an English script, what Hilmy refers to as dynamic equivalence.

When American film star Bette Davis died in 1989, the Latvian Service told its listeners: "The star corps beyond the sun [a Latvian figure of speech for having died] was joined today at the age of eighty-one in Paris, by the unforgettable American movie star Bette Davis."[21]

WORDS NOT ONLY MATTER, BUT CAN BE CRUCIAL

During the first hundred days of the second Bush administration, the collision of an American reconnaissance plane with a Chinese fighter jet over the South China Sea was the new president's first major foreign policy test. It was also a powerful reminder of the central role that words can play, both in diplomacy and in international broadcasting.

John Pomfret, the Associated Press correspondent expelled from Beijing in 1989 with VOA's Alan Pessin, was back in the Chinese capital, this time with the *Washington Post*. In April 2001, the crisis erupted over the release of twenty-four American servicemen and -women who had been aboard the surveillance plane when it made an emergency landing on the southern Chinese island of Hainan. "In the end," Pomfret wrote, "it was a matter of what the United States chose to say and what the Chinese chose to hear."[22]

VOA's Mandarin Chinese Service obviously had to be precise—that is, achieve complete equivalence—in translating the language of the crucial letter handed by the American ambassador in Beijing to the Chinese foreign minister. That letter led to the release of the American crew, which had been held for eleven days on Hainan. China had demanded an apology, which the United States declined to give because, it said, the accident had occurred over international waters when the Chinese fighter jet had buzzed and struck the slower-moving U.S. Navy EP-3E Aires II surveillance plane. Secretary of State Colin Powell said flatly: "There's nothing to apologize for."

Marathon negotiations were held to secure the release of the crew. They focused on language in the letter; its words would be digested, interpreted, analyzed to the last syllable and character in both Washington and Beijing. In English, the American letter said that the United States was "very sorry" for the loss of the Chinese pilot and "very sorry" that the reconnaissance plane had had to enter Chinese airspace to make an emergency landing without express verbal clearance (although Lieutenant Shane Osborn, the pilot, had repeatedly sought permission but never got a response from the Chinese airport control tower on the island of Hainan).

The double "very sorry" was at the heart of conflicting interpretations. VOA's Mandarin Chinese Service, on the air twelve hours a day, was careful to render these phrases as *feichang wanxi* (great sorrow and sympathy) in referring to the loss of the Chinese pilot and *feichang baoqian* (extremely sorry) in citing the letter's reference to the emergency landing. There was no suggestion of an apology in either translation, and both matched precisely ones issued by the American embassy in the Chinese capital.[23] Elsewhere in Beijing, however, the official Foreign Ministry statement and the state-controlled media used the term *shenbiao qianyi* (deep expression of apology or regret) in quoting the U.S. letter. The VOA Mandarin Service broadcast a report contrasting the Chinese-language interpretations of the letter by the United States and China.

Presentation of official renderings from both sides was in line with the charter: it made VOA news accurate, objective, and comprehensive.[24] "We believe that if we can give an audience the full story," VOA director Sanford Ungar said in connection with the United States–China crisis, "they will be able to draw their own conclusions."[25]

Two issues concerning language use surfaced in VOA's Arabic Branch during the Persian Gulf crisis and war of 1990/1991.

• The Foreign Broadcast Information Service is an unclassified unit of the Central Intelligence Agency that shares monitoring of media around the world with the BBC World Service. At the time of the Gulf crisis, it was issuing a terminology guide for translators: *No Uncertain Terms*, or *NUTS*. Its purpose was to help its staff with particular problems in translating other languages into English or, in some cases, simply in making sense of expressions in those other languages. A case in point was the use by Iraqi state-controlled media of the phrase "the mother of all battles" (*umm-al-ma'arik*). *No Uncertain Terms* pointed out that this was a literal translation that made no sense in English because, as the booklet said, the word "mother" can refer to a female bearer of offspring, a creative or an environmental source or origin, or qualities attributed to a mother. None of these applied to a battle. *NUTS* said that Saddam Hussein's use of the expression was a metaphor that should be translated as "battle of all battles."[26]

• As the Gulf crisis began in the autumn of 1990, President George Bush decided to deliver a message directly to the Iraqi people to explain that the buildup of coalition forces in the region was not aimed at them, but at their leader, whose army had occupied Kuwait about six weeks earlier. How best to get the message to Iraq? The answer: VOA's Arabic Branch. But this was no routine exercise. Near East and South Asia Division chief Sam Hilmy obtained a text of Bush's address and noticed that it quoted several sentences from Saddam himself. Hilmy, a longtime American citizen who happens to have been born in Iraq, would not permit his staff to translate President Bush's remarks until he had the actual Arabic text of Saddam's original words. A translation from Arabic to English and back to Arabic would have been fraught with peril, and VOA's use of such a double adaptation might have opened it up to ridicule if Hilmy had not insisted on this precaution (chapter 15).

SADDAM VERSUS SADDAM

President George Bush, in his address beamed to the Iraqi people in Arabic by VOA, told them:

> When we stand with Kuwait against aggression, we stand for a principle well understood in the Arab world. Let me quote the words of one Arab leader, Saddam Hussein himself: "An Arab country does not have the right to occupy another Arab country. God forbid, if Iraq should deviate from the right path, we would want Arabs to send their armies to put things right. If Iraq should become intoxicated by its power and move to overwhelm another Arab state, the Arabs would be right to deploy their armies to check it."
>
> Those are the words of your leader, Saddam Hussein, spoken on November 28, 1988, in a speech to Arab lawyers. Today, two years later, Saddam has invaded and occupied a member of the United Nations and the Arab League. The world will not allow this aggression to stand. Iraq must get out of Kuwait for the sake of principle, for the sake of peace, and for the sake of the Iraqi people.*

*White House, official text of President Bush's address to the Iraqi people, September 16, 1990. According to an Associated Press report from Washington, the address was videotaped in the nation's capital and accompanied by Arabic subtitles and by a voice-over translation into Arabic, both provided by VOA.

Translators (or adapters), the BBC's John Tusa said, have a most complex task. They are "jugglers, conjurers, mind readers, psychologists, games players, poets, social scientists. At the end," he wrote, "they are cultural porters, offering the users of one language an imaginative equivalence of the meaning expressed in another. The question is not whether they get it wrong. The wonder is that so much of it is right."[27]

13

Music

THE UNIVERSAL LANGUAGE

The language of music is common to all generations and nations. It is understood by everybody, since it is understood with the heart.

—Gioacchino Rossini

Jazz is a classical parallel to our American political and social system. We agree in advance on the laws and customs we abide by, and having reached agreement, we are free to do whatever we wish within these constraints. It's the same with jazz. The musicians agree on the key, the harmonic changes, the tempo and the duration of the piece. Within these guidelines, they are free to play what they want. And when people in other countries hear that quality in the music, it stimulates a need for the same freedom in their lives.

—Willis Conover

Music is *the* universal language, ideal for a global broadcast network. At VOA, it has taken many forms over the years. One of the Voice's first directors of music, Bess Lomax, recalled in 1945: "An especially interesting bit of testimony has come to us from the leader of a group of Frenchmen who had been smuggling allied fliers out of France. While listening to the radio on a ship carrying him to the United States, he heard *Yankee Doodle*. He jumped up and said: 'That is the song that kept us alive during the occupation. That was the one radio voice that we could always trust, and that we listened to faithfully.'" Lomax went on to counsel programmers of music at the Voice "to sample every kind of music which is truly part of the American scene . . . as well as music of your target area. . . . We can create a bond of friendship by telling our audience in effect: 'We in America know your music as well as our own.'"[1]

"THIS IS JAZZZZZ"

Over the years, the music gurus of the Voice have attempted to offer a full range of American music and, in some regions, indigenous songs and ballads to an eager listening public around the world. The best-known VOA effort, clearly, has centered on jazz, that unique blend of ragtime and blues combining American with African and Caribbean musical traditions. It also became celebrated in much of the twentieth century as the "music of freedom."

"However far away from home I've traveled covering the news these many years," ABC's Peter Jennings told his listeners in 1996, "there has remained a constant: the voice of Willis Conover via the Voice of America saying: 'This is jazzzzz.'"[2]

The *Reader's Digest* called Willis "the world's favorite American."[3] The famed host for more than four decades before his death in 1996 was

---

THE POWER OF WILLIS CONOVER

"The small hall of the Composer's Union was packed to the rafters," recalled USIA foreign service officer Robert McCarthy, who was stationed in Moscow in the early 1980s.

> The square outside [was] filled with people still hoping to get inside. A shadowy figure strode across the darkened stage to the microphone. "Good evening . . ." he began in the distinctive Conover rumble and got no further. A deafening ovation split the air. People stood on chairs, clapped, screamed, cheered. It lasted a good ten minutes. Why? I asked. They had listened to Willis for thirty years, recorded American jazz off the air when it was a semi-subversive act, learned to play by listening to him, and here he was in Moscow.*

*Robert E. McCarthy, "The Power of Willis Conover," in *United States Information Agency: A Commemoration* (Washington, D.C.: United States Information Agency, 1999), 54.

virtually unknown in his own country because of Smith-Mundt Act provisions prohibiting the distribution of VOA broadcasts in the United
States. But abroad, he was better known than many American secretaries
of state. His deep, mellifluous voice and measured delivery cut through
static and jamming. His personal accounts of encounters with jazz giants
inspired tens of millions over the years—politicians, soldiers, diplomats,
as well as musicians.

"If Conover has been a prophet unheard in his own land," *Down Beat*
magazine said, "he has been a jazz messiah 'round the globe, the best-
known and best-loved ambassador for America's art form since Louis
Armstrong and Dizzy Gillespie."[4] Congress passed a resolution in 1993
saluting Willis. President Reagan, congratulating Conover on his ten
thousandth VOA broadcast, recalled the words of two Bulgarian listeners who had come to the United States: "We are two lucky escapees from
behind the Iron Curtain . . . and we have been living for years with you,
your voice, your music. There is absolutely no way that we can describe
what enormous importance you have for somebody living back there. . . .
You are the music, you are the light, you are America."[5]

How exactly did Willis, to paraphrase Rossini, "touch hearts" in so
many faraway places? In the mid-1950s, Adam Makowicz, a world-
famous jazz pianist, was fourteen years old and studying classical music in
Poland. One night, Makowicz recalled,

> a friend brought [in] a shortwave radio, a scarcity at the time, and
> a group of us congregated around it to listen to that new, enchant-
> ing, improvised music, coming from Willis' program on the Voice
> of America.
>
> We were hooked! From then on, every night at 11 P.M. sharp,
> we were tuned to shortwave to await, with anticipation, what
> would follow the famous "Take the 'A' Train" theme, and the
> announcement *This is Music USA—Jazz Hour*. Willis spoke to us
> distinctly and slowly, so that even those of us who knew very little
> English could understand. . . . That music, open to improvisation,
> coming from a free country, was "our hour of freedom": music we
> had not known before; it was our hope and joy which helped us
> to survive dark days of censorship and other oppression.[6]

Jazz touched the lives of professionals other than musicians. The
music stirred souls in countries where it was officially considered

---

"THE SAME FREEDOM THAT
PEOPLE EVERYWHERE SHOULD ENJOY"

Willis Conover was on the air during the administrations of eight U.S.
presidents, and he was master of ceremonies at White House concerts
for several of them. "Every emotion—love, anger, joy, sadness," he once
said, "can be communicated with the vitality and spirit that characterizes jazz and our country at its best. Which, of course, is the same
freedom that people everywhere should enjoy."

"decadent" or "forbidden fruit." ABC's Peter Jennings, in a tribute the
week after Willis died, recalled: "In the midst of the Cold War, Conover
landed at the Moscow airport and was greeted by a line of generals who
proudly showed him the medals covering their jackets. Only underneath
the medals, the Russians wore buttons which read *Jazz USA*."[7]

In faraway Vladivostok, the Russian Far East, a VOA monitor and jazz
enthusiast, Taroslav Balagush, wrote on learning of Willis's death that his
program was "the first radio school of jazz for Russia. . . . Its graduates are
still grateful to Mr. Conover for teaching them jazz long distance, although
a great part of his pupils never saw their teacher in person. Duke Ellington,
Louis Armstrong, Count Basie, Charlie Parker, and John Coltrane are the
greatest jazz masters, and Willis Conover served as a link between them
and jazz listeners all over the world . . . this is why I think that his place
should be right beside Satchmo, Duke, Count and the Bird."[8]

For a man unknown to many in his own country, Conover did pretty
well. His powerful ego over the years was seasoned with increasing dashes
of paranoia. He remained a contractor, not an employee, to retain what
he regarded as his independence in musical selections. At times, as when
Program Manager Barry Zorthian insisted that he play music other than
jazz for diversity, Willis was insufferable. Yet Willis—in his prime—was a
polished and witty master of ceremonies. Conover hosted programs far
away from Washington, at the Newport Jazz Festival and at huge concerts
in Moscow and Warsaw, years before the end of the Cold War.

CBS commentator Charles Osgood remarked shortly after Willis's
death: "Probably it would be too much to say that the sweet clarion call
of all of those trumpets and saxophones, the joyful noise of the piano,
bass, drums and other instruments caused the collapse of communism in

eastern Europe. So maybe Willis Conover was not exactly Joshua. But in a sense, he was. Because finally, after all that music all those years, the walls did come tumbling down."[9]

MUSIC OF, BY, AND FOR THE PEOPLE

Jazz, however, was only part of the story of music at VOA. In the 1980s and 1990s, American country music began to captivate overseas audiences. I recall one afternoon in 1992 when VOA music director Judy Massa was frantically busy making arrangements for a special VOA fiftieth-anniversary concert with Kenny Rogers and others. Some visitors came to the Voice. Judy didn't really have time, but took the time, to talk to them.[10] She told them about a month-long worldwide contest that she had organized a few years earlier on her weekly program *Country Music USA*. Listeners were asked to write to Judy on the theme "What Country Music Means to Me."

There were 3,000 entries, in just twenty-eight days. The reward was a free round trip for two to Nashville and to VOA in Washington (transportation and accommodations privately donated). The winner was Zhou Zuo-Ren, a twenty-three-year-old international-business student and broadcaster on the Shanghai People's Broadcasting Station in China.

"Country music," Zhou had written, "means music of the people, composed by the people, sung by the people. It offers romantic longing, mystical transcendence, Western imagery. . . . Let it be said loud and clear: country music is forever a mirror reflecting American people's ideals, ambitions, depressions and hopes. . . . I believe it is not only the treasure of American people, but the treasure of all country music fans in the world."[11]

After a delay of months, China granted Zhou a visa. Massa arranged for him and his traveling companion to attend the Nineteenth International Country Music Fan Fair in Nashville. She flew there to meet them and escort them to the fair and around the city. Zhou, a cherub-faced scholar with huge glasses, got off the plane with a slightly balding man who might have been his older brother. The contest winner immediately requested a private huddle with Massa in the lounge. "Look, Judy," he said, "this man is from PRC security. He's my 'minder' they've sent along. He knows nothing about country music."

Judy immediately calmed her guest. "We'll be okay," she reassured him.

They had a fabulous time in Nashville, driving around to see great artists in Music City, USA. They chatted with legendary musician Chet

Atkins. They heard Reba McIntyre, Barbara Mandrell, Randy Travis, and the Oak Ridge Boys, to name just a few. As Judy drove her two guests from place to place, Zhou sat in the front seat and the security man, Zheng Rong Xin, sat behind. Judy, of course, had the radio on, all the time. On the third day of the journey, she suddenly heard a tapping noise back there. The "minder" was tapping his foot in perfect rhythm on the floor.

A week later, the dream trip ended, after Zhou (by then nicknamed Willie after Willie Nelson) and Zheng (nicknamed John) had visited VOA in Washington. Judy said goodbye to her guests at Dulles International Airport. "Willie" graciously hugged her. "John" broke into tears! He had caught the spirit and tasted the "freedom that people everywhere should enjoy."

Massa had joined VOA in the early 1960s. She blossomed into a globally known program host and friend of major artists after VOA director Kenneth Y. Tomlinson plucked her from relative obscurity twenty years later. She retired, looking remarkably youthful still, in January 2001. Over the years, Massa traveled to more than thirty countries to emcee concerts, some of them live—including ones in India, Vietnam, and Kazakhstan.[12] She brought country and pop singer Garth Brooks to the Voice, and featured him on her new weekly music request program of the 1990s, *Border Crossings*. She and Brooks appeared on a VOA worldwide call-in program. During the same visit, they cohosted what *USA Today* called "a foot-stomping music bash" in the VOA auditorium as Brooks unveiled his album *Fresh Horses* in November 1995.[13]

Massa noted that at one time, sixteen VOA language services had country music programs. She attributes the popularity of the music to several things: "Listeners hear the emotion inherent in the music. It deals with the common themes of everyday life—love lost, love found, one's job, the difficulties that life brings to everyone. There's something universal in the simplicity of the melodies. The songs are usually accompanied by a string instrument, which nearly every culture has. Many people are people of the soil. You feel as if you could talk with them, about anything. And young people like country music because it's great to dance to."[14]

"A JACK OF ALL TRADES"

About the time that Judy Massa joined the Voice, United States Information Agency director Edward R. Murrow made a trip to Conakry, Guinea. He decided to meet an American musicologist he had heard a lot about. Murrow and Bill Atwood, U.S. ambassador to Guinea, emerged from a meeting with President Sekou Touré and went to an apartment building just across the street from the presidential palace. As usual, the elevator wasn't working. So they climbed six flights of stairs to the apartment of Leo and Mary Sarkisian.

Murrow, just lighting up a cigarette, introduced himself. "Hi, I'm Ed Murrow. I've heard a lot about Leo's work."[15] Sarkisian then was on a field assignment as music director and sound manager for a Hollywood recording firm. The surprise interview went very well. Murrow hired Sarkisian as the music director for a planned VOA program center in Monrovia, Liberia, part of the new Africa Division (chapter 11). Sarkisian traveled widely, collected African indigenous music, and broadcast it back to the continent. Murrow's recruitment effort turned out to be an incredible bargain.

As VOA director Sanford (Sandy) Ungar said forty years later: "Leo has been described by many as 'one of a kind' and 'a jack of all trades.' He is a broadcaster, artist, illustrator, musician, ethnomusicologist, linguist, lecturer and sound engineer. His weekly program, *Music Time in Africa*, with host Rita Rochelle, has been on the air thirty-five years and is one of VOA's strongest and longest running programs."[16] Ungar's remarks were delivered at the opening of an exhibition of Sarkisian's art held at VOA. Seventy-six of his paintings, sketches, drawings, and illustrations were on display in February 2001, just after Sarkisian's eightieth birthday. Another speaker at the occasion was Mark Lewis, VOA pioneer newswriter (chapter 2) and retired USIA Africa area director. He said that Sarkisian's unique combination of expertise on African indigenous music and stunning charcoal portraits of people throughout the continent added up to cultural diplomacy at its finest. In Lewis's words: "They represented, as Mr. Murrow had hoped, our respect for African culture. . . . They show, as George Kennan once said of cultural programs, that 'America has a soul.'"[17]

Sarkisian worked for ten years recording music and drawing portraits in Asia and Africa before joining the Voice. Over the years, he has recorded or received recordings of indigenous music from throughout the continent, including songs from remote villages. Most of these have aired, exclusively, on *Music Time in Africa*. Sarkisian has collected more than 7,000 pieces of music, now housed in a special library of African music at the Voice of America—the only archive of its kind in the world.

Sarkisian has received as many as a thousand letters a month from listeners. The other part of Murrow's great bargain was Leo's wife, Mary.

THE ACOUSTICS WIZARD AT WORK

The irrepressible Leo Sarkisian gathered much of his material in remote areas under rugged conditions, without the aid of electric outlets or power supplies. As a sound technician, however, he insisted on making the highest-quality recordings on his battery-powered portable tape recorders. To do this, he occasionally placed musicians beneath large mango trees and drummers close to walls to ensure the best acoustics. "*Music Time in Africa*," Sarkisian said, "shows our listeners that we do have deep respect for the cultures of other peoples, that we are sincerely friends, and have respect for their aspirations and their way of life."*

*Quoted in Bitrus Paul Gwanma, "Multicultural Programming as a Strategy in Public Diplomacy: Leo Sarkisian and the Voice of America's *Music Time in Africa*" (Ph.D. diss., Ohio University, 1992), 146, 170.

Together, she and Leo have sorted and answered listener mail on their kitchen table each weekend for more than three decades.

Sarkisian the gifted linguist—he speaks Armenian, Arabic, Farsi, French, and Turkish—is also a gifted teacher. His most consistent pupil over the years has been Rita Rochelle, the vivacious copresenter of his program since 1978.[18] Rochelle recalled when Sarkisian, the "hard taskmaster but true Renaissance man," took her to Africa in the mid-1980s. In one village, she said, they were given a gift that was rather difficult to transport: a charming little chimpanzee. In another, residents presented them with a white rooster. The most moving moment, though, was in a third village when Sarkisian gave his usual spirited talk, thumping his feet to the rhythms and beats of music he played on a tape recorder. The children, fascinated to meet VOA's Music Man in person, responded with equal enthusiasm. They sang "The Star-Spangled Banner" for Sarkisian and Rochelle. She broke into tears. At first, the children were crestfallen. Had they done something wrong? Sarkisian quickly explained: "Not at all . . . those were tears of joy."[19]

HOOKED FOR LIFE ON RAGAS AND TALAS

Practicing ethnomusicologists could form a club at America's Voice. Brian Q. Silver, chief of the Urdu Service, is a master among them. He is a scholar of music and South Asian affairs who joined VOA in 1986 after having taught at Harvard and later served as a dean at Duke University. Silver is the most accomplished American-born player of the sitar, a popular stringed instrument in India and Pakistan. He has appeared in many concerts in the United States and in South Asia, often with his wife, Shubha Sankaran, the world's only female player of another concert instrument in the region known as the *surbahar*. In a commentary written for his wife's World Bank *surbahar* performance cosponsored by the embassy of India in 2000, Silver displayed the expertise that has enhanced placement of his Urdu Service programs on radio stations in Pakistan:

> Each performance of Hindustani music is a unique musical experience based on a complex improvisation within traditional forms; in terms of musical possibilities, this improvisation, constrained like a game of chess in ancient rules, is limitless in the hands of a master. The selection of *ragas* (complex, improvised melodic structures) and *talas* (fixed, repeating cycles of a consistent number of rhythmic beats) is up to the melodic soloist, who makes these choices according to the time of day; her own mood and inclination; and sometimes the degree of audience sophistication and knowledge expressed in subtle vocal utterances that outstanding performances bring forth involuntarily from seasoned listeners.[20]

Silver studied South Asian music under a Fulbright grant to India from 1964 to 1966, learning in the traditional fashion under an established master. He recalls how he first became interested:

> As a fledgling teenage Flamenco guitarist, born and raised in Denver, Colorado, I had on one hot summer evening in 1958 checked out two long-playing microgroove records from the Denver Public Library entitled *The Music of India, Volumes One and Two*. After a long bus ride back the next day from my perspiring, droning, daytime summer factory job as an apprentice machinist, I took out the first record from its orange and ochre jacket, and set the stylus of the Rek-o-kut turntable down on the shimmering black vinyl disc. . . . That gave me my first aural glimpse of an entire new world of music.[21]

Over the years, many such worlds came alive in the studios of America's Voice:

- To the South Asian nation of Bangladesh, Dilara Hashem of the Bangla Service presented her weekly *Matir Gan, Manusher Gan* (Songs of the Soil, Songs of the People), based on country and folk music popular in the United States. A published novelist and poet, Hashem translated lyrics of the American songs into Bangla.
- Lyonel Desmarattes of the Creole Service was another poet—one with a light touch—who wrote and voiced *Nouvelles en vers* (News in Verse) each Friday for his listeners in Haiti. "He puts the story of elections in Poland," said *Voice Magazine*, "or the discovery of Neptune's moon into a twelve-syllable classical French-style verse, set to a rhythmic, Caribbean rap background. 'Only about ten percent of the people in Haiti are literate,' Desmarattes noted, 'and this is one of the easiest and most entertaining ways for them to get news.'"[22]
- Roger Guy Folly of the French-to-Africa Branch (chapter 11) defined reggae as "Third World music derived from the West Indies." He, like Leo Sarkisian and Athanase Maijo of the Swahili Service to East Africa, played music unique to their regions and adaptations of reggae in their programs. A form of reggae, according to Maijo, originated as music of social protest in East Africa.
- Hayat al Khateeb of the Arabic Branch used music as a frame in her information program *Ahlan wa Sahlan* (You're Most Welcome). Each program had a theme—for example, labor, family health, or women's issues. Khateeb combined these with Arabic vocals or histories of some of the ancient instruments of the Middle East and North Africa: the *'oud* (lute), *nye* (flute), *kanun* (zither), and drums of various descriptions.
- Vilnus Baumans of the Latvian Service, another announcer-performer, played local folk music in programs he produced from recordings of Latvian-American music festivals. "The original Latvian solo folk song," he explained, "is accompanied by the *kokle*, a 12-stringed zither. Pure folk songs, those not influenced by other traditions."[23]

One of the most innovative music programs at VOA, however, was the revival of *mohlam*, broadcast to the landlocked Southeast Asian nation of Laos. This traditionally had been performed by wandering troubadours of ancient times, whose balladlike songs told stories, legends, and jokes. They once spread news from village to village in Laos and northeastern Thailand, but *mohlam* was banned on the media by the Communist government in Vientiane in the late twentieth century. So the VOA Lao Service decided to revive it and hire singers to convey not only Lao's rich past, but the American story as well. For many years, the service hired a succession of *mohlam* performers in Bangkok, typically consisting of two singers and a player of the *khene*, a reed instrument with fourteen small pipes. Among *mohlam* topics of note was a poetic review of Mark Twain's *Life on the Mississippi*. Another *mohlam* explained the charter on VOA's fiftieth anniversary.[24]

Brian Silver, the musicologist, dreams of when it might be possible to mount a series of concerts in the Washington, D.C., area called "World Music at VOA." Performers would offer samples of the ethnic music just described (singers, instrumentalists, and even dancers). The presentations, Silver believes, would be eagerly cosponsored by appropriate embassies and ethnic community organizations in Washington whose own music would be performed for both local Washington listeners and a worldwide radio and television audience.[25]

A MUSIC MIX FOR THE WORLD

As this century began, much of the VOA music programming in English was passing to new hands. Willis Conover died in May 1996. A live concert tribute at the Voice a week later ended in an impromptu and unforgettable high-decibel jam session. About seven months later, VOA Europe—the vanguard of satellite-fed American contemporary music programming on VOA—was closed for lack of funding and a commercial sponsor to keep it operating in the post–Cold War era. Judy Massa retired. Inevitably, VOA's programming of American music would change, just as the music itself continued to reflect new approaches and a new generation.

VOA Europe, in particular, was to leave a foundation on which to build. At its demise, the "music and more" network had gone global. It had more than 200 affiliated local FM stations, including ones in Chile, Uruguay, Dominica, Iceland, the Azores, Siberia, and Australia. VOA Europe had brought to the Voice such commercial broadcasting techniques as digital production studios and playlists of American pop music. It was essential to preserve these assets.

The decision was made to continue providing the latest popular music to disappointed VOA Europe affiliates. It was called VOA Express. Over the next three years, under the leadership of Worldwide English head and master musician John Stevenson and veteran music-program host and broadcaster Ed Gursky, the concept grew. In April 1999, they began experimenting with a new service beamed via satellite around the clock, seven days a week, to FM affiliates around the world. That program stream, VOA Music Mix, was formally launched on July 4, 1999, and offered a full range of American music. Among the emcees were Ray McDonald (*Top 20 Countdown*, reflecting pop hits), Ray Freeman (*American Gold*, presenting older American pop hits, and *Border Crossings*, a music request program initiated in 1997 by Judy Massa), Mary Morningstar (*Country Hits USA*, Massa's flagship program), Katherine Cole (*Roots and Branches*, a compilation of American folk, rock, and contemporary regional music), and Ed Gursky (*VOA Music Mix Classic Rock Show*).[26]

Russ Davis, a New York expert jazz host, took up where Willis Conover had left off. Davis previously hosted a daily jazz show for

---

BORDER CROSSINGS IN THE "UNIVERSAL LANGUAGE"

"Music," John Stevenson says, "communicates in a special way to people around the world. It really is the universal language. That's why *Border Crossings* is such a perfect title. In Iran, people dedicate songs to listeners in Albania. Brothers and sisters request songs for each other, even though they live in countries thousands of miles apart. *Border Crossings* has established links between pen pals attracted to music which stretches around the world." Stevenson, a prominent bass soloist who performs in Washington musical theaters and has sung at religious services there and around the nation, is constantly amazed at how much music speaks to people who are denied it. He recalls an Afghan's comment in the year 2000 that the listener cherished Western music on VOA—the former Taliban-controlled radios there broadcast only Koranic chants.*

*John Stevenson, interview with author, April 26, 2001. See also John Baily, "Censorship of Music in Afghanistan," April 26, 2001, available at: www.freemuse.org [Freedom of Musical Expression].

WQCD-FM, New York City's top-ranked jazz station, and has produced his own syndicated jazz program heard on FM stations in Japan and Britain. His two-hour weekend VOA Music Mix program, *Jazz America*, was launched on July 4, 1998. It includes exclusive interviews each week with such notables as Billy Taylor, Benny Green, Pat Metheny, and Eliane Elias, a Brazilian-born jazz pianist.[27]

VOA Music Mix, as of 2001, had 160 FM affiliates around the world that took down the programs fed digitally via satellite and rebroadcast them in real time to local audiences. Regions of heaviest pickup were Eastern and Central Europe, with an uncountable additional number downlinking the program streams in Latin America. There, VOA Music Mix was placed on a twenty-four-hour-a-day digital stream called VOASAT and made available to VOA Spanish-language broadcasting partners before and after a few hours daily of Spanish news and features programs.[28]

Gursky, savvy in many aspects of the broadcasting industry, had been a commercial broadcast on-air host and music programmer in Baltimore, Detroit, Pittsburgh, Knoxville, and Washington, D.C., before joining the Federal Communications Commission and, eventually, Radio Martí and VOA. He was my key associate in the VOA Office of Programs in the late 1980s.[29] More than a decade later, he had some insights about music and international broadcasting in the digital era. For one thing, Gursky said, music is still practical on shortwave (despite its less than perfect audibility). There's a thirst for music beyond the big urban FM markets in places like Afghanistan, Tibet, and Laos.

In 2002, the Voice restored some music within evening segments of the VOA *News Now* shortwave and satellite global English program. As a result, American music would have an enhanced shortwave exposure. "The prospects for music programming in English," Gursky concluded, "are getting brighter. We must remember that music, though not regarded as a central programming thrust of most international broadcasters, is valuable entertainment, draws listeners, and in our case reflects a complete picture of American life and culture."[30] VOA director Robert Reilly, along the same lines, brought in outside artists to perform sixtieth-anniversary noontime concerts at the Voice in 2002. These concerts, featuring such artists as concert pianist Byron Janis and the American Boys Choir, were recorded and rebroadcast—VOA's most innovative classical-music programming since the 1960s. And Broadcasting Board of Governors member Norman J. Pattiz, at about the same time, obtained

$36 million from Congress for the inauguration of the heavily pop-music-oriented Middle East Radio Network (MERN), or Radio Sawa—a twenty-four-hour program in Arabic designed to appeal to youth with a combination of Arabic and American pop artists (chapter 20 and Conclusion).

So VOA in its use of the "universal language" had reached back to its origins. MERN and VOA Music Mix, a programming stream mirroring contemporary and past American music, were well launched. Contemporary American music, and the labor of love of musicologists throughout the Voice who mirror the music of others, seemed to fulfill the charge set by Bess Lomax in the OWI Broadcasting Manual more than a half century earlier: to sample every kind of music that is truly part of the American scene and "to establish a bond between our people and the peoples to whom we broadcast" by reflecting their music as well.

14

To the Roof of the World

THE TIBETAN SERVICE MIRACLE

The launch of the VOA's Tibetan service was like daily medicine . . . for the first time, Tibetans . . . were able to get an
alternative perspective on issues that had a direct bearing on
their lives.
— The Dalai Lama, in Buescher, "Ten Years to Tibet"

Not long after Tibetan broadcasts began, a tourist just back
from Tibet wrote: "Throughout Tibet, simply saying that I was
an American often seemed sufficient to bring forth smiles and
voiced convictions that America was 'the best.' As one monk
bluntly put it, VOA is 'the one thing any foreign country has
done for Tibet that is of real value.'"
— John Buescher,
"Tibetans Cannot Stop Listening to VOA"

In the mid-1990s, a National Geographic television crew made a journey
to the high plains of Tibet, close to the roof of the world. It was a journey filled with sights, sounds, and pictures endlessly fascinating to a
Western video production team. One of their most vivid memories was a
visit to the vast kitchen of the Drebung monastery, high in the hills
above the Tibetan capital, Lhasa. The room had a vaulted ceiling and
echoed with sonorous chants. It was cavernous, an ancient mirage and
ideal documentary material. Buddhist monks in saffron-colored sashes
were stirring tea in huge black cauldrons. They were voicing rhythmic
phrases in their mother tongue, with pictures and sound duly recorded
by a crew that had not a clue about the words they were chanting.

After returning to the United States, the production team turned to the Voice of America Tibetan Service for an expert translation. A member of the service attended the viewing of the raw footage, and burst into laughter as he translated from Tibetan to English. "What they're saying," he reported, "is: 'This is the Voice of America in Tibetan, coming to you from Washington.'"[1]

A decade after the Tibetan Service was founded in 1991, nearly half the Tibetan travelers and exiles interviewed by independent research contractors said they listened to the service at least once a week.[2] How the service became the leading international broadcaster to the remote kingdom is something of a miracle.

APPLAUSE BY CANDLELIGHT

I remember when it all started. The project was led by John Buescher, a scholar of Tibet at the National Endowment for the Humanities who had joined the Voice in late 1990 and set about recruiting a staff. Finding educated Tibetans in the United States with journalistic or broadcasting backgrounds and a fluency in English was as difficult as hunting for rare game. The four leading candidates, eventually hired as broadcasters, included a diamond sorter, a man who hand-sewed camera bags, a lathe operator, and a highly educated journalist who had been working in the Office of Tibet in New York City.

Buescher and Executive Producer Hal Swaney judged that the embryonic staff of four, after just about a month of drilling and practice dry runs, would be ready to broadcast on March 31, 1991. The service was poised to meet the target date, when VOA learned that the U.S. ambassador to Beijing had a long-scheduled visit to Lhasa the same day. To launch the West's first Tibetan broadcast then, it was felt, might be needlessly provocative. But Congress and the first Bush administration were on record as saying that VOA would be on the air in Tibetan by the end of March 1991.

There was only one solution: go on the air a week earlier than planned, even with a neophyte staff. After all, the inaugural program was only fifteen minutes long. The broadcast was set to begin on March 25 at 9:00 P.M., Washington time, prime morning time in Tibet the next calendar day.

It was a family affair. Frank Cummins, the program review director, and his wife, Liliane, brought in one of her piping-hot gourmet meat dishes to celebrate. Belinda Buescher, Dot, and I also cohosted. We purposely stayed out of the studio. We were determined to avoid making Buescher, the four Tibetans, and Swaney more nervous than they already were. Besides, we had to set up the modest candlelight supper in the East Asia and Pacific Division conference room afterward. We listened to the program on the strowger. It sounded very professional, you might say, even polished. As Buescher and his team—emcee Tinley Nyandak; readers Yeshe Khedrup, Palmo Khedrup, and Lobsang Tenpa; and producer Hal Swaney—entered the conference room within a minute or so after the program ended, our surprise welcoming committee broke into applause. It is possible that a couple of pairs of Tibetan broadcast hands were still shaking with fright. But their faces were beaming.

Oops!

A decade later, on March 26, 2001, the same team (now veteran broadcasters) stood proudly before a table groaning under the weight of Tibetan delicacies, joined by nineteen colleagues, to celebrate "ten years to Tibet." It was a milestone in the history of the Tibetan Service. Buescher recalled:

> Ten years ago yesterday, a small group of us, filled with expectation, walked down the hall from our office at the end of the building, into a studio that seemed like the bridge of the *Starship Enterprise*, and in a short—but almost infinitely long—fifteen minutes, broadcast the first international radio show in Tibetan, *to Brazil*. There was a slight glitch in engineering, of course.[3]
>
> I don't mind telling this—it's a reminder that, all things aside, radio is a very human and fallible enterprise, just as, no matter how much fancy technology you have, the broadcasts are still, and always will be, one mind and one voice at a time in front of a microphone *here* connecting with one pair of ears and one mind at a time out on the high plains of Tibet.
>
> Anyway, ten years ago *today*, we walked into the same studio and broadcast the first international radio show in *Tibetan* to Tibet. The first few shows were the cause of the first international diplomatic incident that I'd ever been associated with, because we broadcast a series of congratulatory messages from members of Congress, several of whom took the opportunity to wish for the

speedy independence of Tibet. When the Chinese government formally protested these messages, it became quite evident that the broadcasts were going to the region then (and not to Brazil) and that they were being heard loud and clear.[4]

"Peacocks" Exult on the Roof of the World

Listeners in Tibet, elsewhere in the Himalayan region, and at the Dalai Lama's exile home base, Dharamsala in India, responded enthusiastically. They wrote or sent messages saying they were especially impressed that VOA broadcast whatever news there was, no matter who or what might be put in a bad light. One listener wrote: "We are overjoyed on hearing your program; as a Tibetan saying goes, 'Peacocks dance with happiness when hearing thunder.'"[5]

During its first decade on the air, the Tibetan Service developed a cadre of stringers and other sources that enabled it to cover events inside Tibet with accuracy and speed. This isn't easy. The region's communications system is underdeveloped, and the People's Republic of China (PRC) tightly controls the media and other forms of expression. "Not uncommonly," says Buescher, "Tibetans who talk to foreign reporters or news organizations are considered 'counter-revolutionary' and put into a re-education camp. It can even be dangerous for a Tibetan to talk to a tourist."[6]

DETSEN'S STORY

Detsen, a resident of Tibet, knows that he has to be careful, because he is under constant surveillance. His mail is opened, and his telephone tapped. And yet Detsen makes sure he listens to the Voice of America's daily ninety-minute broadcast in the Tibetan language, which provides information on Tibet and the world and the policies of the government-in-exile. "These broadcasts are of inestimable value for Tibet," says Detsen. "They have been our main source of information since they began two years ago."*

*Quoted in Bernard Kurup, "Lives Will Be Lost But So Will Tibet, If We Don't Resist," Deutsche Presse-Agentur, November 2, 1994; Voice of America, Tibetan Service, fact sheet, March 13, 1995, 2.

The service's sources moved it to the forefront of authoritative broadcast information on Tibet and the world travels of its spiritual leader and Nobel laureate, the Dalai Lama. VOA Tibetan had stringers in eleven cities with large Tibetan exile communities—including four cities in India, one in Nepal, and one in Sikkim—and Tibetan-speaking reporters in New York, London, Taipei, Los Angeles, and Toronto.[7]

CHESS PLAYERS AT THE ROOF OF THE WORLD

The long-distance dialogue between Beijing and the exiled Dalai Lama resembles a cat and a mouse playing chess. There can be great subtlety on both sides. At times, the Dalai Lama's crafty preaching of peaceful resistance contrasts sharply with Beijing's use of brutal force. Since the Tibetan leader fled into exile in 1959, the PRC government has alternately cracked down on opposition within Tibet and attempted to relax its oppression there and in surrounding Tibetan-populated regions. It has also promoted ostensibly more moderate Communist leaders or tried to neutralize or buy off the Dalai Lama's key lieutenants and potential successors.

Right beneath His Holiness the Dalai Lama in the religious hierarchy are the Panchen Lama and the Karmapa Lama, the latter recognized by both the Dalai Lama and government authorities inside Tibet as the reincarnated head of one of the most important sects of Tibetan Buddhism. The secret flight from Lhasa into exile of the fifteen-year-old Karmapa in January 2000 was a major setback for Beijing. The PRC had hoped to groom him as a successor to the Dalai Lama more sympathetic to Beijing's aims in Tibet.

A Significant Defection

The young Karmapa, accompanied by a few aides, slipped out of the Tibetan capital and walked several hundred miles over forbidding Himalayan trails in midwinter to reach the sanctuary of Dharamsala in India, headquarters of the Dalai Lama. It was the most significant defection since that of the Dalai Lama forty years earlier. His flight was unknown to the world until VOA's Tibetan Service, tipped off by two independently corroborating sources in the region, reported it twenty-four hours before any other news agency. The service's reputation for accuracy made it the radio of record sought out by those who wanted the story revealed.

In March 2000, a pro-PRC Tibetan leader, Chyali Chambasonam (the so-called Tibetan Living Buddha), speaking at National People's Congress meetings in Beijing, said that the Karmapa Lama's escape to India was a mistaken decision, subtly encouraged by VOA and other foreign broadcasts to Tibet. The Tibetan Living Buddha was quoted as saying that because of Tibet's isolation, a paucity of Chinese television and radio broadcasts, and a limited understanding of Chinese, many Tibetans—including the Karmapa himself—had listened to VOA and what he called Tibetan-language propaganda of the Dalai Lama. The Living Buddha then recommended a massive increase in PRC broadcasts in Tibetan to Tibet.[8]

The government of India handled the Karmapa's unexpected presence in Dharamsala with great caution for fear of upsetting its giant neighbor, China. About a year after the young religious leader's arrival in its territory, there were reports that India had granted him asylum. VOA Tibetan picked up and verified the reports on its evening program to the region on February 1, 2001, again scooping all others. Forty-eight hours after that, Tashi Wangdi of the Tibetan government-in-exile held a news conference in Dharamsala confirming the news.[9]

When in Doubt, Hold Off

The Tibetan Service, while developing and training stringers, made certain that it was guided by VOA's two-source rule. That "safety net" enabled the service to avoid a major error the same week as India's grant of asylum to the Karmapa was announced. Agence France Presse (APF) had misquoted the Dalai Lama as saying in an exclusive interview that he had decided to bequeath his authority (the implication was *all* of his authority) to someone else. In the Tibetan community, the Dalai Lama's authority is both political and spiritual. His spiritual authority is based in Buddhist tradition on the fact that the Dalai Lama is a particular reincarnation and cannot bequeath that authority until he dies and is reborn. VOA Tibetan did not pick up the AFP quote because the service knew that it couldn't be correct. The misleading attribution was disseminated widely by other media, however. The Tibetan government in Dharamsala felt compelled to issue a clarification. In that statement, it made clear that the Dalai Lama's reference was to the election of a prime minister to assume some of his traditional political power. VOA then broadcast the corrected account.[10]

A WINDOW TO THE WORLD FOR A WIDER TIBETAN COMMUNITY

Buescher believes that the Tibetan Service has succeeded because it offers an accurate window not only on Tibetan affairs, but on the world as well, in language its listeners can understand. Between 5 and 6 million people speak Tibetan, about 2 million of them in Tibet and most of the others in Tibetan-populated regions of China to the east or southeast. Depending on where they live, they speak the Kham or Amdo dialect (as mentioned in chapter 12). To serve the widest possible audience, Buescher and his team produce regularly scheduled newscasts in each dialect throughout the broadcast day.

"One of the reasons for the Tibetan Service's success," Buescher wrote in 1992,

> is that subjects such as AIDS, space travel, women's rights, parliamentary reform, and so on, have not been systematically explored in any dialect of Tibetan before. This is great, but we have to fashion a significant amount of our vocabulary as we go along. We try to make our broadcasts "user friendly," but given the rural background of much of our audience, their lack of formal education, and their lack of contact with people outside their small communities, I think the channel of communication between us and our listeners can never be completely clear.[11]

That wider Tibetan community of VOA listeners also included scores of political prisoners. Among them was former monk and teacher Takna Jigme Sangpo, who had been held in Lhasa's Drapchi Prison by Chinese authorities for most of the past forty years. He was serving his latest sentence for "counterrevolutionary" activity after having put up a prodemocracy poster on a temple gate in the Tibetan capital two decades earlier. Sangpo told a VOA interpreter on his release in 2002 that he and other detainees were regular listeners of the Tibetan Service. The seventy-six-year-old prisoner of conscience—finally released for medical reasons after intense pressure from abroad—told a VOA Tibetan interviewer that because of the broadcasts and despite jamming by the Chinese, he and his fellow prisoners were well aware of the international efforts to free them.[12]

THOSE MULE PACKS OVER THE HIMALAYAS

The opening decade of VOA Tibetan-language broadcasts was studded with "firsts." In 1991, its initial interview with the Dalai Lama was the first time people inside Tibet had heard the Nobel laureate's voice in their own language on the radio since he fled into exile in 1959. In 1998, the service conducted the first Tibetan-language interview on television with the Dalai Lama for a satellite broadcast to the kingdom. In the summer of 2000, VOA Tibetan simulcast on both radio and television the Dalai Lama's talk on the Washington Mall at the annual Smithsonian Institution Folklife Festival. Because there are only a few TV receivers in Tibet capable of bringing down overseas programs, the audience there for the video transmissions is relatively small. But the Tibetan government-in-exile was undaunted. Presented with a video-tape copy of the VOA Tibetan TV interview, one of the Dalai Lama's staff told VOA that "for the next six months, every mule going over the Himalayas will have a copy of this tape on its back."[13]

The impact of the Tibetan Service miracle is perhaps best illustrated by Beijing's reaction. The pro-PRC Tibetan Living Buddha's call for an increase in broadcast activity in early 2000 was almost immediately heeded. During the following year, Radio China International was authorized to triple its Tibetan-language staff. Moreover, the PRC constructed high-powered jamming stations, including one on the outskirts of Lhasa, to try to block Tibetan-language programs from abroad. "This," Buescher said, "may certainly be a response to the rapid increase in the number of hours of U.S. broadcasts during 2000 and 2001, during which time VOA increased its schedule from three to four hours daily, and Radio Free Asia from six to eight hours daily." None of these transmissions overlapped, which meant that Tibetan-language broadcasting from U.S.-funded radios to Tibet was available twelve hours daily.

"THE IMPERMANENCE OF THINGS"

John Buescher, however, on the tenth anniversary of the Tibetan Service, urged all international broadcasters to recognize, with humility, that it is an ever-changing world, and an ever-changing media scene:

> In Buddhism, there's a strong recognition of the impermanence of
> things. I think that radio broadcasting is a fine school for the

impermanence of things. The news is always new, the frequencies in shortwave always float, the voice of the broadcaster sends out a stream of sound that's never the same twice. The words hang on the air for a moment and then disappear. They talk about people, governments, and countries that rise and fall. . . . Our next ten years are filled with challenges, with technological and political change, and every day we'll face the wide open and always surprising question of what's happened in the world today, and report to our audience the always incomplete answer we find.[14]

The establishment of the Tibetan Service occurred just nine months before the collapse of the Soviet Union. Its early years coincided with the first post–Cold War decade. The challenges of technical and political change in the 1990s—what Buescher called the ever-fascinating "impermanences" of international broadcasting—are the subject of the remaining chapters in this book.

15

Middle East Flashbacks

THE WARS OF 1967 AND 1991

It was a rare glimpse into the mind of Saddam Hussein. On *ABC Prime Time Live*, as the Persian Gulf crisis escalated in mid-November1990, Peter Jennings interviewed the Iraqi leader and later observed that Saddam seemed exceptionally well informed. He corrected an interpreter about the number of additional U.S. troops ordered to the region a week earlier by President Bush and was aware days in advance that the president would be traveling to the Middle East to visit American troops on Thanksgiving Day. Saddam's interpreter confided to Jennings that the Iraqi president had just come from listening to an Arabic evening broadcast of the Voice of America.

> —Member of the ABC camera crew, in
> "VOA Broadcasting Initiatives in the Middle East"

With war possibly just hours away, Baghdad is an eerie blend of public grit and private desperation. As the Education Ministry announces plans for midyear exams, families pack children off to stay with rural relatives. Iraqis parrot the bellicose words of Saddam Hussein, then nervously tune in the Voice of America to find out what's really happening.

> —Tony Horwitz and Geraldine Brooks,
> "Baghdad Is a Blend of Bravado and Fear"

"The impermanance of things"—John Buescher's eloquent phrase—is also an apt description of one of the world's most volatile regions: the Middle East. Perhaps that's one reason Arabic at the turn of the century was second only to English as an internationally broadcast language.[1]

The year the Cold War really ended, 1991, the United States waged its first hot war since Vietnam. The Persian Gulf crisis and war lasted for seven months—from August 2, 1990, when Iraq's Saddam Hussein invaded and occupied Kuwait, until February 28, 1991, when his forces were driven out after a six-week air and ground war. The West and some Arab world allies successfully drew a line in the sand to prevent the Iraqi dictator from gaining control over the world's richest oil fields.

During the crisis, the Voice of America was tested (and second-guessed) in unprecedented ways, mostly after the coalition victory. Criticism of its Arabic-language broadcasts surfaced in U.S. dailies such as the *Wall Street Journal* and *New York Post*, and also on Capitol Hill.[2] The inspector general of the United States Information Agency (USIA) echoed some of the complaints months after the war ended. But independent experts cleared the Voice of charges that it had tilted toward Iraq during the crisis. The allegations originated in capitals of some Arab allied nations.

The Center for Strategic and International Studies (CSIS) in Washington, D.C., reviewed hundreds of hours of VOA Arabic programming during the conflict and concluded:

> By standard U.S. journalistic practice, VOA, at worst, made some questionable calls. The vast majority of its coverage, however, should be judged as clearly within the boundaries set by the U.S. journalistic canon. It would be wrong to suggest that its coverage was biased against the coalition forces or that it was an unwitting dupe of Saddam Hussein. Neither the qualitative assessment of VOA's overall thoroughness and balance by CSIS analysts, nor the quantitative analysis performed, leads to that conclusion.[3]

During the seven-month crisis, I worked closely with my friend of many years and mentor on Middle East affairs, Salman (Sam) Hilmy, whom we met in chapter 12. In 1990 and 1991, Sam was the chief of the Voice's Near East and South Asia Division and an Arabic Branch veteran. He was among many VOA tutors I had over years of watching a turbulent but endlessly fascinating region. It is necessary to go back to the mid-1960s to retrace these years.

A NICE, QUIET BEGINNING

In January 1965, my young family and I left Washington for Beirut with only a few weeks' notice, just about twenty-six years to the day before the Persian Gulf War began. My first overseas assignment with the Voice was as the director of the Beirut, Lebanon, subcenter of the Rhodes Program Center of the Arabic Branch. The five-member staff all were either older or vastly more experienced in the ways and psychology of their society and culture than their crew-cut, twenty-nine-year-old neophyte boss from the United States. However, they opened their homes and hearts to the Heil family. "Paradise without people," an old Arabic saying goes, "is not worth setting foot in."[4] "People" in this paradise, we soon learned, meant hospitality at its finest.

Those at the Beirut subcenter were a pleasure to work with. We embarked on a radically new course for them, and they patiently accepted change. The office had been established about a decade earlier, to produce mainly nontopical, nonnews material.[5] This consisted largely of Arabic-language entertainment programming, concerts by celebrated singers such as Lebanon's Fairouz, interviews with artists, and other cultural material. The team's new assignment was to produce a range of programming, at times under more rigorous deadlines: up-to-the-minute correspondent reports on the politics and economics of the eastern Mediterranean as well as the traditional cultural programming. The main job was to send programming and daily news spots and recorded features in Arabic to the Rhodes Program Center for broadcast on shortwave and medium wave to the region. A secondary requirement was that I provide reportage to VOA Washington for English broadcasts, spots translated (or adapted) into Arabic by my Beirut colleagues and put on the Rhodes feed.

The staff of the subcenter became my first tutors:

• Ghassan K. Sabbagh, the senior-ranking Arabic-speaking editor, was born in Palestine and known throughout the Arab world. Sabbagh produced a number of the entertainment programs, including a popular Western music–request show, *Chosen for You*, which he emceed himself in the Beirut studios. Sabbagh, brother of a former VOA and BBC veteran broadcaster, Isa K. Sabbagh, later advanced to senior positions in the Arabic Branch in Washington and served there until his retirement in 2002.

• Mohammed Ghuneim was the subcenter's top news reporter and special events interviewer. Ghuneim was born in Jaffa and, in addition to reporting, wrote, narrated, and produced original dramas based on American short stories. This suave, savvy journalist later directed the Arabic Branch's Amman office for many years (for a description of his detention by Syrian authorities in Damascus, see chapter 4). Ghuneim was chief of the VOA Arabic Branch and moderator of its TV programs in Washington before his retirement in 1999. He was highly respected in Western, as well as local, journalistic circles.

• Hassan Abu Nassif, the administrative and budget officer, had a hearty laugh, a sense of humor, and local connections that enabled him to accomplish any and all tasks. Abu Nassif, born in Kab-Elias in the Lebanese Bekaa Valley, was much more than an administrator. He became a skilled reporter and anchor of news programs. Abu Nassif and his family, like the Sabbaghs and Ghuneims, emigrated to the United States and obtained American citizenship during the Lebanese civil war. The Abu Nassif family later returned to Lebanon.

• Rose Manneh, the key office assistant of the Beirut subcenter, later became a translator and adapter in the Arabic Branch in Washington after the program center was relocated there from the island of Rhodes in the late 1970s. Manneh, who was injured during a bombing attack on the American embassy in Beirut during the civil war of 1974 to 1984, became an American citizen after moving to the United States. She was born in the tiny southern Lebanese village of Barty.

As it turned out, the Beirut assignment was the first of four Heil overseas posts during the next six and a half years. The tireless and patient Dot helped manage subsequent family moves to Cairo, the island of Rhodes, and, finally, Athens for the remainder of my time as a VOA foreign correspondent. In these posts and back in Washington, I had more extraordinary teachers:

• Two unfailingly helpful Egyptian assistants at the Cairo subcenter of the Rhodes Program Center were senior editor and master of classical Arabic style Abdel Moneim Ziadi and indefatigable field reporter Fawzi Tadros.

• VOA Middle East bureau chief Walter A. Kohl, my boss and senior foreign correspondent in Athens, later served as VOA's chief diplomatic correspondent, as head of the USIA Foreign Correspondents

Center in Washington, and as USIA public affairs officer in Athens. Kohl specialized in Aegean, Cypriot, and Middle East history and was known fondly in the newsroom as Sir Walter Cool.

• Ismail Dahiyat and Moazzam Siddiqi, both of whom had earned doctorates, were key mentors in my later Washington days as a Middle East watcher. Both served as Near East Division chiefs, and Siddiqi subsequently as head of an expanded post–September 11 South and Central Asia Division. Dahiyat, originally from Jordan, and Siddiqi, from India, were master linguists and area specialists.

THE JUNE WAR

The Heil family was in Lebanon—that once beautiful land—several years before the terrible civil war. The Beirut dream, alas, was too good to last very long. In 1966, VOA decided to transfer us to a larger subcenter in Cairo after just eighteen months. The tour in the Egyptian capital, it turned out, lasted for less than a year. The final three weeks in Egypt are worth recounting.[6]

On the Suez Canal

The VOA Cairo subcenter wangled places aboard the gleaming white USS *Oceanographer*, a research ship sailing the length of the Suez Canal, on May 19, 1967. This was three days before President Gamal Abdel Nasser closed the Gulf of Aqaba to Israeli shipping on the eve of the June war. Weeks earlier, Fawzi Tadros and I had applied for passage on the research vessel to interview Egyptian and American scientists. As it turned out, we now could offer something far more important: eyewitness accounts of the buildup preceding the third Arab–Israeli war since 1948. Our journey from north to south on the canal was delayed at the halfway point as the Qantara al Sharqia rotating drawbridge swung across the waterway to permit the passage of Egyptian armor across it into Sinai. It was an early phase of Nasser's ill-fated mobilization along Israel's southwestern frontier. We filed our reports immediately after docking at Suez.

The Mobilization Gains Momentum

Egypt was brimming with confidence. It had the edge in numbers of troops, and a Cairo weekly magazine showed, in vivid color, a photo of a practice maneuver by an Egyptian soldier with a flamethrower. "The scorching fire he sprays," I wrote at the time, "seems to leap out of the page at the reader." On the Sinai front, Egyptian forces were beginning to dig massive networks of trenches. Our eighteen-year-old gardener, barefoot and always smiling, was drafted during the last week of May. We could imagine him being sent off to the Sinai desert with literally no military training to face whatever the "battle of battles" might bring. On May 28, on orders of a brand-new U.S. ambassador, Dot, Wendy, Susie, and six-week-old Nancy Heil were evacuated by plane to Athens with about a hundred other dependents. I took them to the airport, assured them that we'd be together again after a few days, and stayed behind to report for VOA.

"Hiyya harb!"

Eight days later it was a sultry morning, June 5, 1967, and the fog over the Nile Valley was just beginning to dissipate. At ten o'clock, Ambassador Richard Nolte was scheduled to pay a call on President Nasser to present his credentials. The meeting never took place. At about that hour, I happened to be in the office of none other than VOA pioneer broadcaster Robert Bauer (chapter 2), now the U.S. public affairs attaché in Cairo. We could hear what at first sounded like sonic booms. "Those are no sonic booms," Bauer exclaimed. "Those are bombs." I picked up the phone and called Reuters. The woman on the other end of the line simply shouted: "Hiyya harb!" (This is war!) Israel was making its first air strikes on the runways of airfields at the giant Egyptian base near the capital, Cairo East. I ran to the office, made other quick calls, and filed, with Tadros quickly preparing an Arabic version of the report. During a stroll on Cairo's Kasr el Nil Street near Tahrir Square a few hours later, we could hear Radio Cairo blaring martial music from every window, interspersed with fictional announcements that scores of Israeli planes had been shot down. Air-raid sirens wailed intermittently. There was the distant rat-tat-tat of antiaircraft fire. Above the Nile, an Israeli-piloted fighter jet, a black U.S.-made Phantom outlined against the blazing summer sky, swept down low over the river, dodging the ground fire.

First Signs of Defeat

By dusk this first evening of the Six-Day War, it appeared that the Egyptian army and air force had suffered serious reverses. We had filed reports to Washington at noon, but by sunset, Egyptian authorities severed phones and broadcast lines from the subcenter to Washington and, in fact, all outgoing phone lines from the country. Cairo was plunged into darkness because of a metropolis-wide blackout. For most of the rest of the week, the Cairo office was deserted (war-frightened staff except for Tadros and Ziadi simply decided not to come to work). We could file texts in English only through very busy embassy communications channels.

Early on, I decided that the extravagant United Arab Republic (Egyptian) claims of air "kills" were bogus and avoided statistics in my reporting. It was an unequal contest from the beginning. I saw a soldier-driver of an Egyptian vehicle on the Nile Corniche (shore boulevard) standing beside his vehicle before an overpass, puzzled. His armored personnel carrier wouldn't fit beneath it; someone had failed to calculate the additional height of an antiaircraft rocket mounted on the rear of the APC and consider whether or not it would fit under highway overpasses.

The Torching Begins, and the Guys in the *Gallebiyas* Start to Climb the Walls

Early on the second day, an embassy political officer remarked that it was "all over." He added that the Egyptians were looking for a scapegoat, and in this case it was the United States because of American support for Israel. "We're going to burn to a cinder today," he said. That Tuesday morning, Radio Cairo began broadcasting allegations that American pilots had joined those of Israel in the conflict. By noon, mobs entered the U.S. library and consulate in Alexandria and torched them. The consulate in Port Said was next.

In Garden City, the center of Cairo, enraged crowds tried to scale the wall and come through the barred gates of the embassy compound and the thick glass door in front of the Zahra Building, where the VOA Cairo subcenter was located. I watched them waving clubs and could see them gesturing in rage, only ten or fifteen feet away, as a few courageous Marine guards beat them back. The glass door I was looking through was so thick that I couldn't hear the shouting. It was like being in the front row at a silent movie—too close for comfort. Later in the day, Egypt severed diplomatic relations with the United States. The American embassy became the U.S. interests section of the Spanish embassy at the moment of the diplomatic break with Egypt.

Endgame in Cairo

On Friday, the fifth day of the war, VOA got an unexpected break. Washington was able to get a phone call into Egypt, and we were able to voice four reports. "Travelers returning from Sinai," I said, "told of vast fields of slain soldiers, shattered emplacements, wrecked tanks. Arab residents of Sinai reportedly were streaming across the Suez Canal to escape advancing Israeli columns."[7] The coverage desk in Washington promised to call back at around ten o'clock that Friday evening, after a nationwide address in which President Nasser was expected to inform Egyptians of their stunning defeat.

At dusk, the city went dark again in the nightly blackout. I lit a candle and listened to the English translation of Nasser's speech on a battery-powered radio, taking notes all the while. It turned out to be a "farewell" address of sorts, and the streets of Cairo erupted in a mighty guttural roar of angry voices. The hero of the Arab world had quit, and Egyptians felt compelled to "get" the enemy—in this case, Uncle Sam. Mobs converged on the embassy from all directions. It was pitch black, and I wondered if they would scale the walls this time. They didn't. But the call didn't come through either. Finally, at 10:15, I called the embassy telephone operator to see if Washington had tried to reach me. He explained, a bit sheepishly, that yes, a call had come through a few minutes earlier to his switchboard. However, he had refused to put it through to me because, he said, "we can't tie up the line . . . we're too busy calling all the remaining Americans to tell them they have to gather at the main Cairo rail station for evacuation at 2:00 A.M., and that includes you, too, Mr. Heil."

Disgusted, I drove my car home (where the tapped phones had long been dead). I grabbed the canvas bag that I had packed with a few household belongings; put the house key in an envelope, as instructed, to turn over to the embassy so it could pack up the household furnishings weeks later; drove the car back to the mission compound; deposited the house and car keys at a checkout desk; and signed out. We then were taken by bus to the train station, and hustled aboard for a rail trip to Alexandria.

The Voyage to Piraeus

Just at dawn, the train pulled right up to a huge warehouse-like terminal at the port of Alexandria and deposited all of us with our bags, including

Ambassador-designate Nolte, on the concrete floor under a corrugated tin roof. No air conditioning here, just an occasional waft of Mediterranean breezes. We waited in the giant shed for many hours, until the SS *Carina*, an evacuation ship, was cleared for entry into the port shortly before sunset. Then we boarded it for a twenty-two-hour crossing of the Mediterranean to the port of Piraeus near Athens. The ship was crammed with more than 200 American citizens, and some had to sleep that night on deck chairs. I penned notes on the deck and was ready when the ship pulled into Piraeus. Jack Hooley of the VOA Athens bureau had set up a phone line from a dockside building. Communications again, at last. An hour later, there was a long-awaited family reunion at a suburban Athens hotel and evacuation center in the hills northeast of the city.

There was no rest for the weary, though. We were told to move within thirty-six hours to the island of Rhodes, where I was to be a shift supervisor of expanded VOA Arabic programming. There we were warmly welcomed by old friends, including Sam and Kate Hilmy and broadcaster Gaby Mallides and his wife, Betty. They helped us settle in a vacated house, our home for the next six months.

Upon arriving on Rhodes, I learned that although most of the breaking news reports on the run-up to the war fed to Washington from May 16 through June 5 had been cleared by the VOA Office of Policy in English, less than half of the identical spots adapted into Arabic had been approved for broadcast.[8] A heavy-handed Office of Policy had prevailed. The June war occurred nine years before the charter became law and just over a decade before VOA correspondents began to operate independently of U.S. missions abroad.

FAST FORWARD TO THE PERSIAN GULF WAR

In 1990 and 1991, external pressures on America's Voice seemed somewhat greater during the seven-month Gulf crisis and war than during the June war a quarter century earlier. There were a number of reasons:

• The Gulf War involved many more actors than the conflict in 1967, including a twenty-eight-nation military coalition led by the United States, among whose members were European and Arab allies. Direct American involvement inevitably placed VOA under greater scrutiny by those inside and outside the U.S. government.

• Communications from the war zone were much more sophisticated and included war coverage for the first time by CNN and scores of live military briefings and presidential statements from many venues as well as frontline pool reporting in which VOA was a full participant. No such luck in the Sinai in 1967, at least from Cairo.

• On both the programming and the technical fronts, VOA had far more sophisticated assets in the early 1990s than it had had in the late 1960s. It had seasoned war correspondents like Gil Butler, Mohammed Ghuneim, Laurie Kassman, Jim Malone, Sonja Pace, and Doug Roberts in the Middle East at various times. Moreover, it put together an around-the-clock crisis program, using both VOA and Radio Free Europe/Radio Liberty (RFE/RL) relay stations—the first technical cooperation by the two U.S.-funded networks on such a scale.

• VOA's daily schedule to the Middle East more than doubled in Arabic,[9] increased by 50 percent in English, and rose by 25 percent in Farsi-to-Iran. Each operation had to maintain programming quality and accuracy with few or no staff increases.

• The crisis lasted for months rather than weeks (if you count the buildup to the June 1967 war), increasing the odds for adaptation errors and misjudgments by an overstretched staff. In many ways, VOA—despite the safeguards of the charter and correspondent guidelines—was a more visible, vulnerable target in 1990 and 1991 than it had been in 1967.

Even before the crisis flared, intensive pressures on content surfaced. Just eight days before Saddam Hussein's troops moved into and occupied Kuwait, the Department of State killed a draft U.S. government editorial written for broadcast by VOA. The editorial noted that Iraq had massed "thousands of troops, as well as tanks and missiles, near its border with Kuwait. The U.S. is concerned about the buildup of military forces along the Iraq–Kuwait border. U.S. officials have stressed that there is no place in a civilized world for coercion and intimidation."[10] No reason was given for the State Department's "kill" of the editorial. Press reports were that Washington was reluctant to criticize Saddam because it wanted to maintain good relations with Iraq. Earlier in the year, Baghdad had vociferously protested another U.S. government editorial that placed Iraq in the company of Libya, North Korea, Cuba, and other countries reliant on what the *Washington Times* called "an elaborate, vicious state security apparatus to check dissent and keep their rulers in power."[11]

After the Iraqi invasion of Kuwait, American policy took a 180-degree turn. There was widespread speculation that the earlier timid U.S. official handling of well-documented troop movements and secret-police activities in Iraq might have been among the factors that had led Saddam to miscalculate the consequences of occupying Kuwait.

VOA Responds to the Crisis

A few hours after the Iraqi invasion on August 2, 1990, Director of Programs Sid Davis authorized the first of three Arabic expansions, from seven and a half to nine and three-quarter hours daily. VOA also covered meetings of the United Nations Security Council on the Iraqi invasion

---

A LIFELINE FROM HOME

In times of crisis, VOA broadcasts State Department advisories to American citizens being assembled at staging points for evacuations.* Scores of Americans were trapped in Kuwait or Iraq until nearly the end of 1990. Between October 3 and December 13, VOA also produced a special program in English, *Messages from Home*, which enabled U.S. families with members stranded in the Gulf region to speak directly to their relatives over the airwaves. When, in fact, the Americans finally were freed, several of them said that they first heard of their impending release on VOA.

For its part, the Arabic Branch set up a telephone dial-in center and stocked it with recordings of updated news bulletins every hour or so around the clock throughout the Gulf crisis and war. Incoming calls between August 2 and February 28 were nonstop. VOA Arabic news reports were placed on radio stations in Egypt, Morocco, Jordan, Tunisia, Saudi Arabia, Bahrain, and the United Arab Emirates. Worldwide, VOA news about Desert Shield and Desert Storm was broadcast live or on a delayed basis by 1,800 affiliated radio stations or networks in at least seventy-five countries.

*Other evacuations in which VOA broadcast advisories to American citizens included the withdrawal of nonessential staff and dependents from several Arab countries during the Six-Day War in 1967, from Jordan during its civil war in 1970, from Pakistan during the India–Pakistan conflict of 1971, and from Lebanon during its decade-long civil conflict in the 1970s and 1980s.

---

in all of its forty-three languages. It provided daily reports on the formation and deployment of the twenty-eight-nation U.S.-led coalition military force to the Gulf region. It followed closely the plight of foreigners trapped in Iraq and Kuwait during the early months of the crisis.

On September 5, a VOA satellite-fed, around-the-clock Middle East network was created, the first of its kind in international broadcasting. With the assistance of the White House, State Department, and Board for International Broadcasting, which was the oversight body for RFE/RL at the time, VOA's Office of Engineering arranged for the use of RFE's Portugal transmitters for some VOA broadcasts to Eastern Europe. This freed up VOA transmitters in Greece and Germany for the extraordinary VOA Middle East network. VOA broadcast on forty-five frequencies, both shortwave and medium wave. Listeners tuned in from as far away as Sweden and South Africa, Thailand and Missouri.

Live from Washington and Other Venues

In many ways, the Arabic Branch—back in Washington for thirteen years since the closure of the Rhodes Program Center[12]—was rejuvenated by the Gulf crisis. Its news desk updated the dial-in service around the clock. Moreover, the staff, little practiced at anchoring call-in programs and simultaneous interpretations of presidential news conferences and military briefings, suddenly found itself forced to engage in all these live programs at all hours of the day or night. During the seven-month crisis, there were ninety-one live broadcasts, with Arabic simultaneous interpretations of news conferences by President Bush, UN Security Council sessions, and military briefings at the Pentagon and in Saudi Arabia. Prewar call-in programs featured ambassadors of the United States, Iraq, Kuwait, and Egypt.

Why, some asked, did VOA broadcast a call-in program with the Iraqi ambassador to the United Nations? They were unaware that hard questions were posed to the Iraqi diplomat by the program host and listeners and that his call-in was followed immediately by one with the Kuwaiti ambassador to Washington. Nor were they aware that U.S. ambassador Hume Horan, an accomplished Arabic speaker, fielded questions about the Gulf War in two similar full-hour programs during the crisis. VOA stopped the call-ins when Desert Storm began.

According to Robert Fortner, an analyst with the Center for Strategic and International Studies,

The Gulf war was both a military and a psychological war, a war of soldiers, tanks, warplanes, and a war of words. The conflict raised the stakes for international broadcasters, thinning out the line that separates journalism from propaganda, and led listeners close to the conflict to listen ever more carefully to what was broadcast.

The BBC was criticized for some of the same reasons as VOA. One attack on the BBC's reporting in London claimed that the BBC had failed to "maintain the degree of neutrality" of VOA and Radio Monte Carlo: it had become a tool of Iraq. Arab members of the coalition were sensitive to reports of the war and to public opinion in their own countries opposing their participation. VOA was bound to be criticized.[13]

The Critiques

Criticisms came from three sources, which at times seemed to reinforce or play off one another:

- *The U.S. press.* American dailies became aware of cables from U.S. missions in the Middle East reporting a perception by some (notably in Bahrain, Egypt, and Saudi Arabia) that VOA Arabic was pro-Saddam or, as one Arab coalition official was quoted as saying, "the voice of Baghdad." In January 1991, U.S. reporters began to question USIA and VOA executives about the Arabic Branch's broadcast of Iraqi and Palestinian statements critical of the Gulf coalition and criticisms of the war in branch-prepared roundups of American newspaper opinion.
- *Coalition allies in the Arab world.* The governments of Egypt and Saudi Arabia registered concerns with U.S. embassies that VOA's Arabic broadcasts were tilting toward Iraq. They were judging VOA broadcasts by their own standards; Saudi Arabia's official media, for example, hadn't reported the Iraqi invasion of Kuwait until seventy-two hours after it occurred. Nonetheless, VOA director Richard W. Carlson and his deputy Robert Coonrod immediately organized independent reviews of the programming to determine whether it met charter requirements.
- *The U.S. diplomatic community.* On orders from USIA, several Arabic-speaking agency officers in the Middle East began daily monitoring and critiquing of VOA Arabic broadcasts. A junior officer in

Saudi Arabia was particularly critical, quoting a Saudi Information Ministry official as saying: "We have little sympathy for balanced news about the war. There can't be two sides when we are fighting evil. Did you give equal time to Hitler in World War Two?"[14] USIA director Bruce Gelb asked the agency's Office of the Inspector General (OIG) to review the content of VOA Arabic broadcasts. The request, which was not supported by Gelb's deputy, coincided with a public dispute between Gelb and Carlson over personnel and budget issues.[15]

In February 1991, Coonrod commissioned the Center for Strategic and International Studies in Washington, D.C., and the Hudson Institute in Indianapolis to conduct independent studies of VOA Arabic.[16] Both organizations concluded that VOA gave far more airtime to coalition and procoalition views of the conflict than to Baghdad spokesmen or opponents of the war. A comprehensive survey by VOA's program review unit indicated that more than three-quarters of the Arabic-language interviews conducted in January and February 1991 reflected procoalition or neutral analysts' views—in addition to several hours devoted to live, simultaneous interpretations of presidential addresses and coalition military briefings.[17] On-scene VOA Arabic-language news reports from coalition capitals outweighed those from pro-Baghdad or Palestinian sources by a margin of six to one.[18] Thousands of centrally produced news and background scripts were issued on the crisis, many adapted by the Arabic Branch. The branch was on the air for more than 2,800 hours between August 2, 1990, and February 28, 1991. Some mistakes and errors of judgment were inevitable. These included

• *Handling of press reviews during the second week of the Gulf War.* In press reviews during the week of January 20, ten out of eighteen American newspaper articles selected gave negative views of the United States and its allies. On some days, that reflected the tenor of the U.S. press. The roundups were part of a VOA Arabic program, U.S. Media Mideast and North Africa Watch. During the same week, however, VOA Arabic broadcast a live simultaneous interpretation of President Bush's January 25 news conference; provided live coverage of the Pentagon briefings of January 21, 22, 24, and 25; and reported a Saudi military spokesman's briefing on January 22. VOA Arabic also aired U.S. government editorials harshly critical of the Iraqi occupation of Kuwait and Baghdad's treatment of its own citizens.[19]

- *A heavier-than-usual proportion of anticoalition interviews early in the conflict.* A statistical breakdown revealed that fifteen out of twenty Americans and Arabs interviewed by the Arabic Branch during the week of January 20 criticized U.S. or coalition policies. Mark Blitzer and Neil Pickett of the Hudson Institute found, however, that if there was one recurring critique of VOA Arabic and English programming as a whole, it was that both "tended to rely too heavily on U.S. government and coalition sources and that the views of those who opposed the war or who might be inclined to be critical of both sides in the conflict, were not well represented."[20]

- *Occasional lapses in news sourcing or Arabic Branch omissions in the adaptation of centrally issued news items.* In one instance, the VOA news-room, relying on two Western news agency reports from Damascus, issued an erroneous news item reporting anticoalition demonstrations in that city. This was broadcast in Arabic, but dropped by both the news-room and the branch soon after the mistake was discovered. In a less serious lapse, there was questionable handling of a news item on January 20. The item, issued by the central newsroom, centered on rather large antiwar demonstrations in Spain and Belgium. It mentioned, however, that an opinion poll in Germany showed that 80 percent of people agreed with military action against Iraq. That sentence, marked optional in the newsroom, was omitted in the Arabic translation.[21]

A Postscript

After a review of twenty complaints from USIA Near East area monitors and embassies in other regions plus materials supplied by USIA director Gelb, the OIG recommended that in future crises, VOA management undertake rigorous internal content reviews of services even earlier than it had done in the Gulf War. The OIG was more critical of the VOA programming than were the independent institutes. The inspectors rec-ommended a logging system to ensure that embassy complaints from abroad be shared with VOA in times of crisis. That was reminiscent, many at the Voice felt, of the precharter era. The OIG, however, also seconded VOA decisions to

- Tighten review procedures for press roundups
- Shorten and balance interviews to reflect all sides in a crisis or dispute

- More rigorously review the content of field stringer reports
- Terminate stringers who worked for official media in countries from which they were reporting (the Arabic Branch had stopped using its Baghdad stringer with such ties the day the war started)

The struggle to tell it straight was challenged throughout the crisis on diplomatic and technical, as well as programming, fronts. As the Gulf War approached, USIA put VOA Arabic on a powerful Saudi station at Ras al Zor, in the eastern province, with a strong reach into Iraq and Kuwait. VOA opposed the idea, because it would sandwich Voice programming blocks between transmissions of the clandestine Radio Free Kuwait and of Saudi radio. According to Director of Programs Sid Davis:

> The argument is made that if VOA broadcasts are widely separated in time from those of the Kuwaiti resistance, other transmissions will "buffer" ours from theirs. In our experience, this simply isn't true. On medium wave, 663 kHz is easily accessible and recognizable to all, from Cadillac to camel driver. Listeners will recall, on hearing Radio Free Kuwait, that they heard VOA on the same frequency, regardless of when. And we can imagine that if Saudi radio is "the buffer," it is more likely to resemble the Kuwaiti broadcast than ours. VOA is recognized as a beacon of truth and credibility in the Middle East, an image carved from dedication to high journalistic principles. Linkage with Ras al Zor's broadcasts would weaken and destroy VOA's distinctive place among Arab listeners.[22]

USIA director Gelb was unconvinced. He ordered a transmission of VOA Arabic's highly regionalized *Around the Gulf* program delivered via satellite to United States Information Service Dhahran beginning on December 22, 1990.[23] We suspected why that was, but didn't learn until months later that starting on January 7, 1991, it was relayed and rebroadcast via Ras al Zor to the region.

During the first five months of the Gulf crisis, USIA research documented that listenership to VOA in Saudi Arabia increased by 57 percent, with one in five Saudi adults listening at least once weekly. In some Gulf emirates, the audience increased tenfold from a very small base before the crisis.[24] Listening undoubtedly increased because some coalition governments in the region did not permit their state-controlled

THE LEGACY OF VOA'S CREDIBILITY

In 2002, VOA's new parent organization, the Broadcasting Board of Governors, replaced the Arabic Branch with a new, around-the-clock service in Arabic (FM, medium wave, and shortwave) to attract younger listeners in the historically turbulent region. In the Middle East especially, planners of the program, including board member and creator of the concept Norman Pattiz, recognized that credibility was of utmost importance. Writing a decade earlier, the two broadcast leaders most directly responsible for the Arabic Branch's performance during the 1990/1991 Gulf crisis had sounded much the same sentiment.

According to Sam Hilmy, chief of the Near East and South Asia Division:

> VOA's influence depends on its credibility as an impartial and objective source of information. That is why, as the CSIS report [in 1991] says, VOA reflected American values during the crisis without lowering itself to Middle East media standards. As we all know, people there do not trust their own government media, so much so that over seventy thousand of them, mostly from coalition countries, spent millions of dollars over seven months to call our news hotlines to hear the latest reliable news about events in the Gulf.*

He was seconded by Arabic Branch chief Mahmoud Zawawi:

> The Arabic branch has been subjected to unprecedented pressure in recent months to depart from the principles of the VOA Charter. Most of the pressure came from officials in Arab coalition partner states where the idea of dynamic interplay and discussion of views is totally alien to the governments of those countries. It is impossible to adhere to the legal requirements of the charter and to please these governments. This consistency, this credibility, has been established by VOA over many years. We did not, in the end, bend to pressure. VOA Arabic bolstered its credibility greatly during the Gulf crisis.†

*Sam Hilmy, "Reaction to CSIS Report," memorandum to author, May 28, 1991.
†Quoted in Chase Untermeyer, "Response to Office of Inspector General's Report, 'A Critique of VOA Broadcasts during the Persian Gulf Crisis,'" draft memorandum to Henry J. Catto, September 1992, 9.

media to report in timely fashion the Iraqi invasion of Kuwait, details of the allied bombing raids and casualties, or the Iraqi Scud missile attacks on Israel and Saudi Arabia.

Two vignettes framed the Gulf War. On the day Desert Storm began, VOA director Carlson dropped by the morning programming meeting and told the staff:

> As you know, we are on the brink of war. The deadline is tonight. There is every reason to believe that the U.S. will enter its most serious conflict in decades. The VOA role in this will be the same as it has always been, only more intense and more important than ever: and that is to bring to the world honest and fair depictions of events as they unfold. We will do that as we have always done it, without fear or favor, with honesty and the integrity that has become part of the Voice over the past fifty years.[25]

On the last day of the war, Arabic Branch senior correspondent Mohammed Ghuneim, along with the newsroom's Gil Butler, was among the first reporters to ride into a newly liberated Kuwait. Ghuneim reported:

> The unmistakable evidence of the ferocious war waged for Kuwait over the last few weeks is apparent with the first step across the Saudi–Kuwaiti border. Bulldozers had erased the modern highways. Trenches and minefields took their place. . . . In Kuwait City, everything in sight was a grim reminder of the people's hunger, thirst, and suffering. Further proof came at noon, when a creeping cloud of smoke from burning oil wells eclipsed the sun and devoured the light. Fumbling through pockets and purses, passersby pulled out their battery-operated torches, if only to light the bleakness of the soul. Suddenly it rained, washing away the black veil. . . . Daylight returned and with it, Kuwaitis went on to celebrate their freedom.[26]

16

Into the 1990s

THE BRAVE NEW WORLD
OF MULTIMEDIA

If we had stayed only on shortwave in the Balkans, we'd be
nowhere today.
—Frank Shkreli, interview with Alan L. Heil, Jr.

The Voice of America has a Farsi [radio-TV] call-in show in
which Iranians from all over the country telephone Washington, long distance, just to chat about their problems.
They are knocking at the world's door.
—Thomas Friedman, "Of Body and Soul"

History has a curious way of framing things. When geopolitics and the
multimedia world of the 1990s turned so many things upside down, those
who previously stifled the free flow of information suddenly, themselves,
became utterly dependent on the very sources they once had tried to
block.

Mikhail Gorbachev, a captive of Soviet hardliners and isolated in
a Black Sea villa during the aborted coup of 1991, had his aides rig up a
shortwave radio to find out what was going on. He later credited the
BBC, Radio Free Europe/Radio Liberty (RFE/RL), and VOA with keeping him abreast of events that led to his release after only three days.
Less than five months after that, the Soviet Union and Gorbachev's leadership of it were history.

One evening in April 1998, a white-haired, frail, and dying Pol Pot—
the master architect of the holocaust in Cambodia in the late
1970s—tuned to VOA in a remote jungle outpost there. He listened to

the Voice's Cambodian Service every day at 8:00 P.M. On this particular evening of April 15, a newscast reported that Ta Ma, Pol Pot's trusted lieutenant in the Khmer Rouge's tiny remaining encampment, was prepared to turn him over to international justice. About two hours later, Pol Pot committed suicide. Former Khmer Rouge members told the *Far East Economic Review* that fear of his possible arrest precipitated the action.[1]

Both events illustrated important truths about global media as the century ended: shortwave's "staying power" was significant, and the credibility of the larger international broadcasters established during the shortwave era was an essential foundation for their pursuit of multimedia in the twenty-first century. After the Cold War, with the advent of new technologies, VOA and the BBC had to reach out via television, the Internet (text, sound, and pictures), and local FM stations to stay in the game.

Ernest B. Furgurson of the *Baltimore Sun* described the impact of the new multimedia: "In 1989, it was still impossible to make a phone call at busy hours . . . a mile away across the Berlin Wall, and those lines could be closed at any time. But for the people of the East Germany, Western TV and radio acted as the bulletin boards of the revolution."[2]

The ill-fated Soviet coup by hardliners two years later reflected the striking changes. According to veteran Moscow correspondent David Hoffman, "Antennas and telephones, satellite dishes and fax machines became the tools by which the United States and other countries let Russian Federation President Boris Yeltsin and others resisting the coup . . . know that they were being supported by the outside world. In turn, the channels let Yeltsin and his backers provide important advice to the outside."[3] An aide to Yeltsin sent a fax to Washington, D.C., exclaiming: "It is a military coup! BY [Yeltsin] made an address to the people standing on a tank. . . . The following is BY's address to the Army. Submit it to USIA. Broadcast it over the country. May be Voice of America. Do it! Urgent!"[4]

Christian Science Monitor columnist and former VOA director John Hughes described how new technologies and international broadcasting converged to help thwart the putsch: "When VOA correspondents reporting the crowd scenes around the Russian parliament in Moscow during the recent coup attempt were trapped on the barricades, they pulled out their Finnish-made cellular phones and called in their reports to their Moscow bureau. The bureau transmitted the reports live to VOA headquarters in Washington, which broadcast them almost instantly by shortwave back to millions of listeners across the Soviet Union."[5] "It's

A TIME FOR DEALS

Four years before the attempted coup in Russia, in 1987, the Soviet Union had stopped jamming VOA and BBC Russian broadcasts. In the early 1990s, Kremlin authorities began to permit VOA and other Western broadcasters to place material, live and uncensored, on FM stations in the nation's eleven time zones. If you visited VOA any weekday at 4:00 or 5:00 A.M., Washington time, in 1991 and 1992, you likely would have found USSR Division chief Gerd von Doemming, sipping coffee, tie already loosened, working the phones to local or national networks across the vast country. He was a super salesman in his element. Von Doemming mastered both Russian and Ukrainian. He helped the Office of Engineering lease transmitters in the USSR and its successor states for VOA relays to an arc of nations, extending from North Korea in the east to Iran and Iraq in the west. In less than two years, von Doemming placed VOA on more than twenty FM stations in Russia and its former republics. Supported by VOA director Chase Untermeyer, he also put a weekly Worldnet Television Ukrainian news magazine, *Window on America,* on Ukraine's national network.* It had a peak viewing audience of 8 million Ukrainians.

*Sid Davis and Alan Heil, memorandum nominating Gerd von Doemming for a Superior Honor Award, September 10, 1992, 1–2.

impossible to conceal major events now," observed former NBC News president Lawrence Grossman. "No one can operate in the dark of night anymore."[6]

After the Berlin Wall fell, the United States and most other countries chopped budgets for international broadcasting because of a common misconception that the radios were created solely to fight the Cold War. This occurred as fresh investments were needed to line up new FM affiliates and to launch television and Internet services. Despite this, in the 1990s, VOA and Worldnet Television together built a worldwide system of 1,500 FM and TV affiliated stations. Programs were relayed via satellite and broadcast live, or simulcast, on government or independent FM or medium-wave outlets.

Placement was greatest in Latin America, southeastern Europe, and East Asia, as well as the former Soviet republics. VOA had two FM affiliates in sub-Saharan Africa in 1990; that grew to forty by the end of the decade. In this brave new multimedia world, global public-service networks also beamed TV to rooftop dishes or homes, launched Internet Webcasting, and developed e-mail lists for so-called text-based narrowcasting of program material.

We've seen how VOA Europe supplied FM stations around the clock with live English programming using satellites, beginning in October 1985. The program delivery revolution at VOA spread to other regions. State-of-the-art, real-time simulcasting by local FM outlets began in Latin America and, through the 1990s, reached the Balkans and East Asia.

LATIN AMERICA

Richard Araujo, a young journalist in El Salvador, fled his country after receiving death threats in 1980 because of his reports as a stringer for international news agencies. Araujo recalls listening almost daily in those days to VOA Spanish back in his home country and during his travels, especially the popular morning program *Buenos Días América.* That blend of the latest news and informal banter was hosted by José "Pepe" del Rio, one of VOA's best-known on-air personalities. Araujo joined VOA in 1983 and became its Latin America Division chief three years later. "Little did I dream," Araujo said, "that someday I'd be working directly with Pepe and *Buenos Días América.*"[7]

Del Rio, who worked for commercial Spanish-language stations in San Antonio before joining VOA in 1961, covered Vietnam for the Voice and anchored all the major U.S. space missions, including *Apollo 11* (chapter 10). His adventures and those of his colleague Roland Massa helped establish the Latin America Division's reputation as an honest and reliable source of news and information. That later led to VOA's extensive placement on FM stations in the Western Hemisphere.

Del Rio was well known to peasants as well as to presidents. He particularly remembers a trip to Costa Rica. His United States Information Service (USIS) host insisted that he visit a small farm, only about ten miles from the capital, San José. Del Rio was used to meeting heads of state and cabinet ministers, so it was a welcome treat to arrive at a modest farmhouse surrounded by cornfields. The farmer tipped his broad-brimmed straw hat when he was introduced to del Rio, and his wrinkled, dark face reflected the hard life of a Central American farmer exposed daily to the tropical sun. "You must meet Oscar," the farmer said, and led

---

"HOLD THAT PHONE, JORGE!"

Pepe del Rio was accustomed to calling stringers throughout Central and South America and having them report live from the scene of breaking stories. In 1984 in San José, Costa Rica, stringer Jorge Valverde camped out at the airport to await the arrival of more than fifty Cubans. They had been given permission by the Castro regime—something of a first at the time—to leave their homeland. The stringer found a pay phone at a good vantage point and called del Rio in the studio in Washington to alert him. Del Rio, the producer-anchor with a keen sense of good, live radio, shouted: "Hold that phone, Jorge! We'll pay for the call." Moments later, Costa Rican president Rodrigo Carazo Odio arrived at the gate directly opposite the phone, and del Rio and Valverde knew then that the arrival of the Cubans was imminent. Valverde grabbed the first of them to set foot in the terminal and put them on the phone for a conversation with del Rio. Not to miss out, President Carazo hurried over to the pay phone to get on the line with the famous emcee of *Buenos Días América*.

---

del Rio some distance from the farmhouse. Oscar, it turned out, was a huge ox. The creature, guided by his master, had plowed the fields for years every morning from six to eight o'clock. The farmer had hung a transistor radio from one of the horns of this beast of burden. Del Rio's morning chatter and news was standard fare for both the farmer and Oscar. The trio posed for a picture together.[8]

"Up Tempo" Is In, Shortwave Is Out

The stars of VOA's Latin America Division—in Spanish and in Portuguese-to-Brazil and, after 1986, in Creole—were accustomed to creating a range of lively, conversational programs, including musical offerings, dramatizations, cultural presentations, sports, and other formats. Appealing as the programs were, they were rather lengthy for the market of the mid-1980s and seemed designed for shortwave—not local FM stations. In trips to the region shortly after he was named division chief, Araujo realized that shortwave listening was declining precipitously. More and more people were turning to faster-paced, "up-tempo" Latin American networks and community stations, mostly on FM. Like the Africa Division, services to Latin America were shipping hundreds of tapes a month to USIS posts in the area to place on local networks or stations. That seemed obsolete in a satellite age.

Araujo went to work. He and Neils Lindquist of the Brazilian Branch found their talented staff receptive to feeding a faster paced, "up-tempo" style of program, via satellite, to affiliates throughout the hemisphere. They launched a VOA simulcast on Saturday mornings of an hour-long news and music program on the São Paulo–based Bandeirantes network in Brazil. This program was called *Um Sabato Allegre* (One Happy Saturday). It preceded a weekly live soccer match on the network. Brazilians noted the happy coincidence of its initials, USA.

Araujo, Lindquist, and the vivacious new staff of the Creole Service to Haiti including Sandra Dominique, cultivated the first affiliates as early as 1987. Brazilian satellite placement began in 1988, and Spanish in 1989. The team came up with the moniker VOASAT for the first international-broadcast network digital satellite system for feeding programs in Spanish to the hemisphere, even before Univision. By 1990, VOA had 100 affiliates in the Spanish-speaking countries and more than a score of stations in Brazil. By the beginning of the twenty-first century, the Latin America Division had more than 600 affiliates, and some stations were downlinking from VOASAT as many as ten or twelve VOA newscasts in Spanish each weekday. There were more Voice placements in the Western Hemisphere than anywhere else. Despite that, the Brazilian Branch was abolished for budget reasons during its fortieth year, in 2001.

The Latin America Division was also among the first to produce call-ins featuring Spanish- or Portuguese-speaking specialists in the United States. Topics included HIV/AIDS and the sensitive problem of domestic abuse. A call-in program on the latter issue won an award from the International Radio Festival in New York City. The division also took on the topic of street children in Guatemala and Brazil, unique among international broadcasters then.[9] Many stations in Latin America asked the division for spot news during the disputed Florida recount after the 2000 U.S. presidential election. The news during the shortwave years helped whet their appetites in a multimedia age.

THE BALKANS

For nearly a half century, Stalinist Albania was one of the darkest corners of Europe and the world. However, the contagion of democratic change in the rest of Eastern and Central Europe was infectious there, too. In March 1991, elections were held in Albania, followed by a general strike and street demonstrations that forced the all-Communist cabinet to resign. The Communist Party renamed itself the Socialist Party and renounced the ideology of longtime dictator Enver Hoxha.

Veterans of VOA's Albanian Service (first established forty-eight years earlier) could at last visit a country where authorities previously had banned virtually all contact with the outside world. Two of them—Frank Shkreli, later the director of the European Division, and longtime scholar of Albania and Albanian Service chief Elez Biberaj—were able to travel to the Albanian capital of Tirana in March 1991.

Upon his arrival at the Hotel Dajti in the Albanian capital, Shkreli (originally from Kosovo) turned in his passport to the hotel clerk, who looked him in the eye intently but said nothing. Fifteen minutes later, the clerk stopped Shkreli in the lobby and said: "I couldn't greet you earlier because there were people around here who would not like that. Now that they are gone, I would like to shake your hand. It's really nice seeing you after having listened to you for so many years."

Later, after a mass in the northern Albanian city of Shkoder, a huge crowd gathered around Shkreli when they learned that he was from VOA. All of a sudden, the crowd made room as an elderly blind man was led toward him. The blind man said: "I've been listening to you for the last fifteen years or so. VOA has been our light and guidance throughout these years. We couldn't have achieved these reforms without VOA."[10]

Shkreli and Biberaj said that Albanian opposition leaders also told them that VOA was an important factor in the country's swift adoption of democratic reforms in 1990 and 1991. Every Albanian they met (or who greeted a U.S. congressional delegation visiting at the time) said that at six and eight o'clock each evening, the streets became almost deserted in Tirana because people were at home listening to the Voice.[11]

New Challenges in Southeastern Europe

Of course, VOA senior managers of the 1990s and European Division chiefs Oksana Dragan, John Lennon, and Shkreli realized that as Albania opened up, its citizens depended much less on shortwave than they had for the previous half century. There would have to be new multimedia delivery systems for Albania, its troubled Balkan neighbors, and, for that matter, all of Eastern Europe.[12]

Milosevic, Tudjman, and the Gathering Storm

Albania's larger neighbor, Yugoslavia, was disintegrating. Beginning in 1989, Slobodan Milosevic began to fan the flames of Serbian national-ism and ethnic hatred to boost his own tenuous hold on power in Belgrade. In the nearby Croatian capital of Zagreb, Milosevic's archfoe Franjo Tudjman followed suit. Clashing nationalisms spawned four wars in the 1990s (Slovenia, Croatia, Bosnia, and Kosovo).The wars in Croatia and Bosnia from 1991 to 1995 and in Kosovo in 1999 were espe-cially devastating.

VOA recruited new staff and new leaders for its half-century-old Serbo-Croatian Service, and directed it toward new multimedia opera-tions. Most of the electronic media in the Balkans were state-controlled or run by nationalist political leaders, but independent FM radio and television stations were springing up as well. In Serbia alone, more than 300,000 homes had personal computers by the mid-1990s; one-tenth of the residences had home dishes. To meet the challenges and successfully rebroadcast its programming, VOA decided to create separate Serbian, Croatian, and Bosnian Services.

Winds of Change on the Danube

The war in Bosnia ended in stalemate, and there was a U.S.-brokered and internationally supervised cease-fire in 1995. However, Milosevic continued to consolidate his hold in Serbia. In 1996, though, there were signs of growing "people power" there. Opposition parties won elections in fourteen municipalities. Milosevic's handpicked supreme court annulled the results. Protest demonstrations erupted in Belgrade and other cities, widely reported by independent stations in Serbia as well as by VOA, the BBC, and RFE. The most popular local radio outlet was an independent Belgrade FM station, B-92.

Milosevic was determined to stamp out dissent. He shut down B-92 in November 1996, and 250,000 citizens rallied in the streets to protest the supreme court's cancellation of the local election results and the closure of the station. One morning in November 1996, the young and energetic new leader of the Serbian Service, Maja Drucker, came up with a simple but revolutionary idea. She noted that some VOA Serbian Service stringers in Belgrade were editors and reporters for B-92. They were off the air locally. Drucker asked: Why not put them on VOA for reports, interviews, and extended question-and-answer sessions? All the standard sourcing and editing guidelines would apply. The plan was implemented a few hours later.

The B-92 reporters then were no longer heard just in Belgrade. They were broadcast by the Voice throughout Serbia and the entire Balkans.[13] In just nineteen hours, Milosevic reversed himself. B-92 was back on the air. "If it weren't for you guys," B-92's courageous director, Veran Matic, faxed VOA's Serbian Service, "this victory for press freedom would never have happened."

Video as well as Voice

A week later, VOA launched the first internationally broadcast Serbian nightly radio–television simulcast to the Balkans, *America Calling Serbia*. It went on the air at 11:00 P.M., local time, and was jointly produced by Worldnet Television and VOA's Serbian Service. At first, it was essentially a radio program videotaped in a studio and put up on a satellite live. The simulcast grew into an increasingly sophisticated production over the years. It was accessible on rooftop home receiver dishes tuned to an Astra satellite channel as well as to affiliated TV stations. It eventually was rechristened *Open Studio* and offered updates each weekday evening of

- The anti-Milosevic street demonstrations during the winter of 1996/1997
- The Kosovo crisis in 1998 and 1999 and the ensuing seventy-eight-day NATO air action against Serbia
- The plight of the 800,000 Kosovar Albanian refugees who had fled Serbian repression in the province before returning in record time and in record numbers
- The dramatic events fifteen months later, including the election and Milosevic's ouster by a "people's revolution" on October 5, 2000

Within a few hours after the storming of the parliament in Belgrade by Milosevic opponents, *Open Studio* had an exclusive Voice interview in the Yugoslav capital with the new president, Vojislav Kostunica. *Open Studio* also had on-scene reports from the Balkans, newsmaker interviews, in-studio panel discussions, and reportage from the war crimes tribunal in The Hague on the genocide trial of Slobodan Milosevic.

In 1993, VOA's language services to southern Europe had just two affiliate stations. Eight years later, division director Shkreli said, those services had 185 FM or TV outlets in Albania, Bosnia, Croatia, Macedonia, and Serbia (including Montenegro). In Serbia and Montenegro alone, around thirty affiliates downlinked VOA programming from the satellite feed system—half of them FM radio, and the other half TV outlets.

Shkreli said that the various media streams developed by the Balkan services reinforced one another. He noted that in a single week in early 2001, leaders of Albania, Macedonia, Cyprus, and Serbia all were in Washington and asked to visit VOA. "They requested interviews on radio and TV in their own languages," Shkreli added, "and in other languages in the Balkans, those of their adversaries. They asked to see us because they know people are listening or watching on television, in all languages."[14] (Other European Division initiatives had included the startups of Bosnian and Albanian Service radio–TV simulcasts in 1997 and 1999, respectively.) Research surveys reflected the impact:

- During the NATO bombings from March through early June 1999, nearly 80 percent of Kosovar Albanians listened at least once weekly to VOA for latest news of the crisis.[15]
- During the October 2000 election and Milosevic's subsequent resignation, one out of five Serbian adults surveyed said that they regularly tuned into VOA Serbian Service broadcasts.

On-scene reportage encouraged stations to rebroadcast VOA. Ilir Ikonomi of the Albanian Service and the ubiquitous Gil Butler of VOA's newsroom were among the first reporters to ride into Kosovo right behind NATO convoys on June 12, 1999. Ikonomi recalls that what was normally a fifty-minute drive from the Macedonian border to the Kosovo capital city of Prishtina took eight hours because of stops to ensure that land mines were cleared from the roads. He and two European journalists finally reached Prishtina and drove their rented car, unescorted, into the city:

> I will never forget the eerie feeling I experienced. I took out my satellite phone, placed it on the hood of the derelict Lada my colleague had rented in Skopje, and filed a short report for the Albanian Service. "I am in Prishtina and the city looks quiet," I said, as I looked carefully around me. . . . Prishtina was like a ghost town. I looked for a friend's apartment where I would go and stay overnight. The first thing I asked was: "What's happening here?"

He told me that the Albanian inhabitants had either left or were huddling in the basements of their homes listening to Western radios, primarily VOA, for word of NATO troops entering the province. Later, I met many people who knew the names of all the people in our service.[16]

There were other landmarks in the shift of VOA Balkan services from shortwave to other delivery systems. The International Broadcasting Bureau (IBB) Office of Engineering in 1995 leased medium-wave or FM transmitters in Romania, Bulgaria, Bosnia, and Albania to supplement its own facilities in Greece and Germany. In practical terms, Shkreli told Reuters in 1996, reaching the region in medium wave meant that people could listen to the Voice on their car radios as well as at home or in their offices.[17]

In 1998, the Broadcasting Board of Governors assembled a network of four FM stations ringing Serbia. For the first time, VOA, RFE, BBC, Deutsche Welle, and Radio France International coordinated schedules to use this around-the-clock FM service. Expanded Web sites of the international broadcasters and independent radio stations helped opposition parties reach potential voters in 2000, a factor in Kostunica's surprise victory over Milosevic in the September election.

Cuts and Conversions

Inevitably, a decade after the Berlin Wall fell, VOA scaled back thirteen of its language broadcasts to the former Soviet Union and Eastern Europe while maintaining or enhancing services to the Balkans (the Macedonian Service was inaugurated in 2000).[18] Under Shkreli and division executive producer Sheila Gandji, nine of the reduced services were converted to small multimedia units capable of producing brief reports or news roundups in area languages, for radio, television, and the Internet (texts and audio, even occasional video streaming for affiliate stations). The long-range effectiveness of such "spot" programming remained to be tested. But VOA was keeping a presence in the greatly reduced languages and could expand one or more of them if necessary again.

ASIA

In Asia, too, VOA expanded into multimedia in the 1990s. Unlike in Europe, greater resources were available (particularly to the Chinese

Branch) for advance planning of integrated live coverage in the region on radio, television, and the Internet. Events included Britain's hand-over of the Crown Colony of Hong Kong to China on July 1, 1997, and the Taiwan presidential election of March 18, 2000.

VOA director Chase Untermeyer, about three years after Tiananmen, had envisioned an enhancement for VOA that he called the "China acorn." It laid out a long-range plan for

- Reestablishment of a VOA office in Hong Kong, which had been closed earlier for budgetary reasons
- Assignment of more Chinese-speaking stringers and reporters there, in the People's Republic of China (PRC), in Taiwan, and in other places in Asia and the United States with large Chinese communities
- Creation of a modest area research unit for the East Asia and Pacific Division to better identify and share the rapidly expanding informa-tion riches of the Internet

The "acorn" enhancement, driven onward by VOA director Geoffrey Cowan, was a unique multimedia and interactive approach to interna-tional broadcasting in a single region.

The British Leave Hong Kong

The Hong Kong handover was a classic example. A weekly VOA sum-mary[19] reported that for the first time ever, IBB engineers linked correspondents (Chinese and English) via video for VOA–Worldnet Television simulcasts, live, of an overseas event. The four-hour Mandarin program included call-in segments, simultaneously interpreted, with Ambassador Richard Solomon, director of the U.S. Institute of Peace and an expert on Asia; Fred Bergsten, an internationally known econo-mist; Yaoru Jin, a political commentator and former editor in chief of the Hong Kong newspaper *Wen Wei Pao*; and Donald Anderson, a former U.S. consul general in Hong Kong. They fielded questions from listeners in Hong Kong, China, and Taiwan.

On the scene, VOA Hong Kong bureau chief Fred Cooper coordi-nated the work of a multilingual reportorial team (English, Mandarin, Cantonese, and Russian). Back in Washington, Peter Chen and a nine-member Cantonese Service staff produced a special of their own. Current Affairs Division writer and former Beijing correspondent Stephanie

Mann Nealer researched and wrote a series of nine *Closeup* documentary scripts for all VOA services. Topics included prospects for press freedom in Hong Kong, the security dimension, corruption, the impact of the events of June 30 on business confidence, and the implications of the Hong Kong reversion for Taiwan.

The China Acorn Becomes an Oak

The Taiwan election nearly three years after the Hong Kong turnover reflected another milestone in modern Asian history. For the first time in millennia, the leader of a ruling Chinese party had been voted out of office in a freely contested election accompanied by a peaceful turnover of power. The victory speech of the new president, forty-nine-year-old Chen Shui-Bian, was broadcast, telecast, and Webcast by VOA and Worldnet Television live throughout the Chinese-speaking world. It was Saturday evening, Taipei time, and Saturday morning in Washington.

The drama was broadcast as the returns came in, not only back to Taiwan but to mainland China. As East Asia and Pacific Division program manager Jay Henderson saw it, the concession speech of the ruling Nationalists was unique in Chinese history: "I'm terribly proud of getting that into China live. Anybody can air the victory speech but only in a pure democracy does the loser get a chance to speak on national media."[20]

"I can recall," I wrote at the time,

being awed only eleven years ago by the sight of a single television camera outside a studio, with Mandarin Chinese–speaking assistants painstakingly scrolling copy by hand at the bottom of a screen. We thought then that was something of a miracle.

But on this Saturday morning, March 18, 2000, we saw an operation involving a staff of at least twenty Worldnet and VOA producers [along with technicians] and camerapersons manning the big Ikegamis [video cameras] in the heart of a fully outfitted studio with two separate sets. Many others supported the effort from distant places. There were stringers and reporters in twenty cities feeding reports and reaction into a globe-girdling technical delivery network assembled for the occasion.[21]

In the John Chancellor TV studio at the Voice, three experts on Asia responded live to listeners' and viewers' questions: Senator Chuck Hagel

(Republican of Nebraska), chairman of the Senate Subcommittee on East Asia; Robert Suettinger of the Brookings Institution; and Shelly Rigger, a professor at Davidson College in North Carolina. Rigger was linked up via an ISDN television line to the studio from a vantage point halfway around the world in Taipei.

The matrix of lines, circuits, and satellite paths included video feeds and e-mail links to VOA's 35,000 Mandarin Chinese–language recipients in the People's Republic of China, Taiwan, and the rest of the Chinese-speaking world. There were live audio and video hookups to Taipei radio and TV. Added to that, there were specially leased lines to Eastern TV in Taipei, bringing millions of VOA listeners and viewers via remote trucks to four different venues in the city, including the headquarters of Taiwan's three principal presidential candidates.

"The atmosphere here," Rigger said, "has been electric throughout the weekend. Fireworks have been going off everywhere this evening, and we've seen an unprecedented level of competition in a presidential race." Another expert in the VOA studio describing the returns, Nancy Bernkopf Tucker, commented: "As a democracy, Taiwan has truly arrived."

THE INTERMINABLE LABOR PAINS OF VOA-TV

As the Hong Kong and Taiwan specials demonstrated, television emerged during the 1990s as essential to VOA's transformation into a full-service, multimedia international broadcasting network. The core problem was merging two distinct organizational cultures.[22] Worldnet Television, created by USIA director Charles Z. Wick in the early 1980s, was controlled largely by agency foreign service or policy officers who felt that most of its programs should be designed primarily to articulate U.S. policies. This was despite congressional passage in 1987 of a law applying the VOA Charter, verbatim, to Worldnet Television—including its mandate of objective news.[23]

As late as 1995, I spent a day at Worldnet Television headquarters and observed a zealous agency policy officer kill an obituary profile of humanitarian actress Audrey Hepburn (who had spent much of her life helping impoverished children in the Horn of Africa). The spot had been scheduled for the Worldnet Television daily newsfile. The policy officer vetoed the profile because, he said, it didn't advance U.S. objectives. I was told that this happened frequently. Was it possible to consolidate two such different organizations as Worldnet Television and VOA?

Those who wanted to combine the two had several things in mind. The Voice, they felt, had to become more multifaceted and to begin to "think TV" as a way of reaching wider, or different, audiences. In an increasingly video-oriented world, this was essential. Worldnet Television, conversely, should "think journalism and mass audiences," recognizing that telling it straight to viewers was the only way to stay relevant in a 500-channel world. Furthermore, Worldnet could benefit from VOA's multicultural journalistic expertise, and VOA could benefit from Worldnet's finely honed television production skills. Until the late 1990s, most of Worldnet Television had supported overseas U.S. missions with interactives and newsfile feeds aimed specifically at advancing public diplomacy goals defined in USIA country plans.

Those Clashing Cultures

The debate intensified as merger prospects accelerated. VOA journalists (including those in language services) resisted what they saw as "contamination" by a policy-freighted approach. They worried, too, about spreading VOA resources too thin in order to develop and produce television programs when budgets cuts already had forced them to abandon needed modernization and even reduce on-air hours. Moreover, unions fought the idea of a "compleat" international broadcaster, a radio professional who would add video photojournalism to his or her skills with little or no additional pay. From Worldnet's perspective, the idea of being swallowed up by what some of the staff regarded as an impoverished, overstretched leviathan inclined to ignore U.S. foreign policy in the name of good journalism was repugnant (VOA was about six times as large as the television operation). One Worldnet Television executive compared the situation to being inside a besieged stockade. "There's ten of them for every one of us," he said. "We have to make every shot count."

Merger moves began in the summer of 1990, when USIA director Bruce Gelb agreed with VOA director Richard W. Carlson that Worldnet Television would become part of the agency's Bureau of Broadcasting. (USIA Television, several times earlier in the agency's history, had been under VOA and now—in theory—would again report to Carlson as associate director of the agency rather than to Gelb.)

Worldnet Television was located across the Washington Mall from VOA, and many agency officers and area specialists at the television service were concerned. They opposed what they saw as a "freewheeling" Voice assuming a greater role in USIA TV programming. The agency's oversight body, the Advisory Commission on Public Diplomacy, however, viewed the creation of a television capability for VOA and the reallocation of resources from radio to television as the wave of the future. In the mid-1990's, USIA director Joseph Duffey invited agency-wide comment on the future of TV, despite his own reservations about VOA-TV.

In late 1993 and early 1994, VOA had worked with Worldnet to develop a pilot weekly television news and discussion program in Mandarin Chinese called *Pacific Horizons*. However, the attempt was scuttled when USIA's Office of East Asian Affairs insisted on approving topics for the program and selecting guests for it. Bureau of Broadcasting director Joseph B. Bruns and Director of Programs Sid Davis refused on principle to move forward with the project. Throughout his seven years as the Voice's longest-serving director of programs, Davis stood firm in resisting external attempts to impose policy controls on the Voice.

In 1994, VOA's new director, Geoffrey Cowan, used his contacts at the White House to accelerate the move toward television. President Bill Clinton announced in May 1994 that he would ask Congress to approve permanent normal trade relations with China but wanted to separate that policy from, or balance it with, a focus on human rights violations in the PRC. The president announced the expansion of VOA Chinese programming by an hour daily, and the inauguration of a VOA Chinese television program to China. USIA and Worldnet Television then had to comply with production on the Voice's terms.

A weekly televised call-in was launched by VOA's Chinese Branch in September 1994, and at the outset, it drew more calls from viewers than listeners. Cowan built on that success. In early 1996, he became director of both VOA and IBB, overseeing it and Worldnet Television. During the next two years, producers expanded VOA Chinese offerings and added VOA radio–television simulcasts or weekly discussion programs in Serbian and Bosnian, as described earlier, and in Farsi, Arabic, Spanish, and Russian. Cowan pressed for the construction of a fairly large TV studio at the Voice, to be run by Worldnet production staff in cooperation with VOA newsroom and language service talent. The deadline for completion was early November 1996, in time for the presidential

---

"You've Just Given Me the Greatest Gift of All!"

Observing the inaugural broadcast from the new television studio at the Voice was like being in NASA mission control. The scene: VOA's first radio–TV simulcast to Iran of the VOA Farsi weekly call-in program, *Roundtable with You.* The date: October 18, 1996. A Farsi-speaking expert on satellite TV reception, Ali Karimi, was the guest. But division director Ismail Dahiyat, Farsi Service chief Bill Royce, emcee Ahmed Baharloo, and Worldnet Television producers had no idea whether the people of Iran could actually watch—as well as hear—this weekly Friday broadcast. Had word spread that it was up on a satellite for TV home dishes? Finally, at precisely thirty minutes past the hour, Mehrdad, of Tehran, called in. He exclaimed somewhat excitedly that it was great to "see" Baharloo; he had *heard* him for years, but had never *watched* him! The control room erupted in applause. The broadcaster offered to send his first viewer a prize. "No need," responded Mehrdad. "You've just given me the greatest gift of all!"*

*Adapted from Alan L. Heil Jr., "Address at Fifty-fifth Anniversary Ceremony, VOA," February 24, 1997, 1–2.

---

election. The construction crew finished the work two weeks ahead of time.

The new basement facility became very busy as the venue for VOA-TV simulcasts. Other events, too, pushed VOA and Worldnet Television closer to consolidation:

• *The departure of USIA foreign service and policy officers from Worldnet.* In 1996 and 1997, all these officers rotated either to the agency or to their next foreign assignments, and the last of them left in early July 1997. For the first time since Worldnet Television had been established in the early 1980s, its own professionals—a number of whom were committed journalists—were free to develop programming without on-scene USIA oversight.

• *The sudden vacancy of huge areas of the VOA headquarters building.* The Wilbur J. Cohen Building had been occupied by both the Voice and the primary tenant of many years, the Department of Health and Human Services. But the department's staff had been reduced substantially during the Clinton administration budget cuts of the 1990s, leaving many empty offices. IBB planners realized that Worldnet might eventually be relocated to share the building with the Voice.

• *The reconstruction at the Worldnet headquarters building across the Mall from VOA.* The television operation was forced to move to different floors in its headquarters building during renovation. It had no desire to move anywhere else, especially not to VOA. But twice in 1996, pieces of the ceiling fell during construction and nearly struck Worldnet producers. The second accident occurred two weeks after Geoffrey Cowan returned to academic life.[24] Acting IBB director Janie Fritzman moved quickly. She persuaded USIA director Duffey that to ensure employee safety, Worldnet could be moved at fairly modest cost into the vacant space in the VOA headquarters building.

Soon, the VOA and Worldnet Television staffs were under the same roof, squeezed into much more limited studio space than the TV professionals had been accustomed to. From early 1997 into the twenty-first century, additional facilities were gradually built. That, painstakingly slow in the view of some, was the easy part. Moving bureaucratic mastodons was much more difficult. A VOA–Worldnet merger required approval both by the executive branch and by Congress and required countless clearances and union meetings. The final consolidation was delayed for years, partly because USIA managers (except for those in broadcasting) were preoccupied by the prospect of their reintegration into the Department of State.

As the new century began, IBB created a small VOA-TV unit headed by Worldnet and VOA veteran Lisa Keathley, and the number of VOA languages doing television simulcasts expanded to around a dozen. The consolidation of VOA and Worldnet seemed inevitable and was the subject of protracted conversations among the Broadcasting Board of Governors, IBB, and interested members and staff on Capitol Hill (where reorganizations must be approved by those funding U.S. government activities). However, successive administrations and Congresses had been slow to focus on the benefits of a VOA–Worldnet merger. It stretched out for more than a decade and was still not completed when the Voice marked its sixtieth anniversary in February 2002. One disheartened former executive of the television service lamented the fact that the "organization still known for awhile as Worldnet continues to struggle along, facing only legislated extinction and the dispersal of its assets as a reward for putting its own and VOA's mission-driven programming on the air."

In 2000 and 2001, VOA director Sandy Ungar and his director of programs, Myrna Whitworth, worked with European Division management to create a multimedia unit of eleven reduced but more versatile language services (radio, TV, and Internet). Planners also pressed ahead with the construction of a huge new central newsroom, a VOA Multimedia Broadcast Center (MBC) on the first floor of the VOA headquarters building. The MBC was to assign coverage of events on radio, television, and Internet and to edit or adapt incoming reports for all three media. A visitors' center was being designed to view the floor of this busy state-of-the-art newsroom. Its entrance on Independence Avenue SW in Washington, D.C., was to be readily visible to tourists visiting the Capitol and the Smithsonian Air and Space Museum across the street. The idea was that America's "best kept secret" was to be a secret no more.

THE EMERGENCE OF VOANEWS.COM

Although VOA was the first international broadcaster to put texts of its correspondents' reports on the Internet on January 31, 1994, it wasn't until six years later that VOA and IBB management were able to overcome substantial budget cuts and administrative obstacles to launch a VOA news Web site. Voanews.com went on-line on November 1, 2000, just in time for the contested election of President George W. Bush. Director Sandy Ungar had pressed for the site, aided by Director of Programs Myrna Whitworth and IBB director of Internet development Connie Stephens.

A fifteen-member unit was established to run the Internet site, an energetic group consisting of newsroom, language service, television, and technical staff who volunteered for the twenty-four-hour-a-day operation. The site is a blend of the latest headlines, rewritten reports from VOA correspondents around the world, and photos acquired through news agency subscriptions or taken by the correspondents themselves. During the first few months of voanews.com, London correspondent Laurie Kassman and Mexico City correspondent Greg Flakus took photos for the Web site while covering Israeli–Palestinian strife and the march of the Zapatistas on Mexico City.

Pointing to the future, the Web site featured audio and video in English, including the weekday *Talk to America* call-in and the half-hour-weekly news and magazine program *This Week,* produced by the VOA-TV staff. That program, plus video Internet relays of *Straight Talk Africa* and other regularly recurring language division call-ins, anticipated the day when many stations around the world might pick up and relay the programs. VOA services that created successful early Web sites included Mandarin, Russian, Spanish, Arabic, Indonesian, Korean, Albanian, and Farsi. Some of the small multimedia units in the European Division planned to follow suit. New Indonesian Service chief Norman Goodman used both the Internet and TV very effectively as the Djakarta placement market opened up. Mandarin, in addition to a Web site, created e-mail lists for news and for English lessons (together, the e-mail "narrowcasts" reached an estimated 200,000 users in the PRC). VOA was registering about 3 million page views a month soon after the inauguration of voanews.com. According to Connie Stephens, the average stay on the site was thirteen minutes—indicating a fairly high interest in exploring its content.[25]

A year after the inaugural radio–television simulcast of the Farsi Service *Roundtable with You,* there was a reception to mark the anniversary. The Iranian government in 1997 had felt compelled to sweep rooftops and residences to confiscate TV receiver dishes. There were reports that 1,700 of them had been seized and stored in a Tehran warehouse. The attempt to seal off Iran electronically failed. *Roundtable with You* was watched and heard in living rooms as far dispersed as Mashhad, Bandarabass, Shiraz, Isfahan, and Tabriz. It was a weekly conversation with the West. As columnist Thomas Friedman noted in the *New York Times,* Iranians "want to be part of the most profound global trends—from open trade to civil society to cultural experimentation—and they demonstrated that by electing the first Iranian president [reformer Mohammad Khatemi] with his own website."[26] It was an embodiment, in multimedia, of John Chancellor's charge to the broadcasters of the Voice years earlier: "Our assignment is to bring the bright dream of a new day into the dark corners of the world."[27]

17

The Struggle
to Get It Straight

INDEPENDENCE AT
THE NEW MILLENNIUM

For freedom's battle once begun,
Bequeathed by bleeding sire to son,
Though baffled off, is ever won.
                    —Lord Byron, on a Solidarity poster

October 1, 1999, is an historic day for us all as the U.S.
Information Agency merges with the Department of State,
and U.S. international broadcasting remains under the
Broadcasting Board of Governors as an independent federal
entity. The landmark reorganization today re-affirms the journalistic integrity of U.S. international broadcasting and sets us
on a clear course to pursue excellence in new programming
and public service information in an increasingly unpredictable world.
                    —Broadcasting Board of Governors

The final two decades of the twentieth century—from the dawn of the
Solidarity movement in Poland to the reorganization of America's overseas information program—culminated in significant changes in U.S.
international broadcasting. Just a dozen weeks before the year 2000, the
Voice of America and the other publicly funded overseas civilian networks achieved organizational (or nominal) independence.

The endgame, however, was strikingly different from VOA's very public, failed autonomy struggle of the 1970s. It began with the activities of opposition movements in Communist Eastern Europe and ended with a post–Cold War review of all of America's overseas information and cultural activities. VOA was only a relatively small part of that reappraisal. One executive even termed the reorganization of international broadcasting "independence on little cat feet."[1]

THE HARBINGERS OF CHANGE

In 1980, Lech Walesa and his union co-workers in Poland became the first mass opposition movement to mount a sustained challenge to a Moscow-supported Warsaw Pact regime. Before the decade was over, Solidarity had gained significantly in the first free elections behind the Iron Curtain—heralding the end of the Cold War. This stimulated serious discussion about the future of U.S. international broadcasting. Congress, which long had viewed the overseas networks as instruments to win the Cold War, severely cut their resources and operations. Because of budget reductions, VOA already had lost more than 120 broadcast positions between 1986 and the end of the decade.[2]

A Contentious Streamlining

From December 1990 until February 1, 1991, United States Information Agency (USIA) director Bruce Gelb proposed organizational changes to streamline the agency. These included abolishing six VOA language services and merging the VOA budget and personnel offices with those of USIA. But Gelb had to face a VOA leadership duo consisting of Director Richard W. Carlson and his deputy, Robert T. Coonrod. Carlson publicly opposed the plan.

Gelb said the six VOA language services (Greek, Lao, Slovene, Swahili, Turkish, and Uzbek) would have to go off the air to meet USIA budgetary requirements because they had relatively small audiences or were directed to mostly smaller countries. Fifty-seven broadcasters would lose their jobs because of the cuts. Carlson voiced serious misgivings. "We are going to do to ourselves," he said, "what thirty years of Soviet jamming couldn't do. This is the toughest and saddest day of my professional life."[3]

A Town Meeting to Remember

Against the advice of both the White House and Carlson,[4] Gelb insisted on a public town meeting in the VOA auditorium to explain his plan. Carlson shared the stage with him and said he was "ordered to implement the plan [to consolidate budget and personnel operations] even though I did not think it was in the best interests of VOA or USIA to do so."[5] There was enthusiastic applause.

The press reported this most serious public dispute between USIA and VOA directors since the days of James Keogh and Kenneth Giddens. Gelb withdrew the proposed changes, but it was too late. The White House reassigned him as ambassador to Belgium. Gelb demanded Carlson's ouster, too, and several months later, the VOA director was named ambassador to the Seychelles. Carlson went there late in the summer of 1991, and returned to Washington a year later as president of the Corporation for Public Broadcasting, which grants funds to the PBS and National Public Radio (NPR).

THE GENESIS OF RADIO FREE ASIA

The Bush administration reacted to turmoil at USIA and questions about the need for international broadcasting after the Cold War. It launched the first of two studies of the future of VOA, Radio Free Europe/Radio Liberty (RFE/RL), and Radio-TV Martí by bipartisan panels of private citizens:

- The first eleven-member body, the President's Task Force on U.S. Government International Broadcasting, was named on April 29, 1991. It was to look at ways of combining all these overseas networks into a single entity, and to examine new technologies and delivery systems.
- The second eleven-member panel, advocated by Senator Joseph R. Biden, Jr. (Democrat of Delaware), was selected by the president and Congress. This Commission on Broadcasting to the People's Republic of China was to study the feasibility of a new grantee surrogate language broadcasting service to the PRC.[6] (It was later expanded during a Senate–House conference on the 1992/1993 State Department authorization bill to include broadcasts in Korean, Burmese, Cambodian, Vietnamese, Tibetan, and Lao.)

A COMMON MYTH ABOUT AMERICA'S VOICE

According to the minority report of the President's Task Force:

> A common misconception, often repeated in the press, runs
> to the effect that VOA, by its Charter (Public Law 94-350), is
> constrained from doing targeted programming [news broad-
> casts of particular interest to or about the country on the
> receiving end]. Such programming, so it goes, must be done by
> surrogate broadcasters. To the contrary, the Voice [does] tar-
> geted broadcasting and makes good use of it, particularly in
> times of crises. The VOA's coverage of the Tiananmen Square
> uprising was a classic of targeted broadcasting, during which
> two VOA correspondents were thrown out of the country, and
> people all over China were listening to get the details of what
> was actually happening. The same was true of its coverage to
> the Middle East during the Gulf War, and to Russia during the
> failed coup in Moscow in August. We examined the subject
> matter [during] an average month of VOA's programming to
> China and found dozens of examples of targeted broadcasting.*

*Department of State, A Report of the President's Task Force on U.S.
Government International Broadcasting, publication no. 9925 (Washington,
D.C.: Department of State, 1991), 19.

VOA was broadcasting in all these languages then. As of 2002, it
remained the most-listened-to international station in China, in
Cambodia, and among Tibetans surveyed in India. But many in Congress
felt that only surrogate (or alternative broadcasting clearly separated
from the federal government and acting as free media in the countries
reached) could bring about change in Beijing and other Communist
regimes in Asia. Both panels were chaired by John Hughes, a nationally
known columnist of the Christian Science Monitor, a former State
Department spokesman, and, for five months during 1982, the VOA
director (chapter 9).

Hughes, however, was attracted to surrogate broadcasting. Majorities
on the task force and on the commission voted with him to recommend
the establishment of Radio Free Asia (RFA). Several members of both
panels dissented, favoring instead a strengthened VOA Chinese Branch.

The task force had unanimously agreed that the first priority ought to be building up the Voice and making it a truly global service. "Siphoning off its transmitter capacity for other purposes," the minority report said, "is inconsistent with that primary goal."[7]

The task force released its report in December 1991 and the commission in September 1992. Lobbying by Radio Free Asia advocates intensified on Capitol Hill. Senator Biden had introduced legislation to create the station as early as the Tiananmen massacre in June 1989. "This is going to be an interesting part of the whole China debate," said Biden aide John Ritch. "It's going to be hard to oppose it. Who could be against spreading the word of human rights when we have a billion people under tyranny?"[8]

YET ANOTHER LOOK AT THE OVERSEAS NETWORKS

At the Voice, meanwhile, the struggle continued to resist pressures on news and programming in other regions. The Creole Service to Haiti obtained an interview with exiled Haitian president Jean-Bertrand Aristide, which the Department of State considered too inflammatory. VOA director Chase Untermeyer, on January 17, 1993, rejected a request by Assistant Secretary of State Bernard Aronson to kill the tape of Aristide. Untermeyer told him that VOA had a responsibility to broadcast the interview, and it was aired almost immediately.

That was just three days before the inauguration of President Bill Clinton. The new administration was determined to take yet another post–Cold War look at international broadcasting. Clinton aides initially recommended that RFE/RL be phased out by September 30, 1995, and that their European operations and the highly respected RFE/RL Research Institute in Munich, Germany, be shut down.

RFE/RL supporters were outraged. They launched an intense lobbying campaign for the radios' survival in the winter and spring of 1993. There was an avalanche of protests against closure by the presidents of East European nations, sympathetic members of Congress, and writers of op-ed articles in the American press. Events of the next ten months shaped the future of U.S. international broadcasting for years to come:[9]

June 15, 1993: The White House issued a statement keeping RFE/RL alive. The president's aides the same week raised the possibility of placing those networks under the federal civil service. Senator Biden vehemently opposed that solution. The Clinton administration mandated the coordination of VOA and RFE/RL schedules, the consolidation of their separate relay station systems, and the startup of Radio Free Asia under the bipartisan Broadcasting Board of Governors (BBG). The White House said: "The new Board, which the President shall appoint with the advice and consent of the Senate, will ensure independence, coherence, quality and journalistic integrity in our surrogate and other broadcast services."[10]

Mid-July 1993: The Senate Foreign Relations Committee, for the first time, established a consolidated budget line item for broadcasting distinct from USIA. The bill combined accounts for VOA, VOA engineering, and the Board for International Broadcasting (BIB), which in 1993 granted funds to RFE/RL. Senator Biden continued to oppose federalizing RFE/RL. He eventually prevailed.

April 30, 1994: Congress passed and President Clinton signed the United States International Broadcasting Act of 1994 (Public Law 103-236).[11] The legislation established within USIA the nine-member bipartisan Broadcasting Board of Governors to oversee (1) VOA, the Martís, Worldnet Television, and associated engineering and support operations under the new International Broadcasting Bureau (IBB), and (2) RFE/RL (the nonfederal, privately incorporated grantee network).

The legislation, in section 305, stated: "The Director of the United States Information Agency and the Board, in carrying out their functions, shall respect the professional independence and integrity of the International Broadcasting Bureau, its broadcasting services and grantees." The act also mandated the creation of Radio Free Asia.

Take a Look at the Fine Print

That was the first time the long-sought "I" word, "independence," had been applied by law to America's Voice. The first three principles for all of U.S. broadcasting outlined in the act were clearly derived from the VOA Charter:

- News that is consistently reliable and authoritative, accurate, objective and comprehensive
- Balanced and comprehensive projection of United States thought and institutions, reflecting the diversity of United States culture and society

- Clear and effective presentation of the policies of the United States Government and responsible discussion and opinion on those policies

VOA remained part of USIA. But about a week before the act was passed, a reader of the fine print noted that Public Law 94-350, the VOA Charter, had been abolished along with other past laws applying to broadcasting. It was too late to revise the language. President Clinton signed the International Broadcasting Act of 1994, minus the charter, the day after Congress acted. Some congressional aides said that the omission of the charter was unintentional. Besides, they added, its points were in the "broadcasting principles" section. In the words of one drafter: "It's no big deal."

The Struggle to "Repeal the Repeal" Begins

Voice professionals, however, regarded it as a very big deal. The charter, after all, hung on every office wall at VOA. Its principles guided all of Voice journalism in the central and language services and were regarded by the staff as a shield as well as a requirement. The charter was, to quote former senator Charles Percy, "holy writ . . . a firewall against bureaucratic and political intrusion into VOA's reporting of the news."[12]

A struggle to restore the charter lasted for many weeks. By midsummer, there had been no action on Capitol Hill. It appeared that the charter would be forgotten as other technical amendments to the International Broadcasting Act were adopted.

VOA director Geoffrey Cowan contacted Scott Cohen, a former aide to Percy and one of the prime movers in the enactment of the charter as law in 1976 (chapter 7). Cohen suggested that Percy (long ago retired from the Senate) contribute an op-ed column in the *Washington Post* focusing on the need to resurrect the charter. Percy cited crises in that summer of 1994 in Haiti, the Balkans, Rwanda, Somalia, Sudan, the Koreas, and the former Soviet republics. "America's Voice," he wrote, "must maintain its most important asset—its credibility—if we are to communicate successfully with the peoples of those trouble spots and with others elsewhere in the world."[13]

A few weeks later, the charter—minus a reference to VOA as the broadcasting service of USIA—was included among the act's technical amendments.

The House Acts, but Then?

The House approved the amendments in September, but then they languished in the Senate. October rolled around, and Congress prepared to recess as the 1994 midterm election approached. I recall checking on the progress of the charter amendment on Friday, October 8, during the last few hours before the recess. There still had been no action. It now seemed certain that the senators would leave town, the 103d Congress would end its second session, and the restoration move would be stalled for several months until it could be debated in 1995 by a new Congress, if at all.

Shortly after eight o'clock the following Monday morning, the phone rang in my office. It was USIA congressional liaison officer Jon Beard, who reported that the Senate had passed all the amendments by voice vote the preceding Friday evening, just minutes before recessing for the year. President Clinton signed the restored charter, Public Law 103-415, on October 25, 1994. Director Cowan thanked Percy for his pivotal contribution to the turnaround.

THE VOICE'S RENAISSANCE IN THE 1990S

Once again, this time in the 1990s, the program review process revitalized VOA. A new director of program review, veteran broadcaster Frank Cummins, set enthusiastically about the task. In 1993, Cummins and his deputy Ismail Dahiyat brought in more than a score of outside journalists, writers, and producers to share their expertise on all aspects of broadcasting. Guest speakers and analysts at the expanding workshops included former White House press secretaries, professors of journalism and area studies, NPR anchorman Scott Simon, and award-winning CBS broadcast writer Ed Bliss. The quality and intellectual depth of the reviews, with Cummins and Dahiyat leading the analysis team, improved greatly. There was a renewed zeal to produce better programming.

Geoffrey Cowan (whom we met briefly in chapters 7, 11, and 16) became VOA's twenty-second director, in March 1994. Cowan's thirty-two months at the Voice were in many ways the most innovative, program-wise, since the era, four decades earlier, of Henry Loomis and Barry Zorthian. In the central newsroom, Cowan became known as the "Energizer bunny." Programming ideas tumbled from his lips, exhausting all those charged with implementing them. The *New Yorker* said that Cowan "can easily be identified not only by his thatch of gray hair but

---

The VOA Journalistic Code

Under Geoffrey Cowan's leadership, a housewide committee drafted VOA's first journalistic code, which defined what application of the charter to programming meant in practice. Its main point: "Accuracy, balance, comprehensiveness, and objectivity are attributes audiences around the world have come to expect of VOA broadcasters and their product."

The code said that the Voice—including all its language services, newsroom reporters, and correspondents—"would be alert to, and reject, efforts by special interest groups, foreign or domestic, to use its broadcasts as a platform for their own views." It said this applied to opinion or press roundups, call-in programs, and any other format where charges against another party or parties might be expressed. VOA interviewers or editors had an obligation, the document said, to ensure that opposing views were reflected. The code also set broad standards for sourcing, accuracy and balance, fairness, context, and comprehensiveness. (For the complete text of the code, see appendix A.)

---

also by his seemingly inexhaustible enthusiasm." That enthusiasm was infectious. It carried forward a family tradition. Geoff's father, Lou Cowan, was VOA's second director. His sister, Holly Cowan Shulman, wrote a history of the Voice during World War II (chapter 2).[14]

Cowan's programming innovations included[15]

- Expansion of the Worldwide English call-in program *Talk to America* to every weekday of the year and creation of regularly recurring call-in programs in ten other languages
- Conversion of more than half the Worldwide English prerecorded programs to a live news and features format
- Creation of new cultural and public-affairs programming, including a revival of the celebrated CBS program *This I Believe*, narrated at VOA by Charles Kuralt
- Production of long-form radio dramas in collaboration with the Smithsonian Institution and Los Angeles Theater Works[16]
- Live concerts, one in tribute to Willis Conover after his death in 1996, and another to help launch a new Garth Brooks album (chapter 13)

- Outreach activities, including (1) a nationwide essay contest for high-school students cosponsored with the National Endowment for the Humanities, (2) the restoration and dedication of a corridor at VOA containing Depression-era master Ben Shahn's art of the period, and (3) new grants by the Carnegie Corporation and USAID to enhance VOA programming in Africa and South Asia

Cowan fought his battles, too. In 1995, VOA—for the first time in fifty years—faced the prospect of being phased out. Cowan spent much of early 1995 defending the Voice's budget and ensuring its survival. *Newsweek* columnist Robert Samuelson called for the abolition of VOA, as well as Amtrak, the Corporation for Public Broadcasting, and the National Endowment for the Arts.[17] The House Budget Committee circulated a document proposing that the new Republican majority in Congress close VOA and a dozen other federal agencies.[18] Liberal Democrat Cowan cultivated friends on both sides of the aisle on Capitol Hill. He and allies in the IBB Office of Policy close to conservative Republicans (including future VOA director Robert Reilly) fought off substantial cuts advocated by the Clinton administration. He and Joseph Bruns, the director of the Bureau of Broadcasting (later the IBB), defended the organization in their paper "Why the United States Still Needs the Voice of America." Cowan and Bruns said: "China, North Korea, and Cuba still attempt to jam international broadcasting in hopes of staving off collapse from within. By beaming uncensored news and information about developments in these countries and the rest of the world, VOA helps keep hopes for freedom alive among these still oppressed peoples. History has not ended, and the U.S. should not unilaterally disarm in the continuing war of ideas."[19]

VOA survived practically intact, but had to fire twenty-eight broadcasters in early 1996 to meet its budget targets (those affected were mostly in the East European services). That was part of a series of international-broadcast reductions affecting both VOA and RFE/RL (which cut its staff from 1,700 to 500 in the mid-1990s and relocated its headquarters from Munich, Germany, to Prague in the Czech Republic to reduce costs).

BACK ON THE ROAD TO CONSOLIDATION

Congress continued to look for savings, as did Vice President Al Gore in his quest to reinvent government. Between 1994 and the end of 1996, the overall international broadcasting budget (VOA, RFE/RL, and Radio-TV Martí) declined from $487 million to $350 million annually, with a reduction in VOA and RFE of about 1,500 broadcast jobs.[20] All that occurred as hiring began for Radio Free Asia in 1996.

Fifteen months after the passage of the International Broadcasting Act of 1994, the nine-member Broadcasting Board of Governors was appointed by the White House and confirmed by the Senate. VOA and RFE/RL staffs, meanwhile, met a tight 120-day deadline for preparing a plan to merge their relay station operations and eliminate overlaps in their broadcast schedules. Reorganization and technical consolidation were accelerating:

September 6, 1995: The Broadcasting Board of Governors, chaired by David Burke of Massachusetts, a former ABC News executive, was sworn in and held its first organizational meeting in the basement conference room at VOA headquarters. For the first time, all publicly funded civilian U.S. government international broadcasting was brought under a single organization, nominally within USIA (under the International Broadcasting Act, the former BIB overseeing RFE/RL was phased out). The board's major initiatives during the first year were

- Accelerating a quest for independence of VOA and the other U.S. government civilian overseas networks
- Backing the Balkans broadcast expansions of both VOA and RFE/RL
- Creating Radio Free Asia, which went on the air on September 29, 1996

Behind-the-Scenes Moves for Independence

December 1996 through April 1997: Board chairman Burke, a Democrat, and the board's ranking Republican member, Tom Korologos, held a series of meetings with Senate Foreign Relations Committee chairman Jesse Helms or his staff.[21] Burke and Korologos stressed the importance of independence to the credibility of the broadcasting entities, federal and grantee. Burke, regarded initially with suspicion by the Helms aides as "a Kennedy man," handled the meetings adroitly. The North Carolina senator's aides had two concerns:

- They did not want to create a new federal agency, while eliminating others to reduce bureaucracies.

- They did not want Burke to halt VOA broadcasts of U.S. government editorials. Helms considered them important because they articulated the nation's foreign policy, at times sharply, and were produced in an IBB office organizationally distinct from VOA.

Burke assured Helms and his aides that he had no interest in building an empire. He said he would resign once legislation keeping the broadcasters out of the State Department was signed into law. He added that although he disliked the U.S. government editorials that VOA was required to broadcast, because in his view they damaged the Voice's credibility,[22] he would leave them alone if that were the price of journalistic independence for the remainder (and bulk) of the programming. Burke eventually resigned as board chairman, for unrelated personal reasons, in late 1998.

March 7, 1997: In a surprise move, USIA director Joseph Duffey, fighting for the agency's survival, appealed during a Senate Foreign Relations Committee hearing for a reexamination of the BBG's "authorities." He wondered if this might not be a basis for revisiting the International Broadcasting Act of 1994. Senator Biden, absent from the hearing, soon entered the room, furious. He accused Duffey of breaking their agreement of 1994. He said that he would recommend that USIA be put back into the State Department and that all the broadcasters, including VOA, be separated and made independent under a board whose authorities would remain intact.

Clinton Moves to Reorganize the Foreign Affairs Agencies

April 18, 1997: The White House announced its support for a comprehensive reorganization of the foreign affairs agencies. This decision followed a series of meetings between Secretary of State Madeleine Albright and Senator Helms. The chairman long had advocated the consolidation of USIA and the Arms Control and Disarmament Agency (ACDA) into the State Department and a tightening of the department's control over USAID. Senator Biden posed no objection to the overall concept. The reorganization plan, however, was unclear about the future of broadcasting.

From the perspective of VOA and the other overseas networks, this was potentially a serious hazard. What if USIA, absorbed into the State Department, should take all of the radios with it? This, the broadcasters felt, would have been devastating to listeners' perceptions of their objec-tivity. The House of Representatives soon passed a bill that would do precisely that: put the USIA and the BBG within the State Department.

Another High Noon in the Senate Foreign Relations Committee

June 14, 1997: A showdown debate on the future of U.S. international broadcasting occurred in the Senate Foreign Relations Committee between two of its Democratic members: Joseph Biden, then the ranking minority member of the committee, and Russell Feingold of Wisconsin. Biden and Chairman Helms introduced a bill that would consolidate USIA into the State Department but place VOA, the Martís, and the surrogate grantees under a separate board. Feingold attacked Helms and Biden's authorization measure. He noted that several years earlier under the Board for International Broadcasting, RFE/RL had spent extrava-gantly on executive salaries (some of its top managers then earned in the range of $200,000 to $300,000 a year, including allowances). Yet now, Feingold added, the Senate was being asked to support the creation of another board and a new federal agency (the Broadcasting Board of Governors) while abolishing USIA and ACDA. This, said Feingold, represented a foolish retreat at a time of fiscal austerity. The Wisconsin senator introduced a bill in the committee placing VOA, RFE/RL, RFA, and the Martís in the State Department along with USIA.

Biden argued that broadcasting expenditures would be far more visible as a separate broadcasting line item than if they were buried in an $18 billion State Department budget. Feingold, he added, could then "watch a separate broadcasting budget with his binoculars." Moreover, Biden said, placing the radios in the State Department would ruin their credibility and render them ineffective. If this should happen, he concluded, the nation might as well not waste taxpayers' money on them at all.

After an hour of debate, the Senate Foreign Relations Committee voted 14–3 against the Feingold amendment. The Helms–Biden bill then was approved in its stead to submit to the Senate as a whole. Biden's fundamental interest was protecting the journalistic integrity of the grantee international broadcasting networks: Radio Free Europe/Radio Liberty and Radio Free Asia. VOA, in effect, was the caboose on the independence train.

June 17, 1997: Helms and Biden introduced their bill, the Foreign Affairs Reform and Restructuring Act of 1997, on the floor of the Senate. It incorporated USIA and ACDA into the State Department, with the board and all its broadcast networks (including VOA) as a separate entity outside the department. The secretary of state or her or his designee was one of nine board members. Helms and Biden's authorization measure passed handily, after another attempt by Feingold on the Senate floor to incorporate the broadcast networks into the State Department failed by a 3–1 margin.

Report language (a discussion of reasoning behind introduction of the proposed law) said: "The rationale for having an arms-length distance from State is two-fold: (1) to provide 'deniability' for the State Department when foreign governments voice their complaints about specific broadcasts; and (2) to provide a 'firewall' between the Department and the broadcasters to ensure the integrity of the journalism."[23]

A Tough Washington Infighter Enters the Struggle

VOA director Evelyn S. Lieberman (1997–1999), a Clinton appointee, worked quietly behind the scenes to keep the Voice out of the State Department. She canvassed her predecessors for support. Among those joining the effort were Ken Tomlinson (1982–1984) and Gene Pell (1985), both Reagan appointees. Lieberman, a former aide of Senator Biden and former White House deputy chief of staff, used her powerful connections at both ends of Pennsylvania Avenue. She headed off additional efforts to trim VOA's budget. This no-nonsense executive aided the independence quest and succeeded in persuading Congress to raise its appropriation for international broadcasting by $10 million in 1998.

Months passed. Senate–House conference sessions included international broadcasting aspects of the Foreign Affairs Reform and Restructuring Act. An unusual bipartisan congruence of interests was at work here. Helms was eager to consolidate USIA into the State Department; Biden wanted to keep the broadcasters out of the department. By working together, the two senators got what each wanted. Earlier deal making seemed to play out in the conference sessions held during the summer and fall of 1997.

November 9, 1997: The Foreign Affairs Reform and Restructuring Act was further refined to

- Require the inclusion of U.S. government editorials in VOA programming
- Mandate that broadcasters offer a surge (expansion) capability "to support United States foreign policy objectives during crises abroad"
- Authorize the secretary of state to use Worldnet Television for policy-oriented interactives between overseas embassies and Washington
- Ensure that the State Department inspector general respects the journalistic integrity of VOA and the other international broadcasters by refraining from content analyses
- Establish targeted RFE/RL broadcasts in Arabic to Iraq and Persian (Farsi) to Iran (despite the fact that VOA had first established both Arabic and Farsi in 1942)[24]

Deadlock in Congress

The 105th Congress then adjourned for the winter, having taken no action on the consolidation act. Political and policy impasses unrelated to broadcasting caused the deadlock. These included a dispute between Congress and the White House over abortion restrictions in international family-planning aid and payment of back dues to the United Nations. Nonetheless, many expected that the consolidation of USIA and the ACDA into the State Department would eventually happen. But there was always the chance that the move would collapse.

FRESH TEST FOR THE FIREWALL

Within days after Congress adjourned, the People's Republic of China released its most celebrated dissident, Wei Jingsheng, for health reasons and sent him into exile. This set in motion disputes over broadcast content, which involved the White House, the Department of State, the American embassy in Beijing, USIA, the Broadcasting Board of Governors, the International Broadcasting Bureau, Worldnet Television, and VOA.

The American embassy in Beijing learned that Wei planned to visit VOA on December 10 and grant both radio and television interviews. Ambassador James Sasser objected, saying that the PRC would regard an interview at VOA and on Worldnet Television as a violation of an agreement made in connection with Wei's release. In that agreement, the envoy noted, the United States had promised not to "exploit" the freeing of the dissident. Sasser also maintained that the broadcast of the interview might jeopardize future releases of dissidents. He called the National Security Council at the White House to voice concern.

In Washington, there was agreement that Public Laws 94-350 and 103-415 (the VOA Charter) made use of the Wei interview on VOA's Mandarin or English Service mandatory, if it met editorial standards. However, USIA director Duffey and others felt that Worldnet Television remained under the control of the agency, not the Board of Governors, and that USIA could order that the interview not be telecast.[25]

The phone lines were hot, between the National Security Council, the USIA director's office, the International Broadcasting Bureau overseeing the Voice, and, not least, Worldnet Television. John Lennon, then acting Worldnet director, received a call from Duffey at 11:45 P.M. the evening before Wei arrived at the Voice. The USIA director asked that no TV footage of Wei be aired—even a brief news clip—on the grounds it might make the ambassador's position in Beijing untenable.

The next day, Wei arrived at VOA headquarters as scheduled. It was December 10, 1997—by sheer coincidence, United Nations Human Rights Day. There were these developments:

- Acting on Duffey's instructions, Worldnet Television did not include Wei in its daily news file, even though it had videotaped an exclusive VOA Chinese Branch interview with the dissident earlier in the day in the VOA–Worldnet studio.
- Ten minutes before a VOA–Worldnet radio–TV simulcast of the midday English program, *Talk to America*, a Worldnet producer rushed into the studio and pulled a one-minute statement that Wei had videotaped for rebroadcast on the talk show. "If VOA programming can be compromised because it is also airing on Worldnet Television," said VOA producer Dick Bertel, "we should cease simulcasts at once. I think this is a serious threat to the integrity of the Voice of America."[26]

Earlier that day, media had been present for Wei Jingsheng's taping in the newly dedicated John Chancellor VOA–Worldnet studio. Associated Press news video cameras were rolling. "I was healthy and strong when I went into prison," Wei said in a review of his eighteen-year jail experience in China. "It is hard for ordinary people to imagine how cruel the methods [in prison] are unless one has experienced them in real life. Now my health is ruined and most of my teeth are gone. What you see are my dentures."[27] Within twenty-four hours, four major Hong Kong TV stations had telecast the interview in Chinese and English. Suddenly, the klieg lights of the world were turned on the Wei Jingsheng affair. The BBG and the IBB were determined to permit the interview to be seen on U.S.-funded Worldnet Television, as it had been heard on VOA.

Board chairman David Burke was adamant, saying that "it's disgraceful that anyone in government would circumvent the Board of Governors, which was designed to be a firewall against that kind of pressure."[28] VOA director Lieberman—pressed by the National Security Council not to air the interview because of its possible negative foreign policy implications—stood firm in advocating its use in Mandarin Chinese on the next available scheduled VOA-TV simulcast to East Asia. A decision was made to include the videotaped conversation on the VOA Mandarin Chinese weekly call-in program, China Forum, the following Monday, December 15.

Duffey appealed the decision. He wrote a letter to IBB director Kevin Klose, one final stab at preventing the use of Wei's interview on VOA-TV. Klose responded in what Duffey described as "a polite letter . . . saying he'd been instructed by the Broadcasting Board to release it [the controversial TV interview with Wei]. We agree to disagree on this issue."[29] The interview was telecast on China Forum, five days after it was recorded.

The Wei incident was reported in the Wall Street Journal, Washington Post, and Washington Times, and by the Associated Press the week of the interview. Senator Biden's reaction was predictable. "This incident," he said, "underscores the need to pass legislation I authored, along with Chairman Helms, to strengthen the journalistic independence of the U.S. government's international broadcasting programs."[30]

A HOSTAGE OF POWERFUL FORCES

The second session of the 105th Congress convened in January 1998. The Foreign Affairs Reform and Restructuring Act remained a hostage of the struggle between Congress and the administration over the same abortion and United Nations financing issues that had stalled it the year before. But behind the scenes, the architects of the act were fine-tuning it to sharpen the emphasis on autonomy for the international broadcasters.

THE FIREWALL

Drafts of the Foreign Affairs Reform and Restructuring Act were shaped partially by two energetic veterans of such legal maneuverings: Brian McKeon, senior Biden aide on the Senate Foreign Relations Committee staff, and John Lindburg, counsel and later acting BBG executive director.

Lindburg, in a briefing paper circulated in both the executive branch and Congress, summed up the "firewall provisions" designed to shield the broadcasters from ambassadorial or area office interference with responsibly sourced news or the travel of VOA correspondents to war zones:

a. Broadcasting the whole truth consistently, not just when convenient, is essential to the credibility and effectiveness of U.S. international broadcasting. It also significantly enhances long-term U.S. national interests (promotes democracy, peace, free markets, and understanding of the United States).

b. By practicing (in federally funded journalism) what it preaches, the U.S. becomes a model for the world.

c. The Broadcasting Board of Governors was created by law to act as a firewall to protect against interference with the principle of truth.

d. Foreign policy information and concerns may be brought to the attention of the Board.

e. Many broadcasting activities using Worldnet personnel and equipment are clearly under the Board's authority and are protected by statutory protections for journalistic independence and integrity. Such protection should have been afforded in the Wei incident.

On March 10, 1998, Senate and House conferees published their report on the joint version of the act agreed on for a final vote in the two chambers. The Senate version—seeking separation of VOA, the surrogate networks, and Worldnet Television from the Department of State—prevailed over the House legislation, which would have put them into the department. It vested supervisory authority over the broadcasters exclusively in the independent Broadcasting Board of Governors.[31]

More months of waiting followed. The deadlock over unrelated issues developed into a deep freeze. Congress also appeared to be increasingly paralyzed as autumn came, eager to adjourn for election campaigning critical to the future of every member of the House in the 1998 midterm election. Once again, it looked like the foreign affairs consolidation and reorganization measure would have to wait—this time for a new Congress in 1999.

ANOTHER GOVERNMENT SHUTDOWN?

But the Senate and House faced pressures on another front: the budget. Members could hardly go home to their districts without taking action on the thirteen major pending appropriations bills to fund federal government operations. Congress still had not approved $500 billion of appropriations affecting most cabinet departments. There was talk of tacking the Foreign Affairs Reform and Restructuring Act onto a huge appropriations bill. A Senate aide who was close to the final deliberations recalls:

> The endgame of getting international broadcasting separated from State/USIA was really not all that difficult. We watched to see when the entire foreign affairs consolidation bill would be attached to the omnibus budget bill and just made sure that broadcasting, as defined in the Senate–House conference report, was included. To be sure, we kept quiet about what we were doing and USIA was taken by surprise. I think they expected, as did many others, that the entire consolidation package would be held over until the 106th Congress when they thought they might be able to prevent its passage.[32]

October 20, 1998: The House passed the $500 billion Omnibus Consolidated and Emergency Supplemental Appropriations Act for the fiscal year 1999 (Public Law 105-277). It incorporated all the latest wording of the Foreign Affairs Reform and Restructuring Act and provided for the organization of the broadcasting networks under the Broadcasting Board of Governors distinct from the Department of State as of October 1, 1999. That same day, USIA and ACDA were to be absorbed into the department.

October 21, 1998: The Senate passed and President Clinton signed the omnibus emergency appropriations act and its landmark foreign affairs reorganization provisions (division G of Public Law 105-277).

Independence at last, "on little cat feet."

In many ways, it happened because of a juxtaposition of factors:

- The end of the Cold War, which demanded a serious fresh look at U.S. government–funded civilian international broadcasting
- Helms and Biden's agreement to work together, each to advance his own long-range goals, in reorganizing the foreign affairs agencies
- The arrival on the scene of Secretary of State Albright, eager to establish warm relations with Senator Helms in order to gain more support for Clinton administration foreign affairs goals such as payment of UN dues
- USIA's focus, because of these alliances of convenience, on ensuring its own survival rather than on preventing a separation of broadcasting from other overseas information and cultural programs
- A growing desire by a few senior State Department officials, in the words of one of them, "to set broadcasting free." Some professional diplomats for years had felt that "deniability" by the State Department of programming content heard on VOA, as well as RFE/RL, could be an advantage[33]
- Budgetary pressures—both in the early 1990s, which forced consolidation economies in U.S. nonmilitary international broadcasting, and at the end of the decade, when senators and representatives were eager to avoid the negative impact of another U.S. government shutdown on their reelection prospects

A year of intense negotiation followed, involving USIA, the BBG, and IBB/VOA. Support services for VOA previously handled by USIA (contracting, some budget functions, security, and payroll, for example) had to be transferred to the BBG. Engineering support and the worldwide relay station system for all the radios had been an IBB responsibility since the mid-1990s. The transition occurred relatively smoothly on October 1, 1999.

But for the Voice, how much had actually changed? The journalists and many on the language service staff continued to find the daily U.S. government editorial distasteful. However, VOA broadcast of the editorials now was mandated by law, much as the charter had been a quarter of a century earlier. The editorial, since the early 1980s, had enabled policymakers to fulfill point 3 of the charter without dabbling in news and programming content. Interferences in programming were few, compared with the first thirty-five years of VOA history before the charter first became law. USIA in its waning years had granted a large measure of programming autonomy to the Voice. Its focus on Worldnet Television during the Wei Jingsheng incident reflected that.

THE SPECIAL CASE OF AFGHANISTAN

At the time of independence, U.S. ambassadors in Pakistan much of the time barred travel to Afghanistan by the VOA correspondent in Islamabad. They cited the Foreign Service Act of 1980 and Diplomatic Security Act of 1986, which gave them authority to clear trips to strife-ridden Afghanistan by most U.S. government employees, including VOA correspondents. They usually denied clearance because, they said, travel was too dangerous for the correspondent.

The BBG, in response, noted that a VOA correspondent's presence on the scene in war zones is essential to the accuracy and credibility of the news that he or she gathers. The board cited its "firewall" authority under the International Broadcasting Act of 1994 and the Foreign Affairs Reform and Restructuring Act of 1998. "It simply makes no sense [for the acts] to prohibit the Department of State from interfering with the content of news," the board said, "yet allow interference in the gathering of it."[34] Eventually, however, many Voice reporters went to Afghanistan during the 2001/2002 military campaign against the Taliban and Al Qaeda terrorists. But the struggle was ongoing to clarify the conflicting pieces of legislation.

THE CURTAIN RISES ON A NEW ERA

A low-key ceremony was held in the VOA auditorium in mid-October 1999 to take note of the newly won independence. The board was in charge and planned the event to encompass all the U.S. government overseas broadcast networks. BBG chairman Marc Nathanson called it "a historic day for all of us" and cautioned that while "change is never easy . . . there are so many opportunities [ahead] to bring truth to the people of the world who cannot hear alternative voices, whether they're in Cambodia, Pakistan, Rwanda, or Serbia."[35]

Senator Biden, a critic of VOA journalism over the years because its editors, correspondents, and broadcasters were federal employees, also spoke.[36] Voice veterans were pleased that Biden apparently had come to see their struggle to get it straight in a new light. He noted that Congress had been the key force in establishing a separate entity for international broadcasting and added:

> This result was not foreordained. In the spring of 1997, for example, many people in the State Department and elsewhere in the government wanted broadcasting to be folded into State along with the rest of USIA. Senator Helms and I convinced our colleagues that placing broadcasting inside the State Department would be the equivalent of a death sentence, threatening both the budget and the journalistic integrity of all the services. . . . Cynics and the ill-informed often proclaim, usually without offering a shred of evidence, that the broadcast services represented here today engage in "propaganda." It is amazing to me that people still believe such nonsense. Although the government pays your salary, you are all *journalists* and don't let anyone tell you differently. It is no accident that VOA employees keep the VOA Charter and its mandate of objectivity posted in the newsroom. Credibility and accuracy must remain the watchwords of all of you.[37]

18

America's Voice

A VOICE FOR THE VOICELESS

Clearly, what you do here on a daily basis enlightens the prospects for all of us. We must defend the truth when we see it trampled. Human rights are African rights, Asian rights, European rights, American rights. Unfortunately, there are governments which choose to forget that the Universal Declaration belongs to everyone, everywhere.
> —Nancy Rubin, U.S. envoy to the
> United Nations Human Rights Commission

Not even the toughest totalitarian state can isolate itself from ideas in the information age.
> —Stephen Rosenfeld, address to the
> USIA alumni association

As the Voice marked its sixtieth anniversary, it remained as Jeffersonian as ever in its resolve to report events in what John Chancellor had called "the dark corners of the world." It covered wars, disease, natural disasters, and human rights violations everywhere, striving to be both a town crier to the world and "an alarm bell of civilization." It was never an easy task. Rung carelessly, the "alarm bell" could become a self-fulfilling prophecy. In Bernie Kamenske's memorable phrase, it was not only a struggle to get it straight. It was a struggle not to get it wrong.

The standard—exemplified in the two-source rule at VOA—was well ingrained. As the Founding Fathers said in their famous declaration: "Let Facts be submitted to a candid World." As we've seen, that tradition was alive and well at VOA two centuries later. Bernie had a framed portrait of Thomas Jefferson on the wall of his office, a portrait he took down when he left on the last day of 1981. Nearly twenty years later, his eighth successor in the glass-walled suite, Andre DeNesnera, pointed with pride to a portrait of Jefferson he had just put up. It was, he explained, in exactly the same spot where—years earlier as a newswriter trainee—he had seen the BHK original.

In DeNesnera's time, submitting facts to a candid world was more challenging than ever: global terrorism, genocide and ethnic cleansing, forced expulsions of people from their homes, the HIV/AIDS pandemic, post-Communist governments seeking to become democratic. In the United States, there were debates about the economy, corporate ethics, capital punishment, and the role of the United States in the world. In this kind of world, Václav Havel once said, VOA was needed more than ever. Nothing more vividly demonstrated the Voice's post–Cold War role than its human rights and humanitarian reporting.

THE COWAN AWARD

Geoffrey Cowan, the Voice's twenty-second director and later dean of the Annenberg School for Communication at the University of Southern California, considered the Voice's reportage about the world's oppressed and disadvantaged among its greatest contributions. On November 15, 1996—his last day at VOA—Cowan's family and friends surprised him by establishing the Cowan Award for Humanitarian Reporting. It was created to honor Cowan and his father, Lou (VOA's second director, 1943–1944). The award was to be issued annually to VOA broadcasters judged by a panel of prominent journalists or area specialists to have produced the best, most effective original programming on humanitarian issues.

Two of the first three awards were shared by a diminutive, unassuming, sari-clad broadcaster named Rashmi Shukla of the Hindi Service to India and her chief, Jagdish Sarin. In the first program to be honored, Shukla interviewed many young people in India. These children, she told VOA listeners, had been "robbed of their childhood, prematurely forced into adulthood, working nonstop fifteen to eighteen hours a day, selling their labor for negligible wages, deprived of the blessings of basic education, play, laughing, and dreaming of faraway homes." In the documentary, fourteen-year-old Nandlal recalled how it had all begun for her: "We were playing in our front yard. Four men came in a jeep and offered us some cookies and invited us to a movie. We were taken to a house far away from home and the next morning one of them informed us that we would not be able to return home and would have to work for him." And ten-year-old Raj Kumar explained how a typical boss in a child labor factory treated his charges: "He didn't provide any medication. When I went to show him my fingertips, bleeding from weaving carpets for many hours, he burned them with his cigarette. If I did not start work right away, he beat them and didn't let me cry."[1]

Shukla discovered that two organizations in India, the South Asian Coalition on Child Servitude and the Bonded Liberation Front, were working to rescue children from such appalling conditions. The two groups, founded in the 1980s, had by the mid-1990s rescued about 50,000 of the more than 55 million child laborers in India. Senator Paul Harkin (Democrat of Iowa), Shukla reported, had introduced legislation that "would forbid entry into this country of any article that is the product of any foreign industry that employs child labor, in whole or in part." Shukla's overall conclusion: "People of conscience have raised their voices to help these children."[2]

Two years later, Shukla won the 1999 Cowan Award for a searching inquiry into the coercive practice of dowry, outlawed in India but still associated with beatings and punishment of women by husbands or their in-laws. It's estimated that one woman dies every hundred minutes in India because of dowry-related abuses. More young brides than ever before, the seven-part documentary concluded, are demanding their rights and rejecting the dowry system.[3]

TOWN CRIER TO THE WORLD

On health issues, too, VOA has been a town crier to the world, particularly in the realm of disease prevention and diagnosis. It has done so through public-service announcements and special programming. On a single Saturday in April 1998, 120 million children in India were vaccinated against polio, as part of Rotary International's campaign to eliminate the disease. USAID provided funds to help promote this unprecedented strike against polio in India. VOA public-service announcements in Hindi on the inoculations helped produce the record turnout.

VOA also reported one of the deadliest medical scourges of our times, HIV/AIDS. In 1992, VOA News Division assignments editor Carolyn

A WORLDWIDE CONFERENCE CALL ON AIDS

For many years, Traffic Chief Jim Cowgill was among the most active technical specialists at VOA headquarters. On election nights, he could be seen bounding down the corridors, double-checking hundreds of incoming and outgoing audio lines to ensure that all was in order. Cowgill was challenged in an unprecedented way on September 30, 1997, when four U.S. Public Health Service (USPHS) specialists came to VOA to conduct a worldwide clinical conference call on HIV/AIDS. The highly technical roundtable was designed to enable physicians at more than 600 sites in the United States and abroad to compare notes on the prevention and treatment of a pandemic that had shattered 30 million lives in Africa alone by the end of the twentieth century.

Working with Dr. Abe Machen of the USPHS, Cowgill learned that many doctors in rural clinics in the developing world had no way of hearing this medical tutorial via standard telephone conference-call links. So Cowgill arranged for fourteen shortwave frequencies to make this advanced medical school conference call available virtually everywhere. Hundreds of physicians sent advance e-mail questions for the expert panel to consider. Countless others in remote areas without electricity or modems could hear the discussion, even those who had only battery-powered transistor radios. The USPHS transcribed the two-hour session, and physicians everywhere with on-line access could read-in just a day or so later. Vital diagnostic information was shared in a global multimedia assault against HIV/AIDS.*

*VOA, weekly look-ahead, September 29, 1997, 1. Abe Machen also appeared on the VOA weekday worldwide call-in program, *Talk to America*, to promote the global conference call for specialists.

Naifeh produced a documentary series on the disease. She traveled to Brazil, Uganda, Romania, Thailand, and several cities in the United States to assess its devastating effects. In a hospital in Romania, she saw a three-year-old infected with AIDS who, Naifeh recalled, "was the size of an infant." In Uganda, she met Catholic missionaries who had clinics for teenagers on the perils of premarital sex. In Thailand, Naifeh said, government officials who wanted to ignore the problem were at war with young physicians who wanted to confront it head-on. "Again," she added, " the church was a big help . . . monks opened their monasteries to people dying of AIDS."[4]

VOA reflected the medical, social, and economic impact of HIV/AIDS in programming to all regions of the world, but nowhere quite as dramatically as Africa. A Worldnet Television call-in program called *Africa Journal*, hosted by Maimouna Mills of French-to-Africa, was simulcast on VOA and tackled HIV/AIDS-related issues from many angles, including the opinions of policy makers, activists, and average citizens in Africa and the United States. VOA and Worldnet video journalists traveling in Africa and equipped with handheld cameras added powerful images for TV to their correspondent reports on HIV/AIDS. VOA joined forces with the Confederation of East and Central Africa Football Associations and Johns Hopkins University to broadcast public-service messages by celebrity soccer players in Africa on ways to prevent the disease.

THE BETTER ANGELS OF THEIR NATURE

Occasionally, the focus on humanitarian programming brought VOA broadcasters face to face with individual victims of disease, disasters, or those displaced from their homes. For many—program hosts, producers in Washington, correspondents in the field—this meant, at times, lending a helping hand.

- Dr. Irene Kelner, host of the Russian Branch's program *Health and Medicine*, received a desperate letter in December 1988 from a Moscow grandmother seeking help. The writer sought assistance for her one-year-old grandson, Kirill, whose brain tumor was spreading. The baby's doctors had told her that the infant faced certain death. Kelner immediately got on the phone and put together a coalition of American foundations and doctors who brought Kirill to the Montefiore Medical Center in the Bronx. There, the child underwent life-saving surgery in August 1989. Kelner kept her listeners informed of the boy's progress throughout the operation and his recovery. Even more far-reaching, the initiative inspired a Dallas philanthropist involved in the project, Marcy Rogers, to establish a medical exchange program to help other needy patients in cooperation with a Russian children's fund and the Ministry of Health in Moscow.[5] Kelner worked closely for years with Irina Burgener, the award-winning coproducer of the VOA weekday call-in program *Talk to America,* to seek donations of medical equipment and supplies for the Soviet Union.

• Judith Latham, a writer and reporter for *Dateline,* a weekday in-depth feature on *VOA News Now,* for years has studied and assisted the oppressed and often forgotten Roma, or Gypsies, of Europe. There are an estimated 9 million Roma in Europe, scattered among nearly forty countries.[6] Latham helped the Roma arrange a concert recorded in the VOA auditorium one evening in November 1996. She also enabled a Romani-speaking American human rights activist, Paul Polansky, to speak on VOA in 1999 about Kosovar Albanian oppression of the shrinking Roma communities in Kosovo. Polansky had spent weeks in temporary Roma settlements assisting them and easing their plight as they were moved from camp to camp in the aftermath of the Kosovo war. Working under the auspices of the United Nations High Commissioner for Refugees (UNHCR), Polansky noted that four out of five Roma in Kosovo had fled or had been forced from their homes during the first year after the UN and the international Kosovo Force (KFOR) took control of the province.

• Negussie Mengesha, Amharic Service chief and later program manager of the Africa Division (chapter 11), conducted an interview in East Africa in 1985 with a dramatic sequel. During a visit to the Umgulja refugee camp in Sudan that year, Mengesha met a refugee woman from Ethiopia at a feeding station and recorded her story for VOA Amharic. The woman—who had lost her husband before fleeing into exile—had four children. Mengesha was astonished to discover that although she was destitute, she had in effect adopted three of them. Out of sheer compassion, she had agreed to take one of the children, a newborn baby, shortly after its mother died. The other two were left with her by their father, a widower, who asked her to keep them for a while so he could go to Khartoum and earn some money. That was months earlier, and the refugee mother had no hope that the father (who seemed to have abandoned his children) would ever return. Mengesha broadcast the interview, and the staff of the Amharic Service took up a collection to help the destitute mother. Three months later, Mengesha received a letter from the father, who wrote that he had heard the interview on VOA Amharic and was ashamed. The father then returned to the camp, picked up his children, and took them to his new home elsewhere in Sudan.[7]

• Sonja Pace, VOA correspondent in Paris, was assigned in the summer of 1994 to cover the refugee crisis in eastern Zaire following the terrible Rwandan genocide earlier that year (chapter 11). She and several other journalists drove to the outskirts of Goma to investigate shooting in the region and word that waves and waves of refugees were on the roads, fleeing for their lives. Pace will never forget what happened there:

> We saw a young woman who was dead—it looked like she had been trampled to death—and next to her was a very small baby. And the baby was still alive, and we picked up the baby. What do you do? We decided we would take it to the orphanage, and a Zairean soldier brought us another baby to take with us too. Again, the mother was dead, and the baby had been scratched up a bit, but miraculously had not been wounded badly.
>
> On the way back to the car as we carried the two babies, we were walking along the road and I noticed two little girls were following me. I would say one of them was about ten years old, and the other maybe five or six. And very silently, they never said a word, they ran after me to make sure they didn't lose me in the crowd. And I looked down and I realized that the whole front part of the older girl's arm was missing; it had been ripped open by shrapnel. And the other girl, the five- or six-year-old, had a big hole in her cheek where she'd been hit by a bullet. And they just sort of went after me, and I bundled them in the car and I took these four children out to the French military hospital at the airport.[8]

As we learned earlier, thousands of lost relatives in Central Africa were reunited via the family reunification hotline of the Kinyarwanda-Kirundi Service. The chairman of the board of Human Rights Watch in New York, Robert L. Bernstein, wrote to VOA director Cowan that even before that hotline was established, international broadcast news reports in French were the only other source of information that the Rwandan people had at the time of their infamous bloodbath in 1994. He added: "Human Rights activist Monique Mujawamaria, feared killed as the fighting started, told *Ms. Magazine* in an interview that when she escaped to Belgium, 'through the Voice of America, I let my children know that I was safe.' . . . Human Rights Watch has counted on the Voice of America for almost twenty years. We hope to be able to do so for many years to come."[9]

A GLOBAL SCAN OF THE HUMAN CONDITION

Around the world, VOA and its correspondents—by reporting humanitarian issues candidly and comprehensively—focused on the need for reforms of potential benefit to thousands of people.

- In Honduras, dozens of street children were picked up by police in the early 1990s and thrown into jail with adults. There, they became defenseless prey. Covenant House, a Miami-based human rights organization, tried for months to get an appointment with Honduran president Carlos Roberto Reina to seek separate facilities for juveniles. The watchdog group never succeeded in getting past the presidential gatekeepers.

In early 1995, VOA Central America correspondent Bill Rodgers became aware of this situation and interviewed Covenant House representatives and others. His report was broadcast back to the region in both Spanish and English. The very next morning, President Reina's office phoned Bruce Harris, executive director of Covenant House Latin America, seeking an urgent appointment. "The very first line the president stated in opening the meeting," Harris told Rodgers, "was that 'it makes me very upset that I have to hear on the Voice of America that Honduras is abusing the rights of children.'"[10] Reina said that he would introduce legislation for separate detention facilities for children in the very next session of parliament.

- In Bulgaria, VOA Central Europe correspondent Barry Wood visited a Sofia hospital in 1997 where there was a shortage of medical supplies and patients had to bring along their own food:

This outpatient ward at Sofia's First City Polyclinic Hospital resembles a waiting room at a train station. Dozens of mostly elderly people sit hunched over and sick on the oversized benches in the middle of the room of tall ceilings. From doors on either side of this cavernous chamber, nurses or doctors in white smocks occasionally emerge to escort a waiting patient inside. Radosvet Gornev is a thirty-five-year-old surgeon assigned to the hospital. He earns the equivalent of less than $35 a month. But he considers himself lucky, compared to the patients. Dr. Gornev says the state hospital system in Bulgaria is broke and there is a desperate shortage of medicines, particularly antibiotics.

TAPE/GORNEV: If I need antibiotics for ten patients, I may have enough for two. There is a big problem. We have help from international organizations now, from Germany, from England. But it isn't enough.

A man named Ivan says the food problem in hospitals is well known.

TAPE/IVAN: I hear that they must bring their own food. Their relatives come and bring them food because there is not enough here.

All of the former communist countries have experienced problems with adjusting their health care systems from the old model where everything was paid for by the state. But here in Bulgaria, where the old system is still pretty much in place, the state has run out of money. Dr. Gornev says the situation was worse two months ago, but shortages remain. He is hopeful that the pro-Western, proreform government that has just been elected in Bulgaria will move quickly to improve the health care system.[11]

• In Burma, VOA Southeast Asia correspondent Dan Robinson (who later became Burmese Service chief) reported from Rangoon in August 1994. Robinson told his listeners what had changed—and had not changed—since his one earlier visit there:

After some of the heaviest rains many Rangoon residents remember, I am driving past the famous Shwedagon Pagoda in the Burmese capital. It is hard not to mention the Buddhist shrine in a story about Burma. An amazing bejeweled spire of gold, it dominates the city of lakes, grabbing rays of the sun and shooting them off in all directions.

Since my first visit almost three years ago, the city seems to be bursting with economic activity. There are more consumer goods, new shops, and more cars and trucks on the streets. Not long ago, large billboards warned against such things as the products of imperialists and their minions. The signs are gone, for the most part, replaced by advertisements for Kodak, Sony, Daewoo, Pepsi, and a variety of foreign beers.

Despite the new economic activity, one impression I find difficult to avoid on this and previous visits is the degree to which Burma today remains a military dictatorship. There is no freedom of expression here. Burmese get their news from VOA, BBC, and other sources.

In local media, there is of course, no mention of yet another reality. This is the continuing presence and widespread popularity of Aung San Suu Kyi, the 1991 Nobel Peace Prize laureate and daughter of Burma's independence hero. When or whether senior military leaders do talk directly with Aung San Suu Kyi, a number of questions come to mind. Are yearnings for democracy being replaced by a rush for money? And, will economic development lead to political change—a theory Burma's southeast Asia neighbors use to support their engagement of, and investment in, the Rangoon junta?[12]

- In China, VOA Beijing correspondent Stephanie Ho traveled to a remote, arid northern region to examine the plight of citizens, many of whom appeared to be exiles in their own country:

From the airplane window, ripples can be seen down below in the shadow of the early morning sun. For a split second, I almost think it could be water, but then I remember that I am in arid Ningxia Hui Autonomous Region and the sun's light shows the ripples to be windblown sand. Ningxia is not the poorest region in China, but dry corn stalks rustling in the wind tell the story of a harsh and desolate place.

For hundreds of years, Chinese emperors used the area where Ningxia is now as a place of exile. That sort of banishment did not change much under the communist government that took over the country in 1949. Walking along the streets of Ningxia's capital, Yinchuan, all of the people I met were from somewhere else. At a resettlement village in the region, a young girl talks about her hometown, more than three hundred kilometers away, and [describes] a famous poem by Tang dynasty poet Li Bai.

TAPE/CHINESE GIRL: (*in Mandarin Chinese*)

This poem expresses Li Bai's longing for his old home far away. It is also relevant to the thousands of Chinese who were sent by the government to Ningxia from provinces to the east, when the region was first established in 1958 or during the Cultural Revolution from 1966 to 1976. For these people, home is still Shaanxi, Henan, Shandong, Liaoning, or Jiangsu province. Other

Yinchuan residents dream of their old homes in one of China's two most famous cities, Beijing and Shanghai.

One phrase that is used to describe residents of Yinchuan who could not return to their homes is *zhizu changle*, literally, "if you know what is good enough, you will always be happy." This can be interpreted in two ways. It could support an attitude of complacency, by providing an excuse for a person to accept his fate and not try to improve his situation. Or, it could have just the opposite effect: providing justification that you are not where you belong, and that, someday, you can return home.[13]

• Of course, in its scan of the globe, VOA also has focused over the years on human rights issues in the United States, including programming on the history of slavery, the civil rights revolution, the treatment of Native Americans, and capital punishment. The execution by lethal injection of Oklahoma City bomber Timothy McVeigh on June 11, 2001, once again stimulated debate on the death penalty. McVeigh confessed to having set off the explosion that killed 168 people. A year before the Oklahoma City bomber was put to death, the United States ranked third behind China and Saudi Arabia in the number of executions, barely edging out Iran.[14] Correspondent Jim Malone spoke with several specialists on capital punishment:

Recent public opinion polls indicate that 75 to 80 percent of Americans support Timothy McVeigh's execution. Pro–death penalty activists insist that the McVeigh execution will bolster public support for capital punishment. But anti–death penalty groups are working hard to counter that view.

Several polls indicate that generic public support for the death penalty has slipped [in the U.S.] in recent years, from about 77 percent five years ago to about 63 percent today. Ajamu Baraka directs an anti–death penalty program for Amnesty International. He predicts the McVeigh case will do little to alter the current debate. Mr. Baraka also expects a negative international reaction to the McVeigh execution that he believes could help death penalty opponents in the long run.

"So there is a clear trend in the international community away from the use of the death penalty," he says. "And therefore, the argument made by U.S. authorities that McVeigh has to be executed because of [the enormity of] his crime does not really set well with our European allies and many people around the world."

Attorney General John Ashcroft postponed McVeigh's execution for one month after the discovery of FBI evidence that was withheld from defense attorneys. Some legal experts believe the problems highlighted in the McVeigh case could cause prosecutors to be more careful with evidence in future death penalty cases.

Paul Heath is one of the leaders of the Oklahoma City Survivors Association. Although he personally opposes the death penalty, he expects a small measure of satisfaction from Timothy McVeigh's death. Death penalty supporters contend McVeigh's execution will bring closure and peace to those who lost loved ones in Oklahoma City. Paul Heath says he has no such illusions.[15]

RELIEF FOR THE CAPTIVES

In other countries, the seizure of hostages—Americans and other nationalities—are followed closely by the Voice. During the crisis preceding the Gulf War of 1991, VOA's Worldwide English Division recorded messages from families in the United States to their loved ones prevented from leaving Iraq or Kuwait by Saddam Hussein.

Later in the 1990s, a North Carolinian named Ray Rising was kidnapped by rebels in Colombia and was held for 810 days before his release on June 17, 1996. After he was freed, Rising wrote to VOA's Tom Crosby to tell him that he was allowed during the latter part of his captivity to listen to the radio, including Crosby's award-winning evening news hour, *Report to the Americas*. Rising thanked Crosby. How he tuned in was nothing short of awe inspiring:

> I had only a small Walkman AM/FM radio that wouldn't pick up signals except at night. So I took it apart and connected a small wire to the tuning capacitor. Then using a scouring pad, I unwound the wire the pad is made of. There is about seventy feet of a very fine wire in one of those scouring pads. Connecting a stick at one end, I threw the wire up into a palm tree and then connected it to the receiver. Wow! Lots of stations, day and night! At night, I could hear shortwave stations. By carefully tuning, I was able to listen to

Report to the Americas. So every night for eleven months, I laid on my bed of sticks and leaves and listened to VOA.[16]

Yet another hostage situation, this one in Africa, illustrated how VOA broadcasters to different regions, working together, can achieve remarkable results reportorially. In June 2001, Idrissa Fall of the French-to-Africa Branch was checking out the story of twenty-four forestry workers from Thailand held by Mai Mai rebels in the northeastern jungles of the Democratic Republic of Congo. Fall knew that this would be of interest to the VOA Thai Service and contacted its dynamic senior editor, Nittaya Maphunphong. He explained that he could reach the rebels at their cell-phone number, at the jungle hideout where the hostages were held. Maphunphong wasted no time in getting on the phone and interviewing hostage Akom Pangsri. He revealed that several of his colleagues had malaria, but that they were being cared for by the rebels' doctor and being fed by people in the village where they were detained. The hostage quoted their captors as saying that they would be released soon. The Thai Service fed the interview to Thailand, and sixty-seven radio station affiliates throughout the Southeast Asian kingdom rebroadcast it immediately after receiving it from Washington.[17]

JUST THE FACTS, PLEASE

Straight reporting, just the facts, offers the most credible programming about democracy, human rights, or humanitarian issues.

"It is counterproductive," said VOA East Asia and Pacific Division program manager Jay Henderson, "for us to report on human rights as if it were our moral mission to do so. The better way for VOA to nurture human rights is to report violations as we would anything else and stick as close to the truth—straight news and description—as possible."[18]

"I agree," added Africa Division director Gwen Dillard, "that VOA's ability to warn about ethnic violence is one of its most important functions. One of the best deterrents to genocide or mass killings," Dillard added, "is to help listeners see and understand some of the underlying forces in their society that lead to violence. Providing more thorough background," she concluded, "can help people understand, recognize warning signs, and develop their own safeguards against similar events in the future."[19]

All Ears for Democratic Reforms

In Europe and in Asia, international broadcasts have helped expand democracy's reach through years of accurate reportage, analysis, and live coverage. Soviet affairs specialist Paul Goble said that VOA's reporting over many years of elections in America and the West were a major factor in legitimizing the process in Warsaw Pact countries following the collapse of the Berlin Wall in 1989.* Historian and author Betty Bao Lord, a charter member of the Broadcasting Board of Governors, lived in Beijing in the early 1990s and was in frequent touch with young Chinese intellectual dissidents. They were electrified, she said, by just six words they heard on VOA. It was during a live broadcast of the 1992 presidential debate between the President George Bush and Democratic candidate Bill Clinton. The words, spoken by the debate moderator, were: "Mr. President, your time is up!" Lord said that her Chinese acquaintances found it profoundly striking that in a democracy, the leader of the Free World was subject to the same rules as everyone else.†

*United States Information Agency, Bureau of Broadcasting, *Annual Report for 1993: Looking Toward Tomorrow* (Washington, D.C.: United States Information Agency, Bureau of Broadcasting, 1993), 24.
†Betty Bao Lord, interview with author, Washington, D.C., April 10, 2002. Lord, a leading proponent of Radio Free Asia, was in Beijing with her husband, Winston, U.S. ambassador to China in the late 1980s and later assistant secretary of state for East Asian affairs.

WARNING SIGNS WRIT LARGE: GIVING VOICE TO THE VOICELESS

In the Africa that Gwen Dillard knows so well, an on-scene report from Brazzaville in 1997 by VOA correspondent Alex Belida illustrates what both she and Jay Henderson were saying. The veteran VOA foreign correspondent's eye for detail was as sharp as a video camera, combined with a sensitivity to human suffering honed over many years of travel in the continent:

I am standing in a rubble-strewn Brazzaville street as the city returns cautiously to life after a bloody civil war. Armed men are all around me, most of them looting, occasionally firing off bursts of bullets in celebration.

But I am not concentrating on this any more. Instead, with the hand holding my microphone limp by my side, my tape running senselessly, I am looking at another corpse—this one of a man, perhaps in his twenties, his legs charred.

I know there will be no voice to record. But his lips are apart, his arms outstretched, fingers together, as if in prayer. It seems another one of Africa's dead is trying to speak to me. And I feel I owe him this one last consideration. I think maybe he wants to share his anguish, his despair, or maybe a last word to a parent or a child. I feel badly, because I do not know for sure.

I do know though that I have seen corpses like this before, victims of war, or of genocide, or of famine, or of sickness. A symbolic path of the dead now runs through my mind—a personal collection reflecting the real path their corpses have left across much of Africa: from arid Somalia in the northeast, across Sudan and into northern Uganda, down through steamy Rwanda, Burundi, and Congo in the center of the continent.

Some have been young men in uniform, their bodies shattered by a bullet or a shell. Some have been old men, thin beyond belief, weakened by hunger or disease. Some have been women, their dresses in tatters, their faces etched in silent agony. Some have been children, too young to die, their skulls cleaved in half.

Some I have met in battle-scarred streets, some in burned-out buildings. Some I have seen sprawled amidst flowers in an open field, some floating, limbs bound, in muddy water. Some I have found in groups thrown into a dirt pit, some alone in the aisles of a gutted church.

I have, at times, had imaginary conversations with these dead I have met—their unrecorded voices playing on endlessly inside my head, sometimes loud, sometimes just a whisper. I tell them I am sorry and if it were in my power, I would restore them to life. But I can't. It's not in my power. Perhaps the only help I can give is to try to tell their story.[20]

19

Yearning to Breathe Free

TALES OF GREAT VOA ESCAPES

Give me your tired, your poor,
Your huddled masses yearning to breathe free,
The wretched refuse of your teeming shore.
Send these, the homeless, tempest-tost to me,
I lift my lamp beside the golden door.
                    —Emma Lazarus, "The New Colossus"

Listening clandestinely to the Voice of America in their God-
forsaken village in Albania, the [Islami] sisters never imagined
that one day they themselves would be the "voice of truth" to
their countrymen.
    —VOA, "VOA's Voices: Life Stories of VOA Broadcasters"

You have seen in chapter 1 how the lady with the lamp, shining over
New York Harbor, inspired the prodemocracy demonstrators in
Tiananmen Square. The light of her torch attracted several generations
of VOA broadcasters or their parents as well. You do not have to go to
detention centers in China, remote reaches of Africa, or other dark
corners of the world to hear descriptions of war, famine, and tyranny by
people who experienced it firsthand and were driven, against great odds,
to escape it. Wander around the halls of America's Voice near the foot of
Capitol Hill in Washington, D.C., and you hear story after story of how
staff members or their families fled their home countries to seek a better
life in the West. Remarkable courage and determination to "breathe
free" brought them, over the years, to VOA. Here are a few of their personal accounts.

GEORGE BERZINS: LATVIAN SERVICE AND CHIEF, EAST ASIA BRANCH

It was February 13, 1995. The trio in the carpool—Frank Cummins, George Dzintars Berzins, and the author—was moving at a snail's pace through gridlock along North Washington Street in Old Town Alexandria, Virginia, during our commute to work. We were riveted to the radio. This was truly inspired public-service broadcasting. National Public Radio was airing a minidocumentary on the fiftieth anniversary of the Allied firebombing of the German city of Dresden toward the end of World War II. The NPR reporter described a city that on a night of hell a half century earlier had become a raging inferno of flying objects and collapsing buildings. "That's exactly the way it was," George exclaimed. We had an eyewitness as a passenger!

The traffic that winter morning suddenly seemed inconsequential. George recalled that he was five years old at the time of the Dresden tragedy, a refugee in that flaming city while fleeing with his family from Latvia. By the winter of 1944/1945, Adolf Hitler's armored units were in full retreat as the Soviet army advanced. Miraculously, the Berzins family was able to stay ahead of the onrushing USSR units. Throughout their eight-month flight to freedom, George and his one-year-old brother, Gunars, were sitting atop a farm cart full of the Berzinses' household possessions. George, whose leg had been badly injured in a bike accident the previous summer in Latvia, was unable to walk. His courageous father, Ludvigs, pulled that green cart across Central Europe as his mother, Austra, pushed it. The heroic parents bore their family to freedom in an exhausting journey of more than 800 miles, as the crow flies.

It was winter most of the time. Ludvigs had to hide during the day in forests near the highway for fear of being caught, drafted into the German army, and sent eastward to the Russian front. At one point, he even buried himself in a snowbank to escape detection. The front, it seemed, was never that far away. Should the Russian forces overtake them, the Berzins parents knew, Ludvigs probably would be deported to Siberia. His name had been spotted on a list of prospective exiles prepared by the Soviets when they briefly occupied Latvia from 1939 until 1941. Then the Germans pushed the Red Army eastward (and out of Latvia) during the ill-fated Nazi drive toward Stalingrad and Moscow. In 1944, the Russians struck back. They expelled the Germans from Latvia in their final drive to Berlin. The Berzins family decided to flee when they heard the big Russian and German guns roar close to the Latvian capital, Riga, in October 1944.

"It Was Dante's Inferno"

The most dangerous hours for the Berzins family lay ahead. Ludvigs finally was seized by the Germans. He was forced to work in a factory in Dresden, making porcelain parts to be used for communications gear by the failing Nazi war machine. The family settled in a walk-up apartment in the middle of the city. Dresden was quiet, its historic buildings untouched by war. Then suddenly, in mid-February, the first air-raid sirens sounded. British Lancaster bombers raided the city in two huge waves on the night of February 13. The planes dropped tons of bombs and incendiaries. American B-17s bombed by day. The aerial bombardments started a firestorm that killed an estimated 50,000 people and transformed Dresden, the city of fine china, into a massive heap of charred rubble on the banks of the Elbe River.

On the evening of February 13, the Berzins family was crouched in a cellar as the air raids became more and more intense. Ludvigs decided that "if we stay here, we won't survive." He led the family into a courtyard next to the apartment. They quickly loaded up the green wagon. The din of sirens and falling bombs was earsplitting. They ventured forth, from the courtyard through a wooden gate, into one of Dresden's major thoroughfares.

They were greeted by sounds and sights that young George recalled a half century later as if it were yesterday. "It was hell outside," he remembered. "There was this incredible whining and whistling as the bombs came down . . . it was Dante's inferno as glowing timbers crashed down from buildings across the street and burning mattresses disgorged from flaming buildings hurtled down the street like flaming rockets. Dad said: 'We're going to get out of here.'"

Ludvigs spotted a German farmer with a flatbed truck full of milk cans riding through the inferno and the noise. The driver's eyes were dazed; his face was frozen in fear. Quickly, as had often happened on this trek, Ludvigs got permission to hitch the green wagon to the rear of the slow-moving vehicle, and the family climbed aboard the truck. "We were sitting among jiggling milk cans," George remembered, "as the farmer kept his truck putt, putt, putting at a maddeningly slow pace toward the edge of Dresden." Miraculously, they made it to the countryside.

No Place to Hide

The ordeal was not over, however. It was dawn. They unhitched from the rescue truck. Ludvigs decided that they must get off the open highway—none too safe as the Allied sorties continued. They resumed pulling the green wagon toward a nearby farmhouse but stopped short in their tracks. The farmhouse apparently was a suspected hideout for German forces, and the Allied bombers immediately obliterated it in a rain of deadly fire. The family gazed back at Dresden, a huge, flaming urban pyre.

The battered green wagon resumed its journey west, Ludvigs pulling, Austra pushing. The family hitched the wagon to other vehicles from time to time, and camped at night in barns, in cellars, and in monasteries. George remembers getting something like pneumonia in the dead of winter and being nursed for a couple of days by a nun in a convent in the German town of Fraunenstein, as the family stood by and waited for him to get better. "The nun slept on the floor of her bedroom," he said, "gave me her bed and covered me with blankets. My mother later told me that nun saved my life."

Crossing the Lines to Freedom

One morning in April 1945, as the war in Europe was sputtering out, the Berzins family had their first glimpse of what was for them a long-cherished and beautiful sight: the first American soldiers. They were hustled onto a boxcar with other war refugees and taken by rail to Hanau, just east of Frankfurt-am-Main. There, they stayed in a former German army garrison that had been converted into a displaced-persons camp administered by the U.S. Army. The long wait then began for an American sponsor, there and at another camp in Stuttgart. A sponsor was found, four years later.

The Berzins family set sail from Bremerhaven on the troop-transport ship USS *General Stewart* on August 25, 1949. The vessel sailed into New York Harbor at dusk on September 4, 1949, and there—fully illuminated and towering above the waves—was the lady with the lamp. The incredible lights of Manhattan, the largest city the family had ever seen, glistened on the opposite shore. Ludvigs, Austra, George, and Gunars, thrilled beyond measure, remained aboard and then were cleared by immigration the next morning to set foot for the first time on U.S. soil. But there was yet another setback. They learned to their dismay that their sponsor had changed his mind.

Then American churches stepped in to help. The Berzins family first was transported to a church refugee-resettlement center in New Windsor, Maryland. The Church of the Brethren soon got Ludvigs a job in Lebanon County, Pennsylvania, and the family later moved to nearby Lancaster. There, Ludvigs Berzins founded the Latvian Relief Fund of America, which at one time had 15,000 members. George, who was attracted to local commercial broadcasting as an adolescent, joined VOA's Latvian Service in 1967 after serving in the U.S. Army in Korea. He later drew from his knowledge of that country and its people to become head of the Korean Service and then VOA's East Asia Branch. The rest, as they say, is history.[1]

JOSEPH BUDAY: NEWS DIVISION AND EUROPEAN DIVISION

Joseph Buday was seven years old, living happily in the farming village of Balassagyarmat in northeastern Hungary, when World War II began in Europe. He attended the Benedictine school there, but soon his world began to fall apart. Troops of the German Wehrmacht passed through the village in 1941 en route to the Balkans. It was 5:30 or 6:00 o'clock one morning when they marched in, fully armored, and began to occupy public places, including school buildings and Hungarian military installations. This was a day that Buday will never forget:

> The Benedictine headmaster called a special meeting about 8:30 that morning. He was our Hungarian and Latin teacher, the two most important subjects at the Benedictine School. I was nine years old at the time, and his words made a profound impression. "Something terrible happened during the night," the headmaster said. "Foreign German troops entered our town. I just want you young masters to be aware that this is a sad day for us. Don't be impressed by the mighty military machine you see, and if I catch any of you lifting a finger to help the Germans, you'll flunk both Hungarian and Latin."

That was only the beginning of horrific years for young Joe. In 1942, his father, Joszef, was killed in an Allied air raid. The Germans, who had marched through in 1941, returned as an occupation force in early 1944. Their goal was to secure the borders of Axis allies Hungary and Romania against the Russian advance from the east. To escape the occupation, Joe's mother, Eugenia, took the boy to Vienna. When the Soviet army reached Vienna in April 1945 and the war ended, the Budays decided to return to Balassagyarmat so that Joe could complete his schooling.

They moved back home in 1946. It was a different Hungary than they once had known. The Communist Party, aided by the presence of occupying Soviet soldiers, assumed control of the Interior Ministry and was about to win a rigged election and take over the government. Joe and his mother were summoned to the local police station for interrogations. Sometimes the sessions lasted for four or five hours. Questions centered on their loyalty to the Soviets and the Communist Party, where their relatives lived, what they thought of their "liberators." A sympathetic young policeman warned Joe and his mother that their deportation to a labor camp might be imminent.

The Budays knew that they had to leave. In August 1947, they applied to the authorities for permission to attend Joe's grandmother's funeral in southern Hungary. Instead, they headed by train to northeastern Hungary and the border town of Sopron. On a bright, sunny Sunday morning that August, they set out through the forests near the town toward the heavily guarded Austrian frontier. They carried small suitcases with all their belongings, fully aware of the risk they were taking. The Hungarian border guards were prepared to arrest anyone caught fleeing the country, and guns were poised to shoot anyone daring to cross the no-man's-land separating Hungary from Austria.

A Forest Hike to Remember

They noticed that two men were following them. Joe and his mother stepped up their pace. So did the two men. They walked even faster. So did their pursuers. Finally Joe, then sixteen, said: "Let's just stop and take a rest and see what happens." The two men quickly caught up with them and explained that they were out in the forest bird-watching, as members of what might be called the Hungarian equivalent of the Audubon Society. They asked where the Budays were headed. When told, they warned Joe and his mother not to continue along the present path. "It leads straight to a checkpoint," they said. "You should head out another way."

One of the bird-watchers immediately assumed the role of an advance sentinel. They devised a unique signal system. The lead man would make a bird call, if the way ahead was clear. His partner would scan the right and left flanks for any sign of security police and whistle back if the way was indeed clear for a further advance. Using the system, the pair led the Budays forward toward a deserted stretch of the frontier. Finally, all four reached it—a flat meadow about 500 yards wide. The two bird-watchers explained that this was as far as they wanted to venture. Should the group be spotted in the free-fire zone, they said, it would be fatal for all.

Joe and his mother, crouching low, headed across the meadow and made it to Austria. Their harrowing eight-hour hike to freedom took them to the border town of Deutschkreuz, about ten miles west of Sopron. They immediately caught a train destined for Vienna, a train, they discovered once aboard, with a most curious route. It *circled back through Hungary* in a loop, passing through Sopron, before heading west to Vienna. During its passage through Hungary, the doors of the train were sealed so that no one could get on or off. As it slowed down to go through the station at Sopron, the Budays glanced out the window. The two bird-watchers were there, beside the track, staring intently at the passing train. They waved a final farewell from Hungary to Joe and Eugenia Buday.

Another Lucky Break, Good for a Lifetime

The Budays settled in Vienna for several years. Joe became a German-language tutor for the son of an American colonel stationed in what was then a city controlled under a postwar four-power agreement by the United States, the Soviet Union, Britain, and France. The colonel took a liking to Joe and helped him enroll in a school in Switzerland. From there, in 1949, the Budays emigrated to the United States. Joe enrolled at George Washington University in the nation's capital and became an American citizen in 1954. He enlisted in the U.S. Army and served as a German-language translator for the army in Germany in the mid-1950s. When he returned to civilian life, he became a translator for the USIA Library Service and research unit back in Washington, D.C. He transferred to VOA's Hungarian Service from there, and felt a sense of awe working beside former Hungarian justices, novelists, authors, and well-known journalists such as László Boross and Paul Nadanyi. After a three-month stay in the service, Joe was selected as a News Division writer trainee. Later, he advanced through the newsroom ranks to become a duty editor (shift supervisor), deputy division chief, and eventually deputy chief of the VOA European Division.

During his military service in Germany, Joe listened frequently to Radio Budapest Hungarian broadcasts at its Stalinist worst. Years later, he remained among the Voice's most avid daily "tasters" of European electronic media. During the early-morning hours, he would spin the dial, taking in the BBC, various German broadcast outlets, and, of course, Radio Budapest during and after the Cold War. His instincts as a journalist bridging languages and cultures were invariably up to the minute. Joe retired from VOA in the late 1990s.[2]

HAMED HOSSEINI AND SPOZHMAI MAIWANDI: AFGHAN SERVICES

VOA's two language services to Afghanistan are Pashto, directed to Pashtuns, who mostly live in southern and eastern Afghanistan and northern Pakistan; and Dari, a variant of Persian (Farsi) that is understood by most Afghans in the cities and in the north and west and by inhabitants of the surrounding areas of Iran and Central Asia. The VOA Dari Service was established in September 1980, just nine months after the Soviet invasion of Afghanistan. VOA Pashto went on the air on July 4, 1982.[3]

The staffs of both services consisted of people who had fled for their lives from occupation, civil war, and deprivation after King Zahir Shah was forced into exile in 1974. Many of these VOA broadcasters came from prominent families or were intellectual leaders in their tragically stricken land: poets, judges, teachers, students. How they fled is a fascinating glimpse of Afghanistan in the early 1980s. Hamed Hosseini initially joined the Dari Service and later moved to the centrally located audio services unit at the Voice. Spozhmai Maiwandi made her first broadcast in the Pashto Service two days after it went on the air and eventually became the service chief. Their recollections of their respective flights to freedom follow, in chronological order.

The Hosseini Story

Hamed Hosseini was born on May 1, 1937, son of a high-ranking Afghan diplomat stationed at the time as his country's representative to the League of Nations in Geneva, Switzerland. Hamed's mother and wife, both named Habiba, were connected to the Afghan royal family. After graduating from university, Hosseini joined the Afghan foreign service and served as second secretary in Afghan embassies: Ankara (1967–1970) and London (1974–1978). Eight months after Hamed and his family returned to Kabul following the latter posting, his world came crashing down—as it did for thousands of other Afghans. Prime Minister Mohammed Daoud and his family were murdered in a Communist-led coup d'état, and the new regime launched purges against favored elites of the old order. "We decided from day one," Hosseini recalled, "to get out. We knew we had to leave. It was only a question of how, and when."

It took the new rulers several months to reorganize the civil and foreign services. Hamed was demoted from deputy director of information in the Foreign Ministry to a series of lesser posts in the Justice Ministry. He considered himself fortunate to have a job at all. The family lived in a house near the airport in Kabul.

The Soviets Move In

On the morning of December 26, 1979, Hamed noticed that air traffic increased dramatically on the runways near their home. "I sensed that something was up," he remembered. "I could hear one transport plane or another landing every minute or so." Within twenty-four hours, the Soviet invasion of Afghanistan became clear. Russian soldiers were patrolling the streets of Kabul, their small tanks omnipresent in the center of the city.

"We knew it was an invasion by listening to the official radio," Hosseini said. "They put the new prime minister, Babrak Karmal [the Soviet puppet leader], on the air even before he arrived to take over the government." The new Soviet-controlled regime, however, promulgated a law that eventually enabled the Hosseini family to finance their escape. For the first time since 1978, private citizens were permitted to sell their homes. The income from the sale, Hamed said, could be used to "buy" their way out of Afghanistan. Smugglers hauling electronic equipment, farm machinery, and even drugs across the border to Pakistan had discovered another lucrative cargo: people. For a price, whole families could be "helped" to the frontier and freedom. The house fetched the equivalent of about $15,000. "We sold it," Hamed said, "to get out."

Endgame, and Escape

Arrangements were made, quietly. In June 1980, the Hosseinis were on the move, in Kabul. They stayed successively in at least three houses, those of relatives and those they rented. The idea was to take no chance of being arrested because they were in one place for too many nights. Shortly before dawn on Friday, July 4, a taxi picked up Hamed and his family at their last residence in Kabul. The others in the group were his mother, wife, and two children, Alina (eighteen) and Haider (eight). The taxi took them to another part of Kabul, where they switched to a second taxi. It drove them to a bus stop outside the city. There were other rides, in nearly a half-dozen taxis and buses, throughout the day. It was a Friday, the Muslim holy day, when there was less traffic on the roads, apparently selected by the handlers to minimize the chances of detection. At one point, the Hosseinis had to go by foot for seven or eight miles across flatlands in Paktia Province to avoid checkpoints and get to their next connection.

Into a Battle Zone

When they were in a caravan of trucks in a mountainous part of the province, fighting suddenly erupted between rebels and Communist forces in a narrow pass. The entire party, including the Hosseinis, had to hide in the bushes to avoid being detected or getting hit by flying bullets. Eventually, the battle subsided, and they went on toward the Pakistani border. Finally, they made it and crossed a lightly patrolled section of the frontier with little difficulty.

Two Pakistani frontier guards were there, wandering about. They each happily accepted a very modest "tip" by Hamed and permitted the family to cross into the neighboring country. It was late afternoon when the family hailed a minibus and headed for the town of Para Chinar. They had traveled approximately a hundred miles to reach freedom that Fourth of July. Three weeks later, papers quickly in order, they took a flight from Pakistan to Dulles International Airport near Washington, D.C. Hamed joined the brand-new Dari Service of VOA about a year later.[4]

The Maiwandi Story

Spozhmai Safi Maiwandi was born in Kabul in 1952. She and her family, like the Hosseinis, decided that they had to leave their homeland after the Soviet-backed government took power in late 1979. But it was three years before they were able to do so. By then, security was so tight that they had to leave one by one, or not more than a group of two, to be sure of avoiding detection by Soviet-trained police. Spozhmai was thirty years old, was married, and had a seven-year-old son and a six-year-old daughter when they fled.

Maiwandi, too, came from a family of distinguished Afghan diplomats. Her father, Hassan Safi, had served as the king's ambassador to Indonesia and Czechoslovakia. When in high school in Kabul, Spozhmai was inspired to learn English and study America by a Peace Corps teacher named Mary. That was in the 1960s. Maiwandi said that her father, a daily listener to VOA, and her brother, Elum, a mujahideen opposition fighter in Soviet-occupied Afghanistan, encouraged the family to leave their homeland. Elum, listening to the Voice out in remote areas of the country where Afghan irregulars were ambushing Soviet troops, lamented that he could not hear it in Pashto. Nearly 40 percent of the Afghans, he said, were Pashtuns, and for many, radio was the only link they had with the outside world. He urged his sister, an administrative assistant at the American embassy in Kabul, to advocate a VOA Pashto Service. Maiwandi did that, took a VOA language translation test (English to Pashto), and passed easily. The Maiwandi family obtained an American visa, and decided to evade the authorities and flee. There was a deadline: VOA Pashto was to make its inaugural broadcast on July 4, 1982.

A FATHER'S BLESSING

It was tradition. Spozhmai Maiwandi felt that she must ask her father's permission to leave their homeland. Hassan Safi inquired if she was going to the United States to make money. Spozhmai replied that the main reason for leaving was so she could take a job at VOA. "That's commendable," the father said. "You're going because you want to tell our people about democracy." Spozhmai never saw her father after leaving Afghanistan. But she knew that he heard her, on America's Voice. Shortly before his death in a Kabul hospital in the 1980s, Hassan Safi requested a shortwave transistor radio to listen to VOA in Pashto and other languages. Maiwandi learned later that during his final days in his hospital bed, he would place the radio on his chest and listen regularly to the news.

The Maiwandi family had next to deal with the smugglers to get across the border to Pakistan. They decided to go in stages, to avoid detection. The smugglers agreed to take seven-year-old Ajmal first. When the smuggler/truck driver passed the security checkpoint at the Afghan–Pakistan border, the lad was in the back, seated atop a pyramid of sacks full of wheat and other food supplies. "Who's that?" a guard asked.

"That's my nephew," the driver replied.

"He doesn't look like you. He's fair-skinned. He looks like a city boy," growled the skeptical guard.

Another member of the border police quickly interjected to his colleague: "Why are you harassing this poor boy?" With that, the truck was waved through, and Ajmal became the first in his family to slip out of Afghanistan.

A few days later, it was Spozhmai's turn, and that of six-year-old Zarina. The two decided to flee together, their identities concealed somewhat by *burkas*, the traditional veil worn by Afghan women. They reached the Torkham crossing point, after a truck ride of some hours from Kabul. Again, a suspicious border guard actually pulled mother and daughter out of the vehicle and began to question Spozhmai persistently about the girl she said was her niece. It didn't help that Zarina had cut her hair short, like a city girl. This aroused suspicions when her *burka* was removed. The questioning was intense. Two giant tears rolled down Zarina's tiny cheeks. A second guard—apparently the interrogator's boss—intervened angrily. He turned to the two Maiwandis and shouted: "Run toward the border, and don't look back!" Spozhmai was sure that they would be shot in the back as they ran a hundred yards toward the Pakistani border station. But the supervisor at the checkpoint turned out to be a savior, not a satan. Spozhmai had to pay a small bribe to waiting Pakistani guards, but she and Zarina a few hours later joined Ajmal at the smuggler's home in Pakistan.

The final family member in the exodus, Spozhmai Maiwandi's husband, Ahmad, was delayed during questioning in Jalalabad, Afghanistan, for several days. But he, too, finally talked his way out and made it through. (Ahmad became a successful businessman in the Washington, D.C., area; Zarina, a Ph.D. graduate in English from Columbia University in New York; and Ajmal, an architect in London.)

The Maiwandis got a flight to Washington, D.C., and arrived on the Fourth of July—just hours after the inaugural VOA Pashto broadcast

---

AFGHAN-BORN WOMEN AT AMERICA'S VOICE

Afghanistan dominated the headlines in late 2001, when U.S. and coalition air and ground forces attacked that terrorist haven after the single worst terrorist attack on American soil in the nation's history (chapter 20). Two of the Voice's best-known broadcasters to Afghanistan at the time were women. Spozhmai Maiwandi of the Pashto Service, as we've seen, and Shukria Raad of the Dari Service spoke daily to a country where women had been severely repressed by the ruling Taliban.

Raad's escape from Afghanistan in 1980 in many respects resembled the flights to freedom of others working at VOA. Raad and her family also fled the country in stages. Her husband, Azim—a famous playwright in Afghanistan—walked over the mountains to Pakistan to get out in March 1980.*

*Shukria Raad, interview with author, Washington, D.C., November 12, 2001. See also Frank Ahrens, "Crackling Signals: Voice of America Is Pulled Between Journalism and Propaganda," *Washington Post*, November 10, 2001, C4.

---

went on the air. At 3:00 A.M. during their first night in the United States, the Maiwandis were jolted from their deep sleep by loud booms like gunfire in suburban Maryland. "It was like what we had become accustomed to back in Kabul," Maiwandi recalled, "but it was actually only fireworks for the Fourth." Spozhmai reported for duty at VOA less than forty-eight hours later, on July 6. "Each time I sit behind the mike," she said, "I think of those people back in Afghanistan. I breathe, I eat, and I sleep VOA—and it all seems very worthwhile."[5]

TUCK OUTHUOK: CAMBODIAN SERVICE

Tuck Outhuok and his family were among the few survivors of the horrific Khmer Rouge killing fields in Cambodia in 1975. During a terror-filled month after the fall of Phnom Penh, Tuck used VOA as a lifeline to the outside world. That was thirteen years before Tuck's first thrilling appearance before a VOA microphone half a world away.

The amiable, trim, and youthful-looking Tuck said that his first encounter with the Voice was when he listened as a teenager to Willis

Conover in the 1950s, captivated by the sound of jazz. "His was an awesome voice, a powerful voice," he recalled. Listening to Willis encouraged him to seek English lessons at American centers in Phnom Penh and eventually to win a scholarship to the University of Georgia. He studied there from 1961 to 1965 and earned a B.S. in forestry.

Upon returning to Cambodia in the late 1960s, Tuck joined the Ministry of Forestry and was employed there when the Khmer Rouge encircled and occupied the capital, Phnom Penh, on April 17, 1975. He; his wife, Hory; his three-year-old daughter, Thilda; and other relatives were ordered by Pol Pot's victorious troops to leave their homes and go to the countryside (chapter 7): "We left, without food, without water, with nothing except what we could put in our car. But there were so many hundreds of thousands being forced out of the city, we had to push the car. I saw people dying on the street, and some of them were shot by the Khmer Rouge for some reason I didn't know. It was very hot. I was trying to get water from a well. We found a human head in the bottom of the well, but were so thirsty and exhausted, we had no choice but to drink the water."

The exodus was on a highway south of Phnom Penh. Ten miles down the road, the Khmer Rouge armed escorts ordered the Outhuoks and hundreds of others into an open field. Those still together at this point scavenged for food to survive, desperately seeking even grass, leaves, roots, and snakes to eat. During the next horrible days, countless men and their families were led away by their captors. Most never returned. At midnight on the tenth day, it was the Outhuoks' turn. The Khmer Rouge soldiers took Tuck, his wife, his daughter, and his father-in-law to the top of a dike on the edge of the field, blindfolded them, and began interrogating Tuck. They accused him of being an American "imperialist lackey, a CIA agent." The questioning got rougher and rougher: "It was terrifying, especially when I could feel the cold steel of a rifle pressed against my temple. I knew I was going to die. Hory and Thilda were quiet . . . they were beyond weeping."

Blindfolded and threatened with execution, Tuck and his father-in-law began to hear arguing atop the dyke. A third Khmer Rouge soldier had come up, and begged the others to let the family go. Tuck recognized the voice as that of a former neighbor in Phnom Penh. "I guarantee," this nocturnal savior told the others, "that if this family betrays the revolution, I will give you my life." The arguing subsided. The Khmer Rouge tormenters walked away. The Outhuoks were suddenly free to take off their blindfolds and roam the countryside. It was nearly dawn.

Tuck, late at night soon afterward, found his car nearby, abandoned in a ditch by the Khmer Rouge. At the risk of capture again, he tuned the car radio to VOA and heard that Saigon had not yet fallen. "We knew we had to get there," he recalls. And so they began their long march, eluding the Khmer Rouge (except when Tuck was retaken for a few hours and bound with rope in a pagoda, from which he escaped because the guards were diverted). The Outhuoks made it across the Mekong River to Vietnam, which by then had fallen to the Communists. They spent three years there, living "hand to mouth" and wandering from Saigon to Hue before obtaining a French visa arranged by Hory's relatives in Paris. From there, it was on to the United States.

In 1988, Tuck reported for work in the VOA Cambodian (Khmer) Service. The very first week, he visited the messy studio of Willis Conover, stacked high with tapes. Willis warmly welcomed yet another of his many fans, now a colleague! "That," Tuck said, "was a high point . . . my dream had come true." But an even greater thrill lay ahead. That was when he received a letter from a Cambodian acquaintance saying that he had heard Tuck on the air and was relieved that the Outhuoks had survived the holocaust.[6]

THE ISLAMI SISTERS: ALBANIAN SERVICE

The Islami sisters in the Albanian Service—Isabela and Zamira—were born in Stalinist Albania in the decade after World War II. That tiny Adriatic police state then was one of the most repressive and isolated anywhere. It was full of informers, who routinely reported their friends to the security forces of dictator Enver Hoxha. One day in 1975, according to newspaper accounts and the VOA Web site, Klement Islami, Isabela's and Zamira's brother, made some antigovernment remarks to a friend. Within hours, he was arrested and the whole family was banished to the remote village of Cerme, a farming community of about 5,000 inhabitants in southern Albania. The Islamis were confined to an isolated hamlet on the outskirts of Cerme, a cluster of about a dozen heavily guarded buildings.

For the next nine years, they worked in a state labor camp called Cerme 2—a kind of agrarian gulag—digging canals, tilling rocky soil, and doing other chores demanded by security police. "It was sort of like house arrest," Isabela recalled. "We were paid the equivalent of $1 to $2.50 a day but prohibited from ever leaving the compound." The family had no hope of returning to Tirana, continuing their education, or even marrying (Isabela was twenty-two years old when they were deported; Klement, twenty; and Zamira, eighteen).

The family had been on the regime blacklist in Albania for years. The siblings' grandfather, the second highest Muslim cleric in the country, had been executed by the Communists shortly after World War II. Their mother had spent ten years in prison after the war. After nine years in Cerme, Klement convinced his sisters that their only chance to build a decent future was to try to flee by swimming out on the Ionian Sea. Their parents agreed, and urged all three to escape. They were fully aware that they probably would never see their children again.

Swimming to Freedom

The two sisters and brother scouted the situation on the last evening of July 1984. They went to the rocky coast of Cerme after darkness fell, around nine o'clock. "We thought that night we'd jump in the water and leave," Isabela recalled. "But then, searchlights of the security forces began to play on the waters, and we decided not to risk it. We waited to see how often they used these, and noticed that they came back with the searchlights at around eleven." (Things seemed always to be on schedule in the martial atmosphere of Communist Albania.)

The next evening—August 1, 1984—the two sisters and brother were in their bathing suits. It was ten o'clock, between searchlight sweeps. They had left their clothes under rocks on the coast. The girls had a little jewelry on. They dived off a rocky bluff at Cerme 2 and began their marathon swim on this moonless night. "We agreed to stick together," Isabela said. They swam for many hours, and all three became exhausted. Isabela was able to keep going longer than her siblings, and paddled between them to offer encouragement as they drifted wider and wider apart on the dark sea.

Somewhat past dawn, around 7:30 or 8:00, Isabela saw land ahead, and reckoned that it was the island of Corfu. "I could see a man walking his dog on the shoreline," she said. Suddenly, she spotted an Italian yacht and swam toward it. The ship picked her up, and she pleaded with the captain to launch a search for her sister and brother. "I realized how exhausted I was," Isabela said, "once I was on the boat." The ship quickly picked up Zamira, who was by then too tired to swim another stroke. Klement was nowhere to be seen, although he had kept up with his sisters for most of the way. He simply vanished, and hasn't been seen to this day.

From Cerme to America's Voice

The two sisters were then taken to Corfu. The Greek government immediately granted them political asylum. A Roman Catholic relief organization took them in. Just a month after their arrival in Corfu, VOA Albanian Service chief Frank Shkreli learned about Isabela and Zamira during a trip to Athens. He interviewed them and urged them to study English. The sisters made their way to the United States the following year and settled in Detroit. They learned English very quickly at the International Institute of Languages in Michigan, and less than a year and a half later joined VOA.

"The excitement of working here, and broadcasting back to Albania, was exhilarating," Isabela remembered. "We used pseudonyms at first, to protect our families back at home." (The parents were immediately redeported, they learned later, to Puk, a remote village in northern Albania far away from the coast.)

Two or three letters a year got through to the United States from the elder Islamis, and one mentioned the death of their father in the late 1980s. In response, they kept the family informed of their movements in the United States. Isabela and Zamira knew that their voices were recognized on the air instantly back in their native country, where, they learned later, "people could hardly wait till the 1800 news on VOA . . . everybody was listening."

"It Must Be Mom!"

The year 1990 turned out to be pivotal for the sisters. In Tirana, the regime was finally coming unraveled, and news of the fall of the Berlin Wall broadcast by VOA—then the only U.S. broadcaster in Albanian to the Balkans—accelerated the process of change.

One morning in April 1990, at two o'clock, Isabela was awakened by a phone call. It was long distance, a faint voice saying "Hello." She thought for a second that it was one of her friends in Britain or Greece. "Then, I realized it was in Albanian," she recalled, wiping tears from her eyes. "It must be Mom!" They talked for five or ten minutes, and Isabela urged her mother to somehow get to Italy and apply for a visa to the

United States. On July 19, 1990, Isabela and Zamira became citizens of the United States. On November 1, their mother arrived in Italy and eventually joined them in Washington.

In the decade that followed, both sisters were married, and each had two children. Zamira, now Zamira Edwards, termed this the best of both worlds: broadcasting news from America and the region back to her country of origin, and then going home to her American husband and children, Mary and Mason. Isabela, now Isabela Cocoli, has two sons, Thomas and Eric. Her elder, it turned out, was christened in the best VOA tradition. Thomas was named after none other than the drafter of the Declaration of Independence of Isabela's newly adopted country, Thomas Jefferson.[7]

20

The Struggle Goes On

VOA AT THE DAWN OF THE TWENTY-FIRST CENTURY

When war is declared, truth is the first casualty.
—Hiram Johnson, to the Senate

Our liberty depends on the freedom of the press, and that cannot be limited without being lost.
—Thomas Jefferson

The most frequently asked question about the Voice of America in the 1990s was: Why is VOA still needed? The Cold War is over.

The answer came swiftly, as the new century dawned, on a bright and beautiful Tuesday morning in the second week of September 2001. Within just two hours, about 3,000 innocent civilians were killed, including Americans and those of more than eighty nations. Terrorists had hijacked four commercial airliners, including one in the skies over Pennsylvania; toppled the twin towers of the World Trade Center in New York City; and destroyed a section of the Pentagon outside Washington. The worst act of terrorism on American soil changed geopolitics for years to come.

A SECOND DAY OF INFAMY

September 11, 2001, was—after December 7, 1941—another much remembered day of infamy, the onset of a global struggle against terrorism. It dramatized, as nothing else could, that "empires of the future," to quote Winston Churchill's famous phrase, "are empires of the mind."

Empires in the minds of the great law-abiding majorities, and empires in the twisted minds of those in terrorist cells girdling the globe. For VOA, this presented an unmatched challenge, and obligation, to tell the story—and tell it straight.

What happened on September 11 illustrates how a multimedia Voice responded in a world seemingly gone mad. VOA reached into the heart of Afghanistan, then the epicenter of world terrorism, as no other U.S. institution could—via tiny shortwave radios. It broadcast in three languages widely understood in Afghanistan: Pashto, Dari, and Farsi (Persian). Four out of five adult Afghan men tuned in VOA once a week, two-thirds of them daily.[1] Yet, as days passed, there were new pressures on the Voice to suppress facts on the grounds that the United States was engaged in a new kind of war of ideas critical to its survival.[2]

VOA mobilized swiftly on September 11, after tragedy struck. The 9:30 A.M. editorial meeting at the Voice that day set a record for brevity. Acting Director Myrna Whitworth had the newsroom give a quick rundown of events during the past forty minutes—by then, the tops of the twin towers in lower Manhattan were plumes of deadly flame and smoke. Whitworth ordered all programs to shift to all-news formats. In less than five minutes, Voice senior managers, the directors of central news and the language services, VOA-TV, and the Internet Web supervisors rushed back to their offices and studios to deal with the rapidly unfolding events.

Veteran start-up anchors Barbara Klein and Russ Woodgates of *VOA News Now* already were on the air to begin live worldwide coverage. Less than a half hour after the second World Trade Center tower was hit, they reached terrorism expert Brian Jenkins and put him on live by phone from the West Coast.

VOA's New York bureau was on the thirtieth floor of a federal office building only eight blocks from Ground Zero, with a narrow view of the twin towers from a southwest window. Klein and Woodgates got through to reporter Barbara Schoetzau at about 9:45. She described apprehensively what it had been like down on the street on her way to work shortly after American Airlines Flight 11 crashed into the north tower. Minutes after Schoetzau's live debriefing, the bureau's phone lines went dead. The bureau at 26 Federal Plaza was evacuated. The financial district was shut down. VOA's New York staff had to relocate to its satellite space at United Nations headquarters on the East River uptown or voice reports from home. The staff soon found communications via conventional phone lines utterly unreliable and via cell phones difficult. This, in the nation's commercial and communications capital.

The Terrorist Carnage Continues

Back in Washington, a third hijacked commercial airliner crashed into the Pentagon at 9:45 A.M. Airports were closed, and federal buildings throughout the nation's capital were being evacuated. That is, all except the headquarters of America's Voice, humming with activity as hundreds of broadcasters once again worked against deadlines to cover a crisis. Whitworth and her associates obtained extra frequencies—some volunteered by Radio Free Europe/Radio Liberty—to expand VOA Arabic programming by two hours daily and Farsi by one hour each day. Both VOA services went on the air much earlier than usual for their evening programs, late morning in Washington. The following week, broadcasts were expanded by a half hour daily in Dari and Pashto (to Afghanistan) and Urdu (to Pakistan). As they had since the mid-1990s, broadcasts in fifty other languages surged into the heavens to every point on Earth through the International Broadcasting Bureau's (IBB) huge parabolic dish antennas atop the roof of the VOA building.

Not that getting the facts was all that simple. New York coverage had to be reinforced. Air traffic was halted, nationwide. Amtrak rail travel was uncertain. VOA national correspondent Jim Malone jumped into his car and drove north. He stopped periodically along the way to gather local reaction and file back to Washington via cell phone. He was the first of three sent to Manhattan to augment the staff and help cover rescue operations in the smoldering ruins at the southern end of the island. "In their own way," Malone reported,

> New Yorkers struck back at terrorism Wednesday [September 12]. Scores of city residents gathered along the main rescue route on Manhattan's lower west side to cheer every official vehicle that passed by . . . from ambulances, to military humvees, to dump trucks laden with debris from the World Trade Center. . . . Many New Yorkers say that the city is bloody, but unbowed. . . . But that resolve will be sorely tested in the days ahead, as rescue teams seek to recover the bodies of victims from the worst terrorist attack in U.S. history.[3]

A crew of VOA *News Now* broadcasters happened to be in Michigan on September 11 for a week-long series of live broadcasts. The team canceled all plans and drove nonstop back to Washington, pausing briefly every so often to report the shock and growing grief of communities along the way.

During the forty-eight hours after the hijackers first struck, Voice journalists in the central services and around the world produced 140 reports, backgrounders, and roundups of U.S. and world opinion about the tragedy.[4] There was reaction from across America and overseas, from Beijing to Buenos Aires, Cairo to Copenhagen, New Delhi to New York. The language divisions produced scores of additional reports and interviews tailored for their specific audiences, including eyewitness accounts of victims' relatives and of rescue workers. VOA covered the statements of President Bush and his secretaries of state and defense as the United States built a global coalition against terrorism. This included live broadcasts in English and simultaneous translations in Arabic, Pashto, and Dari (to Afghanistan) and Urdu (to Pakistan) of the president's address to a joint session of Congress on September 20. VOA-TV was on the air with its own productions in English and a dozen other languages the week of the disaster. Correspondent Malone, on television as well as radio, said that there were "no cars in Manhattan's lower west side . . . no planes in the sky . . . New York is forever changed. The nation is forever changed." And Near East Division director Ismail Dayihat told viewers of the VOA-TV program *News Review* on September 14: "There's a great deal of apprehension on a popular level here in the United States. Passions and emotions are exceedingly high."[5]

"She Said He Called to Say Goodbye"

VOA's Will Marsh, an assistant in the VOA director's office, documented some of the most poignant personal stories of the week:

> In one instance, the Urdu Service talked to a Pakistani American who was on the eighty-second floor of the World Trade Center when the hijacked plane ripped into his building. Joined by his wife on the telephone, he described his ordeal and narrow escape. Then there was the heartrending account of an Albanian woman who told VOA Albanian about her final conversation with her

husband, a window cleaner who called her from the 105th floor of the World Trade Center after it was hit. She said he called to say goodbye, realizing the building was about to collapse and that there was little chance he and the three hundred other victims on that floor could survive. Eyewitnesses to the hellish destruction in Manhattan and Washington continued to talk to VOA (and its listeners around the world) in Amharic, Chinese, Hindi, Kurdish, Turkish, Ukrainian, and other languages.

A Bangla interview with a Bangladeshi-American paramedic who had been working at the disaster scene in New York for fourteen hours was among the many VOA interviews on the heroic efforts of rescue workers and firefighters. The Mandarin Service interviewed a Chinese embassy spokesman and a consulate official who confirmed that eighteen Chinese companies had offices in the World Trade Center before the attack and that three PRC nationals were confirmed dead. There were interviews with relatives and friends as they sought information at the command post for missing persons on Manhattan's Lower East Side. VOA also talked to those who held vigils in front of the Pentagon, hoping for signs of life amid the rubble.[6]

VOA's veteran reporters were at work. In Arlington, Virginia, Pentagon correspondent Alex Belida was among a small group of journalists allowed inside the heavily guarded perimeter around the crash site there. He described "a horrible, blackened, five-story-high gash of twisted metal and collapsed masonry." He quoted an army sergeant major as saying: "When you looked at the destruction in there, it was like walking into hell."[7] In Washington, VOA correspondent Stephanie Mann Nealer interviewed a Japanese embassy spokesman who said that scores of his compatriots working in the World Trade Center were missing and presumed dead. Among other countries with offices in the towers were Britain, Canada, Chile, France, Germany, Lebanon, Mexico, South Korea, and Thailand.[8] VOA Mexico City correspondent Greg Flakus, on home leave, went to George Washington University Medical Center in the nation's capital to report on blood donations. One of those he encountered was historian David McCullough, who observed: "To me, perhaps, it is even worse than Pearl Harbor because . . . this comes out of the blue on a perfectly gorgeous summer morning, coordinated, planned, vicious . . . madness. . . . We are tough. We are resilient. We will come back. We will clean it up. We will build again. We will go to work. What we have as an open society is very valuable. It is essential. It is all the more reason to understand how we got to where we are and what other sacrifices were made to maintain an open society."[9]

Elsewhere in Washington, William Chien, Chinese Branch senior editor and congressional reporter, was busy. Chien was conducting the first of forty interviews with members of the Senate and House broadcast on America's Voice during the first month after September 11. Chien, who did a remarkable number of these interviews himself, spoke with Senator Kay Bailey Hutchinson (Republican of Texas). "America," Hutchinson told Chinese listeners around the world, "will not let thousands of innocent people die for nothing. There will be retribution."[10]

A MIRROR TO THE NATION AND TO THE WORLD

VOA, in that second week in September 2001, was good, solid, interactive radio. The weekday talk show, *Talk to America,* was expanded from one to three hours on September 11, and one to two hours on September 12 and 13, to broadcast samplings of reaction to the terrorist attacks in the United States. The programs were simulcast by VOA-TV and Worldnet Television, and video streamed on the voanews.com Web site. Hits on that site tripled on September 11, from around 320,000 to slightly more than 1 million.

What was the impact of this multimedia effort? Before the attack, VOA's Arabic-language Web site received an average of fifty to eighty e-mail messages daily. The week of September 11 to 18, that number doubled, most of the messages containing expressions of sadness and sympathy. There were only three exceptions. An e-mail from Saudi Arabia lauded Osama bin Laden and added: "The Americans are now tasting what the Palestinians have been tasting for so long under U.S.-supported Israeli attacks." However, Islamic organizations, including Egypt's Al-Azhar University and the banned Muslim Brotherhood, sent e-mails condemning the attacks on innocent civilians. They stressed that Islam strongly rejects violence and terrorism.[11]

And from Iran: "The Iranian nation loves the American people. I, my family, my friends, are very sorry about this horrible event which happened in New York City and Washington, D.C. I hope God helps us all through these catastrophic events. This is what I wanted to say."[12]

The incredible unifying force of this unparalleled catastrophe was perhaps most eloquently reflected in an e-mail to VOA's Russian Branch:

They don't sell American flags in our small town. But believe me that in Russia these days there are a lot of people who would hang an American flag alongside the Russian one in their window. No, I'm not talking about exporting American flags to Russia. We'll find them, make them and color them. In our town of 64,000 people, there are people of 62 nationalities, including Arabs, but I haven't heard any malicious words or seen joy in the eyes glued to the TV screens carrying devastating pictures of your tragedy. Our thoughts are with you. You've suffered for the whole of humanity, for us and our children. We wish you courage, fortitude and consolation.[13]

A HOT WAR THREATENS A FIREWALL

The Cold War was truly over, succeeded by a hot war against global terrorism. Overnight, there was a renewed strategic need for an American Voice to reflect the nation's suffering and its response during that long struggle. But it didn't take long for the "war on terrorism" to generate ancien régime–like pressures from the U.S. government on VOA once again to curb its reporting.

A harbinger of things to come surfaced in a column by conservative *New York Times* columnist William Safire on September 17. He focused on a VOA correspondent's two-minute dispatch from London. The report included an excerpt from an interview with Yasir al-Serri, the exiled leader of Egypt's Islamic Group (Gama'a Islamiyya). The VOA account had omitted mention that the group—one of the country's most notorious terrorist units—was responsible for the killing of fifty-eight tourists and four Egyptians in Luxor in 1997 and that al-Serri was under a death sentence in Cairo. That, in the view of Broadcasting Board of Governors (BBG) chairman Marc Nathanson, "was a serious omission." Morever, Nathanson told a congressional hearing, the use of al-Serri's recorded comment and excerpts from an interview with Taliban leader Mullah Muhammad Omar a few days later amounted to "less than three minutes of broadcast time, out of thousands of hours. Focusing on these incidents," Nathanson said, "runs the risk of obscuring the critical role U.S. international broadcasters have played in this crisis."[14]

On September 21, VOA obtained the controversial interview with Mullah Omar. It was the first significant test in this century of VOA's credibility and culture of responsible journalism. (The Taliban held about 90 percent of Afghanistan territory at the time and steadfastly refused to surrender the suspected mastermind of the assault on America, Osama bin Laden.)

The VOA decision on when and how to broadcast Mullah Omar's comments was not as simple as it might have appeared at first. One thing was certain: VOA journalists had no intention of permitting the mullah to use the Voice, unchallenged, as a forum for widely disseminating his radical views. Excerpts of what he had to say—in response to President Bush's address to a joint meeting of Congress—had to be balanced, editors felt, with other perspectives.[15] That would be consistent with both the charter and the journalistic code of VOA.

Associates of King Zahir Shah of Afghanistan, for many years an exile in Rome, signaled that the aged monarch might be amenable to a Voice interview. The VOA News Division wanted to pair recorded excerpts of the mullah's and the king's interviews in a single, balanced report. (VOA Pashto Service chief Spozhmai Maiwandi had obtained Omar's interview on the telephone, and turned it over to veteran News Division background writer Ed Warner.) The same day, September 21, VOA ordered its Brussels correspondent, Roger Wilkison, to fly to Rome for the interview with Zahir Shah. The plan was to broadcast a roundup incorporating excerpts of both interviews (Mullah Omar's and the king's). This would be balanced, exclusive reaction to President Bush's address already broadcast live by VOA to Afghanistan in the local languages.

As luck would have it, however, two events complicated the situation:

- The king backed away from a VOA interview. By Monday, September 24, it was obvious that he was not going to grant it.
- VOA acting director Myrna Whitworth came under enormous pressure on September 21 from the State Department to kill Mullah Omar's interview. Some members of the Broadcasting Board of Governors, in a series of conference calls that Friday, agreed with the State Department.

Whitworth stood astride John Chancellor's fabled "crossroads of journalism and diplomacy." VOA News people were pressing her to release the Taliban leader's comment; members of the foreign affairs and national security communities were insisting that she discard it. On top of that, several board members earlier in the week had expressed displeasure about the VOA report from London. Lacking support from the board and—as of that Friday—suitable balancing material for the Warner roundup, Whitworth decided to hold off on the Omar exclusive. According to the *Washington Post* in an article on Sunday, September 23, her decision came after objections to the use of Omar's comments by Deputy Secretary of State Richard Armitage and the National Security Council. The administration's reasoning was that a taxpayer-supported network should not become a "platform" for broadcasting terrorist views back into Afghanistan.[16]

Members of the BBG, already shell-shocked by Safire's column, appeared initially to agree with the State Department. Because of the "hold," Omar's interview was inaudible to the world and not even quoted in text form in VOA newscasts, although the *Washington Post* obtained and ran the full text of the interview on its Web site on September 23. The much-vaunted firewall protecting the Voice's journalistic integrity had collapsed under pressure, just ten days after the twin towers had been reduced to a pile of rubble. As one observer put it, the board "was not structurally equipped to handle emergency decisions such as this." In any case, there was no consensus to stand firm and support the Voice's broadcast of Mullah Omar's comments once balancing reaction could be obtained. That weekend of September 22/23, it appeared that VOA's edifice of truth—so painstakingly built over six decades—was once again in danger of being breached.

But the *Washington Post* story on pressure to kill Mullah Omar's interview attracted considerable media attention. On Monday, September 24, the controversy surfaced at State Department spokesman Richard Boucher's midday press briefing:

> QUESTION: On Mullah Omar specifically, can you explain the rationale that this building [the State Department] had when it expressed its opposition to VOA broadcasting portions of an interview with Mr. Omar?
>
> BOUCHER: I'd be glad to. We didn't think it was right. We didn't think that the American taxpayer, the Voice of America, should be broadcasting the voice of the Taliban. We were informed that the Voice of America intended to accept an offer from Mullah Omar to be interviewed. We indicated at that time we thought it would be inappropriate for a number of reasons. One is that his commentaries have already appeared on other broadcasters . . . carrying the

interview would be confusing to the millions of listeners to what is essentially a U.S. government broadcast, paid for by the U.S. government. So we—State Department has a seat on the board—we talked to other members of the Broadcasting Board of Governors about this and indicated we felt as a matter of policy, the board should not—that the Voice of America shouldn't be making these broadcasts, putting this man's voice on our radio. And we think, whether it was the Board of Governors or the Voice of America that ultimately made this decision, it was the right decision, and we think good sense prevailed.

QUESTION: But do you still maintain that VOA has editorial independence?

BOUCHER: We recognize the independence of the Voice of America . . . the VOA works according to its charter. Its charter says that they should explain U.S. government policy and present responsible discussion about it. We don't consider Mullah Omar to be responsible discussion.[17]

As Boucher noted, the State Department had known about the interview with Omar even before it was recorded. The interview had been announced as a "likely possibility" at the VOA morning editorial meeting on September 21. An unidentified source at the meeting stepped into a nearby office and alerted the State Department moments later. This fueled even more questions at the briefing:

QUESTION: Richard, can I go back to the VOA thing for a second? Are you saying that the State Department was aware before the VOA did this interview with Mullah Omar that he was not going to make any news?

BOUCHER: We're saying that we had no indication that he was going to make any particular new statements.

QUESTION: So the VOA Charter doesn't protect them from prior restraint?

BOUCHER: The VOA Charter describes what they're supposed to be doing. We think that these decisions not to broadcast are entirely consistent with the VOA Charter, which is, again, what I said. Read it. You can look it up on the web. President Ford signed it. It's out there. It says to explain—among other things—to report on the news and to explain U.S. government policy and present responsible discussion thereof . . . and we frankly don't consider Mullah Omar to be responsible discussion of U.S. policy.

QUESTION: What can you say to VOA listeners out there who now may have questions about whether the news that they're listening to is going to be impartial and present all sides to the story?

BOUCHER: I'm going to say: "You're going to get the news, as you always have, from VOA."

QUESTION: Unless the State Department objects to it.[18]

Back at the Voice, meanwhile, the newsroom's Ed Warner was lining up an interview with a leading American scholar of Islam, John Esposito, and obtained tape of a news conference in Pakistan held by a representative of the Afghan opposition Northern Alliance, Dr. Abdullah Abdullah. The elements were falling together—even without the exiled king's comments—for a comprehensive backgrounder such as had been originally planned.

Late on September 24, VOA News director Andre DeNesnera circulated an e-mail to his staff that said, in part:

Instead of praising the work of VOA journalists (you don't get an interview such as this overnight, you need to cultivate sources for a long, long time) we got muzzled, big time. The State Department quashed the interview, using the dubious reasoning that "you don't give a platform to terrorists."

Of course you don't—and the journalists here agree. But Mullah Omar's statements were important strictly for their newsworthiness aspect and we were obliged to get them out.

The State Department's decision is a totally unacceptable assault on our editorial independence, a frontal attack on our credibility. As you know only too well, it takes a long time to build up credibility—and an instant to lose it. This certainly was a dark, dark day for those of us who have—for years—fought to uphold journalistic ethics, balance, accuracy and fairness. The State Department's big foot approach begs the question: where was our much-heralded firewall? The silence is deafening.

Having said that, I want to commend you for the sterling work all of you have done during these trying times—and I urge you

NOT to fall under the spell of "self censorship." If you do, "they" have won. All of you have an important job to do: continue to present balanced, objective reports—and continue to interview ANYONE, ANYWHERE. It is essential for us to do so.[19]

Meanwhile, a petition was circulating within the Voice, declaring: "As President Bush has said repeatedly, America stands for freedom. Central to our democracy is freedom of the press. As America's Voice to the world, the Voice of America has a duty to exemplify that principle." The petition eventually amassed more than 200 signatures.

Tuesday, September 25, dawned. Acting Director Whitworth decided that Warner's roundup—beginning with an excerpt from the president's address, followed by Omar's response and comments putting it into perspective—met journalistic standards consistent with the charter and the code. She told members of the Broadcasting Board of Governors that it was time to move. Three of the six had said over the weekend that they would be fully supportive of Whitworth's decision to issue it on the VOA house wire.

Warner's background report was issued on the VOA wire shortly before 5:00 P.M. on September 25. It was broadcast on *VOA News Now* in English, and by the Afghan, South and Central Asia, and Middle East Services. DeNesnera summed it up with eloquent simplicity: "We've done it. Article One of the Charter remains intact. At least for today."[20]

The morning after the backgrounder was broadcast, DeNesnera, Whitworth, and News Division assignments editor Jack Payton were concluding a planning meeting in the news director's office. A staff member interrupted and asked them to come out of DeNesnera's glass-walled suite into the newsroom. As they walked up the ramp into the room, journalists at every desk rose to their feet and gave their leaders a standing ovation.

Two floors below, Spozhmai Maiwandi and her eight Pashto Service colleagues were scrambling that morning of September 26 to wrap up the second of four daily broadcasts. The airshow was to be broadcast at 10:15 A.M. (6:45 P.M. Kabul time). Maiwandi's grueling day, because of the crisis, now typically began at 4:00 A.M., Washington time, and ended at 10:00 P.M. She felt responsible, as senior editor, for all blocks of VOA Pashto airtime to Afghanistan, scattered nearly around the clock. A somewhat similar schedule was in place for the Dari Service.

Maiwandi had abundant evidence that the broadcasts were getting through. The day the four hijacked airliners crashed into U.S. buildings and rural Pennsylvania, the Pashto Service had gone live with descriptions

Omar's Forty Seconds on VOA

In Ed Warner's backgrounder based partly on Spozhmai Maiwandi's interview, the Taliban leader said: "This is not just an issue of Osama bin Laden. This is an issue of Islam, Islam throughout the world. Islam's prestige is at stake; so is Afghan tradition. Whether Afghans uphold their tradition and protect their honor is another issue." Omar, in expressing publicly his first doubts about his country's resolve, also said that Afghanistan was ready to face a U.S. attack (it occurred twelve days later). He repeated that bin Laden would not be turned over to the West, and said that the Taliban was prepared for war. About forty seconds of the mullah's interview was used, in a four-minute report.

John Esposito of Georgetown University had a contrasting perspective. "As many Muslim scholars and others have pointed out," he said, "the Taliban's interpretation, whether it has to do with their support of radical groups or their policies with regard to women and other actions, are not in conformity with mainstream Muslim interpretations around the world." Warner's backgrounder concluded with the Northern Alliance spokesman's assertion: "It is the Taliban which has provided the opportunity for the terrorist network in Afghanistan not only to be able to terrorize our nation, but also to commit criminal acts against people all over the world."*

Seven months later, the University of Oregon announced that its annual Payne Award for Ethics in Journalism had been given to VOA. School of Journalism dean Tim Gleason praised the Voice's handling of the Omar story, and added: "Consider this award an exclamation point for courage."†

*Quoted in Ed Warner, "Mullah Omar Replies," VOA background report 5-50203, datelined Washington, D.C., September 25, 2001, 1–3.
†Timothy Gleason, congratulatory call to Andre DeNesnera, April 16, 2002. See also University of Oregon, School of Journalism and Communication, "Payne Awards for Ethics in Journalism Honor Joy Harris, Voice of America, and KOMU-TV," press release, April 16, 2002. Two days later, DeNesnera learned that he also had received the 2002 Tex Harris Award of the American Foreign Service Association for "integrity, intellectual courage, and constructive dissent."

of the carnage. The service broadcast reaction reports from around the world, and President Bush's expression of determination to combat the evil of world terrorism. Within hours, an e-mail arrived from an Afghan listener addressed to Maiwandi: "Hello, dear sister. Although there were huge buildings falling and a fearful situation in the United States, you broadcast the news with confidence. I was in [the village of] Laghman with many others, and we all listened. We admired your courage."[21]

Those sheltering Osama bin Laden were listening, too. The day after the American and British airstrikes commenced against Taliban military targets in Afghanistan, Taliban Information Minister Qatradullah Jamal accused Western broadcasters, including VOA and the BBC, of waging a propaganda war against the Afghan leadership. "Every night in their Pashto and Dari Services," he said, "they are talking about different options."[22]

"Why Are You Interviewing Me? You'll Never Use It"

Maiwandi recalled that in early 2001, several months before Afghanistan made daily headlines around the world, the Taliban representative in New York had told her that Mullah Omar "never misses a single VOA or BBC broadcast." The envoy added that the mullah advised members of his cabinet to listen faithfully, as well. When the Pashto Service chief recorded Omar's remarks on September 21, he inquired: "Why are you interviewing me? You'll never use it."

"Of course we'll use it," Maiwandi responded. "VOA believes in freedom of the press, in giving all sides of the story."[23] Only gritty determination by VOA's leadership during the four days that followed eventually proved her thesis correct. Maiwandi, however, was removed from her job as Pashto Service chief two months later by new VOA management and temporarily promoted to a desk job, that of program coordinator for VOA's South and Central Asia Division.[24] "Maiwandi's reassignment," according to Ann Cooper, president of the Committee to Protect Journalists, "suggests that VOA is sacrificing its hard-earned reputation as a reliable and independent news source to short-term political considerations."[25] Al Cross, president of the Society of Professional Journalists said, "Punishing a VOA employee in this fashion does incalculable damage to VOA's credibility, which must be maintained in order to achieve its mission."[26]

ALL AFGHANISTAN WAS LISTENING

From the Taliban heartland in the south, to the opposition Northern Alliance frontline positions and Panjshir valley in the north, Afghan warriors at the peak of the crisis pointed their shortwave radio aerials skyward.

- As reported in the *Guardian*, Bagram, Afghanistan, September 24, 2001: "Street urchins in the villages of the valley accost strangers with yelps of 'America, America.' Their parents stroll around with tiny radios glued to their ears listening to the BBC, Voice of America, or Iranian radio, desperately seeking clues to what may be about to befall them."[27]
- From the *New York Times*, Quetta, Pakistan, September 30, 2001: "Television is banned in Afghanistan. Word of the attacks on America and the potential reprisal was broadcast on the Voice of America and the BBC World Service. [Homayoun] Barak [director of a nonprofit medical service that runs clinics in Quetta, Pakistan, and Kandahar, Afghanistan] said that when he left Kandahar a few days ago, stores had sold virtually every radio set to nervous residents."[28]
- And from Reuters, Sari Sayad, Afghanistan, October 8, 2001: "Just behind the front line, a group of opposition fighters huddled around a Soviet army jeep listening to President Bush's speech interpreted into Persian (Dari) on Voice of America shortwave radio. They laughed, and repeated the list of Taliban-held cities that had been struck. Two small boys, porters for the Northern Alliance army, wrestled giggling in the dust."[29]

Over many years, the major international broadcasters had built a following among listeners in Afghanistan by airing what one writer called "a subversive diet of news, cultural discourse, and music that are not filtered through the unyielding Islamic doctrine of the Taliban." An Afghan engineering professor expelled from his homeland in 1998 said that VOA and the BBC "are the only sources that people trust" there. A spokesperson for the United Nations High Commissioner for Refugees (UNHCR) added: "The two radio stations probably have got more influence in Afghanistan than any foreign media has in any other country."[30]

The Rebirth of Radio Free Afghanistan

As the American and British air strikes began on October 7, there was serious talk in Congress about reviving a second U.S.-funded international broadcast service to the region: Radio Free Afghanistan. The proposed network was placed under Radio Free Europe/Radio Liberty, where it had been a decade earlier. VOA, on September 11, had the highest audience of any media outlet in Afghanistan—including the Taliban state radio. Yet just three days after the allied bombing raids began against Taliban military targets, Representative Edward R. Royce (Republican of California) announced at a House hearing that he had thirty-three bipartisan cosponsors of Radio Free Afghanistan legislation.[31] In December, Congress appropriated $19.2 million as part of a Department of Defense bill to start the service. Radio Free Afghanistan was inaugurated on January 30, 2002, and later combined with VOA in an around-the-clock Dari/Pashto network.

The Birth of Radio MERN (Radio Sawa)

At almost the same time, Congress voted $34.6 million for the pet project of BBG member Norm Pattiz: the Middle East Radio Network (MERN), in Arabic, of pop music and news using some techniques that were successful in Pattiz's own Westwood One syndicated music service. The new network began phasing in its broadcasts on March 23, 2002. Initially, most of its airtime consisted of the pop-music offerings of such artists as the Backstreet Boys, Egyptian rock idol Amer Diab, and Lebanese pop queen Nawal Zoghby.[32] The idea, Pattiz said, was first to appeal to a new generation of Arab listeners with popular music, and later add news and information. MERN is a state-of-the-art, around-the-clock FM and medium-wave service with regionalized content, including local Arabic dialects and reportage targeted to Iraq and the Gulf region, and envisioned for the West Bank/Gaza, Egypt, and Sudan. MERN replaced the sixty-year-old VOA Arabic Branch, which made its final broadcast on April 20, 2002. The old service had been on shortwave and medium wave (from Rhodes and Kuwait) for seven hours a day and, according to Pattiz, attracted only 1 to 2 percent of adult Arab listeners. In MERN, all references to VOA were dropped.

At its launching, MERN adopted the on-air brand name of Radio Sawa, which means "together" in Arabic. It was, however, a world apart from normal Voice programming. It did not use VOA central news (MERN staff members transferred from VOA prepared brief, fast-paced news summaries from wire service and Internet reporting, some of them single-sourced). MERN's first month on the air coincided with the Palestinian suicide bombing of a Passover seder in Netanya, Israel, and

Israel's devastating retaliatory assaults on Jenin, Nablus, and other West Bank towns and cities. Ordinarily (as in 1956, 1967, 1973, and the Gulf crisis and war) VOA Arabic would have expanded its news, analysis, and in-depth programming—typical Voice programming at a time of crisis. In 1990 and 1991, it broadcast live simultaneous interpretations in Arabic of more than forty U.S. presidential statements of direct relevance to the region (chapter 15). During the Israel–Palestine carnage in April 2002, however, only one-tenth of Radio Sawa's airtime was news and reportage. This mostly consisted of brief summaries that included fast-paced, sound-bite-length (forty- to fifty-second) field reports from stringers. Sawa did broadcast President Bush's entire statement on the Middle East on April 4 and, later, an exclusive interview with Secretary of State Colin Powell, but most of the remainder of the programming was pop music. BBC Arabic, meanwhile, switched to an all-news format. But Pattiz predicted that more substantive fare eventually would become a feature of MERN, which was aimed at young, educated Arabs under thirty—future leaders. Pattiz envisioned eventual expansion on the new network of targeted reportage from a state-of-the-art news center in Dubai. He told a House subcommittee after one month on the air: "Accurate, fair, objective news will be the lifeblood of MERN, and we hope, will do much to combat hate media and misinformation."[33] MERN began to expand its news windows about seven weeks after its inaugural broadcast.

SLAVING AWAY ON THE STRAIGHT STORY

Three blocks away from Capitol Hill, Voice broadcasters continued on their sixtieth anniversary to broadcast to a curious world. With overstretched staffs, cramped quarters, and pressures on content, VOA reflected the state of the U.S. overseas information and cultural program at the beginning of the twenty-first century.

"Public diplomacy has not been an American priority," observed Robert Kaiser in the *Washington Post*. He cited extensive cuts in the foreign service during the 1980s and 1990s, "which included elimination of the United States Information Agency." He also mentioned "what experts describe as an insignificant effort by the Voice of America in the Middle East."[34] Throughout the late 1980s and 1990s, the VOA Arabic audience had declined because of budget cuts. Successive administrations and Congress had failed to invest in expanded reportage in Arabic or to build new facilities (with the notable exception of a new medium-wave relay station in Kuwait).

Could this be corrected? Clearly, as Henry Hyde (Republican of Illinois), chairman of the House International Relations Committee, asserted at its October 10 hearing, "we must accept that there can be no quick fixes."[35] The ranking minority member of the committee, Representative Tom Lantos (Democrat of California) cited the appropriation by Congress in late September 2001 of $40 billion in emergency funds to fight terrorism. He called on President Bush "to allocate from these funds whatever is required to increase dramatically U.S. broadcasting to Afghanistan and throughout the Arab and Muslim world."[36]

CALLS TO ACTION, WITH CREDIBILITY THE KEY

After the September 11 atrocities, the United States appeared to have been jolted into recognition that neglect of its overseas information programs—including international broadcasting—left it extremely vulnerable in an era of hijackings, bombings, and anthrax threats. As Lantos put it: "The United States spends on international broadcasting a sum that I can only describe as paltry and shameful. . . . We are spending $2.2 billion on chewing gum, $75 billion on cigarettes, and $400 million on the [international] public broadcasting establishment."[37] Experts agreed, though, that changing anti-American attitudes in the Islamic world over time was going to be exceedingly difficult, if not impossible. As Ambassador William A. Rugh, a Middle East specialist and former USIA area director, put it: "I think it's very late in the game."[38]

In the autumn of 2001, as the debate on public diplomacy expanded, there was an unusually intense media focus on VOA and its proper role at a time of war. Among those covering or assessing the issue were the Associated Press, Reuters, and Agence France Presse; the New York Times, Washington Post, Baltimore Sun, Philadelphia Inquirer, Christian Science Monitor, Chicago Tribune, Houston Chronicle, Fort Worth Star-Telegram, and Los Angeles Times; and National Public Radio, NBC's Today, PBS, CNN, and C-SPAN.

On October 12, 2001, Bush appointee and political conservative Robert Reilly became VOA's twenty-fifth director. Recognizing the growing public awareness of America's Voice, Reilly said that he was determined to protect the organization's professional integrity and garner more resources. In his words: "This is VOA's hour."[39] Reilly had served in the IBB Office of Policy for a decade until his appointment as director on the eve of the Voice's sixtieth anniversary. He soon would face serious challenges—inside and outside VOA—from the administration, from Congress, from the Broadcasting Board of Governors, from his longtime allies in a policy office heavily influenced by conservatives in the Republican Party, and from his new associates in the VOA journalistic and broadcasting community. In his first message to the staff, Reilly defined his mission in the context of the antiterrorist campaign: "One of the many differences that characterize our side in the war of ideas is that we are not afraid to tell the truth. Telling the truth requires a great deal more than simply recounting the positions of various sides in a dispute. It requires an act of discernment as to the veracity of the contending claims. In order to tell the truth, we must know it. In reporting it, our stories must point our audiences in its direction."[40]

The pressures that Reilly would face surfaced soon after his appointment. Senator Jesse Helms, the ranking minority member of the Foreign Relations Committee, said that Secretary of State Powell "should, and must be, in charge of U.S. international broadcasting" when the United States is at war against terrorists. The North Carolina senator assailed the interview with Mullah Omar, which, he said, the Voice broadcast while "ignoring repeated requests from senior U.S. government officials that VOA not do so. . . . International broadcasting," he added, "is intended to be an important instrument in promoting American values, interests and perspectives. If it is to be merely an international version of National Public Radio, it might as well be shut down."[41]

About a month later, a conference committee of the Senate and House issued its own statement: "The conferees expect that the VOA will not air interviews with any official from nations that sponsor terrorism or any representative or member of terrorist organizations, or otherwise afford such individuals opportunities to air inaccurate, propagandistic or inflammatory messages."[42] Reilly, in a message to the staff, said that whenever questions arise about the applicability of the conference language, then "VOA service directors are immediately to report via division directors to the Office of the Director of VOA for a determination."

Like the war on global terrorism, the struggle to tell it straight appeared to be never-ending. In the VOA newsroom and language services, it was—as it had been for decades—a struggle to get it right. For those shielding the Voice, it was a struggle against attempts from any quarter to distort at VOA what Edward R. Murrow once called on all journalists in free societies to offer: "an honest mirror of events in the world, to report without fear or favor."[43]

Editorials and op-ed columns in American newspapers, too, reflected all sides of the debate over VOA's proper role in a time of war. Most came down on the side of journalistic integrity in international broadcasting:

- From the *New York Times*: "Since the end of the cold war, the Voice of America's radio programs have metamorphosed from government echo into real journalism. . . . The VOA today is an independent agency, but it is government-funded and still susceptible to State Department and Congressional pressure. The advent of war should be an occasion to strengthen its independence."[44]

- From the *Wall Street Journal*: "There will always be room for argument about how and what any news service reports in wartime. But the VOA is not *60 Minutes*; it is a service paid for by American taxpayers."[45]

- From the *Chicago Tribune*: "Pressure is mounting on Voice of America to behave less like a news network and more like a megaphone for U.S. government policy. Such pressures, which typically arise during wartime, could cost the agency its credibility as a reliable news source. That loss would be a bad bargain for the taxpayers who fund it."[46]

- From Kenneth Y. Tomlinson, in a *Washington Times* op-ed column, months before he became BBG chairman: "No journalistic entity—be it VOA or the *New York Times*—would have gone with an interview with Benito Mussolini or Hideki Tojo on the issues behind World War II. News balance is not halfway between good and evil. . . . Obviously, VOA should not be broadcasting an interview with this guy [Mullah Omar]."[47]

- From Sanford J. Ungar, twenty-fourth director of VOA, in a *New York Times* op-ed column: "Now, more than ever, the Voice of America has important work to do. It must be able to interview anyone anywhere at any time, without fear of rebuke or reprisal, in order to provide honest and full coverage of momentous events. The State Department should keep its hands—and editing pencils—off the news."[48]

Professional journalistic organizations agreed that VOA, even in wartime, should be shielded from pressures to alter its news content.

- At a meeting in Bellevue, Washington, the 2001 national convention of the Society of Professional Journalists (Sigma Delta Chi) condemned "the efforts that were made to prevent the VOA from carrying out its mission of responsible, objective and comprehensive reporting." The society said that it would continue to monitor the Voice and oppose "any attempt by the U.S. government to curb or sway free and fair news reporting and discussion" prescribed in the VOA Charter.[49]

• The International Press Institute, based in Vienna, wrote to VOA News director Andre DeNesnera "to express its unconditional support" for VOA's decision to air excerpts of Mullah Omar's interview. Because the United States is a leading democracy, the letter said, the institute was deeply concerned that State Department efforts to kill the Omar inter-view might provide "active encouragement for governments in other countries to apply pressure on their own public service broadcasters or analogous institutions."[50]

• Ian Williams, of the London-based Institute for War and Peace Reporting, added:

> If the government-owned [media] institutions are regarded as just mouthpieces of their government, then it means they're not going to be listened to. . . . You identify correctly what the other side is doing and what it's saying. And then, you can roll out the full details and even condemnations [precisely the way VOA handled the Omar interview]. But, the basic point is always that you should tell the truth. . . . It's pointless fighting for freedoms if in the very act of fighting you destroy those freedoms.[51]

As founding BBG chairman David Burke put it: "Censorship is not the answer. What the Afghan people most need and want are unimpeded flows of accurate and objective news and information. They can smell propaganda a mile away; the Taliban and other regimes have rubbed their nose in it for years. They look to America for a beacon of freedom. Fortunately, they find this beacon in VOA, and they listen to it."[52] Board member Norm Pattiz said of VOA's decision on Mullah Omar: "I happen to believe that any legitimate news organization in the world would do that interview. And if the United States is going to be a proponent of a free press, it has to walk the walk."[53]

Despite its initial hesitance to defend the Voice during the Omar flap in September 2001, the BBG two months later reinforced its determina-tion to shield U.S. international broadcasters. In a note to the staff, the board said:

We would like to reassure all of you that the Board takes seriously its legislated role as a "firewall" to protect the journalistic integrity of all our broadcasting services. We unanimously support your efforts, as mandated by Congress, to provide accurate, objective and comprehensive news and information about America and the world. . . . For nearly sixty years, the Voice of America and its sister broadcasting organizations have served as shining examples of a free press in the American tradition. This is a treasured legacy that we must all strive to uphold and defend.[54]

At the October 10, 2001, hearing of the House International Relations Committee, Representative Lantos recalled a day he had spent many years earlier with legendary broadcaster Edward R. Murrow in Geneva:

Ed Murrow, who knew more about this incredibly important instrument than anyone, taught not just the importance but the essentiality of making our public diplomacy credible. So I would like to conclude by quoting the great Edward R. Murrow, whose contributions to American society are gigantic. "To be persuasive," he said, "we must be believable. To be believable, we must be credible. To be credible, we must tell the truth." American public diplomacy will have to be truthful. We cannot match—nor should we—the latter-day Goebbelses in their lies and distortions. Our story sells itself, if it is told powerfully, accurately, and with credibility.[55]

Conclusion

Knowledge will forever govern ignorance, and people who mean to be their own governors must arm themselves with the power that knowledge gives.
—James Madison

And let thy feet—millenniums hence—be set in knowledge.
—Alfred, Lord Tennyson

The appetite for accurate world and U.S. news and information is timeless, as the campaign against terrorism—military and diplomatic—has so vividly reminded us. It is incalculably greater in the twenty-first century than it was at the founding of the republic or even when the Berlin Wall tumbled down. Long before the invention of radio and long before the Cold War, Thomas Jefferson, James Madison, and Ralph Waldo Emerson spoke of the power of facts and ideas to transform lives. VOA has tried to embody that principle for more than six decades.

KNOWLEDGE BROKERS IN A CANDID WORLD

With the nation's support, the Voice's burden of truth—never easy to bear—will continue. It will, in a sustained struggle to get the facts straight, seek to enhance a free flow of knowledge in a world where many in the post–Cold War years still are not only information deprived, but, to quote former BBC managing director John Tusa, "information impoverished."[1] In its ideal form, VOA today is a multimedia model of what a free press can achieve. Half the world's people have yet to make their first telephone call. Many, however, have access to tiny world-band shortwave radios. They continue to seek accurate information in today's increasingly crowded spectrum of media voices. This is especially so as the United States reengages itself in the dangerous world of terrorism and nuclear proliferation beyond its borders.

Ian O. Lesser, a senior analyst at RAND in Washington, D.C., put it bluntly: "Many of the world's leading proliferators of ballistic missiles are arrayed in an arc stretching from Libya to South Asia. Iran and Iraq are both pursuing the acquisition of weapons of mass destruction—nuclear, chemical, and biological—and the means for their delivery with greater accuracy at longer ranges."[2] (In 2002, North Korea was, as well.)

As VOA director Geoffrey Cowan once said: "In such a period of history, it's in some ways more important than ever to have a voice of sanity in the world, and that's what the VOA tries to represent. . . . It's probably the least expensive way that America has of helping to introduce models of freedom, democracy, and the diversity of cultures in a world in which people from different religious and ethnic and national backgrounds are at war."[3]

Writing in *Foreign Affairs* in 1996, Joseph S. Nye, Jr., and William A. Owens described a new force in the century ahead. They called it "soft power." By that, they meant the capability of nations to project ideas combined with "hard power" military strength in a communications age: "Knowledge more than ever before is power. . . . Information is the new coin of the international realm and the United States is better positioned than any other country to multiply the potency of its hard and soft power resources through information." The advantage of information as a power resource, Nye and Owens added, is that it also almost inevitably democratizes societies.[4]

In the words of VOA director Mary G. F. Bitterman:

I see the primary post–Cold War role of the Voice to be what has always been its role—to be an authoritative source of news and information about the world, to paint a balanced and diverse picture of American life, and to present American policy in a manner which allows for responsible discussion of that policy. I grant that communication links are far greater now than at the time of VOA's founding and that many formerly closed societies have access to a larger view of the world. Nonetheless, I am disturbed by the closing of numerous American network overseas bureaus and the changes at CNN. Increasingly, it will be difficult for audiences abroad to have a clear understanding of the American perspective in all its diversity.[5]

"Why" some ask, "is VOA needed today when there is a CNN?" The founding chairman of the Broadcasting Board of Governors (BBG), David Burke, has a ready answer: "CNN can be seen in hotel lobbies; VOA can be heard in refugee camps."[6] And, he might have added, after the watershed events of September 11, 2001, listening is even more intense than before in the widely dispersed clandestine cells of world terrorism. Terrorists, too, listen to world-band radio and might be deterred by what they hear. In remote caves and hideouts the world over, it sometimes is their best, or only, source of reliable information.

Four-fifths of VOA's listeners tune in to its language services. Because of the portability of shortwave radios, as we've seen, VOA reaches listeners in war-ravaged villages in the Balkans, in rebel-held hideouts in Colombia, in mountainside monasteries in Tibet, and in columns of humanity in strife-torn regions of Central Africa. It will be light-years, if ever, before CNN considers it commercially feasible to broadcast in Tibetan or Kurdish or in Pashto and Dari to Afghanistan. And where technologies are more advanced or used by elites, Voice transmissions are available not only on radio, but on television, the Internet, and local FM stations on car radios.

There's a distinct difference between commercial broadcasting designed largely to attract an American audience and public-service broadcasting beamed overseas. Publicly funded international broadcasting, through accurate and comprehensive news reporting, provides a context and a framework necessary to empower budding democrats, in Madison's phrase, "who mean to be their own governors." The purpose of international public-service broadcasting is to offer information across cultures, not to sell a product.

"The marketplace that matters now is not the souk with its bootlegged copies of American CDs and sneakers," says Columbia University professor of journalism Samuel Freedman. "It is the marketplace of ideas."[7]

THE CHALLENGES AHEAD

If VOA is to build on the foundation chronicled in these pages, its directors and governing board must take the lead. They must explain to successive administrations and Congresses that uncensored news, information, and public-affairs programming delivered under a well-established brand name, the Voice of America, inherently serves the national interest.

The agenda for VOA and the BBG is a full one: mission, programming, technologies, structure, and, most important, audiences.

Mission

The United States International Broadcasting Act of 1994 (Public Law 103-236) cites two principal purposes of America's publicly funded civilian overseas broadcasting:

- To promote the right of freedom of expression, including the freedom "to seek, receive and impart information and ideas through any media, regardless of frontiers," in accordance with Article 19 of the Universal Declaration of Human Rights
- To communicate information and ideas among peoples, which, the law says, contributes to international peace and stability and therefore is in the U.S. interest[8]

In advancing the free flow of information around the world, VOA and the other U.S.-funded international broadcasting organizations strive to

- Provide audiences with accurate, objective, and comprehensive news and information
- Represent American society and culture in a balanced and comprehensive way
- Present U.S. policies clearly and effectively, with responsible discussion of those policies
- Reach audiences in the languages, media, and program formats that make the most sense in their region of the world
- Retain flexibility to quickly expand their programming, known as "surge broadcasting," in times of world or national crisis
- Encourage development of free and independent media through training and exchanges
- Use research to understand audiences and their programming preferences[9]

The mission and strategy are a blend of audience and U.S. national interests. The combination is consistent with both American journalism and diplomacy. As a "full-service" global network guided by its charter,

VOA is challenged as never before to fulfill its complex mission in a multimedia age. Its journalists pursue the facts, wherever the pursuit may lead them. VOA at the same time reflects—more than its international broadcast cousins at home and abroad—American society in its diversity and U.S. policies and debate on those policies.

Programming

Jonathan Marks of Radio Netherlands once told the very valuable Radio Canada International biannual conference on global broadcasting that in today's brave new world of digital communications, international broadcasters "are knowledge brokers. They must share information, not shout it."[10] They must eschew any semblance of Cold War preaching, shed all appearances that they exist to promote a government "line," if they are to compete effectively. In this century, there is a growing global recognition of the necessity of telling it straight. Almost immediately after the collapse of the Berlin Wall, Radio Prague International—the external broadcaster of what had been a Warsaw Pact regime—rejected as no longer necessary the Czechoslovak government–produced commentaries and editorials of the Cold War era.

Experts in international broadcasting have identified a number of trends in programming of the future.

The Signal Importance of News

Audience research indicates that accurate, reliable news and the on-scene presence of correspondents are consistently the most important factors in building listenership to the larger international broadcasters. In 2001, the Office of Program Review of the International Broadcasting Bureau (IBB) made suggestions to guide VOA news in the years ahead.[11] The unit surveyed VOA broadcasters who produce news and those who put it on the air.

A high priority at the Voice, those questioned said, is rebuilding a newsroom staff that declined from sixty-two to forty-nine between 1999 and 2001. This staff operates around the clock and produces a news file cross-checked and rewritten from hundreds of thousands of words daily. The central newsroom managing editor said: "We are critically understaffed." This is also the case at the smaller news desks in a number of language services.

With sufficient numbers, an expanded corps of central and language news writers could once again concentrate on building up regional coverage and developing more area expertise and research on America and the world. The language services, at the same time, could increase "tips" to the newsroom about breaking stories they uncover. With greater online research resources, a strengthened newsroom could also offer more in-depth reporting and analysis. International broadcasters, and public broadcasters in general, air longer reports with more depth, dimension, and presence than their commercial counterparts. VOA central news, adequately staffed and funded, could produce more of the in-depth pieces so avidly sought by listeners and viewers in a "sound bite" age.

Diversity Programming

There is a need for programming that educates, enlightens, and explores culture, new ideas, humanitarian themes, matters of faith, and issues of interest to youth and women. In short, this means the creation of public-service programming of a nonpolitical nature that offers information useful to citizens in their daily lives and essential in building civil societies. Information can be healing. In September 2001, a priest, a rabbi, and an imam appeared on the VOA's *Talk to America* (radio, television, and Internet) during the world day of prayer for victims of terrorism just three days after the skyjackers struck. VOA programs such as *Kaleidoscope* and *Coast to Coast* (English), *Cultural Odyssey* (Chinese), and *New American Voices* (on immigrant communities in all languages) blend American and world cultural diversity in contemporary formats.

Interactive Programming for International Audiences

Increasingly, broadcasting across borders is two way, and so are live dialogues with listeners via phone, Internet, and fax.[12] "International broadcasting is much more democratic than it used to be," observes BBG strategic planner Sherwood Demitz. "A major shift of power is under way . . . from the broadcaster to the listener." Straight talk across borders may even help stem potential wars and perhaps enhance trade and contacts. A recent example was joint live simulcasts by the VOA Greek and Turkish Services, broadcast by FM affiliates in Athens and Istanbul, in which politicians and artists from both sides of the Aegean questioned one another.

VOA's Albanian, Chinese, English-to-Africa, Farsi (Persian), and Indonesian Services also use call-ins to stimulate debate and dialogue between listeners and experts in the United States, as does the weekday *Talk to America* English call-in. According to Intermedia Survey, a Washington, D.C.–based research firm, international broadcasters can appeal to youth by addressing issues that directly affect their lives: educational, environmental, and health concerns—if they are part of a contemporary-sounding programming mix that includes call-ins and some FM popular music.[13]

At VOA in 2002, a key question was: How much pop music in the FM formats, how much substance? Some agreed that there was a need to appeal to a new generation reflected in the cross-cultural blend of Arabic and Western music offered by Norm Pattiz's Middle East Radio Network (MERN), or Radio Sawa (Together). Others, however, expressed hope that the Voice's traditional news and reportage and its current affairs, public-service, and humanitarian programming would eventually reassert itself within MERN. Such in-depth programming would speak to Arab government leaders and educated elites—an essential audience today—as well as to youth. And even the relatively sophisticated youth in much of the Arab world may listen to Radio Sawa more to be entertained than to be informed. Two months after Radio Sawa went on the air, columnist Ayman el-Amir wrote in the Cairo newspaper *Al Ahram*: "The chances are the Arab youth themselves will split the strategy: take the U.S. sound and discard the U.S. agenda."[14]

Innovative Expansion of the "University of the Airwaves"

Over the years, there have been many long-range planning committees at the Voice. At one such brainstorming session in 2000, there was a proposal for program-enriching agreements between VOA and universities across America. Universities would benefit as well as the Voice, by providing their specialists in international and U.S. affairs with worldwide exposure. Furthermore, if funding permitted, a university affiliate could nominate one or two graduating interns each year to work at VOA. The Voice would gain from an infusion of fresh talent and direct access to expertise about specific regions in the nation it reflects to the world.

During my final year at the Voice, two university presidents, William E. Kirwan II of the University of Maryland, College Park, and Nannerl

THE CHARLES KURALT AND
MARC NATHANSON FELLOWSHIPS

Thanks to leadership by the School of Journalism at the University of
North Carolina and the Broadcasting Board of Governors, in 1997
VOA established an intern program at the university, named for CBS
correspondent Charles Kuralt. Nearly every summer since, it has
brought a graduate journalist to the VOA newsroom for a year as a
trainee, after which he or she could move on to a permanent post.
Intern Challis McDonough, for example, later became VOA bureau
chief in Johannesburg, South Africa.

At VOA's sixtieth anniversary celebration, the VOA and the
University of Southern California's Annenberg School for Communication announced the creation of the Nathanson Fellows Program,
to commence in 2003. Under that five-year internship program,*
endowed by retiring BBG chairman Marc Nathanson, four students
selected by Annenberg School faculty spend several weeks each
summer working at the VOA news bureau in Washington, Hong
Kong, or London.

*George Mackenzie, "Nathanson Fellows to Get VOA Internships in Joint
Project with USC Annenberg School for Communication," International
Broadcasting Bureau, press release, February 25, 2002.

Keohane of Duke University, appeared on *Talk to America*. In both
instances, the telephone switchboard lit up with calls. Queries from
younger listeners ranged from trends in U.S. higher education to specific
requests for scholarship information.[15] It was another indicator of the
potential value of partnerships between universities and what one listener called America's "university of the airwaves, VOA."

One of the Voice's most versatile broadcasters from the 1970s
through the 1990s was Paul Francuch. For years, he ran the Chicago
bureau and ranged widely across the Plains states to report and reflect on
what some have called "the real America." Francuch counseled VOA
senior managers in 1997 to assign more reporters on even brief trips to
the American heartland, including its new generation. "Just send the
broadcasters out there to cover what's happening," he said, "and not
wonder too much how. They're good. They'll dig up the stories. Our

programs and most important, our listeners, will be richer for it." A relatively new VOA English program, *Coast to Coast*, is a twenty-first-century embodiment of Francuch's suggestion.

Former BBC managing director John Tusa agrees with the concept. "Unlike commercial radio or television," he says, "the Voice offers the world something of American values. Is the United States to be defined by Coca Cola and McDonalds, by the advertising of the giant multinationals, or by something more?"[16] VOA's twenty-fifth director, Robert Reilly, adds: "That is why the VOA was never envisaged as simply a news organization. We have the duty to reflect the character of the American people in a way that the underlying principles of American life are revealed."[17]

Technologies

As one ponders the century ahead, technical options abound for international broadcasters in general, and the Voice in particular. The IBB's Office of Engineering provides technical services to VOA and other U.S. international broadcasters. It has been retooling for the demands of the multimedia age.

The possibilities stir the imagination: radio, television, wireless, the Internet, cell phones, alert systems, search engines—all interacting with one another. "Is this a new portal-based era?" asks one specialist. "It's easier than ever to lose your audience," says Gavin Starks of the International Broadcasting Association, "with all these interactive media choices."[18] International broadcasters must deploy different sets of technological combinations in different areas of the world, depending on the resources they are given by their funders and, of course, the media used by their particular audiences. Europe, Japan, Australia, and most of the Americas and Middle East are awash with new technologies. Shortwave is declining in those regions, but it will remain dominant for some years to come in Africa and in areas of East, South, and Central Asia. Information "haves" and "have-nots" live on either side of what professional communicators call "the digital divide." Multimedia international broadcasters must serve both.

More money is essential if international broadcasters are to meet the many demands. Some governments want to deny their citizens access to the world of ideas by using new technologies to block new international broadcast delivery systems. For years, the government of China jammed

VOA shortwave in Chinese; more recently, it ordered Internet service providers within the People's Republic to block access to news on VOA Web sites in Mandarin as well as English. The IBB's Office of Engineering has established an Internet unit to help get through. The hope is that e-mail address lists or mirror sites can help impede Beijing's electronic Great Wall by permitting Chinese citizens to access VOA and Radio Free Asia (RFA) Web sites.[19] To quote IBB and VOA director Evelyn S. Lieberman: "No matter how they try to jam us, block us, or silence us, the people of China find us."[20]

The Promise—and Limitations—of New Delivery Systems

Many international broadcasters are fascinated these days as the Internet and other delivery systems replace shortwave in affluent societies. As the communications digital divide sharpens, however, shortwave still reaches huge audiences in Africa and large areas of Asia. It is the most inexpensive technology for the consumer. There are 600 million to 1 billion radios in the world capable of pulling down a shortwave or medium wave signal but incapable of accessing satellites or digital radio. "Replacing six hundred million of anything," one communications expert has noted, "takes a long time."[21]

The Internet

The emergence of the Internet is expected to hasten the convergence of many media—radio, TV, wireless, and electronic newspapers. A few communications gurus have predicted that all these may be available someday on a single, fixed platform "box" or screen, accessing the Internet, high-density television, and digital radio on demand. Others say that media consumers will want more portable digital delivery systems: world-band radios, laptops, and mobile phones. At its sixtieth anniversary, VOA was concluding two long-sought multimedia technical projects:

- The final organizational merger of VOA and Worldnet Television into a VOA-TV
- The establishment at the Voice of the Multimedia Broadcast Center (MBC), to commission and edit news stories for use on radio, television, or the Internet

The Internet challenge posed for VOA and other international broadcasters is to retain adequate news coverage and quality programming at the radio core of the operation while investing in and sustaining new, constantly expanding multimedia delivery systems. In an unstable world, shortwave also must be maintained to reach crisis-plagued regions and, as necessary, inform American citizens abroad in critical need of information about emergency evacuations.

The Internet, as of 2001, according to David Colker of the *Los Angeles Times*, "was not quite ready for prime time."[22] Radio Netherlands director general Lodewijk Bouwens says that on the Internet, "the current streaming technology is useless at coping with the peak demands of serious live broadcasting. For every 100,000 listeners over the air at any moment," Bouwens notes, "there are only a few thousand capable of hearing the broadcasts simultaneously on the web . . . webcasting is expensive, it is often congested during a crisis, there are copyright restrictions."[23] That is changing as bandwidth expands. Meanwhile, the Internet continues to find a niche not so much as a broadcaster, but as a medium for short, on-demand, timely bursts of information. It has been used to organize "rallies on demand" via cell phones, such as those that disrupted several international financial gatherings at the beginning of the century and helped lead to the ouster of Philippines president Joseph Estrada.

Television

Television is expensive, too, for both the producer and the viewer. Bruce Gregory, a Washington, D.C., public diplomacy specialist, notes that in a television age, U.S. government international broadcasters still spend about eleven times as much on radio as they do on TV. "Radio continues to be an important instrument of public diplomacy," he says. "We must continue to invest in radio where media research shows it to be cost effective and where listening rates are high, as in Afghanistan, China, Ethiopia, and Nigeria. But we must invest much more in television in the twenty-first century. Radio is important," Gregory adds, "but it is not eleven times more important than television."[24]

The potential of publicly funded international TV is widely recognized. It can be rebroadcast by terrestrial affiliates, video streamed on the Internet to TV stations and Internet cafés, or downlinked direct to homes (DTH) free of local censorship. Research revealed that it helped to double VOA audiences in Indonesia and the Balkans between 1996 and 2001. Production costs and a succession of bureaucracies have impeded expansion of U.S.-funded overseas television since 1990 (chapter 16). That could change in the aftermath of the 2001 terrorist attack on the United States. Immediately after the tragedy, Congress was studying a multimillion-dollar international broadcasting expansion to the Islamic world. The so-called Initiative 911 included an around-the-clock Arabic-language TV network initially estimated to cost $62 million.

Digital Radio

Promising tests of digital shortwave and medium wave to replace traditional analog delivery systems took place in 2000 and 2001. The experiments were organized by a consortium of international and regional broadcasters from more than sixty nations and several radio-receiver manufacturers. The new system is called Digital Radio for the World (or Digital Radio Mondiale [DRM] in French). IBB engineer Don Messer was among the leading organizers in the DRM pilot experiments.

International broadcasters are attracted to DRM because most shortwave transmitters built since 1990 can be converted easily to transmit digital programming. Moreover, the fuel cost for shortwave transmitters converted to digital can be cut in half. The estimated cost of digital radio receivers ($50 to $100) is competitive, even in the developing world. Best of all, the signal is crystal clear, free of the fades and imperfections long associated with shortwave.

The Digital Revolution in Program Production

Within the VOA headquarters building and at the BBC World Service, conversions were under way at the beginning of the century from the use of antiquated recording tape in analog production to a state-of-the-art, all-digital, computerized system for preparing programs. In the words of the IBB *Tune In* newsletter: "Take a long look at VOA employees pushing tape carts through hallways or broadcasters staring at spinning reels. Memorize these soon-to-be-quaint scenes, if only to tell your grandchildren about the old times. VOA's familiar way of handling audio—by analog tape—is going by the wayside. In its place will be the world's largest, fully-integrated, digital broadcasting network, known as IDAPS (short for Integrated Digital Audio Production System)."[25]

IDAPS encompasses more than a thousand workstations and enables VOA to acquire, schedule, produce, store, and broadcast news, sound archives, and music.

Direct Broadcasting by Satellite

In the early 1990s, Noah Samara founded the WorldSpace Corporation in the United States. It has since launched satellites over Africa and Asia capable of beaming radio signals via multiple channels to homes in a global footprint inhabited by more than 4.2 billion potential users.[26] WorldSpace disclosed at a London conference in 2001 that it already had deployed 100,000 new radios and had 300,000 more on order. That number is small, however, in a world where an estimated 330 million people regularly tune in to international broadcasts. The first direct broadcasting via satellite (DBS) receivers also were expensive, around $190 to $200 a radio. As of 2002, WorldSpace had yet to report an annual profit.

Rebroadcasting (or Placement) on Local Television and FM Radio Stations

As we have seen, the placement of programs was given a substantial boost as VOA and Worldnet Television's use of satellites took root in the mid-1980s. By December 2000, around 1,500 radio and TV stations worldwide were downlinking and rebroadcasting their programs. The BBC World Service had committed itself to being present on local or national FM affiliate stations in 135 countries by 2003 or 2004. A recent estimate was that more than a quarter of its global audience listened to World Service programming via rebroadcasts. Awakening to the importance of FM rebroadcasting, IBB lately has invested in VOA leases on a number of local FM and medium-wave outlets in the Arab world, Afghanistan, and Africa. Long-needed funding, denied until the September 11 tragedy, has helped.

BBG member Norm Pattiz said that after September 11, his appeals to Congress to fund the Middle East Radio Network became a "slam dunk."[27] A $34 million supplemental appropriation enabled the BBG to put MERN on FM stations in the Arab world, using FM and medium-wave relays that the IBB had never been able to afford for the soon-to-be replaced VOA Arabic Branch. There were plans, as well, for a $62

A Test of War?

A year and a half before the 2003 war in Iraq and even before the demise of VOA Arabic, Norman Pattiz envisioned MERN as "a potential organizational model."* Shortly after MERN went on the air as Radio Sawa, IBB director Brian Conniff predicted: "As this network expands and gains new listeners every day, its success will provide a blueprint for the future operations of both the VOA and IBB."† But how would MERN sound when the nation was at war?

Coalition forces entered Iraq in March 2003, seven months after the installation of the third BBG chairman, Kenneth Y. Tomlinson, and on Sawa's first anniversary. By then, Sawa had been an instant success with youth in Jordan and some Gulf states. In December 2002, the BBG had launched a similar network in Persian, Radio Farda (Tomorrow), to replace a highly respected RFE/RL Persian service. VOA's Persian Service was retained, but reduced and on shortwave only. During the war, Sawa and Farda did double the normal news and information content in their 24/7 schedules, but remained two-thirds pop music. A revived VOA Arabic Web site, RFE/RL's twelve-hour Radio Free Iraq in Arabic, and VOA's Persian Service offered on-scene reports, live broadcasts of presidential addresses and military briefings, and in-depth analyses typical in wartime. During the war, however, television was dominant in a Middle East hungry for real-time news images.

*Norman J. Pattiz, testimony submitted for the record to the House, Committee on International Relations, 107th Cong., 1st sess., November 14, 2001, 4.
†Brian Conniff, "A Note from the IBB Director," *Tune In*, April 2002, 1.

million around-the-clock U.S.-funded Arabic-language satellite TV service to compete with the popular Al Jazeera in Qatar. As it went on the air, the Middle East Radio Network expanded at considerable cost to other U.S. international broadcast services. At the BBG's insistence, Sawa's predominantly pop-music service on April 28, 2002, replaced

- VOA Kuwait medium-wave transmissions in Farsi to Iran in prime morning time

- VOA *News Now* and Special English medium wave on both the Rhodes and Kuwait transmitters, in effect eliminating medium-wave transmissions in English to much of the Middle East[28]
- Radio Free Europe/Radio Liberty's (RFE/RL) Radio Free Iraq in Arabic aimed at Baghdad from Kuwait on medium wave

The substitutions were in line with Pattiz's insistence that in order to build an audience, his network must be on a continuous frequency twenty-four hours a day. Not only did MERN replace VOA Arabic, but the damage to VOA Farsi was significant. A survey in Tehran two months after the September 11 terrorist attack indicated that about a third of VOA listeners there tuned into medium wave.[29]

The establishment of new separate networks, in whatever form, posed a number of questions:

- Would VOA survive in regions where the new BBG-funded networks were established? Its Arabic Service, as we've seen, was abolished in the spring of 2002.
- Would the U.S.-funded civilian overseas broadcasters (VOA, RFE/RL, RFA, and the Martís) be permitted to retain their distinct missions and on-air brand names?
- Would the new regional networks, light on talk and heavy on music, serve as reliable and respected sources of in-depth information amid the national and global debate over war in Iraq? Would these new networks still be closely tied to the VOA central newsroom? (MERN was prohibited from using VOA central news.) What about the two-source rule so vital to VOA's record of accuracy over the years?

VOA advocates of "independence" could scarcely have imagined this turn of events.

The year 2002 was a busy one for the BBG and the Voice. As the U.S. military action in Afghanistan subsided, they arranged for around-the-clock satellite-fed transmissions in Afghan languages from Washington and Prague to an FM outlet in Kabul. The service was launched on August 4 and consisted of broadcasts of VOA Dari and Pashto and of RFE/RL's new Radio Free Afghanistan. This Afghan Radio Network Initiative (ARNI) was also available on shortwave. The launching followed months of negotiations with the new Afghan government

VOICE PIONEERS ON THE CLOSURE OF VOA ARABIC

A task force of the nongovernmental Council on Foreign Relations issued a report on July 30, 2002, on reform of the U.S. overseas information and cultural programs in an age of terrorism. The report applauded the MERN initiative. But two task force members and Voice pioneers we met in chapters 2 and 3, Barry Zorthian and Walter Roberts, viewed the elimination of VOA Arabic as a "mistake" and counseled caution.

According to Zorthian, "The Task Force endorsement of MERN as a prospective model for other areas should not be interpreted to support the elimination of core VOA language broadcasts. The Voice of America and its hard-earned record of credibility, represents sixty years of investment by the United States and is an asset that should not be discarded readily."

Roberts added, "Elimination of VOA in Arabic makes no sense since the only segment of Arab society now being reached by U.S. broadcasts is the young generation. American broadcasts during the Cold War that proved very effective were directed at the intellectuals of the Soviet Union and Eastern Europe. VOA in Arabic should be reinstated and should include programs devoted to establishing meaningful dialogue with Arab intellectuals."*

*Quoted in Council on Foreign Relations, *Public Diplomacy: A Strategy for Reform* (New York: Council on Foreign Relations, 2002), 28.

involving the BBG, IBB, VOA, and American embassy in Kabul. Afghanistan and the United States also signed an agreement for the construction by the United States of two 400-kilowatt medium-wave transmitters to be heard throughout Afghanistan, one for ARNI and the other for Afghan state radio.[30]

Structure

As it entered its seventh decade, VOA had been able to resist, much of the time, outside pressures to shape its programming content, except for congressionally mandated U.S. government editorials written elsewhere in IBB and cleared by the State Department. For 96 percent of the on-air product—news, features, and other programming fare—the BBG had available the firewall mechanism (described in chapters 17 and 20) to help keep VOA programming journalistically sound.

As we've seen from the four-day broadcast delay in airing portions of an interview with Taliban leader Mullah Omar, however, the pressures not to get it straight still loomed large from time to time. Even before the war on terrorism, the board and its staff had to periodically investigate a complaint and/or handle a postbroadcast criticism of content from the media, a foreign government, the administration, Congress, or a U.S. mission abroad. For some years before September 11, 2001, the central newsroom rarely heard of these complaints (except for those surfacing in the media). That, perhaps, made the State Department's attempt to kill Omar's interview seem even more threatening to VOA journalists.

Chairman Marc Nathanson, in an interview, called VOA "the main linchpin of our system. Its task," he said, "is to work within the framework of U.S. international broadcasting to be a vital U.S. link to people unserved by free and open media around the world."[31] Both Nathanson and his predecessor, David Burke, deemed nominal organizational independence as an important board achievement in its early years. Burke cited legislation passed during his tenure that prevents the State Department inspector general from subjecting VOA content (aside from the government editorials) to a policy litmus test. "I wouldn't have tolerated her [the inspector general] coming into the newsroom," Burke said, "and telling news professionals what to write."[32]

Looking Ahead

VOA continued to face a number of administrative challenges as the twenty-first century began. The management vision group mentioned earlier assessed them in 2001. It stated that VOA wants a BBG that continues to be an advocate, a firewall, and a sounding board, but one whose members and staff leave most day-to-day programming and operational decisions to VOA and the other U.S.-funded overseas networks. It suggested better communications between the BBG and VOA. "Multiple policies [of different board members]," it said, "are transmitted through multiple channels [to VOA] and are often filtered through [BBG] staff members, leading to misunderstandings."[33] The group also suggested more dialogue among executives of VOA, RFE/RL, and RFA.

I asked a number of international-broadcasting specialists to assess the challenges VOA faces in the years ahead. They identified six.

- *Continuity in top management.* Since 1965, the VOA director has been appointed or approved by the White House. Although most directors have fully subscribed to the charter, many also have been short term. During the first sixty years of VOA operations, there were twenty-five directors—an average length of service of less than two and a half years.[34] Somehow, the White House and board should work together to recruit future directors on a longer-term basis, preferably nonpartisan executives influential in both the executive branch and Congress, with credentials in broadcasting, journalism, and foreign affairs, as well as past successes in heading a large organization.

- *Accountability of support services.* During the 1990s, most of VOA's support resources gravitated—under first the United States Information Agency (USIA) and later the Broadcasting Board of Governors—to the International Broadcasting Bureau or the BBG. Their staffs, as of February 25, 2002, totaled nearly 300. Now, the Voice director in effect runs only programming: he or she does not control engineering, personnel, administration, the budget, marketing, program placement, international training, headquarters of nontechnical facilities, program evaluation, research, or strategic planning. All these responsibilities are within the International Broadcasting Bureau, successor to the USIA's Bureau of Broadcasting, which used to be synonymous with the Voice. Because of divided authority, flexibility is hampered.

One solution might be the restoration of some or most support functions to the VOA.[35] RFE/RL and RFA, for example, are largely self-contained. Having most functions under a single CEO enables their presidents to administer the organizations in a coordinated way. If more support services were returned to the Voice, board members and staff could then concentrate on larger strategic issues as Congress intended. As the history of the USIA–VOA relationship has shown, the more administrative autonomy the Voice had (professional managerial independence, if you will), the better it served the national interest.[36]

- *Increased funding and balanced resource allocations.* The global struggle against terrorism dramatizes the dire need for increased investment in international broadcasting (chapter 20). This is essential to pay for expanded broadcasts to the Middle East and Islamic world and for multimedia modernization. As the experience of the VOA Arabic Branch illustrates, one can produce solid, original radio programming, but if transmission facilities are inadequate or if program promotion and advertising are lacking, listenership can be relatively small. Throughout VOA, budget exercises lately (even before the BBG assumed its responsibilities) tended to reduce frontline broadcast talent with small audiences. But the delivery system and other support may, in some cases, have been as much or even more responsible for low listenership as the programming. Nearly all VOA employees terminated for budget reasons between 1995 and 2001 were on-air broadcasters or producers, most of them in language services. Future reviews should consider qualitative measures of both support and programming.

• *Broad-based strategic planning.* In a wider context—that of the national interest—there should be serious, extended consultations among the BBG, Department of State, National Security Council, appropriate congressional committees, and international broadcast networks affected before international broadcast languages are added or deleted. Editorial independence is essential to credibility, as we've seen. But the radios (federal and grantee) are there to serve the national interest. That should be given greater weight in determining which languages go, which remain, and which are added. In early 2001, VOA broadcasts in Brazilian Portuguese were abolished, and those in Armenian, Azerbaijani, Bulgarian, Georgian, Romanian, Slovak, Turkish, and Uzbek substantially reduced. Turkey, Brazil, and Uzbekistan, according to a *Wall Street Journal* editorial, appeared to be extremely important to U.S. interests, and the *Journal* criticized the cuts in broadcasts to those countries.[37] Not surprisingly, the VOA programs to Turkey and Uzbekistan were restored to their earlier levels after September 11. RFE/RL inaugurated Radio Free Afghanistan on January 30, 2002, even though most area specialists felt that Afghanistan already was free and VOA could have expanded its highly successful Pashto and Dari Services. Between 1990 and 2002, largely because of congressional insistence, U.S. government surrogate networks launched seventeen language services that already were on the air at VOA.[38] The missions of the grantees and the Voice are in many instances complementary. But the structure and complexities of international broadcasting operations—particularly launching new services and eliminating old ones—require a more coherent approach.

• *Sustained and coordinated expansion of audience research.* To its credit, the board expanded research substantially during the late 1990s. Expenditures on listener surveys increased fivefold. In 2001, Intermedia Survey of Washington, D.C., was contracted to coordinate about 400 new audience studies for VOA, the Martís, and the grantees by a consortium of research firms with global experience. As part of the initiative, the BBG moved to gauge the popular-music preferences of young Arab listeners. These surveys preceded the introduction of the multimillion-dollar MERN. The board contracted Edison Research to carry out extensive field studies and focus groups of young Arabs, distinct from the work in other regions assigned to Intermedia Survey.

• *Revisions in the Smith-Mundt Act.* Various legal challenges have been made over the years to provisions in the Smith-Mundt Act (chapter 2) that prohibit the distribution of VOA broadcasts and scripts within the United States. One-quarter of a century after the charter became law, and in the age of the Internet and the bipartisan BBG's legislated firewall, congressional concerns about the use of VOA to "propagandize" the American public appear to be outmoded. As recently as 1997, White House spokesman Mike McCurry, speaking informally at a briefing to reporters, called the Smith-Mundt clause preventing the dissemination of Voice scripts and broadcasts within the United States "a crocodilian piece of legislation dating back to the 1940s."[39]

Time for Yet Another Sweeping Reorganization?

As VOA approached its sixtieth anniversary, there were calls for changes in the organization of international broadcasting. Former VOA program manager Barry Zorthian (chapter 3) proposed a single, powerful senior executive reporting to the BBG. He or she would be appointed for a lengthy term (perhaps six years to ensure continuity) as CEO for all U.S. government–funded civilian international broadcasts.

A glance at various organizational charts illustrates the need for streamlining (appendix C). As VOA marked six decades on the air, what clearly was not needed was more proliferation of separate regional networks and their attendant managements. Pioneer broadcaster and producer Tibor Borgida noted on VOA's fiftieth anniversary: "Not many voices of America . . . just one . . . just one."[40]

Kim Andrew Elliott is a widely published international broadcasting research specialist who joined the Voice staff in the 1980s and subsequently was editor and host of its weekly program, *Communications World*. Speaking as a private citizen, he laments the proliferation of America's voices and management superstructures since the Cold War and says that they can adversely affect U.S. overseas broadcasting in the years ahead:

> Americans generally assume that their long-term national interest is supported by the truth and feel that providing accurate and balanced reporting to the world is a worthwhile endeavor. Yet the current institutional structure and content of some nonnews programs in U.S. international broadcasting prevent it from building the image of reliability it deserves. Operating an international radio station is much like a chess game. The director must have access to all his/her pieces to win. There is the programming knight and the transmission bishop. However, with VOA/IBB/ BBG, there are three players on one side of the table, the VOA director moving the knights, the IBB director moving the bishops—not always in full consultation—and the BBG standing behind them, and with increasing frequency, overruling both. A recent example was the Board's decision to remove VOA Farsi and RFE/RL's Radio Free Iraq in Arabic from the Kuwait medium wave, costing those services valued listeners.[41]

Despite the adversities of "independence," the Voice—with solid management, streamlined support, and a propensity to reinvent and rejuvenate itself—can continue to be what a presidential task force in 1991 called "the great overarching voice of our country in the world."[42] The director of the Voice then, Chase Untermeyer, notes that structure in an organization is never as important as the people in charge of making it work. "It's not so much the firewall," he says, "but the firefighter that counts." Mary Bitterman agrees: "It is not the organizational structure which permits creativity and integrity, but the character of the people involved in oversight."

Untermeyer assesses the impact of the Voice between its fiftieth and sixtieth anniversaries this way: "The primary post–Cold War role for the VOA has been to carry out the mandate of the charter as broadly and audibly as possible. In the process, it has served to encourage the growth of democracy, pluralism and free markets by an honest recounting of the experience (both good and bad) of the United States and other nations, including the nations in which the listeners reside."[43] Today, Untermeyer says, "the Voice desperately needs a better understanding of its role on Capitol Hill, especially since the older generation that instinctively knew and valued that role has passed."

Audiences

In the end, the listener decides. Eric Sevareid once counseled: "Never underestimate your listener's intelligence, or overestimate your listener's information." That's sound advice for VOA and other U.S. publicly funded international broadcasters. Their programming must serve both the listeners who hear it and the nation that offers it. Therein lies the heart of the ongoing debate within and beyond VOA. Do audiences tune in because of its journalistic integrity, or because of its reflection of America and American foreign policies? Or do they listen for all these reasons?

Toward the end of the 1980s, Conrad Kiechel of the VOA's Office of Policy wrote in a letter to the editor of the *Wall Street Journal:* "My job— writing [U.S. government] editorials that legally can't be sent to Mom, in prose plain enough to be translated into 44 languages—may not be everyone's idea of fun. But there are those of us who think it is important for people abroad to understand our country's views. And perhaps as long as the U.S. taxpayer is footing the bill for more than a thousand hours each week of news and entertainment, it's not unreasonable to include an occasional word from the sponsor."[44] Many experienced diplomats and even some former VOA broadcasters like Walter Roberts (chapter 2) would agree. Roberts—throughout his career an advocate of truthful news on the Voice—adds: "If the U.S. government is paying for the broadcasts, it ought to expect to have its view articulated. Otherwise, why should the government pay for it?"[45]

Others say that airing accurate, objective, complete information does the job. By simply broadcasting straight news and balanced analysis to a candid world, they maintain, the United States over time builds an edi- fice of credible soft power. "The idealism of our system is our ideology," Bernie Kamenske is fond of saying. "I mean by that the ideas of Mason, Madison, Jefferson, Lincoln, the Roosevelts—a laissez-faire, honest pro- vision of facts and ideas which empower the listener to make his or her own judgments." He added, in assessing the events of September 2001: "I regard that first five or ten minutes of the VOA newscast as sacrosanct and inviolate . . . they are a sacred pledge to the listener."[46]

"If you have faith in the American concept and position," adds Barry Zorthian, "then you've got to believe that an objective picture serves the U.S. interest, simply because it is believable and portrays U.S. and world developments in balance."[47] Examples in VOA programming include

- The live broadcast each year of the president's State of the Union Address, along with the response of the opposition party, whether Democratic or Republican
- The full range of opinion on Capitol Hill and in American media about administration domestic policies (pro and con)
- Reports of anti-American statements (such as those by terrorists, for example), contrasted with other statements placing them in context, which might include support for the United States in the war against terrorism and the views of mainstream Islamic religious and secular leaders, in the United States and the Muslim world
- Vignettes of America's lively debates in all their diversity, a nation of immigrants whose story, honestly told, is endlessly fascinating to millions around the globe

To quote Geoffrey Cowan:

It's remarkable that you can have an organization financed by the government, legally controlled by the government, run by someone appointed by the president of the United States, and still have it be accurate, balanced, and comprehensive. People don't really believe it. But because of the charter and because we prove day after day that even government-financed broadcasters can achieve its highest standards, we are saying implicitly to people who work at and listen to other government-controlled and financed networks around the world: even you can hold yourself to the high standards embodied in the Voice of America Charter.[48]

Cambodia, a decade after the Cold War ended and two years after the death of Pol Pot (chapter 16), offered an example of the need for those high journalistic standards in twenty-first-century international broadcasting. A report commissioned by the BBG said:

Cambodia's ingrained history of power patronage is manifest in today's media market. The majority of outlets are owned by politicians, their political parties, or at least are under their influence. . . . The result has been a local media widely recognized for a lack of accuracy and objectivity, for taking sides in debates, and for ignoring, delaying, or only partially reporting issues and events. Cambodians rely on the foreign broadcasters, in particular VOA and the lesser-known RFA, for accurate news and analysis of domestic political events. An often-heard phrase in fieldwork [is]: "They dare to speak the truth" . . . in their coverage of events in Cambodia and beyond.[49]

"We're in It for the Long Run"

Richard W. Carlson, VOA's twentieth director, was interviewed by *American Legion Magazine* in the late 1980s:

QUESTION: Critics are asking: wouldn't it be in our best interests to tone down sensitive reporting—even if it's true and objective—just to improve the climate a bit?

CARLSON: There are perfectly sound arguments that short-term gains could be made from doing that, no question. We don't do that because we're in it for the long run. We feel that the confidence of our audience is dependent on the belief that you tell the truth all the time, that you don't pull your punches, even when it's convenient. . . . We just don't feel it's in the interest of the listeners or the American people to spin any news stories to effect short-term gains.*

In the words of a veteran VOA observer and senior IBB official: "That, it seems to me, is the remarkable enduring pattern of VOA. There have always been people, even well-intentioned and decent ones, who believed that it was necessary to manipulate the news or at least to modify it for reasons of state. But in the end, the organization always returned to its original journalistic principles. Even today, VOA is sticking to them."†

*Richard W. Carlson, "The War of Words," *American Legion Magazine*, July 1987, 20.
†Chris Kern, e-mail to author.

When the tiny VOA Thai Service faced possible abolition in early 2001, the owner of a ceramic factory in the northern Thai city of Chiang Mai telephoned the service and begged it to stay on the air. "It's an educational service," he said. Every morning, he added, 400 workers in his plant listened to VOA Thai piped onto the factory floor as it was rebroadcast live by a local FM affiliate station.[50]

Joseph S. Nye, Jr., notes that the quest for credibility becomes an even more important soft power attribute today because of "the deluge of free information and the 'paradox of plenty' in an information age." The BBC, Nye writes, has more competitors than ever, but to the extent that it maintains credibility in what he termed "an era of white noise, its value as a power resource may increase. . . . If the U.S. government thought in these terms, it would invest far more than it now does in instruments of soft power (such as the information and cultural exchange programs) and be less likely to try to constrain the Voice of America as it did in September 2001."[51] In international broadcasting, accurate, comprehensive, and honest reportage is a force multiplier of soft power.

A pioneering executive and news director of CBS, Paul White, noted that the quest for truth is common but challenging: "Complete journalistic objectivity is only an ideal, but the fact that it is difficult if not impossible to attain does not seem to me to impair the ideal itself, or excuse the broadcaster from a constant and vigilant effort to try for it. The Golden Rule is unattainable, too."[52] Reaching for the ideal over the long run sometimes has totally unexpected endings.

In May 1997, a listener from northeastern China called the VOA Chinese Branch hot line and identified himself as one of the soldiers involved in carrying out martial law orders at Tiananmen Square eight years earlier:

> How should I put it? Well, as a soldier, my gun was not aimed at the enemy but at my compatriots, the students. I felt ashamed of myself. . . . What happened in Tiananmen was not what the Chinese government claimed, [to put down] rioters and lawless people. They said that only to hide the real purpose of the action. . . . I can tell you that ever since then, I have always felt guilty. I did open fire but I shot into the air. I felt very shocked and anguished. That is why I'm calling you today. I am just an ordinary person without much education or influence, just a faithful listener, you might say.

Ding Zilin, a former professor at a university in Beijing, heard the soldier's confession. Her son, Jiang Jielan, was among the prodemocracy demonstrators killed in the square:

> Up until now, I have located the families of more than 150 victims and have learned how they died. . . . I could not help but think, over eight years: there were so many soldiers in the martial law operation . . . the day would come when I would hear a soldier talk. Under the present circumstances, when the government still holds on to lies about the June fourth event . . . that took real courage.[53]

And so, we come full circle. VOA is interactive. Among its listeners is a new generation. Shortwave and medium wave survive despite FM, television, the Internet, and the end of the Cold War. There are still 330 million listeners to international broadcasts, and professionals at America's Voice and elsewhere are learning how to harness a variety of multimedia delivery systems around the vital "radio informational base." Now, in an era of globalization, the Voice remains the nation's broadcaster of record to the world. It serves listeners, young and old, on both sides of the great communications digital divide. It, like radio everywhere, remains at its best an intensely personal medium in an increasingly impersonal "high-tech" age. It has receivers that can be carried and heard anywhere, from a workbench in a crowded Thai ceramic factory to the horn of a solitary farmer's plow-pulling ox. It can master the challenges before it and inform listeners wherever they may be. That will be so, as long as it is left intact to broadcast straight, unvarnished facts and fair, reasoned analysis. Then, America's Voice will fulfill its founders' dreams and serve, as only it can, as a steady and faithful mirror of the nation and of the world.

Appendix A

VOA JOURNALISTIC CODE, APRIL 12, 1995

PREAMBLE

Since 1942, the Voice of America has built a global reputation as a consistently reliable source of news and information. Accuracy, balance, comprehensiveness and objectivity are attributes audiences around the world have come to expect of VOA broadcasters and their product. These standards are legally mandated in the VOA Charter (Public Laws 94-350 and 103-415). Because of them, VOA has become an inspiration and information lifeline to nations and peoples around the world.

SUMMARY

Adhering to the principles outlined in the Charter, VOA reporters and broadcasters must strive for accuracy and objectivity in all their work. They do not speak for the U.S. government. They accept no treatment or assistance from U.S. government officials and agencies that is more favorable or less favorable than that granted to staff of private sector news agencies. Furthermore, VOA professionals, careful to preserve the integrity of their organization, strive for excellence and avoid imbalance or bias in their broadcasts.

The Voice of America pursues its mission today in a world conflict ridden and unstable in the post–Cold War era. Broadcasting accurate, balanced, and complete information to the people of the world, and particularly to those who are denied access to accurate news, serves the national interest and is a powerful source of inspiration and hope for all those who believe in freedom and democracy.

THE CODE

All staff who report, manage, edit, and prepare programming at VOA in both central and language services therefore subscribe to these principles:

Sourcing

- VOA news and programming must be rigorously sourced and verified. VOA normally requires a minimum of two independent (non-VOA) sources before any newswriter, background writer, political affairs writer, correspondent, or stringer may broadcast information as fact in any language.

- The only exceptions to the double-source requirement are facts directly confirmed by a VOA journalist or significant news drawn from an official announcement of a nation or an organization. In those rare instances when a secondary source offers exclusive news (e.g., a verified news agency exclusive interview with a chief of state or prominent newsmaker), this story is attributed to the originating agency by name.

Accuracy and Balance

- Accuracy and balance are paramount, and together, they are VOA's highest priority. Accuracy always comes before speed in VOA central service and language programming. VOA has a legal obligation to present a comprehensive description of events, reporting an issue in a reliable and unbiased way. Though funded by the U.S. government, VOA airs all relevant facts and opinions on important news events and issues. VOA corrects errors or omissions in its own broadcasts at the earliest opportunity.
- VOA is alert to, and rejects, efforts by special interest groups, foreign or domestic, to use its broadcasts as a platform for their own views. This applies to all programs and program segments, including opinion or press roundups, programs discussing letters, listener comments, or call-in shows. In the case of call-ins, views of a single party must be challenged by the interviewer if alternative opinions are unrepresented. In interviews, points of possible discussion are submitted in advance if requested by an interviewee of stature (e.g., a chief of state).
- VOA journalists (including correspondents, news and language stringers, political affairs writers, and program hosts) avoid at all times the use of unattributed pejorative terms or labels to describe persons or organizations, except when the individuals and groups use those labels to describe themselves or their activities.
- In news, features, and current affairs programming, VOA broadcasters will meticulously avoid fabricating, distorting, or dramatizing an event. If sound at an event illustrates the reporter's account of that event and is edited for time, the remaining sound effect reflects what occurred in an accurate and balanced way. If there is a risk of misleading the audience, no use will be made of sound effects not actually recorded at the event being described.

Context and Comprehensiveness

- VOA presents a comprehensive account of America and the world, and puts events in context. That means constant vigilance to reflect America's and the world's political, geographical, cultural, ethnic, religious, and social diversity. VOA programming represents the broadcast team's best effort to seek out and present a comprehensive account of the event or trend being reported.
- VOA broadcasters will avoid using announcing or interviewing techniques that add political coloration or bias to their reportage or current

affairs programming. Music will not be used to make editorial statements. VOA journalists and all those preparing news and feature programming avoid any action or statement that might convey the appearance of partisanship.

Procedures

- When performing official duties, VOA broadcasters leave their personal political views behind. The accuracy, quality, and credibility of the Voice of America are its most important assets, and they rest on listeners' perception of VOA as an objective source of world, regional, and U.S. news and information. To that end, all VOA journalists will:

  1. Always travel on regular, nondiplomatic passports, and rely no more and no less than private-sector correspondents on U.S. missions abroad for support, as set out in the guidelines for VOA correspondents.
  2. Assist managers whose duty is to ensure that no VOA employee, contract employee, or stringer works for any other U.S. government agency, any official media of another state, or any international organization, without specific VOA authorization.
  3. Adhere strictly to copyright laws and agency regulations and always credit the source when quoting, paraphrasing, or excerpting from other broadcasting organizations, books, periodicals, or any print media.

- In addition to these journalistic standards and principles, VOA employees recognize that their conduct both on and off the job can reflect on the work of the Voice of America community. They adhere to the highest standards of journalistic professionalism and integrity. They work to foster teamwork, goodwill, and civil discourse in the workplace and with their colleagues everywhere in the world, all to enhance the credibility and effectiveness of the Voice of America.

Appendix B

KEY LEGISLATION AFFECTING VOA IN ADDITION TO THE CHARTER

INTERNATIONAL BROADCASTING ACT OF 1994 (PUBLIC LAW 103-236)

Section 305. Authorities of the Board
(the Broadcasting Board of Governors)

(a) Implementation. The Director of the United States Information Agency and the Board, in carrying out their functions, shall respect the professional independence and integrity of the International Broadcasting Bureau, its broadcasting services, and grantees.

FOREIGN AFFAIRS REFORM AND RESTRUCTURING ACT OF 1998 (PUBLIC LAW 105-277)

A reorganization plan and report of the Department of State following adoption of Public Law 105-277 states:

> Under the Foreign Affairs Reform and Restructuring Act of 1998, the Broadcasting Board of Governors will become an independent federal entity by October 1, 1999. Consistent with the Act, international broadcasting will remain an essential instrument of U.S. foreign policy. The Board (including the Secretary of State who will be a statutory member of the Board) and State will respect the professional independence and integrity of U.S. international broadcasting.*

Pursuant to the Act, the BBG will become an independent Federal entity. This provides a "firewall" between State and the broadcasters to ensure the integrity of journalism. The Act thus ensures that the credibility and journalistic integrity of broadcasting will be preserved and enhanced. The Act also provides "deniability" for State when foreign governments complain about specific broadcasts.

*Under the 1998 act, the secretary of state or his or her designee replaced the director of the United States Information Agency. The agency was abolished in the act.

Appendix C

TABLES AND CHARTS

Table C.1 VOA Direct Broadcast Hours per Week, 1985 and 2002

Language	1985	2002	
	Radio	Radio	Television
Afan Oromo-to-Ethiopia		1.25	
Albanian	10.50	11.75	2.50
Amharic-to-Ethiopia	7.00	6.00	
Arabic[a]	66.50	49.00	1.00
Armenian	8.75	7.00[e]	
Azerbaijani	7.00	3.50[e]	
Bangla	14.00	10.50	
Bosnian[b]		2.50	2.50
Bulgarian	10.50	1.25[e]	
Burmese	7.00	10.50	
Cantonese-to-China		14.00	
Creole-to-Haiti		9.50	
Croatian[b]		10.50	
Czech[c]	10.50	1.25[e]	
Dari-to-Afghanistan	14.00	21.00	
English[d]	398.00	378.00	16.00
Estonian	8.75	3.75[e]	
Farsi-to-Iran	24.50	45.50	3.00
French-to-Africa	38.50	22.50	0.50
Georgian	5.25	3.50[e]	
Greek	3.50	10.50[e]	
Hausa-to-Nigeria, Niger	7.00	9.50	
Hindi-to-India, Pakistan	10.50	10.50	
Hungarian	17.50	1.25[e]	
Indonesian	24.50	18.75	1.50
Khmer-to-Cambodia	10.50	10.50	
Kinyarwanda-Kirundi-to-Central Africa		7.00	
Korean	10.50	10.50	
Kurdish-to-Iraq, Iran, Turkey, Syria		7.00	
Lao	7.00	3.50	
Latvian	8.75	2.50[e]	
Lithuanian	8.75	1.50[e]	
Macedonian		6.25[e]	
Mandarin-to-China	63.00	84.00	7.00
Pashto-to-Afghanistan	14.00	21.00	
Polish	49.00	1.25[e]	
Portuguese-to-Africa	10.50	16.50	
Portuguese-to-Brazil	14.00	[f]	
Portuguese-to-Portugal	7.00	[f]	
Romanian	12.25	1.25[e]	
Russian	119.00	34.00	1.00
Serbian[b]		14.00	2.50
Serbo-Croatian[b]	8.75		
Slovak[c]	10.50	1.25[e]	
Slovene	3.50	1.25[e]	
Spanish-to-Americas	52.50	34.50	4.00

Language	1985	2002	
	Radio	Radio	Television
Swahili-to-East and Central Africa	7.00	9.00	
Thai	7.00	8.50[e]	
Tibetan		28.00	
Tigrigna-to-Ethiopia, Eritrea		1.25	
Turkish	7.00	7.00	
Ukrainian	35.00	14.00	1.00
Urdu-to-Pakistan, India	10.50	17.50	
Uzbek	14.00	7.00	
Vietnamese	21.00	17.50	
Totals	1204.75	1030.75	42.50

Note: Hours calculated as of February 25, 2002.

[a]VOA's Arabic Branch was abolished on April 20, 2002, and replaced by MERN (Radio Sawa), broadcasting 168 hours weekly.

[b]VOA's Serbo-Croatian Service was divided in 1992 into Serbian and Croatian Services to better deal with the wars that accompanied the dissolution of Yugoslavia. In 1996, the Serbian Service began simulcasting radio and television for a half hour daily, as did a newly formed Bosnian feed unit the following summer. A Macedonian feed service was established in January 1999.

[c]The combined Czechoslovak Service broadcast for twenty-one hours weekly in 1988. When the Czech Republic and Slovakia formed separate countries in 1992, the service split into separate Czech and Slovak units. In 2000 and 2001, they were converted to smaller multimedia feed services.

[d]The total for English in 1988 includes some satellite feeds by VOA Europe. In 2002, the total for English includes satellite feeds by VOA Music Mix, Special English, and some English-language instruction programs. The specialized English-to-Africa broadcasts are included in both totals.

[e]Reduced to satellite feed or multimedia unit, transmitting materials by means other than direct over-the-air broadcasts to affiliate radio or television outlets, audio, video and Internet.

[f]VOA's Portuguese Services to Portugal and to Brazil were abolished in 1987 and 2001, respectively.

Sources: Barbara L. Schiele, "VOA Broadcast Hours History," Office of Programs, December 1988, 8; Broadcasting Board of Governors, annual report, 1999–2000; Norma Morrison and Ronald J. Tripp, VOA traffic schedule, February 25, 2002; Lisa Keathley, interview with author, March 25, 2002.

Table C.2 Voice of America Directors, 1942–2002

1. John Houseman	February 1942–July 1943
2. Louis G. Cowan	August 1943–August 1945
3. John Ogilvie	September 1945–January 1946
4. Charles Thayer	January 1948–October 1949
5. Foy David Kohler	October 1949–September 1952
6. Alfred Morton	October 1952–April 1953
7. Leonard Erikson	July 1953–April 1954
8. John R. Poppele	May 1954–July 1956
9. Robert E. Button	July 1956–July 1958
10. Henry Loomis	July 1958–March 1965
11. John Chancellor	August 1965–June 1967
12. John Charles Daly	September 1967–June 1968
13. Kenneth R. Giddens	September 1969–April 1977
14. R. Peter Straus	July 1977–October 1979
15. Mary G. F. Bitterman	March 1980–January 1981
16. James Conkling	August 1981–March 1982
17. John Hughes	March 1982–August 1982
18. Kenneth Tomlinson	December 1982–September 1984
19. Gene Pell	June 1985–October 1985
20. Richard W. Carlson	November 1986–September 1991
21. Chase Untermeyer	September 1991–January 1993
22. Geoffrey Cowan	March 1994–November 1996
23. Evelyn S. Lieberman	March 1997–March 1999
24. Sanford J. Ungar	July 1999–June 2001
25. Robert Reilly	October 2001–August 2002
26. David Jackson	August 2002–

Source: Voice of America, *Voice of America: A Brief History* (Washington, D.C.: Voice of America, Office of External Affairs, 1998).

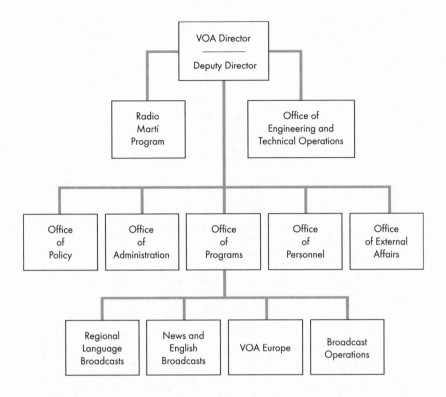

Figure C.1 Voice of America organizational chart, 1990

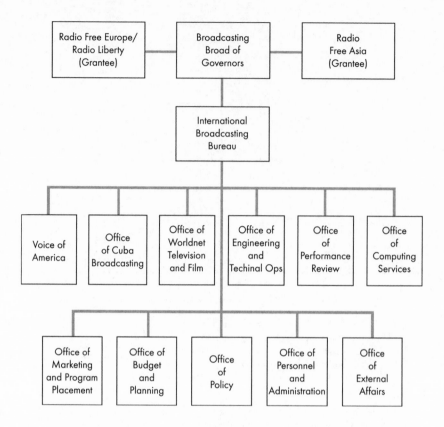

Figure C.2 Organization of United States publicly funded civilian international broadcasting, 2002

Appendix D

SELECTED STATEMENTS ABOUT VOA BY PRESIDENTS

In 1946, the United Nations General Assembly passed a resolution, reading in part: "Freedom of information is a fundamental human right," and the touchstone of all the freedoms to which the United Nations is consecrated. This is our touchstone as well, this is the code of the Voice of America. We welcome the view of others, we seek a free flow of information across national boundaries and oceans, across iron curtains and stone walls. We are not afraid to entrust the American people with unpleasant facts, foreign ideas, alien philosophies and competitive values. For a nation that is afraid to let its people judge the true and the false in an open market is a nation that is afraid of its people. The Voice of America thus carries a heavy responsibility. Its burden of truth is not easy to bear.

— JOHN F. KENNEDY, 1962

Several principles guided me in shaping this reorganization plan. Among the most important were keeping the Voice of America's news gathering and reporting functions independent and objective. . . . Under this administration, VOA will be solely responsible for the content of its news broadcasts—for there is no more valued coin than candor in the marketplace of ideas.

— JIMMY CARTER, 1977

To millions in closed societies, your broadcasts are . . . the voice of truth. We in America believe every man, woman and child has the right to free sources of information. We do not think a mind can or should be imprisoned. . . . Let us remember that many listeners, listeners in these closed societies, tune in to VOA at grave personal risk. I said several years ago that I attach the kind of importance to modernizing the Voice that President Kennedy gave to the space program. I want to renew that pledge to you today.

— RONALD REAGAN, 1987

Throughout its history, the Voice of America has applied the power of technology to the advance of liberty. It has used every means possible—shortwave, television, and now the Internet—to bypass the barriers of tyrants. Radio waves are not hindered by borders, and as technology improves, the Internet will become less vulnerable to the censor's hand. No one knows what new information technologies will be available sixty years from now, but two things we do know. First, that the Voice of America will find a way to use them, and second, through these means—though these means of delivery may change— the message never will. It's a simple message. It's a message of freedom, and freedom is worth defending. And the truth, no less than the force of arms, is needed for its defense.

— GEORGE W. BUSH, 2002

Notes

Introduction

1. Douglas A. Boyd, *Broadcasting in the Arab World: A Survey of the Electronic Media in the Middle East*, 3d ed. (Ames: Iowa State University Press, 1999), 290.

2. James Reston, "The Voice of America," *New York Times*, March 12, 1978, A27.

3. The others, besides the Voice of America and Worldnet Television (VOA-TV), are the U.S. government–funded surrogate networks: Radio Free Europe/Radio Liberty (RFE/RL), broadcast to Eastern Europe, the former Soviet Union, and southern Central Asia; Radio Free Asia (RFA), broadcast to China and other Communist or dictatorial regimes in East Asia; and Radio-TV Martí, broadcast to Cuba. These other networks serve as alternative media to their target countries, uncensored by local authorities. The Voice of America offers "full-service" programming, containing news and information about its listeners' own countries, as well as regional, world, and U.S. news of interest to them via radio, television, and local FM relays—and on the Internet, to a global audience.

1. Tiananmen: The Burden of Truth

1. Alan Pessin, interview with author, Washington, D.C., June 29, 1999; Betty Tseu, interview with author, Washington, D.C., April 6, 1998; Ivan Klecka, "Impact of VOA Broadcasting to China," memorandum to Richard W. Carlson (director, VOA), May 14, 1989.

2. Shen Tong, remarks at "International Broadcasting in a Changing World," symposium cosponsored by the Voice of America and the Smithsonian Institution, Washington, D.C., January 23, 1992.

3. Alan Pessin, "Behind the Story: Tiananmen Square, a Reporter's Perspective," *Voice Magazine* [magazine for Voice of America audience], October–November 1989, 8.

4. At VOA, the larger language units are called branches (Arabic, Chinese, English-to-Africa, French-to-Africa, Russian, Spanish, and Ukrainian). The Chinese Branch consists of two services: Mandarin and Cantonese. Some units, such as Russian in 1947, began as services and later became branches. The News Division began as a branch and grew later into a division.

5. Pessin, "Behind the Story," 8.

6. Pessin, interview.

7. Pessin, "Behind the Story," 8.

8. Tseu, interview.

9. Ibid.

10. Author's notes, May 10–14, 1989.

11. Klecka, "Impact of VOA Broadcasting to China."

12. Tseu, interview.

13. Steven Mufson, "Documents Reveal Top Chinese Split Before Crackdown," *Washington Post*, January 6, 2001, A1. According to leaked Chinese documents, hardliner Li Peng accompanied Zhao Ziyang to the meeting with the students.

14. Pessin, "Behind the Story," 8.

15. Mufson, "Documents Reveal Top Chinese Split Before Crackdown," A1.

16. The extent of the jamming was detailed in memoranda from the VOA Office of Engineering to Carlson and in operational memoranda shared with Sid Davis, director of programs, May 21–28, 1989.

17. Richard Baum, "International Broadcasting to Asia" (paper presented at a symposium of the Broadcasting Board of Governors, Annenberg School for Communication, University of Southern California, Los Angeles, November 18, 1997).

18. Office of the President, "Statement by the White House Press Secretary on Student Demonstrations in China," May 23, 1989, 1.

19. The sequence of events is reconstructed from operational mail notes from the VOA Office of Engineering and Office of Programs, May 24–28, 1989.

20. Jay Mathews, "Movement Taps American Influences," *Washington Post*, May 25, 1989, A16.

21. Philomena Jurey, with Stephanie Mann Nealer, newsroom directive, June 2, 1989.

22. Alan Pessin, interview with author, Washington, D.C., September 14, 2000.

23. Author's recollections and memoranda recapping technical and programming events surrounding the massacre; Voice of America, Office of Programs, "Chronology of Events in the PRC and VOA Responses," October 1, 1989, 1–3.

24. Transcript of monitoring report on Radio Beijing's English Service, relayed via a leased transmitter in Spain. The monitor was Tom Gavaras of Minnetonka, Minnesota, at 0300 UTC, June 4, 1989, on 9690 kHz, shortwave. The announcer's fate was reported by a friend of the author at Radio Canada International.

25. John Harbaugh (editor, Chinese Branch), memorandum to Sid Davis (director of programs), June 4, 1989; Jacqueline Trescott, "Signals of China's Hope and Turmoil," *Washington Post*, June 8, 1989, B12.

26. Trescott, "Signals of China's Hope and Turmoil," B12.

27. VOA, Office of Programs, "Chronology of Events," 1.

28. Nicholas D. Kristof, "Army Rift Reported in Beijing; Shooting of Civilians Goes On; Bush Bars Arms Sales to China," *New York Times*, June 6, 1989, A1.

29. VOA, Office of Programs, "Chronology of Events," 2.

30. Alan Pessin, "A 'Brazen' Violation," *Gannett Center Journal*, fall 1989, 117–118.

31. Jay Henderson, "VOA Reviewed in the Tiananmen Papers," advisory to Sanford J. Ungar and other senior managers, January 11, 2001.

32. Pessin, "'Brazen' Violation," 125.

33. Pessin, interviews.

34. Alan Pessin, telex to Philomena Jurey, June 10, 1989.

35. Pessin, "'Brazen' Violation," 118–120, 122.

36. Alan Pessin, remarks at Hong Kong airport, June 17, 1989, in Harry Miles Muheim and Jerry Krell, *The Voice* (Washington, D.C.: Worldnet Television, 1992), a television documentary for the fiftieth anniversary of VOA.

37. David Lawsky, Reuters, June 14, 1989.

38. Kelu Chao, interview with author, Washington, D.C., September 17, 2000.

39. Jay Henderson, interview with author, Washington, D.C., July 8, 2000.

40. David Hess, memorandum to Sid Davis, Bob Knopes, and Alan L. Heil, Jr., August 2, 1989, 1.

41. Alan Pessin, address at the annual conference of the National Association of Government Communicators, Arlington, Va., December 8, 1989, 11.

42. Gerald (Jerry) Stryker, interview with author, Alexandria, Va., September 19, 2000.

2. The Struggle to Get It Straight: The Early Years

1. Quoted in International Broadcasting Bureau, *Voice of America: A Brief History* (Washington, D.C.: International Broadcasting Bureau, Office of External Affairs, 1998), 1.

2. William Benton, quoted in Robert William Pirsein, *The Voice of America: An History of the International Broadcasting Activities of the United States Government, 1942–1962* (New York: Arno Press, 1979), 2.

3. Ibid., 6.

4. John Houseman, "Excerpts from John Houseman's Speech," *USICA World*, April 1982, 6.

5. Holly Cowan Shulman, *The Voice of America: Propaganda and Democracy, 1941–45* (Madison: University of Wisconsin Press, 1990), 41.

6. Ibid., 7.

7. Houseman, "Excerpts from John Houseman's Speech," 6.

8. Quoted in Pirsein, *Voice of America*, 53; Marcel Fodor, "VOA History (1942–1967)" (manuscript, 1967), chap. 4, p. 7.

9. Robert Bauer, interview with author, Washington, D.C., October 6, 2000.

10. Quoted in Michael A. Hanu, "My Two Close Encounters of the Third Kind with John Houseman," *USICA World*, April 1982, 7.

11. Quoted in Martin Manning, "VOA Studio Dedicated to Houseman," *USIA World*, May 6, 1990, 6.

12. Eugene Kern, letter to author, September 25, 2000.

13. Holly Cowan Shulman, "John Houseman and the Voice of America: American Foreign Propaganda on the Air," *American Studies*, spring 1988, 31.

14. Quoted in Shulman, *Voice of America*, 49.

15. Hanu, "My Two Close Encounters," 7.

16. Walter Roberts, address at the inauguration of the John Houseman memorial studio, Voice of America, Washington, D.C., February 23, 1990.

17. Shulman, *Voice of America*, 194.

18. Walter Roberts, oral-history interview by Cliff Groce, Washington, D.C., September 10, 1990.

19. Ed Goldberger was head of the New York office some years after the Voice headquarters moved to Washington, D.C. He had superb judgment in shaping both news and cultural programs and retired in 1972.

20. Eugene Kern, oral-history interview by Cliff Groce, New York, December 12, 1986; Ed Goldberger, oral-history interview by Cliff Groce, New York, December 12, 1986.

21. Walter Roberts, interview with author, Washington, D.C., March 28, 2000.

22. Quoted in Pirsein, *Voice of America*, 76.

23. Quoted in Shulman, *Voice of America*, 98.

24. Ibid., 95.

25. As a primary source of information on the "Moronic Little King" flap, Shulman cites Joseph Barnes's reminiscences, Oral History Collection, Columbia University, New York (*Voice of America*, 46).

26. Shulman, *Voice of America,* 101–102.

27. Ibid., 109.

28. Pirsein, *Voice of America,* 82.

29. Robert A. Bauer, "D-Day, June 6, 1944," in United States Information Agency, *United States Information Agency: A Commemoration* (Washington, D.C.: United States Information Agency, 1999), 8.

30. Pirsein, *Voice of America,* 91–92.

31. Quoted in Thomas C. Sorensen, *The Word War: The Story of American Propaganda* (New York: Harper & Row, 1968), 231.

32. Pirsein, *Voice of America,* 81.

33. William Winter, "Voice of an American" (manuscript, 1990), 3.

34. Shulman, *Voice of America,* 112.

35. Quoted in International Broadcasting Bureau, *Voice of America,* 5.

36. Quoted in Pirsein, *Voice of America,* 114.

37. Ibid., 111.

38. Ibid., 113–133.

39. Michael A. Hanu, "Some of Our Yesterdays" (transcript of VOA fiftieth-anniversary documentary, January 30, 1992), 5.

40. Quoted in U.S. Congress, House, *United States Information and Educational Exchange Act of 1948,* 80th Cong., 2d sess., *Congressional Service* (St. Paul, Minn.: West, January 26, 1948), 1:4–12.

41. Quoted in Pirsein, *Voice of America,* 146.

42. Ibid., 145.

43. Ibid., 156.

44. The Ring Plan was so named for two reasons: it had been designed by an engineering consultant named Andrew Ring, and its intent was to build facilities that could "ring" the Soviet Union.

45. Quoted in Pirsein, *Voice of America,* 221.

46. Fodor, "VOA History (1942–1967)," chap. 20, p. 4.

47. Earl Latham, *The Communist Controversy in Washington: From the New Deal to McCarthy* (Cambridge, Mass.: Harvard University Press, 1966), 323.

48 Pirsein, *Voice of America,* 274.

49. Quoted in ibid., 255.

50. Robert Goldmann, interview with author, New York, September 4, 2000. See also Goldmann, *Wayward Threads* (Evanston, Ill.: Northwestern University Press, 1996), 166–168.

51. Goldmann, *Wayward Threads,* 167–168.

52. Ed Kretzman, "McCarthy and the Voice of America," *Foreign Service Journal,* February 1967, 26.

53. Quoted in Pirsein, *Voice of America,* 236.

54. Henry Loomis, in Hans N. Tuch and G. Lewis Schmidt, eds., "Ike and USIA" (summary of proceedings at the Eisenhower Centennial Symposium, National War College, Washington, D.C., October 11, 1990), 45.

55. International Broadcasting Bureau, *Voice of America,* 7.

3. The 1950s and 1960s: Forging a More Credible Voice

1. Robert Goldmann, interview with author, New York, September 4, 2000.

2. U.S. Congress, House, Committee on International Relations, *Proceedings of the HIRC*, 95th Cong., 1st sess., June 8–24, 1977, 472; Abbott Washburn to House Committee on International Relations, June 23, 1977. Washburn wrote to the committee as a member of the Federal Communications Commission.

3. Barry Zorthian, interview with author, Arlington, Va., July 11, 2000, and various USIA oral histories.

4. Robert Goldmann, *Wayward Threads* (Evanston, Ill.: Northwestern University Press, 1996), 49–50, 115–116.

5. Henry Loomis, curriculum vitae, Voice of America, 1992; author's recollections.

6. Zorthian, interview; Goldmann, interview.

7. Edgar Martin, oral-history interview by Cliff Groce, Washington, D.C., February 5, 1988.

8. Author's conversations over many years and personal recollections. Groce was one of my first editors at VOA.

9. This biographical sketch is based on many daily and nocturnal phone conversations with Bernie Kamenske over the years and on Kamenske, interview with author, Bethesda, Md., September 3, 2000.

10. Quoted in Voice of America, transcript of "Twentieth Anniversary of the Signing of the VOA Charter," symposium, Washington, D.C., July 12, 1996, 3.

11. The citation of key figures in the "greening" of the Voice is based on Goldmann, interview; Kamenske, interview; and Zorthian, interview.

12. Jack O'Brien, oral-history interview by Cliff Groce, Washington, D.C., February 8, 1988.

13. Barry Zorthian, interview with author, Arlington, Va., April 3, 2001.

14. Ibid.

15. Quoted in VOA, "Twentieth Anniversary."

16. Jack O'Brien, oral-history interview by Hans N. (Tom) Tuch, February 5, 1988. See also O'Brien, in VOA, "Twentieth Anniversary."

17. Henry Loomis, "Farewell Address to the Voice of America Staff," March 4, 1965, 14.

18. Barry Zorthian, in Voice of America, transcript of fortieth-anniversary celebration of VOA Special English, December 1, 1999.

19. Ernest Acquisto, interview with author, Falls Church, Va., August 18, 2001. Acquisto later became chief of the Technical Operations Division at VOA headquarters (1978–1986). Beginning in 1983, Acquisto and his able executive officer, Agnes Timcheck organized well-attended annual VOA alumni gatherings.

20. "ANTA, Voice of America Bring Class to Global B'cast of 'Our Town,'" *Variety*, June 19, 1957, 1; Eugene Kern, oral-history interview by Cliff Groce, New York, December 12, 1986; Ed Goldberger, oral-history interview by Cliff Groce, New York, December 12, 1986. *American Theater of the Air* notes are based on e-mail exchanges with Kern and a list supplied by Goldberger, September 2000.

21. Barry Zorthian, in Hans N. Tuch and G. Lewis Schmidt, eds., "Ike and USIA" (summary of proceedings at the Eisenhower Centennial Symposium, National War College, Washington, D.C., October 11, 1990), 17.

22. Stanley Cloud and Lynne Olson, *The Murrow Boys* (Boston: Houghton Mifflin, 1996), 353.

23. Jon Elliston, *Psywar on Cuba: The Declassified History of U.S. Anti-Castro Propaganda* (New York: Ocean Press, 1999), 30.

24. George V. Allen, "USIA: The Big Problem Is Belief," *New York Herald Tribune*, August 4, 1963, 8.

25. Quoted in Elliston, *Psywar on Cuba*, 34–35.

26. Ibid., 34.

27. Harry Miles Muheim and Jerry Krell, *The Voice* (Washington, D.C.: Worldnet Television, 1992), a television documentary for the fiftieth anniversary of VOA.

28. Elliston, *Psywar on Cuba*, 135.

29. Quoted in Ibid., 141.

30. Ibid., 135.

31. The strowger was an internal monitoring system on which a broadcaster could access different field and studio audio sources via an elaborate switching device. VOA's Chris Kern reports that Almon B. Strowger, an American telephone engineer, patented the device in 1891. The term "strowger" was widely used at VOA until the late 1980s. Recent generations of VOA staff have come to refer to updated boxes as "monitrons."

32. VOA carried live the swearing in of President Lyndon B. Johnson and the funeral observances for John F. Kennedy at the Capitol, the White House, St. John's Church, and Arlington National Cemetery. The special broadcast ended on November 27, 1963, shortly after the new president addressed Congress.

33. O'Brien, interview.

34. I recall hearing about the letter from the VOA audience mail department at the time.

35. Muheim and Krell, *The Voice*.

36. Ibid.

37. Carl Rowan, "Why Henry Loomis Left the Voice of America," *Washington Evening Star*, April 2, 1969, A23.

38. Ibid.

39. Mary McGrory, "'Voice' Chiefs Chafe at Curbs," *Washington Evening Star*, March 7, 1965, A23.

40. Ibid.

41. Loomis "Farewell Address," 5–6.

42. Quoted in Muheim and Krell, *The Voice*.

43. Loomis "Farewell Address," 6–8.

44. Henry Loomis, address at the National Press Club, Washington, D.C., February 21, 1962, 9–10.

4. The VOA Correspondent: To the Ends of the Earth

1. Author's notes, September 28–October 15, 1970. Among sources during the coverage of Jordan were Bahi Ludgham, the prime minister of Tunisia (chairman of the Arab peacekeeping mission in Jordan), and spokesmen for King Hussein's Bedouin army and the fedayeen.

2. I watched Jesse Helms make his challenge. Associate gallery access was granted to VOA a few days later. Its reporters, however, were barred from seeking office in either the House or the Senate press association.

3. Voice of America, press release, August 1, 1994.

4. Mohamed Ghuneim, interview with author, Arlington, Va., June 15, 2000. See also Jack Anderson and Joseph Spear, "Syrians Detained VOA Correspondent," *Washington Post,* January 27, 1987, B16.

5. The excerpted correspondents' reports in this section originated from the places indicated and were distributed by the VOA News Division on the dates noted, from 1975 to 2000.

6. Mort Rosenblum, "The John Peter Zenger Award for Freedom of the Press and the People's Right to Know" (address at the John Peter Zenger Award ceremony, University of Arizona, Tucson, April 24, 1991), 8–9. In 1990, the award was given to Terry Anderson, the AP correspondent held hostage in Lebanon.

7. Alan L. Heil, Jr., "VOA Correspondents Ace a Story," in *United States Information Agency: A Commemoration* (Washington, D.C.: United States Information Agency, 1999), 47.

5. From Here to Everywhere: Building a Global Network

1. The Greenville Relay Station was named after Edward R. Murrow, the USIA director at the time of its dedication. I visited there and interviewed staff members on February 19–21, 1998.

2. Vicki Brimmer and Terry Balazs, "The Technical Magic of the IBB's Office of Engineering," *Tune In* [internal newsletter of International Broadcasting Bureau], February 1999, 9.

3. Lord Byron Van Wagenen, interview with author, Greenville, N.C., February 20, 1998.

4. "The Next Internet," *The Economist,* December 1999, 111.

5. Michael Nelson, *War of the Black Heavens: The Battles of Western Broadcasting in the Cold War* (Syracuse, N.Y.: Syracuse University Press, 1997), 1.

6. Edwin F. Burgeni, George Jacobs, and Edgar T. Martin, "The Voice of America—A Generation of Growth," *Cathode Press* 22 (1965): 1–12.

7. Robert William Pirsein, *The Voice of America: An History of the International Broadcasting Activities of the United States Government, 1942–1962* (New York: Arno Press, 1979), 3.

8. Ibid., 78–79.

9. Ibid., 82–83.

10. Ibid., 193–169.

11. Vicki Brimmer and Fred Wulff, "A Technical History of the VOA Network" (internal unclassified paper, International Broadcasting Bureau, Office of Engineering, October 25, 1995), chap. 2, p. 9.

12. Ibid., 1–11.

13. Edgar T. Martin, oral-history interview by Cliff Groce, Washington, D.C., February 12, 1988, 7.

14. Ibid., 54.

15. Barry Zorthian, interview with author, Arlington, Va., July 21, 2000.

16. Quoted in Eugene S. Reich, "The Wall of Noise" (script of VOA *Studio One* documentary, February 1, 1987), 10.

17. Henry Loomis, "Farewell Address to the Voice of America Staff," March 4, 1965, 2–3.

18. James Wood, *History of International Broadcasting* (London: International Institute of Engineers/Science Museum, 2000), 2:110.

19. Office of the President, "Statement by President Reagan upon Signing the U.S.–Moroccan Relay Station Agreement," March 1, 1984.

20. Wood, *History of International Broadcasting,* 189.

21. "VOA Modernization Under Fire," *Broadcasting Magazine,* September 28, 1987, 65–66.

22. Voice of America, Office of Engineering, "Voice of America Engineering Modernization/Refurbishment Program: Recent Accomplishments," October 1989, 2–3.

23. Quoted in Alan L. Heil, Jr., notes on the Radio Canada International Challenges II conference, Quebec City, Quebec, Canada, March 1992.

24. Quoted in Alan L. Heil, Jr., notes on the Radio Canada International Challenges V conference, Ottawa, Ontario, Canada, May 25, 1998.

25. International Broadcasting Bureau, Office of Research, "VOA's Global Audience" (research memorandum, August 1999), 5. In this survey, VOA's total audience was estimated at 91 million listeners, about two-thirds of them in Africa, the Middle East, and South Asia. In 1987, the audience had been estimated at 130 million, about two-thirds of them in the Soviet Union, Eastern Europe, and China.

26. Brimmer and Balazs, "Technical Magic," 8; Wood, *History of International Broadcasting,* 120–123.

27. This account of VOA's technical comeback in Africa is based on Vicki Brimmer, interview with author, Washington, D.C., December 8, 2000, September 14, 2001; Robert Everett, interview with author, Washington, D.C., October 10 and 18, 2000; Bruce Hunter, interview with author, Washington, D.C., February 10 and 20, 1998, March 6, 2000; Gaines Johnson, interview with Vicki Brimmer, Washington, D.C., January 11, 2001; Samuel K. Paye, interview with author, Washington, D.C., October 29, 2000; Cliff Weese, interview with author, Washington, D.C., November 17, 2000; Gary Wise, interview with author, Washington, D.C., November 29, 2000; and on e-mail notes from Brimmer, Everett, and Jan Hartman between October 18 and November 29, 2000.

28. Kenneth Stern, "Broadcasting into the New Millennium," memorandum to the Broadcasting Board of Governors, August 27, 1999, 1.

29. Richard W. Carlson, "The War of Words," *American Legion Magazine,* July 1987, 20.

30. Author's notes, 1993.

6. Into the Citadel of "Ramshackle Excellence": A Portrait

1. Author's notes on VOA's fiftieth anniversary. See also United States Information Agency, Bureau of Broadcasting, *Annual Report for 1993: Looking Toward Tomorrow* (Washington, D.C.: United States Information Agency, Bureau of Broadcasting, 1993), 18.

2. Marian Burros, "Eating Well: At the Voice of America, a Feast of 46 Cultures," *New York Times,* March 18, 1992, C4.

3. John Chancellor, "The Intimate Voice," *Foreign Service Journal,* February 1967, 19.

4. Margaret Jaffie, interview with author, Falls Church, Va., September 16, 2001.

5. Visitors to VOA see the radio and television studios and the multimedia news center as well as watch the broadcasters prepare their programs and news reports. Tours are available on weekdays, except for holidays, at 10:30 A.M., 1:30 P.M., and

2:30 P.M., or at other times by special arrangement for groups. To make reservations, call (202) 619-3919.

6. The descriptions of the VOA communities are based on author's notes and recollections and on Jack O'Brien, oral-history interview by Cliff Groce, Washington, D.C., February 8, 1988, 44–48.

7. Chancellor, "Intimate Voice."

8. I attended hundreds of program reviews between 1973 and 1997. These profiles of the geographic divisions are a compilation of information gleaned during those sessions.

9. The South Asian services later became part of the South and Central Asia Division, which inherited some of the language units of the former USSR Division and the Near East and South Asia Division as well.

10. The USSR Division was renamed the Eurasia Division after the collapse of the Soviet Union in December 1991.

11. Cliff Groce, untitled paper, 1968.

12. Cable News Network, "Jonestown Massacre + 20: Questions Linger," November 18, 1998 (available at: www.cnn.com/us/9811/18/jonestown.anniv.01/).

13. Fred Collins, "Further Implications of the Guyana Study," memorandum to R. Peter Straus, April 17, 1979, 2, 7.

14. Frank Cummins, recollection to author, 1997.

15. Author's notes, 1981.

16. Douglas B. Roberts, interview with author, Washington, D.C., October 3, 2000. See also David Hirst, "'If We Die—We Die Together'—She Embraced Us," *Guardian*, March 26, 1978, 18.

17. Charlene Porter, "Words Can Not Explain: Communications Problems Defying Translation in a Multi-Lingual, Multi-Cultural Workplace" (paper for a course in public administration, University of Maryland, 1995), 22.

7. The Struggle to Get It Straight: The Charter as Law

1. Quoted in Voice of America, transcript of "Twentieth Anniversary of the Signing of the VOA Charter," symposium, Washington, D.C., July 12, 1996, 1–2. By coincidence, John Chancellor died on this anniversary date at his home in Princeton, New Jersey, after a long struggle with stomach cancer.

2. Thomas C. Sorensen, *The Word War: The Story of American Propaganda* (New York: Harper & Row, 1968), 245.

3. Paul Modic, interview with author, Bethesda, Md., October 11, 2000.

4. Quoted in Associated Press, "Daly," unsigned dispatch, AO 39WX, May 31, 1967, 4:27 P.M. EDT.

5. Quoted in U.S. Congress, House, Committee on International Relations, *Hearings on Public Diplomacy and the Future*, 95th Cong., 1st sess., June 16, 1977, 460.

6. Lois Roth, "Public Diplomacy and the Past: The Studies of U.S. Information and Cultural Programs (1952–1975)" (paper presented at the twenty-third session, Executive Seminar in National and International Affairs, Department of State, Foreign Service Institute, Washington, D.C., 1980–1981), 2.

7. Gerald (Jerry) Stryker, interview with author, Alexandria, Va., September 15, 2000.

8. Maureen Jane Nemecek, "Speaking of America: The Voice of America, Its Mission and Message, 1942–1982" (Ph.D. diss., University of Maryland, 1984), 280.

According to Nemecek, VOA faced a potential budget cut of 30 percent in 1972 (a reduction from thirty-six to eleven languages), when Senator J. William Fulbright called the VOA "a Cold War relic." Fulbright's measure was rejected. In 1975, Congress proposed a 14 percent cut in VOA operations. VOA director Kenneth Giddens had bipartisan support, however, and the 1975 cuts were averted.

9. Panel on International Information, Education, and Cultural Relations (Stanton Commission), *International Information Education and Cultural Relations: Recommendations for the Future* (Washington, D.C.: Center for Strategic and International Studies, 1975), iii.

10. G. Lewis Schmidt, John R. O'Brien, and Edmund Schechter, "Management Report on VOA" (internal unclassified paper, April 22, 1974), 50–53.

11. George Jacobs, "Testimony on Soviet Jamming of Radio Broadcasts" (paper prepared for the Commission on Security and Cooperation in Europe, Washington, D.C., October 29, 1985), 6.

12. Michael Nelson, *War of the Black Heavens: The Battles of Western Broadcasting in the Cold War* (Syracuse, N.Y.: Syracuse University Press, 1997), 149.

13. James Keogh to Representative Robert L. F. Sikes, March 5, 1974.

14. Author's notes and Kingsley's talking points, February 26, 1974.

15. The United States Information Agency was known overseas as the United States Information Service (USIS).

16. "Muted Voice of America," *Time*, December 16, 1974, 80–81.

17. Mark Hopkins, fax to author, September 30, 2001.

18. "Muted Voice of America," 81.

19. News and Current Affairs (NCA) logs, February 9, 1977.

20. "Muted Voice of America," 81.

21. Philomena Jurey, *A Basement Seat to History: Tales of Covering Presidents Nixon, Ford, Carter, and Reagan for the Voice of America* (Washington, D.C.: Linus Press, 1995), 60.

22. Quoted in Nemecek, "Speaking of America," 286.

23. Ibid., 260.

24. Jack Shellenberger, interview with author, Washington, D.C., July 13, 2000.

25. The description of VOA coverage of Richard Nixon's resignation is based on Shellenberger, interview; Bernard Kamenske, interview with author, Bethesda, Md., February 7, 2001; Chris Kern, "Watergate Chronology," August 8, 1974; and author's notes.

26. Shellenberger, interview.

27. Pham Tran, interview with author, Alexandria, Va., February 13, 2001.

28. Quoted in Nemecek, "Speaking of America," 302–303.

29. Ibid.

30. The slot note, issued on April 14, 1975, read: "In relation to the question of evacuation or phasedown of Americans and Vietnamese associated with them from Vietnam, we are to use only official statements of the White House, and Departments of State or Defense, and Congressional *actions* (e.g., a vote) until further notice. This instruction stems from a very volatile situation in Saigon which raises concern for the lives and safety of these individuals and recognition of a responsibility to protect them."

31. Quoted in Cheryl Arvidson, "Voice of America—Lids Off on U.S. Government's Radio Message to the World," United Press International, July 8, 1975.

32. Ibid.

33. Pham Tran, interview.

34. Author's notes; Alan L. Heil, Jr., memorandum to Hans N. Tuch and Jack Shellenberger, April 3, 1975.

35. Slot note, issued on April 26, 1975, rescinding the one issued twelve days earlier.

36. The evacuation of P. T., My Binh, and their families was carefully orchestrated at every step by Kamenske. This account is pieced together from Pham Tran, interview; Bernard Kamenske, interview with author, Bethesda, Md., January 9, 2001; and author's notes.

37. Kamenske, interview, January 9, 2001.

38. Wayne Corey, e-mail to author, February 14, 2001.

39. William Cohen to James Keogh, May 6, 1975, 1; Lloyd Bentsen to James Keogh, April 10, 1975; Charles Percy to James Keogh, May 8, 1975.

40. NCA logs, 1974–1975.

41. Because of the two-source rule, errors were relatively rare in a news file that was global in scope. In their study, Schmidt, O'Brien, and Schechter estimated that the NCA file was distilled from source material of 750,000 words daily ("Management Report on VOA," 50). The most serious error during my eight years there was when a stringer on the Pakistan–Afghanistan border, one with a sound reportorial record of accuracy, mistakenly reported the defection of an Afghan education minister and VOA broadcast a news item on this. The error was discovered a few hours later, and a retraction was broadcast. It was that stringer's last report for VOA.

42. Kamenske, interview.

43. Public Law 94-350, sec. 206, 94th Cong., 2d sess. (July 12, 1976), VOA Charter, 9–10. See also U.S. Congress, Senate, Committee on Foreign Relations, Foreign Relations Authorization Act, Fiscal Year 1977, 94th Cong., 2d sess., S. 3168, report no. 94-703, 1976, 11–12. The bill amended the Smith-Mundt Act of 1948 by adding this charter text.

44. Quoted in VOA, "Twentieth Anniversary," 4.

45. Robert S. Fortner, International Communications: History, Conflict, and Control of the Global Metropolis (Belmont, Calif.: Wadsworth, 1994), timeline on inside cover.

8. The Independence Debate: To the Brink and Back

1. Richard Weintraub, "Voice of America—Its Own: Law Lets Radio Resist Pressures," Washington Post, August 1, 1976, A1, A14. Director Kenneth R. Giddens was quoted as calling the enactment of the charter as law "an immense step forward."

2. The sequence of events is pieced together from NCA logs, September–October 1976.

3. Quoted in H. D. S. Greenway, "U.S. Officials Forbid VOA to See PLO," Washington Post, October 9, 1976, A1.

4. Hans N. (Tom) Tuch, oral-history interview by Cliff Groce, Washington, D.C., February 24, 1988, 16–17.

5. Bella Abzug to James Keogh, October 12, 1976, 1–2.

6. Richard Weintraub, "U.S. Officials Back Ambassador on VOA Reporting Curb," Washington Post, October 27, 1976, A5. On July 13, 1977, David Nalle, USIA Near East and South Asia area director, wrote a memo to Tuch saying he believed that "VOA reporters should be specifically exempted from the

no-PLO-contact policy. Credibility," he added, "is the essence of VOA's value in this delicate phase of the Middle East peace process." The ban on VOA contacts, nonetheless, remained in force with occasional exceptions until September 1993 and the signing of the Oslo accords by Israel and the Palestine Liberation Organization.

7. VOA's Cairo office was reestablished in 1978.

8. Charles Percy, "Percy Calls for Independent Voice of America," press release, November 30, 1976, 2.

9. Author's notes, March 1977.

10. U.S. Congress, Senate, Committee on Foreign Relations, *Hearings of Subcommittee on International Operations on the Foreign Relations Authorization Act of 1978*, 95th Cong., 1st sess., S. 1190, April 29, 1977, 237–287.

11. Ibid., 238–239, 268.

12. Ibid., 276.

13. Ibid., 281. The correspondent I referred to was John Bue, a French and British citizen who headed the VOA Paris bureau for about three decades before his retirement in the late 1970s. Bue made the comment during a visit to Washington in 1976 to observe the national election.

14. U.S. Congress, Senate, Committee on Foreign Relations, *Markup Session of Full Committee on Foreign Relations Authorization Act of 1978*, 95th Cong., 1st sess., S. 1190, May 4, 1977, 37.

15. Walter Roberts, interview with author, Washington, D.C., July 7, 2000.

16. John Reinhardt, memorandum to Hans N. Tuch (acting director, VOA), May 4, 1977, 1.

17. Elmer Staats, *Public Diplomacy in the Years Ahead—An Assessment of Proposals for Reorganization*, Comptroller General's report no. ID-77-21 (Washington, D.C.: General Accounting Office, May 5, 1977), 28–33.

18. Quoted in Senate Committee on Foreign Relations, *Markup on Foreign Relations Authorization Act of 1978*, May 10, 1977, 168.

19. Ibid., 172

20. Ibid., 175–176.

21. Scott Cohen, interview with author, Washington, D.C., April 29, 1999.

22. Quoted in Senate Committee on Foreign Relations, *Markup on Foreign Relations Authorization Act of 1978*, May 10, 1977, 179.

23. Ibid., 183.

24. The final recast amendment to S. 1190, as it pertained to VOA programming, read: "That global broadcasting by the Voice of America, in addition to constituting a significant international news source, is both an important cultural activity serving to portray American values in society and also an important medium for the articulation of official U.S. policy; and that these potentially conflicting roles can be better reconciled and the stature and credibility of Voice of America broadcasts enhanced if the Voice of America has a clear mandate to broadcast accurate, objective and comprehensive news, to represent American society in its totality, and to provide such airtime as is necessary for the articulation by Executive Branch spokesmen of official United States policy."

25. Roberts, interview.

26. Chalmers Roberts, *Report of the Panel to Study the Role of the Foreign Correspondents of the Voice of America* (Washington, D.C., March 9, 1978), 1–7. Besides Roberts, Pauline Frederick, and E. W. Kenworthy, the other members of the panel

were Franklin H. Williams, former ambassador to Ghana, and S. William Scott, vice president for radio news operations for Westinghouse Broadcasting.

27. Department of State. "Guidelines and Operating Procedures for VOA Foreign Correspondents," joint cable with the International Communication Agency (formerly USIA), signed by Warren Christopher and John Reinhardt, to all U.S. embassies and missions, June 28, 1978.

28. Eva Jane Fritzman, "Administrative Procedures Governing VOA Correspondents," September 28, 1978.

29. Tuch, interview, 24–25.

30. Jodie Lewinsohn, memorandum to Harold Schneidman (assistant director for policy and plans, USIA), copied to R. Peter Straus and Hans N. Tuch, January 4, 1978, 2–3.

31. Hans N. Tuch, memorandum to Jodie Lewinsohn, January 9, 1978, 2.

32. David Williams, interview with author, Falls Church, Va., March 17, 2001.

33. Barbara Schiele, "VOA Languages 1942–1982," April 3, 1981, 6.

34. Tuch, interview, 31.

35. Mary G. F. Bitterman, letter to author, August 13, 2001.

36. Author's notes, 1980.

37. Gary Sick, *All Fall Down: America's Tragic Encounter with Iran* (New York: Random House, 1985), 337, 340–341.

38. The "double lead," Reagan's inauguration and the release of the hostages, topped the 12:30 P.M. VOA news summary of January 20, 1981.

39. Alan L. Heil, Jr., memorandum to the files, November 10, 1981, 2.

40. Williams, interview.

41. The State Department and ICA also lifted the ban on VOA news analyses about China when Beijing and Tokyo signed a peace treaty on August 12, 1978. The United States and China established full diplomatic relations on January 1, 1979.

42. John Reinhardt, memorandum to R. Peter Straus, August 14, 1978, 1.

43. Tuch, in Jack O'Brien, oral-history interview by Hans N. Tuch, Washington, D.C., February 5, 1988, 24.

9. The Tumultuous 1980s: A Lost Horizon Regained

1. Mary G. F. Bitterman, farewell remarks to the Voice of America staff, January 28, 1981, 2, 4.

2. Quoted in Marguerite Michaels, "The Surprising Success of Charles Wick," *Parade*, March 31, 1985, 8.

3. Philip Nicolaides, memorandum to Charles Z. Wick (director, USIA), October 20, 1981, 4. At that time, Nicolaides was adviser to Wick on VOA policy. He was later named VOA deputy director of programs for commentary and analysis, a post he held from late 1981 until late February 1982.

4. Charles Fenyvesi, "I Hear America Mumbling," *Washington Post Magazine*, July 19, 1981.

5. Carnes Lord, "The Past and Future of Public Diplomacy," *Orbis*, January 1998, 51.

6. Quoted in ibid., 52.

7. NCA log, August 18, 1981. The report in *Far East Economic Review* also attracted congressional interest. I was summoned to testify on October 5 before the House International Relations Committee on the implications of U.S. refugee reset-

tlement policies and programs. A few weeks earlier, VOA correspondent Wayne Corey (chapter 7) had been questioned by a congressional delegation that was visiting Hong Kong. Asked by a delegation member if an interagency task force should vet VOA news on the flight of boat people, Corey said that if that became policy, he would resign immediately. Congress, apparently satisfied that VOA had played the issue straight, dropped the matter.

8. Mark Willen, in *Room News*, September 9, 1981, 1. Willen was a duty editor in the VOA newsroom who handled the assassination attempt against President Reagan on March 31, 1981, with exceptional sensitivity and skill. He refused, for example, to authorize the broadcast that afternoon of an erroneous commercial-network report that the president had been shot in the heart and carefully placed in context Secretary of State Alexander Haig's assertion that he was "in charge."

9. Ernest B. Furgurson, "VOA," *Baltimore Sun* News Service, September 9, 1982.

10. Fitzhugh Green, *American Propaganda Abroad: From Benjamin Franklin to Ronald Reagan* (New York: Hippocrene Books, 1988), 90–91.

11. Quoted in Willen, in *Room News*, 5.

12. Michael Getler, "Weinberger," *Washington Post* News Service, September 23, 1981.

13. Philip Nicolaides, memorandum to Charles Z. Wick, September 21, 1981, 5, 7.

14. Nicolaides, memorandum to Wick, October 20, 1981, 2.

15. Bill Read was assigned back at the Voice six months later to complete the strategic plan. Although promised a permanent position, he soon was transferred back to the agency a second time and later resigned.

16. Francis X. Clines and Bernard Weinraub, "Briefing," *New York Times*, November 4, 1981, A20.

17. Steve Bell's commentary was broadcast on the ABC radio network on November 19, 1981.

18. Quoted in Robert Leonard, "Charles Percy Comments on VOA," VOA correspondent report no. 2-8133, November 17, 1981.

19. The resolution was adopted by acclamation at Sigma Delta Chi's national convention, November 14, 1981.

20. Bernie Kamenske became a senior editor at CNN. Five and a half months later, he spoke at a symposium, "Voice of America at the Crossroads," Media Institute, Washington, D.C., June 24, 1982, 10, 11, 14.

21. Editorial, *New York Times*, December 24, 1981, A22.

22. John Trattner, "America's Voice," *New York Times*, February 6, 1982, A23. Earlier in his career, Trattner was a colleague of Frank Cummins and the author, as an editor in VOA Worldwide English of a program to Europe.

23. Laurien Alexandre, *The Voice of America: From Détente to the Reagan Doctrine* (Norwood, N.J.: Ablex, 1988), 88. See also Edward DeFontaine (chief, News and Current Affairs) to newspaper editors, July 3, 1986, on the tenth anniversary of the signing of the VOA Charter as law.

24. Bernard Weinraub, "Panel Urges Reagan to Guard Credibility of Voice of America," *New York Times*, July 20, 1982, A1.

25. Government editorials broadcast on VOA included "By Hook and Crook," July 29, 1983; "Shave Closer, Sleep Better," January 11, 1984; and "Comrade, Can You Spare a Dime?" August 16, 1986.

26. Michael Nelson, *War of the Black Heavens: The Battles of Western Broadcasting in the Cold War* (Syracuse, N.Y.: Syracuse University Press, 1997), 176–177;

Carolyn Weaver, "When the Voice of America Ignores Its Charter," *Columbia Journalism Review,* November–December 1988, 36–37.

27. Chinese, for example, has thousands of characters, far beyond the capability of a single keyboard. SNAP was designed for an adapter in the Chinese Branch to type in the approximate sound of the Chinese word into his or her computer in pinyin, a Roman-alphabet equivalent of the intended word or phrase. Then a hierarchical search begins, until the proper Mandarin Chinese character pops up on the screen. The search occasionally can extend to seven levels. Before 1986, scripts were handwritten and edited. SNAP immensely improved the appearance of scripts and significantly aided Chinese Branch announcers (frequently different from the writers and editors of the scripts) during their live reading of news in studios.

28. Chris Kern, "SNAP: A Five Year Retrospective," USIA Technology Forum internal newsletter, December 1991, 1, 6–7.

29. Greg Flakus, "Behind the Story: Reporting from Cape Canaveral," *Voice Magazine,* June–July 1986, 4.

30. Transcript of Reagan's remarks, Voice of America live broadcast that began at 1830 UTC, January 28, 1986.

31. Lawrence Mosher, "VOA Handles a Touchy Issue . . . The Way Other Media Do," *National Journal,* January 24, 1987, 206–207.

32. Voice of America, Office of External Affairs, *Voice of America: A Brief History* (Washington, D.C.: Voice of America, Office of External Affairs, 1998), 18.

33. "Helms, Conservatives, Put Kibosh on Sheehan VOA Bid," *Broadcasting Magazine,* March 17, 1986, 94.

34. John E. Lennon, "A Pilot Study of Differences Between the Carter and Reagan Administrations' Influence on Voice of America News, 1977–1985" (master's thesis, University of Maryland, 1993), 50, 81–83.

35. Author's notes, December 1981.

36. Carlson, interview, 30.

37. Maureen Jane Nemecek, "Speaking of America: The Voice of America, Its Mission and Message, 1942–1982" (Ph.D. diss., University of Maryland, 1984), 413.

38. "If the World Is to Listen" [editorial], *Christian Science Monitor,* November 16, 1981.

10. The Epochal Years: 1969 and 1989

1. Philomena Jurey, *A Basement Seat to History: Tales of Covering Presidents Nixon, Ford, Carter, and Reagan for the Voice of America* (Washington, D.C.: Linus Press, 1995), 355. Reuel Zinn's photo of the inscription appears in Jurey's fascinating account of her years as VOA's White House correspondent.

2. Voice of America, Office of Programs, "VOA Coverage on the Flight of *Apollo XI,*" September 11, 1969.

3. Rhett Turner, interview with author, Washington, D.C., March 29, 2001.

4. Citation of the Peabody Awards committee, University of Georgia School of Journalism, 1970.

5. Michael A. Hanu, "Eagle on the Moon" (transcript of documentary on the *Apollo* moon landing, July 25, 1969). Quotes from President Kennedy come from two speeches: to a joint meeting of Congress, May 25, 1961 (available at: www.cs.umb.edu.jfklibrary/j52561.htm), and at Rice University, September 12, 1962 (available at: www.rice.edu/fondren/woodson/speech.html).

6. Michael Nelson, *War of the Black Heavens: The Battles of Western Broadcasting in the Cold War* (Syracuse, N.Y.: Syracuse University Press, 1997), xiii.

7. Ibid., xvi.

8. Quoted in Marcel Fodor, "VOA History, 1942–1967" (manuscript, 1967), chap. 23, p. 12.

9. Quoted in Francis Ronalds, "VOA at 45" (script of VOA focus documentary, February 23, 1987), 7.

10. David K. Shipler, *Russia: Broken Idols, Solemn Dreams* (New York: Times Books, 1983), 35.

11. Quoted in author's prepared remarks for briefing of visitors to VOA, summer 1982, 2.

12. Quoted in Michael Dobbs, "In the Service of the Motherland: Soviet Society Bears Wounds of the Afghan War," *Washington Post*, February 14, 1989, A17.

13. Judith Latham, "Russian Branch: A Profile," *Voice Magazine*, June–July 1989, 6.

14. Mark Hopkins, interview with author, Washington, D.C., September 20, 2001.

15. Andrei Sakharov, interview with Zora Safir-Hopkins (translated by Bill Skundrich and Tom Gilfether), January 8, 1987.

16. Quoted in Alan L. Heil, Jr., "VOA Builds Democracy in Closed Societies," in *United States Information Agency: A Commemoration* (Washington, D.C.: United States Information Agency, 1999), 52.

17. Misha Glenny, "Spring Fever: The Momentous Events in Czechoslovakia," *Listener* [news magazine for BBC audience], November 30, 1989.

18. George H. W. Bush, address to the annual convention of the National Association of Broadcasters, Atlanta, Ga. April 2, 1990, 4.

19. Barbara J. Tripp, "Programming Effectiveness Report," memorandum to Joseph B. Bruns, July 20, 1993, 1.

20. Kenneth Y. Best, statement submitted for the record to the House, Committee on International Relations, Subcommittee on Africa, 105th Cong., 1st sess., July 15, 1997, 2, 10. Best was the editor of a newspaper in Liberia that had been shut down five times by the regime of Samuel Doe, and he was imprisoned three times. Later, he established the first independent newspaper in the West African country of Gambia, but was deported after a military coup there in 1992. Despite these setbacks, Best told the subcommittee, both papers later resumed publication.

11. Out of Africa: The Triumph of Straight Talk

1. Connie Stephens, interview with author, Washington, D.C., January 5, 1999. Stephens provided a wealth of detail on internal Africa Division dynamics and was among its most talented managers over the years.

2. Stephens, interview.

3. Gwen Dillard, interview with author, Washington, D.C., November 21, 2002.

4. This account is based on Sonja Pace, interview with author, Washington, D.C., August 23, 2000; her telexed message to the VOA newsroom in April 1987; and a diary she wrote shortly after returning to Abidjan from her mission in the Sahara, April 13, 1987.

5. Margaret Binda, weekly report to Sid Davis, August 20, 1993, 1–2.

6. Ferdinand Ferella, interview with author, Washington, D.C., April 25, 2001; Gwen Dillard, fax to author, April 23, 2001. Ferella initially tried to get into Kigali from Nairobi, but fighting between the Rwandan Patriotic Front (RPF) and the

Hutu extremists at the airport prevented his entry for several days. So Ferella flew to neighboring Burundi and crossed the border to accompany the RPF, which was moving on Kigali. After a week or so, the RPF expelled the Hutu-led extremists, and Ferella was able to report from Kigali. Dillard was chief of the French-to-Africa Branch in 1994 and familiar with details of the coverage.

7. Larry James, e-mail to Mark Hopkins (director, VOA London Regional Center), August 19, 1994, 1.

8. Dillard, fax.

9. Voice of America, "VOA Africa Broadcasts Fact Sheet," January 1997, 1; author's notes.

10. Quoted in Douglas B. Roberts, "Reporter's Notebook: Rwanda/Refugees," current affairs feature no. 3-26330, December 3, 1996, 4–5.

11. For a description of the annual Cowan Award for Humanitarian Reporting, see chapter 18. Scott Stearns won the award in 1999 for his coverage of Central and East Africa.

12. Voice of America, weekly report summary, March 18, 1997.

13. This summary of coverage of the election in South Africa by the Africa Division is pieced together from Geoffrey L. Cowan, remarks at swearing-in ceremony as Voice of America twenty-second director, April 26, 1994, 7, and Deborah Block, "VOA Covers the South African Elections," *On the Air* [internal newsletter of Bureau of Broadcasting], October 1994, 14–15, an account of on-scene coverage.

14. This account is based on logs and extensive notes of the meeting of the Board of Broadcasting Governors, subcommittee on Africa, that I attended.

15. Broadcasting Board of Governors, "Horn of Africa Broadcasting," in *U.S. Broadcasting Board of Governors Handbook* (Washington, D.C.: Intermedia, 1997), 4.

16. Pace, interview.

17. Mimi Sebhatu, interview with author, Washington, D.C., September 9, 1999. Mimi's sighting on Ethiopia's northern frontier occurred on June 6, 1998.

18. Evelyn S. Lieberman, "VOA Africa Projects Underway or Already Completed" (briefing paper, Voice of America, Africa Division), prepared for the House, Committee on International Relations, Subcommittee on Africa, 105th Cong., 1st sess., July 1997.

19. VOA's Portuguese-to-Africa Service was the prime source of independent news in that civil war–torn nation for many years.

20. Gwen Dillard, "Globalization, the U.S. Media, and the Voice of America's Coverage of Africa" (address presented at "The Challenges and Opportunities of Globalization at the Dawn of the New Millennium," symposium, Howard University, Washington, D.C., April 12, 2001).

21. Ousmane Mahamane's rule, and democracy in Niger, were short lived. In January 1996, the president was overthrown in a military coup and the constitution suspended.

22. The number of conflicts in Africa doubled between 1989 and 2000, from eleven to twenty-one, according to Tim Docking, *Peacekeeping in Africa*, special report (Washington, D.C.: U.S. Institute of Peace, 2001), 5.

12. On Language: Words and Their Stories

1. Chase Untermeyer, "Comments by Prince Norodom Ranaridh," memorandum to Sid Davis (director of programs), October 4, 1991.

2. Mark Lewis, "Voice of America's Special English Fortieth Anniversary," *ESL Magazine*, September–October 1999, 16. Lewis compares reading speeds: U.S. commercial broadcasting, 150 words a minute; VOA standard English, 130 words a minute; VOA Special English, 90 words a minute.

3. Voice of America, Special English briefing paper prepared for a program review, January 1990, 1.

4. Quoted in Voice of America, transcript of fortieth-anniversary celebration of VOA Special English, December 1, 1999, 1.

5. Dick Borden, after launching Special English, became editor of regional programs in the Worldwide English Division. He taught many who later were to leave their imprint on America's Voice, including Jack Shellenberger, Frank Cummins, John Trattner, Lee Hall, Ray Kabaker, Irving Lind, and the author.

6. Quoted in Michael A. Hanu, "The Biography of an Experiment" (transcript of VOA documentary on Special English, October 1994), 11.

7. Ibid., 13.

8. Lewis, "Voice of America's Special English Fortieth Anniversary," 17.

9. Hanu, "Biography of an Experiment," 15.

10. George Grow and David Jarmul, "This Is America no. 468—Thirtieth Anniversary of Special English" (script of VOA feature, October 16, 1989), 3.

11. Ibid., 4.

12. Frank Beardsley, "An Idea Whose Time Had Come—30 Years Ago" [letter to the editor], *Washington Post*, August 2, 1989, A22.

13. VOA, Special English briefing paper, 5; Lewis, "Voice of America's Special English Fortieth Anniversary," 18.

14. Dobrin Tzotzkov to VOA Special English writing competition, 1993.

15. Quoted in VOA, Special English briefing paper, 6.

16. One possible explanation for this expression comes from New England in the late eighteenth century: after a day on the battlefields, Revolutionary War militiamen would retire to a tavern for ale. They discovered that they could get an extra "kick" from their drink by stirring it with a hot poker, known as a "logger," from the nearby fireplace. The extra "kick" led to loud arguments and even fistfights among the militiamen, who were said to be "at loggerheads." See also Barry Newman, "World Speaks English, Often None Too Well; Results Are Tragicomic," *Wall Street Journal*, March 22, 1995, 1.

17. John Tusa, *A World in Your Ear* (London: Broadside Books, 1992), 107.

18. Author's recollections from several Hausa-language program reviews, 1980–1997. The precise equivalent in Hausa is *jirqin sama mai sauk'ar ungulu*.

19. John Buescher, remarks at a Tibetan Service program review, October 9, 1992.

20. Of course, John Buescher notes, the phrase "most favored nation" was not really accurate in English either. In practice, it meant "normal" trade relations. VOA Tibetan later changed the term to reflect current common usage, permanent normal trade relations (PNTR). Buescher believes that the Dalai Lama has as well.

21. Voice of America, translation of Latvian Service script, October 7, 1989, 1.

22. John Pomfret, "Resolving Crisis Was a Matter of Interpretation," *Washington Post*, April 12, 2001, A1.

23. Interestingly, the American embassy in Beijing, before issuing its official translation of the letter, checked with the VOA Chinese Branch in Washington to be sure that the letter was correct in Mandarin Chinese.

24. At times, traditional translations or adaptations become so ingrained that it is difficult or impractical to change them. Chinese offers one example. Even before VOA existed, according to East Asia and Pacific Division managing editor Jay Henderson, Chinese used the term *guo wu yuan* (state affairs council) to describe the Department of State. That gives it the appearance, in Chinese, of a somewhat higher status than other cabinet-level departments in the U.S. government. It is not really an accurate adaptation. But the weight of historical precedent and usage, Henderson says, has caused the staff of the Chinese Branch to stay with the traditional terminology on the assumption that most listeners do indeed understand that the State Department is equivalent to a Ministry of Foreign Affairs and not a cabinet or prime minister's office.

25. Sanford J. Ungar, "News and Views Got Inside China During the Airplane Crisis," *Nieman Reports*, summer 2001, 89.

26. Foreign Broadcast Information Service, "Battle over Mother of Battles," in *No Uncertain Terms* (Langley, Va.: Foreign Broadcast Information Service, 1990), 10.

27. Tusa, *World in Your Ear*, 109.

13. Music: The Universal Language

1. Bess Lomax, *OWI Broadcasting Manual* (Washington, D.C.: Office of War Information, Committee on Broadcasting Operations, 1945), installment 7, pp. 1–2.

2. Peter Jennings, remarks on ABC Information Network, May 23, 1996. Jennings, a foreign correspondent before he became ABC-TV's senior news anchor, broadcast a tribute to Willis Conover shortly after the jazz host's death.

3. Lawrence Elliott, "The World's Favorite American," *Reader's Digest*, July 1985, 94.

4. Fred Bouchard, "Willis Conover, the Voice Heard Round the World," *Down Beat*, September 1995, 28.

5. Quoted in W. Royal Stokes, "Willis Conover: Voice of Jazz Abroad," *Jazz Times*, July 1986, 12.

6. Adam Makowicz, "Willis Conover Remembered" (manuscript, September 1996).

7. Jennings, remarks.

8. United States Information Service, Moscow, e-mail to Sherwood (Woody) Demitz (chief, Eurasia Division), May 31, 1996.

9. Quoted in Voice of America, "Tribute to Willis Conover, 1920–1996" (program for VOA memorial concert, June 5, 1996). Performing were Keter Betts, Charlie Byrd, Paquito D'Rivera, Billy Taylor, and Joe Williams.

10. This account is based on Judy Massa, "A Dream Come True: Contest Winner Comes to America," *Voice Magazine*, October–November 1988, 6–8, and Alan L. Heil, Jr., "VOA Builds Democracy in Closed Societies," in United States Information Agency, *United States Information Agency: A Commemoration* (Washington, D.C.: United States Information Agency, 1999), 70.

11. Quoted in Massa, "Dream Come True," 8.

12. Voice of America, press release on Massa's retirement, January 22, 2001.

13. Evelyn Tan Powers, "World Audiences Attuned to U.S. Country Music," *USA Today International Edition*, November 29, 1995, 8.

14. Quoted in Brian Q. Silver and Judith Latham, "World Music on VOA," *Voice Magazine*, winter 1990, 6.

15. USIA Archives, "Edward R. Morrow Recruits Leo Sarkisian for VOA," in United States Information Agency, *United States Information Agency: A Commemoration* (Washington, D.C.: United States Information Agency, 1999), 27.

16. Sanford J. Ungar, remarks at the opening of Leo Sarkisian's "Faces of Africa" art exhibition, Voice of America, Washington, D.C., February 21, 2001.

17. Mark Lewis, remarks at the opening of Leo Sarkisian's "Faces of Africa" art exhibition, Voice of America, Washington, D.C., February 21, 2001. See also Lewis, "Leo Sarkisian: Music Man of Africa," *Monitoring Times*, October 2000, 18–20, and "The Music Man: LEO SARKISIAN," *Beat* 19 (2000): 12.

18. Leo Sarkisian writes and produces *Music Time in Africa*. He appears in nearly every program as an expert interviewee to explain selections from his rare collection. He is a member of the Society of Ethnomusicology, the Asia Society, and the Center for Black Music Research at the University of Chicago.

19. Author's notes of Rita Rochelle, remarks at the opening of Leo Sarkisian's "Faces of Africa" art exhibition, Voice of America, Washington, D.C., February 21, 2001.

20. Brian Q. Silver, "A Surbahar Concert" (notes for a program for Embassy of India and World Bank/International Monetary Fund Club concert, World Bank, Washington, D.C., April 29, 2000), 1, 3.

21. Brian Q. Silver, "Another Musical Universe: The American Recording Industry and Indian Music, 1955–1965" (paper presented at a seminar on Indian music and the West, sponsored by the Sangreet Research Academy, National Centre for the Performing Arts, Mumbai, India, November 29–December 1, 1996), 225–226.

22. Silver and Latham, "World Music on VOA," 8.

23. Ibid., 7.

24. Ibid., 8.

25. Brian Q. Silver, interview with author, Washington, D.C., April 17, 2001.

26. Ed Gursky, interview with author, Washington, D.C., April 25, 2001. Ed produced a four-hour music programming block for VOA Music Mix, and used the on-air name Ed Kowalksi. He became fascinated with radio and programming of radio music while recovering from measles as a twelve-year-old in Manhattan in the mid-1940s. His father, an engineer, owned all the latest electronic devices, including early TV receivers. They were out of order during Ed's bout with the measles, however, and he turned, of necessity, to the radio. The rest is history.

27. John Stevenson, interview with author, Washington, D.C., April 26, 2001.

28. For more details about the pioneering work of the Latin America Division in satellite distribution of real-time news in Spanish and Portuguese to the Western Hemisphere, see chapter 16.

29. Gursky credits VOA Europe with being extremely important in shaping the musical programming of the Voice in the twenty-first century. He notes that the two pioneer operations managers of VOA Europe, Terry Hourigan and John Stevenson, launched it on October 15, 1985, with only about eight weeks' notice.

30. Gursky, interview.

14. To the Roof of the World: The Tibetan Service Miracle

1. Author's notes, 1997.

2. International Broadcasting Bureau, Office of Research, "International Media Use by Tibetan Exiles and Travelers" (research memorandum, March 26, 2001), 1.

Forty-five percent of the adults questioned said that they had listened to VOA Tibetan at least once weekly. Other services mentioned were Radio Free Asia, 22 percent, and All India Radio, 21 percent. About 500 adult travelers from Tibet were interviewed in Dharamsala and Bodhgaya, India, and in Kathmandu, Nepal. Opinion sampling within Chinese-occupied Tibet is impossible.

3. The Network Control Center in Washington on this first Tibetan transmission had inadvertently reversed two broadcast paths, sending Portuguese broadcasts intended for Brazil to Tibet, and Tibetan broadcasts to Brazil.

4. John Buescher, "Ten Years to Tibet" (program and remarks for the tenth anniversary of VOA Tibetan Service, March 26, 2001).

5. Quoted in John Buescher, "Tibetan Service Profile" (script for VOA Current Affairs, May 12, 1992), 2.

6. John Buescher, "Tibetans Cannot Stop Listening to VOA," *Tune In*, October 2000, 3.

7. John Buescher, "VOA Tibetan Service" (profile prepared for a Tibetan Service program review, December 2000), 1.

8. Chyali Chambasonam (Tibetan Living Buddha), cited in Jay Henderson (managing editor, East Asia and Pacific Division), "The Real Reason the Karmapa Left Tibet," e-mail to author, March 13, 2001, based on a report on Chinesenewsnet.com, March 7, 2000.

9. Jay Henderson, "VOA Tibetan Uses Opposite Methods to Score Back to Back Successes," e-mail to author, February 6, 2001.

10. Henderson, e-mail, March 13, 2000.

11. John Buescher to Bob Knopes (chief, East Asia and Pacific Division), 1992.

12. Kelu Chao, "VOA Report on Tibetan Dissent," e-mail to Robert Reilly, July 16, 2002.

13. Buescher, "Ten Years to Tibet," 5.

14. Ibid.

15. Middle East Flashbacks: VOA and the Wars of 1967 and 1991

1. Douglas A. Boyd, *Broadcasting in the Arab World: A Survey of the Electronic Media in the Middle East*, 3d ed. (Ames: Iowa State University Press, 1999), 5.

2. In June 1991, the *Wall Street Journal* alleged in an article that "Saddam Hussein received an unexpected boost during the Gulf War from the Voice of America." For contrast, see Tony Horwitz and Geraldine Brooks, "Baghdad Is a Blend of Bravado and Fear," *Wall Street Journal*, January 15, 1991, 1.

3. Harold F. Radday (director of communications, Center for Strategic and International Studies) to Elizabeth Borst, *New York Post*, June 21, 1991.

4. Isa Khalil Sabbagh, *"As the Arabs Say . . ."* (Washington, D.C.: Sabbagh Management Corporation, 1983), 27. Isa Sabbagh was a commentator and broadcaster on both the BBC and VOA Arabic Services in the 1940s and 1950s who later became a senior U.S. diplomat and liaison with the royal families of Libya and Saudi Arabia. He explains the Arabic saying about people being an indispensable part of paradise: "the oft-cited generosity of the Arabs stems directly from their instinctive love of company, of people to talk to, and of guests to visit and share a meal or an event."

5. An exception was when U.S. Marines landed in Lebanon in 1958 in response to a brief civil war fomented by Nasser-led Arab nationalists who were determined

to upset the country's carefully balanced confessional political power-sharing arrangement among Christians, Sunni, Shia Muslims, and Druze. Then, the Beirut operation was the hub for a time of VOA's around-the-clock Lebanese crisis broadcasts.

6. This account is based on the author's notes. Some facets of the brief history are drawn from my VOA correspondent reports of May 19, 22, 31 and June 5–10, 1967.

7. Excerpted from Alan L. Heil, Jr., VOA correspondent report, datelined Cairo, June 9, 1967.

8. Alan L. Heil, Jr., to William Minehart (chief, Near East and South Asia Division), June 1967. The total output of the Cairo subcenter from May 16 until it ceased operations on June 10 was 144 reports and interviews.

9. Normally, Arabic was on the air for seven and a half hours a day; this grew to fifteen and a half hours daily during Operation Desert Storm, with a few days' expansion (depending on events) up to eighteen and a half hours. Increases in broadcasts in English to the region were from ten to fifteen and a half hours, and in Farsi to Iran from three to four hours daily.

10. "New Persian Gulf Threats" [government editorial], July 25, 1990, 1.

11. "The VOA Under Siege," *Washington Times*, July 2, 1992, G2.

12. The advent of satellites led to the center's closure in 1977. The technical quality of transmissions via satellite was such an improvement over shortwave that it was no longer necessary to have a more expensive overseas programming unit near the relay station to produce music programming of acceptable audio quality for the medium-wave transmitters in Rhodes.

13. Robert S. Fortner, *Analysis of Voice of America Broadcasts to the Middle East during the Persian Gulf Crisis* (Washington, D.C.: Center for International and Strategic Studies, 1991), 56.

14. Chase Untermeyer, "Response to Office of Inspector General's Report, 'A Critique of VOA Broadcasts during the Persian Gulf Crisis,'" draft memorandum to Henry J. Catto (director, USIA), September 1992, 5.

15. United States Information Agency, Office of Inspector General, "Inspection of Allegations Concerning VOA Arabic Broadcasting during the Persian Gulf Crisis" (draft report, July 29, 1991), 1.

16. Fortner, *Analysis of Voice of America Broadcasts to the Middle East*; Mark Blitzer and Neil Pickett, *Review of VOA Programming During the Persian Gulf War* (Indianapolis: Hudson Institute, 1991).

17. The precise number of interviews: procoalition, 242; pro-Iraq, 64; neutral, 33 (Voice of America, Arabic Branch, "Interviews Conducted during January, 1991," and "Interviews Conducted during February, 1991" [surveys prepared for independent reviewers, March 1991]).

18. Voice of America, Office of Programs, "Point by Point Discussion of VOA Gulf Crisis Coverage" (talking paper, June 24, 1991), 2.

19. Ibid., 4.

20. Blitzer and Pickett, *Review of VOA Programming*, 1.

21. VOA, Office of Programs, "Point by Point Discussion," 5.

22. Sid Davis, memorandum to Richard W. Carlson (director, VOA), October 2, 1990.

23. Authorization for VOA Arabic TVRO feed for USIS Dhahran, Saudi Arabia, December 21, 1990.

24. United States Information Agency, Office of Research, "Foreign Radio Listening Rates High in Four Arab Gulf Nations; VOA Increases Audience during Crisis" (research memorandum, February 14, 1991), 1.

25. Richard W. Carlson, remarks to Voice of America staff on the eve of the Gulf War, January 15, 1991.

26. Mohammed Ghuneim, VOA correspondent report translated from Arabic, March 1, 1991.

16. Into the 1990s: The Brave New World of Multimedia

1. For a detailed initial account of Pol Pot's last hours, see Nate Thayer, "Dying Breath: The Inside Story of Pol Pot's Last Days and the Disintegration of the Movement He Created," *Far East Economic Review*, April 30, 1998 (available at: www.cambodian.com/polpot). Subsequently, Thayer quoted former Khmer Rouge officials as confirming that their leader had taken a lethal cocktail of antimalarial pills and tranquillizers to avoid being taken alive. His follow-up account appears in *Far East Economic Review*, January 21, 1999 (available at: www.feer.com/breaking_news/pol). See also Keith Richburg, "Pol Pot's World Ended with a Whimper," *Washington Post*, April 30, 1998, A28.

2. Ernest B. Furgurson, "We Start to Be Mankind," *Baltimore Sun*, August 23, 1991, 9A.

3. David Hoffman, "Global Communications Network Was Pivotal in Defeat of Junta." *Washington Post*, August 23, 1991, A27.

4. Series of messages to Allen Weinstein (president of the Center for Democracy), in "Make It Known," *Washington Post*, August 20, 1991, A15.

5. John Hughes, "Moscow Witnesses an Information Revolution," *Christian Science Monitor*, August 29, 1991, 11.

6. Quoted in Tony Mauro, "Freedom's Voice Proved Impossible to Silence," *USA Today*, August 22, 1991, 3.

7. Richard Araujo, interview with author, Washington, D.C., February 28, 2001.

8. José "Pepe" del Rio, interview with author, Washington, D.C., May 17, 2001. These anecdotes are based on his recollections of high points in his quarter-century career at VOA.

9. Araujo, interview.

10. Quoted in Devorah Goldburg, "Albanian Anecdotes," *USIA World*, July–August 1991, 6.

11. Research conducted by the United States Information Agency in Albania in 1993 indicated that more than 60 percent of adult Albanians were regular listeners to VOA, one of the highest audience ratings in its history. Elez Biberaj, one of the nation's leading scholars on Albania, later anchored a VOA-TV daily broadcast widely watched in Albania and Kosovo.

12. Much of this account is based on the author's notes.

13. Radio Free Europe's South Slavic Service also began relaying B-92 material a few hours after VOA.

14. Frank Shkreli, interview with author, Washington, D.C., May 7, 2001.

15. Janice Bell and Dina S. Smeltz, comps., "Kosovo Albanians Relied on Albanian TV and Foreign Radio During Crisis" (survey report compiled for the Department of State, Office of Research, November 24, 1999), 3.

16. Ilir Ikonomi, "Reporting from Kosovo," *Tune In*, August 1999, 3.

17. Unsigned Reuters article, datelined Washington, D.C., December 4, 1996.

18. From 1999 to 2001, those VOA services reduced and converted into multimedia production units (radio, television, and Internet) included Armenian, Azerbaijani, Bulgarian, Czech, Georgian, Hungarian, Latvian, Lithuanian, Polish, Romanian, Slovak, Slovene, and Uzbek.

19. I wrote "weekly look-aheads," journal style, to alert senior management to key issues and, with mixed results, to keep action items moving in the complex maze of VOA, IBB, and BBG administrative clearances in the mid- to late 1990s.

20. Jay Henderson, "Look Back at Taiwan Election," e-mail to author, May 9, 2001.

21. Author's account of the multimedia production.

22. Much of this account is based on John E. Lennon, interview with author, Washington, D.C., September 26, 2000, combined with my own notes on VOA perspectives.

23. Public Law 100-204, title II, 100th Cong., 1st sess. (December 22, 1987), *VOA Charter Applied to Worldnet TV.* See also United States Information Agency, Worldnet Television, press release, February 25, 1988.

24. Geoffrey Cowan became the dean of the Annenberg School for Communication at the University of Southern California, Los Angeles.

25. Connie Stephens, interview with author, Washington, D.C., April 20, 2001.

26. Thomas Friedman, "Of Body and Soul," *New York Times,* July 17, 1997, A23.

27. John Chancellor, September 1, 1965. This statement by the former VOA director was cited at the dedication of a radio and television studio named in his honor at VOA headquarters, Washington, D.C., September 4, 1997.

17. The Struggle to Get It Straight: Independence at the New Millennium

1. Kevin Klose (director, International Broadcasting Bureau), remarks at a town meeting for International Broadcasting Bureau and Voice of America employees with Evelyn S. Lieberman (director, VOA), October 30, 1998.

2. Alan L. Heil, Jr., talking points for Voice of America senior managers on the impact of budget cuts, May 23, 1990, 2.

3. Quoted in Ruth Sinai, "VOA Cuts," Associated Press, February 1, 1991.

4. Richard W. Carlson, interview with author, McLean, Va., May 14, 2001.

5. Voice of America, Office of Broadcast Operations, tape of town meeting of Voice of America staff with Bruce Gelb and Richard W. Carlson, January 7, 1991.

6. Grantee international broadcast networks are so named because they receive U.S. federal grants to operate. However, they are privately incorporated organizations—not, like the Voice of America, federal agencies. Radio and TV Martí, although surrogate in nature, like the grantees, are anomalies because they are part of the International Broadcasting Bureau, as is VOA. Radio Martí was advocated by powerful Cuban-American political leaders in southern Florida and backed by conservatives in the Reagan administration. The radio network was created in 1982 and began broadcasting three years later; TV Martí was established in 1990. In the mid-1990s, the same lobbies successfully pressed for the move of the headquarters of Radio and TV Martí from Washington to Miami.

7. Department of State, *A Report of the President's Task Force on U.S. Government International Broadcasting,* publication no. 9925 (Washington, D.C.: Depart-

ment of State, 1991); Department of State, *The Commission on Broadcasting to the People's Republic of China*, publication no. 9997 (Washington, D.C.: Department of State, 1992). Those in the minority on the task force were Rita Crocker Clements, Rozanne L. Ridgway, Viviane M. Warren, and Abbott McC. Washburn. Dissenting members of the commission were Donald Anderson, Nien Cheng, Merle Goldman, and Gene P. Mater.

8. Quoted in George Lardner, Jr., "'Free China' Radio Backed by Senators," *Washington Post*, June 10, 1989, A16.

9. The remaining dated entries in this chapter are drawn from a chronology of steps toward international broadcasting reorganization that I compiled in October 1999.

10. William J. Clinton, "Statement on International Broadcast Programs," June 15, 1993, in *Public Papers of the Presidents of the United States*, book 1, *January 20–July 31, 1993* (Washington, D.C.: Government Printing Office, 1994), 857–858.

11. Public Law 103-236, title III, secs. 301–314, 103d Cong., 2d sess. (April 30, 1994), *United States International Broadcasting Act*.

12. Charles H. Percy, "Bring Back the VOA Charter," *Washington Post*, July 14, 1994, A23.

13. Ibid.

14. "The Voice of the V.O.A.," *New Yorker*, September 18, 1995, 41.

15. Much of this summary is drawn from Geoffrey Cowan, "Message for the IBB Community," November 8, 1996, a summary of the highlights of his thirty-two months as director of the Voice of America and, for the last ten months of his tenure, as director of the International Broadcasting Bureau as well.

16. As of the year 2001, VOA and its partners had recorded seventeen plays in the "Radio Theatre—Live!" series, including Mr. *Rickey Calls a Meeting*, *The Heiress*, *Barefoot in the Park*, *The Diary of Anne Frank*, *The House of Blue Leaves*, *Caine Mutiny Court Martial*, and *Seven Days in May*, and featuring such artists as Ed Asner, Paul Winfield, and Julie Harris. The performances were recorded and then broadcast worldwide on VOA and nationwide on National Public Radio.

17. Geoffrey Cowan, message to the Voice of America staff, January 1995, 1.

18. "Selected Programs the GOP Might Eliminate," *Wall Street Journal*, May 10, 1995.

19. Geoffrey L. Cowan and Joseph B. Bruns, "Why the United States Still Needs the Voice of America" (International Broadcasting Bureau and Voice of America summary, June 1995), 1–2.

20. Jonathan Landay, "Former Cold War Warrior Tunes into New World Order," *Christian Science Monitor* News Service, December 24, 1996.

21. This account is based on a series of conversations that the author had with David Burke on November 1, 1998, and a number of members of the Board of Governors, International Broadcasting Bureau, and Senate Foreign Relations Committee staff between January 28, 1998 and August 2, 1999.

22. At the turn of the century, the U.S. government editorials were prepared in the International Broadcasting Bureau, Office of Policy, which was distinct from VOA, and were carefully separated in broadcasts from other Voice programming. They were clearly labeled as government policy statements, usually were read by staff not heard elsewhere on the program, and made up about 2 percent of VOA airtime, subsequently increased in 2001 to around 4 percent. The Office of Policy also produced a discussion program, *On the Line*. It featured American policymakers as well as other specialists and was issued in shortened text form for adaptation by the language services.

23. *Foreign Affairs Reform and Restructuring Act of 1997*, "Report Together with Additional and Minority Views," 105th Cong., 1st sess., report no. 105-28 (Washington, D.C.: Government Printing Office, June 13, 1997), 15.

24. Proceedings and debates of the 105th Cong., 1st sess., *Congressional Record* 143, no. 158, November 10, 1997, S12363–S12364, S12383.

25. This account is based on program logs and on John E. Lennon, e-mail to Kevin Klose, December 10, 1997, 1–2. In that message, Lennon wrote: "Despite the nearly four-year-old International Broadcasting Act of 1994 which puts Worldnet squarely under the Charter with VOA, not enough has been done to separate Worldnet from its past; television at USIA is equated in most minds and places with policy explication, rather than news reporting and public affairs discussions."

26. Dick Bertel, e-mail to author, December 11, 1997.

27. Quoted in Ben Barber, "VOA Panel Spurns White House Bid, Airs Chinese Dissident's Interview Despite Plea Not to Embarrass Beijing," *Washington Times*, December 17, 1997, A15.

28. Quoted in Phil Kuntz, "U.S. Officials Tried to Stop Broadcast of Wei into China," *Wall Street Journal*, December 17, 1997, A24.

29. Quoted in Barber, "VOA Panel Spurns White House Bid," A15.

30. Joseph R. Biden, Jr., press release, December 17, 1997.

31. *Foreign Affairs Reform and Restructuring Act*, 105th Cong., 2d sess., conference report no. 105-432, joint explanatory statement submitted by Representative Benjamin Gilman (Republican of New York) (Washington, D.C.: Government Printing Office, March 10, 1998), 125–129.

32. Anonymous aide, interview with author, Washington, D.C., December 21, 1998.

33. In the mid-1970s, Ambassador Edmund Gullion had said that he doubted that the State Department really wanted to "be hitched to a radio station" chartered to broadcast accurate, objective, and comprehensive news.

34. Quoted in John Lindburg to Dawn Jensen (acting assistant attorney general), July 31, 1997, 1–12. The board and the State Department had turned to the Department of Justice for a ruling on the conflict between the diplomatic security acts and the firewall provisions in the broadcasting acts of the 1990s.

35. Marc B. Nathanson, remarks at ceremony marking the independence of U.S. government international broadcasting, October 13, 1999, 1, 5.

36. Biden had said on a number of occasions that "a government journalist is an oxymoron."

37. U.S. Congress, Senate, Committee on Foreign Relations, "Remarks by Senator Joseph R. Biden, Jr., at the International Broadcasting Independence Ceremony," October 13, 1999, 1–2.

18. America's Voice: A Voice for the Voiceless

1. Rashmi Shukla and Jagdish Sarin, "Child Laborers" (script for VOA broadcast, April 12, 1994), 2–3.

2. Ibid., 8.

3. Joseph D. O'Connell, Jr., "VOA's Rashmi Shukla and Jagdish Sarin Win the Cowan Award for Humanitarian Reporting on the Dowry System in India," Voice of America, press release, September 22, 2000, 1.

4. Carolyn Naifeh, e-mail to author, August 26, 2001.

5. William G. Blair, "Plea Saves Soviet Boy in Need of Surgery," *New York Times,* November 24, 1989, B1–B2.

6. European Roma Rights Center, report based on data compiled by the High Commission for National Minorities of the Organization for Security and Cooperation in Europe, Budapest, Hungary, 1999.

7. Negussie Mengesha, interview with author, Washington, D.C., June 4, 2001.

8. Tom Mahoney, "The Rwandan Refugee Tragedy" (script of VOA Current Affairs focus documentary no. 4-07581, July 24, 1994), 7–8. Sonja Pace turned over the two babies to some Rwandan women who were caring for orphans, and subsequently returned to the hospital to check up on the two older girls. The older one was able to keep her arm; emergency surgery prevented it from having to be amputated. The younger one, with the face wound, was expected to fully recover.

9. Robert L. Bernstein to Geoffrey Cowan, May 31, 1995, 1–2.

10. Bruce Harris to Bill Rodgers, June 9, 1995.

11. Barry Wood, "Sofia Hospital," VOA correspondent report, datelined Sofia, April 21, 1997, 1–3.

12. Dan Robinson, "Burma Impressions," VOA correspondent report, datelined Rangoon, August 4, 1994.

13. Stephanie Ho, "Reporter's Notebook: Ningxia, China," October 31, 1998.

14. Peter Ford, "A World Shift from Execution," *Christian Science Monitor,* June 8, 2001, 8.

15. Jim Malone, "Opinion Polls Indicate High American Support for McVeigh Execution," Washington, D.C., June 8, 2001, 0827 UTC.

16. Ray S. Rising to Tom Crosby, November 7, 1996.

17. Jay Henderson, "Weekly Report of VOA East Asia and Pacific Division," June 5, 2001, 1–2.

18. Jay Henderson, "On Whether Covering Human Rights Should Be Routine Reporting or a Moral Mission," e-mail to author, September 20, 2000.

19. Gwen Dillard, fax to author, April 23, 2001, 1–2.

20. Alex Belida, "Reporter's Notebook: Congo/Dead," VOA background report no. 5-37947, October 31, 1997.

19. Yearning to Breathe Free: Tales of Great VOA Escapes

1. George Berzins, interview with author, Alexandria, Va., July 31, 2001. George was also director of operations of TV Martí and, earlier, VOA deputy chief of information.

2. Joseph Buday, interview with author, Bethesda, Md., August 9, 2001.

3. Barbara Schiele, "VOA Broadcast Hours History, 1955–1989," February 25, 1992, 4, 11. Schiele's regularly updated histories were drawn from the records of Voice of America, Network Traffic; United States Information Agency; archivist Martin Manning; agency historians Bruce N. Gregory and Murray Larson; and Robert William Pirsein, *The Voice of America: An History of the International Broadcasting Activities of the United States Government, 1942–1962* (New York: Arno Press, 1979).

4. "Life Stories of VOA Broadcasters," July 25, 2001 (available at: voanews.com); Hamed Hosseini, interview with author, Washington, D.C., August 14, 2001.

5. Spozhmai Maiwandi, interview with author, Washington, D.C., October 14, 2001.

6. Tuck Outhuok, interview with author, Washington, D.C., April 7, 2002. See also Oksana Dragan, "From Cambodia's Killing Fields to VOA," English programs feature no. 7-36052, March 18, 2002.

7. Pierre Thomas, "To Albanian Sisters, Freedom at a Cost," *Washington Post*, July 20, 1990, B1; "Life Stories of VOA Broadcasters"; Isabela Cocoli, interview with author, Washington, D.C., August 5, 2001.

20. The Struggle Goes On: VOA at the Dawn of the Twenty-first Century

1. William Bell, interview with author, Washington, D.C., October 2, 2001.

2. This account is assembled from many interviews of Voice of America staff, monitoring of VOA from September 11 to 14, 2001, and a review of scripts available at voanews.com during the same period.

3. Jim Malone, "Defiant New York," VOA background report no. 5-501131, datelined New York, September 12, 2001, 1–3.

4. Voice of America, newswire log, September 11–13, 2001.

5. I watched a VOA-TV program, *News Review*, in a control room at Voice of America, 3:30 P.M. EDT, September 14, 2001.

6. William Marsh, "VOA Crisis Programming: Attack on the United States, the Aftermath, September 12–13," September 13, 2001, 2. See also Voice of America, East Asia and Pacific Division, report, September 13, 2002. The Chinese presence in the World Trade Center and casualties were reported by Wei Lin of VOA's Mandarin service.

7. Alex Belida, "Pentagon Eyewitness," VOA correspondent report no. 2-280307, datelined Arlington, Va., September 11, 2001.

8. Stephanie Mann Nealer, "Global Impact," VOA background report no. 5-50121, datelined Washington, D.C., September 13, 2001.

9. Quoted in Greg Flakus, "Terrorism/McCullough," VOA correspondent report no. 2-280322, datelined Washington, D.C., September 11, 2001.

10. Quoted in William Chien, e-mail to William Baum (chief, Chinese Branch), September 11, 2001. Chien interviewed more than 500 of the 535 members of Congress between 2000 and 2002. It was a tutorial in democracy, reflecting for listeners to Voice of America in Chinese and other languages the way in which Congress goes about its work and the legislative issues it faced. Chien's wife, Yang Yang, had been a paramedic in rural China during the Cultural Revolution. She left the PRC in 1988 and joined VOA three years later. Her specialty is science and medicine. She traveled to Taiwan in 2001 to do general reporting and cover the growing HIV/AIDS crisis there.

11. Marsh, "VOA Crisis Programming," 6.

12. Quoted in Dan Noble, "Listeners' Reactions," English programs feature no. 7-35264, September 12, 2001, 1.

13. Yuri Ustinov, e-mail to VOA, Russian Branch, September 14, 2001, courtesy of Myrna Whitworth (acting director, VOA).

14. Marc B. Nathanson, testimony submitted for the record to the House, Committee on International Relations, 107th Cong., 1st sess., October 10, 2001, 3.

15. Ed Warner, telephone interview with author, September 27, 2001.

16. Ellen Nakashima, "Broadcast with Afghan Leader Halted," *Washington Post*, September 23, 2001, A9.

17. Department of State, transcript of daily briefing by spokesman Richard Boucher, Federal News Service, September 24, 2001, 13.

18. Ibid., 15–16.

19. Andre DeNesnera, "Some Thoughts on Credibility," e-mail to VOA News Divsion staff, September 24, 2001, 1–2.

20. Andre DeNesnera, "Mullah Omar Piece Is Released," e-mail to author, September 25, 2001.

21. Spozhmai Maiwandi, interview with author, Washington, D.C., October 14, 2001.

22. Quoted in "Armed Forces Send Out Pro-US Messages," Associated Press, October 8, 2001.

23. Maiwandi, interview.

24. Robert Reilly, message to the International Broadcasting Bureau staff, December 5, 2001, 1. A month later, former acting director and program director Myrna Whitworth retired.

25. Quoted in Committee to Protect Journalists, press release, January 17, 2002, 1.

26. Quoted in Society of Professional Journalists (Sigma Delta Chi), press release, February 8, 2002, 1.

27. Ian Traynor, "Trapped in the Dark Ages, a Ragtag Army Welcomes the US Bombs," *Guardian*, September 24, 2001 (available at: www.guardian.co.uk).

28. Douglas Frantz, "Refugees from Afghanistan Flee Out of Fear and Find Despair," *New York Times*, September 30, 2001, B7.

29. "Exuberant Opposition Battles Taliban After Attack," Reuters, October 8, 2001 (available at: http://library.northernlight.com).

30. Quoted in David Folkenflik, "Afghans Flock to Western Radio," *Baltimore Sun Journal*, October 7, 2001 (available at: www.sunspot.net).

31. U.S. Congress, House, Committee on International Relations, *Hearing on Public Diplomacy and the Anti-Terrorism Campaign*, 107th Cong., 1st sess., October 10, 2001, 8–9.

32. Janine Zacharia, "Tuning into the Voice of Freedom," *Jerusalem Post*, April 25, 2002 (available at: http://www.jpost.com/).

33. Quoted in Joyce Howard Price, "U.S. to Go on Air in Arabic to Counter Propaganda," *Washington Times*, April 25, 2002, A9.

34. Robert G. Kaiser, "U.S. Message Lost Overseas: Officials See Immediate Need for 'Public Diplomacy,'" *Washington Post*, October 15, 2001, A8.

35. House Committee on International Relations, *Hearing on Public Diplomacy and the Anti-Terrorism Campaign*, 2.

36. Ibid., 3.

37. Ibid.

38. Kaiser, "U.S. Message Lost Overseas," A8.

39. Robert Reilly, interview with author, Washington, D.C., October 15, 2001.

40. Robert Reilly, "Message to the Staff from the New VOA Director," October 18, 2001.

41. Jesse Helms, "Censor Broadcasts to the World" [op-ed piece], *USA Today*, November 8, 2001, 14A.

42. Robert Reilly, "Interviews with Members of Terrorist Organizations," memorandum to Voice of America division directors, December 12, 2001.

43. A. M. Sperber, *Murrow: His Life and Times* (New York: Freundlich Books, 1986), 111.

44. "Censorship in Pashto and Arabic" [editorial], *New York Times*, October 10, 2001, A22.

45. "A New Voice for America" [editorial], *Wall Street Journal*, October 3, 2001.

46. "Balance Under Fire at VOA" [editorial], *Chicago Tribune*, October 10, 2001.

47. Kenneth Y. Tomlinson, "VOA Led Astray?" *Washington Times*, October 14, 2001, B3.

48. Sanford J. Ungar, "Afghanistan's Fans of American Radio," *New York Times*, October 6, 2001, p. A23.

49. Society of Professional Journalists (Sigma Delta Chi), "Resolution No. 8 Commending the Voice of America" (resolution submitted by the International Journalism Committee and adopted at the national convention, Bellevue, Wash., October 6, 2001).

50. Johann P. Fritz (director, International Press Institute) to Andre DeNesnera, October 2, 2001, 1–2.

51. Quoted in Judith Latham, "Reporting in Time of War," VOA script no. 7-35427, datelined Washington, D.C., October 15, 2001, 8.

52. David Burke, "A Truthful Voice" [op-ed piece], *Washington Post*, October 10, 2001, A23.

53. Quoted in Felicity Barringer, "State Department Protests Move by U.S. Radio," *New York Times*, September 26, 2001, B3.

54. Broadcasting Board of Governors, "The Firewall," memorandum to Voice of America and International Broadcasting Bureau staff, December 14, 2001.

55. House Committee on International Relations, *Hearing on Public Diplomacy and the Anti-Terrorism Campaign*, 3.

Conclusion

1. John Tusa, interview with author, London, May 28, 2001.

2. Ian O. Lesser, *Missile Proliferation and Security in the Eastern Mediterranean*, strategic regional report (Washington, D.C.: Western Policy Center, 2001), 1.

3. Robert Scheer, "Eyewitness: Geoffrey Cowan," *Online Journalism Review*, Annenberg School for Communication, University of Southern California, Los Angeles, June 20, 1994 (available at: www.robertscheer.com/3_scheerbytes).

4. Joseph S. Nye, Jr., and William A. Owens, "America's Information Edge," *Foreign Affairs*, March–April 1996, 20–36.

5. Mary G. F. Bitterman, letter to author, August 13, 2001, 2.

6. David Burke, telephone interview with author, Eastham, Mass., June 18, 2001. Burke originally made the statement when testifying before Congress as board chairman in 1996.

7. Samuel G. Freedman, "What U.S. Image Will Linger?" *USA Today*, January 2, 2002, 9A.

8. Public Law 103-236, title III, sec. 302, 103d Cong., 2d sess. (April 30, 1994), *United States International Broadcasting Act*, 133.

9. This list is drawn largely from Broadcasting Board of Governors, *Mission and Strategic Goals*, annual report, 1999–2000 (Washington, D.C.: Broadcasting Board of Governors, December 1, 2000), 2.

10. Quoted in Alan L. Heil, Jr., notes on the Radio Canada International Challenges V conference, Ottawa, Ontario, Canada, May 25, 1998, 2.

11. International Broadcasting Bureau, Office of Program Review, "VOA Central News File Program Review," June 21, 2001.

12. Alan L. Heil, Jr., "Report on Challenges VI: Programming: The Heart of Radio" (notes on the Radio Canada International Challenges VI conference, Montreal, Quebec, Canada, May 22–25, 2000), 8.

13. Alan L. Heil, Jr., "International Broadcasting in the Twenty-first Century: Can It Survive in the Digital Age?" *Channel* [magazine of the Association for International Broadcasting], May 2000, 3; November 2000, 4. This was a two-part series.

14. Ayman el-Amir, "Filtering the Propaganda," *Al Ahram Weekly*, no. 586, May 16–22, 2002 (available at: www.ahram.org.eg/weekly/2002/586/fel.htm).

15. My cousin, William "Brit" Kirwan, subsequently served as president of Ohio State University in Columbus.

16. Tusa, interview.

17. Robert Reilly, "Message from the VOA Director," e-mail to Voice of America staff, January 17, 2002, 3. See also Robert Reilly, "Winning the War of Ideas: VOA Can Deploy America's Truths," *Washington Times*, January 28, 2002, A17.

18. Alan L. Heil, Jr., notes on the World Radio Network Conference, London, May 31, 2001.

19. Broadcasting Board of Governors, "FY 2002 Budget Request," July 2001, 4.

20. Lieberman's comment came during a visit by President Clinton to VOA on October 24, 1997. There, Clinton made a major foreign policy address on Sino-American relations on the eve of talks at the White House with Chinese president Jiang Zemin.

21. Tom Rogers, remarks to panel on international communications at "Turning Up the Volume on International Radio," symposium, Center for Strategic and International Studies, Washington, D.C., May 23, 1991.

22. David Colker, "From Shortwave to New Wave," *Los Angeles Times*, May 22, 2001, A1.

23. Radio Netherlands, "Press Release Announcing the Inauguration of Shortwave Broadcasts to North America," July 1, 2001, 2.

24. Bruce Gregory, interview with author, Washington, D.C., April 25 and May 26, 2002.

25. *Tune In*, July 2001, 4.

26. A third satellite was scheduled for launch over the Caribbean and South and Central America.

27. Mark O'Keefe, "Radio Sawa Exports U.S. Values to Young Arabs," Newhouse News Service, May 3, 2002 (available at: www.newhouse.com/archive/story/la050302.html).

28. Norma Morrison, "Kuwait MW Implementation Notice," VOA Traffic operational notice, April 26, 2002.

29. International Broadcasting Bureau, "Iran Media Survey" (research memorandum, November 2001), 9. According to a four-city survey conducted by the International Broadcasting Bureau in June and July 2001 in Iran, VOA had more annual listeners on medium wave (41 percent of adults) than did either the BBC (31 percent) or the Persian Service of RFE/RL (25 percent). See also International Broadcasting Bureau, Office of Research, "Media Use in Iran: Program Review Notes for VOA Farsi" (research memorandum, January 31, 2002).

30. Joan Mower, interview with author, Washington, D.C., July 24, 2002.

31. Marc Nathanson, telephone interview with author, Aspen, Colo., July 3, 2001.

32. Burke, interview.

33. Voice of America, "VOA Challenges and Opportunities" (informal vision group talking points, August 2001), 3.

34. Robert Reilly, the director at the time of VOA's sixtieth anniversary, was replaced by the Broadcasting Board of Governors after only ten months in office. His successor was veteran *Time* journalist David Jackson.

35. An exception would be the Office of Engineering and Technical Services, which supports the grantees as well as VOA, VOA-TV, and the Martís. Because the VOA director usually is a presidential appointee, he or she might be able to work closely with the IBB director to ensure accountability and responsiveness of support services. Two VOA heads, Geoffrey Cowan and Evelyn S. Lieberman, served for a number of months as both VOA and IBB directors.

36. Under section 305 (d) of the Foreign Affairs and Restructuring Act of 1998 (PL 105-277), the board, as well as the State Department, is legally obligated to "respect the professional independence and integrity of the International Broadcasting Bureau, its broadcasting services and grantees" (see appendix B).

37. "America, Signing Off?" [editorial], *Wall Street Journal,* June 14, 2001.

38. Most of these were congressionally mandated. The so-called overlap languages inaugurated since 1990 are Albanian, Arabic, Bosnian, Burmese, Cambodian, Cantonese, Croatian, Dari, Farsi, Korean, Lao, Macedonian, Mandarin, Pashto, Serbian, Tibetan, and Vietnamese. Dari and Pashto are used by the RFE/RL-run Radio Free Afghanistan.

39. Quoted in David Gollust (White House correspondent), e-mail to Sonja Pace (chief, News Division), October 23, 1997.

40. Harry Miles Muheim and Jerry Krell, *The Voice* (Washington, D.C.: Worldnet Television, 1992), a television documentary for the fiftieth anniversary of VOA.

41. Kim Andrew Elliott, interview with author, Washington, D.C., May 30, 2002. See also Elliott, "Too Many Voices of America?" *Foreign Policy,* winter 1989–1990.

42. Department of State, *A Report of the President's Task Force on U.S. Government International Broadcasting,* publication no. 9925 (Washington, D.C.: Department of State, 1991), 5.

43. Chase Untermeyer, letter to author, June 26, 2001, 1.

44. Conrad Kiechel, "Voice of America Speaks Up," *Wall Street Journal,* January 28, 1988, 17.

45. Walter Roberts, interview with author, Washington, D.C., July 7, 2000.

46. Bernard H. Kamenske, telephone interview with author, Bethesda, Md., October 9, 2001.

47. Barry Zorthian, interview with author, Arlington, Va., July 11, 2000.

48. Voice of America, transcript of "Twentieth Anniversary of the Signing of the VOA Charter," symposium, Washington, D.C., July 12,1996, 5. See also Bernard H. Kamenske and Alan Heil, "A Brief History of the VOA Charter," *Tune In,* October 1998, 6.

49. International Broadcasting Bureau, Office of Research, "Cambodian Audience Research: Focus Groups in Phnom Penh, May 2000" (research memorandum, March 2001), 2–3. A parallel quantitative survey in urban Cambodia estimated that 40 percent of international radio listening is to Voice of America; 5 percent to Radio Free Asia; and about 1 percent to Radio France International.

50. Nittaya Maphungphong, interview with author, Washington, D. C., June 21, 2001. The Broadcasting Board of Governors later announced that the Thai Service would be extended at least until 2002.

51. Joseph S. Nye, Jr., *The Paradox of American Power: Why the World's Only Superpower Can't Go It Alone* (New York: Oxford University Press, 2002), 68.

52. Edward Bliss, Jr., *Now the News: The History of Broadcast Journalism* (New York: Columbia University Press, 1991), 141.

53. Voice of America, East Asia and Pacific Division, "Chinese Soldier Expresses Remorse for His Role in Tiananmen Crackdown" (division summary for Evelyn S. Lieberman, VOA director, June 1, 1997), 1–2.

Glossary

ABSIE. American Broadcasting Station in Europe. This offshoot of the **OWI** was established in London in 1944, as the Allies began to gain footholds in southern Europe toward the end of World War II.

AFP. Agence France Presse, the French news agency.

airshow. A radio program on the Voice of America.

AM. Amplitude modulation, associated with the widely used original standard broadcast bands (550–1600 MHz on the radio dial in the United States). The term "AM" is often used interchangeably with "medium wave" in international broadcasting circles. It is capable of reaching listeners within 50 to 100 miles of the transmitter during the day and beyond 1,000 miles at night, when its signal may be reflected from the ionosphere. Shortwave broadcasting uses several variations of AM, higher frequencies, and the "bounce" off the ionosphere to reach listeners across oceans. *See also* **FM, frequency band, hertz,** and **megahertz.**

AP. Associated Press.

barrage broadcasting. The massing of transmitters and added frequencies to overcome **jamming.**

BBC. British Broadcasting Corporation.

BBG. Broadcasting Board of Governors. This body oversees all U.S. government publicly funded civilian international broadcasting, including the federal civil service networks—VOA, Radio-TV Martí, and Worldnet Television—and the privately incorporated grantees: **RFE/RL** and **RFA.**

BOB. Bureau of Broadcasting. One of four directorates of the **USIA** before USIA's incorporation into the Department of State in 1999: VOA, Worldnet Television, Radio-TV Martí, and the Office of Engineering. From 1978 to 1993, the VOA director was also the USIA associate director for broadcasting.

branch. In VOA parlance, a broadcasting or central support service unit that usually has twenty or more people. In 1947, for example, the small Russian Service was established. The unit grew to more than fifty broadcasters and was redesignated a branch. *See also* **service.**

CIAA. Coordinator of Inter-American Affairs. This U.S. government agency headed by Nelson Rockefeller provided publications and broadcasts in Central and South America beginning in 1940 through the end of World War II. It mounted the first regularly scheduled international broadcasting activities of the United States, even before VOA.

CPJ. Committee to Protect Journalists. This private New York–based organization is dedicated to shielding journalists everywhere from danger and detention and to promoting press freedom.

DBS. Direct broadcast satellites.

DRM. Digital Radio Mondiale. This consortium of international broadcasters, international broadcasting service providers, and receiver manufacturers is committed to developing and fostering digital AM—that is, medium-wave and shortwave broadcasting—worldwide.

DW. Deutsche Welle, the German publicly funded international broadcasting network.

FBIS. Foreign Broadcast Information Service. This unclassified service of the Central Intelligence Agency monitors foreign broadcasts in many languages at stations around the world and exchanges English texts of these broadcasts with **BBC** World Service Monitoring in Caversham, England.

FIS. Foreign Information Service. During World War II, this New York–based office was responsible for distributing U.S.-funded media (including posters, pamphlets, and shortwave broadcasts) to all areas of the world except Latin America. VOA was a component of the FIS, first reporting to the wartime Coordinator of Information and, after June 13, 1942, as part of the **OWI**.

FM. Frequency modulation. FM radio broadcasts have a sound quality better suited to the transmission of music than medium-wave or shortwave transmissions. The key to success for major international broadcasters today, in addition to high-quality news and programming, is the creation of a global network of terrestrial FM relays. FM uses a wider band than AM (short- and medium wave), producing higher fidelity for music programming. It is limited to listeners from near the transmitter to slightly over the horizon because of the characteristics of this frequency band. *See also* **AM, frequency band, hertz,** and **kilohertz.**

frequency band. Parts of the electromagnetic spectrum, including bands where a radio or television program can be received. Units of frequency in the spectrum include **hertz** (Hz), **kilohertz** (kHz), **megahertz** (MHz), and gigahertz (GHz). The individual bands extend from those for subaudible frequencies through those for low-frequency radio waves, to those used for most radio and television broadcasting, to those of very high-frequency cosmic rays. Bands most often mentioned in this book are medium frequency (medium wave or standard AM, 300 kHz to 3 MHz) and high frequency (shortwave, 3 MHz to 30 MHz). In general, the higher the frequency, the shorter the radio wave. *See also* **hertz, kilohertz,** and **megahertz.**

FY. Fiscal year, in U.S. federal budgets. Currently, the fiscal year begins on October 1 and ends on September 30. For example, FY 2002 started on October 1, 2001, and ended on September 30, 2002, three months before the end of calendar year 2002.

GAO. General Accounting Office. This audit agency of Congress analyzes U.S. government operations, often at the request of Congress, and issues reports on its findings. Major GAO reports are issued by the comptroller general and may be published under his name.

GMT. Greenwich Mean Time. The mean solar time at Greenwich, England, is used as the prime standard time throughout the world in many international broadcasts. The abbreviation "GMT" is synonymous with **UTC.**

hertz. The unit of frequency in an electromagnetic field of one cycle per second. *See also* **frequency band, kilohertz,** and **megahertz.**

IBB. International Broadcasting Bureau. This federally funded body, established in the late 1990s as a successor to the **BOB**, performs many VOA nonprogramming support functions: budget, administration, strategic planning, program evaluation, marketing, computing services, and research. Its Office of Engineering and Technical Services provides transmission of broadcasts for **RFE/RL, RFA,** and Radio-TV Martí, as well as VOA. The IBB director reports to the **BBG.**

ICA. International Communication Agency. In 1978, following a reorganization early in the Carter administration, the **USIA** was renamed the ICA. The original name was restored in 1982.

IIA. International Information Administration. This agency, in the Department of State, included VOA after World War II. Many of its functions were transferred in 1953 to the new **USIA,** VOA's parent body.

Initiative 911. A global project for expanded U.S. government international broadcasting proposed after the September 11, 2001, terrorist airline hijackings and mass fatalities in New York, Washington, D.C., and Pennsylvania. Under the initiative, U.S. government civilian overseas broadcasting would expand in twenty-six existing or newly established language services.

IPI. International Press Institute. This Vienna-based nongovernmental organization seeks to advance a free flow of information via print and electronic media throughout the world.

ITU. International Telecommunication Union. This Geneva-based body fosters international cooperation in the use of a broad range of telecommunications activities, coordinates use of radio and television frequencies, promotes safety measures, and conducts research.

jamming. Deliberate interference with a radio signal using another signal on the same frequency. Jamming is a violation of a number of international agreements.

jamming, groundwave. Local interference on a shortwave or medium-wave frequency intended to block an incoming signal in a city and its suburbs. Groundwave jamming usually has a daylight range of around twenty miles.

jamming, skywave. Deliberate interference with a skywave high-frequency radio signal using another skywave signal on the same frequency. Skywave signals are those traveling extraordinarily long distances—continent to continent—at times depending on a series of bounces off the ionosphere to reach listeners. In skywave jamming, a government uses in-country transmitters to obstruct an external shortwave signal after it is reflected off the ionosphere close to the target region. This technique prevents normal access by the originating nation to listeners in a closed society.

kilohertz. One thousand **hertz.** *See also* **frequency band, hertz,** and **megahertz.**

kilowatt. One thousand watts, a unit of measure of power. In broadcasting, transmitters are designed to achieve specific power outputs for both medium-wave and shortwave broadcasting. Superpower high-frequency transmitters exceed 250 kilowatts. Most commercial AM radio stations in large cities in the United States have a maximum power of 50 kilowatts. *See also* **megawatt.**

MBC. Multimedia Broadcast Center. In 2000, construction began on this state-of-the-art central newsroom for VOA, combining radio, TV, and Internet intake and editing capabilities, and was slated for completion in 2003.

megahertz. One thousand **kilohertz,** or 1 million **hertz.** *See also* **frequency band, hertz,** and **kilohertz.**

megawatt. One thousand **kilowatts,** or 1 million watts. Several international broadcasters, including VOA, use these transmission leviathans. Such **IBB** medium-wave transmitters in the Philippines and Thailand carry powerful signals to listeners in East and South Asia.

MERN. Middle East Radio Network. This project, launched in 2001 to greatly expand U.S. government Arabic-language programming and transmission capability in the Middle East, centered largely on Iraq, the Persian Gulf, the Levant, Egypt, and Sudan. The on-air identification of MERN is Radio Sawa (Together).

monitron. A dial-up audio monitor available in nearly every program production office in VOA. It enables broadcasters to listen to line feeds from remote locations or studios. *See also* **strowger.**

OCB. Office of Cuba Broadcasting. This umbrella organization administers Radio-TV Martí. The OCB director supervises the network offices in Miami and reports to the **BBG.**

OWI. Office of War Information. This was the parent agency of VOA through most of its World War II years.

pigeoning. A technique of bygone days (discontinued with the advent of satellite telephones and PCs), by which foreign correspondents in inaccessible places or war zones sometimes filed their dispatches or audio tape via airplane.

RCI. Radio Canada International. The official Canadian external-broadcasting network, based in Montreal, broadcasts in seven languages. Every two years, from 1990 to 2000, it sponsored a major conference bringing together all international broadcasters to discuss audiences, programming, and technical innovations in the field.

RFA. Radio Free Asia. This U.S.-funded grantee surrogate network, established in 1996 and based in Washington, D.C., broadcasts in ten languages to information-denied areas of East Asia. It reports to the **BBG.**

RFE/RL. Radio Free Europe and Radio Liberty. This U.S.-funded grantee surrogate network, with headquarters in Prague, broadcasts in more than thirty languages to the former Soviet republics and to South and South Central Asia, including recently established services to Iran, Iraq, and Afghanistan. It reports to the **BBG.**

RFI. Radio France Internationale. The official French external-broadcasting network, with headquarters in Paris, broadcasts in sixteen languages.

rigger. A maintenance and construction engineer who works on the high pylons of shortwave or medium wave-transmission antennas, sometimes hundreds of feet above the ground.

satphone. A satellite telephone used by foreign correspondents for filing reports from any place in the world to their home offices. They came into wide use in the 1990s.

service. A smaller VOA broadcasting unit or support organization. *See also* **branch.**

slewing. The ability to direct a signal from a transmission antenna at a variety of angles.

stringer. A contract reporter.

strowger. A dial-up monitoring system for access to field remotes and studios in wide use at VOA from the 1950s through the 1980s. *See also* **monitron.**

switch matrix. A device in a building with transmitters that can direct transmission antennas in the vicinity to specific broadcast target areas.

UNHCR. United Nations High Commissioner for Refugees.

UPI. United Press International.

USIA. United States Information Agency. From 1954 to 1999, this independent U.S. government agency, which reported directly to the president, administered the nation's overseas broadcasting, information, and (after a reorganization in 1978) cultural-exchange programs. It was consolidated into the Department of State on October 1, 1999. Overseas, USIA offices were known as the United States Information Service (USIS).

UTC. Universal Time, Coordinated. The standard time for international broadcasts and scheduling of frequencies and transmissions. The abbreviation "UTC" is synonymous with **GMT.**

webcasting. Increasingly, radio and television programs are available on Internet Web sites, as an alternative to the long-established mode of reception: the airwaves. Even a tiny nation such as Fiji in the South Pacific, for example, can become an international broadcaster by including its radio program in English or local languages on the Internet, accessible anywhere in the world.

Bibliography

BOOKS

Alexandre, Laurien. *The Voice of America: From Détente to the Reagan Doctrine*. Norwood, N.J.: Ablex, 1988.

Bliss, Edward, Jr. *Now the News: The History of Broadcast Journalism*. New York: Columbia University Press, 1991.

Bliss, Edward, Jr., ed. *In Search of Light: The Broadcasts of Edward R. Murrow, 1938–1961*. New York: Da Capo Press, 1997.

Boyd, Douglas A. *Broadcasting in the Arab World: A Survey of the Electronic Media in the Middle East*. 3d ed. Ames: Iowa State University Press, 1999.

Browne, Donald R. *International Radio Broadcasting: The Limits of the Limitless Medium*. New York: Praeger, 1982.

Elliston, Jon. *Psywar on Cuba: The Declassified History of U.S. Anti-Castro Propaganda*. New York: Ocean Press, 1999.

Fortner, Robert S. *International Communications: History, Conflict, and Control of the Global Metropolis*. Belmont, Calif.: Wadsworth, 1994.

Fortner, Robert S. *Public Diplomacy and International Politics: The Symbolic Constructs of Summits and International Radio News*. Westport, Conn.: Praeger, 1994.

Goldmann, Robert. *Wayward Threads*. Evanston, Ill.: Northwestern University Press, 1996.

Green, Fitzhugh. *American Propaganda Abroad: From Benjamin Franklin to Ronald Reagan*. New York: Hippocrene Books, 1988.

Houseman, John. *Front and Center*. New York: Simon and Schuster, 1979.

Jurey, Philomena. *A Basement Seat to History: Tales of Covering Presidents Nixon, Ford, Carter, and Reagan for the Voice of America*. Washington, D.C.: Linus Press, 1995.

Latham, Earl. *The Communist Controversy in Washington: From the New Deal to McCarthy*. Cambridge, Mass.: Harvard University Press, 1966.

Lomax, Bess. *OWI Broadcasting Manual*. Installment 7. Washington, D.C.: Office of War Information, Committee on Broadcasting Operations, 1945.

Mickelson, Sig. *America's Other Voice: The Story of Radio Free Europe and Radio Liberty*. New York: Praeger, 1983.

Nelson, Michael. *War of the Black Heavens: The Battles of Western Broadcasting in the Cold War*. Syracuse, N.Y.: Syracuse University Press, 1997.

Neuman, Johanna. *Lights, Camera, War*. New York: St. Martin's Press, 1996.

Nye, Joseph S., Jr. *The Paradox of American Power: Why the World's Only Superpower Can't Go It Alone*. New York: Oxford University Press, 2002.

Pirsein, Robert William. *The Voice of America: An History of the International Broadcasting Activities of the United States Government, 1942–1962*. New York: Arno Press, 1979.

Rosenblum, Mort. *Coups and Earthquakes*. New York: Harper & Row, 1979.

Sabbagh, Isa Khalil. *"As the Arabs Say . . ."* Washington, D.C.: Sabbagh Management Corporation, 1983.

Shipler, David K. *Russia: Broken Idols, Solemn Dreams*. New York: Times Books, 1983.

Short, K. R. M. *Western Broadcasting over the Iron Curtain*. London: Croom Helm, 1986.

Shulman, Holly Cowan. *The Voice of America: Propaganda and Democracy, 1941–45*. Madison: University of Wisconsin Press, 1990.

Sick, Gary. *All Fall Down: America's Tragic Encounter with Iran*. New York: Random House, 1985.

Sorensen, Thomas C. *The Word War: The Story of American Propaganda*. New York: Harper & Row, 1968.

Sperber, A. M. *Murrow: His Life and Times*. New York: Freundlich Books, 1986.

Tusa, John. *A World in Your Ear*. London: Broadside Books, 1992.

United States Information Agency. *United States Information Agency: A Commemoration*. Washington, D.C.: United States Information Agency, 1999.

Voice of America. *Special English Word Book*. Washington, D.C.: Voice of America, 1987.

Voice of America. *Voice of America: A Brief History*. Washington, D.C.: Voice of America, Office of External Affairs, 1998.

Voice of America. *Voice of America Programming Handbook*. 3d ed. Washington, D.C.: Voice of America, 1993.

Wood, James. *History of International Broadcasting*. Vol. 2. London: International Institute of Engineers/Science Museum, 2000.

Zorthian, Barry, and Hal Berman. *This Is Your Job*. Voice of America, News Branch, stylebook. Washington, D.C.: Voice of America, 1963.

DOCUMENTS, MEMORANDA, TRANSCRIPTS, ARTICLES, AND LEGISLATION

Baily, John. "Censorship of Music in Afghanistan," April 26, 2001. Available at: www.freemuse.org [Freedom of Musical Expression].

Bauer, Robert A. "D-Day, June 6, 1944." In United States Information Agency, *United States Information Agency: A Commemoration*. Washington, D.C.: United States Information Agency, 1999.

Baum, Richard. "International Broadcasting to Asia." Paper presented at a symposium of the Broadcasting Board of Governors, Annenberg School for Communication, University of Southern California, Los Angeles, November 18, 1997.

Bell, Janice, and Dina S. Smeltz, comps. "Kosovo Albanians Relied on Albanian TV and Foreign Radio During Crisis." Survey report compiled for the Department of State, Office of Research, November 24, 1999.

Best, Kenneth Y. Statement submitted for the record to the House, Committee on International Relations, Subcommittee on Africa, 105th Cong., 1st sess., July 15, 1997.

Bitterman, Mary G. F. Farewell remarks to the Voice of America staff, January 28, 1981.

Blitzer, Mark, and Neil Pickett. *Review of VOA Programming During the Persian Gulf War*. Indianapolis: Hudson Institute, 1991.

Boucher, Richard. Daily press briefing, Department of State, September 24, 2001.

Brimmer, Vicki, and Fred Wulff. "A Technical History of the VOA Network." Internal unclassified paper, International Broadcasting Bureau, Office of Engineering, October 25, 1995.

Broadcasting Board of Governors. "Amharic Broadcasting" In *U.S. Broadcasting Board of Governors Handbook*. Washington, D.C.: Intermedia, 1997.

Broadcasting Board of Governors. "Fiscal Year 2002 Budget Request," July 2001.

Broadcasting Board of Governors. "Horn of Africa Broadcasting." In *U.S. Broadcasting Board of Governors Handbook*. Washington, D.C.: Intermedia, 1997.

Broadcasting Board of Governors. *Mission and Strategic Goals*. Annual report, 1998. Washington, D.C.: Broadcasting Board of Governors, November 1998.

Broadcasting Board of Governors. *Mission and Strategic Goals*. Annual report, 1999–2000. Washington, D.C.: Broadcasting Board of Governors, December 1, 2000.

Broadcasting Board of Governors. Statement to the International Broadcasting Bureau staff, December 15, 2001.

Broadcasting Board of Governors. "Summary of Broadcasting and Staff Realignments, BBG 2000/2001 Language Service Review," January 19, 2001.

Buescher, John. Remarks at a Tibetan Service program review, October 9, 1992.

Buescher, John. "Ten Years to Tibet." Program and remarks for the tenth anniversary of VOA Tibetan Service, March 26, 2001.

Buescher, John. "Tibetan Service Profile." Script for VOA Current Affairs, May 12, 1992.

Buescher, John, "VOA Tibetan Service." Profile prepared for a Tibetan service program review, December 2000.

Burgeni, Edwin F., George Jacobs, and Edgar T. Martin. "The Voice of America—A Generation of Growth." *Cathode Press* 22 (1965): 1–12.

Bush, George H. W. Address to the annual convention of the National Association of Broadcasters, Atlanta, Ga., April 2, 1990.

Carlson, Richard W. Remarks to the Voice of America staff on the eve of the Gulf War, January 15, 1991.

Carlson, Richard W. "The War of Words." *American Legion Magazine*, July 1987.

Chao, Kelu. "VOA Report on Tibetan Dissent." E-mail to Robert Reilly, July 16, 2002.

Clinton, William J. "Statement on International Broadcast Programs," June 15, 1993. In *Public Papers of the Presidents of the United States. Book 1, January 20–July 31, 1993*. Washington, D.C.: Government Printing Office, 1994.

Collins, Fred. "Further Implications of the Guyana Study." Memorandum to R. Peter Straus, April 17, 1979.

Cowan, Geoffrey L. Remarks at swearing-in ceremony as twenty-second director of Voice of America, April 26, 1994.

Cowan, Geoffrey L. "The Role of International Public Broadcasters in Shaping the Global Information Marketplace." Address presented at the twenty-fifth annual conference of the Institute of International Communications, Tampere, Finland, September 7, 1994.

Cowan, Geoffrey L., and Joseph B. Bruns. "Why the United States Still Needs the Voice of America." International Broadcasting Bureau and Voice of America summary, June 1995.

DeNesnera, Andre. "Some Thoughts on Credibility." E-mail to VOA News Division staff, September 24, 2001.

Department of State. *The Commission on Broadcasting to the People's Republic of China*. Publication no. 9997. Washington, D.C.: Department of State, 1992.

Department of State. "Guidelines and Operating Procedures for VOA Foreign Correspondents." Joint cable with the International Communication Agency (formerly USIA), signed by Warren Christopher and John Reinhardt, to all U.S. embassies and missions, June 28, 1978.

Department of State. *A Report of the President's Task Force on U.S. Government International Broadcasting*. Publication no. 9925. Washington, D.C.: Department of State, 1991.

Dillard, Gwen. "Globalization, the U.S. Media, and the Voice of America's Coverage of Africa." Address presented at "The Challenges and Opportunities of Globalization at the Dawn of the New Millennium." Symposium, Howard University, Washington, D.C., April 12, 2001.

Docking, Tim. *Peacekeeping in Africa*. Special report. Washington, D.C.: U.S. Institute of Peace, 2001.

Elliott, Kim Andrew. "Too Many Voices of America?" *Foreign Policy*, winter 1989–1990.

Fodor, Marcel. "VOA History (1942–1967)." Manuscript, 1967.

Fortner, Robert S. *Analysis of Voice of America Broadcasts to the Middle East During the Persian Gulf Crisis*. Washington, D.C.: Center for Strategic and International Studies, 1991.

Fritz, Johan P. Letter to Andre DeNesnera, October 2, 2001.

Fritzman, Eva Jane. "Administrative Procedures Governing VOA Correspondents" September 28, 1978.

Giddens, Kenneth R. Statement before the House, Committee on International Relations, Subcommittee on International Relations, 95th Cong., 1st sess., April 5, 1977.

Gwanma, Bitrus Paul. "Multicultural Programming as a Strategy in Public Diplomacy: Leo Sarkisian and the Voice of America's *Music Time in Africa*." Ph.D. diss., Ohio University, 1992.

Hanu, Michael A. "The Biography of an Experiment." Transcript of VOA documentary on Special English, October 1994.

Hanu, Michael A. "Eagle on the Moon." Transcript of VOA documentary on the *Apollo* moon landing, July 25, 1969.

Hanu, Michael A. "Some of Our Yesterdays." Transcript of VOA fiftieth-anniversary documentary, January 30, 1992.

Heil, Alan L., Jr. "Address at Fifty-fifth Anniversary Ceremony, VOA." February 24, 1997.

Heil, Alan L., Jr. Notes on World Radio Network Conference, London, May 31, 2001.

Heil, Alan L., Jr. "VOA Builds Democracy in Closed Societies." In *United States Information Agency: A Commemoration*. Washington, D.C.: United States Information Agency, 1999.

Heil, Alan L., Jr. "VOA Correspondents Ace a Story." In *United States Information Agency: A Commemoration*. Washington, D.C.: United States Information Agency, 1999.

Henderson, Jay. "Look Back at Taiwan Election." E-mail to author, May 9, 2001.

Henderson, Jay. "On Whether Covering Human Rights Should Be Routine Reporting or a Moral Mission." E-mail to author, September 20, 2000.

Henderson, Jay. "The Real Reason the Karmapa Left Tibet." E-mail to author, March 13, 2001.

Henderson, Jay. "VOA Tibetan Uses Opposite Methods to Score Back to Back Successes." E-mail to author, February 6, 2001.

Henderson, Jay. "Weekly Report of VOA East Asia and Pacific Division," June 5, 2001.

Hilmy, Salman. "Reaction to CSIS Report." Memorandum to author, May 28, 1991.

International Broadcasting Bureau, Office of Program Review. "VOA Central News File Program Review," June 21, 2001.

International Broadcasting Bureau, Office of Research. "Cambodian Audience Research: Focus Groups in Phnom Penh, May 2000." Research memorandum, March 2001.

International Broadcasting Bureau, Office of Research. "International Media Use by Tibetan Exiles and Travelers." Research memorandum, March 26, 2001.

International Broadcasting Bureau, Office of Research. "Iran Media Survey." Research memorandum, November 2001.

International Broadcasting Bureau, Office of Research. "Media Use in Iran: Program Review Notes for VOA Farsi." Research memorandum, January 31, 2002.

International Broadcasting Bureau, Office of Research. "VOA's Global Audience." Research memorandum, August 1999.

Jacobs, George. "Testimony on Soviet Jamming of Radio Broadcasts." Paper prepared for the Commission on Security and Cooperation in Europe, Washington, D.C., October 29, 1985.

Jacobs, George. "Why Shortwave?" Remarks at a symposium of the Center for Strategic and International Studies, Washington, D.C., May 23, 1991.

Kamenske, Bernard H. Remarks at "Voice of America at the Crossroads." Symposium, Media Institute, Washington, D.C., June 24, 1982.

Keogh, James. Statement before the House, Committee on International Relations. *Hearings on Public Diplomacy and the Future*, 95th Cong., 1st sess., June 16, 1977.

Kern, Chris. "SNAP: A Five Year Retrospective." USIA Technology Forum internal newsletter, December 1991.

Klecka, Ivan. "Impact of VOA Broadcasting to China." Memorandum to Richard W. Carlson, May 14, 1989.

Lennon, John E. "A Pilot Study of Differences Between the Carter and Reagan Administrations' Influence on Voice of America News, 1977–1985." Master's thesis, University of Maryland, 1993.

Lesser, Ian O. *Missile Proliferation and Security in the Eastern Mediterranean*. Strategic regional report. Washington, D.C.: Western Policy Center, 2001.

Lewis, Mark. Remarks at the opening of Leo Sarkisian's "Faces of Africa" art exhibition, Voice of America, Washington, D.C., February 21, 2001.

Lindburg, John. Letter to Dawn Jensen, July 31, 1997.

Loomis, Henry. "Farewell Address to the Voice of America Staff," March 4, 1965.

Markov, Sergei. "Soviet Media Say Little About Events in China." USSR Division content analysis, May 23, 1989.

Marsh, William. "VOA Crisis Programming: Attack on the United States, the Aftermath, September 12–13," September 13, 2001.

McCarthy, Richard E. "Idioms in the News (2)." Script of VOA, East Asia and Pacific Division, *English, American Style*, no. 260, May 11, 1993.

McCarthy, Robert E. "The Power of Willis Conover." In *United States Information Agency: A Commemoration*. Washington, D.C.: United States Information Agency, 1999.

McKinney, Jerry. "The Voice of America Correspondents Corps Reporting the World." *Voice Magazine*, August–September 1989.

Muheim, Harry Miles, and Jerry Krell. *The Voice*. Documentary. Washington, D.C.: Worldnet Television, 1992.

Mytton, Graham, and Carol Forrester. "Audiences for International Radio." *European Journal of Communication* 3 (1988): 458–481.

Nathanson, Marc B. Remarks at ceremony marking the independence of U.S. government international broadcasting, October 13, 1999.

Nathanson, Marc B. Testimony submitted for the record to the House, Committee on International Relations, 107th Cong., 1st sess., October 10, 2001.

Nemecek, Maureen Jane. "Speaking of America: The Voice of America, Its Mission and Message, 1942–1982." Ph.D. diss., University of Maryland, 1984.

Nicolaides, Philip. Memoranda to Charles Z. Wick, September 21, October 20, 1981.

Nye, Joseph S., Jr., and William A. Owens. "America's Information Edge." *Foreign Affairs*, March–April 1996, 20–36.

O'Connell, Joseph D., Jr. "VOA's Rashmi Shukla and Jagdish Sarin Win the Cowan Award for Humanitarian Reporting on the Dowry System in India." Voice of America, press release, September 22, 2000.

Office of the President. "Statement by President Reagan upon Signing the U.S.–Moroccan Relay Station Agreement," March 1, 1984.

Office of the President. "Statement by the White House Press Secretary on Student Demonstrations in China," May 23, 1989.

Panel on International Information, Education, and Cultural Relations (Stanton Commission). *International Information Education and Cultural Relations: Recommendations for the Future.* Washington, D.C.: Center for Strategic and International Studies, 1975.

Percy, Charles. "Bring Back the VOA Charter." *Washington Post*, July 14, 1994, A23.

Percy, Charles. "Percy Calls for Independent Voice of America." Press release, November 30, 1976.

Pessin, Alan. Address at the annual conference of the National Association of Government Communicators, Arlington, Va., December 8, 1989.

Porter, Charlene. "Words Can Not Explain: Communications Problems Defying Translation in a Multi-Lingual, Multi-Cultural Workplace." Paper for a course in public administration, University of Maryland, 1995.

Public Law 402, section 502. 80th Cong., 2d sess., 1948. *United States Information and Educational Exchange Act (Smith-Mundt Act).*

Public Law 94-350. 94th Cong., 2d sess., July 12, 1976. *VOA Charter.*

Public Law 100-204, title II. 100th Cong., 1st sess., December 22, 1987. *VOA Charter Applied to Worldnet TV.*

Public Law 103-236, title III, sections 301–314. 103d Cong., 2d sess., April 30, 1994. *United States International Broadcasting Act.*

Public Law 103-236. 103d Cong., 2d sess., October 25, 1994. *Restoration of VOA Charter.*

Public Law 105-277. 105th Cong., 2d sess., October 21, 1998. *Foreign Affairs Reform and Restructuring Act.*

Reilly, Robert. "Message to the Staff from the New VOA Director," October 18, 2001.

Reinhardt, John E. Memorandum to Hans N. Tuch, May 4, 1977.

Reinhardt, John E. Memorandum to R. Peter Straus, August 14, 1978.

Roberts, Chalmers. *Report of the Panel to Study the Role of the Foreign Correspondents of the Voice of America.* Washington, D.C., March 9, 1978

Rosenblum, Mort. "The John Peter Zenger Award for Freedom of the Press and the People's Right to Know." Address at the John Peter Zenger Award ceremony, University of Arizona, Tucson, April 24, 1991.

Rosenfeld, Stephen. Address to the alumni association of the United States Information Agency, Fort McNair, Washington, D.C., September 19, 2000.

Roth, Lois. "Public Diplomacy and the Past: The Studies of U.S. Information and Cultural Programs (1952–1975)." Paper presented at the twenty-third session, Executive Seminar in National and International Affairs, Department of State, Foreign Service Institute, Washington, D.C., 1980–1981, 2.

Schiele, Barbara. "VOA Broadcast Hours History, 1955–1989," February 25, 1992.

Schiele, Barbara. "VOA Languages 1942–1982," April 3, 1981.

Schmidt, G. Lewis, John R. O'Brien, and Edmund Schechter. "Management Report on VOA." Internal unclassified paper, April 22, 1974.

Silver, Brian Q. "Another Musical Universe: The American Recording Industry and Indian Music, 1955–1965." Paper presented at a seminar on Indian music and the West, sponsored by the Sangreet Research Academy, National Centre for the Performing Arts, Mumbai, India, November 29–December 1, 1996.

Silver, Brian Q. "A Surbahar Concert." Notes for a program for Embassy of India and World Bank/International Monetary Fund Club concert, World Bank, Washington, D.C., April 29, 2000.

Society of Professional Journalists (Sigma Delta Chi). Press release [on political pressures at VOA], February 8, 2002.

Society of Professional Journalists (Sigma Delta Chi). "Resolution No. 8 Commending the Voice of America." Resolution submitted by the International Journalism Committee and adopted at the national convention, Bellevue, Wash., October 6, 2001.

Staats, Elmer. *Public Diplomacy in the Years Ahead—An Assessment of Proposals for Reorganization.* Comptroller General's report no. ID-77-21. Washington, D.C.: General Accounting Office, May 5, 1977.

Stern, Kenneth. "Broadcasting into the New Millennium." Memorandum to the Broadcasting Board of Governors, August 27, 1999.

Stiglitz, Joseph. "Free Markets and Free Press: What's the Connection?" Paper presented at the Broadcasting Board of Governors Public Forum on International Broadcasting, Chicago, Ill., June 17, 1999.

Tuch, Hans N., and G. Lewis Schmidt, eds. "Ike and USIA." Summary of proceedings at the Eisenhower Centennial Symposium, National War College, Washington, D.C., October 11, 1990.

Ungar, Sanford J. "HIV-AIDS in Africa: Steps to Prevention." Testimony before the House, Committee on International Relations, Subcommittee on Africa, 107th Cong., 1st sess., September 27, 2000.

Ungar, Sanford J. "News and Views Got Inside China During the Airplane Crisis." *Nieman Reports*, summer 2001.

Ungar, Sanford J. Remarks at the opening of Leo Sarkisian's "Faces of Africa" art exhibition, Voice of America, Washington, D.C., February 21, 2001.

United States Information Agency, Bureau of Broadcasting. *Annual Report for 1993: Looking Toward Tomorrow.* Washington, D.C.: United States Information Agency, Bureau of Broadcasting, 1993.

United States Information Agency, Office of the Inspector General. "Inspection of Allegations Concerning VOA Arabic Broadcasting during the Persian Gulf Crisis." Draft report, July 29, 1991.

United States Information Agency, Office of Research. "Foreign Radio Listening Rates High in Four Arab Gulf Nations; VOA Increases Audience during Crisis." Research memorandum, February 14, 1991.

United States Information Agency, Office of Research. "Listeners' Views on the Use of Correspondents by International Broadcasters," January 31, 1978.

University of Oregon, School of Journalism and Communication. "Payne Awards for Ethics in Journalism Honor Joy Harris, Voice of America, and KOMU-TV." Press release, April 16, 2002.

Untermeyer, Chase. "Comments by Prince Norodom Ranaridh." Memorandum to Sid Davis, October 4, 1991.

Untermeyer, Chase. "Response to Office of Inspector General's Report, 'A Critique of VOA Broadcasts during the Persian Gulf Crisis.'" Draft memorandum to Henry J. Catto, September 1992.

U.S. Congress. House. *United States Information and Educational Exchange Act of 1948*, 80th Cong., 2d sess., H.R. 3312, January 26, 1948.

U.S. Congress. House. Committee on International Relations. *Hearings on Public Diplomacy and the Anti-Terrorist Campaign*, 107th Cong., 1st sess., October 10, 2001.

U.S. Congress. House. Committee on International Relations. *Hearings on Public Diplomacy and the Future*, 95th Cong., 1st sess., June 8–24, 1977.

U.S. Congress. Senate. Committee on Foreign Relations. *Foreign Relations Authorization Act, Fiscal Year 1977*, 94th Cong., 2d sess., S. 3168, report no. 94-703, 1976.

U.S. Congress. Senate. Committee on Foreign Relations. *Hearings of Subcommittee on International Operations on the Foreign Relations Authorization Act of 1978*, 95th Cong., 1st sess., S. 1190, April 29, 1977.

U.S. Congress. Senate. Committee on Foreign Relations. *Markup Session by Full Committee on Foreign Relations Authorization Act of 1978*, 95th Cong., 1st sess., S. 1190, May 4 and 10, 1977.

U.S. Congress. Senate. Committee on Foreign Relations. "Remarks by Senator Joseph R. Biden, Jr., at the International Broadcasting Independence Ceremony," Washington, D.C., October 13, 1999.

Voice of America. "The Challenges and Opportunities of Globalization at the Dawn of the New Millennium." Symposium, Howard University, Washington, D.C., April 12, 2001.

Voice of America. "International Broadcasting in a Changing World." Symposium cosponsored with the Smithsonian Institution, Washington, D.C., January 16–February 20, 1992.

Voice of America. "Tribute to Willis Conover, 1920–1996." Program for VOA memorial concert, Voice of America, June 5, 1996.

Voice of America. Transcript of fortieth-anniversary celebration of VOA Special English, December 1, 1999.

Voice of America. "Twentieth Anniversary of the Signing of the VOA Charter." Symposium, Washington, D.C., July 12, 1996.

Voice of America. "VOA's Voices: Life Stories of VOA Broadcasters." Available at: voanews.com.

Voice of America. *Voice of America Broadcasting for the 90s*. Annual report. Washington, D.C.: Voice of America, 1990.

Voice of America, Africa Division. Division briefing paper for Evelyn S. Lieberman, VOA director, April 7, 1997.

Voice of America, East Asia and Pacific Division. "Chinese Soldier Expresses Remorse for His Role in Tiananmen Crackdown." Division summary for Evelyn S. Lieberman, VOA director, June 1, 1997.

Voice of America, Office of Broadcast Operations. Tape of town meeting of Voice of America staff with Bruce Gelb and Richard W. Carlson, January 7, 1991.

Voice of America, Office of Director. VOA *Annual Report*. Washington, D.C.: Voice of America, 1988.

Voice of America, Office of Director. "Why the Voice of America?" Fact sheet, 1991.

Voice of America, Office of Engineering. "Voice of America Engineering Modernization/Refurbishment Program: Recent Accomplishments," October 1989.

Voice of America, Office of Programs, "Chronology of Events in the PRC and VOA Responses," October 1, 1989.

Voice of America, Office of Programs. "Point by Point Discussion of VOA Gulf Crisis Coverage." Talking paper, June 24, 1991.

Voice of America, Office of Programs. "VOA Broadcasting Initiatives in the Middle East," November 20, 1990.

Voice of America, Office of Programs. "VOA Coverage on the Flight of *Apollo XI*," September 11, 1969.

Willen, Mark. Articles and interviews in *Room News*, June 1, 1981–January 20, 1982.

Winter, William. "Voice of an American." Manuscript, 1990.

INTERVIEWS AND CORRESPONDENCE

Acquisto, Ernest (former chief, VOA Technical Operations Division). Interview with author, August 18, 2001.

Araujo, Richard (director, VOA Latin America Division). Interview with author, February 28, 2001.

Balazs, Terry (assistant to director, IBB, Office of Engineering and Technical Services). Interview with author, December 8, 2000; August 14, 2001.

Bauer, Robert (pioneer broadcaster, VOA German Service). Interview with author, October 6, 2000.

Bell, William (director of research, IBB). Interview with author, October 2, 2001.

Berzins, George (former director of operations, TV Marti, and chief, VOA East Asia Branch). Interview with author, July 31, 2001.

Biberaj, Elez (chief, VOA Albanian Service). Interview with author, January 22, 2001.

Bitterman, Mary G. F. (president and CEO, James Irvine Foundation, San Francisco and Los Angeles, and former VOA director). Letter to author, August 13, 2001.

Brimmer, Vicki (archivist, IBB, Office of Engineering and Technical Services). Interview with author, December 8, 2000; September 14, 2001.

Buday, Joseph (former deputy chief, VOA News and European Divisions). Interview with author, August 9, 2001.

Burke, David (former chairman, BBG). Telephone interview with author, June 18, 2001.

Carlson, Richard W. (former VOA director). Interview with author, May 14, 2001.

Chao, Kelu (director, VOA East Asia and Pacific Division). Interview with author, September 17, 2000.

Cocoli, Isabela (senior editor, VOA Albanian Service). Interview with author, August 5, 2001.

Cohen, Scott (former senior administrative assistant for foreign affairs, Senator Charles Percy of Illinois). Interview with author, April 29, 1999; September 24, 2001.

Corey, Wayne (former chief, VOA Saigon, Beijing, Bangkok, and Geneva bureaus). E-mail to author, February 14, 2001.

Cummins, Frank (former chief, IBB, Office of Program Review; VOA deputy director of programs for operations; and editor in chief, *Voice* magazine). Interview with author, January 25, 1999; March 15, October 29, 2001.

del Rio, José "Pepe" (former anchor, *Buenos Días América*). Interview with author, May 17, 2001.

DeNesnera, Andre (director, VOA News Division, and former chief, VOA Geneva and Moscow bureaus). Interview with author, June 4, September 25, 2001; May 8, 2002.

Dillard, Gwen (director, VOA Africa Division). Fax to author, April 23, 2001.

Dillard, Gwen. Interview with author, November 21, 2002.

Elliott, Kim Andrew (research analyst, IBB, Office of Research, and writer/anchor, *Communications World*). Interview with author, May 30, 2002.

Everett, Robert (former site manager, São Tomé Relay Station). Interview with author, October 10 and 18, 2000.

Ferella, Ferdinand (senior field correspondent, VOA French-to-Africa Branch). Interview with author, April 25, 2001.

Freund, Lawrence S. (former chief, VOA New York bureau, and correspondent, Belgrade and London bureaus). Interview with author, October 1 and 7, 2001.

Ghuneim, Mohamed (former chief, VOA Arabic Branch, and chief, Amman bureau). Interview with author, June 15, 2000.

Goldberger, Ed. Oral-history interview with Claude (Cliff) B. Groce, December 12, 1986.

Goldmann, Robert (former chief, VOA News Division). Interview with author, September 4, 2000.

Gregory, Bruce (lecturer, George Washington University, and former executive director, U.S. Advisory Commission on Public Diplomacy). Interview with author, April 25, May 26, 2002.

Groce, Claude (Cliff) B. (former VOA deputy program manager, and deputy director, Worldnet Television). Interview with author, February 12, April 4, July 16, September 17, 2001.

Groce, Claude (Cliff) B. Oral-history interview by Jack O'Brien, Washington, D.C., February 24, 1988.

Gursky, Ed (producer-director, VOA Music Mix). Interview with author, April 25, 2001.

Hartman, Jan (former public affairs officer, Libreville, Gabon). E-mail to Bob Everett, October 13, 2000.

Heintzen, Harry (former director, VOA International Media Training Center). Interview with author, June 14, 2001.

Henderson, Jay (program manager, VOA East Asia and Pacific Division). E-mail to author, September 20, 2000; February 6, March 13, May 9, 2001.

Henderson, Jay. Interview with author, July 8, 2001.

Hilmy, Sam (former chief, VOA Near East and South Asia Division). Interview with author, July 5, 2001.

Ho, Stephanie (former correspondent, VOA Beijing bureau). Interview with author, February 14, 2002.

Hopkins, Mark (former chief, VOA Belgrade, Munich, Moscow, Beijing, Boston, and London bureaus). Fax to author, September 30, 2001.

Hosseini, Hamed (former broadcaster, VOA Dari Service). Interview with author, August 14, 2001.

Hunter, Bruce (former director, Greenville Relay Station). Interview with author, February 19 and 20, 1998; March 6, 2000.

Jacobs, George (George Jacobs and Associates, and former chief, VOA Frequency Division). Interview with author, May 11, 2001.

Jaffie, Margaret (former escort, VOA Public Affairs). Interview with author, September 16, 2001.

Johnson, Gaines (former manager, Belize and São Tomé Relay Stations). Interview with Vicki Brimmer, January 11, 2001.

Kamenske, Bernard H. (former chief, VOA News Division). Interview with author, September 3, 2000; January 9, February 7 and 15, October 9, 2001.

Keathley, Lisa (director, VOA-TV). Interview with author, March 25, 2002.

Kelly, Sean (former VOA correspondent, Africa, Latin America, and Indochina). E-mail to author, June 2, 2002.

Kennedy, Charles Stuart. Oral-history interview with Richard W. Carlson, Foreign Service Institute, Arlington, Va., March 2, 1993.

Kern, Christopher (director, IBB, Computing Services). Interview with author, September 27, 2000; May 2, 2001.

Kern, Eugene (Gene) (former chief, VOA New York and Munich Program Centers). Letter to author, September 25, 2000.

Kern, Eugene (Gene). Oral-history interview with Claude (Cliff) B. Groce, December 12, 1986.

Lennon, John E. (director, IBB, Office of Program Review; former acting director, Worldnet Television; and chief, VOA South European Division). Interview with author, November 4, 1998; September 26, 2000; August 15, 2002.

Lindburg, John (former acting executive director and chief counsel, BBG). Interview with author, February 12, August 23, 1999; June 15, 2001.

Lord, Bette Bao (charter member, BBG). Interview with author, April 10, 2002.

Maiwandi, Spozhmai (chief, VOA Pashto Service). Interview with author, October 14, 2001.

Manolescu, Nicolae (editor, *România literară*). Interview with Dorin Tudoran, April 10, 1990.

Maphungphong, Nittaya (chief, VOA Thai Service). Interview with author, June 21, 2001.

Martin, Edgar. Oral-history interview with Claude (Cliff) B. Groce, February 5 and 12, 1988.

Mengesha, Negussie (program manager, VOA Africa Division). Interview with author, June 4, August 2, 2001.

Modic, Paul (former program manager, VOA). Interview with author, October 11, 2000; July 13, 2001.

Mower, Joan (press spokeswoman, BBG). Interview with author, July 24, 2002.

Mytton, Graham (former director, International Broadcast and Audience Research, BBC World Service). Interview with author, May 31, 2001.

Naifeh, Carolyn (former assistant to VOA director, and to assignments editor, VOA News Division). E-mail to author, August 26, 2001.

Nathanson, Marc (chairman, BBG). Telephone interview with author, July 3, 2001.

Nelson, Michael (former general manager, Reuters). Interview with author, May 28, 2001.

O'Brien, Jack. Oral-history interview by Claude (Cliff) B. Groce, February 8, 1988.

O'Brien, Jack. Oral-history interview by Hans N. Tuch, February 5, 1988.

O'Connell, Joseph D., Jr. (director, IBB, Office of External Affairs). Interview with author, September 24, October 23, 2001.

Outhuok, Tuck (editor, VOA Cambodian Service). Interview with author, May 7, 2002.

Pace, Sonja (former director, VOA News Division, and former chief, Moscow bureau). Interview with author, August 23, 2000.

Paye, Samuel K. (former acting manager, Liberia Relay Station). Interview with author, November 29, 2000.

Pessin, Alan (correspondent, VOA Beijing bureau). Interview with author, June 29, 1999; September 14, 2000.

Raad, Shukria (broadcaster, VOA Dari Service). Interview with author, November 12 and 13, 2001.

Reilly, Robert (former VOA director). Interview with author, October 18, 2001.

Roberts, Douglas B. (former VOA correspondent, Middle East). Interview with author, October 3, 2000; August 8, 2001.

Roberts, Walter (pioneer VOA broadcaster, and member, U. S. Advisory Commission on Public Diplomacy). Interview with author, March 28, July 7, 2000; August 9, 2001.

Roberts, Walter. Oral-history interview with Claude (Cliff) B. Groce, September 10, 1990.

Sarkisian, Leo (musicologist, VOA Africa Division). Interview with author, May 2, 2001.

Sebhatu, Mimi (correspondent, VOA Horn of Africa Service). Interview with author, September 9, 1999.

Shellenberger, Jack (former VOA program manager). Interview with author, July 13, 2000.

Shkreli, Frank (director, VOA European Division). Interview with author, January 22, May 7, 2001.

Silver, Brian Q. (chief, VOA Urdu Service). Interview with author, April 17, 2001.

Stephens, Connie (director, IBB, Internet development, and former deputy chief, VOA Africa Division). Interview with author, January 5, 1999; April 20, 2001.

Stevenson, John (chief, VOA Music and Special English Division). Interview with author, April 26, 2001.

Stryker, Gerald (Jerry) (former VOA chief of policy and retired foreign service officer, USIA). Interview with author, September 19, 2000.

Tran, Pham (assignments editor, VOA News Division). Interview with author, February 13, 2001.

Tseu, Betty (correspondent, VOA Chinese Branch). Interview with author, April 6, 1998.

Tuch, Hans (Tom) N. (former VOA deputy director). Interview with author, March 2, 2000; April 6, 2001.

Tuch, Hans (Tom) N. Oral-history interview by Claude (Cliff) B. Groce, Washington, D.C., February 24, 1988.

Turner, Rhett (former VOA science and space reporter and anchor). Interview with author, March 29, 2001.

Tusa, John (former managing director, BBC World Service). Interview with author, May 28, 2001.

Ungar, Sanford J. (former VOA director). Interview with author, December 6, 2000.

Untermeyer, Charles (Chase) (former VOA director). Letter to author, June 26, 2001.

Van Wagenen, Lord Byron (antenna rigger, Greenville Relay Station). Interview with author, February 20, 1998.

Warner, Ed (senior background writer, VOA News Division). Telephone interview with author, September 27, 2001.

Weese, Cliff (IBB, Office of Engineering and Technical Services). Interview with author, November 17, 2000.

Whitworth, Myrna (former VOA director of programs). Interview with author, October 5, November 9, 2001.

Williams, David (former chief, VOA Africa Division, and chief, Nairobi and London bureaus). Interview with author, March 17, 2001.

Wise, Gary (director, Greenville Relay Station). Interview with author, November 29, 2000.

Zorthian, Barry (former VOA program manager). Interview with author, July 11, 2000; April 3, 2001.

Index

Photographs are indicated by page numbers in italics.